THE

CAUS

OF

GOD AND TRUTH

In Four Parts

WITH A

VINDICATION OF PART IV

FROM THE CAVILS, CALUMNIES, AND DEFAMATIONS, OF MR. HENRY HEYWOOD

BY JOHN GILL, D.D.

A NEW EDITION

BAKER BOOK HOUSE
Grand Rapids, Michigan 49506

Reprinted 1980 by
Baker Book House Company
from the 1855 edition published by
W. H. Collingridge, London

ISBN: 0-8010-3761-1

PHOTOLITHOPRINTED BY CUSHING - MALLOY, INC.
ANN ARBOR, MICHIGAN, UNITED STATES OF AMERICA

PREFACE

It should be known by the reader, that the following work was undertaken and begun about the year 1733 or 1734, at which time *Dr. Whitby's Discourse on the Five Points* was reprinting, judged to be a masterpiece on the subject, in the English tongue, and accounted an unanswerable one ; and it was almost in the mouth of every one, as an objection to the Calvinists, Why do not ye answer Dr. Whitby ? Induced hereby, I determined to give it another reading, and found myself inclined to answer it, and thought this was a very proper and seasonable time to engage in such a work.

In the year 1735, the First Part of this work was published, in which are considered the several passages of Scripture made use of by Dr. Whitby and others in favour of the Universal Scheme, and against the Calvinistical Scheme, in which their arguments and objections are answered, and the several passages set in a just and proper light. These, and what are contained in the following Part in favour of the Particular Scheme, are extracted from Sermons delivered in a Wednesday evening's lecture.

The Second Part was published in the year 1736, in which the several passages of Scripture in favour of special and distinguishing grace, and the arguments from them, are vindicated from the exceptions of the Arminians, and particularly from Dr. Whitby, and a reply made to answers and objections to them.

The Third Part was published in 1737, and is a confutation of the arguments from reason used by the Arminians, and particularly by Dr. Whitby, against the above doctrines ; and a vindication of such as proceed on rational accounts in favour of them, in which it appears that they are no more disagreeable to right reason than to divine revelation ; to the latter of which the greatest deference should be paid, though the Rationalists of our age too much neglect it, and have almost quitted it ; but *to the law and to the testimony, if they speak not according to this word, it is because there is no light in them.*

In this part of the work is considered the agreement of the sentiments of Mr. Hobbes and the Stoic philosophers with those of the Calvinists, in which the difference between them is observed, and the calumny removed ; to which is added, a Defence of the Objections to the Universal Scheme, taken from the prescience and the providence of God, and the case of the Heathens.

The Fourth Part was published in 1738, in which the sense of the ancient writers of the Christian Church, before the times of Austin, is given ; the importance and consequence of which is shown, and that the Arminians have very little reason to triumph on that account.

This work was published at a time when the nation was greatly alarmed with the growth of Popery, and several learned gentlemen were employed in preaching against some particular points of it ; but the author of this work was of opinion, that the increase of Popery was greatly owing to the Pelagianism, Arminianism, and other supposed rational schemes men run into, contrary to divine revelation, This was the sense of our fathers in the last century, and therefore joined these and Popery together in their religious grievances they were desirous of having redress- ed ; and indeed, instead of lopping off the branches of Popery, the axe should be laid to the root of the tree, Arminianism and Pelagianism, the very life and soul of Popery.

This *new edition*, with some alterations and improvements, is now published by request.

CONTENTS

PART I.

EXAMINATION OF

PART II.

PART III

PART IV

A

TABLE OF THE SCRIPTURES

EXPLAINED IN THIS WORK

CAUSE OF GOD AND TRUTH

SECTION I

If thou dost well, shalt thou not be accepted?
&c.—Gen. iv. 7.

I. It will be proper to inquire, whether a wicked, an unregenerate man, as was Cain, can perform good works. To which may be answered,

1. Adam had a power to do every good work the law required; which men, since the fall, have not. Men indeed, in an unregenerate state, might do many things which they do not; such as reading the Scriptures, attending on public worship, &c. No doubt but the persons in the parable, who were invited to the dinner, could have gone to it, had they had a will, as well as the one did to his farm, and the other to his merchandise. Men have an equal power, had they an heart, a will, an inclination, to go to a place of divine worship, as to a tavern, or alehouse; but it is easy to observe, that persons oftentimes have it in the power of their hands, when they have it not in the power of their hearts, to do a good work; as a rich man to give alms to the poor. Unregenerate men are capable of performing works, which are in a natural and civil, though not in a spiritual sense, good. They may do those things, which externally, in appearance, and as to the matter and substance of them, may be good; such as hearing, reading, praying, giving alms to the poor, &c., when the circumstances requisite to good works are wanting; for whatsoever is done as a good work, must be done in obedience to the will of God; from a principle of love to him; must be performed in faith; in the name of Christ, and to the glory of God by him. Therefore,

2. It must be denied, that wicked, unregenerate men, have a power to perform good works in a spiritual manner; which is evident from their natural estate and condition, according to the scriptural representation of it, which is this: that the bias of their minds is to that which is evil, and to that only; that they are wholly carnal, and mind nothing else but the things of the flesh; that they are weak and strengthless, yea, dead in trespasses and sins; nay, that they are under an impossibility to do that which is spiritually good; *There is none that doeth good, no, not one* of them, nor are they able; they are *not subject* to the law of God, nor can they be. When the *Ethiopian changes his skin, and the leopard his spots, then may they also do good, who are accustomed to do evil.* Men may expect as soon to *gather grapes of thorns, or figs of thistles,* as good fruit to grow upon, or good works to be performed by, unregenerate men; no, they must be *created in Christ Jesus,* have the Spirit of Christ put into them, and his grace implanted in them; they must be believers in him, before they are capable of doing that which is spiritually good. And even believers themselves are not able to think a good thought or perform a good work of themselves; it is God who works in them both *to will and to do of his good pleasure.* Sometimes when they have a will to that which is good, yet how to perform they know not; they can do nothing without Christ, though all things through him, who strengthens them; much less then have unregenerate persons either a power or a will to that which is spiritually good. Nor,

3. Is there any foundation for such a proposition in these words, which are hypothetically expressed, and therefore nothing absolutely to be concluded from them; that is to say, we are not to argue from God's saying to Cain, *If thou dost well,* therefore Cain had a power to do well, or to do that which is spiritually good, well; much less should we infer from hence, as one does, that "God could not have proposed the doing of good as a condition, if he had not given Cain sufficient strength whereby he was capable to do good."* Since God could not only have proposed the doing of good, but have required it according to his law, without being under obligation to give sufficient strength to obey; for though man by his sin has lost his power to obey the will of God in a right manner, yet God has not lost his authority to command; which he may use without obliging himself to find man sufficient strength to act in obedience to it. Besides,

4. These words regard doing well, not in a moral, but in a ceremonial sense. Cain and Abel were very early taught the necessity, manner, and use of sacrifices; and in process of time they brought their offerings to the Lord, each according to his different calling and employment; the one brought of the fruit of the ground, the other of the firstlings

---

* Barclay's Apology, p. 151.

of his flock. Now to Abel and his offering the Lord had respect, that is, he accepted him and his offering; but to Cain and his offering he had not respect; which made Cain very wroth, and his countenance fell; upon which the Lord expostulates with him after this manner, *Why art thou wroth? and why is thy countenance fallen? If thou dost well,* ἐὰν ὀρθῶς προσενέγκης, *If thou hadst offered rightly,* as the Septuagint renders the words; which though it is not a proper literal translation of them, yet agreeable enough to their sense, *shouldst thou not be accepted?* Cain failed either in the matter or manner of his sacrifice; probably in the latter; since the author of the Epistle to the Hebrews observes, that *by faith, Abel offered a more excellent sacrifice than Cain.** Cain offered his sacrifice without faith, without any view to the sacrifice of Christ: he performed this his sacrifice hypocritically, in show and appearance only; he acted from no right principle, nor to any right end; and therefore his works, whatever show of righteousness they might have, are, by the apostle John,† rightly called *evil;* as are also all the works of wicked and unregenerate men. I proceed,

II. To consider whether man's acceptance with God is on the account of his good works.

1. There is a difference between the acceptance of men's works, and of their persons for them: there are many actions done by men, which are acceptable and well-pleasing to God, when they themselves are not accepted by him, on account of them. Besides, no man's works are accepted by him whose person is not previously accepted: God first had respect to the person of Abel, and then to his offering; which shows that his person was not accepted for the sake of his offering. The best works of the saints are imperfect, and attended with sin, and are only acceptable to God through Jesus Christ, in whom, and in whom only, who is the beloved, their persons are accepted and well-pleasing to God. No man can be justified or saved by his works, and therefore no man can be accepted with God on that account; which is the current doctrine of the sacred writings: this will help us to understand the true sense of such passages, as Acts x. 35, Rom. xix. 18, 2 Cor. v. 9, compared with Eph. i. 6, 1 Pet. ii. 5.

2. Nor do these words suppose that man's acceptance with God stands upon the foot of works. The Hebrew word שאת, for there is but one word in the original text, which our translators render, *shalt thou not be accepted?* signifies either excellency, as in Psal. lxii. 4, and may design the dignity of primogeniture, or honour of birth-right, as it does in Gen. xlix. 3, and so be rendered, *shalt thou not have the excellency?* that is, shall not the right of primogeniture continue with thee? shall not the honour and privilege of being the first-born abide with thee? thou needest not be afraid that this shall be taken from

thee, and given to thy younger brother, who is willing to be subject to thee, and ready to serve thee; which well agrees with the latter part of the text, *and unto thee shall be his desire, and thou shalt rule over him;* or the word signifies an *elevation,* or *lifting up;* and is to be understood as Aben Ezra‡ observes of שאת פנים, a lifting up of the countenance, which was fallen, ver. 5, 6, and then the sense is, if thou hadst done well, when thou broughtest thine offering, thou mightest have *lift up thy face without spot,* and doubtless thou wouldst have done so; but inasmuch as thou hast sinned and done evil, and which is to be seen in thy fallen countenance, sin lies at the door of thy conscience; which, when once opened, it will enter in, and make dreadful work; as it did a little after; which made him say, *My punishment is greater than I can bear.* But admitting that the word signifies acceptance, and be rendered, *shall there not be an acceptance?* it is to be understood, not of an acceptance of his person, but of his sacrifices and services.

III. It remains to be considered, whether Cain had a day of grace,§ in which it was possible for him to be accepted with God.

1. There is no acceptance of any man's person, but as he is considered in Christ the Mediator. Now as there is no reason to believe that ever Cain, who was of the wicked one, the devil, was ever in Christ, or ever considered in him; so there is no reason to conclude, that he either was, or that it was possible for him to be, accepted with God.

2. The text does not speak of his doing well in a moral or spiritual, but in a ceremonial way; and not at all of the acceptance of his person, on the foot of so doing; but at most, only of the acceptance of his sacrifice and ceremonious services, supposing them rightly performed

3. These words are not expressive of a day of visitation in a way of grace and mercy to him; but are to be considered as an expostulation with him for his wrath, fury, and fallen countenance, and an upbraiding of him with his evil doing, in order to awaken his conscience, and bring him to a full sense of his sin; which was so far from proving a day of grace to him, that it quickly issued in the utmost distress of mind, torture of conscience, and black despair.

SECTION II

And the Lord said, my Spirit shall not always strive with man, for that he also is flesh; yet his days shall be an hundred and twenty years.—Gen. vi. 3.

IT will be necessary, in order to understand the sense of this text, to inquire,

I. Who is meant by the Spirit of God; and whether the Holy Ghost, the third Person in the Trinity, is designed or not.

1. Some of the Jewish writers‖ think, that the soul of man is intended; which is

---

* Heb. xi. 4.

† 1 John iii. 12.   ‡ In loc.

§ So says Barclay in his Apology, p. 154.

‖ R. Levi Ben Gersom, R. Aben Ezra, &c., in loc.

called not only the spirit of man, but also the Spirit of God; as in those words of Job, *All the while my breath is in me, and the Spirit of God is in my nostrils.*[*] Some of them † derive the word יָדוֹן, translated *strive*, from נָדָן, which signifies the scabbard of a sword, and say, what the scabbard is to the sword, that the body is to the soul; and give this as the sense of the words; "My Spirit, or the soul which I have put into man, shall not always abide in him as a sword in its scabbard; I will unsheath it, I will draw it out; he shall not live always, seeing he is flesh, corrupt, given up to carnal lusts; yet his days, or term of life, which I will now shorten, shall be one hundred and twenty years." Another of them ‡ delivers the sense of the words to this purpose; "My Spirit, which I have breathed into man, shall not be any more in contention with the body; for it does not delight in nor receive profit from the desires of the body; for the body is drawn after beastly desires, and that because it is flesh, and its desires are plunged and fixed in the propagation of the flesh; however, I will prolong their days one hundred and twenty years; and if they return by repentance, very well; but if not, I will destroy them from the world." The Targum paraphrases the words thus, "This wicked generation shall not be established before me for ever."

2. Others, as Sol. Jarchi, understand it of God himself, thus saying, within himself, "My Spirit, which is within me, shall not always be, as it were, in a tumult, or contention about man, whether I shall spare him, or destroy him, as it has been a long time, but it shall be no longer so; I will let man know that I am not fluctuating between mercy and judgment, but am at a point, being determined to punish him, since he is wholly given up to carnal pleasures, when I have spared him an hundred and twenty years more."

This sense of the words much obtains among learned men.§ And if either of these senses be received, the reasonings of the Arminians from these words, in favour of any branch of their scheme, fall to the ground; but I am willing to allow,

3. That by the Spirit of God, we are to understand the Holy Ghost; so Jonathan Ben Uzziel, in his Targum, expressly calls him; and I am the rather induced to believe this to be the meaning of the phrase; since the apostle Peter, when he speaks of Christ being *put to death in the flesh, and quickened by the Spirit*, which is to be understood of the Holy Spirit, adds, *by which*, that is, by which Spirit, *also he went and preached unto the spirits in prison, which sometimes were disobedient, when once the long-suffering of God waited in the days of Noah;*‖ which words refer to those in Genesis, and are the best

key unto them, and comment on them. I proceed to consider,

II. Whether the Holy Spirit was in the men of the old world, since, as it is observed,¶ the words may be rendered, *My Spirit shall not always strive in man;* and whether it may be concluded from hence, that the Spirit of God is in every man, from whom he may wholly remove through man's misconduct.

1. The Spirit of God is every where, in every creature, and so in every man, as he is the omnipresent God; hence says the Psalmist, *Whither shall I fly from thy Spirit?*[**] He may also be in some persons by his gifts natural or divine, and that either in an ordinary or in an extraordinary way, or by some operations of his on the mind; which are not of a saving nature, nor designed to a saving purpose; and in one or other of these senses, the *manifestation of the Spirit is given to every man to profit withal;*†† and the Spirit may be said to be both in the men of the old world, and of this. But,

2. That he is in every man in a way of special grace, and to saving purposes, provided they behave well, must be denied; for every unconverted man is destitute of the Spirit; were the Spirit, in this sense, in every man, the indwelling of the Spirit would be no evidence of regeneration; the difference between a regenerate and an unregenerate man lying in this, the one has, the other has not the Spirit of God. Hence,

3. It is easy to judge in what sense the Spirit of God does, and does not depart where he once is. Where he is only by his gifts or external operations, he may wholly remove, he may take away those gifts, or cease from those works; and men, notwithstanding these, may be everlastingly lost; but where he is by his special grace, he never totally departs, though he may withdraw his gracious presence for a time; his people may not be indulged with his joys and comforts, and in their apprehension he may seem to be taken away from them, yet he always abides in them; otherwise Christ's prayers for his perpetual continuance with his people would not be answered; nor would the Spirit's indwelling be a security of the saints' perseverance, nor any certain pledge of their future glory. To add no more, the words of the text speak not of the Spirit's being in the men of the old world, but of his striving with them. Wherefore the next inquiry

III. Is, what is meant by the strivings of the Spirit? and whether through man's neglect of him, or opposition to him, he may strive to no purpose.

1. The Hebrew word דין, here used, signifies to *judge*, to *execute judgment*, or *punish* in a righteous way; and so some‡‡ read the words, *My Spirit shall not judge these men*

---

* Job xxvii. 3.   † So Some in R. Aben Ezra, iu loc. R. Hona in Bereshit Rabba, fol. 22, 3.   ‡ R. Joseph. Kimchi in R. David Kimchi, lib. Shorash, rad. דין.

§ Vid. Fuller. Miscell. Sacra, 1, 5, c. 5; and Vatablus, and Capellus, iu loc.   ‖ 1 Pet.

iii. 18—20.   ¶ Barclay's Apology, p. 154.
** Ps. cxxxix. 7.   †† 1 Cor. xii. 7.
‡‡ So Symmachus, Hieron. Trad. Heb. tom. iii. p. 66; R. Juda Bar Elhai in Bereshit Rabba, fol. 22, 3.

for ever ; I will not reserve them to everlasting torments ; I will punish them here in this world ; for they are flesh, frail sinful creatures ; *I will not contend for ever, neither will I be always wroth ; for the spirit should fail before me, and the souls which I have made ;*[*] or rather the sense is according to this version, My Spirit shall not exercise judgment on them for ever,[†] that is, immediately, directly, at this very instant ; though they are so corrupt, I will give them the space of one hundred and twenty years to repent in ; and after that, if they repent not, I will deliver them up to destruction ; which accordingly was the event of things.

2. The word here translated *strive*, signifies also to *litigate* a point, or *reason* in a cause ; before it is ripe for judgment, or the execution of it. Now the Spirit of God had been litigating and reasoning with these men in the court and at the bar of their own consciences, about their sins, by one providence or another, and by one minister or another ; particularly by Noah, a preacher of righteousness, and that to no purpose ; hence he determines to go on no longer in this way, but to proceed to pass and execute the sentence of condemnation on them, since they were so very corrupt, being nothing else but flesh. However, to show his clemency and forbearance, he grants them a reprieve for one hundred and twenty years ; which is that *long-suffering of God* the apostle speaks of, *that waited in the days of Noah, while the ark was preparing.*[‡] Hence it appears, that the strivings of the Spirit of God with these men, were only by the external ministry of the word, and in a way of moral suasion, which came to nothing. This may lead us to observe the insufficiency of moral suasion and the external ministry of the word, without the powerful and efficacious grace of the Spirit.

3. It is now easy to discern in what sense the Spirit of God may be opposed and resisted, and strive to no purpose, and in what sense not. The things of the Spirit of God are disagreeable to a natural man : it is no wonder that the external ministry of the word and ordinances are despised, opposed, and resisted. The external call may be rejected ; yea, some inward motions and convictions may be overruled, stifled, and come to nothing : nay, it will be granted, that there may be and is an opposition and resistance to the work of the Spirit of God in conversion ; but then the Spirit cannot be so resisted in the operations of his grace, as to be obliged to cease from his work, or to be overcome or or hindered in it ; for he acts with a design which cannot be frustrated, and with a power which is uncontrollable ; were it otherwise, the regeneration and conversion of every one must be precarious, and where the grace of the Spirit is effectual, according to the doctrine of free-will, it would be more owing to the will of man than to the Spirit of God.

IV. It may be asked whether the old world had a day of grace,[§] and so all mankind, in which they might be saved if they would ; during which time the Spirit strives with man ; and when that is expired he strives no longer.

1. The space of one hundred and twenty years allowed the old world for repentance was indeed a favour, and indulgence of divine Providence, a time of God's long-suffering and forbearance ; but it does not follow, that because they had such a space allotted to them, in which, had they repented, they would have been saved from temporal ruin ; that therefore all mankind have a day of grace, which if they improve, they may be saved with an everlasting salvation. For,

2. If by a day of grace are meant the means of grace, the external ministry of the word and ordinances, these are insufficient to salvation, without the efficacious grace of God ; and besides, these are not enjoyed by all mankind. Every man has not a day of grace in this sense. Sometimes the means of grace have been confined to one particular nation, and all the rest of the world have been without them for a considerable number of years. This was the case of all the nations of the world whom God suffered to walk in their own ways ; overlooked them, took no notice of them, gave them no day of grace ; while his worship was only kept up in the land of Judea. And since the coming of Christ, the administration of the word and ordinances has sometimes been in one place, and sometimes in another, when the rest of mankind have been without them : so that every man in this sense has not had a day of grace.

3. The whole Gospel dispensation in general may be called a day of grace ; but this day does not expire while men live, or at their death ; it reaches from the coming of Christ, unto the end of the world ; it will continue until all the elect of God are gathered in : nor can it be said of any man, that, he has outlived or outsinned this day of grace ; for still it is said, *To-day if ye will hear his voice;*[||] *Now is the accepted time, now is the day of salvation.*

4. The open special day of grace to God's elect, begins at their conversion, which will never end, never be over with them ; though may have their clouds and darkness, until it is changed into the everlasting day of glory.

SECTION III.

O that there were such an heart in them that they would fear me, and keep all my commandments always, that it might be well with them, and with their children for ever.
—Deut. v. 29.

1. THESE vehement desires of God for the good of these people, are said to be irreconcileable with his decrees of election and reprobation ; and supposing those decrees,

---

[*] Isa. lvii. 16.   [†] Vid. Fuller. Miscell. Saer. l. 5. c. 5.   [‡] 1 Peter iii. 20.

[§] See Barclay in his Apology, pp. 153, 154.
[||] Heb. iii. 7 ; 2 Cor. vi. 2.

they are represented* to be hypocritical: to which may be replied;

1. For God passionately to wish good things, even salvation itself, for some, and not for all, is no ways contrary, but perfectly agreeable to the doctrine of election. If any thing is said to the purpose, as militating against that doctrine, it ought to be said and proved, that God has vehemently desired the salvation of all mankind; of which these words can be no proof, since they only regard the people of Israel, who were the *fewest of all people*. As for those scriptures which represent God as willing *all men to be saved*,† and *not willing that any should perish*, they will be considered in their proper places.

2. It might seem repugnant to these decrees, and to imply hypocrisy and guile, could any instance be produced of God's passionately wishing the salvation of such whom the Scriptures represent as rejected of him, given up to a reprobate mind, and as vessels of wrath fitted for destruction, or who are not eventually saved; but none will say, such were the people whose good and welfare are vehemently desired in this passage of Scripture. For,

3. These are the most improper instances that could have been pitched upon: since they were a peculiar people to the Lord, whom he had *chosen to be a special people to himself, above all people upon the face of the earth.*‡

II. These passionate wishes also, supposing the doctrine of particular redemption, are said to represent§ God as full of guile, deceit, insincerity, dissimulation, and hypocrisy; to which I answer,

1. The doctrine of particular redemption is the doctrine of the Scriptures. Christ died not for all men, but for some only; who are called his people, his sheep, his church, unless all men can be thought to be the people, sheep, and church of Christ.

2. The blasphemous charge of guile, deceit, insincerity, dissimulation, and hypocrisy, ought to be removed from God, who cannot lie, deceive, dissemble, or deny himself; who is a God of truth, and without iniquity; just and right is he. Nor,

3. Does such a passionate wish for the good of these people, whom God had so great a regard for as to redeem from Egyptian bondage, imply any thing of this nature, supposing the doctrine of particular redemption: for, as has been observed in answer to the former question, it ought to be proved, that God has ever used such expressions of desire for the salvation of all mankind, and particularly of such who are not saved; in which number none will choose to put the people of Israel, especially since it is said,‖ that *all Israel shall be saved*. And,

4. After all, these words do not express God's desire of their eternal salvation, but only of their temporal good and welfare, and that of their posterity; for their eternal salvation was not to be obtained by works of righteousness done by them, by their fear or worship of God, or by their constant universal obedience to his commands. They were saved by the grace of the Lord Jesus Christ, even as we. Their fear of God, and obedience to his will, issued indeed in their temporal prosperity, and on this account were strictly enjoined them; that so they might live, and it be well with them, and they prolong their days in the land they were going to possess, as appears from ver. 33; and with a view to this, God so ardently desired these things in them, and to be done by them.

III. Such pathetic¶ expressions are thought to imply, that God gives to all men sufficient grace for conversion, and to militate against the necessity of the unfrustrable operation of his grace in that work.

1. Admitting that the saving work of conversion is here wished for; such a wish does not necessarily suppose that sufficient grace for that work either was or would be given; and if the thing wished for was effected, it does not follow from hence, that this was not performed by the unfrustrable operation of God's grace.

2. Allowing that this grace, an heart to fear the Lord, and all that is requisite to it, were given to the Israelites; it ought not to be concluded from hence, that all men have the same, or that God wishes the same to all men.

3. We are not to imagine that such vellieties and wishes are strictly and properly in God; who here speaks, as R. Aben Ezra** observes, כלשון בני אדם, by an anthropopathy, after the manner of men; such desires are ascribed to him in the same way as human passions and affections are; as anger, grief, repentance, and the like: nor do such wishes and desires declare either what God does or will do; but what he approves of, and is grateful to him; as are an heart to fear him, and a constant and universal obedience to his commandments.

4. The words are so rendered by some, as that they express no wish or desire in God, but rather what was to be desired by the Israelites themselves; so the Arabic version, *it should be wished for by them, that such an heart would continue in them;* that is, such an heart as they professed to have in ver. 27, when they said to Moses, *Go thou near, and hear all that the Lord our God shall say; and speak thou unto us all that the Lord our God shall speak unto thee, and we will hear it, and do it.* The Lord takes notice of this declaration, in ver. 28: *I have heard*, says he, *the voice of the words of this people, they have well said all that they have spoken;* and then adds, according to this version, that a continuance

---

* Curcellæ, Relig. Christ. Inst. l. 6, c. 6, sect. 7, p. 370; Whitby's Discourse on the Five Points, pp. 77, 197; edit. 2. 76, 193.   † 1 Tim. ii. 4; 2 Peter iii. 9.   ‡ Deut. vii. 6.

§ Whitby, p. 179, 181; ed. 2. 175, 177. ‖ Rom. xi. 26.   ¶ Whitby, p. 235; ed. 2. 230.   ** In loc.

of such an heart to hear and do, should be very desirable by them. Moreover, the words מי יתן, may be rendered as they are by the Septuagint, τίσδώσει, *who will give?* and so be considered as an inquiry, as Dr. Whitby himself says :* who will give them this heart? they could not give it themselves: no creature could give it them; only God could give them such an heart as this. And perhaps this mode of expression may be used on purpose to convince them of their want of such an heart, and of the necessity of such an one, and that God only could give it to them; and therefore they should apply to him for it, and not presume, as they seemed to do, to hearken to his commandments, and obey them in their own strength, and without the assistance of his grace. Or,

5. These words may be considered as an upbraiding of these people with the want of an heart to fear the Lord, and with want of ability to keep all his commandments, and that always, notwithstanding the vain boasts and empty resolutions they had just now made. In the same manner are we to consider other pathetic expressions of the like nature; such as Deut. xxxii. 28, 29, Psal. lxxxi. 11—13.

SECTION IV

And thou shalt remember all the way which the Lord thy God led thee these forty years in the wilderness, to humble thee, and to prove thee, to know what was in thine heart, whether thou wouldest keep his commandments or no—Deut. viii. 2.

It is said,† that it is evident from this and other passages of Scripture, that the state of man in this world, is a state of trial or probation. It will be proper therefore to make the following inquiries:

I. What this state of probation is, or what is meant by it.

1. This state of trial is not of men's graces, as faith, patience, &c., by afflictive dispensations of Providence; for men in general are not in such a state, since all men have not grace to be tried; nor is the state of every man an afflicted one in this life: this is a state peculiar to the people of God, and to them only when converted: for before conversion they have no graces to be tried; and with some of them, this state is very short, and so far from being the state of man whilst in this world; and yet, as will be seen hereafter, the proof of the state of probation pretty much depends on passages of Scripture which relate to the exercise of the graces of the saints by afflictions, temptations, &c.

2. This state of trial, if I understand it right, is of man's obedience and conduct towards God during his life; according to which conduct and behaviour God acts towards him, both in this and the other world; his state, as to happiness or misery, being yet unfixed: so that whilst this state lasts, it is uncertain whether he will be saved or lost.

II. What proof is given of the state of man in this world, being such a one.

1. All those scriptures are urged,‡ which speak of God's proving the children of Israel when in the wilderness, and in their own land, whether they would walk in his statutes, and keep his commandments, or no; such as Exod. xvi. 4, xx. 20; Deut. viii. 2, and xiii. 3; Judg. ii. 21, 22, and iii. 1, 4. It ought to be observed, that these people were under a *theocracy*, or the immediate government of God as their King, who gave them laws, according to which they should act; to which they readily promised a cheerful and universal obedience; on condition of which obedience, they were to enjoy and continue in their enjoyment of the land of Canaan. Therefore, before they entered into the land, and when in it, God was pleased to try them, sometimes in one way, and sometimes in another, whether they would yield that obedience to his commands which he required, and abide by the promises which they themselves had made, or no; all which he did not for his own sake, who knows all things, but that their obedience or disobedience might be made manifest, and he be justified in all his dealings with them. This trial of their obedience was not in order to their salvation in another world, but to their temporal good in this; for such of them as were saved with an everlasting salvation, were saved not by their obedience to the commands of God, but by the grace of the Lord Jesus Christ. Besides, the scriptures produced, speak only of the people of Israel, and of what was their state and case as a politic body, under the immediate government of God, in a certain period of time; and not of all mankind; and so fall abundantly short of proving that the state of man in this world, is such a state of probation as before described.

2. This is attempted§ to be proved from all those places in which God is said to try men, their works and graces, by afflictions, persecutions, temptations, and the like; as 1 Cor. iii. 13; 2 Cor. viii. 2; 1 Pet. i. 7, and iv. 12; Jam. i. 3; Rev. ii. 10, and iii. 10; Psal. lxvi. 10; Dan. xi. 35, and xii. 10; Zech. xiii. 9. What I have said in answer to the first query, is a sufficient reply to what is alleged from these passages; since these only speak of the saints, and of the trial of their grace, who only have grace to be tried, and that not in order to fix and settle the affair of their salvation; nor are these trials mere experiments of the truth and constancy of their graces; but are also designed for the further exercise and increase of them; the issue of which is their own spiritual good, and God's glory. Hence it must follow that these scriptures are insufficient proofs of every man's being in a state of probation, and in order to everlasting happiness or misery.

3. This is said‖ to be evident from all the promises and threats recorded in the Scripture, to engage all men to repent, and turn to God; for it is added, no such thing is or can

---

* Page 235; ed. 2. 230. † Whitby p. 305, 314; ed. 2. 297, 306. ‡ Whitby, p. 305, 314; ed. 2. 297, 306. § Ibid. p. 306; ed. 2. 298. ‖ Ibid. p. 306; ed. 2. 298.

reasonably be offered to them who are already in a fixed state either of happiness or misery. To which I reply, that the promises and threats recorded in the Scripture, which relate to men's spiritual and eternal good, may be reduced to and comprehended in these words, *He that believeth, and is baptized, shall be saved; he that believeth not, shall be damned;* which was the substance of the gospel ministry the apostles had in commission from Christ to fulfil, and which might be exercised fully and thoroughly, supposing a fixed state of happiness or misery; since such a ministry might be, and is used, through the grace of God, to bring those who are designed for happiness, into a state of grace meet for the same; and to leave others inexcusable, to discover the more the corruption and vitiosity of their nature, and so to justify the righteous proceedings of God against them.

4. This is argued for * from all the exhortations of the holy Scripture to men to watch and pray, that they enter not and are not led into temptation, and from such scriptures which suppose men to be in danger by temptation; the passages referred to are, Matt. vi. 13, and xxvi. 41; Luke viii. 13; 1 Thess. iii. 5; which only regard the saints, or such who profess to be so, and not all mankind. Besides, if God has put all men into a state of probation, and this designed by temptation, how should any watch and pray not to enter or be led into it? Moreover, this state of probation, is either a good one, or a bad one; if a good one, why should men watch and pray against it? if a bad one, can it be reasonably supposed, that God has put men into it, in order to their everlasting good? and why then should it be contended for?

5. This is said to be evident † from the temptations of Satan, who *goes about continually seeking whom he may devour;* and it is added, to what end should he tempt, or endeavour to destroy the elect, or strive to hinder the progress of the gospel, or the conversion of any man; when supposing a fixed state by the decrees of God, and a divine unfrustrable operation on the hearts of men, he must know that his labour will certainly be in vain? to which I answer, that Satan has not the book of life in his keeping; nor does he know who are and who are not the elect of God, until this appears by the unfrustrable operation of God's grace on their hearts, and it may be, not even then: so that it is no wonder that he tempts, strives, and endeavours to hinder the success of the gospel in their conversion, and to destroy them; and when he does know who they are, endeavours to distress them by his temptations, though he cannot destroy; and in ten thousand instances will show his malice, when he cannot show his power. Besides, the text referred to in 1 Pet. v. 8, carries in the sense of it the doctrine of a fixed state; when it supposes that there are some whom Satan may devour, and leaves a plain intimation that there are ohers whom he may not and cannot devour;

who are the sheep of Christ, and being in his hands, neither man nor devil will ever be able to pluck from thence. This is the sum of the proof offered in favour of this notion, by a celebrated writer, which how pertinent it is, must be left to the consideration of others.

III. What reason there is to conclude that the state of man in this world is not such a state.

1. Angels and man both, have been in a state of probation already, in which their free-will, and power to obey the commands of God, have been sufficiently tried; which trial has issued in the fall and ruin of a large number of angels, and of the whole race of mankind: and therefore it is not reasonable to suppose that God would put man into such a state again; but rather provide in another way for the good of those he designed to bring to everlasting happiness.

2. If men were in a state of probation, they ought to be on equal ground, enjoying equal privileges and advantages; whereas this is not the case; some have only the dim light and weak law of nature, whilst others enjoy the gospel revelation; and of these some have larger, and others lesser, means of grace, light, and knowledge; some have the grace of God itself bestowed upon them, others have it not. Now were all men in such a state of probation as is pleaded for, is it reasonable to suppose that there would be such an inequality among them?

3. This state of probation, which renders salvation precarious and uncertain, is contrary to God's foreknowledge and decree of election; for God, according to his foreknowledge, has chosen and predestinated a certain number of men to eternal life and salvation, by which their state is fixed, and their salvation sure, for *the purpose of God according to election* shall *stand. Whom he did foreknow, he also did predestinate; whom he did predestinate, them he also called; and whom he called, them he also justified; and whom he justified, them he also glorified.* Rom. ix. 11, and viii. 29, 30.

4. This notion puts man's salvation on the foot of his obedience and works, contrary to the Scriptures, to the merits of Christ, and to the grace of God; it ascribes more to the free-will of man than to the free grace of God, and lays a foundation for boasting in the creature.

5. Such a state of probation is contrary to all those scriptures which represent the saints to be now in a saved state, and as having everlasting life; such as Eph. ii. 8, John v. 24, and vi. 47.

In a word, it destroys the doctrine of assurance, and leaves the saints themselves in a most uncomfortable condition, because it leaves them in a most precarious, unsettled, yea, dangerous one.

SECTION V

I have set before you life and death, blessing and cursing; therefore choose life, that both thou and thy seed may live.—Deut. xxx. 19.

THESE words are frequently made use of

---

* Whitby, p. 306; ed. 2. 298.

† Ibid. p. 307; ed. 2. 299.

by the patrons of* free-will, in favour of it, and its power, to do that which is spiritually good. I shall briefly consider this so-much-controverted subject, by considering the following things:

I. What free-will is, or what is the nature of the liberty of the human will.

1. The will of man, though it is free, yet not independently and absolutely so; it is dependent on God, both in its being and acting; it is subject to his authority and command, and controllable by his power. *The King's heart*,† and so every other man's, *is in the hand of the Lord: as the rivers of waters, he turneth it whithersoever he will.* The will of God is only free in this sense; he is not subject to a superior being, and therefore acts without control, according to his will, in the armies of the heavens, and among the inhabitants of the earth: hence those great swelling words of vanity, αὐτεξούσιον, *liberum arbitrium*, which carry in them the sense of self-sufficiency, despotic, arbitrary liberty, are improperly given to the human will, though agreeable enough to the language of some free-willers; such as Pharaoh, who said, *Who is the Lord that I should obey his voice, to let Israel go?‡ I know not the Lord, neither will I let Israel go.* Others have said, *Our lips are our own; who is Lord over us?§*

2. The liberty of the will does not consist in an indifference to good and evil, or in an indetermination to either; otherwise the will of no being would be free; for God, as he is essentially and naturally good, his will is determined only to that which is so; nor does he nor can he do anything evil; and yet in all he does, acts with the utmost freedom and liberty of his will. The will of the good angels, though in their state of probation, was left mutable and liable to change; yet in their confirmed state, is impeccable, wholly turned unto and bent upon that which is good, and yet all the services they perform to God and man, are done with the greatest readiness, cheerfulness, and willingness, without any force or compulsion. The will of the devil is biassed only to that which is evil, without the least inclination to that which is good; and yet moves freely in the highest acts of sin and malice. The will of man, considered in every state he has been, is, or shall be in, is determined to good or evil, and does not stand in *equilibrio*, in an indifference to either. The will of man, in a state of innocence, was indeed mutable, and capable of being wrought upon and inclined to evil, as the event shows; yet during that state, was entirely bent on that which is good, and acted freely, and without any co-action, in obedience to the commands of God. The will of man, in his fallen state, is wholly addicted to sinful lusts, and in the fulfilling of them takes the utmost delight and pleasure. Man, in his regenerate state, though he is inclined both to good and evil, which arises from the two different principles of corruption and grace in him; yet both move freely, though determined to their several objects. The flesh, or corrupt part, is solely determined to that which is evil; grace, or the new creature, to that which is spiritually good; so that with the flesh, the regenerate man serves the law of sin, and with his mind the law of God. The will of the glorified saints in heaven is wholly given up to spiritual and divine things, nor can it be moved to that which is sinful; and yet as they serve the Lord constantly, so with all freedom and liberty. Consider, therefore, the will in every rank of beings, its liberty does not consist in an indifference or indetermination to good and evil.

3. The liberty of the will is consistent with some kind of necessity. God necessarily, and yet freely, hates that which is evil, and loves that which is good. Christ, as man, was under some kind of necessity of fulfilling all righteousness, and yet performed it voluntarily. The will of man is free from a physical or natural necessity; it does not act and move by a necessity of nature, as many creatures do. So the sun, moon, and stars, move in their course; fire, by a physical necessity, burns; light things ascend upwards, and heavy bodies move downwards. Moreover, it is free from a necessity of coaction or force; the will cannot be forced; nor is it even by the powerful, efficacious, and unfrustrable operation of God's grace in conversion; for though before, it is unwilling to submit to Christ, and his way of salvation, yet it is made willing in the day of his power, without offering the least violence to it; God working upon it, as Austin says, *cum suavi omnipotentia et omnipotenti suavitate*, with a sweet omnipotence, and an omnipotent sweetness: but then the will of man is not free from a necessity of obligation; it is bound to act in obedience to the divine will; though it is free, it is not free to act at pleasure, without control; though the sinful, corrupt will of man, breaks out in despite of the laws of God, and chooses its own ways, and delights in its abominations; yet this is not properly liberty, but licentiousness. And though a good man looks upon himself under a necessary obligation to act agreeable to the will of God, yet this necessity is not contrary to the liberty of his will; for he *delights in the law of God after the inner man.* Moreover, there is a kind of necessity which the school-men call a necessity of immutability; which respects the divine decrees, and their necessary, unchangeable, and certain events, that is consistent with the liberty of man's will: for though the decrees of God are necessarily fulfilled, yet these do not infringe nor hinder the liberty of the creature in acting; for instance, the selling of Joseph to the Ishmaelites, by whom he was brought to Egypt, was according to the decree

---

* Erasmus in Luther. de Servo Arbitr. c. 95 and 97, pp. 145, 148; Curcellæi Institut. Rel. Christian. l. 6, c. 13, sect. 2, p. 400; Limborch. Theolog. Christ. l. 4, c. 13, sect. 22, p. 376,

Whitby, pp. 317. 318; ed. 2. 309, 310.
† Prov. xxi. 1.   ‡ Exod. v. 2.
§ Psalm. xii. 4.

and purpose of God, who sent him thither, and designed it for the good of others, and yet his brethren in the whole of that affair, acted with the utmost deliberation, choice, and freedom of their wills imaginable. Nothing was more peremptorily decreed and determined by God than the crucifixion of Christ, and yet men never acted more freely, as well as more wickedly, than the Jews did in all the parts and circumstances of that tragical scene. So that the liberty of the will is consistent with some kind of necessity, yea, even with some kind of servitude. A servant may serve his master freely and voluntarily, as the Hebrew servant who was unwilling to part from his master when his time of servitude was expired. A wicked man, who commits sin, gives up himself wholly to it, is a servant of it, yet acts freely in all his shameful and sinful services; even at the same time he is a slave to those lusts and pleasures he chooses and delights in; which made Luther call free-will *servum arbitrium*.

4. The consideration of the will of man in the several states of innocence, the fall, regeneration, and glorification, serves much to lead us into the true nature and notion of the liberty and power of it. Man, in his state of innocence, had both a power and will to do that which was naturally and morally good; though his will was left mutable, and so through temptation might be inclined to evil, at which door came in the sin and fall of man. Man, in his fallen state, is wholly under the power and dominion of sin, is a captive under it, and a slave unto it, and has neither a power nor will to that which is spiritually good. Man, in a state of regeneration, is freed from the dominion of sin, though not from the being of it; his will is sweetly and powerfully wrought upon, and inclined to what is spiritually good, though he finds a body of sin and death about him, which much distresses and hinders him in the performance of it. The saints in heaven are freed both from the being and dominion of sin; and as they have a will solely inclined, so they have full power, to serve the Lord without ceasing.

5. The distinction between the natural and moral liberty of the will is of great service in this controversy;* though these two are artfully confounded together; and because the one is denied by us, it is concluded that the other is also; whereas we affirm, that the natural liberty of the will is essential to it, and always abides with it in every action and in every state of life. A wicked man, in the highest degree of servitude to sin, his will acts as freely in this state of bondage as Adam's will did in obedience to God, in a state of innocence; but the moral liberty of the will is not essential to it, though it adds to the glory and excellency of it; and therefore may and may not be with it, without any violation to, or destruction of, the natural liberty of the will. The moral liberty of the will to that which is good was with Adam in a state of innocence; this was lost by the fall; hence man in a state of corruption and unregeneracy is destitute of it; in the regenerate state it is implanted in the will by the Spirit and grace of God, and in the state of glorification will be in its full perfection; so that the controversy ought to be not about the natural but moral liberty of the will, and not so much about free-will itself, as the strength and power of it; which leads me to the consideration of the next inquiry, which is,

II. What is the strength and power of man's free-will; or what it is that the will of man itself can will or nill, choose or refuse, effect and perform.

1. It will be allowed that the human will has a power and liberty of acting in things natural, or in things respecting the natural and animal life; such as eating, drinking, sitting, standing, rising, walking, &c. The external parts, actions, and motions of the body, generally speaking, are subject to, and controllable by the will; though the internal parts, motions, and actions of it, are not so, such as digestion of food, secretion of it to various purposes and uses, nutrition and accretion of the several parts of the body, circulation of the blood, &c., all which are performed without the consent of the will.

2. The will of man has a liberty and power of acting in things civil, such as relate to the good of societies, in kingdoms, cities, towns, and families; as obedience to magistrates, lawful marriage, education of children, cultivation of arts and sciences, exercise and improvement of trades and manufactures, and every thing else that contributes to the good, pleasure, and advantage of civil life.

3. Man has also a power of performing the external parts of religion, such as praying, singing the praise of God, reading the scriptures, hearing the word of God, and attending on all public ordinances. So Herod heard John gladly, and did many things in a religious way, externally. Men may also give to every one their own, do justice between man and man, love such as love them, live inoffensively in the world, appear outwardly righteous before men, and do many things which have the show of moral good, as did the heathen and publicans, and the apostle Paul before conversion.

4. Man has neither will nor power to act of himself in things spiritually good, or in such as relate to his spiritual and eternal welfare; as conversion, regeneration, faith, repentance, and the like. Conversion is not the work of a creature, but of God, even a work of his almighty power; by which men are turned from sin and Satan to him, are delivered from the power of darkness, and translated into the kingdom of his dear Son. Regeneration, or a being born again, is expressly denied to be of the will of the flesh, or of the will of man, and is ascribed to God himself. All men have not faith in Christ; and such who have it, have it not of themselves; it is the gift of God, the operation of his Spirit, the fruit and effect of electing and efficacious grace. Evan-

---

* Vide Gale's Court of the Gentiles, part iv. b. 3, c. 1, sect. 4, pp. 13, 14.

gelical repentance, which is unto life, is not in the power of man; man, in a state of nature, has no true sense of his sins; nor will any means of themselves bring him to repentance for them, without the efficacious grace of God. True evangelical repentance is God's free-grace gift.

5. That there is no power naturally in the will of man, to will, choose, and effect things spiritually good, does not only appear from all experience of human nature, but also from all those scriptures which represent men as polluted, wholly carnal, given up to sin, slaves unto it, and dead in it; and not only impotent unto, but under an impossibility to do that which is good; and from all those scriptures which declare the understanding, judgment, and affections, to be corrupt, by which the will is greatly influenced and directed; and from all such scriptures which intimate that every good gift and spiritual blessing come from God, and that the saints themselves only will and act through the power, and under the influence of the grace of God, *who works in them both to will and to do of his good pleasure.* I proceed,

III. To inquire whether the words of the text under consideration assert the power and liberty of the will of man in choosing that which is spiritually good. To which I answer,

1. Supposing what is here proposed to be chosen is spiritually good, and what to be refused is spiritually evil; it does not follow from hence that man has a power to choose the one and refuse the other; for, as Luther* says, "The words are imperative, they assert nothing but what ought to be done; for Moses does not say, thou hast a power of choosing, but choose, keep, do. He delivers precepts of doing, but does not describe the power of man."

2. Life and death, blessing and cursing, are to be taken in a civil sense, and design the external dispensations of God's providence, with respect to temporal good or evil, which should befal the people of Israel, according to their civil behaviour and conduct. That people were under the immediate government of God; he was their political king and head. Moses, from him, gave a system of laws to them as a body politic; according to their obedience to which laws, they and their seed were to live and dwell in and enjoy all the temporal blessings of the land of Canaan, as appears from ver. 16, 20; but if they disobeyed, they were to expect cursing and death, captivity and the sword, and not prolong their days in the land they were going to possess, as is evident from ver. 17, 18. Therefore Moses advises them to choose life, that is, to behave according to those laws given them as a commonwealth; that so they, under the happy government they were, might comfortably live, and they and their posterity enjoy all the blessings of a civil life in the land of promise. What comes

nearer to such a case, and may serve to illustrate it, is as if a person should represent the wholesome constitution laws of Great Britain, preserved under the government of his majesty king George, with all the consequent blessings and happiness thereof, and also the sad and miserable condition it would be in under a popish Pretender; and then observe that it would be most desirable, advisable, and eligible peaceably to continue under the government of the one, than to receive the yoke of the other. To choose the one is to choose liberty and property, blessing and life, and everything that is valuable, in a civil sense; to choose the other, is to choose slavery and arbitrary power, cursing and death, and everything that is miserable and destructive. Now it is allowed that man has a power of willing and nilling, choosing and refusing, acting and not acting, in things of a civil nature; therefore these words can be of no service, nor ought they to have a place or concern in the controversy about the power and liberty of the will in things spiritual.

SECTION VI

O that they were wise, that they understood this, that they would consider their latter end.—Deut. xxxii. 29.

THESE words were made use of to contradict the doctrines of absolute election, particular redemption, and unfrustrable grace in conversion; it is intimated,† that, on supposition of these doctrines, they would represent the God of sincerity and truth as full of guile and hypocrisy, when he earnestly wishes and desires the welfare of men, and that they have spiritual wisdom; and yet he himself has decreed to leave them without a Saviour, and without means of being spiritually wise; which is all one as though he had passionately wished they had been of the number of his elect, when he himself, by an absolute decree from all eternity, had excluded them out of that number. In answer to which, let it be observed,

I. That it ought to be proved that God does passionately wish the spiritual and eternal welfare of all mankind; or desires that every individual of human nature might have spiritual wisdom to know his spiritual estate, and consider his latter end; since it is evident that he does not afford to every son of Adam the means of being spiritually wise, and it is certain that these words to not express such an universal wish; for they only regard a part of mankind, either the people of Israel, or the adversaries of Israel, as will be seen hereafter; and therefore, being spoken only of some, and not of every individual of men, cannot militate against the election and redemption of some only.

II. It ought to be proved that God wishes or desires the spiritual welfare of, or spiritual wisdom for any, but those whom he has cho-

---

* *Verba adducta sunt imperativa; nihil dicunt, nisi quid fieri debeat; neque enim Moses dicit, eligendi habes vim, vel virtutem; sed elige, serva, fac. Praecepta faciendi tradit, non autem describit hominis facultatem.*—Luther, de serv. arbitr. c. 97, p. 148.   † Whitby, p. 181, 222, 223; ed. 2. 177, 216, 217.

sen to eternal life, whom Christ has redeemed by his blood, and to whom the Spirit of wisdom and revelation in the knowledge of themselves and Christ is given ; or in other words, that God wishes and desires the spiritual welfare of such, and spiritual wisdom for such, who, in the event, are not eternally saved.

III. It ought to be considered whether these words regard the spiritual welfare of any, or contain in them a wish for wisdom and understanding in spiritual things ; or rather, whether they do not only regard things temporal, and the knowledge of them, as will quickly be made to appear.

IV. Supposing the words to contain a wish for wisdom and understanding in spiritual things, such a wish must be ascribed to God, not properly, but by an anthropopathy, or after the manner of men ; wishes and velleities are improperly, or in a figurative way, attributed to God ; nor do they suppose any imperfection in him, nor sufficiency in his creatures ; nor do such necessarily imply that it is his will to give that wisdom he wishes for ; nor do they lay him under obligation even to afford the means of spiritual wisdom ; but as a man wishes for that which is grateful and agreeable to him, so when God wishes for spiritual wisdom in men, it only implies that such wisdom in them would be well-pleasing to him. Besides, such a mode of speaking may be used either by way of complaint of ignorance, or as expressing pity for it, or as upbraiding with it ; and that in order either to bring to a sense of it, and encourage to apply to him for wisdom, who gives it liberally, or to leave inexcusable. But,

V. The words are not delivered in the form of a wish, but are an hypothetical proposition. The Hebrew word לו signifies *if**, and the whole verse should be rendered thus :—*If they were wise, they would understand this, they would consider their latter end ;* and supposing them to be understood in a spiritual sense, the meaning is, had they been wise to do good, as they are to do evil, they would have understood the things that belong to their spiritual peace and welfare, and would have seriously considered the last issue and end of all things, and themselves ; but they are not wise in things divine and spiritual, and therefore have no understanding of them ; nor do they consider the end of their sinful actions ; nor the end of their days, how short it is, how nigh at hand ; nor that awful judgment that will follow after death ; nor their final doom, nor whither they shall go, to heaven or hell. Though,

VI. After all, the words are to be understood of things temporal, and not of what concerns the spiritual and eternal welfare of any. Instances of God's goodness to the

people of Israel are at large recited in ver. 7—14. After that, their many sins against God and great ingratitude to him are mentioned in ver. 15—18, which drew God's resentment and indignation against them, expressed in threatenings of many severe judgments, ver. 19—25, which he would have executed on them, but that he *feared the wrath of the enemy, lest their adversaries should behave themselves strangely, and lest they should say, Our hand is high, and the Lord hath not done all this* (ver. 27), for he knew that *they were a nation void of counsel : neither was there any understanding in them* (ver. 28), for *if they* had been *wise, they would have understood this,* that the destruction of the people of Israel was of God, and not of them ; for otherwise,† *how should one chase a thousand,* that is, one *Gentile* a thousand *Israelites ; and two put ten thousand to flight, except their Rock had sold them, and the Lord had shut them up ?* (ver. 30.) They would also have considered their own end, or what must befal them in length of time ; that as God had cut off and destroyed his people Israel for their sins, so they might expect the same destruction for iniquities of a like kind. Now since this is the plain and obvious sense of the words, they cannot be used with any propriety in the controversy about the doctrines of distinguishing grace.

SECTION VII

O that my people had hearkened unto me, and Israel had walked in my ways ; I should soon have subdued their enemies, and turned my hand against their adversaries.—Psalm lxxxi. 13, 14.

THIS passage is produced by the Remonstrants, to prove the resistibility of the grace of God in conversion ;‡ in favour of the defectibility of the saints ; and by a late writer,§ as irreconcilable with God's decrees of election and reprobation, and the doctrine of particular redemption ; and as proving that men have a sufficiency of ability to do what God wishes they would do. But let it be considered,

I. That, admitting the words contain a wish and desire of God for the spiritual welfare and conversion of men, such a wish can only be ascribed to him in a figurative sense, as has been observed under the preceding section. Wishing cannot be attributed to God in such sense as it is to man, who often wishes for that which is not in his power to perform, and therefore desires it to be done by another, which cannot be said of God without impeaching his omnipotence. When God is said to wish for and desire, as we will suppose here, the conversion and obedience of men, it only

---

* The three Targums of Onkelos, Jonathan, and Jerusalem, render it by אין, if ; as do also R. Sol. Jarchi, R. Aben Ezra, and R. Levi ben Gersom, in loc. So Noldius in Concord. partic. Ebr, Chal. p. 503, translates the words, *Si saparent-intelligerent ista ;* so the Arabic and Syriac versions. The Septuagint seems to have read לא for

לו, since they render them οὐκ ἐφράνησαν συ ιέναι, *they were not wise to understand:* so the Samaritan version.

† Vid. Vatablum in loc.   ‡ In Coll. Hag. art. iii. iv. p. 216, 219 ; art. v. p. 15, ed. Bert.   § Whitby, p. 77, 181, 222 ; ed 2. 76, 177, 216.

implies that these would be grateful and well-pleasing to him; and not that either is in the power of men to convert themselves, and obey the commands of God, or that it is the determining will of God that every individual of mankind should be converted and obey his commands in a way acceptable to him; for then every man would be converted and obey: therefore, such a wish, suppose it as universal and extensive as you please, does not militate against the distinguishing grace of God, in choosing, redeeming, and calling some only; since such a wish only declares what God approves of, and not what he determines shall be.

II. The wish for the spiritual welfare of the persons here mentioned, supposing it to be one, is only for the people of Israel, God's professing people, and whom he calls *my people*, and not all mankind, or every individual son of Adam, as it ought to have been, could it be thought to militate against the election, redemption, and effectual vocation of some particular persons only; and besides, it would be difficult to prove that these persons spoken of, notwithstanding all their perverseness, rebellion, and misconduct, were not chosen of God, redeemed by Christ, and savingly wrought upon by the power of divine grace, and finally saved.

III. The words, if duly examined, will appear not to contain any wish at all, but an hypothesis, or supposition; being to be read thus, If my people had hearkened unto me, and Israel had walked in my ways, I should, &c.   R. Sol. Jarchi interprets לו by אם, and R. Aben Ezra by אילו, and the Septuagint by εἰ; all which signify *if*: so the Syriac, Arabic, Ethiopic, Vulgate Latin, Junius, and Tremellius, read the words; therefore, as the* Contra-Remonstrants have rightly observed, it does not follow from hence, that these people could obey the commands of God; or that the performance of obedience depended on their will; no more than it would follow from such a proposition, if a man keeps the law of God perfectly, he shall be justified by it: therefore it is in the power of man to keep the law of God perfectly; or from this, if a man believes he shall be saved; therefore, faith depends on man's will, or is in man's power.   Besides,

IV. The words are not to be understood of the internal work of grace and conversion, and of spiritual and evangelical obedience springing from it, which would have been attended with spiritual and eternal blessings; but of an external obedience to God's commands, which would have been followed with temporal favours; such as subduing their enemies under them, feeding them with the finest of the wheat, and satisfying them with honey out of the rock; in the same sense are we to understand the words in Isa. xlviii. 18, which usually go in company with these under examination, and are also to be read conditionally; *If thou hadst hearkened to my commandments, then had thy peace been as a*

river; as they are by the Targum, the Septuagint, and Arabic versions, by R. David Kimchi, Junius, and Tremellius; and neither the one nor the other regard the spiritual, but temporal welfare of God's people Israel; nor do they contain a wish for that, but a declaration or an asseveration of it, on condition of their obedience to God's commands.   The passage in Hos. xi. 8, which is sometimes joined with this, is a human way of speaking, as R. Aben Ezra on the place observes; and expresses God's compassionate concern for the temporal welfare of Ephraim and Israel, and not transports of affection, and desire after the spiritual welfare of any, much less of all mankind.

SECTION VIII

For the rod of the wicked shall not rest upon the lot of the righteous, lest the righteous put forth their hands unto iniquity.—Psalm cxxv. 3.

THESE words are made use of† to prove, that " saints, or true believers, or men once truly good, may cease to be so: for it is said, that they seem plainly to insinuate, that great and long impressions might have this effect upon them; and surely that which God is thus careful to prevent, might possibly befal the righteous: there being no need of care to prevent that which he hath absolutely engaged to preserve them from."   Strange ! seeing,

I. The doctrine of the saints' final perseverance is so plainly intimated in the two preceding verses of this psalm: *They that trust in the Lord shall be as mount Zion, which cannot be removed, but abideth for ever.   As the mountains are round about Jerusalem, so the Lord is round about his people, from henceforth even for ever.*   If they that trust in the Lord, who are saints, true believers, men truly good, are as mount Zion; then they cannot be removed neither from the heart of God, nor out of the hands of Christ; but will abide there for ever, and consequently cannot cease to be what they are.   If, as the mountains are round about Jerusalem, so the Lord is round about the same persons before described, who are his people, and that even for ever; how is it possible that they should ever perish?

II. These words are strictly connected with the former, and express a certain effect that should surely follow from the safe state and happy situation of such who trust in the Lord, כי *for*, or *because* it is so and so with them; *therefore the rod of the wicked*, the tyrannical government, oppressions and persecutions of wicked men, to which the saints are often subject, *shall not rest*, always continue and abide, *upon the lot*, not the *back*, as Dr. Whitby cites the words, *of the righteous;* meaning either their persons or their goods; *lest the righteous*, who are made so by the righteousness of Christ, *put forth their hands unto iniquity;* that is, lest through the op-

---

* In Coll. Hag. art. iii. iv. p. 232.   † Whitby, p. 436; ed. 2. 425.

pressions of wicked men, the instigation of Satan, and their own hearts, they should be moved to that which would dishonour God, bring a reproach on his ways, and wound their own souls; all which they may do, and yet not cease to be saints, true, believers, truly good men; as the instances of David, Peter, and others, fully make appear. The righteous may put forth their hands unto iniquity, and fall into great sins, and yet not totally fall away, or so fall as to be lost and perish: total apostacy is not intended by putting forth their hands unto iniquity.

III. It is stranger still, that the care of God to prevent the righteous putting forth their hands unto iniquity, should be improved into an argument against their perseverance, and in favour of their apostacy. It will be readily allowed, that what God is thus careful to prevent, even suppose a total apostacy was meant, might possibly befal the righteous, should they be left to themselves, destitute of the powerful protection of God; nor would there be a possibility of its being otherwise; but since the care and power of God are so greatly employed about their preservation, it is impossible that it should befal them.

IV. It is an egregious mistake to say, that "there is no need of care to prevent that which he (God) absolutely hath engaged to preserve them from;" since God's engagement to preserve his people, is the true reason of the employment of his care about them; which is necessary to prevent their doing the iniquity, which otherwise would be done by them: God having absolutely resolved, determined, and engaged, that those that trust in him should not be removed, but abide for ever; therefore he will be round about them for ever, and take care of them, that nothing hurt or destroy them; he will keep them by his power through faith unto salvation.

SECTION IX

The Lord is good to all, and his tender mercies are over all his works.—Psalm cxlv. 9.

THE doctrines of election and reprobation, and of particular redemption, are represented as contrary to the general mercy and goodness of God expressed in this passage: with a view to these doctrines, it is asked by one writer,[*] "Why is it said, that *his tender mercies are over all his works*, if they are so restrained from his most noble creatures?" And it is observed by another[†], "That it should not be said, *his tender mercies are over all his works*: but his cruelties are over all his works." To which I reply,

I. That the said doctrines do not restrain the tender mercies of God in a providential way, of which this text only speaks, as will be shown hereafter, from any of his creatures; no, not even from the non-elect, or those who have no share in the special grace and favour of God, and who are not eventually saved;

though these should not be reckoned God's *most noble creatures*:[‡] for surely they are not more noble than the elect of God, or those who are saved with an everlasting salvation; or more noble than the angels, who stand, and never left their first estate in which they were created. Admitting also that these doctrines carried in them ideas of cruelty, and want of compassion in God to those who are rejected by him, and excluded from redemption by Christ; yet it should not be concluded from hence, that the cruelties of God are over *all* his works; since, according to the known tenor of these doctrines, some of God's creatures are chosen by him to eternal life, redeemed by the blood of Christ, and shall be certainly and eternally saved.

II. The said doctrines are not expressive of cruelty in God to mankind, nor inconsistent with his goodness and mercy; nor do they represent God less good, or less merciful, than the doctrines of conditional election and universal redemption do; nay, they represent him more merciful than these do, since they ascertain the salvation of some, whereas these leave the salvation of every man precarious and uncertain, if not impossible, depending upon the mutable will of the creature.

III. These words are to be understood not of special mercies, or saving benefits, bestowed by God upon any of his creatures; but of his providential goodness, which extends to them all, even to the brutal world, to all irrational as well as rational creatures, as appears from ver. 15, 16, compared with Psalm cxlvii. 8, 9, who have no concern in election and redemption; so that if these words should be so understood, as to relate to the blessings of spiritual and eternal salvation, they would prove too much, more than our opponents desire; namely, that these blessings are provided for, and extend unto irrational creatures, yea, even to all the works of God, of every kind and sort. Therefore,

IV. The said doctrines are not at all repugnant to these universal expressions of God's goodness and mercy; since the non-elect, or such who have no saving benefit by the death of Christ, have a share in the providential goodness and tender mercies of God; who *makes his sun to rise on the evil and on the good, and sendeth rain on the just and on the unjust, and is kind to the unthankful and to the evil*: nay, oftentimes the worst of men have the greatest share of the good things of this world; *their eyes stand out with fatness, and they have more than heart could wish*: their temporal mercies are oftentimes larger than those that the dear children of God enjoy; and therefore are not what they have in common with the brutes that perish;[§] God takes more care of them than of oxen, or the fowls of the air, in a providential way; though they *despise the riches of his goodness and forbearance, and long-suffering*; *not knowing that the goodness of God leadeth them to re-*

---

* Whitby, p. 159; ed. 2, 155.   † Curcellæ Relig. Christ. Inst. l. 6, c. 6, sect. 8, p. 370.

‡ Whitby, p. 159, 177; ed. 2. 155, 173.
§ Vid. Whitby, p. 159; ed. 2. 155.

pentance ; but after their *hardness and impenitent heart, treasure up unto* themselves *wrath against the day of wrath, and revelation of the righteous judgment of God.*

SECTION X.

How long, ye simple ones, will ye love simplicity? Turn ye at my reproof, &c.—Prov. i. 22—30.

THESE are the words of Christ, who, under the name of *Wisdom*, is represented crying *without*, and uttering his *voice in the city, in the streets, in the chief place of concourse, in the opening of the gates;* which is to be understood of the public preaching of the word, either by Christ himself, or by his ministers. What is advanced from these passages in favour of any part of the Arminian scheme, will be considered in the following order :

I. It is said,* that from hence " it is very evident, that it was primarily the counsel and will of God, that even they who would not turn, would not repent and accept of salvation, should believe and come to repentance, and be made partakers of it : " in which I observe,

1. That this writer, with the Remonstrants, supposes an antecedent and consequent will in God, when he says, that it was *primarily* the counsel and will of God, &c., as if what was once the will of God is not now his will ; which is contrary to the immutability of his nature and will ; who *is in one mind; and who can turn him? and what his soul desireth, even that he doth.* What is once his will, is always so; nor can it be made null and void by the will of man.

2. That he mistakes the counsel of God here, as also in Luke vii. 30, for the intentional will of God, respecting the faith, repentance, and salvation of persons; when it designs in both places, God's will of command and approbation ; and is expressive, not of what God intended and designed concerning these persons; but of what was their duty, and which would be grateful to him, and approved of by him : for had it been his intentional determining will that these persons, who rejected and despised his counsel, should believe, repent, and be saved, they would have believed, repented, and been made partakers of salvation; for *who hath resisted his will?*

II. It is intimated from hence, that man does not lie under a disability to believe, repent, and turn to God; and it is asked,† "To what purpose did wisdom say to them, who were thus disabled, *Turn you at my reproof?* Or could she, without insulting over the misery of fallen man, thus laugh at the calamity they could never prevent?" To which I reply,

1. That the exhortation, *Turn ye at my reproof,* is not to repentance and conversion, but to an attendance to the external ministry of the word. *Reproof* is the same with *counsel*, in ver. 25, 30, where they are joined to-

gether, and put for each other, and design the word preached, which reproves of sin, righteousness, and judgment; and it is not turning *at*, but *to* this reproof, which is exhorted to; for the תשבו לתוכחתי, should not be rendered, *turn ye at*, but *to my reproof;* so Arias Montanus, Mercerus, Gejerus, Junius, and Tremellius, read them ; and the meaning is either as the Targum interprets them תחפנון למכסנותי, *turn your face to my reproof*, and not your backs; or as Aben Ezra, *turn ye*, that is, your ears, *to hear my reproof;* and do not pull away the shoulder, or stop your ears. Now it is certain, that man does not lie under a disability to turn his face and ears to the external ministry of the word; though so depraved are the inclinations and will of man, and such a lover is he of simplicity and scorning, and such a hater of true, useful, and spiritual knowledge, that he had rather hear an idle story told, or the Scriptures burlesqued, than an honest, serious sermon, which is reproving, searching, and informing.

2. The calamity of these persons did not arise from a disability to do what they were exhorted to, but was owing to a neglect of what they might have done : for they could have attended the ministry of the word, observed ordinances, and turned their faces and ears to the reproof of Wisdom; but they hated knowledge, and the means of it; they despised sermons, laughed at ordinances, and treated with the utmost contempt every admonition, counsel, and reproof; *therefore they did eat of the fruit of their own ways,* and were *filled with their own devices,* ver. 31; there was a just retaliation made to them; they were paid in their own way; it was a righteous thing with Wisdom, and no insult on their misery, to laugh at their calamity, and mock when their fear came upon them.

III. This passage is produced in favour of sufficient grace given to men, to repent, believe, and convert themselves ;‡ and to prove that God's calls, invitations, and messages, by his prophets, are sufficient inducements to procure reformation and repentance. To which I answer,

1. It is plain that the persons here spoken of, called unto, exhorted, and threatened, had not sufficient grace; since they are represented as fools, scorners, lovers of folly, haters of knowledge; who despised the counsel of Wisdom, and rejected her reproof.

2. Nor should this be concluded from the encouragement that Wisdom gives, to *turn* to her *reproof;* saying, *Behold, I will pour out my spirit unto you;* since this is not to be understood of the Holy Ghost, and of the dispensation of his extraordinary gifts, or of saving grace; for when he is promised in either of these senses, it is expressed by a different phrase than what is here used; he is promised to be *poured out upon*, and not as here, *unto* the sons of men: see Isa. xliv. 3 ; Ezek. xxxix. 29 ; Joel ii. 28. I observe that Dr. Whitby, whenever he cites the passage

---

* Whitby, p. 72 ; ed. 2. 71.   † Ibid. p. 252 ; ed. 2..246.

‡ Whitby, p. 250, 251 ; ed. 2. 244, 245.

before us, inadvertently transcribes it as though it was read,* *I will pour out my Spirit upon you*, when it is *unto you*. By the *Spirit*, we are to understand the mind of Wisdom; so the word רוח is used in Prov. xxix. 11; and by *pouring* it *out*, a large and full revelation of it to the sons of men, as it is explained in the next clause, *I will make known my words unto you*.

3. This external revelation of the mind of Christ, ought not to be called sufficient grace; it is indeed the means of conveying and implanting grace, when it comes not in word only, but the Holy Ghost and with power: it is not sufficient means of grace to all men; for all men have it not, nor is it so to all that have it; for to some it is the *savour of death unto death*, whilst it is to others the *savour of life unto life*; nor is it of itself sufficient means to any, without the efficacious grace of God. Hence,

4. Though the calls, invitations, and messages of God to men, by his ministers, may be sometimes (for they are not always) sufficient inducements to procure an external reformation, an outward repentance, as in the people of Nineveh; yet these are not sufficient of themselves, without powerful grace, to produce true faith in Christ, evangelical repentance towards God, and new spiritual obedience, in life and conversation.

IV. These words, *I have called, and ye refused; I have stretched out my hand, and no man regarded*, are used † to prove the resistibility of the grace of God, and that an irresistible power is not necessary to the conversion of a sinner. But,

1. It ought to be observed, that there is a twofold call; the one is internal, which is by the powerful operations of the Spirit of God on the soul, either with or without the word; which cannot be so resisted, as to be made to cease, to become void, and of no effect; the other is external, by the ministry of the word; and may be resisted, rejected, and despised, and become useless: now it is of the latter call, and not of the former, that the text speaks, and therefore no way militates against the irresistible, unfrustrable grace of God in conversion: and in this sense are we to understand some other places of Scripture, as Prov. ii. 3, 4, and xi. 3, 4; Isa. lxv. 2; Matt. xx. 16.

2. It is said,‡ that "were such an irresistible power necessary to the conversion of a sinner, no man could be converted sooner than he is; because before this irresistible action came upon him, he could not be converted; and when it came upon him, he could not choose but be converted." To which I reply, I see no absurdity in the consequence; for, as all our times are in the hands of God, a time to be born, and a time to die; so likewise the time of conversion, which is called a time of love, Ezek. xvi. 8. Now as a man cannot be born sooner or later than he is, nor

die sooner or later than he does; so neither can he be converted sooner or later than he is. But then,

3. It is objected,§ that if this be the case, "no man could reasonably be blamed that he lived so long in his impenitent and unconverted state." To which I answer, that living in an impenitent and unconverted state, is living in sin, and therefore blameworthy. And though man, by sinning, has involved himself in a state, out of which he cannot extricate himself; yet is he not the less culpable on that score for living in it.

4. It is further objected,‖ that if man cannot be converted sooner than he is, God must unreasonably make these inquiries, *How long, ye simple ones, will ye love simplicity?* with others, in the following places, Exod. xvi. 28; Numb xiv. 11; Jer. iv. 14, and xiii. 27. In answer to which, it will be enough to say, that these passages speak not of conversion, but of external obedience and reformation; which might be sooner done, though conversion cannot.

5. It is said,¶ that if it is so, "it would not be praiseworthy in persons that they were then converted, it being not in their power then to be otherwise; since an unfrustrable operation is that which no man can frustrate." It is very true; for all the praise of conversion is due to the powerful and efficacious grace of God, and none to the power and will of man.

6. It is asked,** "If there be some physical and unfrustrable operation on God's part, necessary to the new birth, why is the want of this new birth and spiritual renovation imputed to men's voluntary want of consideration, to their *rejecting the counsel of God*, and *not choosing the fear of the Lord?*" Prov. i. 24, 25, 29, 30. I reply, that the want of the new birth and spiritual renovation, is not the thing spoken of in the place referred to; but a non-attention to, and a contempt of, the ministry of the word, though these indeed are a sign of it; much less is this imputed to men's rejecting the counsel of God, and not choosing the fear of the Lord; for the tables must be turned; and if we speak truth, we must say, that man's rejecting the counsel of God, and not choosing the fear of the Lord, are owing, and to be imputed, to a want of the new birth and spiritual renovation. Besides, as the new birth and spiritual renovation are the effects of, and owing to the Spirit and grace of God, and therefore called a being *born of water and of the Spirit*, and *the renewing of the Holy Ghost;* so a want thereof is owing to a man's not having that grace which is in the power of God only to bestow upon him.

SECTION XI

Wash ye, make you clean, &c.—Isa. i. 16, 17.

THESE words are supposed to express the power of man, and contradict the necessity of

---

* Ibid., p. 181, 251; ed. 2. 177, 245.
† Remonstr. in Coll. Hag. art. iii. iv. p. 215.
‡ Ibid. art. iii. iv. p. 221; Whitby, p. 260;

ed. 2. 254.
‖ Ibid.
** Ibid. p. 224, 257; ed. 2. 218, 251.

§ Whitby, ib.
¶ Whitby, p. 261; ed. 2. 255.

unfrustrable grace in conversion: the argument from them is formed in this manner ;* " If conversion be wrought only by the unfrustrable operation of God, and man is purely passive in it, vain are all these commands and exhortations directed to wicked men." The weakness of which conclusion will appear by considering particularly each command or exhortation.

1. *Wash ye, make you clean ;* these two are to be regarded as one, since they intend one and the same thing; and suppose, that men, in a state of nature, are polluted and unclean; and indeed their pollution is of such sort, and to such a degree, that they cannot cleanse themselves, either by ceremonial ablutions, or moral services, or evangelical ordinances; for, *who can say, I have made my heart clean ; I am pure from my sin ?*† This is God's work only, as appears from his promises to cleanse his people from their sins; from the end of Christ's shedding his blood, and the efficacy of it; from the sanctifying influences of the Spirit; and from the prayers of the saints‡ to God, that he would *create* in them *clean hearts, wash them thoroughly from* their *iniquity*, and *cleanse* them *from* their *sin*. But if this be the case, that it is God's work alone, and that man is incapable to cleanse himself from sin, it will be said, to what purpose are such exhortations? I answer, to convince men of their pollution, and that they stand in need of being washed and cleansed, of which they are naturally ignorant : there are two many who are *pure in their own eyes, and yet not washed from their filthiness ;*§ as also, to bring them to a sense of their own inability to cleanse themselves; which seems to be the particular design of them here; since these Jews thought to have washed themselves from their immoralities by their ceremonial services, and which are therefore rejected by God, ver. 11—15; and they, notwithstanding all their legal purifications, are called upon to wash and make clean : besides, such exhortations may be useful to lead persons to inquire after the proper means of cleansing, and so to the fountain of Christ's blood, in which only souls being washed are made clean. These exhortations then are not in vain; though conversion is wrought only by the unfrustrable operation of God, and man is purely passive in it. This view of them will help us to understand aright some parallel places; such as Jer. iv. 14, xiii. 27 ; 2 Cor. vii. 1; James i. 21, and iv. 8, which commonly go in company with these.

2. *Put away the evil of your doings from before mine eyes.* Evil is said to be put away from a nation, when it is punished in the doer of it; see Deut. xiii. 5, and xvii. 7, 12 ; and from a family and particular persons, when discouraged and abstained from, Job xi. 14, and xxii. 23. But it ought to be observed, that the exhortation here is not barely to put away their doings, but the evil of them ; and that not from themselves, but from before the

eyes of God. Now to put away sin in this sense, is to take it away, to remove it, as that it is pardoned, and men acquitted and discharged from it ; but this is impracticable to men, and is the act of God only ; as is evident from his promises to remove the sins of his people ; from the end of Christ's sacrifice which was to put away sin for ever ; and from the prayers of the saints, who desire that God would *take away all iniquity, and receive graciously.* But why then is such an exhortation given ? First to convince men, that the putting away of sin from the eyes of God's vindictive justice, is absolutely necessary to salvation ; and then that men cannot by all their ceremonial and moral services do this ; for *it is not possible that the blood of bulls and goats should take away sin ;*‖ as also to lead and direct their views to the sacrifice of Christ, which effectually does it ; and without which, *to what purpose is the multitude of sacrifices ?* and vain are all *oblations,* ver. 11, 12.

3. *Cease to do evil ;* which regards either a cessation from ceremonial works, which being done with a wicked mind, were an abomination to the Lord, ver. 13, 14, or an abstinence from outward immoralities ; such as shedding innocent blood, oppressing the fatherless and widow, ver. 15, 17. Now a natural man may be able to abstain from such external enormities of life, without supposing a power in him to do that which is spiritually good ; or that the unfrustrable grace of God is unnecessary in conversion.

4. *Learn to do well ;* that is, to do acts of justice, beneficence, liberality, and charity, such as are here mentioned ; *seek judgment, relieve the oppressed, judge the fatherless, plead for the widow ;* all which are very commendable, and may be performed by men in an unconverted state ; and no way militate either against man's passiveness, or the necessity of God's efficacious grace in the work of conversion.

SECTION XII

Come now and let us reason together ; If ye be willing and obedient, &c.—Isa. i. 18, 19.

I. THE eighteenth verse is considered in strict connection with the words preceding and following ; from whence it is concluded, that to *cease to do evil,* and *learn to do well,* to *be willing and obedient,*¶ are qualifications for the pardoning mercy of God, and conditions of obtaining it ; the promises of pardon, life, and salvation, being made to persons of such characters. But,

1. Let it be observed, that the eighteenth verse may be read in a parenthesis, without any connexion with or dependence on either the preceding or subsequent verses ; being thrown in on purpose to comfort the people of God, oppressed with a sense of their sins, whilst he is expressing his just resentment and indignation against the sins of others.

2. Admitting it to be in strict connexion

---

* Ibid. p. 237 ; ed. 2. 231.   † Prov.
xx. 9.   ‡ Psalm li. 2, 7, 10.
§ Prov. xxx. 12.   ‖ Heb. x. 4.

¶ Whitby, p. 181, 242, 298 ; ed. 2. 177
236, 291.

with the context, it contains a free declaration of pardoning grace and mercy, without any conditions annexed to it; it is not expressed in a conditional form; it is not said, if ye *cease to do evil,* and *learn to do well,* then *though your sins be as scarlet, they shall be as white as snow;* nor is it said, *if ye be willing and obedient,* then *though your sins be red like crimson, they shall be as wool,* but *ye shall eat the good of the land.*

3. God's promise of pardon is free, absolute, and unconditional; it is expressed in this manner; *I will be merciful to their unrighteousness, and their sins and their iniquities I will remember no more;*[*] and made to persons guilty both of sins of omission and commission; who had *bought* him *no sweet cane with money; neither* had *filled* him *with the fat of sacrifices;* but had *made* him *to serve with* their *sins,* and had *wearied* him *with* their *iniquities.*[†]

4. Pardon of sin is never ascribed to any condition performed by men, but to the free grace of God, streaming through the blood of Christ; which was shed to obtain it, and in whose gift it is, being *exalted to be a Prince and a Saviour, to give repentance unto Israel, and forgiveness of sins;*[‡] and which is often given to persons without any conditions previously qualifying them for it.

5. Obedience is not the condition of pardon, though a declaration of pardon is an excellent motive to induce to obedience; evangelical obedience springs from, and is influenced by, discoveries of pardon, but is neither the cause nor condition of it.

II. It is here promised to such who are *willing and obedient,* that they *shall eat the good of the land;* and threatened to the disobedient, that they *shall be devoured with the sword;* from whence it does not follow, that it is in the power of man to do what is spiritually good, much less that eternal happiness depends upon, or is to be obtained by, man's obedience. For,

1. The voluntary obedience here encouraged, is to things civil; such as to *relieve the oppressed, judge the fatherless, and plead for the widow,* ver. 17, which it is allowed are in the power of a natural man to perform; and might be reasonably expected from a professing people, as these were to whom these exhortations were given.

2. What is here promised, is not of a spiritual or eternal, but of a temporal nature; *ye shall eat the good of the land;* that is, of the land of Canaan; the possession of which they held by their obedience to those laws of a moral, civil, and ceremonial kind, which God gave them as a body politic; and which, so long as they observed, they were continued in the quiet and full enjoyment of all the blessings of the good land, flowing with milk and honey, as were promised to them; see Deut. v. 32, 33, and vi. 24, 25, and xxviii. 1

—14; Lev. xxvi. 3—10. But when they refused and rebelled it was otherwise with them. And therefore,

3. The punishment threatened to their disobedience and rebellion is temporal; *ye shall be devoured with the sword, for the mouth of the Lord hath spoken it;* as he had in Lev. xxvi. 25, 33, and so it was frequently with this people, when they broke the laws of God, transgressed his commands, and rebelled against him, the enemy was let in upon them, the sword was drawn against them, and they destroyed by it, or carried captive.

SECTION XIII.

*What could have been done more to my vineyard, that I have not done in it? Wherefore when I looked, &c.—*Isa. v. 4.

No one place of Scripture is more frequent in the mouths and writings of the patrons of free-will,[§] and adversaries of the grace of God, than this; which is used by them, to prove that God gives sufficient grace for the conversion of such who are not converted; and that he does not effect that work by an irresistible power, by an unfrustrable operation; which operation, it is said, "if necessary to produce the expected fruits, and not vouchsafed, it must follow, that this vineyard had not grace sufficient to answer her Lord's expectations; and if so, he must unreasonably complain, that she brought forth wild grapes, and more unreasonably expect good grapes, and most unreasonably punish her for not doing what he would not give her grace sufficient to perform."[||] To which I reply,

1. These words are part of a parable, representing the state and condition of the people of the Jews. Now, parabolical divinity is not argumentative; nor ought parables to be stretched beyond their scope and design; the intent of this is to show the ingratitude of the Jews, in the midst of many favours bestowed on them, and the patience and long-suffering of God towards them, and to vindicate his justice in their ruin as a nation.

2. Seeing there is a particular application of this parable to the people of Israel and Judah, ver. 4; *The vineyard of the Lord of Hosts is the house of Israel, and the men of Judah his pleasant plants;* who were favoured with peculiar blessings above all people on the face of the earth; it can be no proof of any blessing or grace common to all mankind; or in other words, it can be no proof that God gives to all men sufficient grace for conversion, though not effectual, through their perverseness.

3. It does not appear from hence that God gave to all the men of Israel and Judah, grace sufficient for conversion; which is not a national, but a personal blessing; and it is evident, that some among them had not restraining grace, no sense of sin in them, nor fear

---

* Heb. viii. 12.   ‡ Isa. xliii. 24, 25.
† Acts v. 31.   § Remonstr. in Coll.
Hag. art. iii. iv. p. 216, 219; Act. Synod. p. 89, &c; Curcell. Christ. Institut. l. 6, c. 13, sec.

3, p. 400; Limborch. l. 4, c. 13, sect. 2, 3, 4, p. 369.
|| Whitby, p. 334; ed. 2. 229.

of God before their eyes; they *drew iniquity with cords of vanity, and sin as it were with a cart rope;* they said, *Let him make speed, and hasten his work, that we may see it; and let the counsel of the Holy One of Israel draw nigh and come, that we may know it; they called evil good, and good evil; put darkness for light, and light for darkness,* ver. 18, 20. Nor was every man in Israel and Judah capable of judging whether God had given sufficient grace or no, to any, or all among them.

4. These words, *What could have been done more to my vineyard, that I have not done in it;* cannot be understood of God's having done all that was sufficient and necessary to the saving conversion of those who are designed by the vineyard; for a reply to the question, taken in this sense, might easily be made after this manner: that God could have made of this bad vine a good one, which was absolutely necessary to its bringing forth good grapes; he could by internal grace have effected the saving work of conversion; to which, external means, without it, were insufficient; he could have removed the veil from their understandings, and have taken away the stony heart, and given an heart of flesh; all which are requisite to the real work of conversion.

5. The similitudes in the parable only regard the external culture of the vineyard, and can only, at most, design the outward means of reformation, which these people enjoyed; such as the mission of the Lord's prophets to them, the ministry of the word, admonitions, exhortations, reproofs, &c., when it might be expected that a people enjoying such privileges, would behave well in their moral conversation; and instead of being guilty of rapine, oppression, luxury, drunkenness, pride, and contempt of God himself, sins which they are in this chapter charged with; they would have done common justice between man and man, would have sought judgment, relieved the oppressed, judged the fatherless, and pleaded for the widow; all which they might have done, without supposing them to have grace sufficient to saving conversion, and though this might be withheld from them, and therefore it was not unreasonable in the Lord to expect good grapes of this kind from them, nor to complain of their wild grapes, nor to punish them for them.

6. If the parable is narrowly examined, it will be found, that the good things which God had done for his vineyard, the men of Israel and Judah, were of a civil nature, and which regarded their civil constitution and settlement as a body politic; such as the planting of it *in a very fruitful hill,* in the land of Canaan, a land flowing with milk and honey; *fencing* it with good and wholesome laws, which distinguished and kept them separate from other nations, as well as with his almighty power and providence; especially at the three yearly festivals, when all their males appeared at Jerusalem; *gathering out the stones,* casting the heathen out, and dri-

ving Canaanites before them; *planting it with the choicest vine,* such having fallen in the wilderness who murmured and rebelled against God; *building a tower in it,* expressive of divine protection: and placing *a winepress,* which may either mean plenty of temporal blessings, or the prophets, who were placed among them to stir up and exhort the people to a regard to the laws of God.

7. God's *looking* or *expecting* that this vineyard should bring forth grapes, is not to be taken properly but figuratively, after the manner of men; for, from such a well-formed government, from such an excellent constitution, from a people enjoying such advantages, might it not be reasonably expected that the fruits of common justice and equity would have appeared? might not *judgment* have been *looked* for instead of *oppression,* and *righteousness* instead of a *cry?* but alas! it proved just the reverse.

9. The interrogation ought not to be rendered as it is by our translators, *What could have been done more to my vineyard?* nor as Dr. Whitby reads it, *What was there more to do for my vineyard?* &c., but מה־לעשות עוד לכרמי should be translated, *What is to be done here, after to my vineyard?* &c., and so designs not any thing past, but something to come; and is to be understood not of good things bestowed before, but of punishment hereafter to be inflicted, as evidently appears from the answer to it, ver. 5, 6:—*And now go to, I will tell you what I will do to my vineyard; I will take away the hedge thereof, and it shall be eaten up, and break down the wall thereof, and it shall be trodden down, and I will lay it waste,* &c., which was fulfilled in the destruction of the land by the Chaldeans, a punishment God never inflicted to that degree before on that people; and so the words have much the same meaning with those in Matt. xxi. 40, 41:—*When the Lord therefore of the vineyard cometh, what will he do unto these husbandmen? they say unto him, He will miserably destroy those wicked men, and let out his vineyard to other husbandmen, which shall render him the fruits in their seasons;* for the question must be of the same nature with the answer; and if it be so, the words are far enough from proving that grace sufficient for conversion is given to some who are not converted, or from contradicting the doctrine of unfrustrable grace in conversion.

SECTION XIV

For thus saith the Lord, the Holy One of Israel; In returning and rest shall ye be saved; in quietness and in confidence shall be your strength; and ye would not.—Isa. xxx. 15.

THESE words are cited in* favour of free-will, as proving that men's impotency to that which is good, is not owing to any disability by the fall of Adam, but to other causes acquired by, and not born with them; such as evil dispositions, customs, prejudices, hard-

---

* Whitby, pp. 261, 262; ed 2. 255.

ness of heart, or blindness wilfully contracted; and therefore irresistible and unfrustrable grace is not necessary to the conversion of a sinner; but of what service they are in this cause will be better understood when the following things are observed.

1. Admitting that the words regard the spiritual and eternal salvation of men, then they are expressive of the way and manner in which God saves such who are saved. *In returning and rest shall ye be saved*, that is, by faith and repentance; repentance may be meant by *returning*, and faith by *rest*; or by *returning and rest*, may be designed returning to rest, that is, to Christ, who is the only rest to weary souls; *in quietness and confidence shall be your strength*. *Quietness* may intend peace of conscience, and *confidence* assurance of faith, which make men strong Christians, though their strength does not barely lie in these graces, but in the object of them. Now faith and repentance are blessings of the covenant, gifts of God; the graces of the Spirit go together in the doctrine of salvation, and have a great concern in it; though they are not meritorious, procuring causes, nor conditions of it, yet in this way God brings his people to salvation; they enter into and are descriptive of the character of such that are saved; there is so close a connexion between these and salvation, that none are saved without them.

2. If we take this to be the sense of the words, then the last clause, *and ye would not*, shows, that God's way of saving men through repentance and faith, by going to Christ alone for rest, by placing all confidence in, and deriving all peace and comfort from him, is disagreeable to unregenerate men; which is a proof of the wretched depravity, corruption, and perverseness of the will. Hence this scripture, viewed in this light, with Jer. vi. 16, 17, and xiii. 11, 27, and xviii. 12, and xxix. 19, Ezek. xx. 8, Hos. v. 4, stand on record, as so many lasting reproaches to the will of man.

3. Let this depravity, corruption, perverseness, and obstinacy of the will, proceed from what cause soever, whether from any thing born with men, or acquired by them; such as evil dispositions, customs, prejudices, hardness and blindness of heart; what else can conquer these evil dispositions, break such customs, destroy such prejudices, and remove this blindness and hardness of heart, but the almighty power and efficacious grace of God? How necessary therefore are the irresistible and unfrustrable operations of the Spirit of God to the conversion of such sinners; when can it be reasonably expected they should be *willing* to be saved by Jehovah in his own way, but *in the day of* his *power* on their souls? who must *work in* them both *to will and do* of his *good pleasure*, if ever the perverseness of their wills is cured. But,

4. Though, no doubt, the depravity and stubbornness of the will is increased by prejudices, customs, &c., yet to what can its first taint be ascribed, or from whence had it its first blow, and received its original disability, but from the fall of Adam? Does not the Scripture, according to this doctrine, furnish us with the best account of the origin of moral evil? Does not the apostle* attribute men's conversation in *the lusts of the flesh*, their *fulfilling*, τὰθελήματα τῆς σαρκὸς *the wills of the flesh, and of the mind*, to their being *by nature children of wrath*? Why is it *the wicked will not hearken to the voice of the charmer, charm he never so wisely*; but because they *are estranged from the womb, they go astray as soon as they be born speaking lies*?† And what else can be the source and spring of such early practices in iniquity, but the corruption of nature, owing to the fall of man, they bring into the world with them? Do we not read ‡ of some whose *neck* was *an iron sinew*, and their *brow brass*; whose obstinacy, disobedience, and treacherous dealing, are accounted for by their being *called transgressors from the womb?*

5. After all, the words are not to be understood of the spiritual and eternal salvation of men, but of the temporal safety and happiness of the people of Israel, had they acted according to the advice given them; *in returning and rest shall ye be saved*; that is, if ye return from the evil *counsel* which ye have taken, which is *not of me*, saith the Lord, ver. 1, and rest quietly in your own land, and do not *walk to go down into Egypt*, nor seek to Pharaoh for help, ver. 2, 3, *ye shall be saved*; you shall be in safety, no enemy shall break in upon you, or disturb you: *in quietness and in confidence shall be your strength*; your *strength is to sit still*, ver. 7, quietly to abide in Jerusalem, in your own cities, and trust in my power and protection, then ye need not fear any enemy; *and ye would not*; *but ye said*, for we will flee סוס על, *unto horses*, to Egypt for horses, or *upon horses*, which we have had from thence; *therefore shall ye flee*; *we will ride upon the swift*; *therefore they that pursue you shall be swift*, meaning the Chaldeans; one thousand shall flee *at the rebuke of one, at the rebuke of five shall ye flee, till ye be left as a beacon upon the top of a mountain, and as an ensign on an hill*. Now as this appears from the context to be the plain and genuine sense of the words, they can be of no use to prove what they are cited for, and ought to have no place in the controversy about free-will, and efficacious grace.

SECTION XV

Ho, every one that thirsteth, come ye to the waters, and he that hath no money; come ye, buy, and eat, yea, come, buy wine and milk without money and without price.— Isa. lv. 1.

1. THESE words are no call, invitation, or* offer of grace to dead sinners, since they are spoken to such who were *thirsty*, that is, who, in a spiritual sense, were thirsting after pardon of sin, a justifying righteousness, and salvation by Christ; after a greater knowledge of him, communion with him, confor-

---

* Eph. ii. 8.   † Psalm lviii. 8, 5,   ‡ Isa. xlviii. 4, 8. § Whitby, p. 341; ed. 2. 358.

mity to him, and enjoyment of him in his ordinances, which supposes them to be spiritually alive; for such who are dead in sin, thirst not after the grace of God, but the lusts of the flesh; they mind and savour the things of the flesh, and not the things of the Spirit; only new-born babes, or such who are born again, are quickened and made alive, desire Christ, his grace, and *the sincere milk of the word*, that their souls may grow thereby; besides, the persons called unto, are represented as having *no money;* which, though true of unconverted persons, who have nothing to pay off their debts, or purchase any thing for themselves; yet they fancy themselves to be *rich*, and *increased in goods*, and *stand in need of nothing;* whereas the persons here encouraged are such, who not only have no money, but know they have none; who are *poor in spirit*, and sensible of their spiritual poverty; which sense arises from the quickening influences of the Spirit of God upon their souls; nor are Isa. i. 18, 19, Luke xiii. 3, John iii. 16, and viii. 24, any offers of grace, as they are with this represented to be.

2. They do not express any power or ability in unconverted persons to come to Christ, seeing they are not directed to such, as is before observed; besides, neither Christ, nor the grace of Christ, are designed by *the waters*, but the ordinances; the allusion being, as is thought by some,* to maritime places, or sea-ports, where ships of merchandise unload their traffic, and people resort to buy things necessary for them. Now where should hungry and thirsty souls, and such that have no money, attend, but on the ordinances, the means of grace? where they may expect to meet with Christ, and *of his fulness receive*, even *grace for grace*. Nor,

3. Do they declare any self-sufficiency in creatures to procure any thing for themselves by their works; for the things to be bought, *wine and milk* suitable to thirsty persons, signify either the doctrines of the gospel, or the blessings of grace, both which are freely given. *Buying* here is to be taken not in a proper sense, for no valuable consideration can be given to God for his grace; but in an improper one, the manner in which these things were to be bought, being *without price;* and besides, the persons who are called upon to buy, are said to *have no money*. This explanation of the words in the several parts of them, will help us to understand the advice and invitation given in other places; such as Rev. iii. 18, and xxii. 17.

SECTION XVI

Seek ye the Lord while he may be found, call ye upon him while he is near.—Isa. lv. 6.

THIS passage of Scripture is no proof of a day of grace, which, if men improve, they may enjoy the favour of God; but if they let it slip, if it is once elapsed, there is no more opportunity of meeting with him.

1. They are an exhortation to public wor-

ship, signified by *seeking the Lord and calling upon him;* the time for which, with the Jews, was on the seventh day of the week, and with us Christians, on the first; these being *times in which he might be found*, it became the Jews of old, and us now, to attend public ordinances, in expectation of meeting with God; since he has promised his people to be in the midst of them, when they are met together.

2. The words may be so rendered, as that they may be understood of place as well as time; *Seek ye the Lord*, בהמצאו, *in his being found, call ye upon him*, קרב בהיותו, *in his being near;* that is, in the place where he is to be found, and in the place where he is near. Now, though God is everywhere, and in all places, yet, in the Old Testament dispensation, there was a particular place for public worship appointed, where God vouchsafed his presence, and where it was both the duty and interest of his people to attend; and though under the gospel dispensation, all places are alike, yet where the saints agree to meet together, there God has promised to be in the midst of them; and, therefore, there should he be sought and called upon.

3. The words may have a particular regard to Christ's being on earth in the land of Judea, seeing he is spoken of under the name of David, ver. 3, and is promised to be *given for a witness to the people, a leader, and commander of the people*, ver. 4, and it is prophesied of him, that there should be a large concourse of the Gentiles to him, ver. 5, who are here encouraged, or rather the Jews, to seek unto him, and call upon him, while he was in their land, near unto them; when they had the advantage of his personal presence, ministry, and miracles.

SECTION XVII.

Let the wicked forsake his way, and the unrighteous man his thoughts, and let him return unto the Lord, and he will have mercy upon him, and to our God, for he will abundantly pardon.—Isa. lv. 7.

I. THESE words are represented † as a promise of pardon, on condition of forsaking sinful ways and thoughts and turning to the Lord; which, if not in man's power to perform, is to promise on an impossible condition, and that is, indeed, to promise nothing. To which may be replied,

1. That forsaking sin, and turning to the Lord at first conversion, or returning to him after backslidings, which perhaps may be here meant, are not owing to the power of man, but to the efficacious grace of God. None can truly forsake sin, or heartily turn to the Lord, but such who are influenced by the Spirit of God; hence says Ephraim, *Turn thou me, and I shall be turned.*‡

2. That the promise of pardon is free, absolute, and unconditional, not depending on any condition whatever to be performed by men; forsaking sinful ways and thoughts, and returning to the Lord, are not here pro-

---

posed as conditions of obtaining mercy, and receiving pardon; but the declarations of pardoning grace and mercy here made, are made on purpose to encourage souls sensible of the wickedness of their ways, and unrighteousness of their thoughts, to return to the Lord, who is a God of grace and mercy.

3. Though faith and repentance are not conditions of pardon, nor in the power of man, of himself, to perform; yet as pardon is promised to such who repent, believe, and turn to the Lord, so all such, to whom God makes the promise of pardon, he gives the graces of faith and repentance; hence his promise is not vain, empty, and delusory.

II. It is said,* that " if conversion is wrought only by the unfrustrable operation of God, and man is purely passive in it, vain are the promises of pardon, such as this; for no promises can be means proper to make a dead man live, or to prevail upon a man to act, who must be purely passive." To which I answer,

1. That these words contain no promise to dead men, but a declaration of pardoning grace to sensible sinners; who were wicked and unrighteous in their own apprehensions, being represented as thirsty, ver. 1, seeking after the way of life and salvation; though they took the wrong way, and had their thoughts wrongly turned to *spend money for that which is not bread*, and their *labour for that which satisfieth not*, ver. 2, and therefore remained oppressed with a sense of sin; hence they are here encouraged to quit their own *way* of salvation, and all *thoughts* of their own righteousness, and alone to seek the Lord for mercy and pardon; since his *thoughts* were *not as* their *thoughts*, nor his *ways as* their *ways.*

2. Admitting them to be a promise of pardon made to dead men; it may be thought to be a proper and sufficient means in the hand of God, under the mighty influences of his Spirit and grace, to make dead men live; since *the gospel is the power of God unto salvation*, the *ministration of life*, yea, *the savour of life unto life ;*† and especially when it is observed what is said in ver. 10, 11. *For as the rain cometh down, and the snow from heaven, and returneth not thither, but watereth the earth, and maketh it bring forth and bud, that it may give seed to the sower, and bread to the eater; so shall my word be that goeth forth out of my mouth*, now at this present time delivered, in ver. 7—9; *it shall not return unto me void, but it shall accomplish that which I please, and it shall prosper in the thing whereto I sent it.*

3. Though man is passive in regeneration, yet he is active in forsaking sin and turning to the Lord. Promises of pardon may, through the grace of God, prevail on such to act in these instances, who have been passive in the work of regeneration; for regeneration antecedes these; forsaking sin, and turning to the Lord, follow upon, and rise from regenerating grace. No man can truly

do these, until he is regenerated by the Spirit of God. It follows, then, that men may be prevailed upon, by the promises of pardon, to act, who have been passive in regeneration.

III. It is intimated, that such who are in the Calvinistical way of thinking, say, that God promises pardon and life to the non-elect, on condition of their faith and repentance :‡ and it is asked, " How can a God of truth and sincerity be said to promise to them pardon and salvation, seriously and in good earnest, who are, by his own act of preterition, infallibly and unfrustrably excluded from it ?" I answer,

1. Who the men are that say so, I do not know, and must leave them to defend their own positions, who only are accountable for the consequences of them; for my own part, I utterly deny that there is any promise of pardon made to the non-elect at all, not on any condition whatever. The promise of pardon is a promise of the covenant of grace, and which is made to none but to such who are in that covenant, in which the non-elect have no share; to whom the blessing of pardon belongs, to them only is the promise of it made: the blessing of it only belongs to such for whom Christ died, whose blood was shed for the remission of sin; and these are the elect of God only: and though the gospel declaration of pardon is made in indefinite terms, to every one that believes; the reason is, because all those who are interested in the covenant of grace, and for whom Christ died, God does in his own time, give faith and repentance, and along with them forgiveness of sins.

2. This passage of Scripture now under consideration, is no promise of pardon to the non-elect; for the words *wicked* and *unrighteous*, are not peculiar to them; God's elect are so in their state of nature, and in their own sense and apprehension, when the Spirit of God convinces them. Besides, the persons spoken to, appear from the context, to be such towards whom God's *thoughts* had been from everlasting, ver. 8, 9 ; and who were to partake of the blessings of joy and peace for ever, ver. 12, 13.

SECTION XVIII

Circumcise yourselves to the Lord, and take away the foreskins of your heart, ye men of Judah, and inhabitants of Jerusalem; let my fury come forth like fire, and burn that none can quench it; because of the evil of your doings.—Jer. iv. 4.

THESE words, with Deut. x. 16, which express much the same thing, in almost the same words, are thought to disprove man's passiveness and the unfrustrable operation of God in conversion; or that that is God's work alone; which, if true, it is said,§ vain are all such commands and exhortations as these : on which, let the following things be observed :

---

* Whitby, pp. 237, 242 ; ed. 2. 231, 236.
† Rom. i. 16. 2 Cor. ii. 16, and iii. 6.

‡ Whitby, p. 243 ; ed. 2. 237.
§ Whitby, pp. 237, 287; ed. 2. 231, 280.

1. That it is questionable whether these figurative expressions are to be understood of internal conversion,* or the first work of it on the soul; since they are directed to backsliding Israel and Judah; and may not rather design a national repentance and reformation of them, as God's professing people, that they might be saved with a temporal deliverance from temporal judgments; with which they are threatened throughout this chapter.

2. Admitting that they are to be understood of the internal, spiritual, and saving work of conversion; since *he is a Jew who is one inwardly; and circumcision is that of the heart, in the spirit, and not in the letter, whose praise is not of men, but of God;*† this sense of the word carries the things expressed by them still farther out of the power of man, and into the hands of God alone; seeing this is the *circumcision made without hands,*‡ that is, without the power, help, and assistance of men. Circumcision of the flesh was typical of that of the spirit, and fitly expresses the passiveness of men in it; for as the infant was entirely passive and not active in circumcision, so is man in regeneration and first conversion; not to take any notice of, or insist upon the word הזלל, being of a passive form, and rendered by the Septuagint, πεοιτμηθητε, and by the Vulgate Latin, *circumcidimini, be ye circumcised.*

3. What God here requires, commands, and exhorts unto, he elsewhere promises to do himself, saying; *The Lord thy God will circumcise thine heart, and the heart of thy seed, to love the Lord thy God, with all thine heart, and with all thy soul, that thou mayest live;*§ which at once discovers the inability of man, and the necessity of the grace of God; for if man could do this of himself, there would be no need of God's doing it for him: since this is the case, we may say, as Austin did, *Domine, da quod jubes, et jube quod vis; Lord, give what thou commandest,* and *command what thou wilt.*

4. Such commands and exhortations are not in vain, supposing man's passiveness in this work of conversion, and the unfrustrable operation of God in it; seeing such exhortations may be useful to convince men of the corruption of their nature; the necessity of a spiritual circumcision, without which there can be no salvation; their own disability, and the need of the power and grace of God to effect it.

SECTION XIX

But when the righteous turneth away from his righteousness, and committeth iniquity, and doth according to all the abominations that the wicked man doth, shall he live? all his righteousness that he hath done shall not be mentioned; in his trespass that he hath trespassed, and in his sin that he hath sinned, in them shall he die.—Ezek. xviii. 24.

THIS scripture is placed at the front of those which are ‖ said " expressly to assert the possibility, that true believers, true penitents, men truly just and righteous, may fall from their righteousness, and die in their iniquity." But,

1. The man here spoken of, is not one truly just and righteous; seeing he is denominated righteous from *his* own righteousness in which he trusted, and from which he is supposed to turn. Now none are truly, and in an evangelic sense, righteous by their own righteousness; only such are, who are made so by the obedience of Christ; and these never can, nor shall they *turn* from this righteousness, which is the righteousness of God, an *everlasting* one, and is *revealed from faith to faith;* nor do they *commit sin,* that is, make a trade of sinning, live in a course of it; much less do they *according to all the abominations of the wicked;* nor can it be said of them, that their *righteousness shall not be mentioned,* since it *endures for ever;* and they, on the account of it, *shall be in everlasting remembrance.* Nor can they ever die, in the Arminian sense of the phrase here used; for they are justified by Christ's righteousness from all their sins, and therefore shall not die in them; they live by faith on it, and shall never die the second death; there is more virtue in the righteousness of Christ to justify them, than 'there is in all their sins to condemn them; their justification and glorification are inseparably connected together. Besides, such are the love, care, and power of God, which are engaged on their side, and exercised towards them, that it is impossible they should everlastingly perish.

The man here designed, is one that is *outwardly righteous before men;* who imagines himself to be so; *trusteth to his own righteousness;*¶ concludes, that what he suffered was owing to his father's sin, and not any iniquity of his own; and therefore complains of injustice in God; whose folly, vain opinion of himself, and unrighteous notions of God's providence, are fully and justly exposed in this chapter. The righteousness from which he is denominated righteous, is *his* own, and not another's, and what *he* himself *hath done,* and not what Christ hath done for him: a mere moral righteousness, consisting of some negative holiness, and a few external, moral performances, as appears from ver. 5—9; from such a righteousness a man may turn, commit iniquity, sin and die; but then this is no proof or instance of the apostacy of the saints, of true believers, true penitents, men truly just and righteous.

It is indeed said, " that the righteous man here spoken of, is one truly righteous; for he is one who *sinneth not, committeth not iniquity, and turneth not away from his righteousness;* one who walketh in God's statutes, and keeps his judgments, yea, who *walketh in the*

---

* Vid. Remonstr. in Coll. Hag. art. iii. and iv. p. 265.   † Rom. ii. 29.
‡ Col. ii. 11.   § Deut. xxx. 6.
‖ Remonstr. in Coll. Hag. art. v. p. 14; Act

Synod. p. 218; Limborch. l. 5, c. 81, sect 1, p. 705; Whitby, p. 401, ed. 2. 390.
¶ Ezek. xxxiii. 13. ** Whitby, p. 402, ed. 2. 3.

statutes of life, without committing iniquity; and therefore assuredly is one, who is truly and inwardly righteous, and not in outward profession only." To which I answer; the texts referred to in chap. xxxiii. 12, 13, and xviii. 9, 17, 19, say not any one of these things concerning the righteous man; but on the contrary, suppose he may sin, commit iniquity, and turn from his righteousness; and indeed, there is not *a just man*, one that is truly so, *that lives and sins not;* nor is any man righteous in the sight of God by virtue of his inward holiness, or outward walk; besides, the same author contradicts himself in the next page,* when he says, " the righteous man who turneth away from his righteousness, is one who *committeth iniquity and doth according to all the abominations which the wicked man doth;* and therefore must be one to whom belongs the portion of the wicked, which is death eternal." It is further objected† from Dr. Prideaux, that " should he (the righteous man) only turn from his counterfeit and hypocritical righteousness, should he not rather live than die; inasmuch as he would put off the wolf, to put on the lamb?" which will be fully answered by observing the horrid blunder, and wretched mistake, that one doctor has made, and another by him is led into; for the turn is not from a counterfeit and hypocritical righteousness to a real one; but from a mere external moral righteousness, which had some appearance and degree of obedience in it, to an open, shameful, and abominable course of sinning; which is so far from putting off the wolf to put on the lamb, that it is just the very reverse; it is to put off the lamb or sheep's clothing, in which he appeared, to put on the wolf he really was; and consequently such an one should rather die than live.

2. The death threatened to the righteous man that turns from his righteousness, is not an eternal death, or the death of the soul and body in hell; since this death was then upon them, what they were complaining of, imagining it came upon them for the sins of their parents; and besides, they might have been recovered from it by repentance and reformation. *Have I any pleasure at all that the wicked should die?‡ saith the Lord God; and not that he should return from his ways and live? For I have no pleasure in the death of him that dieth; wherefore turn yourselves, and live ye;* all which cannot be said of an eternal death; dying *in his iniquity*, is the same with dying *for his iniquity*, as it is rendered in ver. 26, and designs some severe temporal calamity or affliction; which is often in Scripture called a *death*, Exod. x. 17, 2 Cor. i. 10, and xi. 23; such as captivity, in which the Jews then were, of which they were complaining, what was owing to their sins, and from which they were capable of being recovered. " This answer, it is said,§ contradicts the express words

of the prophet about twenty times;" though not one single instance of it is given. Wherefore,

3. Admitting that the truly just and righteous man is here intended; it is no proof of a possibility of his turning away from his righteousness and sinning, so as to be finally lost and perish; only so as to be afflicted, or suffer in a general calamity; besides, the words are delivered in a conditional form, being to be read thus: *If the righteous man turneth away from his righteousness.* Now *suppositio nil ponet in esse, a supposition puts nothing in being,* is no proof or instance of matter of fact. But this is said‖ to be " flying for refuge to a mere mistake; the words in the original being not *if*, but *beshub,* ἐν ᾗ ἂν ἡμέρα ἐπιστρέψῃ, *in the day that he turns away from his righteousness.*" To which I reply, that the word בשוב *beshub* may be rendered, *if he turns;* as it is by the Vulgate Latin and Pagnine¶ here and by our translators in chap. xxxiii. 19, agreeable to the like forms of expression in other places; as Ps. xlvi. 2, *Therefore will not we fear* בהמיר ארץ, *though,* or *if the earth be removed,* ובמוט הרים, and *though,* or *if the mountains be carried into the midst of the sea.* Nor does the Greek version of the Septuagint read the words, ἐν ᾗ ἂν ἡμέρα ἐπιστρέψῃ, *in the day that he turns away;* but ἐν δε τῳ ἀποστρέψαι, *in his turning,* or *when he turns.* Add to this, that a conditional form is not only signified by *if,* but by *when.* And whereas it may be said, as it is, that such a form of words suppose something in possibility, though not in being, as it does in a wicked man's turning from his wickedness, opposed unto; it will be allowed that there is a possibility of a truly righteous man's falling away, was he left to himself, and not kept by the power and grace of God; and therefore such a supposition as this may be designed for, and made use of, as a means to show him his weakness, make him cautious of his walk, and lead him wholly to rely and depend on superior help and assistance, and so consequently be the means of his final perseverance.

SECTION XX

Therefore I will judge you, O house of Israel, every one according to his ways, saith the Lord God: repent, and turn yourselves from all your transgressions; so iniquity shall not be your ruin.—Ezek. xviii. 30.

THESE exhortations are represented as contrary to the doctrines of absolute election and reprobation, and of unfrustrable grace in conversion. The argument from them stands thus;** " He who would have all men, to whom the gospel is vouchsafed, to come to repentance, hath not prepared this saving grace only for some few Christians, leaving the rest under a necessity of perishing for the

---

* Ibid. p. 403; ed. 2. 392.   † Ibid. p. 402; ed. 2. 391.   ‡ Ezek. xviii. 23, 32.   § Whitby, p .402; ed. 2. 391.   ‖ Whitby, p. 403; ed. 2. 392.   ¶ So

even Vorstius reads the words, and argues from them for a conditional decree in God. Amic. Collat. cum Piscator, sect 4, p. 10.
** Whitby, p. 70; ed. 69.

want of it; for to all such persons he hath promised, that they shall not perish." And elsewhere it is said,* that "such delude men with vain words, who teach, that a God of truth, and of sincerity, and of great goodness, should say to persons with such symptoms of passionate concern, *Repent, and be converted from all your transgressions; so iniquity shall not be your ruin;* when he himself had from eternity appointed them to ruin, and purposed to withhold from them that grace, without which it was impossible they should repent, or be converted;" and that,† "if conversion be wrought only by the unfrustrable operation of God, and man is purely passive in it, vain are all such exhortations." To all which I reply,

1. That these exhortations are not made to all men, but only to the house of Israel; and therefore do not contradict the preparation of saving grace for some few only, as the Israelites were; nor do we say, that God has prepared saving grace only for some *few Christians*, but for all Christians; that is, all that are Christ's; nor are any of them left under a necessity of perishing for the want of it, since it is given to them, and they have it, as their character supposes: and whereas it is said, that to all such persons God has promised, that they shall not perish; it is readily granted, and by the way, is an acknowledgment of the doctrine of the saints' final perseverance; which is elsewhere greatly objected to. Moreover, inasmuch as they were *the house of Israel*, and *every one* of them, that are here spoken to, they are the wrong persons pitched upon to contradict the decrees of election and reprobation; for who will say of every one of them, that they were doomed to eternal death, or appointed to everlasting ruin, who were chosen to be a peculiar people? It ought to be shown, if anything is done to purpose, that God has somewhere or other expressed himself in such language to all men, and particularly to such as shall not eventually be saved, as is here used to his professing people.

2. The *repentance* here exhorted to, is not to be understood of an evangelical one, which is a *repentance unto life*, and *unto salvation;* but of a national one, for national iniquities, and to prevent national judgments, with which they are here threatened; seeing it is the whole *house of Israel*, the whole nation, and every one of them, who are exhorted unto it. Now, though there can be no true evangelical repentance without the unfrustrable grace of God, yet there may be a national external repentance without it; as in the case of the Ninevites. Besides, was an evangelical repentance designed here, an exhortation to it being made to the people of God, as the house of Israel were, could only be to the exercise of it, the grace itself having been wrought in them by the power of God: or admitting that the words are spoken to such

who had not the grace itself; such an exhortation might not be in vain, supposing the necessity of an unfrustrable operation; seeing it might be made use of to convince such of the necessity of repentance, and of their want of it; and so God may in this way bring his elect to it, according to his eternal purposes and designs. Moreover, *turning from transgression*, does not intend the first work of internal, saving conversion, which is wrought by the powerful and efficacious grace of God, and in which men are purely passive; but an external reformation, or a bringing forth *fruits meet for repentance*, in which persons may be, and are active; since it is not reasonable to suppose that the *house of Israel*, and *every one* of them, should be in an unconverted state. Besides, some give the sense of these words thus: not *turn yourselves*, but *turn others*, every man his neighbour, or his brother; so R. Sol. Jarchi, R. David Kimchi, R. Sol. Ben Melec, and some Christian interpreters.

3. The *ruin* the house of *Israel* was in danger of through iniquity, and which they might escape by repentance and reformation, was not eternal but temporal; *so iniquity shall not be your ruin*, למכשול *a stumbling-block to you;* an hindrance, an obstruction, lying in the way of your enjoyment of temporal blessings; therefore, cast away from you all your transgressions. This sense of the words may be confirmed from the advantages proposed to such who turned from their sins and transgressions, ver. 27, 28, as that such an one *should save his soul alive;* not with an everlasting salvation, for no man can save his soul alive in that sense; but with a temporal one, as did the Ninevites, by their repentance and reformation: it is also said, that he *shall surely live*, not a spiritual and eternal life; for he is said ‡ to *live by* his doing *that which is lawful and right;* whereas, no man can live spiritually and eternally by so doing; but it intends a civil life, in the comfortable enjoyment of outward mercies. It is moreover added, *he shall not die*, which is to be understood not of an eternal death, but of a temporal one, or of a death of afflictions, as has been observed under the preceding section.

SECTION XXI

Cast away from you all your transgressions, whereby ye have transgressed, and make you a new heart and a new spirit; for why will ye die, O house of Israel? For I have no pleasure in the death of him that dieth, saith the Lord God: Wherefore turn yourselves, and live ye.—Ezek. xviii. 31, 32.

THIS passage of Scripture is frequently used by the § patrons of free-will, and opposers of God's grace; in which they imagine the power of man in conversion is strongly asserted, and the doctrine of reprobation suffi-

---

* Ib. p. 34; ed. 2. 33.   † Whitby, pp. 237, 242; ed. 2. 231, 236.

‡ Ezek. xxxiii. 19.   § Remontr. in Coll. Hag. art. iii. iv. p. 216; Act. Synod. p. 78, &c.;

Curcell. l. 5, c. 6, sect. 1. p. 363; et. l. 6, c. 14, sect 8, p. 408; Limborch. l. 4, c. 5, sect. 2, p. 331, &, 31. p. 374.

ciently disproved; but whether they are, or are not, we shall be better able to judge when the following things are considered.

1. That the exhortation to *cast away* their *transgressions from* them, regards either their *sins* themselves, which they had committed, and shows, that they were not only unprofitable, but pernicious, and so to be disliked and abhorred, as such things are that are proper to be cast away; or else the *punishment* due to their sins, which they might have removed and cast off from them by their repentance and reformation, and is the sense Kimchi gives of the words; or rather those things, particularly their *idols, by which they transgressed.* Now let it be observed, that this phrase of *casting away transgressions,* is no where else used, is peculiar to Ezekiel, and so may be best interpreted by chap. xx. 7, 8. *Then said I unto them, Cast ye away every man the abominations of his eyes,* &c. Now these idols were the abominations of their eyes, were the cause of their transgressions, or that *by which they transgressed, which* their *own hands had made unto* them, *for a sin :** and what they had power or were able to cast away from them; and no ways militates against the necessity of an unfrustrable operation in conversion.

2. The other exhortation, to *make* them *a new heart and a new spirit,* admitting that it designs a renewed, regenerated heart and spirit, in which are new principles of light, life, and love, grace, and holiness, it will not prove that it is in the power of an unregenerate man, to make himself such a heart and spirit; since from God's commands, to man's power, *non valet consequentia,* is no argument: God commands men to keep the whole law perfectly; it does not follow from hence that they can do it; his precepts show what man ought to do, not what he can do. Such an exhortation as this, to *make a new heart,* may be designed to convince men of their want of one, and of the importance of it, that without it is no salvation; and so be the means, through the efficacious grace of God, of his elect enjoying this blessing; for what he here exhorts to, he has absolutely promised in the new covenant ;† *A new heart also will I give you, and a new spirit will I put within you.* Though it ought to be observed, that these words are not spoken to unconverted persons, but to *the house of Israel, every one* of them; who cannot be thought, especially all of them, to have been at that time in an unregenerate state; and therefore must not be understood of the first work of renovation, but of some after renewings, which were to appear in their external conversation; and so the words have the same sense as those of the apostle Paul to the believing Ephesians,‡ *Be ye renewed in the spirit of your minds ; and put on the new man, which after God is created in righteousness and true holiness.* Moreover, by a *new heart,* and a *new spirit,* may be

meant, as the Targum of Jonathan Ben Uzziel renders them, לב דחיל ורוח דחלא, *a fearing heart,* and *a spirit of fear,* that is, a heart and spirit, to fear, serve, and worship the Lord, and not idols. And it is observable, that wherever a new heart and spirit are spoken of, they stand opposed to idols, and the service of them; so that the exhortation amounts to no more than this, that they yield a hearty reverential obedience to the living God, and not to dumb idols. Besides, what is here called a *new heart,* is, in chap. xi. 9, called *one heart,* that is, a single heart, in opposition to a double or hypocritical one; and so may design sincerity and uprightness in their national repentance and external reformation, which they are here pressed unto.

3. The expostulation, *Why will ye die ?* is not made with all men; nor can it be proved that it was made with any who were not eventually saved, but with *the house of Israel,* who were called the children and people of God; and therefore cannot disprove any act of preterition passing on others, nor be an impeachment of the truth and sincerity of God. Besides, the death expostulated about, is not an eternal, but a temporal one, or what concerned their temporal affairs, and civil condition, and circumstances of life; see chap. xxxiii. 24 to 29. Hence,

4. The affirmation, *I have no pleasure in the death of him that dieth,* which is sometimes introduced with an oath,§ *as I live, saith the Lord God, I have no pleasure in the death of the wicked,* does not in the least militate against an act of preterition; whereby any are left by God justly to perish in and for their iniquities; or the decree of reprobation, whereby any, on the score of their transgressions, are appointed, or fore-ordained to condemnation and death; and therefore all the reasonings|| made use of to disprove these things, founded on this passage of Scripture, are vain and impertinent; for a death of afflictions is here intended, as has been already observed, which the house of Israel was groaning under, and complaining of; though it was wholly owing to themselves, and which was not grateful to God, and in which he took no pleasure : which is to be understood, not simply and absolutely, and with respect to all persons afflicted by him; for he delights in the *exercise of judgment and righteousness,* as well as in showing mercy, and *laughs at the calamity* of wicked men, and *mocks when* their *fear cometh ;*¶ but it is to be taken comparatively; as when he says,** *I will have mercy, and not sacrifice ;* that is, I take delight in mercy rather than in sacrifice; so here, *I have no pleasure in the death of him that dieth :* in his afflictions, distresses, calamities, captivity, and the like; but rather, that he would *return from his ways,* repent and reform, and *live* in his own land; which shows the mercy and compassion of God,†† who *does not afflict willingly, nor grieve the*

---

* Isa. **xxxi.** 7.   † Ezek. **xxxiv.** 26.   32, 156, 192, 193.   ¶ Jer. ix. 24 ; Prov.
‡ Eph. iv. 23, 24.   § Ezek. **xxxiii.** 11.   i. 26.   ** Hos. v. 6.   †† Lam. iii.
|| See Whitby, pp. 3, 33, 160, 196, 197 ; ed. 2. 3,   33.

children of men. Wherefore he renews his exhortation, *Turn yourselves, and live ye.* The sum of all this is, you have no reason to say, as in ver. 2, *The fathers have eaten sour grapes, and the children's teeth are set on edge;* or as in ver. 25, that *the way of the Lord is not equal;* seeing it is not for the sins of your parents, but your own, that the present calamities you are complaining of lie upon you; for my part, I take no delight in your death, in your captivity; it would be more agreeable to me, would you turn from your evil ways, to the Lord your God, and behave according to the laws I have given you to walk by, and so live in your own land, in the quiet possession of all your goods and estates. But what has this to do with the affairs of eternal life, or eternal death?

SECTION XXII.

Because I have purged thee, and thou wast not purged, thou shalt not be purged from thy filthiness any more, till I have caused my fury to rest upon thee.—Ezek. xxiv. 13.

THESE words are represented as irreconcilable with God's decrees of election and reprobation as inconsistent with the doctrine of particular redemption, and in favour of sufficient grace given to all men.[*] But,

1. The words are not spoken to all men, nor do they declare what God hath done for, or what he would have done by all men; but are directed only to Jerusalem, or the house of Israel, whose destruction is here represented under the parable of a boiling pot; and do not discover any design of God, or steps that he has taken towards the purgation of all mankind, and therefore no ways militate against the decrees of election and reprobation.

2. This purgation of Jerusalem, and the inhabitants thereof, is to be understood either of ceremonial purifications, or of an external reformation of life and manners, and not of an internal cleansing of them, much less of all men, from sin, by the blood of Jesus; and so is no ways inconsistent with the doctrine of particular redemption.

3. These words do not express what God had done, and was not done; which is a contradiction in terms; nor what he had done sufficient for their purgation, but was obstructed by their obstinacy; or that he would have purged them, and they would not be purged; for *our God is in the heavens; he hath done whatsoever he pleased,*[†] but what he commanded to be done, and was not done; for so the words should be rendered; as they are by Pagnine, *Jussi ut mundares te, et non mundasti te, I commanded that thou shouldest purge thyself, and thou hast not purged thyself;* to which agrees the note of Junius on the text. *Verbo præcepi te mundari et toties et tamdiu per prophetas imperavi, I have in my word, and by my prophets, so often and so long*

commanded thee to be purged. The sense of them is, that God had commanded either ceremonial ablutions and purifications, or a moral, external reformation, and they had not obeyed; and therefore threatens to leave them in their filthiness, and pour out all his fury on them; and so are no proof of God's giving sufficient grace, or sufficient means of grace to all men. The text in Jer. ii. 9, *We would have healed Babylon, but she is not healed,* is very improperly joined with this, since they are not the words of God, expressing any kind intentions, or sufficient means of healing, which were obstructed, as through mistake, they are represented by a learned writer;[†] but of the Israelites, or others, who were concerned for the temporal welfare of Babylon, though in vain, and to no purpose.

SECTION XXIII

Ye are the salt of the earth; but if the salt have lost its savour, wherewith shall it be salted? It is thenceforth good for nothing, but to be cast out, and to be trodden under foot of men.—Matt. v. 13.

THIS is one of the places which, it is said,[§] "do plainly suppose that saints, or true believers, or men once truly good, may cease to be so; for sure, good salt must signify good men; nor can this salt lose its savour, and become good for nothing, but by ceasing to be good salt." To which I reply,

1. That the text speaks not of men as saints or true believers, comparable to salt, for the truth and savour of the grace of God in them: but as ministers and preachers of the Gospel, who, by their savoury doctrines and conversations are *the salt of the earth,* the means of purifying and preserving the world from corruption. Now some men may be good preachers, and so good salt, and yet not be good men, or true believers; and therefore, when any of these drop the savoury truths of the word, and fall off from the seeming conversation they have maintained, they are no proofs nor instances of the final and total apostacy of real saints. If it should be said, that those who are here called *the salt of the earth,* were the disciples of Christ, and therefore good men, as well as good preachers; it may be replied, that there were many who were called the disciples of Christ, besides the apostles; and some there were who, in process of time, drew back from him,[||] and *walked no more with him.* But allowing the twelve apostles are particularly designed, there was a Judas among them, who Christ might have a special eye to; for he *knew from the beginning who they were that believed not, and who should betray him;*[¶] that one of those whom he had *chosen* was *a devil;* that he would lose his usefulness and his place; that he would be an unprofitable wretch; and, at last, be rejected and despised of men. Admitting further, that the true and sincere apostles of Christ are here intended; yet this

---

[*] Whitby, pp. 77, 160, 204, 251, 252, 447; ed. 2. 76, 156, 199, 245, 246, 452.

[†] Psal. cxv. 3.   [‡] Whitby, pp. 204,

477; ed. 2. 199, 456.   [§] Ibid. p. 435; ed. 2. 424.   [||] John. vi. 66.

[¶] John vi. 64, 70.

of losing their savour is only a supposition, which *nil ponit in esse*, puts nothing in being, proves no matter of fact, and may be only designed as a caution to them, to take heed to themselves, their doctrines, and ministry, to which they are advised in many other places; see Matt. xvi. 6, 12, and xxiv. 4, 5; Luke xxi. 34—36; though there was no possibility of their final and total falling away.

2. The *savour* here supposed, that it may be lost, cannot mean *the savour* of true grace, or true grace itself, which cannot be lost, being an incorruptible seed; but either gifts, qualifying men to be good and useful preachers, which gifts may cease; or the savoury doctrines of the gospel men may depart from; or their seeming savoury conversations they may put away; or that seeming savour, zeal, and affection, with which they have preached, and which may be dropped; or their whole usefulness, which they may lose; for all these things men may have and lose, who never really and truly tasted that the Lord is gracious: and, generally speaking, when such men lose their usefulness, it is never more retrieved; they become and remain unprofitable, are despised and trodden under foot of men: but these instances are no proofs that saints, or true believers, or men once truly good, may cease to do so.

The similitude in which our Lord saith,[*] that *a piece of new cloth is not to be put to an old garment, lest the rent be made worse; nor new wine into old bottles, lest the bottles burst;* no more plainly supposes this, than the former metaphor of *salt:* for be it that the design of this to show,[†] that Christ's "young disciples must not presently be put upon severe duties, lest they should be discouraged and fall off from him." It shows indeed their weakness and danger of falling, and yet, at the same time, the care and concern of Christ in the preservation of them; and therefore ought not to be improved into an argument against their final perseverance: though the plain design of the similitude seems, from the context, to be this, that it would be equally as absurd for the disciples to fast and be sad, while Christ, the bridegroom, was with them, as it would be to put new cloth into an old garment, or new wine into old bottles.

Nor does the commination against them, who shall *offend one of Christ's little ones believing in him,[‡]* viz. that *it were better for him that a mill-stone was hanged about his neck, and he cast into the midst of the sea,* plainly suppose that saints, or true believers, may cease to be so; for the word σκανδαλίζειν, here used, does not signify an *offending* of them, so as to be the occasion of their falling off from the faith to their eternal ruin, but stands opposed to *receiving* of them, in ver. 5, and is explained by despising them, in ver. 10, and at most, can only mean the *laying of an offence,* scandal, or stumbling-block in

their way; which might be of bad consequence, considering their weakness and the wickedness of men, were it not for the care, power, and grace of God, which are concerned for them: and since *the angels,* who are their guardians on earth, *always behold the face of Christ's Father in heaven,* ver. 10; and seeing *the Son of man,* who also is the Son of God, *is come to save* such *lost* ones, ver. 11, and especially since *it is not the will of* our *Father which is in heaven, that one of these little ones should perish,* ver. 14. It is not false but true, that they who do truly believe in Christ, are of the number of those whom God would not have to perish, cannot be so offended as to fall off from the faith to their ruin: nor do the pathetic discourses, and dreadful woes and punishments denounced, imply the contrary; seeing they are used to show the care of God over his people, and the natural tendency to ruin such offences might have, was it not prevented by his power; and consequently their attempts that way are not less sinful and criminal. As for Rom. xiv. 20; 1 Cor. viii. 9, 11; Psal. cxxv. 3; which are urged to the same purpose; see in sections VIII., XXXVI., and XXXVII.

SECTION XXIV

Wo unto thee, Chorazin! wo unto thee, Bethsaida! for if the mighty works which were done in you had been done in Tyre and Sidon, they would have repented long ago in sackcloth and ashes. And thou, Capernaum, which art exalted unto heaven, shalt be brought down to hell: for if the mighty works which have been done in thee had been done in Sodom, it would have remained until this day.—Matt. xi. 21, 23.

THESE words are frequently insisted on[§] as proving man's ability to repent, believe, and convert himself; and that unfrustrable and irresistible grace is not necessary to these things; and that faith, repentance, and conversion, are not produced by it. But,

1. Here is no mention made of faith and conversion, only of repentance; and that not spiritual and evangelical, but external and legal; such as was performed in *sackcloth and ashes,* and by virtue of which *Sodom* might have *remained unto this day;* for though a repentance is not unto eternal salvation, yet it is often attended with temporal blessings, and is the means of averting temporal judgments, as in the case of the Ninevites, and may be where the true grace of God is not; with the want of this Christ might, as he justly does, upbraid the cities where his mighty works had been done, and the Jews, in Matt. xii. 41, and xxi. 31, 42,[||] which might have been performed by them, though they had no power to repent in a spiritual and evangelical sense, to which more is required than the bare performance of miracles. See Luke xvi. 31.

---

* Matt. ix. 16, 17.   † Whitby, p. 435; ed. 2. 426.   ‡ Matt. xviii. 6.   § Remonstr. in Coll. Hag. art. iii. iv. p. 218; Act. Synod. p. 120,

&c; Limborch. l. 4, c. 13, sect. 6, p. 370; Whitby, p. 173; ed. 2. 169.

|| Whitby, p. 174; ed. 2. 170.

2. These words are to be understood, as Grotius * observes, in a popular sense, and express what was probable, according to a human judgment of things ; and the meaning is, that if the inhabitants of Tyre, Sidon, and Sodom, had had the advantages of Christ's ministry, and of seeing his miracles, as the inhabitants of Chorazin, Bethsaida, and Capernaum had, it looks very likely, or one would be ready to conclude, they would have repented of their flagitious crimes, which brought down the judgments of God upon them in such a remarkable manner ; as these ought to have done, particularly of their sin of rejecting the Messiah, notwithstanding all the evidence of miracles, and convictions of their own consciences, and so probably sinned the sin against the Holy Ghost. And therefore,

3. The words are an hyperbolical exaggeration of their wickedness, such as those in Ezek. iii. 5—7, showing that they were worse than the Tyrians and Sidonians, who lived most profligate and dissolute lives ; than the inhabitants of Sodom, so infamous for their unnatural lusts ; yea, than any others, if there were any worse than these under the heavens ; and therefore would be punished with the worst of punishments, ver. 22, 24. In much the same way are we to understand, Matt. xii. 14, and xxi. 31, 32, where Christ upbraids the Jews with the want even of an external repentance for their sin of rejecting him, though they had such a full proof and demonstration of his being the Messiah ; and therefore were worse than the men of Nineveh, who repented externally at the preaching of Jonah ; yea, worse, notwithstanding all their pretended sanctity and righteousness, than the publicans and harlots, who went *into the kingdom of God*, attended on the outward ministry of the word, *believed John the Baptist*, and gave at least an assent to what he said concerning the Messiah as true.

4. These words can be no proof of God's giving sufficient grace equally to all men, which is in some effectual to conversion, and in others not ; seeing the men of Tyre, Sidon, and Sodom, had not the same advantages and means, or the same grace, as the inhabitants of these cities had, if the mighty works done among them are to be called so. Besides, where persons have the same external means of grace, and the same outward advantages, and one truly repents, believes, and is converted, and another not ; this is owing not to the will of man, but the sovereign grace of God, as appears from ver. 25, 26 :—*At that time Jesus answered and said, I thank thee, O 'Father, Lord of heaven and earth, because thou hast hid these things from the wise and prudent, and hast revealed them unto babes ; even so, Father, for so it seemed good in thy right.*

SECTION XXV

O Jerusalem, Jerusalem, thou that killest the prophets, and stonest them which are sent unto thee, how often would I have gathered thy children together, even as a hen gathereth her chicken under her wings, and ye would not !—Matt. xxiii. 37.

NOTHING is more common in the mouths and writings of the Arminians than this Scripture, which they are ready to produce on every occasion, against the doctrines of election and reprobation, particular redemption, and the irresistible power of God in conversion, and in favour of sufficient grace, and of the free-will and power of man,† though to very little purpose, as will appear when the following things are observed.

1. That by Jerusalem we are not to understand the city, nor all the inhabitants ; but the rulers and governors of it, both civil and ecclesiastical, especially the great Sanhedrim, which was held in it, to whom best belong the descriptive characters of *killing the prophets*, and *stoning* such as were *sent* to them by God, and who are manifestly distinguished from their *children* ; it being usual to call such who were the heads of the people, either in a civil or ecclesiastical sense, *fathers*, Acts vii. 2, and xxii. 1, and such who were subjects and disciples, *children*, xix. 44, Matt. xii. 27, Isa. viii. 16, 18. Besides, our Lord's discourse, throughout the whole context, is directed to the Scribes and Pharisees, the ecclesiastical *guides* of the people, and to whom the civil governors paid a special regard. Hence it is manifest, that they are not the same persons whom Christ would have gathered, who *would not*. It is not said, *how often would I have gathered you, and you would not*, as Dr. Whitby‡ more than once inadvertently cites the text ; nor, *he would have gathered Jerusalem, and she would not*, as the same author§ transcribes it in another place ; nor, *he would have gathered them, thy children, and they would not*, in which form it is also sometimes‖ expressed by him ; but *I would have gathered thy children, and ye would not*, which observation alone is sufficient to destroy the argument founded on this passage in favour of free-will.

2. That the *gathering* here spoken of does not design a gathering of the Jews to Christ internally, by the Spirit and grace of God ; but a gathering of them to him internally, by and under the ministry of the word, to hear him preach ; so as that they might be brought to a conviction of and an assent unto him, as the Messiah ; which, though it might have fallen short of saving faith in him, would have been sufficient to have preserved them from temporal ruin, threatened to their city and temple in the following verse—*Behold, your house is left unto you desolate :* which

---

* In loc.   † See Whitby, p. 13, 77, 162, 204, 222, 358 ; ed. 2. 13, 76, 158, 199, 216, 349 ; Remonstr. in Coll. Hag. art. iii. iv. p. 215 ; Act. & Script. Synodalia circa art. iv. p. 64 ; Curcell. Relig. Christ. l. 6, c. 6, sect. 7, p. 370,

and c. 13, sect. 5, p. 402 ; Limborch, l. 4, c. 13, sect. 7, p. 371.
   ‡ Whitby, pp. 13, 162, 201 ; ed. 2. 13, 158, 197.   § Ibid. p. 77 ; ed. 2. 76.
   ‖ Ibid. p. 222 ; ed. 2. 216.

preservation is signified by the *hen gathering her chickens under her wings,* and shows that the text has no concern with the controversy about the manner of the operation of God's grace in conversion; for all those whom Christ would gather in this sense were gathered, notwithstanding all the opposition made by the rulers of the people.

3. That the will of Christ to gather these persons is not to be understood of his divine will, or of his will as God; *for who hath resisted his will?* this cannot be hindered nor made void; *he hath done whatsoever he pleased;* but of his human will, or of his will as man; which though not contrary to the divine will, but subordinate to it, yet not always the same with it, nor always fulfilled. He speaks here as a man and *minister of the circumcision,* and expresses a human affection for the inhabitants of Jerusalem, and a human wish or will for their temporal good, instances of which human affection and will may be observed in Mark x. 21, Luke xix. 41, and xxii. 42. Besides, this will of gathering the Jews to him was in him, and expressed by him at certain several times, by intervals, and therefore he says, *How often would I have gathered,* &c. Whereas the divine will is one continued invariable and unchangeable will, is always the same, and never begins or ceases to be, and to which such an expression as this is inapplicable; and therefore this passage of Scripture does not contradict the absolute and sovereign will of God in the distinguishing acts of it, respecting election and reprobation.

4. That the persons whom Christ would have gathered are not represented as being *unwilling* to be gathered; but their rulers were not willing that they should. The opposition and resistance to the will of Christ, were not made by the people, but by their governors. The common people seemed inclined to attend the ministry of Christ, as appears from the vast crowds which, at different times and places, followed him; but the chief priests and rulers did all they could to hinder the collection of them to him; and their belief in him as the Messiah, by traducing his character, miracles, and doctrines, and by passing an act that whosoever confessed him should be put out of the synagogue; so that the obvious meaning of the text is the same with that of ver. 13, where our Lord says, *Wo unto you, scribes and Pharisees, hypocrites; for ye shut up the kingdom of heaven against men; for ye neither go in yourselves, neither suffer ye them that are entering to go in;* and consequently is no proof of men's resisting the operations of the Spirit and grace of God, but of obstructions and discouragements thrown in the way of attendance on the external ministry of the word.

5. That in order to set aside and overthrow the doctrines of election, reprobation, and particular redemption, it should be proved that Christ, as God, would have gathered, not Jerusalem and the inhabitants thereof only, but all mankind, even such as are not eventually saved, and that in a spiritual saving way and manner to himself, of which there is not the least intimation in this text; and in order to establish the resistibility of God's grace, by the perverse will of man, so as to become of no effect, it should be proved that Christ would have savingly converted these persons, and they would not be converted; and that he bestowed the same grace upon them he does bestow on others who are converted; whereas the sum of this passage lies in these few words, that Christ, as man, out of a compassionate regard for the people of the Jews, to whom he was sent, would have gathered them together under his ministry, and have instructed them in the knowledge of himself as the Messiah; which, if they had only notionally received, would have secured them as chickens under the hen from impending judgments which afterwards fell upon them; but their governors, and not they, would not, that is, would not suffer them to be collected together in such a manner, and hindered all they could, their giving any credit to him as the Messiah; though had it been said *and they would not,* it would only have been a most sad instance of the perverseness of the will of man, which often opposes his temporal as well as his spiritual good.

SECTION XXVI

The parable of the talents.—Matt. xxv. 14—30.

I. It is not to be concluded from this parable that sufficient grace is given to all men, by which they may be saved if they will. For,

1. All men are not designed by the *servants* to whom the talents were committed; these are not all Christ's servants, nor so called; much less with an emphasis *his own servants.* No more can be included under this character here than belong to *the kingdom of heaven,* the visible gospel church-state, the subject of this parable, which does not consist of all mankind; yea, even all the elect of God are not intended; for though they are the servants of Christ, and his own servants, whom the Father has given him, and he has purchased by his blood, and subjects to himself by his grace, yet all that come under this character here, were not such; for one of them is represented as a *wicked and slothful servant,* and to be justly *cast into outer darkness;* but the servants of the *man travelling into a far country,* meaning Christ, are the ministers of the gospel, who are, in a peculiar sense, the servants of Christ; and who, whether faithful or slothful, are in a lively manner described in this parable, which is a distinct parable from that which is delivered in the preceding part of this chapter; for as that gives an account of the several and different members of the visible church, so this of the several and different ministers in it; and being spoken to the disciples, was an instruction, direction, and caution to them, and not only to them, but is so to all the ministers of the word in succeeding ages.

2. Sufficient grace is not intended by the *talents*, but gifts; and these not merely the gifts of natural and acquired knowledge, of wealth, riches, and honour, of the external ministry of the word, gospel ordinances, and opportunities of enjoying them; but spiritual gifts, or such as fit and qualify men to be preachers of the gospel, as appears from the *name*, *talents*, these being the greatest gifts for usefulness and service in the church, as they were the greatest of weights and coins among the Jews; from the *nature* of them, being such as may be improved or lost, and for which men are accountable; from the *persons* to whom they were delivered, the servants of Christ; from the *time* of the delivery of them, when Christ went into a far country, into heaven, when he ascended on high, and received gifts for men, and gave them to men; and from the *unequal distribution* of them, being given to some more, and to others less; all which perfectly agree with ministeral gifts. Now these may be where grace is not; and if they are to be called grace because freely given, yet they are not given to all men, and much less unto salvation, for men may have these and be damned. See Matt. vii. 22, 23; 1 Cor. xiii. 1, 2. And therefore,

II. It is not to be established from hence that a man has a power to improve the stock of sufficient grace given him,[*] and by his improvement, procure eternal happiness to himself; since such a stock of grace is not designed by the talents, nor is it either implanted or improved by man; nor does the parable suggest that men, by their improvement of the talents committed to them, do or can procure eternal happiness. *Good and faithful servants* are indeed commended by Christ, and he graciously promises great things to them, which are not proportioned to their deserts; for whereas they have been *faithful over a few things*, he promises to make them *rulers over many things*, and bids them enter *into the joy of* their *Lord;* into the joy which he of his grace and goodness had provided for them, and not which they had merited and procured for themselves.

III. It is not to be inferred from hence that true grace once given or implanted may be taken away or lost; for the parable speaks not of what is wrought and implanted in men, but of goods and talents, meaning gifts, bestowed on them, committed to their trust, and received by them; which may be lost, or taken away, or be wrapped up in a napkin, and lie useless by them; when true grace is the incorruptible seed which never dies, but always remains that good part which will never be taken away nor lost, but is inseparably connected with eternal glory.

SECTION XXVII

And when he was come near, he beheld the city, and wept over it, saying, If thou hadst known, even thou, at least in this thy day, the things which belong unto thy peace: but now they are hid from thine eyes.—Luke xix. 41, 42.

THESE words' are often made use of to disprove any decree of reprobation in God, Christ's dying intentionally, for some only, the disability of man, and in favour of a day of grace. But,

I. It should be observed that they are not spoken of all mankind, only to Jerusalem and its inhabitants, and regard not their spiritual and eternal salvation, but their temporal peace and prosperity; and therefore ought not to have a place in our controversies about these things. That the words relate only to Jerusalem and the inhabitants thereof, will not be disputed; and that they design their temporal prosperity, which Christ was concerned for, and was almost at an end, appears from the following verses, 43, 44, *For the days shall come upon thee*, &c. Add to this, this one observation more, that Christ here speaks as a man, expressing his human affection for the present temporal good of this city, as is evident from his *weeping* over it on his near approach to it. Hence,

2. There is no foundation in this text for such an argument as this:[†]—"Christ here taketh it for granted that the people of Jerusalem, in the day of their visitation by the Messiah, might savingly have known the things belonging to their peace. Now, either this assertion, that they might savingly have known these things, was according to truth; or his wish, that they had thus known the things belonging to their peace, was contrary to his Father's will and decree; which is palpably absurd. And seeing the will of Christ was always the same with that of his Father, it follows also that God the Father had the same charitable affection to them; and so had laid no bar against their happiness by his decrees, nor withheld from them any thing on his part necessary to their everlasting welfare." But it was not their everlasting welfare, or that they might savingly know the things which belong to eternal peace, but their outward prosperity, which he as a man, and one of their own nation, was concerned for; and such a human compassionate regard for them he might have and show, notwithstanding any decree of his Father's, respecting the eternal state of some or all of these people, or any other part of mankind. It does not follow that, because Christ as a man had a charitable affection for the inhabitants of Jerusalem, God the Father bore an everlasting love to them; or, because he showed a goodwill to their temporal welfare, that the Father had at heart their eternal salvation. Christ's human affections and will were not always the same with his Father's: he beheld the young man mentioned by the evangelist,[‡] *and he loved him*, as man; but it does not

---

* Vid. Whitby, pp. 30, 175; ed. 2. 30, 171.
† Whitby, p. 13, 14, 236, 237; ed. 2. 13, 14, 231.   ‡ Mark x. 21.

follow from hence that God the Father loved him, and gave him or did every thing necessary to his everlasting welfare. The sufferings and death of Christ were absolutely and peremptorily decreed by God, and yet Christ as man desired that, if it was possible, the cup might pass from him; and so he might wish as man for the temporal happiness of this city, though he knew that *the desolations determined would be poured upon the desolate*,[*] both in a temporal and spiritual sense; and yet his tears over them are tears of charity and true compassion, and not crocodile's tears, as they are impiously called,[†] on a supposition of God's decree of reprobation, or act of preterition. Hence,

3. We shall not meet with so much difficulty to reconcile these words to the doctrine of particular redemption, as is suggested,[‡] when it is said, "You may as well hope to reconcile light and darkness, as these words of Christ with his intention to die only for them who should actually be saved;" unless it can be thought irreconcilable, and what implies a contradiction, that Christ as man should wish temporal good to the inhabitants of Jerusalem, and yet not intentionally die for all mankind: should he intentionally die for them who are not actually saved, his intentions would be so far frustrated, and his death be in vain.

4. It does follow from hence that, because these people might have known the things which belonged to their temporal peace, though they were now in a judicial way hid from their eyes, therefore men may of themselves, and without the powerful and unfrustrable grace of God working upon their hearts, and enlightening their understandings, know the things that belong to their spiritual and eternal peace, seeing it is said of natural men, *the way of peace they have not known;*[§] and could these words be understood of the things belonging to spiritual and eternal peace, they would only prove that these Jews had the means of the knowledge of them, which they despising, God had given them up to blindness of heart; and so Christ's words are to be considered, not so much as pitying them, but as upbraiding them with their ignorance, unbelief, neglect, and contempt of him, his miracles, and doctrines; therefore God was just, and they inexcusable.

5. The time in which Christ was on earth was a day of light, of great mercies and favours, to the Jews; but it does not follow that, because they had such a time, therefore all men have a day of grace, in which they may be saved if they will. Besides, the phrase *this thy day* may respect *the time of her (Jerusalem's) visitation*, ver. 44, which was a day of vengeance, and not of grace, that was hastening on, and near at hand, though hid from her, and was the occasion of Christ's compassionate tears and wishes.

SECTION XXVIII

The same came for a witness, to bear witness of the light, that all men through him might believe.—John i. 7.

A CONSIDERABLE argument in favour of the extent of Christ's death to all men is thought to arise from the obligation which is, and always was, upon all persons to whom the Gospel is or was revealed, to believe in Christ, that he came to save them, and died for them; for if he died not for them, they are bound to believe a lie; and if condemned for not believing, they are condemned for not believing an untruth.|| I observe,

1. That the argument is most miserably lame and deficient. The thing to be proved is, that Christ died for every individual man and woman that have been, are, or shall be in the world. The medium by which this is attempted to be proved is, the obligation that lies on such to whom the Gospel is revealed, to believe that Christ died for them; and the conclusion is, that therefore Christ died for all men. Now the Gospel has not been nor is it revealed to all men, only to some; wherefore was there any truth in the medium, the conclusion would not follow. The argument stands thus: all men to whom the Gospel is revealed are bound to believe that Christ died for them; some men have the Gospel revealed to them, therefore Christ died for all men. The weakness and fallacy of such an argument must be seen by every one; a most miserable argument this, which proceeds upon a partial revelation of the Gospel to an universal redemption. I observe,

2. That the obligation to believe in Christ, and so the faith to which men are obliged, are in proportion, and according to the nature of the revelation of the Gospel, which obliges them. Now the Gospel revelation is either external or internal: the external revelation is by the word, and the ministry of it; which respecting Christ, lies in these things, that he is really and properly God, and truly man; that he is the Son of God, and the Mediator between God and men; that he is the Messiah, who is actually come in the flesh; that he died and rose again the third day; is ascended into heaven, and sits at the right hand of God, and will come a second time to judge the world in righteousness; and that by his obedience, sufferings, and death, he is become the Saviour of sinners, and that none can be saved but by him. Now let it be observed, that this revelation is general, and not particular, and does not necessarily oblige persons to whom it comes to believe that Christ is their Redeemer and Saviour, and that he died for them particularly, though the Spirit of God may and does bless it to many for the begetting special faith; and it may and does lay a general foundation for special and appropriating acts of that grace, yet it only requires an historical faith, or bare assent to the truth of the said propositions. Now such a faith is not saving;

---

* Dan. ix. 26, 27.　　　† Curcellæi Relig. Christ. Inst. l. 6, c. 6, sect. 7, p. 470, and c. 13, sect. 5, p. 402.

‡ Whitby, p. 162; ed. 2, 158.　　§ Rom. iii. 17.　　|| Ibid., p. 143, 144, 146; ed. 2. 140—142.

men may have this, and yet be damned; yea, the devils themselves have it. It follows that men may be obliged to believe, and yet not to the saving of their souls, or that Christ died for them. Besides, this revelation is not made to all men; and therefore all men, such as Indians, and others, are not obliged to believe in Christ, nor even to give a bare assent to the truth of the abovesaid things, much less to believe that Christ died for them; and indeed, *How shall they believe in him of whom they have not heard? and how shall they hear without a preacher?** And perhaps all are not obliged to believe who live in a land where this revelation does come; as those who have not their natural reason and hearing, or the due and proper use and exercise of the same, such as infants, idiots, madmen, and those who are entirely deaf; only such to whom this revelation is made, and are capable of hearing and understanding it, are obliged to have faith in Christ by it, as were the Jews of old, who were condemned for their unbelief, not because they did not believe that Christ died for them, to which they were not obliged, but because they did not believe him to be God, the Son of God, the true Messiah, and Saviour of sinners. The internal revelation of the Gospel, and of Christ through it, is by *the Spirit of wisdom and revelation in the knowledge of him;* whereby a soul is made sensible of its lost state and condition, and of its need of a Saviour; is made acquainted with Christ as the alone Saviour, both able and willing to save to the uttermost all that come to God by him; whence it is encouraged to venture on him, rely upon him, and believe in him to the saving of it: now such an one ought to believe, and none but such, that Christ died for them. This faith all men have not; it is the faith of God's elect, the gift of God, the operation of his Spirit, and the produce of almighty power.

Now, according to the revelation is the faith men are obliged to, and what is produced by it: if the revelation is external, or the Gospel comes in word only, the faith men are obliged to is only an historical one, nor can any other follow upon it; and that Christ died for every individual man is no part of the revelation. If the revelation is internal, a special spiritual appropriating faith is the result of it; but then this revelation is not made to all men, nor are God's elect themselves, before conversion, bound to believe that Christ died for them; and when they are converted, to believe that Christ died for them is not the first act of special faith; it is the plerophory, the full assurance of faith, to say, *He hath loved me, and hath given himself for me.*† Hence,

3. Since there is not a revelation of the Gospel made to all men, and all men are not bound to believe in Christ, much less to believe that Christ died for them; it follows that no such absurdity can attend the denial of universal redemption, that some more are bound to believe a lie; nor will it be the condemnation of the heathens that they believe not in Christ, but that they have sinned against the light, and broken the law of nature; nor will any persons enjoying a revelation be condemned for not believing that Christ died for them, but for the breach of God's laws, and neglect and contempt of his Gospel; nor is there any danger of any one person's believing a lie, since all those who do truly believe in Christ, and that he died for them, shall certainly be saved, which is the fullest proof that can be of his dying for them. Christ dying for an unbelieving Christian, and a Christian being under a condemnatory decree, are unintelligible phrases, mere paradoxes, and contradictions in terms.‡

4. John the Baptist's bearing witness of Christ, the light, and true Messiah, *that all men through him might believe,* respects not all the individuals of human nature, since millions were dead before he began his testimony, and multitudes since, whom it never reached; nor can it design more than the Jews, to whom alone he bore witness of Christ; the faith which he taught, and required by his testimony, was not to believe that Christ died for them, who as yet was not dead, but an assent unto him as the Messiah. This was *the work,* will, and command of God, *that they should believe on him,* in this sense, *whom he had sent.* This is what Christ often called for from them, declaring, that if they believed not that he was the Messiah, they should die in their sins; and this was what the Spirit of God *reproved the world of the Jews* for, by bringing down the wrath of God in temporal ruin and destruction, upon their persons, nation, city, and temple. Since then this text, with multitudes of others, which speak of believing in Christ, only regards the people of the Jews, and designs only a bare assent to him as the Messiah, which would have preserved that people and nation from temporal ruin; it does not follow that all men are bound to believe in Christ, that he died for them, and consequently can be of no service to the doctrine of universal redemption.

SECTION XXIX

But these things I say, that ye might be saved.
John v. 34.

This passage of Scripture is often produced§ as a proof of Christ's serious intention to save some who are not saved, to whom he gave sufficient means of salvation, which they refused; and consequently that his Father had made no decree, whereby they stood excluded from salvation; that he did not die intentionally only for such who are actually saved, and

* Rom. x. 14.

† Gal. ii. 20.   ‡ Whitby, p. 146; ed. 2. 142.

§ Remonstr. in Coll. Hag. art. iii. iv. p. 216;

Act Synod. p. 81; Curcell. l. 6, c. 13, sec. 6, p. 402; Limborch. l. 4, c. 13, sect. 13, p. 373; Whitby, p. 13, 73, 135, 162; ed. 2. 13, 72, 132, 158.

that the work of conversion is not wrought by an irresistible and insuperable power. To which I reply,

1. It is certain that the Jews, to whom Christ here speaks, had not means sufficient to salvation; for though the testimonies of his Father, of John the Baptist, and of his own works and miracles, which he produced, were proper means to induce them to believe that he was the Messiah, yet not means sufficient to salvation; for to salvation, an internal work of grace, the regeneration of the Spirit, are absolutely requisite and necessary; without which no man can be saved. Now it is evident, that they wanted these, since they had not the love of God in them, ver. 42; nor his word abiding in them, ver. 38; nor so much as the knowledge of Christ's divinity, or of his being the true Messiah, ver. 18.

2. It is taken for granted, that these words regard a spiritual and eternal salvation; whereas they may very well be understood of a temporal one; and the sense of them be this; *these things I say*, that is, these testimonies of my Father, and of John, I produce, not so much for my own honour and glory, as for your good; that ye, through these testimonies of me, may believe that I am the true Messiah, and so be *saved* from the temporal ruin and destruction, which will otherwise come upon you and your nation, for your disbelief, neglect, and contempt of me. But,

3. Admitting that Christ spoke these words with a view to the spiritual and eternal salvation of his audience; it should be observed, that he is here to be considered as a preacher, a minister of the circumcision, sent to the lost sheep of the house of Israel, for whose welfare he had a compassionate regard and concern; and therefore published the things concerning his person, office, and grace, indefinitely to them all, that he might gain some, not knowing as man, though he did as God, who were chosen, and who were not; which consideration of him is neither injurious to God nor to him.

4. It will be difficult, if not impossible, to prove, that the persons to whom Christ spoke these words, were not eternally saved; though at the present time they were unbelievers, and destitute of the grace of God, yet might hereafter be converted and enabled to go to Christ for life and salvation; or at least, there might be some among them who were the elect of God, and sheep of Christ; for whose sake Christ might express himself in this manner, in order to bring them to the knowledge of him, and salvation by him; and therefore do not militate either against any decree or act of preterition passed by God, respecting any part of mankind, or the doctrines of particular redemption and unfrustrable grace in conversion.

SECTION XXX

And ye will not come to me, that ye might have life.—John v. 40.

THESE words are usually cited together with the former, and are urged for the same purposes; particularly to show that Christ seriously intended the salvation of such who would not come to him for it ; and that man does not lie under any disability of coming to Christ for life; did he, his not coming to Christ would not be criminal in him; nor would he be blame-worthy for what he could not help.[*] To which I answer,

1. That what Christ intends, he intends seriously; but it does not appear from these words, that he did intend the salvation of these persons who would not come to him, but rather the contrary; since they look more like a charge exhibited against them, for their neglect of him, as the way of life and salvation, and trusting to the law of Moses, and their obedience to it, and therefore did not receive him, or believe in him; and though Christ declined bringing in an accusation directly and in form against them, yet he acquaints them that there was one that accused them, even Moses, in whom they trusted; and therefore their future condemnation would be justifiable upon their own principles, and by the very writings they had such an opinion of; since these testified of him, and of eternal life by him, which they rejected.

2. These words are so far from being expressive of the power and liberty of the will of man to come to Christ, that they rather declare the perverseness and stubbornness of it; that man has no desire, inclination, or will, to go Christ for life; but had rather go any where else, or trust to any thing else, than to him. Man is *stout-hearted*, and *far from the righteousness* of Christ, and submission to it; is not *subject to the law of God*, nor the Gospel of Christ; nor *can he be*, till God works in him both *to will and to do of his good pleasure;* or until he is made *willing in the day of his power*. No one *can come to Christ, except the Father draw him;* nor has he a will to it, unless it be wrought in him.

3. Though man lies under such a disability, and has neither power nor will of himself to come to Christ for life; yet his not coming to Christ, when revealed in the external ministry of the Gospel, as God's way of salvation, is criminal and blame-worthy; since the disability and perverseness of his will are not owing to any decree of God, but to the corruption and vitiosity of his nature, through sin; and therefore, since this vitiosity of nature is blame-worthy; for *God made man upright*, though *they have sought out many inventions*, which have corrupted their nature; that which follows upon it, and is the effect of it, must be so too.

---

* Whitby, p. 52, 73, 358; ed. 2. 51, 72, 349.

SECTION XXXI

And I, if I be lifted up from the earth, will draw all men unto me——John xii. 32.

THOUGH this text is not produced by the principal writers in the Arminian controversy, nor by the Remonstrants formerly, nor by Curcellæus, nor by Limborch, nor by Whitby of late; yet inasmuch as it it is urged by others,* in favour of universal redemption, that he who draws all men to him by his death, must needs die for all men; it will be proper to consider the import of it, and the argument upon it. And,

1. It is certain, that the death of Christ, and the very kind of death he should die, is intimated by his being *lifted up from the earth;* since the evangelist observes in the next verse, that *this he said signifying what death he should die;* and it must be owned, that the *drawing of all men to Christ,* is here represented as a fruit of his death, or as what should attend it, or would follow upon it; *and I εἀν ὑψωθῶ, when I am lifted up from the earth, will draw all men to me.* And therefore,

2. The sense of these words pretty much depends on the meaning of the word *draw:* which either designs a collection of a large number of people to him, and about him, when he should be lifted on the cross, some against, others for him; some to reproach, and others to bewail him; or rather of *the gathering of the people to him,* through the ministry of the apostles; and so of their being enabled, through the power of divine grace, to come unto him, and believe on him for eternal life and salvation; for all those whom God has loved with an everlasting love, and Christ has died for, are, sooner or later, *with loving-kindness drawn unto him;* in this sense Christ uses the word in this Gospel;† *no man can come unto me, except the Father which hath sent me draw him.* Now,

3. It is most evident, that all men, that is, every individual of human nature, every son and daughter of Adam, have not faith, are not drawn, or enabled to come to Christ, and believe in him. There were many of the Jews who would not, and did not *come to Christ, that they might have life;* who, instead of being drawn to him in this sense, when lifted up on the cross, vilified and reproached him; nay, at this time, here was a *world* spoken of in the preceding verse, whose *judgment,* or condemnation, was now come; and besides, there was then a multitude of souls in hell, who could not nor never will be drawn to Christ; and a greater number still there will be at the last day, to whom, instead of drawing to him in this gracious way and manner, he will say,‡ *Depart from me, ye workers of iniquity.* Christ died, indeed, for all men who are drawn unto him; but

this is not true of all men that are, were, or shall be in the world. Add to this that the *men* is not in the Greek text; it is only πάντας, *all;* and some copies read πάντα, *all things;* ‡ so Austen read it formerly, and so it was in an ancient copy of Beza's. But not to insist on this;

4. By *all men,* is meant some of all sorts, all the elect of God, *the children of God, that were scattered abroad;*‖ and particularly the Gentiles as well as the Jews, as Chrysostom and Theophylact§ interpret the words; which interpretation is perfectly agreeable with ancient prophecy; that when Shiloh was come,¶ *to him should the gathering of the people, or Gentiles, be;* and with the context, an occasion of these words, which was this; *certain Greeks* that were *come up to worship at the feast,* desired to *see Jesus;* of which when he was apprised by his disciples, he answered, that the *hour* was *come* in which he *should be glorified,* and that as a *corn of wheat falls into the ground and dies,* so should he: and though he tacitly intimates, that it was not proper to admit these Greeks into his presence now, yet when he was *lifted up from the earth,* or after his death, his Gospel should be preached to them as well as to the Jews; and that large numbers of them should be drawn unto him, and brought to believe in him; agreeable to which sense of the words is Dr. Hammond's paraphrase of them: " And I being crucified, will, by that means, bring a great part of the whole world to believe on me, Gentiles as well as Jews." And to the same purpose is the note of Dr. Whitby on the text.

SECTION XXXII

Repent ye therefore, and be converted, that your sins may be blotted out, when the times of refreshing shall come from the presence of the Lord.—Acts iii. 19.

IT is concluded from hence,†† that repentance and conversion are in the power of men, and not wrought by the unfrustrable grace of God; that there is no such thing as an absolute election, nor special redemption of particular persons; since all men are exhorted to repent and be converted, and that in order to procure the remission of their sins. But,

1. It should be observed, that repentance is either evangelical or legal, and this either personal or national. Evangelical repentance is not in the power of a natural man, but is the gift of God's free grace. Legal repentance may be performed by particular persons, who are destitute of the grace of God, and by all the inhabitants of a place, as the Ninevites, who repented externally at the preaching of Jonah, though it does not appear that they had received the grace of God, since destruction afterwards came upon that city for its iniquities; and such a repentance these Jews

---

* Vid. Polani Syntag. Theolog. l. 6, c. 18, p. 398.   † John. vi. 44.

‡ Matt. vii. 23, and xxv. 41.   § Vid. Bezam in loc.   ‡ John. xi. 52. The Persic version, in Lond. Bibl. Polyglott, reads

the words thus: *And I, when I am lifted up from the earth, will draw my friends unto me.*

‖ In Beza in loc.   ¶ Gen. xlix. 10; Isa. xi. 10.   ** Limborch, l. 4, c. 13, sect. 16, p. 374; Whitby, p. 70, 88, 153; ed. 2. 69, 87, 149.

are here exhorted to, on the account of a national sin, the crucifixion of Christ, with which they are charged, ver. 14—18, and in the guilt and punishment of which they had involved themselves and all their posterity, when they said, *His blood be upon us, and upon our children.** Likewise the conversion here pressed unto us, is not an internal conversion of the soul to God, which is the work of almighty power, but an outward reformation of life, or a bringing forth fruit in conversation meet for the repentance insisted on. Besides, exhortations to any thing, be it what it will, do not necessarily imply that man has a power to comply with them. Men are required to believe in Christ, to love the Lord with all their heart, to make themselves a new heart and a new spirit, yea, to keep the whole law of God; but it does not follow that they are able of themselves to do all these things. If, therefore, evangelical repentance and internal conversion were here intended, it would only prove that the persons spoken to were without them, stood in need of them, could not be saved unless they were partakers of them, and, therefore, ought to apply to God for them.

2. These exhortations do not militate against the absolute election nor particular redemption of some only, since they are not made to all men, but to these Jews, the crucifiers of Christ; and were they made to all men, they should be considered only as declarations of what God approves of, commands, and requires, and not what he wills and determines shall be; for then all men would repent and be converted; *for who hath resisted his will?* Besides, in this way God may and does bring his elect to see their need of repentance, and to an enjoyment of that grace, and leaves others inexcusable.

It is said, that if Christ died not for all men, God could not equitably require all men to repent: and it is asked, What good could this repentance do them? what remission of sins could it procure? and therefore must be in vain; yea, that it would follow from hence, that no impenitent person can be justly condemned for dying in his impenitent estate. To which I reply; it does not become us to fix what is, and what is not equitable for God to require of his creatures, on supposition of Christ's dying or not dying for them; this is limiting the Holy One of Israel. Supposing Christ had not died for any of the sons of men; have they not all sinned and transgressed the commands of God? and should they not be sorry for these sins, and repent of the same, being committed against the God of their mercies? and might not God equitably require this at their hands, though he had not given his Son to die for them? and though such a repentance would not procure remission of sins, which is not to be procured by any repentance whatever; nor is it by the repentance of those for whom Christ has died, but by his precious blood, without

which there is no remission; yet it might be the means of enjoying a present temporal good, and lessening the aggravation of future punishment; as in the case of the Ninevites. Nor does it follow from Christ's not dying for all men, that no impenitent person can be justly condemned for dying in his impenitent estate; since the providential *goodness of God leads to repentance;†* and therefore such who *despise the riches of his goodness, forbearance, and long-suffering,* do, *after* their *hardness and impenitent heart, treasure up wrath against the day of wrath, and righteous judgment of God;* and since, *as many as have sinned without law,‡* and consequently without the Gospel and the knowledge of Christ, his sufferings, and death, *shall also perish without law; and as many as have sinned in the law, shall be judged by the law.* Besides, as has been observed, the exhortation to repent here made, is not made unto all men, but *to the Jews,* on a very remarkable occasion, and was blessed to many of them, to the turning them away from their iniquities; for *many of them which heard the word, believed; and the number of the men was about five thousand.§*

If it should be replied, that though the exhortation to repentance is not here made to all men; yet it is elsewhere expressly said, that|| *God commandeth all men everywhere to repent.* Let it be observed, that as this command to repentance does not suppose it to be in the power of man; nor contradicts its being a free-grace gift of God; nor its being a blessing in the covenant of grace, and in the hands of Christ to bestow; so neither does it extend, as here expressed, to every individual of mankind; but only regards the men of the then present age, in distinction from those who lived in the former *times of ignorance:* for so the words are expressed: *and the times of this ignorance God winked at;* overlooked, took no notice of, sent them no messages, enjoined them no commands of faith in Christ, or repentance towards God; *but now,* since the coming and death of Christ, *commandeth all men, Gentiles* as *well as Jews, everywhere to repent;* it being his will, that¶ *repentance and remission of sins should be preached among all nations:* but admitting that it has been God's command in all ages, and to all men that they repent,* as all men are indeed bound, by the law of nature, to a natural repentance, though all men are not called by the gospel to an evangelical one; yet I see not what conclusions can be formed from hence against either absolute election or particular redemption.

3. Though there is a close connexion between evangelical repentance, true conversion, and pardon of sin; that is to say, that such who are really converted and truly repent, have their sins pardoned; yet not repentance and conversion, but the free grace of God and blood of Christ are the causes of pardon.

---

* Matt. xxvii. 25.   † Rom. ii. 4, 5.   xvii. 30.   ¶ Luke xxiv. 47.
‡ Ver. 12.   § Acts iv. 4. || Chap.

Forgiveness of sin is indeed only manifested to converted penitent sinners, who are encouraged and influenced to repent of sin, and turn to the Lord from the promise of pardoning grace; hence the most that can be made of such an exhortation is only this; that it is both the duty and interest of men to repent and turn to God, that they may have a discovery of the remission of their sins through the blood of Christ, and not that they shall hereby procure and obtain the thing itself: though, after all, neither evangelical repentance and internal conversion, nor the grace of pardon are here intended; not evangelical repentance and internal conversion, as has been before observed, nor the spiritual blessing and grace of pardon; for, though pardon of sin is signified by blotting it out, Psal. li. 1, 9; Isa. xliii. 25, and xliv. 22; yet forgiveness of sin sometimes means no more than the removing a present calamity, or the averting of a threatened judgment, Exod. xxxii. 32; 1 Kings viii. 33 to 39, and is the sense of the phrase here. These Jews had crucified the Lord of glory, and for this sin were threatened with miserable destruction; the apostle therefore exhorts them to repent of it, and acknowledge Jesus to be the true Messiah; that so when *wrath* should come upon their nation *to the uttermost*, they might be delivered and saved from the general calamity; which, though these would be terrible times to the unbelieving Jews, yet would be *times of refreshing* to the people of God from troubles and persecutions. Though the last clause may be considered, not as expressing the time when their iniquities should be blotted out, but as a distinct additional promise made to penitents, and be read with the other thus: *that your sins may be blotted out, that the times of refreshing may come;* as they are by the Syriac and Arabic versions, and to which the Ethiopic agrees, and is the reading preferred by Lightfoot; and the sense is this, "Repent of your sin of crucifying Christ, acknowledge Jesus as the true Messiah, and you shall not only be saved from the general destruction of your nation, but shall have the gospel and the consolation of Israel with you. Jesus Christ, who was first preached unto you, shall be sent down unto you in the refreshing consolatory ministry of the word, though he in person must remain in heaven, *until the times of restitution of all things.*"

SECTION XXXIII

Ye stiff-necked and uncircumcised in heart and ears, ye do always resist the Holy Ghost: as your fathers did, so do ye.—Acts vii 51.

Though these words are not once cited or referred to by Dr. Whitby, as I remember, yet, inasmuch as the Remonstrants* have never failed to urge them in favour of the irresistibility of God's grace in conversion, and to prove that that work is not wrought by an

irresistible power; and that men may have sufficient grace for conversion who are not converted, it will be proper not to omit them; their argument from them stands thus. If the Holy Spirit may be resisted when he acts in man with a purpose and will to convert him, then he does not work conversion by an irresistible power; but the Holy Spirit may be resisted when he acts in man with a purpose and will to convert him: therefore, &c. But,

1. That the Spirit of God in the operations of his grace upon the heart in conversion may be resisted, that is, opposed, is allowed; but that he may be so resisted as to be overcome, or be hindered in, or obliged to cease from the work of conversion, so as that it comes to nothing, where he acts with purpose and will to convert, must be denied, *for who hath resisted his will?* who, in this sense, can resist it? No one instance of this kind can ever be produced.

2. It should be proved that the Spirit of God was in these persons, and was acting in them with a design to convert them, and that they had sufficient grace for conversion given them, and that that grace was the same with that which is given to persons who are only converted; whereas it does not appear that they had any grace at all, since they are said to be *stiff-necked and uncircumcised in heart and ears.*

3. Supposing the Spirit of God was acting in them with a purpose and will to convert them, it will be difficult to prove that they so resisted, and continued to resist him, as that they were not hereafter converted by him; we are sure that one of these persons, namely Saul, was afterwards really and truly converted; and how many more were so, we know not.

4. The resistance made by these persons was not to the Spirit of God in them, of which they were destitute, but to the Spirit of God in his ministers, in his apostles, and particularly Stephen; not to any internal operation of his grace, which does not appear to have been in them, but to the external ministry of the word, and to all that objective light, knowledge, evidence, and conviction, that it gave of Jesus being the Messiah; in which sense they are said to *reject the counsel of God against themselves,* Luke vii. 30; and to *put from* them *the word of God,* Acts xiii. 46. Such who resist Christ's ministers resist him; and such who resist him may be said to resist his Holy Spirit. Once more,

The word ἀντιπίπτετε, signifies a rushing against, and falling upon, in a rude and hostile manner; and fitly expresses their ill-treatment of Christ and his ministers, by falling upon them and putting them to death, which is the resistance here particularly designed, as is manifest from the following words, ver. 52.

---

* In Coll. Hag. art. iii. iv. p. 215; Acta Synod. p. 70, &c.; Limborch, l. 4, c. 13, sect. 14, p. 373.

SECTION XXXIV

Therefore, as by the offence of one, judgment came upon all men to condemnation, even so by the righteousness of one, the free gift came upon all men to justification of life.—Rom. v. 18.

THESE words stand as a proof of general redemption; and the sense given of them is,[*] that Christ died for the justification of all men; and that justification of life was procured by him for, and is offered unto, all men; it being apparent that the apostle is comparing the condemnation which is procured by the sin of Adam, with the free gift of justification procured by the second Adam, as to the extent of persons concerned in both; *all men*, in the first clause, being to be taken in the utmost latitude, the same word in the latter clause must be taken in the same manner, or the grace of the comparison is wholly lost. To all which I reply;

1. These words say nothing at all about the death of Christ, or of his dying for any persons or any thing, but speak of his righteousness and the virtue of it, to justification of life; by which righteousness is meant his active obedience, as appears from the following verse: nor do the Scriptures anywhere say, that Christ died for our justification, but that he *died for our sins, and rose again for our justification.* It is true indeed that justification is procured by the death, as well as the obedience of Christ; as that we are *justified by his blood* as well as by his righteousness; but it cannot be said, with any propriety, that justification of life is *offered* to any; since justification is a forensic, a law term, and signifies a sentence pronounced, or declared, and not offered. A judge, when he either acquits or condemns, he does not offer the sentence of justification or condemnation, but pronounces either: so God, when he justifies, he does not offer justification to men, but pronounces them righteous, through the righteousness of his Son; and when Christ procured justification, it was not an offer of it, but the blessing itself. These words then are not to be understood either of Christ's dying for justification for any, especially for every individual man; since all men, in this large sense, are not justified; many will be righteously condemned, and eternally punished; and consequently his death, respecting them, must be in vain, were this the case; nor of the procuring of justification, still less of the offer of it, but of the application of it to the persons here mentioned.

2. It is apparent, that the apostle is here comparing the first and the second Adam together, as heads and representatives of their respective offspring, and the effects of sin, to the condemnation of those that sprang from the one, with the grace of God to the justification of such that belong to the other, and not the number of persons concerned in these things. His plain meaning is, that as the first Adam conveyed sin, condemnation, and death, to all his posterity; so the second Adam communicates grace, righteousness, and life, to all his posterity; and herein the latter has the preference to the former, and in which lies *the abundance of grace* here spoken of; that the things communicated by the one are, in their own nature, to be preferred to the other; and particularly, that the righteousness which Christ gives to his, not only justifies from the sin of the first Adam, and secures from all condemnation by it, but also from all other offences whatever, and gives a right to eternal life, wherefore it is called *the justification of life*, which the first Adam *never had.* Were the comparison between the numbers of such who are condemned by the sin of the one, and of those who are justified by the righteousness of the other, the numbers being the same, the grace of the comparison would be wholly lost; for where would be the exuberance when there is perfect equality?

3. Admitting that the apostle is comparing the condemnation which was procured by the sin of Adam with the free gift of justification procured by the second Adam, as to the extent of persons concerned in both; this extent cannot be thought to reach to more than such who respectively spring from them, and belong to them. No more could be condemned by the sin of Adam than those who naturally descended from him by ordinary generation. The angels that fell are not condemned for Adam's sin, from whom they did not spring, but for their own personal iniquities. This sin reached not to the man Christ Jesus, nor was he condemned by it for himself, because he descended not from Adam by ordinary generation; so no more can be justified by the righteousness of Christ, nor does that reach to the justification of more than those who are Christ's, that belong to him, and who are in time regenerated by his Spirit and grace, and appear to be his spiritual seed and offspring.

4. *All men*, in the latter clause of this text, can never design every individual of mankind; for if *the free gift came upon all men*, in this large sense, *to justification of life*, every man would have a righteousness to be justified, be secure from wrath to come, have a right to eternal life; and at last be glorified and everlastingly saved; for such who are *justified by the blood of Christ, shall be saved from wrath through him;*[†] and *whom* God *justifies, them he also glorifies.* Now it is certain, that all men, in the utmost latitude of this phrase, have not a justifying righteousness; there is a set of unrighteous men who shall not inherit the kingdom of God, are not, nor will they ever be justified; but the wrath of God abides on them, and will be their everlasting portion: could it be proved that the righteousness of Christ is imputed by the Father, and applied by the Spirit, to the justification of every man, and that every man will be saved, we shall readily come in to the doc-

---

* Whitby, p. 113, 117, 118; ed. 2. 111, 115, 116.   † Rom. v. 9, and viii. 30.

trine of universal redemption by the death of Christ. But,

5. The apostle is the best interpreter of his own words, and we may easily learn, from this epistle, who the *all men* are, to whom *the free gift* by Christ's righteousness comes, to *justification of life;* they are *the elect* whom God *justifies,* through the righteousness of his Son, and secures from condemnation by his death, chap. viii. 33, 34; they are all the seed to whom *the promise* of righteousness and life belongs, and is sure, chap. iv. 16; they are *the all that believe,* upon whom and unto whom the righteousness of Christ is manifested, revealed, and applied by the Spirit of God, chap. iii. 22; and they are such who *receive abundance of grace and of the gift of righteousness,* chap. v. 17; and, in a word, the gift comes upon all those that are Christ's, and belong to him to justification, even as judgment came upon all to condemnation, through the offence of Adam, that belong to him, or descend from him.

The text in 1 Cor. xv. 22, *for as in Adam all die, so in Christ shall all be made alive,* in which the same comparison is made between the two heads, Adam and Christ, and their different effects, and which is sometimes used in favour of general redemption, is foreign to the purpose, since it speaks not of redemption by Christ, nor of spiritual and eternal life through him, but of the resurrection of the dead, as is evident from the whole context; and that not of every individual man, only of such as *are Christ's,* and who *sleep* in him, of whom he is *the first-fruits,* ver. 20, 23; who will be raised by virtue of union to him, and *come forth unto the resurrection of life;* which all will not, for some will *awake to shame and everlasting contempt,* yea, to the *resurrection of damnation,* which, by the way, is a proof that the word *all* does not always design every individual of mankind.

SECTION XXXV

For God hath concluded them all in unbelief, that he might have mercy upon all.—Rom. xi. 32.

This passage of Scripture is produced as a proof of God's will, that all men should be saved, and to show that he has rejected none from salvation by an absolute and antecedent decree, and consequently that Christ died for all men; seeing as God hath concluded all men in unbelief, none excepted, so, by the rule of opposition, he hath mercy on all, none excepted.* To which I answer:

1. That God shows mercy to all men in a providential way, is granted, for *his tender mercies are over all his works;*† but that all men are partakers of his special mercy through Christ, must be denied, since *the vessels of mercy* are manifestly distinguished from *the vessels of wrath fitted for destruction;* ‡

and certain it is, that there are some whom *he that made them will not have mercy on them, and he that formed them will show them no favour;*§ and where God does extend his special mercy, it is wholly owing to his sovereign will and pleasure, *for he hath mercy on whom he will have mercy, and whom he will he hardeneth.*‖

2. By the rule of opposition, no more can be thought to be the objects of God's mercy than those whom he has shut up in unbelief, which is not true of all men that ever were in the world; for, though all men are, by nature, unbelievers, yet they are not all shut up by God in unbelief. To be *shut up in unbelief,* is the same as to be *concluded under sin,* the meaning of which phrases is, not that God makes men sinners and unbelievers, or puts them into the prison of sin and unbelief, but that he proves, demonstrates, and convinces them, that they are in such a state and condition, as Chrysostom¶ on the other place observes, and which is the sense that Grotius and Vorstius,** who were both on the other side of the question, give of these words; for such who are savingly convinced of sin, are held andbound down by a sense of it in their consciences, that they can find no by-way to creep out, or make any excuse for it. Now, all men are not in this sense concluded under sin, or shut up in unbelief, none but those whom the Spirit of God reproves and convinces of these things; which convictions are wrought in them, on purpose that they may flee, not to their own merits, but to the mercy of God, which they may hope to share in, since *with the Lord is mercy, and with him is plenteous redemption.*††

3. It is not said absolutely, *God hath concluded,* πάντας, *all in unbelief, that he might have mercy,* πάντας, *on all;* but *God hath concluded,* τοὺς πάντας, *them all in unbelief, that he might have mercy,* τοὺς πάντας, *on them all,* which limits and restrains the *all* to the persons the apostle is speaking of in the context; were the elect of God among the Jews and Gentiles, and so designs *the fulness of the Gentiles,* whom God determined to bring in, ver. 25, and especially *that all Israel,* ver. 26, that *shall be saved,* not by their own righteousness, but by the pure mercy and free grace of God. In short, by the *all* whom he has mercy on, and in order to bring them to a sense of their need thereof, concludes in, and convinces of, unbelief, are to be understood all believers, that is, who are eventually so, be they Jews or Gentiles, as Vorstius observes,‡‡ and which is manifest from a parallel text, *The scripture hath concluded all under sin, that the promise by faith of Jesus Christ might be given to them that believe.*§§ Hence this passage neither militates against an absolute election, nor special redemption of particular persons.

---

* Limborch, l. 4, c. 5, sect. 6, p. 333.
† Psalm cxlv. 9.   ‡ Rom. ix. 22,
23.   § Isa. xxvii. 11.

‖ Rom. ix. 18.   ¶ In Pharæus in loc.
** In loc.   †† Psalm cxxx. 7.
‡‡ In loc.   §§ Gal. iii. 22.

SECTION XXXVI

Destroy not him with thy meat, for whom Christ died.—Rom. xiv. 15.

THESE words are frequently* used in favour of universal redemption, and to prove that Christ died not only for the elect, for his sheep, and true believers, but also for them that perish; and the argument from them is formed† thus : "If Christ died for them that perish, and for them that do not perish, he died for all. But Christ died for them that perish, and for them that do not perish; *ergo*, he died for all men. That he died for them that do not perish, is confessed by all ; and that he died for such as may, or shall perish, is intimated in this injunction; *destroy not him with thy meat, for whom Christ died.*" But whether so much is intimated hereby, will be seen when the following things are considered ;

1. That the injunction, *destroy not him with thy meat, for whom Christ died*, does not intend eternal destruction; since that can never be thought to be either in the will or the power of those on whom this is enjoined. Such a degree of malice and wickedness surely can never arise in the heart of any, to wish for, desire, and take any steps towards the eternal damnation of others; what comes nearest to such an instance, is the Jews' prohibition of the apostles, *to speak o the Gentiles, that they might be saved ;‡* which discovered implacable and inveterate malice indeed; but surely nothing of this kind could ever be among brethren of the same faith, and in the same church state; and were any so wicked as to desire the eternal destruction of another, yet it is not in his power to compass it; none can eternally destroy but God ; *fear not them which kill the body, but are not able to kill the soul ;§ but rather fear him which is able to destroy both soul and body in hell*. Besides, is it reasonable to suppose, or conclude, that eternal damnation should follow upon eating and drinking things indifferent, as herbs, meat, and wine, or be caused by an offence given and taken through these things ? Therefore, unless it can be proved, that eternal destruction did or might ensue upon the use of things indifferent; or that weak brethren might or were so ensnared, offended, and stumbled hereby, as to perish eternally, there is no force in the argument.

2. It will appear from the context, that the destruction of the weak brother dehorted from, is not the eternal destruction of his person; but the present destruction, interruption, or hindrance of his peace and comfort. To *destroy* the brother *with meat*, is, by eating it, to *put a stumbling, or an occasion to fall in his way*, ver. 13 ; not to fall from the grace and favour of God; but so as that the peace of his mind may be broken, his affections to the brethren wax cold, and he be staggered in the doctrines of the gospel : hence says the apostle, *It is good neither to eat flesh, nor to drink wine, nor any thing whereby thy brother stumbleth or is offended, or is made weak,* ver. 21; to do which, is contrary to Christian charity ; *if thy brother be grieved with thy meat, now walkest thou not charitably;* yea, it is *destroying the work of God,* ver. 20; not the Christian convert, who is God's workmanship; nor *the good work of grace,* which will be *performed until the day of Christ ;* nor the work of faith, which will never fail;‖ but the work of peace in churches, and particular persons, which God is the author of, and which the things that make for it, saints should follow after, ver. 19. Now a weaker brother, for whom Christ has died, may be thus grieved, distressed, wounded, his peace destroyed, and yet not eternally perish; and so can be no instance of Christ's dying for such as may be or are eternally lost. The apostle's design in this dehortation, is manifestly this ; partly from the interest Christ has in, and the love he has showed to such brethren in dying for them; and partly from the hurt that may be done to their weak minds and consciences, to deter stronger believers from giving them any offence by their free use of things indifferent; though he knew their eternal salvation could not be in any danger thereby.

SECTION XXXVII.

And through thy knowledge shall the weak brother perish, for whom Christ died?— 1 Cor. viii. 11.

THESE words are commonly joined with the former, and produced for the same purposes, both to prove that Christ died for such as perish, and that true believers may totally and finally fall away¶ What has been said under the preceding section, might be sufficient to lead us into the true sense of this text, which is parallel with the other, and so remove any argument or objection taken from hence. But not to let it pass without particular examination, let it be observed;

1. That as the text in Rom. xiv. 15, is a dehortation, or an injunction not to destroy him with meat, for whom Christ died ; this is delivered out in the form of an interrogation; and neither the one nor the other prove matter of fact, supposing they could be understood of eternal destruction and ruin; as that any one brother, who was a true believer, was destroyed, or perished eternally this way; and at most, only imply the danger and possibility thereof, through their own corruptions, Satan's temptations, and the offences given by stronger brethren; were they not preserved by the grace and power of God, through Christ, who died for them, and so will not suffer them to perish.

2. The *perishing* of this weak brother, is to

---

* Remonstr. in Coll. Hag. art. ii. p. 132 ; Act Synod. p. 346, &c.; Curcell. l. 6, c. 4, sec. 7, p. 360 ; Limborch, l. 4, c. 3, sect. 9, p. 321.
† Whitby, p. 138 ; ed. 2. 235.

† 1 Thess. ii. 16. § Matt. x. 28.
‖ Vid. Whitby, p. 436, 442 ; ed. 2. 425, 431.
¶ Whitby, p. 138, 436, 442; ed. 2. 135ᵈ 425, 431. ** In Coll. Hag. art. ii. p. 173.

be understood of, and is explained by, a *defiling* of his conscience, ver. 7; a *wounding* of it, ver. 12; and making him to *offend*, ver. 13, by the imprudent abuse of Christian liberty in those who had stronger faith, and greater knowledge, and by a participation in things offered to idols, in an idol's temple, ver. 7, 10; and not of his eternal damnation in hell, which could never enter into the apostle's thoughts; since he says, ver. 8, *Meat commendeth us not to God ; for neither, if we eat, are we the better ; neither, if we eat not, are we the worse.* Hence we have no need to return for answer, to arguments formed on these texts; that these weak brethren, of whom it is supposed that they might perish, being under a profession of religion, men were obliged, from a judgment of charity, to believe that Christ died for them, though he might not, or that others may be said to destroy, or cause them to perish, though their destruction followed not; because they did all that in them lay towards it, and what in its own nature tended to it; and therefore we are not concerned with the replies made unto such answers, which we shall not undertake to defend.

3. This text proves, that Christ died for weak brethren, whose consciences may be defiled, wounded, and offended, through the liberty others might take, and in this sense, perish; but does not prove that Christ died for any besides his sheep, his church; or those who are eventually true believers; for which the Remonstrants* cite it; for surely a brother who is truly one, though weak, is a sheep of Christ, a member of his church, and a believer; and therefore can be no instance of Christ's dying for any reprobates, and still less for all mankind.

4. Such for whom Christ died, can never finally, totally, and eternally perish; since he has, by his death, procured such blessings for them, as a justifying righteousness, pardon of sin, peace with God, reconciliation to him, and eternal salvation; which will for ever secure them from perishing. Besides, should any of them perish in this sense, his death would be so far in vain; nor could the death of Christ be thought to be a sufficient security from condemnation; whereas the apostle says, *Who shall condemn ? it is Christ that died :* nor a full satisfaction to the justice of God; or God must be unjust to punish twice for the same faults.

SECTION XXXVIII

Wherefore let him that thinketh he standeth, take heed lest he fall.—1 Cor. x. 12.

IT is observed,† that " the apostle here speaks to the whole church at Corinth, and to such who truly thought they stood; and plainly supposes, that he who truly stood, might fall, and would do so, if he used not great diligence to keep his standing; for had not this *taking heed* been the condition of their standing; had they been of the number of those who, by God's decree, or promise, infallibly were assured of standing, this exhortation to take heed, must have been superfluous; since men can need no admonitions to do that which God's decree and promise secure them they cannot omit; much less to do it to prevent what cannot possibly befal them." To which I reply ;

1. That the apostle does not speak these words to the whole church at Corinth; for though the epistle is in general directed to the church, yet there are several things which only respect some particular persons; as the incestuous person; such who went to law with their brethren before unbelievers; some that behaved disorderly at the Lord's table, and others that denied the resurrection of the dead, of and to whom some particular things are spoken, which did not belong to the whole church; and here the apostle exhorts, not such who truly thought they stood; for such do stand in the grace of God, in Christ, and by faith, and shall never finally and totally fall away; but such ὁ δοκῶν,, who seemeth to himself and others, *to stand ;* and manifestly designs such who were swelled with a vain opinion of themselves, of their knowledge and strength, tempted God, and *trusted to* themselves, as the Ethiopic version reads it, and despised weak believers : now such as these may fall, as they often do, from that which they seemed to have, from the truths of the Gospel, and a profession of it, and into scandalous sins, and at last, into condemnation. If it should be asked, why should the apostle concern himself about these persons, or exhort them to take heed to their standing? would it not have been as well, if they had thrown off the mask at once, and have appeared to be what they really were? I answer, that the apostacy of formal professors, is injurious both to the honour and interest of true religion; for the ways of God are evil spoken of, the name of Christ blasphemed, profane sinners hardened, and weak believers stumbled by the falls of formal professors, as of real Christians : besides, it must be worse for themselves, their defection being the means of a more severe punishment : *for it would have been better for them not to have known the way of righteousness, than after they have known it, to turn from the holy commandment delivered unto them.*†

2. Supposing that such who truly taught spoken to; it will be allowed that these may fall into temptation, into snares, into sin, from a degree of steadfastness in the Gospel, and from a lively and comfortable exercise of grace, but not finally, totally, and irrecoverably; since they are enclosed in the arms of everlasting love, secured in the hands of Christ, built on a foundation that will never give way, and kept by an almighty power, which can never be overcome : and though taking heed is not the condition of their standing, but that is secured unto them by the purpose and promise of God, which can never fail; yet such an exhortation is not super-

---

* Whitby, p. 428, 429; ed. 2. 417, 418.

† 2 Pet. ii. 21.

fluous; since though they cannot finally and totally fall, they may fall to the dishonour of God, the reproach of the Gospel of Christ, the grieving of the Spirit, the wounding of their own souls, the stumbling of weak believers, and the strengthening of the hands of the wicked; all which are so many strong reasons and arguments why they should take heed lest they fall; though they can never so fall as to perish eternally: nor are the admonitions needless to that which God's decree and promise secure; since these are often the means in and by which God executes his decree, and makes good his promise; see Acts xxvii. 22, 24, 31. To add no more, these words should never be made use of against the saints' final perseverance, since they are so closely connected with the following verse, which so fully expresses that doctrine: *there hath no temptation taken you, but such as is common to man. But God is faithful, who will not suffer you to be tempted above that ye are able: but will with the temptation also make a way to escape, that ye may be able to bear it.* By this way we may judge of the nature, design, and use of cautions given to the saints not to fall away; which are represented* as evidences and suppositions that they may do so; such as

The caution Christ gave all his disciples, in these words; *Take heed unto yourselves, lest at any time your hearts be overcharged with surfeiting,*† &c. Which only implies, that the apostles, like other men, were subject to infirmities, sins, snares, and temptations: and therefore caution, watchfulness, and prayer, were incumbent on them, that they might not be found in a supine, negligent, sleepy frame, when not the day of judgment, but of the destruction of Jerusalem, came on; and so they might escape the general calamity, and stand before the Son of man, and carry his Gospel into the Gentile world: and is no proof of the possibility or danger of their final falling away; who were chosen of Christ, given him by his Father, and so kept by him, as that none were lost, but the son of perdition.

When the author of the Epistle to the Hebrews cautions the believers he writes unto, to *take heed, lest there be in any of them an evil heart of unbelief, in departing from the living God,* and fall from the promised rest; and to *look diligently lest any man fail of the grace of God;*‡ his design is to expose the sin of unbelief, as what bereaved the saints of much comfort, and God of much glory; every degree of it in that, being a partial, though not a total departure from God, and therefore should be watched against: and it should be observed, that he does not caution them to take heed lest they fell from the rest promised them, but lest they *should seem to come short of it;* which they might do, and yet enjoy it: and when he exhorts them, to *look diligently lest any man fail of the grace of God;* this is not to be understood of the grace and favour of God towards them, nor of the grace of God in them, but of the doctrines of grace which they had received; the duty enjoined them being a mutual one, in which they were ἐπισκόπειν, to act the part of a bishop or overseer over each other.

When the apostle Paul cautions the Colossians,§ *to beware, lest any man should beguile them with enticing words, spoil them through philosophy and vain deceit, and beguile them of their reward;* he does not design a final and total seduction of them from Christ their head, in whom they were complete, ver. 10; not a destruction of grace in them but a corruption of the doctrine of grace received by them; which might be unawares introduced by false teachers, under the specious pretences of humility and holiness.

When the apostle Peter‖ exhorts those he wrote to, to *beware, lest being led away with the error of the wicked,* they *fall from their own steadfastness:* his meaning is, not as though there was danger or a possibility of falling from the *like precious faith* they had *obtained:* but that they might be in danger of falling from some degree of steadfastness in the doctrine of faith, through the ensnaring errors of wicked men; and therefore should guard against it.

Lastly. When the apostle John¶ saith to the children of the elect lady, *Look to yourselves, that we lose not those things that we have wrought, but that we receive a full reward;* it does not follow, that such who have the true grace of God, may lose those things which they have wrought; for it is not what *ye,* but what *we,* have wrought; much less lose what the Spirit of God has wrought; but the caution regards the doctrines and ministry of the apostles, lest that should be in any respect in vain; or a veil be drawn over the glory of it, through those persons any way giving heed to the doctrines of deceivers, ver. 7, 9, 10.

SECTION XXXIX

*For the love of Christ constraineth us, because we thus judge, that if one died for all, then were all dead: and that he died for all, that they which live, should not henceforth live unto themselves, but unto him which died for them, and rose again,—*2 Cor. v. 14, 15.

THIS scripture** never fails to have a place in the controversy about the extent of the death of Christ. Universal redemption is concluded from hence, by the following arguments, now to be examined.

I. The first is taken from the word *all* †† here used, *if,* or *since one died for all.* But it ought to be observed,

1. That the text does not say that Christ died for *all men,* but for *all;* and therefore,

---

* Whitby, p. 429, 430; ed. 2. 418, 419.
† Luke xxi. 34, 36.   ‡ Heb. iii. 12, and iv. 1, and xii. 15.   § Col. ii. 4, 8, 18.
‖ 2 Pet. iii. 17.   ¶ 2 John, ver. 8.

** Remonstr. in Coll. Hag. art. ii. p. 132; Curcellæus, l. 6, c. 4, sect. 6, p. 360; Limborch, l. 4, c. 3, sect. 3, 4, p. 319. †† Whitby, p. 113, ed. 2. 111.

agreeable to other scriptures,* may be understood of all *the people* whom Jesus saves from their sins; of all *the sheep* for whom he laid down his life; of all the members of his *church*, whom he loved, and for whom he gave himself; or of all *the sons* for whom he tasted death, and, as the Captain of their salvation, brings to glory.

2. That it is said in the latter part of the text, that those for whom Christ died, for them also he rose again; who therefore ought to live τῷ ὑπὲρ αὐτῶν ἀποθανόντι καὶ ἐγερθέντι,† *to him that died and rose again for them.* Christ died for no more nor for others than those for whom he rose again; such for whom he rose again, he rose for their justification; if Christ rose for the justification of all men, all men would be justified, or the end of Christ's resurrection would not be answered; but all men are not, nor will be justified; some will be condemned: it follows, that Christ did not rise from the dead for all men, and consequently did not die for all men.

3. That the *all* for whom Christ died, died with him, and through his death are dead, both to the law and sin; *then were all dead.* Besides, the end of his dying for them was, that they might *live, not to themselves, but to him that died for them;* neither of which is true of all mankind; not to take any notice of the nature and manner of Christ's dying for these *all;* which was *for*, in the room and stead of them; and denotes a substitution made, a satisfaction given, which issues in the full discharge, acquittance, and justification of them, and is not the case of every individual of human nature.

4. That the context‡ explains the *all* of such who are in Christ, are new creatures, reconciled to God, whose trespasses are not imputed to them, for whom Christ was made sin, and who are made the righteousness of God in him; which cannot be said of all men.

II. It is observed,§ that " the words, *all weredead*, must certainly be taken in their greatest latitude; wherefore, the words preceding, *if* or *since* Christ *died for all*, from which they are an inference, ought also to be taken in the same extent." To which I reply,

1. The latitude in which the words *all were dead*, are to be taken, must be according to that in which the preceding words, *if one died for all*, are to be taken; by these the extent of the other is fixed, and not the extent of these by them. The apostle does not say, nor is it his meaning, that Christ died for all that were dead; but that all were dead for whom he died; *if one died for all*, then οἱ πάντες ἀπέθανον, *those all were dead;* for the article οἱ is anaphorical or relative, as Beza and Piscator rightly observe: supposing, therefore, that the words *all were dead*, are capable of being taken in such a latitude as to comprehend every individual of mankind, there is no necessity that they should be so taken here, unless it be first proved, that the

preceding words, *if one died for all*, by which the extent of these is fixed, are to be understood in so large a sense; which is the thing in question, and cannot receive any proof from hence; till this is done, it is enough to say, that all for whom Christ died were dead: from whence it does not follow, by any just consequence, that Christ died for all that were dead.

2. It is proper to consider the sense of these words, *then were all dead.* The Remonstrants‖ understand them of a death in sin, which is common to all mankind; and because all men are dead in sin, they conclude that Christ died for all men. Admitting this sense of the words, they prove no more, than that all for whom Christ died were dead in sin; which is very true; for the elect of God are dead in trespasses and sins, whilst in a state of nature, as well as others; but not that Christ died for all that were dead in sin: and therefore, even according to this interpretation, they conclude nothing in favour of universal, or against particular redemption. Though it does not appear that this is the sense of the words, since to be dead in sin is no consequence of the death of Christ, that is, such an one as is depending on it; for it would have been a truth, that all men descending from Adam, were dead in sin, if Christ had never died; or if he had died for some or for none; much less is a death in sin the fruit of Christ's death, or what puts persons in a capacity of living to Christ, which the death here spoken of is intimated to be and do; but, on the contrary, this death is the fruit of sin, and what renders persons incapable, whilst under the power of it, to live to Christ. And therefore,

3. When those for whom Christ died, are said to be dead through his dying for them, the meaning is, either that they were dead with him, or *in him*, as the Ethiopic version reads it, their head and representative; when he was crucified they were crucified with him, and so was their *old man, that the body of sin might be destroyed; that henceforth they should not serve sin;* or that they were *dead to the law by the body of Christ*, as to the curse of it, and condemnation by it; and *dead to sin*, as to its damning power, so that they were acquitted, discharged, and justified from it; the consequence of which is, a deliverance from the reigning power and dominion of it. Hence, being thus dead to the law and sin, they are capable, through the assistance of divine grace, of living unto righteousness, and to the glory of Christ; all which is the saints' privilege, and the fruit and effect of Christ's death. Now as the former sense of the words concludes nothing in favour of Christ's dying for every individual of mankind; this latter sense, which is most genuine, strongly concludes against it; since all men are not, nor will be, dead to the law and to sin.

---

* Matt. i. 21; John x. 15; Eph. v. 25; Heb. ii. 9, 10.   † Repete ὑπὲρ αὐτῶν, *sicut ratio hypozeugmatis requirit;* Vorst. in loc.

‡ Ver. 17, 18, 21.   § Whitby, p. 119; ed. 2. 116.   ‖ In Coll. Hag. art. ii. p. 160, 192.

III. Universal redemption is pleaded for from the end of Christ's death; which is, *that they which live, should not live unto themselves, but unto him that died for them.* Upon which it is observed,* "This sure must be the duty of all Christians in particular (unless there be any Christians not obliged to live to Christ, but rather at liberty to live unto themselves), and so that death, which is the motive to it, must be intended for them all." To this I add, instead of answering, that this is a way of reasoning which cannot be contradicted, certainly it is the duty of all Christians to live to Christ, nor are any at liberty to live to themselves : and it will not be denied, that the death of Christ was intended for them all, since all Christians, who are really such, are true believers, and these are the elect of God. But then there is a wide difference between these two propositions, Christ died for all Christians, and Christ died for all men ; unless it can be thought, that all men, Turks, Jews, and Indians, are Christians. The argument from the end of Christ's death, here mentioned, is formed in a much better manner, and to better purpose, by the Remonstrants,† thus " Those who ought to live to Christ, for them Christ died ; but not the elect only ought to live to Christ, therefore Christ did not die for the elect only." To which I answer, that however plausible this argument may seem to be, yet it has no foundation in the text, which does not say, that Christ died for all them who ought to live to him ; but only, at most, proves, that those for whom he died, ought to live to him : all men ought to live to Christ as God, as their Creator, they are obliged to it by the laws of Creation, and ties of nature, whether he died for them or no, and indeed, supposing he had never died for any; but besides the obligation from creation, there is a fresh one upon such for whom he died to live to him : hence it follows not that " to say‡ that Christ died for some only of all nations, Jews and Gentiles, is to exempt all others of those nations from living to Christ ; " for though they are not bound to live to Christ on the account of redemption by him ; yet, because they are his creatures, and are supplied with temporal mercies from him : and as to what is further observed,§ that " to say he died for all the elect, that they of them who live, might not live to themselves, is to suppose that some of the elect might live, not to Christ, but to themselves ; which cannot truly be imagined of the elect of God." I reply, that there is a proneness in all the elect of God, even after they are made spiritually alive, to live to themselves, and not to Christ ; and therefore, such an argument, taken from Christ's dying for them in particular, is a very proper one to quicken them to their duty, and engage them with all readiness and cheerfulness to seek the glory and honour of their Redeemer.

IV. That Christ died for all men, is argued for from the love of Christ constraining the apostles to preach the Gospel to all ; and it is said,‖ the apostle "declares, that the sense of this love of Christ prevailed upon them to persuade men to believe in him. Now this persuasion they used to every man to whom they preached ; and therefore they persuaded all men to believe that Christ died for them, Col. i. 28." To which I answer ; that it was not the love of Christ, but the terror of the Lord, that prevailed upon them to persuade men, ver. 11, and that it is not said, that they persuaded all men, but men ; for it was not all men they preached unto. Moreover, this persuasion was not to believe in Christ, but a general judgment, to which all will be summoned, ver. 10, much less to believe that Christ died for all to whom they preached ; of which kind of persuasion we have no instance, neither here nor in Col. i. 28, nor in any other passage of scripture.

SECTION XL

To wit that God was in Christ, reconciling the world unto himself, not imputing their trespasses unto them.—2 Cor. v. 19.

THIS text is produced¶ to confirm the truth of general redemption ; and it is said to do it beyond exception ; which, whether it does it does or no, will better appear, when,

I. It is considered, that the word *world* cannot be understood of every man or woman that have been, are, or shall be in the world. For,

1. All and every one of these, are not reconciled to God. The text says, *God was in Christ, reconciling the world unto himself;* which must be understood of his doing it either intentionally, or actually; if intentionally only, that is, if he intended to reconcile the world to himself by Christ, and drew the scheme of reconciliation in him, can intentions be frustrated ? shall not his counsel stand ? will he not do all his pleasure ? shall a scheme so wisely laid by him in his Son, come to nothing; or at least, only in part be executed? which must be the case, if it was his design to reconcile every individual of mankind to himself, since a large number of them are not reconciled : but if the words are to be understood of an actual reconciliation by Christ, which is certainly the sense of the preceding verse, *all things are of God, who hath reconciled us to himself by Jesus Christ ;* then it is beyond dispute, that the word *world* cannot be taken in so large a sense as to include every man and woman in the world ; since there are multitudes who die in their sins, in a state of enmity to God and Christ, whose peace is not made with God, nor they reconciled to his way of salvation by his Son. It is indeed said,** that "the import of these words is plainly this ; he was offering through Christ a reconciliation to the world, and promising

---

* Whitby, p. 119; ed. 2. 116.   † In Coll. Hag. art. ii. p. 132.   ‡ Whitby, p. 119 ; ed. 2. 116.   § Ibid.

‖ Whitby, p. 119 ; ed. 2. 116.   ¶ Whitby, p. 129 ; ed. 2. 124.   ** Ibid p. 136 ; ed. 2. 133.

them who would believe in him, absolution from their past offences." To which I answer; Admitting the ministry of the word is here designed, that is not an offer of reconciliation to the world; but a proclamation or declaration of peace, made by the blood of Jesus, of reconciliation by the death of the Son of God: nor is this ministry of reconciliation sent to all men; millions of people were dead and gone before and since the word of reconciliation was committed to the apostles, who never so much as heard of this ministry; nor did it reach to all that were alive at that present time. Besides, the text does not speak of what God did by the ministry of his apostles, but of what he himself had been doing in his Son, and which was antecedent, and gave rise unto, and was the foundation of their ministry. There was a scheme of reconciliation drawn in God's counsels before the world began, and an actual reconciliation by the death of Christ, which is published in the Gospel by the ministers of it, and which is not published to all mankind; nor did the apostles entreat all men to whom they preached, to be reconciled to God; the exhortation in the following verse, *be ye reconciled to God,* is given not to all men, but to the believing Corinthians, for whom Christ was made sin, and they made the righteousness of God in him.

2. It cannot be said of every man and woman in the world, that God does *not impute their trespasses to them;* whereas this is said of the *world* here: *Blessed* indeed is the man *to whom the Lord will not impute sin;* but does this blessedness come upon all men? *Some men's sins are open beforehand, going before to judgment; and some they follow after.*[*] To say[†] that God is here " promising to them who would believe in him, an absolution from past offences," is putting a wrong construction on the words; which are not a promise of what God would do, did men believe, but a declaration of what he had been doing: besides, if only an absolution from past offences is promised, what must be done with after ones? And after all, they who would or do believe, are not every man and woman in the world.

II. There is good reason to conclude, that the whole *world,* is to be restrained to the elect of God; since these are the persons whose *peace* Christ is, who are reconciled to God by his death, whose sins are not imputed to them, and against whom no charge of any avail can be laid; and perhaps the people of God among the Gentiles, may be more especially designed; since,

1. They are called by the world, who are said to be reconciled, Rom. xi. 12, 15, yea, the whole world, for whose sins Christ is the propitiation, 1 John ii. 2. Nor was any thing more common among the Jews than to call the Gentiles אומות העולם, *the nations of the world.* Dr. Hammond, by the *world,* in this place, understands the greater and worse part of it, the Gentiles.

2. This sense well agrees with the context. In ver. 14, 15, the apostle asserts that Christ died for all, Gentiles as well as Jews, and adds, in ver. 16, *Wherefore henceforth know we no man after the flesh. Yea, though we have known Christ after the flesh, yet now henceforth know we him no more;* that is, we make no difference in our ministry, nor in our esteem, value, and affections for men, with respect to their carnal descent, whether they be born of Jewish or Gentile parents: *yea, though we have known Christ after the flesh;* had a value for him, as a Jew, as one of our own country, entertained gross notions about him, and about a temporal deliverance from the Romans, and a temporal kingdom to be erected amongst us by him; *yet now henceforth know we him no more;* we have quitted our former carnal apprehensions of him, and only look upon him as a spiritual Saviour of Jews and Gentiles; *therefore,* ver. 17, *if any man,* Jew or Gentile, *be in Christ, he is a new creature,* or *let him be a new creature;* which is the main thing we regard; *old things are passed away;* the Old Testament economy is abolished; *behold all things are become new,* under the Gospel dispensation; hence now *in Christ Jesus neither circumcision availeth any thing, nor uncircumcision, but a new creature;* for this is the subject of our ministry, *God was in Christ reconciling the world,* Gentiles as well as Jews, *unto himself.*

3. That reconciliation was made for Gentiles as well as Jews, was not only a reason why the apostles, to whom the word of reconciliation was committed, carried it among the Gentiles, but was also a noble argument to engage the believing Gentiles at Corinth to regard the exhortation made unto them, ver. 20, *be ye reconciled to God,* that is, to his providential dispensations towards them, to the order and ordinances of his house, to the form of discipline he had fixed in the church, and to all the laws of Christ, as King of saints, since he had been reconciling them to himself by his Son, the blessed effects of which they then enjoyed. This exhortation was not made to unconverted sinners, much less to the non-elect;[‡] but to the church of Christ, professing faith in him, and who were reconciled to God's way of salvation by him.

SECTION XLI

We therefore, as workers together with him, beseech you also, that ye receive not the grace of God in vain.—2 Cor. vi. 1.

THIS scripture usually stands[§] among the proofs of the saints' defectibility or apostacy, from whence it is concluded, that a man may receive the true grace of God in regeneration in vain, which may become useless and of no avail, may be lost, and he himself everlastingly perish. But,

---

* 1 Tim. v. 24.

† Whitby, p. 136; ed. 2. 133.

‡ Whitby, p. 2, 6, 75   ed. 2. 2, 6, 74.

§ Remonstr. In Coll. Hag. art. v. p. 14, 78; Limborch, l. 5, c. 83, sect. 1, p. 718; Whitby, p. 423, 461; ed. 2, 412, 441.

1. We are not to understand by *the grace of God*, that grace which is implanted in the souls of men at the time of their regeneration, for that cannot be received in vain; it always produces its proper fruit and designed effect; it begins, carries on, and finishes the work of sanctification; it is an immortal, *incorruptible*, never-dying *seed;* it cannot be lost in any part or branch of it; it is *a well of living water springing up unto everlasting life;* it is closely and inseparably connected with eternal glory; to all those to whom God gives grace he gives glory; whom he calls and justifies, them he also glorifies.

2. The *grace of God* is sometimes to be understood of gifts of grace, and particularly such as qualify men for the work of the ministry, in which sense it is used by the apostle Paul, in Rom. i. 5, and xii. 6; Eph. iii. 8; 1 Cor. xv. 10; of which he had a large measure; nor was the *grace which was bestowed* on him *in vain*, seeing he *laboured more abundantly than all the* rest of the apostles. And it will appear reasonable to take the phrase in the same sense here, if we consider the words as they stand in connexion with the latter part of the preceding chapter, and some following verses in this, after this manner; seeing *the word* and *ministry of reconciliation is committed to us*, and *we are ambassadors for Christ ; we* not only *pray you*, the members of the church at Corinth, to *be reconciled* to the order of the Gospel, and the laws of Christ in his house, but as *workers together*, (not *with him*, that is, God or Christ, which is not in the text,) as fellow-labourers in the Lord's vineyard, as jointly concerned in the same embassy of peace; *we beseech you also*, the ministers of the word in this church, *that ye receive not the grace of God in vain;* that is, that you be careful that the gifts bestowed on you do not lie neglected and useless, but that you use and improve them to the advantage of the church and glory of Christ, by giving up yourselves to study, meditation, and prayer, and by labouring constantly in the word and doctrine; and also, that you have a strict regard to your lives and conversations, *giving no offence in any thing*, laying no stumbling-block in the way of such you are concerned with, *that the ministry be not blamed*, ver. 3 (for ver. 2 is included in a parenthesis), and then adds the apostles, *but in all things approving*, ἑαυτοὺς, *yourselves as the ministers of God in much patience, &c.*

3. The *grace of God* often designs the doctrine of grace, or the Gospel of the grace of God, as in Tit. ii. 11, Heb. xii. 15; Jude, ver. 4; which may be truly so called, since it is a declaration of the love and grace of God to sinful men; it ascribes the whole of salvation to it, and is the means of implanting the grace of God in the hearts of his people in regeneration. Now the grace of God, in this sense, that is, the doctrine of grace, may be received in vain, so as that it may become useless, take no real effect, produce no real fruit; as was the case of such who received seed by the way-side, into stony places, and among thorns; and is the case whenever it comes in *word only;* is received, not into the heart, but into the head only; when the life and conversation is not becoming it; and especially when it is abused to vile purposes, that is, when *men turn* this doctrine of *the grace of God into lasciviousness;* and when besides, they drop, deny, and fall off from those truths of the Gospel they have before professed; and since this too often is the case, an entreaty, an exhortation of this kind made to a visible church, consisting of real and nominal professors, cannot be improper, without supposing that true believers may fall from or lose the true grace of God in regeneration.

SECTION XLII

For I am jealous over you with a godly jealousy! for I have espoused you to one husband, that I may present you a chaste virgin to Christ. But I fear, lest by any means, as the serpent beguiled Eve through his subtlety, so your minds should be corrupted from the simplicity that is in Christ.—2 Cor. xi. 2, 3.

THE fears of the apostle, expressed in these words, and in Gal. iv. 11, 1 Thess. iii. 5, lest pious persons should miscarry, are thought to add farther strength to the argument against the saints' final perseverance ;* "for, it is said, if the apostles, by the dictates of the Holy Spirit, had declared, that God had absolutely promised, that men once truly pious, should persevere to the end, how could they reasonably express their fears, lest it should be otherwise ?" To which I reply,

1. That the fears of the apostle about the persons referred to in these several passages, were not lest they should fall from the love and favour of God, nor from the grace which was implanted in them, and so miscarry of heaven and eternal happiness; but lest, through the subtlety of Satan, and his instruments, false teachers, their minds and judgments should be in any degree corrupted from the purity and simplicity of the Gospel of Christ, and they should any way give into erroneous doctrines, or comply with judaizing practices, and so the labour of him and his fellow-ministers, in instructing and establishing them in Gospel truths, be so far in vain.

2. The fears of the apostle, lest these persons should fall in this sense, yea, even if they could be extended further, are no proofs of fact that these persons did fall away; but only, at most, declare his apprehensions of their danger. And it is certain, that the most eminent saints are in danger through the wiles of Satan, the cunning of false teachers, the persecutions of the world, and and the corruption of their own hearts, of falling from their steadfastness in the faith; and it is owing to the mighty power and grace of God, that they are in any measure pre-

---

served. The apostle might express his fears on account of these things without any contradiction to or hesitation about God's absolute promise of the saints' final perseverance, and his faithfulness in the performance of it.

3. The jealousies and fears of the apostle about these persons, expressed with such a tender and affectionate concern for them, might be purposely directed and powerfully blessed to them by the Spirit, by whom he was assisted, as a means of their preservation from false principles and practices they were in danger of falling into, and thereby God's absolute promise of their final perseverance be accomplished.

Nor does the apostle's fear, jealousy, caution, and watchfulness of himself, expressed in 1 Cor. ix. 27, *lest that by any means, when I have preached to others, I myself should be cast away* imply, any possibility or danger, or supposed danger, of his eternal damnation; since the word ἀδόκιμος, does not design a reprobate,* as that is opposed to an elect person; for the apostle *knew in whom he had believed*, and *was persuaded* that nothing could separate him *from the love of God*; but his concern was, lest he should do any thing that might bring a reproach on the Gospel, and his ministry be justly blamed, and brought under contempt, and so be rejected and disapproved of by men, and become useless.

SECTION XLIII

Wherefore, my beloved, as ye have always obeyed, not as in my presence only, but now much more in my absence, work out your own salvation with fear and trembling.—Phil. ii. 12.

THESE words are represented as militating against God's decree of reprobation, man's passiveness, and the unfrustrableness of grace in conversion, and the final perseverance of the saints.

1. It is asserted,† that "to say God seriously invites, exhorts, and requires *all men to work out their salvation*, and yet, by his decree of reprobation, hath rendered the event, to most of them, impossible, is to make the gospel of Christ a mockery." But it should be observed, that this exhortation is not given to all men, and particularly not to reprobates, but to men already believing and converted, as is ‡ elsewhere owned, even *to all the saints in Christ Jesus, which* were *at Philippi, with the bishops and deacons*, in whom *a good work* of grace was *begun*; to whom it was *given* both *to believe on* Christ, and *suffer for his sake*; who were *beloved* by the apostle, had *always obeyed* the Lord, and in whose hearts he was then *working both to will and to do of his good pleasure*. Now to exhort these, and such as are in the like state and

condition, to *work out their salvation*, who have a principle of spiritual life in them, and have measures of grace and strength given them, answerable to what they are exhorted to, is not to make the gospel of Christ a mockery, since these can never be thought to be reprobates; nor does this contradict the decree of the reprobation of others, which springs from the sovereign and righteous will of God, and which is not, but sin, the cause of man's damnation.

2. It is asked, § "If some physical and irresistible operation were required on God's part, which makes it necessary for us to will and to do, why are we then commanded to *work out our own salvation?* for can we act where we are purely passive?" To which I reply, that these words are spoken to men already converted, in whom the work of regeneration was wrought, in which work they were purely passive; though now, having a principle of spiritual life, and under the influences of the grace of God, were capable of being active in *working out their own salvation*, which is something distinct from conversion and regeneration, and is to be understood, not in such a sense, as though men could procure and obtain spiritual and eternal salvation by their own performances, which is contrary to the Scriptures, which ascribe salvation in whole, and in part, to the free grace of God; contrary to the glory of the divine perfections of wisdom, grace, and righteousness, and inconsistent with the weakness and impotence of believers themselves; besides, the best works of men are imperfect, and, were they perfect, could not be meritorious, since the requisites of merit are wanting in them. Add to this, that salvation is obtained alone by Christ, and is already finished, and not to be wrought out now, either by Christ or believers; and, were it procured by the works of men, the death of Christ would be in vain; boasting in the creature would not be excluded, and men's obligations to God and Christ would be greatly weakened; and, since this sense of the words is attended with such insuperable difficulties, it can never be the true meaning of them. Let it be observed, that the words may be rendered, ‖ *work about your salvation*, that is, employ yourselves in things which, though not essential to, yet do *accompany salvation*, and are to be performed by all those who expect it, though not do be expected for the performance of them; such as hearing of the word, submission to gospel ordinances, a discharge of every branch of spiritual and evangelical obedience, for which the apostle commends them in the beginning of this verse, since they had *always obeyed, not only in* his *presence, but much more in* his *absence*, he exhorts them to go on in a course of cheerful obedience to the close of their days, when they

---

* Vid Whitby, p. 9, 10.

† Whitby, p. 76; ed. 2. 75.   ‡ Ibid. p. 295; ed. 2. 288.   § Ibid. p. 294; ed. 2. 287.

‖ *Nos vertimus, operamini circa salutem vestram,* κατὰ τὴν σωτηρίαν ὑμῶν ὑργάζεσθε; *imo quamvis sine* κατὰ, *dixisset simpliciter,* τὴν σωτηρίαν ὑμῶν ἐργάζεσθε, *sensus non esset, salutem, vestram, efficite, sed idem quam jam nunc dedimus, sicut* 1 Cor. x. 13, Apoc. xviii. 17, and Joan. vi. 27. *Ita et hic* ἐργάζεσθε *aut* κατεργάζεσθε τὴν σωτηρίαν, *non est salutem efficere, sed circa eam operari et laborare, ea tractare, quæ ad salutem facient. De Dieu, in loc.*

should *receive the end* of their *faith*, that which they were aiming at, and looking for, even *the salvation of* their *souls.* The Syriac version, if not a strict translation, yet gives the just sense of the words, by rendering them דחיין פלוחו פולהנא *do the work* or *business of your lives,* that is, your generation work, what God has cut out and appointed for you in this life; do all that *with fear and trembling,* with all humility, not trusting to your own strength, but depending on the grace of God, *who worketh in you both to will and to do of his good pleasure.*

3. This exhortation to *work out salvation with fear and trembling,* being directed to such who were, at present, in a state of favour with God, and in whom God had *begun the good work,* with others, directed to churches and persons, to fear, lest they should fall away, and finally miscarry, such as Prov. xxiii. 17, and xxviii. 14, Rom. xi. 20, Heb. iv. 1, and xii. 28, 1 Pet. i. 17; are improved into an argument against any absolute decree or promise of God, in favour of the saints' final perseverance : * for it is said, " What ground of fear can there be, where God hath absolutely decreed to confer this salvation, and stands obliged by promise to afford those means, which will infallibly produce it ?" To which I answer :

1. The exhortation to the Philippians to work out their salvation *with fear and trembling,* is not to be understood of a slavish fear of hell and damnation, or lest they should fall away and finally miscarry ; since this would have been a distrust of the power and faithfulness of God, and so criminal in them. Nor is it reasonable to suppose that the apostle would exhort to such a fear when he himself was† *confident of this very thing, that he which* had *begun a good work in* them would *perform it until the day of Jesus Christ.* Besides, the exhortation would be very oddly formed, if this were the sense of it, *work out your salvation with fear* of damnation, but as the phrase *with fear and trembling* always designs, wherever used, so here, modesty and humility, and stands opposed to pride and vain confidence ; as in Rom. xi. 20, *Be ·not high-minded, but fear,* which sense perfectly agrees with the apostle's general design in this chapter, which is to engage the saints to a modest and humble deportment in the whole of their conversation with each other, and in every branch of duty ; and which he enforces by the example of Christ, in his incarnation, humiliation, and death ; and in imitation of him, urges to a constant and cheerful obedience, with all humility of soul, without dependence on it, or vain-glory in it ; but ascribing it wholly to the grace of God, who *works in* us *both to will and to do of his good pleasure.*

2. Several of the passages referred to, such as Prov. xxiii. 17, and xxviii. 14, Heb. xii. 28, 1 Pet. i. 17, are to be understood not of a fear

of apostasy, but of a filial, spiritual, and evangelical fear of God ; which is a grace of the Spirit of God, a branch of the new covenant, and of considerable moment to secure the saints from a total and final departure from God ; *I will put my fear into their hearts,* says God, *that they shall not depart from me.*‡

3. The apostle, in Heb. iv. 1, speaks indeed of a cautionary fear of falling ; but yet in that does not exhort the believing Hebrews to *fear lest any of* them *should fall short of entering into rest,* as Dr. Whitby cites the words, but *lest any of* them *should seem to come short of it.* Now, between *coming short* and *seeming to come short* is a great difference ; and though there was no danger of their coming short of heaven, yet, inasmuch as through the disagreeableness of conversation, they might *seem* to others to come short ; therefore, for the glory of God, the honour of the gospel, the credit of religion, and the good of others, it became them to be cautious, wary, and jealous of themselves, and watchful over their conversations, that they gave no occasion to any one to entertain such an opinion of them. Hence it appears that all the reasonings against the doctrine of the saints' perseverance to the end, founded on these scriptural exhortations, *to fear,* are vain and impertinent.

SECTION XLIV

Holding faith and a good conscience, which some having put away, concerning faith have made shipwreck; of whom is Hymeneus and Alexander.—1 Tim. i. 19, 20.

AMONG the instances of the saints' apostasy, stand,

I. Hymeneus, Alexander,§ and their associates, who are here said to *put away a good conscience* and make *shipwreck of faith.* "Now," it is said,‖ "*to put away a good conscience* belongs to them alone who once had, and ought to have retained it ; and to *make shipwreck of the faith,* so as to *blaspheme* the doctrine which they once professed, is surely to fall off from the profession of it." And these instances are represented as a sufficient confutation of all the arguments produced from Scripture for the doctrine of perseverance. But,

1. It should be proved that these men were once good men, and had the truth of grace in them ; otherwise they are no instances of the apostasy of saints. Hymeneus and Alexander, who are mentioned by name, were vile, wicked men ; the one was a *profane* and *vain* babbler, who went not from the truth of grace to a course of sin, but from a lesser degree of impiety¶ to *more ungodliness ;* the other, who seems to be the same with *Alexander the coppersmith,*** did the apostle *Paul much evil,* and not only *withstood* his *words* and doctrines, but also those of others.

2. Their *putting away a good conscience,* does not necessarily imply that they formerly

---

* Whitby, p. 424—426, 480 ; ed. 2. 413—415, 459.   † Phil. i. 6.   ‡ Jer. xxxii. 40.
§ Vide Remonstr. in Coll. Hag. art. v. p. 17 ;   Act. Synod. p. 266 ; Limborch, l. 5. c. 82, sect. 15, p. 716.   ‖ Whitby, p. 411, 412 ; ed. 2. 402.   ¶ 1 Tim. ii. 16, 17.   ** Chap. iv. 14, 15.

had one, since that may be rejected and put away which was never had. Thus of the Jews, who contradicted and blasphemed the word of God, never received it, nor gave their assent to it, the apostle says,[*] *ye put it from you,* πωθεῖαθε, ye rejected it; the same word which is here used, and signifies[†] to refuse, reject anything with detestation and contempt. These men always had an abhorrence to a good conscience among men, and to a good life and conversation, the evidence of it, and at last threw off the mask, and dropped the faith they professed, as being contrary to their evil conscience and practices. But admitting that this phrase does suppose that they once had a good conscience, this is not to be understood of a conscience really purged and cleansed by the blood of Christ; but of a good conscience in external show only, or in comparison of what they afterwards appeared to have. Besides, some men, destitute of the grace of God, may be said to have a good conscience in some sense, or with respect to some particular facts, or to their general conduct and behaviour among men; so the apostle Paul, whilst unregenerate, *lived in all good conscience ;*[‡] and it is said of the unenlightened heathens, that *their conscience also* was *bearing witness, and their thoughts the meanwhile accusing or else excusing one another.*[§] Now, these persons had put away, rejected, and acted contrary to the very dictates of natural conscience; theirs was become *seared with a hot iron,* and so *spoke lies in hypocrisy, giving heed to seducing spirits and doctrines of devils.*[||]

3. It will be granted, that to *make shipwreck of faith,* so as to blaspheme the doctrine which they once professed, is to fall off from the profession of it; but then to fall from the doctrine of the Gospel, and a profession of it, and to fall from the grace and favour of God, or from the grace of faith, are different things. Man may fall totally and finally from the one, but not from the other; and it is not the grace, but the doctrine of faith, that is here designed, and is the sense in which it is often used in this epistle;[¶] though supposing faith as a grace was intended, the phrase, *to make shipwreck of* it, is not strong enough to prove the total and final falling away of true believers, could such be thought to be here meant, since persons may be shipwrecked and not drowned or lost. The apostle Paul *thrice suffered shipwreck,*[**] and yet was each time saved. Besides, as there is a true and unfeigned, so there is a feigned and counterfeit faith, which may be in persons who have no true grace, and may be shipwrecked so as to be lost.

II. The next instances of the saints falling away are Hymeneus and Philetus, of whom the apostle says, that they *erred concerning the*

truth, and overthrew the faith of some.[††] Now,

1. As was before observed, it should be proved that these men were once good men, true believers in Christ; whereas, on the contrary, it appears that they had only a *form of godliness,* but denied *the power thereof,* were *evil men and seducers,* who waxed *worse and worse.*

2. When it is said of them, *who, concerning the truth, have erred;* or, as Dr. Whitby renders the words, *have fallen off from the truth,* for about such a rendering we will not contend; the meaning is not that they fell from the truth of grace in their hearts, which it doth not appear they ever had, but from the truth of the gospel in the profession of it, and particularly from that branch of it which respects the resurrection, *saying, that the resurrection is past already.*

3. When they are said to *overthrow the faith of some,* this is not to be understood of the true grace of faith, *the end* of which is the salvation of the soul, and is not to be overthrown by men or devils, but of a doctrinal faith, or an historical one, which is a bare assent of the mind to some doctrinal proposition, as here, to the resurrection of the dead, and which had a place in some nominal professors, who were *ever learning and never able to come to the* saving *knowledge of the truth ;* and after all these instances of falling from the truth, and of the subversion of faith, the apostle says, *Nevertheless, the foundation of God standeth sure, having this seal, the Lord knoweth them that are his:* so that these are no instances of the apostacy of real saints.

III. Many judaizers in the church of Galatia, appear next much suspected to be in the black list of apostates, of whom it is said[‡‡] that they were *fallen from grace ;* from whence it is argued, [§§] that they therefore must have been formerly in a state of grace, and consequently, that such who were once known of God might fall from his grace and favour. But it should be observed,

1. That as on the one hand, all that is said in this epistle, to that church in general, is not to be applied to every member in particular; as that they had received the Spirit through the hearing of faith, were all the children of God, and the like; so, on the other hand, it is not to be thought that all of them were fallen from grace, but only *whosoever of* them were *justified by the law,* that is, who sought for justification by the works of it; so that they were not the same individual persons who fell, to whom the best characters in the epistle belong.

2. The grace from whence they fell was not the grace and favour of God in his own heart towards them, nor any grace of God wrought in their hearts; but the doctrine of grace,

---

* Acts xiii. 45, 46.

† The Septuagint render the Hebrew word אֵם, by it in Job xxxiv. 33, Jer. ii. 37, Hos. iv. 6, and elsewhere, and also the word בזל, in Ezek. xvi. 45; both which signify to refuse or reject any thing with loathsomeness and contempt.

‡ Acts xxiii. 1.   § Rom. ii. 15.
|| 1 Tim. iv. 1, 2.   ¶ See chap. iii. 9, and iv. 1, and v. 8, and vi. 21.
** 2 Cor. xi. 25.   †† 2 Tim. ii. 18, 19.
‡‡ Gal. v. 4.   §§ Whitby, p. 513; ed. 2. 403.

particularly that of justification by the grace of God, through the righteousness of Christ, which they had formerly professed, but were now going off from it, and embracing the doctrine of justification by works.

IV. To this head of instances of apostacy are referred * the predictions of the Scripture concerning persons who should fall away; such as,

1. The words of our Lord, in Matt. xxiv. 12, 13, are thought to be, *because iniquity shall abound, the love of many shall wax cold; but he that shall endure unto the end, the same shall be saved.* Now these *many* are either hypocrites and formal professors, liable to be deceived by false teachers, ver. 11, and so not the elect of God, who cannot be seduced, ver. 24, and their love is no other than a flashy zeal for religion, which in time, through the subtlety of false teachers, the corruptions of men, and persecutions of the world, abates, waxes cold, and at last disappears, and so no instance of the falling away of the saints; or else these *many* are true believers whose love to Christ, though it may *wax cold* in bad times, yet shall not be lost, even as the church at Ephesus *left*, abated in the fervency of *her first love*, though she did not lose it; which, though a proof of declension, yet not of final and total apostacy.

2. The words of the apostle Paul, in 1 Tim. iv. 1, are produced for the same purpose; *Now the Spirit speaketh expressly, that in the latter times some shall depart from the faith;* but this is to be understood, not of a falling away from the true grace of God, but of a departure from the doctrine of faith; since it follows, *giving heed to seducing spirits, and doctrines of devils, speaking lies in hypocrisy, having their conscience seared with a hot iron, forbidding to marry, and commanding to abstain from meats;* which manifestly point at the general *falling away*† from the truths of the gospel, when *the man of sin*, and *son of perdition*, the Pope of Rome, was *revealed*.

V. This would be a proper place to consider the instances of David, Solomon, Peter, Demas, and others, who are usually alleged ‡ as proofs of the saints' apostacy; but these are not mentioned by the celebrated writer I chiefly attend to. However, I shall just observe, that as to David, though, by his fall, his bones were broken, and the joy of salvation was gone, yet his salvation was safe and secure; and though the graces of the Spirit might lie unexercised by him, yet the Spirit itself was not taken from him, as appears from his own words, when most sensible of his case: *Take not thy Holy Spirit from me; restore unto me the joy of thy salvation, and uphold me with thy free Spirit.*§ As for Solomon, though his backsliding was great, and attended with aggravating circumstances, yet it does not appear to be total,

from some qualifying expressions in the account of it; ‖ as, that *his heart was not perfect with the Lord his God, as was the heart of David his father;* and that he *went not fully after the Lord as did David his father;* nor was it final; which is not reasonable to suppose of one who was so eminent a type of Christ: and besides would be contrary to the promise God made concerning him, saying, *I will be his father, and he shall be my son: If he commit iniquity, I will chasten him with the rod of men, and with the stripes of the children of men; but my mercy shall not depart away from him.*¶ Besides, he had repentance for his sins, and the book of Ecclesiastes was penned by him in his old age, as an acknowledgment and retraction of his former follies: and after his death, some persons are spoken of with a commendation for *walking in the way of David and Solomon.*** As for Peter, his fall was not total; Christ prayed for him, that his faith failed not; nor final, for he was quickly restored by repentance. And as for Demas, who, very probably, was a good man, since he is mentioned with such who were so, Col. iv. 14, Phil. ver. 24; what the apostle says of him,†† as that he had *forsaken* him, *having loved this present world,* is not sufficient to prove him an apostate, any more than Mark's departure from Paul, as others·at Pamphylia; or that too much love of the world, which is to be observed in many otherwise valuable good men, would prove them to be so; however, these instances are recorded in Scripture for our admonition; *that he that thinks he stands,* should *take heed lest he fall.*

SECTION XLV

Who will have all men to be saved, and to come unto the knowledge of the truth.— 1 Tim. ii. 4.

THESE words are often used to oppose God's decree of reprobation,‡‡ and in favour of universal redemption; but with what success will be seen when it is observed,

1. That the *salvation* which God here wills that all men should enjoy, is not a mere possibility of salvation for all, nor putting all men into a salvable state, nor an offer of salvation to all,§§ nor a proposal of sufficient means of it to all in his word; but a real, certain, and actual salvation, which he has determined they shall have, has provided and secured in the covenant of his grace, sent his Son into this world to effect, which is fully effected by him.

2. That the *will* of God, that all men should be saved, is not a conditional will,‖‖ or will that depends upon the will of man, or anything to be performed by him: for if this was the case, none might be saved; and if any should, salvation would be of *him that*

* Whitby, p. 413, 414, 440; ed. 2. 403, 404, 428.　　† 2 Thess. ii. 3.

‡ Vide Act. Synod. p. 252, &c.; Limborch, l. 5, c. 82, p. 712, &c.　　§ Psalm li. 11, 12.

‖ 1 Kings xi. 4, 6.

¶ 2 Sam. vii. 14, 15.　　** 2 Chron. xi. 17.　　†† 2 Tim. iv. 10.　　‡‡ Re-

monstr. in Coll. Hag. art. ii. p. 134; Act. Synod. circa art. ii. p. 321, &c.; Curcellæs, p. 364; Limborch, p. 332; Whitby, p. 29, 30, 74. 120, 121; ed. 2. 29, 30, 33, 117, 118.

§§ Vorst in loc.　　‖‖ Ibid. et Amica Collat. cum Piscator, p. 8, 13, 28; Curcell. Relig. Christ. Instit. l. 6, c. 5, sect. 7, p. 366.

willeth, and of him that runneth, and not *of God that sheweth mercy,* contrary to the express words of scripture * but this will of God, respecting the salvation of men, is absolute and unconditional, and what infallibly secures and produces it : nor is it such a will as is distinguishable into antecedent and consequent : with the former of which it is said, God wills the salvation of all men, as they are his creatures, and the work of his hands ; with the latter he wills or not wills it, according to their future conduct and behaviour : but the will of God, concerning man's salvation, is one entire, invariable, unalterable, and unchangeable will ; *He is in one mind ; and who can turn him ? and what his soul desireth even that he doth.*† Nor is it merely his will of approbation or complacency, being only expressive of what is grateful and well-pleasing to him ; but it is his ordaining, purposing, and determining will, which is never frustrated, but is always fulfilled. I know it is observed by some, that it is not said that God will σῶσαι, *salvos facere,* save all men, as implying what he would do ; but that he would have all men σωθῆναι, *salvos fieri,* to be saved, as signifying their duty to seek after salvation, and use all means for the obtaining of it, which, when effected, is well-pleasing to him. But the other sense is to be abundantly preferred.

3. That the *all men* whom God would have to be saved, are such whom he would also have *to come to the knowledge of the truth ;* that is, not a mere nominal, but experimental knowledge of the Gospel of Jesus Christ, as *the way, the truth, and the life,* or of the true way of life and salvation by him ; and all those whom God saves, they are brought by his Spirit and grace to an acquaintance with these things, which is an act of his sovereign will, and an instance of his distinguishing favour ; for *whilst he hides these things from the wise and prudent, he reveals them to babes : even so, Father,* says Christ, *for so it seemed good in thy sight.*‡ Hence,

4. By *all men* whom God would have to be saved, we are not to understand every individual of mankind, since it is not the will of God that all men, in this large sense, should be saved ; for it is his will that some men should be damned, and that very justly, for their sins and transgressions ; *ungodly men, who were before of old ordained to this condemnation ;*§ and to whom it will be said, *go, ye cursed, into everlasting fire.* Moreover, if it was the will of God that every individual of mankind should be saved, then every one would be saved ; *for who hath resisted his will?* or can do it ? Does he not do *according to his will in the armies of the heavens, and among the inhabitants of the earth ?*‖ Nay, does he not *work all things after the counsel of his own will?* and it is certain that all men, in this large sense, are not saved, for some will *go away into everlasting punishment,* when the *righteous* shall go *into eternal life.*¶ Besides, the same persons God would have saved he would have come to the *knowledge of the truth ;* but this is not his will with respect to every individual of mankind ; were it his will, he would, no doubt, give to every man the means of it, which he has not done, nor does he ; for many hundred years he *suffered all nations to walk in their ways,* and overlooked *the times of their ignorance. He showed his word unto Jacob, his statutes and his judgments unto Israel ; he hath not dealt so with any nation : and as for his judgments, they have not known them.*** From many to whom the Gospel does come, it is hid ; some are given up to strong delusions to believe a lie, and few are savingly and experimentally acquainted with the truth as it is in Jesus.

5. There are indeed†† many things urged in favour of this large sense of the phrase *all men.* As,

1. The exhortation of the apostle, in ver. 1, that *supplications, prayers, intercessions, and giving of thanks, be made for all men.* But surely by *all men,* is not meant every individual man, that has been, is, or shall be, in the world ; millions of men are dead and gone, for whom prayer is not to be made ; many in hell, to whom it would be of no service ; and many in heaven, who stand in no need of it ; nor should we pray for such who have sinned *the sin unto death.*‡‡ Besides giving of thanks, as well as prayers, were to be made for all men ; but certainly the apostle's meaning is not that the saints should give thanks for wicked men, and persecutors, and particularly for a persecuting Nero ; nor for heretics or false teachers, such as Hymeneus and Alexander, whom he had delivered to Satan ; the phrase is therefore to be taken in a limited and restrained sense, for some only, as appears from ver. 2, *for kings and for all in authority ;* that is, for men of the highest, as well as of the lowest rank and quality.

2. This sense is contended for, from the reason given in ver. 5, *for there is one God,* "who is the God of all, the common Father and Creator of all men." Now, "it is said, thus he is the God of all men in particular ; and so this argument must show, he would have all men in particular to be saved." To which may be replied, that God is the God of all men, as the God of nature and providence, but not as the God of grace, or in a covenant way, for then it would be no distinguishing favour or happiness to any people, that the Lord is their God ; he is indeed *the one God and Father of all, who is above all, and through all, and in you all,* meaning believers, to whom the apostle writes ;§§ *the same Lord is rich unto all,* but then it is to them *that call upon him.*

3. This is argued for from *the one Mediator between God and man, the man Christ Jesus ;*

---

* Rom. ix. 16.   † Job xxiii. 13.
‡ Matt. xi. 25, 26.   § Jude 4.
‖ Rom. ix. 19 ; Dan. iv. 35 ; Eph. i. 11.
¶ Matt. xxv. 46,   ** Acts xiv. 16,

and xvii. 30 ; Psalm cxlvii. 19, 20.
†† Whitby, p. 120, 121 ; ed. 2. 117, 118.
‡‡ 1 John v. 16.   §§ Eph. iv. 6 ; Rom. x. 12.

but it should be observed, that he is not said to be the Mediator between God and all men, and much less every individual man; and since he is expressly called, *the Mediator of the new covenant,** he only can be a Mediator for those who are in that covenant; and it is plain, that he has not performed the several branches of his meditorial office, the oblation of himself on the cross, and his intercession in heaven, for every man; and though the nature he assumed is common to all men, was endued with the best of human affections, and subject to the common law of humanity; yet, since it was assumed with a peculiar view to the elect of God, the seed of Abraham, they share all the peculiar blessings and favours arising from the assumption of such a nature.

4. It is observed that Christ is said, in ver. 6, to *give himself a ransom for all,* which is understood of all men in particular; but it should be observed also, that this ransom is ἀντίλυτρον ὑπερ πάντων, a vicarious ransom, substituted in the room and stead of all, whereby a full price was paid for all, and a plenary satisfaction made for the sins of all, which cannot be true of every individual man, for then no man could be justly condemned and punished. The sense of these words is best understood by what Christ himself has said, *The Son of Man came not to be ministered unto, but to minister, and give his life a ransom for many.*† So the Hebrew word כל, *all,* to which this answers, signifies sometimes *many,* a multitude; and sometimes only a part of a multitude, as Kimchi‡ has observed. Wherefore,

5. It is better by *all men* to understand some of all sorts, as Austin§ did long ago, and is the sense in which the word *all* is to be taken in many places; as in Gen. vii. 14; Matt. iv. 23, 24; Joel ii. 28; and is the meaning of it in ver. 1, and well agrees with the matter of fact; since Christ has redeemed some of all nations, some out of every kindred, tongue, and people; and God saves and calls some of every rank and quality, as kings and peasants: of every state and condition, as rich and poor, bond and free; of every sex, male and female; of every age, young and old; and all sorts of sinners, greater and less. It is‖ indeed said, that, according to this limitation and sense of the words, *God is willing some of all kindred and people should be saved;* it may more truly and properly be said, that God would have all men to be damned, and that Christ died for none; since they for whom he died are none, according to this doctrine, comparatively to the greater number for whom he died not. To which I answer, it does not become us to say what might be more truly and properly said by God, or an inspired writer. However, this is certain, that as there is a *whole world that lies in wickedness,*¶ so there is a world that shall be damned; which agrees with what the apostle

Paul says in so many words, that the world shall be condemned, *We are chastened of the Lord, that we should not be condemned or damned with the world.*** Moreover, though they for whom Christ died are but few comparatively, yet they cannot be said, in a comparative sense, or in any sense at all, to be none; and indeed, when considered by themselves, are a number which no man can number. But,

6. I rather think that by *all men* are meant the Gentiles, who are sometimes called the world, the whole world, and every creature, Rom. xi. 12, 15; 1 John ii. 2; Mark xvi. 15; which is the sense, I apprehend, in which it is used in ver. 1, where the apostle exhorts, that *supplications, prayers, intercessions, and giving thanks, be made for all men; for kings, and for all in authority;* which was contrary to a notion that obtained among the Jews, of whom there were many in the primitive churches, that they should not pray for heathens and heathen magistrates.†† The apostle enforces this exhortation from the advantage which would accrue to themselves; *that we may lead a peaceable and quiet life, in all godliness and honesty;* besides, says he, *This is good and acceptable in the sight of God our Saviour, who will have all men,* Gentiles, as well as Jews, *to be saved, and to come to the knowledge of the truth,* and therefore has sent his ministers to preach the gospel among them; and the doctrine of *the grace of God has appeared* to these, *all men,* in order to bring them to it; *for there is one God of Jews and Gentiles,* who, by his gospel, has taken out of the latter a people for his name and glory; *and there is one Mediator between God and man, the man Christ Jesus,* who, not like Moses, who was the Mediator for the Jews only, but is for the Gentiles also; and is become *our peace,*‡‡ *that hath made both one, reconciled both in one body on the cross; preached peace to them that were afar off, and to them that were nigh; through whom,* as the mediator, *both have an access by one Spirit to the Father; who* also *gave himself a ransom for all,* to redeem the Gentiles as well as Jews; which was *to be testified in due time* to them, as it was by the apostle, who adds, *Whereunto I am ordained a preacher and an apostle (I speak the truth in Christ, I lie not,) a teacher of the Gentiles in faith and verity;* and then concludes, *I will therefore that men pray everywhere,* and not be confined to the temple for public prayer, another Jewish notion and practice, *lifting up holy hands without wrath and doubting.* Seeing then there are some Jewish notions pointed at in the context, and the whole is adapted to the state and case of the Gentiles, under the Gospel dispensation, there is a good deal of reason to conclude that they are designed here; whereby another principle of the Jews is confuted, which is, that the Gentiles should re-

---

* Heb. xii. 24.
† Matt. xx. 28.   ‡ In lib. Shorash
rad. כלל.   § Enchirid. c. 103.
‖ Whitby, p. 114; ed. 2. 111. To the same

purpose, Curcellæus, p. 365, and Limborch, p. 332.   ¶ 1 John v. 19.
** 1 Cor. xi. 32.   †† See Lightfoot, vol. i. p. 309.   ‡‡ Eph. ii. 14—18.

ceive no benefit by the Messiah when he came; and is the true reason of most, if not of all, those universal expressions, relating to the death of Christ, we meet with in Scripture.

From the whole, since these words cannot be understood of every individual man, they cannot be thought to militate against God's righte*h*us decree of reprobation, nor to maintain and support universal redemption.

SECTION XLVI

For therefore we both labour and suffer reproach, because we trust in the living God, who is the Saviour of all men, especially of those that believe.—1 Tim. iv. 19.

THESE words stand among others, which are said to contain, in express terms, the doctrine of general redemption. But,

1. If these words represent God, as *the Saviour of all men*, in the sense of a spiritual and eternal salvation, they prove more than any, unless Origen and his followers contend for, namely, an universal salvation. To say that Christ is the Saviour of all men, with respect to the impetration of salvation for them, though not with respect to the application of it to them all, is a distinction which must, in part, make the death of Christ in vain; nor can a mere possibility of salvation, nor a conditional one, nor a putting of men into a salvable state, be intended; for then they that believe, would be only in such a precarious and uncertain state; whereas it is certain, that *he that believeth shall be saved*. Besides, if God is the Saviour of all men, in the sense of eternal salvation, then he must be the Saviour of unbelievers, contrary to many express passages of Scripture; such as John iii. 18, 36, Mark xvi. 16, Rev. xxi. 8.

2. The words are to be understood of providential goodness and temporal salvation; which all men have a share in, more or less, God the Father and not Christ, is here called *the living God*, who is *the Saviour of all men*, that is, *the preserver of all men;* who supports them in their being, and supplies them with all the necessaries of life, and *especially them that believe,* who are the particular care of his providence; for though he is good, and does *good to all men*, yet more *especially to the household of faith;* which was the foundation of the apostles' trust in him, under all their labours and reproaches, which attended the preaching of the Gospel. Which sense of the words is perfectly agreeable both to the analogy of faith, and to the context, and is owned by some† who are on the other side of the question.

SECTION XLVII

For the grace of God that bringeth salvation hath appeared to all men, teaching us, that denying all ungodliness and worldly lusts, we should live soberly, righteously, and

godly, in this present world.—Titus ii. 11, 12.

THIS scripture also appears among the very many clear and express ones,‡ in which the doctrine of universal redemption is thought to be contained. It is§ observed, " That the grace here mentioned, is *the grace of God*, even of that God who *spared not his Son, but freely gave him up for us ;* that it is styled ἡ χάρις ἡ σωτήριος, *saving grace :* and that this grace hath appeared to all men ;" all which is readily granted. The argument formed on these observations stands thus ; " If the apostles did in their preaching tender it (salvation) to all without exception, they either tendered it to them, to whom, by God's intention it did not belong, and so exceeded their commission, or else it belongs to all men ; and since it could only belong to them by virtue of Christ's passion, it follows that the benefit of his passion must belong to all," What foundation there is in the text for such kind of reasonings, will be seen when it is considered,

1. That, by *the grace of God*, we are not to understand the grace which lies in his own heart, or his free love, favour, and good-will to any of the sons of men through Christ ; which, though it is productive of salvation, and instructive in real piety, yet does not appear, nor has it been, nor is it made manifest to all men ; neither is that grace designed by it, which lies in the hearts of believers, being implanted there by the Spirit of God ; for though this also brings salvation, or has it strictly connected with it, and powerfully influences the lives and conversations of such as are partakers of it ; yet it neither has appeared to, nor in all men ; for all men have not faith, nor hope, nor love, nor any other graces of the Spirit ! but, by *the grace of God*, is meant the grace which lies in the Gospel, or which is the Gospel of the grace of God, in which sense it is often used ; as in Acts xx. 24, 2 Cor. vi. 1, Heb. xii. 15 ; and is indeed owned to be the sense of it here by the learned author‖ I am concerned with. Now,

2. This doctrine of the grace of God *bringeth salvation :* it brings the news of it to the ears of men, in the external ministration of it, and brings that itself to the hearts of men, under the powerful influences and application of the Spirit of God ; and so may be rightly called *saving grace,* as being *the power of God unto salvation to all them that believe ;* though it is not, nor was it designed to be so, to all to whom it is externally preached ; nor does the text say that it brings salvation to all men ; and if it did, or if it should be rendered, as it is by some, *the grace of God that bringeth salvation to all men ;* to which agrees the Syriac version, מחיה כל, *that quickeneth or saveth all ;* so the Arabic ; this cannot be understood of every individual person, every man and woman ; for the Gospel has not

---

* Whitby, of Redemption, p. 113 ; ed. 2. 111.
† Volkelius de vera Relig. l. 2, c, 7, p. 10. See also Crellius de Deo, c. 19, p. 133.

‡ Whitby, p. 113, ed. 2. 111 ; Curcellæus, p. 359.   § Ibid. p. 122 ; ed. 2. 119.
‖ Whitby, p. 165 ; ed. 2. 161.

brought salvation to every one, in any sense; not in the external ministry of it, for there have been multitudes who have never so much as heard the outward sound of salvation by Jesus Christ, and fewer still who have had an application of it to their souls by the Spirit of God: to many to whom it has come, it has been a hidden gospel, and *the savour of death unto death.*

3. It is indeed said, that this doctrine of the grace of God *hath appeared to all men;* but by *all men* cannot be meant every man and woman that has been in the world, for it would not be true that the grace of God has appeared to all in this sense. The whole Gentile world, for many hundred years, was in darkness, without the light of the Gospel; it neither shined upon them, nor in them: in the times of the apostles, when the doctrine of the Gospel appeared the most illustrious, and shone out most extensively, as well as most clearly, it reached not every individual person, nor has it in ages since, nor does it in ours, no, not in our own nation; nor in this great city, where the Gospel is most fully preached; for of preachers, they are the fewest who preach the doctrine of the grace of God; and so of hearers, they are the fewest who attend unto and embrace this doctrine; multitudes know nothing of it, are under neither the form nor power of it. Since then, matter of fact stands incontestibly against this sense of the words, we must look out for another. By *all men,* therefore, may be meant all sorts of men, men of every rank and condition of life, high and low, rich and poor, bond and free, masters and servants; which sense of the phrase well agrees with the context, in which the apostle charges Titus to *exhort servants to be obedient to their own masters, and to please them well in all things; not answering again, nor purloining, but showing all fidelity; that they may adorn the doctrine of God our Saviour in all things,* ver. 9, 10; and gives this as the reason of all, *for the grace of God, that bringeth salvation, hath appeared to all men,* servants as well as masters; *teaching us* who have believed, whether we be masters or servants, of whatsoever state or condition, to live a godly and religious life, whilst we are in this world: or by *all men,* we may, with Dr. Hammond, understand the Gentiles, before the times of the apostles. The Gospel was like a candle lighted up in one part of the world, in Judea only; but now it shone out like the sun in its meridian glory, and appeared to all men, Gentiles as well as Jews; it was no longer confined to *the lost sheep of the house of Israel,* but *preached to every creature under heaven;* but though it appeared to all, it was not applied to all, though it shined out upon them all, yet not into the hearts of them all; nor is this universal appearance of the Gospel, in the external ministration of it, any proof of universal redemption, nor was it so de-

signed by the apostle; and it is easy to observe, that when he comes to speak of redemption, and the persons redeemed in ver. 14, he makes use of a different form of expression; where he says, *who gave himself for us,* not *for them,*[*] or for *all; that he might redeem us,* not *them,* or *all men, from all iniquity; and purify unto himself a peculiar,* distinct *people, zealous of good works.* The argument above cited, is founded on a manifest falsehood, that the apostles tendered the saving grace of God to all men, without exception; whereas they tendered it to none, but preached the Gospel to all, without any distinction of persons who came to hear it. The Arminians frequently argue from an universal offer of the Gospel to an universal redemption; such whose ministrations run in the strain of offers and tenders, would do well to consider this, and deliver themselves from this argument, who only are pinched by it.

4. The doctrine of the grace of God is represented as *teaching us to deny ungodliness and worldly lusts, and to live soberly, righteously, and godly, in this present world.* Observe, the apostle does not say, *teaching them,* all men, to whom it appeared, which is the sad mistake of a learned writer;[†] but *teaching us,* to whom it has come, not in word only, but in power; and so taught them not not only doctrinally, but influentially, both negative and positive holiness; which lesson, all who learn will be undoubtedly saved, though not by learning this lesson, or doing these things, but by our Lord's salutary passion; to which things they are obliged by the grace of God and sufferings of Christ; though all men are not obliged by them, of which many are ignorant, but by the law of nature; from whence this absurdity therefore does not follow,[‡] " that there are some yet, yea, the greatest part of Christians, who are not, on the account of this grace appearing to them, or of these sufferings, obliged to the performance of these duties." Since all men are not Christians, and all that are true and real Christians Christ suffered for, and the grace of God appears to with powerful influences, engaging them to the discharge of these things.

SECTION XLVIII
THE EPISTLE TO THE HEBREWS

It is said, " That the Epistle to the Hebrews was manifestly written to prevent the apostacy of the believing Jews: and that as the excellent Dr. Barrow used to say, it was written against the doctrine of perseverance, and that it certainly contains many cogent arguments, against that doctrine, as is evident from the exhortations, cautions, promises, declarations, and threats, to true believers, of whom the apostle there speaks; which suppose that they unquestionably might fall away, both finally and totally."[*]

* Whitby, p. 122; ed. 2. 119.
† Ibid. See also p. 51, 205; ed. 2. 200.
‡ Ibid. p. 123; ed. 2. 120.

§ Whitby, p. 414—417; ed. 2. 404—406, 408.

1. It is very awkwardly expressed, and sounds a little oddly, that this epistle should be written to prevent the apostacy of believing Jews, and yet written against the doctrine of the saints' perseverance, since all means to prevent apostacy tend to establish and secure perseverance, and can never be contrary to the doctrine of it; and among the means of perseverance may be reckoned the exhortations, cautions, promises, declarations, and threats mentioned, and, the refore, ought not to be considered as so many cogent arguments against the doctrine of it. Besides, this church of the Hebrews, like other churches, no doubt, consisted of real and nominal professors, true believers, and hypocrites; and, perhaps, with a particular view to the latter, many of these exhortations, cautions, promises, and threats are given out; and, supposing them to be all true believers, these directions were not unseasonable and improper, but very useful to stir them up to duty, diligence, care, and watchfulness, since there might be danger of a partial, though not of a total and final falling away; and, at most, these can only imply a possibility or danger of such a falling, considered in themselves, and if left to themselves, through sin, Satan, and false teachers, but prove no matter of fact, or furnish out any instance of any one true believer that ever did finally and totally fall away.

2. It seems strange that this epistle should be written against the doctrine of perseverance, when there are so many strong proofs of this doctrine in it; the author of it represents the unchangeableness of God's counsel, purpose, and promise, respecting the salvation of his people, in the strongest light, when he says, *Wherein God, willing more abundantly to show unto the heirs of promise the immutability of his counsel, confirmed it by an oath; that by two immutable things, in which it was impossible for God to lie, we might have strong consolation, who have fled for refuge to lay hold on the hope set before us;* * but where would be the immutability of God's counsel, or the strong consolation of the saints, if the heirs of promise could possibly perish? In it, also †, Christ is set forth as having, *by one offering, perfected for ever them that are sanctified;* as *able,* and as one that will *save to the uttermost, all that come unto God by him;* as one that *ever lives to make intercession* for the saints; and, as the *Captain* of their *salvation,* who has brought, and will bring, *many sons* safe *to glory,* even all the sons of God; for, at the great day, he will say, *Behold, I and the children which God hath given me,* which he would not be able to do should any of them be lost and perish. The graces of the Spirit are spoken of as sure and certain things, *faith* is said to be *the substance of things hoped for, and the evidence of things not seen;* and *hope, as an anchor of the soul, both sure and steadfast;*‡ yea, the apostle says of these believing Hebrews,§ as well as of himself, that they had received a *kingdom which cannot be moved,* and knew in themselves that they had *in heaven a better and a more enduring substance;* that they were *not of them who draw back unto perdition, but of them that believe to the saving of the soul:* and that *the just shall live by faith.* He was *persuaded better things of* them, *and things that accompany salvation,* when such who were not true believers, finally and totally fell away, to whom alone the threats in this epistle are directed. From all which it is plain, that this epistle was not written against the doctrine of perseverance; nor are the exhortations, cautions, promises, and declarations, made to true believers, cogent arguments against it, since these were designed as means to promote and secure it, and do not in the least imply that any of the true believers in this church might, or should, finally and totally fall away.

SECTION XLIX

That he by the grace of God should taste death for every man.—HEB. ii. 9.

THE doctrine of universal redemption is ‖ said to be contained in express terms in these words, and it is observed ¶ upon them, that " here is no restraint at all, nor any seeming limitation of the comprehensive phrase, *he tasted·death for every man,* distributively taken;" and that there is something " which doth seem to strengthen the general intendment of the phrase, for this is said to magnify the grace of God in sending his Son to die for men; now sure the grace of God will be more magnified by this general extent of our Saviour's death, than by contracting the intentment of it to a few; for, if the grace of God be great in sending his Son to die for a few chosen persons, it must be greater in sending him to die for many, and greater still in giving him up to die for us all." To which I reply;

1. That the word *man* is not in the original text; which says not that Christ *should taste death,* ὑπερ παντὸς ἀνθρώπου, *for every man,* but ὑπερ παντὸς, which may be taken either collectively, and be rendered *for the whole,* that is, for the whole body, the church, Eph. iv. 16, for which Christ died, and of which he is the Saviour; or distributively, and be translated *for every one,* that is, for every one of the *sons,* Christ, the Captain of salvation, brings to glory, ver. 10; for every one of the *brethren,* whom he sanctifies, is not ashamed to own, and to whom he declares the name of God, ver. 11, 12; for every one of the members of the *church,* even the general assembly and church of the first-born, whose names are written in heaven, in the midst of which he sang praise, ver. 12, for every one of *the children* God has given to him, and for whose sake he took

---

* Heb. vi. 17, 18.

† Heb. x. 14, and vii. 25, and ii. 10, 13.

‡ Heb. xi. 1, and vi. 19. § Chap. xii. 28, and x. 34, 38, 39, and vi. 9.

‖ Remonstr. in·Coll. Hag. art. ii. p. 134, 135; Curcellæus, p. 360; Limborch, p. 319; Whitby, p. 143; ed. 2. 111. ¶ Ibid, p. 123; ed. 2, 120.

part of flesh and blood, ver. 13, 14; and for every one of *the seed of Abraham*, taken in a spiritual sense, which are Christ's, whose nature he assumed, ver. 16. Moreover, supposing there is a change of number, and that ὑπερ παντὸς, is instead of ὑπερ παντῶν, *for all*, that is, for all men, there is, in the context, a plain restraint and limitation of the phrase, to all the sons, the brethren, the members of the church, the children, the seed of Abraham, for all whom Christ tasted death, that is, he really died, and became the author of eternal salvation to them, which does not in the least help the cause of general redemption.

2. It deserves consideration, whether the words ὑπερ παντὸς γεύσηται θανάτου, may not be rightly rendered, *that he should taste of every death*, or *of the whole of death*. This hint I have received from an author* referred to in the margin. If this reading of the words can be established, as I think it may, agreeably to their grammatical construction, the context, and the analogy of faith, the argument, and any colour of or pretence for one from hence, in favour of the universal scheme, are entirely removed: should it be objected, that if this were the sense of the words, they would have been placed thus, γεύσηται ὑπερ παντὸς θανάτου, and not the verb between the adjective and substantive; it may be observed, that there is in the very text itself a like position of words, as ἠλαττωμένον βλέπομεν Ἰησοῦν; therefore, such an objection would have no weight in it; ὑπερ is sometimes put for περὶ, and signifies *de, of*, instances of which the lexicons themselves will furnish us with; and, though the verb γεύομαι governs a genitive case without a preposition, yet it is well known that the Greek language abounds in pleonasms of this kind. The context also favours this sense of the words; for if they be considered in connexion with the phrase, *made a little lower than the angels*, or that other, *crowned with glory and honour*, they contain a reason for either; for if it should be asked, Why was Christ so greatly depressed and humbled in the human nature? the answer is ready, that he might be capable of tasting of every death, or of the whole of death; and should it be inquired, wherefore he is exalted in such a glorious manner, it may be replied, Because he has tasted it; for, as in ver. 10, *the Captain of salvation* is made *perfect through sufferings*. And it is certain, that Christ has tasted of every death, or of the whole of death, the law required he should, in the room and stead of his people: hence we read of his deaths in the plural number, Isa. liii. 9, *He made his grave with the wicked, and with the rich*, במתיו, *in his deaths;*† he tasted of the death of afflictions, being all his days *a man of sorrows, and acquainted with griefs;* of a corporal death, being *put to death in the flesh*, in the body or human nature; and of eternal death, or what was equivalent to it, when his Father hid his face from him, poured out his wrath upon him, as the surety of his people, whereby his *soul* became *exceedingly sorrowful, even unto death;* he tasted of the whole of death, of the agonies, miseries, bitterness, and curse of it, and so has delivered his people from the sting of it, and from all the wrath which follows upon it.

3. Whereas it is observed, that the scheme of general redemption more magnifies the grace of God than that of particular redemption does; the contrary is most true; for surely that scheme of redemption which provides for the certain salvation of some, which some are a number that no man can number, more magnifies the grace of God, than that scheme which provides a precarious, uncertain salvation for all, giving only a mere possibility of it, with a probability that all of them may perish; leaving multitudes of them without so much as the means of salvation, and entirely without the Spirit of God to apply it to them; putting them only in a salvable state, so that they may be saved if they will; which, if it is effected, must depreciate the grace of God and sufferings of Christ, and exalt the power and free-will of man. The instance of a prince affording an act of grace and idemnity to some rebels, leaving others under condemnation, who would assuredly conceive his grace and favour would be greater were it extended to them also, and not think it the more magnified for being so discriminating, is not to the purpose; for the prince's grace is not to be judged of by the conceptions of such rebels, who are justly left under condemnation; and whatever they think of it, it is certain, that those who are comprehended in the act of grace, look upon their prince's favour to be the greater for being so discriminating, seeing they were equally guilty with such who are left out. The grace of God is magnified, not so much by the number of persons on whom it is conferred, as by the sovereignty of it, the circumstances of the persons interested in it, and the manner in which it is bestowed.

SECTION L.

For it is impossible for those who were once enlightened, and have tasted of the heavenly gift, and were made partakers of the Holy Ghost, and have tasted the good word of God, and the powers of the world to come, if they shall fall away, to renew them again unto repentance; seeing they crucify to themselves the Son of God afresh, and put him to an open shame.—Heb. vi. 4—6.

THIS scripture‡ is often used to contradict the final perseverance of the saints: and it is said, § that "The doctrine of the possibility of the final departure of true believers and penitents from the faith, is fully contained in these words; that it is evident they are spoken of such, from the word φωτισθέντες, *enlightened*, used by the same apostle, speaking to the same persons, in chap. x. 32, who were so en-

---

* Obadiah How's *Universalist Examined*, c. 11, p. 149, 150.   † Vide R. Sol. Jarchi in loc.
‡ *Remonstr. in Coll. Hag. art. v.* p. 18 ; Act. Synod. circ. art. v. p. 235, &c.; Limborch, p. 709, 710.   § Whitby, p. 404—406; ed. 2. 394—396.

lightened as to know they had an inheritance in heaven; and from the words, *it is impossible to renew them again to repentance*, which imply, that they had once truly repented, and were once truly in that state to which they were to be renewed, and their loss of it; and that these must fall totally and finally, because the apostle doth pronounce it a thing *impossible to renew them to repentance*, and, on this account, that they *crucified to themselves afresh the Son of God, and put him to an open shame*. But,

1. Admitting that these words are spoken of true believers, they will bear such a version and sense as will be so far from furnishing out an argument against the saints' perseverance that they will conclude one for it; for they may be rendered thus: *it is impossible that there should be any who have been once enlightened, and have tasted of the heavenly gift*, καὶ παραπέσοντας, *and yet fall away*, that is, it is impossible that such should fall away; agreeable to which is the Syriac version of the words, *it is impossible*, &c., רחוב נחמין, *that they should sin again*, so as to die spiritually, or lose the grace of God, and stand in need of a new work of grace upon them, which would require the crucifying of Christ again, and a re-exposing him to public shame, which latter things are impossible; and, therefore, the former, namely, that they should sin in such a manner; for, according to this version, the several other things mentioned, are connected with the word *impossible*, as it is impossible that they should be renewed again to repentance, that they should again crucify the Son of God, and put him to shame. This sense of the words is also confirmed by the Arabic version. Moreover, should we read the words, *if they fall away*, they do but at most contain a supposition of the saints falling; et suppositio nil ponit in esse, *a supposition puts nothing in being*, proves no matter of fact; nor can it be concluded from hence that any such have fallen away, and are, at most, only expressive of the danger they are in, and of the difficulty of restoring them when fallen even partially; a total and final falling away being prevented by the grace and power of God.

2. It is not evident, from the characters of those persons, that they were true believers; they are said to be *once enlightened*, which some understand of their being once baptized; and it is certain, that φώτισμος and φώτισμα, *illumination*, were used by the ancients[*] for baptism, and φωτιζόμενοι, *enlightened once*, for baptized persons; accordingly, the Syriac version reads the words thus, *who once* נחתו למעמודיתא, *have descended into baptism;* the Ethiopic, *after they are baptized;* and it will not be denied that some such, as Simon Magus, may totally and finally fall away; but not to insist on this sense of the words. There are two sorts of enlightened persons, some who are savingly enlightened by the Spirit of God, to see their lost state and condition, their need of salvation by Christ, and their interest in it,

who shall never perish; others are enlightened only into the doctrines of the Gospel, and some to such a degree as to be able to preach them unto others, and yet entirely destitute of the grace of God; and when such fall away, they are no proofs nor instances of the apostacy of real saints. The enlightened persons in Heb. x. 32, are not the same with these here mentioned; for the believing Hebrews are manifestly distinguished from these, ver. 9; *But, beloved, we are persuaded better things of you, and things that accompany salvation, though we thus speak;* and therefore, though the Hebrews were so enlightened as to know that they had an inheritance in heaven, it does not follow that these were enlightened in the same manner, and so sincere Christians and true believers. They are also said to *have tasted of the heavenly gift*, by which, whether we understand eternal life, or any of the blessings of grace, as a justifying righteousness, or, with the Greek fathers, ἄφεσιν τῶν ἁμαρτιῶν, the remission of sins; the meaning is, that they had some speculative notions about these things, and some desires after them, arising from a natural principle of self-love; or should Christ himself be intended by it, *tasting* of it, stands opposed to eating his flesh and drinking his blood, which is proper to true believers, who feed upon him, internally receive him, and are nourished by him; while hypocrites, and formal professors, only *taste* of him, have a superficial knowledge of him, and gust for him. In the same sense are they said to have *tasted the good word of God*, the Gospel, in the bare form and notion of it, *and the powers of the world to come*, meaning either the state of the church, and the glorious things relating to it, after the first resurrection, which they might have some notional apprehensions of, or the joys and glories of heaven, on which they might be able to make some natural and pleasing reflections; or rather, the δυνάμεις, miracles and mighty works in the former part of the Gospel dispensation, or times of the Messiah, the Jews, עלם הבא *world to come*, which many, as Judas and others, were able to perform, who were not sincere Christians, nor true believers, and yet might be said to be *partakers of the Holy Ghost;* not of his person, nor his grace, but of his extraordinary gifts, in which sense not only Dr. Hammond,[†] but Dr. Whitby himself,[‡] understand the phrase. Now it may be observed, that here is nothing said of these persons but what may be applied to hypocrites, nor any thing that is peculiar to true believers; these are not said to be regenerated, nor sanctified, nor justified, nor adopted, nor sealed by the Holy Spirit of God, all which are true of real saints. Besides, true believers are, in the context, manifestly distinguished from them, and are compared to the fruitful earth, when others are only likened to the barren land, ver. 8, 9; their case is mentioned with a view to stir up the saints to industry and diligence,

---

ver. 11, 12 ; and so be the means of their final perseverance, which they had reason to expect and believe, from the immutability of God's counsel, the safe refuge in Christ, the nature of hope, the anchor sure and steadfast, and the entrance of Christ, their forerunner for them, into heaven, ver. 17—20.

3. The phrase, *it is impossible to renew them again to repentance*, does not imply that they had once truly repented, and their loss of true repentance ; that cannot be lost, it is inseparably connected with life and salvation, and therefore is called *repentance unto life*, and *unto salvation*. The repentance of these persons, like that of Cain, Pharaoh, and Judas, was only a show of one, a counterfeit one ; and consequently, the renewing them again to repentance designs a renovation of them to that which they only seemed to have, and to make pretensions to.

4. It will be granted, that these persons might, and such as these may, fall finally and totally ; but inasmuch as it does not appear that they were true penitents and believers, they are not to be mentioned as, nor allowed to be, instances of the final departure of such from the faith.

SECTION LI

For if we sin wilfully after that we have received the knowledge of the truth, there remaineth no more sacrifice for sins, but a certain fearful looking for of judgment, and fiery indignation, which shall devour the adversaries. He that despised Moses' law, died without mercy, under two or three witnesses : Of how much sorer punishment, suppose ye, shall he be thought worthy, who hath trodden under foot the Son of God, and hath counted the blood of the covenant, wherewith he was sanctified, an unholy thing, and hath done despite unto the Spirit of grace ?—Heb. x. 26—29.

This passage is used on a double[*] account, both to prove that Christ died for some that perish—otherwise, it is asked, " in what tolerable sense can it be said, that no farther *sacrifice for sin* remains to them, for whom no sacrifice was ever offered or intended ; and who were, by God's own decree, excluded from any interest in Christ's death before they came into the world ? how were they *sanctified by the blood of the covenant*, from which they were inevitably excluded from the beginning of the world ?"—and also to prove that true believers, such as these are said to be, from their being *sanctified by the blood of the covenant*, may finally and totally fall away, since they so sinned, and there remained *no more sacrifice for their sin*, and did *despite to the Spirit of grace*. But,

1. It is not evident from what is said of these persons, that they were true believers ; not from the apostles speaking in the first person plural, *we*, which may seem to include himself, who was a true believer, and a chosen vessel of salvation ; since the apostle frequently makes use of this way of speaking, not so much with regard to himself as others ; that so what he delivered might come with greater weight upon them, and be more readily received by them, when they observed he entertained no hard thoughts or jealousies of them ; which would greatly distress the minds of those who were truly gracious ; see Heb. ii. 1, and iv. 1. Besides, it may be observed, that sometimes, when the apostles express themselves in this manner, they do not design themselves at all, but others, who were under the same visible profession of religion, and belonged to the same community of believers as they did ; see 1 Pet. iv. 3 ; Tit. iii. 3 ; Eph. ii. 3 ; compared with Acts xxii. 3, and xxvi. 5 ; Phil. iii. 6. But admitting that the apostle and other true believers are included in these words, they are not a categorical but hypothetical proposition ; which may be true when one or both parts of it are impossible ; the truth of such a proposition consisting in the connexion of the antecedent and consequent ; as when our Lord said to the Jews, *If I should say I know him not, I should be a liar like unto you ;*[†] the proposition is true, when both the parts of it were impossible ; it was impossible that Christ should say, he knew not the Father ; and it was equally impossible that he should be a liar like unto them. So the proposition in the text is true, though it is impossible that true believers should so sin as to perish eternally ; when I say impossible, I do not mean that it is impossible considering their own weakness, and the power of Satan, and should they be left to their own corruptions, and the temptations of the evil one ; but impossible, considering the grace of God, the power of Christ, their security in an everlasting covenant, &c. Hence it follows, that such a proposition neither proves that they could or should, or did sin in this manner. It may be said, that then such a proposition is delivered in vain, and answers no purpose. I reply ; It may be of service, though the condition is impossible, as to illustrate and certify the just punishment of apostates ; for if true believers themselves would be so severely punished, should they, or were it possible they should sin after this manner ; such hypocritical wicked persons, and vile apostates, could not expect to escape divine vengeance ; yea, such declarations may be made use of by the Spirit of God, to stir up true believers to diligence in duty, and watchfulness, against every degree of apostacy, and so be the means of their final perseverance ; and after all, it is plain that the apostle distinguishes true believers, ver. 38, 39 ; from these apostates, whose custom it had been to forsake the assembling of themselves together, ver. 25. Nor does it appear that these were real saints, from their having *received the knowledge of the*

---

[*] Remonstr. in Coll. Hag. art. ii. p. 176, 178. and art. v. p. 18 ; Act. Synod. circa art. ii. p. 346, art. v. p 235, Limborch, p. 322, 709 ; Curcellæus, p. 360 ; Whitby, p. 140, 406, 407 ; ed. 2. 137, 396, 397.

[†] John viii. 55.

truth; whether by *the truth* we understand Jesus Christ, or the Scriptures, or the Gospel, or some particular doctrine of it, especially the principal one, salvation by Christ; which I am inclined to think is intended; since, besides a saving knowledge of these things, which is peculiar to true believers, there is a notional one common to them with others; who may not only give their assent to them as true, but have much light into them, be able to explain them, and preach them to others, and yet be destitute of the grace of God; and therefore if such persons sin, and finally and totally fall away, they are no instances nor proofs of the final and total apostacy of real saints; nor is it manifest that such were the persons here spoken of, from their being *sanctified by the blood of the covenant,* supposing the words are to be understood of them; seeing they have no relation to the inward sanctification of our nature by the Spirit of Christ, as Dr. Whitby* himself owns; who contends that they should be understood of remission of sins, and justification by the blood of Christ, which these persons had received. It is true indeed, that the blessings of pardon and justification, are by and through the blood of the covenant; and are sometimes expressed by sanctifying, purging, and cleansing; see Heb. ix. 13, 14, x. 10, xiii. 12; 1 John i. 7; yet cannot be designed here; for either these persons received a partial remission of sins, and a partial justification from them, or a full remission of all their sins, and a plenary discharge from them, not a partial one; for when God forgives for Christ's sake, he forgives all trespasses, and justifies from all sin: if then these persons had received the forgiveness of all their sins, and were justified from all their iniquities, they would have stood in no need of any more sacrifice for sin; see Heb. x. 18, nor would there be any foundation for punishment of any kind, much less for one so severe as is here represented; see Rom. viii. 1, 30, 33. If then these words are to be considered as spoken of these apostates, the meaning of them is, either that they were sanctified, or separated from others, by a visible profession of religion, had given themselves up to a church, to walk with them in the ordinances of the Gospel, had submitted to baptism, and partook of the Lord's Supper, and drank of the cup, *the blood of the New Testament,* or *covenant;* though they did not spiritually discern the body and blood of Christ in that ordinance; but *counted* the bread and wine, the symbols thereof, as *common* things; or that they professed themselves, and were looked upon by others, to be truly sanctified by the Spirit, and justified by the blood of Christ. Persons are often described, not by what they really are, but by what they are thought to be. Thus the apostle writing to the Corinthians, says of them all, that they were sanctified in Christ Jesus, and by his Spirit, because they professed themselves to be so, and in the opinion of others, were so; though it cannot

be thought that they were all of them really so. But after all, it seems most probable, that not *he that trod the Son of God under foot,* but the *Son of God* himself, is said here to be *sanctified by the blood of the covenant;* which is mentioned as an aggravation of the wickedness of such that count that blood unholy, by which the Son of God himself was sanctified, that is, set apart, hallowed, and consecrated; as Aaron and his sons were by the sacrifices of slain beasts, to minister in the priest's office: Christ, when he had offered himself, and shed his precious blood, whereby the covenant of grace was ratified and confirmed, was, through the blood of that covenant, brought again from the dead, and declared to be the Son of God with power; and being set down at God's right hand, ever lives to make intercession for us; which is the other part of his priestly office he is sanctified by his own blood to accomplish.

2. The crimes which are supposed of these persons, or they are charged with, such as *sinning wilfully;* which is not understood of the common infirmities of life, even grosser acts of sin, which may be voluntarily committed by the saints after regeneration, as were by David, Peter, and others; but of a denial of *the truth* of the Gospel, that salvation is by Christ, against all the evidence of it, and convictions of their own minds: *treading under foot the Son of God,* as much as in them lay, pulling him from his throne, and trampling on him, stripping him of the glory of his person and sacrifice, denying him to be the eternal Son of God; *counting the blood of the covenant an unholy* or *common thing,* putting it upon a level with the blood of a bullock, or at most, counting it, אֵיךְ דכלינש, according to the Syriac version, as the blood of any other man, yea, reckoning it as unclean and abominable; and doing *despite to the Spirit of grace,* rejecting him as a lying spirit, and his gifts, and miracles, as illusions, as Dr. Whitby observes;† I say such crimes as these, are what can never be thought to have been committed, or capable of being committed, by such who have truly tasted that the Lord is gracious.

3. The declaration made to these persons, *there remaineth no more sacrifice for sins;* no more typical sacrifices at Jerusalem, nor any more real sacrifice of the same kind, that has been offered up by Christ, who will not come and die again, and repeat his sacrifice; and therefore, they having denied salvation by him, and the virtue of his former sacrifice, can never expect another; but that when he appears a second time, he will bring on an awful judgment, which will issue in the devouring flames of his wrath and indignation, and be a sorer punishment than the transgressors of Moses' law endured; which was but a temporal, this an eternal death; such a declaration of wrath and vengeance, I say, proves indeed that these persons fell finally and totally; but inasmuch as they cannot be proved to be true believers, it will not be

---

evident from hence, either that Christ died for such as perish; or that those who have truly believed may totally and finally fall away.

SECTION LII

Now the just shall live by faith; but if any man draw back, my soul shall have no pleasure in him.—Heb. x. 38.

THE doctrine of the possibility of the final departure of true believers from the faith, is said* to be still farther evident from these words: Wherefore,

1. For the right understanding of this passage it will be proper to consult the original text in Hab. ii. 4, from whence it is taken. The word עפלה, which the Septuagint have rendered by ὑποστείληται, here used by the apostle, and in our version translated *draw back*, is, according to R. David Kimchi,† עניג גבהות הלב ודרך, expressive of pride and haughtiness of heart: and according to Jarchi‡ is עזות, a word that has the signification of impudence in it; R. Moses Kimchi§ takes it to be the same with עפל, which signifies a tower or fortified place; and thinks it designs one that betakes himself to such a place for shelter from the enemy, and seeks not to God for deliverance; from all which senses or the word we may conclude that such an one is intended who is proud, haughty, vain, and conceited, lifted up with his own righteousness, in which he trusts, and in which he imagines himself to be safe from all evil; and so stands opposed to the *just* man who *lives by faith*, walks humbly with God, in a dependence, not on his own, but Christ's righteousness, in which he is safe from all wrath and condemnation, and secure of the divine favour; while the other will be so far from being the object of God's delight and pleasure, that he will lie under his sad displeasure, and feel his keen and just resentment. The Greek word ὑποστείληται, used by the Septuagint and the apostle, signifies a withdrawing through fear, as Peter withdrew because of the circumcision, Gal. ii. 12, and may here intend a forsaking the assemblies of the saints (ver. 25, which was the manner of some), and all the ordinances of public worship, through fear of reproach, scandal, and persecution, withholding truth, shunning to declare it, or to maintain a profession of it, contrary to what the apostle Paul says of himself, Acts xx. 20, 27, where this word is twice used, and may design one who ὑποκρίνεται, δολιεύεται, *plays the hypocrite*, and *deals deceitfully*, as a late writer‖ observes, the word is rendered by Hesychius and Suidas; than which, to do in religious affairs especially, nothing is more abominable to God; and, in short, may be expressive of an entire departure and total apostacy from the faith, not from true saving faith, but from a mere profession of the grace and doctrine of faith. But then,

2. It must be observed, that ἐὰν ὑποστείληται, *if he* or *any one draws back*, does not refer plainly, as it is said,¶ to the *just man* who *lives by his faith*; for as the drawer back, in ver. 39, stands opposed to him that *believes to the saving of his soul*; so the drawer back, in ver. 38, stands opposed to *the just that lives by faith*, which is owned by the author I refer to, and consequently cannot be the same person; this will still more fully appear from the order of the words in Hab. ii. 4, *he that is lifted up, or withdraws himself,*** *or fails, his soul, that is, God's, shall have no pleasure in him; but the just shall live by his faith;* therefore the words do not plainly suppose, as is asserted,†† that *the just man who lives by that faith*, in which, if he persisted, he would save his soul, may *draw back to perdition;* nor is this evident from the ensuing words, *my soul shall have no pleasure in him,* for they do not plainly intimate, as is affirmed, that God took pleasure in him before his drawing back; since it is not said, *my soul shall have no more, or no further pleasure in him,* but *shall have no pleasure in him;* which does not necessarily suppose that he had any pleasure in him before, but that he should have none in him hereafter. Besides, such who are the objects of God's delight and pleasure are always so; nothing can separate from the love of God, which is always joined with delight in his people.

3. Admitting that the words do plainly refer to the just man that lives by faith, such a one cannot *draw back to perdition;* for that is denied in the following verse; is contrary to an express declaration, *a just man falleth seven times a day, and riseth up again;*‡‡ and consistent with a divine promise, *the righteous shall hold on his way;*§§ and even with this in the text, *the just shall live by faith;* and therefore shall not die the second death, or so draw back as to be eternally lost; though his zeal may abate, his love grow cold, and he fall from some degree of steadfastness in faith; but allowing that drawing back to perdition is here supposed of the just man, it is no more than an hypothetical proposition, which proves not that ever any just man did, could, or should so draw back. The nature and use of such conditional propositions, in which the condition, or thing supposed is impossible, has been shown under the foregoing section. But it is observed,‖‖ that καὶ ἐὰν, may be rendered not hypothetically, *and if,* but *and when he draweth back:* be it so, it is well known that a condition is as well and as frequently expressed by *when*, the *adverb* of time, as by the conjunction *if*, of which numerous instances might be given. The objection from the impossibility of the condition, and the uselessness of threats founded thereon, is answered in the preceding section.

* Whitby, p. 407; ed. 2. 397.   † In loc.
‡ Ibid   § In R. David Kimchi in loc. and in lib. Shorash. rad. עפל.   So Philip Aquinas in Lex. rad, עפל.
‖ Whitby, p. 408; ed 2. 397.   ¶ Ibid.
** Vide Pocock Not. misc. in port. Mosis, p. 43, 44.   †† Whitby, p. 408; ed, 2. 397.
‡‡ Prov. xxiv. 16.   §§ Job xvii. 9.
‖‖ Whitby, p. 409; ed. 2. 398.

4. I see not why the supplement *any man*, should not stand, made by our translators, which the grammatical construction of the words seems to require. Grotius owns the justness of it. Now this carries off the sense from *the just man that lives by faith*, to *any* of those who had made an external profession of religion, but were withdrawing themselves from the communion of the saints, through fear of persecution, who are threatened with the just resentment and displeasure of the Almighty; but lest this should be startling and surprising to true believers, the apostle adds, *but we are not of them that draw back unto perdition, but of them that believe to the saving of the soul.* So far is this from proving the final and total apostacy of real saints, that it establishes the doctrine of their final perseverance; for he that is *just* or righteous by the *everlasting righteousness of Christ*, will ever remain so; who will *live* spiritually, and that by that *faith* which will never fail, and is inseparably connected with salvation, and so he shall never die.

SECTION LIII

Wherefore the rather, brethren, give diligence to make your calling and election sure ; for if ye do these things, ye shall never fall.— 2 Pet. i. 10.

It is said,* "That the election mentioned in the Holy Scriptures is not that of particular persons, but only of churches and nations ; that it is to the enjoyment of the means of grace, which puts them in a capacity of having all the privileges and blessings which God hath promised to his church and people, and is only a conditional one, upon our perseverance in a life of holiness, and is to be made sure unto us by good works, according to this exhortation." But,

1. Though it will be granted that there was a national election of the Jews, who enjoyed the means of grace, the word and ordinances of God, and had peculiar blessings and privileges in consequence of this special choice of them as a nation ; yet this was not an election to salvation elsewhere spoken of, and about which our controversy is, and therefore in vain are so many passages produced by Dr. Whitby,† out of the Old Testament, to prove what nobody denies. And though sometimes whole communities or churches are by the apostles styled the elect of God, as the churches of Colosse, Thessalonica, Babylon,‡ and others, yet they were not chosen as such; nor is it to be thought that all of them were ordained to eternal life, though the apostles speak of them in the bulk as the elect of God, being under a visible profession of religion ; just as they call them all *saints, the sanctified, and faithful in Christ Jesus ;* though it is not to be supposed that all the individual members of these churches were real saints. However, it does not appear that the persons the apostle Peter wrote his epistles to were either a nation or a church, being *the strangers scattered throughout Pontus, Galatia, Cappadocia, Asia, and Bithynia ;*§ they are indeed called *a chosen generation, a royal priesthood, a holy nation, a peculiar people ;*‖ but that is only in allusion to typical Israel, and the shadowy election of that people as a nation. It is certain that these persons were chosen not merely to external means and outward blessings and privileges, but to grace here, and glory hereafter ; for they were *elect according to the foreknowledge of God the Father, through sanctification of the Spirit unto obedience, and sprinkling of the blood of Jesus,* and in consequence of this were *begotten again to a lively hope of an inheritance incorruptible, and undefiled, and that fadeth not away, reserved in heaven,* and were *kept by the power of God through faith unto salvation.*¶ They were a set of particular persons, who *had obtained like precious faith with* the apostles,** and were every one to use *diligence to make sure* their own, and not another's *calling and election ;* and so not a national or church-election, but a personal one.

2. This election it not a conditional one, depending on perseverance in a life of holiness. The text does not say, *if ye do these things* ye shall be elected, or your election shall remain firm and sure, but *ye shall never fall ;* meaning, not into lesser sins and infirmities of life, *for in many things we offend all,* πταιομεν απαντες, *we all fall ;* but into the great evil of a final and total apostacy ; or *ye shall never fall*,†† so as to be lost and perish. The final perseverance of the saints is secured by electing grace ; that is not the cause, but the fruit of election ; election does not depend upon that, but that upon election.

3. *Election and calling* here mentioned with it, are to be *made sure ;* not that they can be made surer in themselves, nor with respect to God, than they are, being both *not according to our works, but according to the purpose and grace of* God, which cannot be frustrated ; and so stand upon a sure foundation, which can never fail, and are inseparably connected with glorification, Rom. viii. 30. Nor are these to be made sure by the saints *to themselves,* for, though they may have some doubts and scruples in their minds about their interest in these things, and an assurance of which may be attained ; yet it is not their work, but the work of the Spirit of God, to certify or assure them of their vocation and election of God. But diligence is to be used by the saints, to make sure their calling and election *to others ;* either to their fellow-Christians, which they may do by conversing with them about the work of grace upon their souls, or rather to the world, and that διὰ των καλων εργων, *by good works ;* as these words are read in two manuscript copies of Beza's, and by the Syriac, Ethiopic, and Vulgate Latin ; and then the meaning is, be careful to maintain good works, be diligent in doing these things, which, through the

---

* Ibid. p. 86 ; ed. 2. 35.   † Pages 37–40 ; ed. 2. 36–39.   ‡ Col. iii. 12 ; 1 Thess. i. 4 ; 2 Thess. ii. 13 ; 1 Pet. v. 13.   § 1 Pet. i. 1.   ‖ Ch. ii. 9. ¶ 1 Pet. i. 2–5.   ** 2 Pet. i. 1.   †† James iii. 2.

grace of God, will not only be the means of your final perseverance, but also of making your calling and election sure to others ; you will hereby certify and assure others, give the best evidence to the world you are capable of giving, or they of receiving, that you are the called and chosen of God you profess yourselves to be.

SECTION LIV

But there were false prophets also among the people, even as there shall be false teachers among you, who privily shall bring in damnable heresies, denying the Lord that bought them, and bring upon themselves swift destruction.—2 Pet. ii. 1.

This passage of scripture is often produced as a proof both of the saints' final and total apostacy,* and of universal redemption ; or that, besides those that are saved, Christ died also for them that perish. Dr. Whitby† mentions the several answers which different men give to these words : one saith, Christ bought these persons only to be slaves ; another, that he died to rescue them from temporal, but not eternal punishments ; a third, that he died for them because he gave a sufficient price for them ; a fourth, that they denied that Lord whom they professed to have bought them ; and a fifth, that they denied him, who, in the judgment of other men, had bought them. Upon which he observes, that they are so extravagant, that it is as easy to confute as to recite them.

1. I do not think myself concerned to defend any of these senses of the text mentioned, judging neither of them to be the meaning of the words, and so have nothing to do with the reasonings made use of in the confutation of them ; though, perhaps, the two latter are not so extravagant as represented. However, in order to give the genuine sense of this text, let it be observed,

2. That Christ is not here at all spoken of ; nor is there one syllable of his dying for any persons, in any sense whatever. The word δεσπότης, Lord, does not design Christ, but God the Father of Christ. The only places besides this where this word is used, when applied to a divine person, are Luke ii. 29, Acts iv. 24, 2 Tim. ii. 21, Jude ver. 4, Rev. vi. 10, in all which places God the Father is plainly intended, and in most of them manifestly distinguished from Christ ; nor is there anything in this text or context which obliges us to understand it of the Son of God ; nor should this be thought any diminution of the glory of Christ, since the word δεσπότης is properly expressive only of that power which masters have over their servants ; whereas the word κύριος, which is used whenever Christ is called Lord, signifies that dominion and authority which princes have over their subjects. Besides, Christ is called *King of kings, and Lord of lords,* and the only *Potentate ;* yea, *God over all, blessed for ever.* Moreover,

3. When these persons are said to be *bought,* the meaning is, not that they were redeemed by the blood of Christ, for, as is before observed, Christ is not intended. Besides, whenever redemption by Christ is spoken of, the price is usually mentioned, or some circumstance or another which fully determines the sense of it ; see Acts xx. 28 ; 1 Cor. vi. 20 ; Eph. i. 7 ; 1 Pet. i. 18—19 ; Rev. v. 9, and xiv. 3—4, whereas here is not the least hint of anything of this kind. Add to this, that such who are redeemed by Christ, are never left to deny him, so as to perish eternally ; for could such be lost, or bring on themselves swift destruction, Christ's purchase would be in vain, and the ransom-price be paid for nought. But,

4. The word *buying* regards temporal deliverance, and particularly the redemption of the people of Israel out of Egypt ; who are therefore called *the people the Lord had purchased.* The phrase is borrowed from Deut. xxxii. 6 ; *Do ye thus requite the Lord, O foolish people and unwise? Is not he thy Father that hath bought thee? Hath he not made thee and established thee?* Nor is this the only place the apostle Peter refers to in this chapter ; see ver. 12, 13, compared with Deut. xxxii. 5. Now the persons the apostle writes to, were Jews, *the strangers scattered throughout Pontus, Galatia, Cappadocia, Asia, and Bithynia,* a people who, in all ages, valued themselves upon, and boasted mightily of their being the *bought, purchased people of the Lord ;* wherefore Peter makes use of this phrase much in the same manner as Moses had done before him, to aggravate the ingratitude and impiety of these false teachers among the Jews ; that they should deny, if not in words, at least in works, that mighty Jehovah, who had of old redeemed their fathers out of Egypt, with a stretched-out arm, and, in successive ages, had distinguished them with peculiar favours ; being *ungodly men, turning the grace,* the doctrine of the grace *of God, into lasciviousness.* Hence,

5. Nothing can be concluded from this passage in favour of Christ's dying for them that perish ; since neither Christ, nor the death of Christ, nor redemption by his blood, are here once mentioned, nor in the least intended. Nor can these words be thought to be a proof and instance of the final and total apostacy of real saints, since there is not anything said of these false teachers, which gives any reason to believe that they were true believers in Christ, or ever had the grace of the Spirit wrought in their souls.

SECTION LV

For if after that they have escaped the pollutions of the world, through the knowledge of the Lord and Saviour Jesus Christ, they are again entangled therein, and overcome ; the latter end is worse with them than the beginning. For it had been better for them

---

* Remonstr. in Coll. Hag. art. v. p. 17, and art. ii. p. 132, 160 ; Act. Synod. circ. art. ii. p. 354, &c. ; Curcell. p. 360 ; Limborch, p. 322.

† Page 141, 142 ; ed. 2. 138, 139.

not to have known the way of righteousness, than after they have known it, to turn from the holy commandment delivered unto them. But it is happened unto them according to the true proverb, The dog is turned to his vomit again; and the sow that was washed, to her wallowing in the mire.—2 Pet. ii. 20—22.

This Scripture generally* stands among the proofs of the apostacy of real saints; and it is said,† that the possibility of the final and total falling away of true believers, may be strongly argued from these words.

1. It will be allowed that the persons here spoken of, finally and totally fell away; since they are not only said *to turn from the holy commandment delivered unto them*, but to *be again entangled in the pollutions of the world, and overcome;* yea, to *turn like the dog to his vomit*, and *the sow to her wallowing in the mire:* so that *the latter end with them is worse than the beginning.* Yet,

2. Nothing is said of them which discovers them to have been true believers. They might have externally *escaped the pollutions of the world*, reformed in their outward lives and conversations, through the national *knowledge of the Lord and Saviour Jesus Christ;* professed *the way of righteousnss*, and for a while, visibly walked in it, and submitted to *the holy commandments* and ordinances of Christ, and yet not have been partakers of the grace of God; nor is it evident that the apostle here speaks of such who had *obtained like precious faith with* them; but of some third persons distinct from them. Perhaps the highest character given them is in ver. 18, which is, that they were such who *were clean,* ὄντως, truly and really, as Dr. Whitby renders the word, *escaped from them who live ἐν πλάνη, in error;*‡ which, he observes, is to be understood not of judgment, but of deceitful lusts. But let it be considered that there are different readings of this text; some copies, instead of ὄντως read ὀλίγως *within a little*, or *almost*, so the Alexandrian MS. in the Polyglott Bible, and two books of Beza's; others ὀλίγον; so the Complutensian edition, and the King of Spain's Bible; agreeably the Vulgate Latin renders it *paululum, a very little*, or *a very little time.* The Syriac version reads it במלא קליל, *in a few words*, or *almost;* and, according to the Ethiopic version, *a few persons* are designed. From all which, this sense of the words may be collected, that there were some few persons, who, in some few instances, had almost, or within a very little, or for a little time, escaped from such who lived in error, being carried away with divers and strange doctrines. But admitting that ὄντως is the true reading, and that πλάνη signifies not error of judgment, but deceitful lusts; it is possible that men may truly and really escape, not only from idolaters and

false teachers, and so have the form of sound doctrine, whilst they deny the power of it, but also reform and withdraw from openly profane and scandalous sinners, and yet not be true believers, as it appears these were not; since they openly turned to, and appeared to be what they really were; as *the dog turns to his own vomit, and the sow to her wallowing in the mire.*

SECTION LVI

The Lord is not slack concerning his promise (as some men count slackness), but is long-suffering to us-ward, not willing that any should perish, but that all should come to repentance.—2 Pet. iii. 9.

This scripture appears among those which are said§ to be very many clear and express ones for the doctrine of universal redemption; and it is observed,‖ " that τίνες, opposed to πάντες, is a distributive of all, and, therefore, signifies, God is not willing that any one of the whole rank of men should perish." But,

1. It is not true that God is not willing any one individual of the human race should perish, since he has *made* and appointed *the wicked for the day* of evil, even *ungodly men*, who are *fore-ordained to this condemnation,* such as are *vessels of wrath fitted for destruction;* yea, there are some to whom *God sends strong delusions, that they may believe a lie, that they all might be damned;* and others *whose judgment now of a long time lingereth not and their damnation slumbereth not.*¶ Nor is it his will that all men, in this large sense, should come to repentance, since he withholds from many both the means and grace of repentance; and though it is his will of precept, that all to whom the preaching of the Gospel is vouchsafed should repent, yet it is not his purposing, determining will, to bring them all to repentance, *for who hath resisted his will?***

2. It is very true that τίνες, *any*, being opposed to πάντες, *all*, is a distributive of it; but then both the *any* and the *all* are to be limited and restrained by the *us*, to whom God is long-suffering; God is not willing that any more should not perish, and is willing that no more should come to repentance than the *us* to whom his long-suffering is salvation. The key, therefore, to open this text lies in these words, εἰς ἡμᾶς, *to us-ward*, or *for our sake;* for these are the persons God would not have any of them perish, but would have them all come to repentance. It will be proper, therefore,

3. To enquire who these are. It is evident that they are distinguished from the scoffers mocking at the promise of Christ's coming, ver. 3, 4, are called beloved, ver. 1, 8, 14, 17, which is to be understood either of their being beloved by God, with an everlasting and unchangeable love, or of their being

---

* Remonstr. in Coll. Hag. art. v. p. 17; Act. Synod. circ. art. v. p. 242, &c.; Limborch, p. 711.   † Whitby, p. 409; ed. 2. 398.
‡ Page 410; ed. 2. 399.
§ Remonstr. in Coll. Hag. art. ii. p. 160, 181,

196; Curcellæus, p. 364; Limborch, p. 333; Whitby, p. 113; ed. 2. 111.   ‖ Whitby, p. 124; ed. 2. 121.   ¶ Prov. xvi. 4; Jude, ver. 4; Rom. ix. 22; 2 Thess. xi. 12; 2 Pet. i. 3.   ** Rom. ix. 19.

beloved as brethren by the apostle and other saints; neither of which is true of all mankind. Besides, the design of the words is to establish the saints in, and comfort them with the coming of Christ, until which, God was long-suffering towards them, and which they were to account salvation, ver. 15. Add to this, that the apostle manifestly designs a company or society to which he belonged, and of which he was a part, and so can mean no other than such who were chosen of God, redeemed from among men, and called out of darkness into marvellous light; and such were the persons the apostle writes to. Some copies read the words δὶ ὑμᾶς, *for your sakes;* so the Alexandrian MS. the Syriac version, מטלחכון, *for you,* or your sakes; the same way the Ethiopic. Now these persons were such who were *elect, according to the forknowledge of God the Father, through sanctification of the Spirit unto obedience, and sprinkling of the blood of Jesus Christ;*[*] and such, as these, or who belong to the same election of grace they did, God is unwilling that any of them should perish, but wills that all of them should have repentance unto life; and, therefore, he waits to be gracious to them, and defers the second coming of Christ. The case stands thus: there was a promise of Christ's second coming, to judge the world, delivered out; it was expected that this would have been very quickly, whereas it has been a long time deferred. Hence scoffers shall arise in the last days, charging the Lord with slackness and dilatoriness concerning his promise, though he is not slack with respect to it, but is long-suffering towards his elect, waiting till their number is completed in effectual vocation, and for their sakes bears with all the idolatry, superstition, and profaneness that are in the world; but when the last man that belongs to that number is called, he will stay no longer, but descend in flames of fire, take his own elect to himself, and burn up the world and the wicked in it.

4. It is indeed[†] said, "that the apostle, by *the elect,* to whom he writes, does not mean men absolutely designed for eternal happiness, but only men professing Christianity, or such as were visible members of the church of Christ: since he calls upon them to *make* their *calling and election sure,* exhorts them to watchfulness, seeing their *adversary the devil goes about seeking whom he may devour,* and to *beware lest* they *fall from their own steadfastness;* yea, he speaks of some of them as having *forsaken the right way;* and also prophesies that *false teachers should make merchandize of them,* neither of which, it is observed, can be supposed of men absolutely elected to salvation; and, also, that the church at Babylon was elected, together with these persons, which could not be known and said of all its members." To all which I reply, that calling upon them to make their election sure, does not suppose it to be a precarious and conditional one, as I have shown in a preceding section;

that exhortations to sobriety, and vigilance against Satan, and cautions about falling, are pertinent to such who are absolutely elected to salvation; for, though Satan cannot devour them, he may greatly distress them; and, though they shall not finally and totally fall from the grace of God, yet they may fall from some degree of steadfastness, both as to the doctrine and grace of faith, which may be to their detriment as well as to the dishonour of God: that it is not true, that the apostle speaks of any of these elect he writes to, that they had *forsaken the right way,* but of some other persons; and though he prophesies that *false teachers* should *make merchandize* of them, the meaning is, that, by their fine words and fair speeches, they should be able to draw money out of their pockets, not that they should destroy the grace of God wrought in their hearts. As to the church at Babylon being said to be elected with them, the apostle might say this of the church in general, as he does, in a judgment of charity, of the church at Thessalonica, and others, though every member of it in particular was not elected to salvation, without any prejudice to the doctrine of absolute election. Besides, the persons he writes to were not visible members of any one particular church or community, professing Christianity, but were strangers scattered abroad in several parts of the world, and were such who had *obtained like precious faith* with the apostles, and is a strong evidence of their being men absolutely designed for eternal happiness. And whereas it is suggested, that these persons were come to repentance, and therefore cannot be the same to whom God is long-suffering, that they might come to repentance; I answer, that though they are not the same individual persons, yet are such who belong to the same body and number of the elect, on whom the Lord waits, and to whom he is long-suffering, until they are all brought to partake of this grace, having determined that not one of them should ever perish.

5. Hence it follows, that these words do not furnish out any argument in favour of universal redemption, nor do they militate [*] against absolute election and reprobation, or unfrustrable grace in conversion; but, on the contrary, maintain and establish them, since it appears to be the will of God, that not one of those he has chosen in Christ, given to him, and for whom he died, shall ever perish; and, inasmuch as evangelical repentance is necessary for them, and they cannot come at it of themselves, he freely bestows it on them, and, by his unfrustrable grace, works it in them; and, until this is done unto and upon every one of them, he keeps the world in being, which is *reserved unto fire, against the day of judgment, and perdition of ungodly men.*

---

* 1 Pet. i. 2. † Whitby, p. 125, 126; ed. 2. 122, 123.

‡ Whitby, p. 13, 75; ed. 2. 74.

SECTION LVII

And he is the propitiation for our sins; and not for ours only, but also for the sins of the whole world.—1 John ii. 2.

A VERY considerable argument for the universal extent of Christ's death is thought to arise * from this passage of scripture, as well as from all those which represent Christ as *the Saviour of the world;* and it is observed, that whereas these scriptures are all, save one, in the writing of St. John, the sense which *the world* beareth in St. John's gospel and epistles, must be esteemed, in reason, the proper import of the word, where it never signifies the elect only, in opposition to the wicked of the world, but the wicked of the world in opposition to the faithful Christian.† To which I answer,

I. That there would be some weight in this observation if the word *world* was always used in one uniform and constant sense in the writings of the apostle John, whereas it admits of a variety of senses; and, therefore, the sense of it in one place cannot be the rule for the interpretation of it in another, which can only be prefixed as the text or context determine: sometimes it signifies the whole universe of created beings, John i. 10; sometimes the habitable earth, John xvi. 28; sometimes the inhabitants of it, John i. 10; sometimes unconverted persons, both elect and reprobate, John xv. 19; sometimes the worse part of the world, the wicked, John xvii. 9; sometimes the better part of it, the elect, John i. 29, and vi. 33, 51; sometimes a number of persons, and that a small one in comparison of the rest of mankind, John xii. 19; in one place it is used three times, and in so many senses, John i. 10; *he,* that is, Christ, *was in the world,* the habitable earth, and *the world,* the whole universe, *was made by him,* and *the world,* the inhabitants of the earth, *knew him not;* and which is not to be understood of them all, for there were some, though few, who did know him: and I will venture to affirm, that the word *world* is always used in the apostle John's writings, in a restricted and limited sense, for some only, unless when it designs the whole universe, or habitable earth, senses which are out of the question, for none will say Christ died for the sun, moon, and stars, for fishes, fowls, brutes, sticks, and stones; and that it is never used to signify every individual of mankind that has been, is, or shall be in the world; in which sense it ought to be proved it is used, if any argument can be concluded from it in favour of general redemption.

II. It is most manifest that the word *world,* used by the apostle John when speaking of redemption and salvation by Christ, is always used in a limited and restrained sense, and signifies some persons only, and not all the individuals of human nature, as will appear from the consideration of the several passages following, as when the Baptist says.

John i. 29, *Behold the Lamb of God, which taketh away the sins of the world!* By the *world* cannot be meant every individual of mankind; for it is not true, it is not fact, that Jesus Christ, the Lamb of God, takes away the sin or sins of every individual man, since there are some who *die* in their *sins,* whose *sins go beforehand to judgment,* and *others they follow after,* for which they will be righteously and everlastingly condemned; which can never be, if Christ has taken away their sin. Should it be said,‡ as it is, "That the Baptist speaks this in allusion to the lambs daily offered up for the sin of the whole Jewish nation; and, therefore, intimates, that as they were offered up to expiate the sins of the whole nation, so was this Lamb of God offered to expiate the sins of the whole world in general;" I reply, that as the lambs daily offered were typical of Christ, the Lamb of God, so the people, for whom they were offered, were typical, not of the whole world in general, but of the true Israel and church of God, for whom Christ gave himself an expiatory sacrifice, and whose sins he so takes away as they shall not be seen any more.

When our Lord says, that *God so loved the world, that he gave his only-begotten Son, that whosoever believeth in him should not perish, but have everlasting life,*§—by the *world* he cannot mean every son and daughter of Adam; for this world is represented as the object of God's *love,* even of his special love, which all men are not: as such to and for whom God has *given his only-begotten Son,* which is not true of all mankind; who are brought to *believe* in Christ, in consequence of God's love, and the gift of his Son, but all men have not faith; as such who shall never *perish,* though it is certain that some men will; and as such who shall have *everlasting life,* whereas some will go into everlasting punishment, and die the second death. The similitude of the brazen serpent lifted up for the preservation of the Jews, is insufficient to prove the redemption of all mankind: nor is it supposed, of this world, so beloved of God, that some would not believe, and therefore perish; and that others would, and be saved; for the phrase *whosoever believeth,* does not design a division of different persons, but a distinction of the same persons; who, in their unconverted state, believe not, but, through the power of divine grace, are brought to believe in Christ for life and salvation; and so it points out the way in which they are secured from perishing, and have everlasting life. Nor will it be the condemnation of infidels among the Heathens that they believed not in Christ, but their transgressions of the law of nature; nor of the unbelieving Jews, that they believed not Christ died for them, but because they did not believe him to be the Messiah: nor do these words, taken in the universal sense, more magnify the love of God than when taken in a more restrained one; since accord-

---

* Remonstr. in Coll. Hag. art. ii. p. 133; Curcellæus, p. 353; Limboren, p. 321.

† Whitby, p. 127, 128, 134; ed. 2. 124, 125, 131.   ‡ Ibid. p. 134.   § John iii. 16.

ing to this general scheme, men may be the objects of God's love, and have an interest in the gift of his Son, and yet finally perish, and come short of everlasting life. The words in the following verse,* and which are elsewhere in the same manner expressed, that Christ came *into the world not to condemn it*, but to *save* it, are designed to point out the different ends of Christ's first and second coming. Again,

When the Samaritans declared their belief in Christ, that he was the *Saviour of the world ;†* and the apostle John says, that *we have seen, and do testify, that the Father sent the Son to be the Saviour of the world ;* by the *world*, cannot be intended every man and woman that has been, is, or shall be in the world, since every one is not saved ; and Christ cannot be the Saviour of more than are saved. Besides, was he the Saviour of the world in this universal sense, he must be the Saviour both of believers and unbelievers, contrary to his own words ; *He that believeth and is baptized, shall be saved ; he that believeth not shall be damned.‡* Moreover,

When Christ says, *The bread of God is he that cometh down from heaven and giveth life to the world ;§* no more can be designed by *the world* than those to whom this bread of God gives life. Now it is certain, that spiritual life here, and everlasting life hereafter, are not given to all men, and therefore all men cannot be intended here ; only such who are quickened by the Spirit of God, and shall enjoy eternal life ; and these are *the world, for the life of* which Christ promised to *give his flesh*, in this same chapter.‖ Now from the consideration of all these passages, it will appear how weak, trifling, and inconclusive is the argument taken from hence in favour of universal redemption. But,

III. It may be said, if the *world* does not include every individual person in it, yet surely the phrase, *the whole world*, must : and when the beloved disciple says, *And he is the propitiation for our sins, and not for ours only, but for the sins of the whole world ;¶* these, his words, will not admit of a restrained sense, but must extend to all men.** To which I reply :

1. The phrase, *the whole world*, is frequently used by the Jews in a limited and restrained sense ; as when they†† report, "That it happened to a certain high priest, that when he went out of the sanctuary, כולי עלמא, the whole world went after him ;" which could only design the multitude in the temple ; and where‡‡ it is said, "כולי עלמא, the whole world has left the *Misnah* and gone after the *Gemara ;*" which at most can only intend the Jews, and perhaps only a majority of their doctors ; and in another§§ place, "כולי עלמא, the whole world fell upon their faces ; but

Raf did not fall on his face ;" where it means no more than the congregation. Once more‖‖ it is said, " When R. Simeon Ben Gamaliel entered, that is, into the synagogue, כולי עלמא, the whole world, that is, all the synagogue, stood up before him." Such phrases as these כולי עלמא לא פליגי, the whole world does not dissent ; כולי עלמא מודי, the whole world confesseth ; and כולי עלמא סברי, the whole world are of opinion, are frequently met with in the Talmud ; by which is designed an agreement among the Rabbins in certain points ; nay, sometimes two doctors only are meant by כולי ע׳מא, the whole world.¶¶

2. This phrase in scripture, unless where it signifies the whole universe, or habitable earth, is always used in a limited and restrained sense ; *a decree went out that all the world should be taxed ;* which was no other than the Roman empire, and such countries as were subject to it. The *faith* of the church at Rome, was *spoken of throughout the whole world*, that is, throughout all the churches, and among all the saints in the world. *All the world* is said *to become guilty before God by the law ;* which can be said of no more than were under that law, and so not true of all mankind ; who, though all guilty by the law of nature, yet not by the law of Moses. The apostle tells the Colossians, that *the gospel* was *come into all the world, and bringeth forth fruit ;* which can design only real saints and true believers, in whom alone it brings forth fruit. An *hour of temptation* is spoken of, *which shall come upon all the world, to try them which dwell upon the earth ;* who can be no other than such who will then be in being, and cannot be thought to include all the individuals that have been in the world. *All the world wondered after the beast ;* and yet there were some who did not receive his mark, nor worship him. Satan *deceiveth the whole world ;* and yet it is certain, that the elect cannot be deceived by him. *The whole world* will be gathered together to the *battle of the great day of God Almighty ;* who are distinct from the saints, whom they will oppose.***

3. This phrase in the writings of the apostle John, is used in a restrained sense, and does not extend to every individual of human nature, that has been, is, or shall be in the world, as it should be proved it does, to conclude an argument from it in favour of universal redemption. Now it is used but in one place besides the text under consideration, when it designs men, in all his writings, and that is in 1 John v. 19. *And we know that we are of God, and the whole world lieth in wickedness ;* where the whole world lying in wickedness, is manifestly distinguished from the saints, who are of God, and belong not to the world ; and consequently the whole world is not to be understood of all the individuals in it. And it

---

* John iii. 17 ; chap. xii. 47. † John iv. 43 ; 1 John iv. 14. ‡ Mark xvi. 16.
§ John vi. 33. ‖ John vi. 51.
¶ 1 John ii. 2. ** Whitby, p. 132 ; ed. 2. 129. †† Talmud. Yoma, fol. 71.

2. ‡‡ Bava Metzia, fol. 33. 2.
§§ Megilla, fol. 22. 2. ‖‖ Horaiot fol. 13.
2. ¶¶ Vid. Mill. Formul. Talmud, p. 41, 42.
*** Luke ii. 1 ; Rom. i. 8, and iii. 19 ; Col. i. 6 ; Rev. iii. 10, and xii. 3, and xiii. 3.

is easy to observe the like distinction in the text before us; for *the sins of the whole world* are opposed to *our sins*, the sins of the apostle, and others to whom he joins himself; who therefore belonged not to, nor were a part of the whole world, for whose sins Christ was a propitiation, as for theirs. That the whole world, for whom Christ is a propitiation, cannot intend every man and woman that has been, is, or shall be in the world, appears from his being their *propitiation;* for, for whose sins he is a propitiation, their sins are atoned for and pardoned, and their persons justified from all sin, and so shall certainly be glorified; which is not true of the whole world, taken in the large sense contended for. Besides, Christ is *set forth to be a propitiation through faith in his blood.** The benefit of his propitiatory sacrifice, is only received and enjoyed through faith; so that in the event, it appears that Christ is a propitiation only for believers, a character which does not agree with all mankind. Add to this, that for whom Christ is a propitiation, he is also an advocate, ver. 1, but he is not an advocate for every individual in the world; yea, there is a world he will not pray for, and consequently is no propitiation for. Once more, the design of the apostle in these words, is to comfort his *little children*, who might fall into sin through weakness and inadvertency, with the advocacy and propitiatory sacrifice of Christ; but what comfort would it yield to a distressed mind, to be told that Christ was a propitiation, not only for the sins of the apostles, and other saints, but for the sins of every individual in the world, even of those that are in hell? Would it not be natural for persons in such circumstances, to argue rather against than for themselves; and conclude, that inasmuch as persons might be damned, notwithstanding Christ's propitiatory sacrifice, that this might and would be their case? But,

4. For the better understanding the sense of this text, it should be observed, that the apostle John was a Jew, and writes to Jews, as Dr. Whitby himself observes,[†] and them chiefly, if not altogether, who were distinguished from the Gentiles, commonly called the world: now, says the apostle, *He is a propitiation for our sins, and not for ours only*, the sins of us Jews, *but also for the sins of the whole world*, the Gentiles. Nothing is more common in the Jewish writings,[‡] than to call the Gentiles עלמא, the world; and כל עולם, the whole world; and אומות העולם, the nations of the world; hence the apostle Paul calls them κόσμος, the world, in Rom. xi. 12, 15. It was a controversy agitated among the Jewish doctors, whether when the Messiah came, the Gentiles, the world, should have any benefit by him; the majority was exceeding large on the negative of the question, and determined they should not; only some few, as old Simeon and others, knew that he should

be *a light to lighten the Gentiles*, as well as *the glory of the people of Israel*. The rest concluded, that the most severe judgments and dreadful calamities would befal them; yea, that they should be cast into hell in the room of the Israelites.[§] This notion John the Baptist, Christ, and his apostles, purposely oppose, and is the true reason of the use of this phrase in the Scriptures which speak of Christ's redemption. Thus John the Baptist, when he pointed out the Messiah to the Jews, represents him as *the Lamb of God, which taketh away the sin of the world*, the Gentiles as well as the Jews; for by the blood of this Lamb, men are *redeemed to God, out of every kindred, and tongue, and people, and nation*. When our Lord was discoursing with Nicodemus, one of their Rabbins, he lets him know that *God so loved the world*, the Gentiles, contrary to their rabbinical notions, *that he gave his only begotten Son, that whosoever* of them *that believeth on him, should not perish*, as they had concluded every one of them should; *but have everlasting life:* and that *God sent not his Son into the world, to condemn the world*, the Gentiles, as they imagined, *but that the world through him might be saved*. When the Samaritans believed in Christ, they declared him to be *the Saviour of the world*, the Gentiles, and so of themselves, who were accounted by the Jews as Heathens; Christ sets forth himself as *the bread of life*, preferable to *the manna*, among other things, from its extensive virtue to the world, the Gentiles: and here the apostle John says, that Christ was not only *the propitiation for the sins of the Jews*, but for the *sins of the whole world*, the Gentiles.[||] This puts me in mind of a passage I have met with in the Talmud,[¶] a saying of Rabbi Jochanan, "Wo, says he, העסל לאומית, to the nations of the world, who are lost, and they know not that they are lost; whilst the sanctuary stood, the altar atoned, or was a propitiation for them; but now who shall be a propitiation for them?" Blessed be God, we know who is the propitiation for us, the nations of the world, one that was typified by the altar, and is greater than that, even the Lord Jesus Christ.

SECTION LVIII

Keep yourselves in the love of God, looking for the mercy of our Lord Jesus Christ unto eternal life.—Jude, ver. 21.

THESE words are thought to represent the saints' continuance in the love and favour of God, as conditional, depending on their obedience, care, and keeping of themselves; and that there is a possibility of their falling from it, and consequently that they are not absolutely elected to everlasting life.[**] To which I reply;

1. That the saints' continuance in the love and favour of God, does not depend on their

---

* Rom. iii. 25.

† Page 466; ed. 2. 446.   ‡ Talmud, Rabbot, and Zohar. Vid. Jarchi in Isa. liii. 5.

§ Vid. Shemot Rabba, fol. 98. 3, and 99. 4: Shirhash, Rab. fol. 24. 1; Jarchi and Kimchi, in

Zech. ix. 1. || John i. 29, and iii. 16, 17, and iv. 42, and vi. 33; 1 John ii. 2.

¶ Succa, fol. 55. 2.

** Whitby, p. 87, 398, 422, 458; ed. 2. 86, 388, 410, 411, 438.

obedience, or on any thing done by them; since his love to them is an everlasting one, which commenced from everlasting, and will continue to everlasting; is prior to all their obedience; was in his own heart towards them, and expressed by several acts before they had done either good or evil; and continued, notwithstanding all their disobedience, in an unregenerate state, and is the source and spring of all their love and obedience to him; nor is there anything in their best works that can entitle them to his favour, or secure the continuance of it; since, when they had done all they can, they are but "unprofitable servants." Nor is there any possibility or danger of real saints falling from the love and favour of God. They may, and sometimes are, left to do those things which are displeasing to him, and, was he a man, or should he act as men usually do in such cases, would at once, and effectually, turn them out of his favour; but the case is, he is *the Lord*, and not man, and *changes not* in his affections as men do; "and therefore the sons of Jacob are not consumed."* In his severest providences towards his people, his love always remains the same, as when he hides his face from them, or chides and chastises them in a fatherly way; should it be otherwise, his love would not be everlasting, unchangeable, and from which there is no separation, as the Scriptures represent it; and besides, would be contrary to the assurances he has given of the continuance of his love, both by word and oath, Isaiah liv. 9, 10.

2. By the *love of God*, in this text, we are not to understand the love which God bears in his own heart to his people, or with which they are loved by him, but rather that love with which they love him, and of which he is the object; see Luke xi. 42, which is a sense some interpreters† on the other side of the question readily allow of; and then the meaning of the exhortation, *keep yourselves*, ἑαυτούς, *one another*, as it may be rendered, *in the love of God*, is, that though this grace of love cannot be lost, yet, inasmuch as the fervour of it may be abated, and the saints grow cold and indifferent in their expressions of it, it becomes them to make use of all proper means to maintain, increase, and inflame it, both in themselves and others, such as are mentioned in the context, as conversing together in an edifying way, about either the grace or doctrine of their *most holy faith; praying* either separately or together, under the influences of *the Holy Ghost*, and *looking* forward *for the mercy of Christ unto eternal life*. All which, with many other things, by the blessing of God, may serve to maintain and revive the grace of love, and blow it up into a flame. Though, perhaps, this phrase may chiefly design that love, peace, and concord, which ought to subsist among saints as brethren, and which they should be careful to preserve. This may be called *the love of God*, just as the same thing is styled *the peace of God*, Col.

iii. 15, because he calls them to it, it is of him, what they are taught by him, and in which he causes them to abound; and then the sense of the exhortation, *keep yourselves*, or *one another in the love of God*, is, *endeavour to keep the unity of the Spirit in the bond of peace; provoke one another to love and good works ;‡ walk in love*, both to God and among yourselves, as ye have Christ for an example; which sense is strengthened by the following words, *of some have compassion, making a difference*, and *others save with fear*. And hence it will appear that this text neither militates against the doctrine of absolute election, nor countenances the doctrine of the possibility of real saints falling from a state of grace and favour with God. But,

3. Admitting that by *the love of God*, is meant the grace and favour of God: the exhortation to the saints, to *keep themselves in* it, is, to set it always before them, to keep it constantly in view, to exercise faith on it, firmly believing their interest in it, and hence keep *looking* and waiting *for the mercy of Christ unto eternal life ;* or to *keep themselves in* it, is to meditate on it, give themselves up wholly to the contemplation of it, and employ their thoughts constantly about this delightful subject, the love of God; which is the foundation of all grace here, and glory hereafter. Once more, the words, ἑαυτοὺς ἐν ἀγάπῃ Θεοῦ τηρήσατε, may be rendered, *preserve yourselves by the love of God*, that is, against Satan's temptations, the snares of the world, and the lusts of the flesh. Whenever Satan solicits to sin, any snare is laid to draw into it, and the flesh attempts to be predominant, betake yourselves to the love of God, as a strong hold, or preservative against sin; and reason thus, as Joseph did, "How then can I do this great wickedness, and sin against God?"§ who, when I look backward, has loved me with an everlasting love; and when I look forward there is *the mercy of our Lord Jesus Christ unto eternal life*. Consider the words in either light, they neither prove a conditional election, nor a possibility of the saints falling from grace; against which, provision is made in Christ, who, in ver. 24, is represented as "able to keep *them* from falling, and to present *them* faultless before the presence of his glory with exceeding joy."

SECTION LIX

REVELATIONS, CHAP. II. AND III.

SEVERAL passages are produced from the epistles to the seven churches of Asia, in favour of the defectibility and total apostacy of real saints. It should be observed, that the churches in all ages, have more or less consisted of true believers and hypocrites, wise and foolish virgins, sheep and goats, wheat and tares, and sometimes are denominated from the better, and sometimes from the worser part; some things in the epistles to them particularly regard true believers

---

* Mal. iii. 6. † Vorstius and Grotius in loc. ‡ Eph. iv. 3; Heb. x. 24; Eph. v. 2. § Gen. xxxix. 9.

and others formal professors among them. This observation will help us to understand the reason and meaning of many commands, cautions, exhortations, and threatenings, not only used in these epistles, but in the rest of the epistles sent to the several churches. Besides, it may be observed, that the whole churches may be unchurched, their church state be dissolved, and yet not one true believer among them be lost or perish, as has been the case of these seven churches, and many others; which is brought about by removing true believers by death, withholding a blessing from the means of grace to the conversion of others; and at length, taking the Gospel wholly from them, and so at last the candlestick is removed out of its place. It is, therefore, to no purpose to urge passages and instances of this kind against the saints' final perseverance; however, we shall consider the several scriptures urged and referred unto. And,

1. The first of this kind to be examined, is in the epistle to the church at Ephesus. *Nevertheless, I have somewhat against thee, because thou hast left thy first love. Remember, therefore, from whence thou art fallen, and repent, and do the first works; or else I will come unto thee quickly, and will remove thy candlestick out of his place, except thou repent.** But neither the complaint lodged against this church, that she had left her first love, proves that she had totally and finally fallen away from grace; since she might leave, that is, abate in the fervency of her love to Christ, though not lose it; which sometimes waxes cold through the prevalence of corruption and the snares of the world, when it is not lost, as it was not in this church; nor can it be lost in any true believer, notwithstanding their desertions, temptations, falls, and backslidings: nor does the exhortation, to *remember from whence* she was *fallen*, prove it, seeing she might be fallen partially, though not totally; and the design of this exhortation be to put her upon comparing her former and present condition together; that her desires, after a restoration to her former lively and comfortable frame, might be quickened, and she be humbled under a sense of her backslidings, and brought to an acknowledgment of the same, which would appear by her doing her *first works:* nor does the threatening to *come unto* her, and *remove her candlestick out of his place,* in case of non-repentance, prove it; seeing this may be understood of his coming to her in a providential way, and either shaking her church state, by suffering persecution or heresy to come in upon her, or by wholly removing it, through withholding a blessing from the means of grace, and entirely taking them away; which might be done without the loss of one true believer, as has been observed. Besides, this church is greatly commended in ver. 2, 3, for her labour, and patience, and zeal

against false apostles; a plain case that she was not finally and totally fallen from grace.

2. The next passage to be considered is the promise made to the church at Smyrna, *Be thou faithful unto death, and I will give thee a crown of life.*[†] It is represented as incongruous with an absolute promise of God, that believers should persevere to the end, to suspend their happiness on condition of their perseverance, which is said to be done in these words. But it should be observed, that the *crown of life,* or eternal happiness, is not a blessing *suspended,* since it never was promised nor ever expected to be enjoyed before death, much less suspended on any condition whatever to be performed by us; since it is a gift, a gift wholly of free grace. Faithfulness unto death is not here made the condition of enjoying the crown of life; but the gift of the crown of life is made the encouragement to faithfulness unto death. In the same light are we to consider James i. 12, and the words of our Lord in Matt. xxiv. 12, 13. *Because iniquity shall abound* (not *because tribulations abound,* as Dr. Whitby cites the words,) *the love of many shall wax cold: but he that shall endure to the end, the same shall be saved;*[‡] where enduring to the end, is not the condition of salvation, but the promise of salvation is the encouragement to endure to the end.

3. A third passage referred to is the exhortation to the church at Pergamos, not Ephesus, as Dr. Whitby, through mistake,[§] calls it: *Repent, or else I will come unto thee quickly, and will fight against them with the sword of my mouth.*[‖] This church is so far from being an instance of the apostacy of real saints, that she is commended for *holding fast* the *name* of Christ, and not *denying* his *faith* in the worst of places, and in the worst of times, *even where Satan's seat* was, and *wherein Antipas,* a *faithful martyr, was slain;* and though there were some among them who held the doctrines and followed the practices of Balaam and the Nicolaitans, which should have been matter of humiliation, and on the account of which Christ exhorts to repentance; and though he says that he will *come to* her *quickly,* that is in a providential way, yet not to fight against her, but them; for he says not, I will *fight against thee,* the church, as Doctor Whitby inadvertently reads the words, but *against them,* the Balaamites and Nicolaitans; and that not with the temporal sword, but with the *sword of his mouth,* the word of God. The passage out of the epistle to the church at Thyatira, being much the same with what is alleged from the epistle to the church at Philadelphia, will be considered with it. I proceed,

4. To examine the instance of the Church at Sardis. There were but few true believers in this church; she had a *name to live,* but was *dead;* she had but a *few names which had not defiled their garments,* and therefore the de-

---

* Rev. ii. 4, 5. Vid. Limborch, l. 5. c. 83, sect. 19, p. 721; Whitby, p. 432, 458; ed. 2. 420, 438.

† Rev. ii. 10. Vid. Whitby, p. 430, 431; ed. 2. 419, 420.   ‡ Ibid. p. 431; ed. 2. 420. § Ibid p. 432; ed. 2. 420. ‖ Rev. ii. 16.

fection of her is no proof of the apostacy of real saints. *The things which remain*, she is called upon to *strengthen*, are not to be understood of the graces of the Spirit in her members; since these are never really wasting and declining, they are always all they were, and never less, but continually on the growing, thriving, and increasing hand; for this *good work* of grace is daily carrying on, whether the saints are sensible of it or no, and will be *performed until the day of Christ*; nor can the graces of the Spirit die, being immortal and incorruptible seeds; nor are they ever *ready to die*, unless in the apprehensions of saints under fits of unbelief. Besides, it is God's work, and not man's, to strengthen these; and should these be intended in this passage, it would be no proof of the real loss of true grace, since these are said not to be dead, but *ready to die*, and recoverable. The τὰ λοιπὰ were the remaining members of this church, which sense is confirmed by the versions of the Syriac, Arabic, Ethiopic, Vulgate Latin, and others. The majority of the members were already *dead*, and many others of them were sickly, and *ready to die;* the angel or pastor of this church is called upon to do his duty, to confirm such as were wavering, and do all that in him lay, by a diligent preaching of the word, and constant administration of ordinances, to preserve them from a more general defection. The threatening, in ver. 3, regards the formal and lifeless part of this church;* and as for the rest, *the few undefiled names in Sardis,* a promise of perseverance and happiness is made unto them :—*They shall walk with me in white, for they are worthy. He that overcometh, the same shall be clothed in white raiment ; and I will not blot out his name out of the book of life, but I will confess his name before my Father, and before his angels.*†

5. When Christ says to the church at Thyatira, *That which ye have already,* not *what thou hast attained to,*‡ as Dr. Whitby cites the words, *hold fast till I come ;*§ and to that at Philadelphia, *Hold that fast which thou hast, that no man take thy crown ;*‖ by what they had, and should hold fast, he does not mean the grace, but the doctrine of faith, the faithful word, the form of sound words, which both ministers and members should hold fast, in opposition to wavering about it, cowardice in it, and a departure from it; and such exhortations, though they may imply that saints may have their temptations to, and there is a possibility that they may, fall from some degree or steadfastness in the doctrines of the Gospel, and therefore should be on their guard, yet not that they may or shall finally and totally let them go. And whereas the saints are stirred up to regard the more such exhortations from this consideration, *that no man take* their *crown :* by which may be meant, either the Gospel, which was their

crown and glory, or the honour they had gained by their faithfulness, and integrity in abiding by it ; or if eternal life is intended by it, it follows not that this is liable to be taken away from or be lost to true believers, though some professors who expect it will be disappointed of it ; but the design of the expression, in allusion to the Olympic games, in which many ran, but *one received the prize,* is to excite the saints to industry, diligence, and watchfulness.

6. When Christ says to the church of the Laodiceans, *Because thou art lukewarm, and neither cold nor hot, I will spue thee out of my mouth,*¶ let it be observed that the state of this church, and the members of it, was such that she was not *cold*, without a principle of spiritual life and love, and a profession of religion; nor *hot*, lively, warm, and zealous in the exercise of grace, and discharge of duty ; but *lukewarm*, indifferent, unconcerned about her own condition, and the honour and interest of Jesus Christ, a frame of soul very disagreeable to Christ, and therefore, to show his resentment of it, he threatens to spue her *out of his mouth*, as men do that which is ungrateful to them : which designs some chastisement or affliction, and that in order to bring her to a sense of her present condition, and out of it; for certain it is he had a love, an unchangeable and everlasting one, to many in this church ; wherefore he says, *As many as I love, I rebuke and chasten ; be zealous therefore, and repent,* ver. 19.

SECTION XL

Behold I stand at the door, and knock : if any man hear my voice, and open the door, I will come in to him, and will sup with him, and he with me.—Rev. iii. 20.

FROM hence it is concluded,** that Christ stands and knocks at the hearts of unregenerate sinners by the ministry of the word, and that they have sufficient grace and strength to open their hearts unto him, or else he knocks in vain; for what wise man would stand at another's door and knock, if he knew there were not any within that could open to him ? and since it is required of men in conversion, to open their hearts to Christ, it follows, that the work is not performed by an irresistible power, or without the consent and co-operation of the will of man. But,

1. It should be proved that the ministry of the word is ever signified by knocking at the hearts of unregenerate sinners, or that God, or Christ, are ever said to knock at men's hearts by the ministry of the word. Men can strike the ear, God only can reach and strike the heart, which is done when the Gospel comes *not in word only, but in power, and in the Holy Ghost;* and when God does this, he does not knock and rap, and then wait till entrance is made from within; but

* Vide Whitby, p. 432, 433 ; ed. 2. 420, 421.
† Rev. iii. 4, 5.　　　‡ Rev. ii. 25.
§ Whitby, p. 422 ; ed. 2. 411.
‖ Rev. iii. 11.　　　¶ Rev. iii. 16. Vide

Remonstr. in Coll. Hag. art. v. p. 14.
** Bellarmin. de Gratia et. Lib. Arbitr. l. 1. c. 11 ; Remonstr. in Coll. Hag. art. iii. and iv. p. 274; Whitby, p. 286 ; ed. 2. 279.

he strikes home, and at once opens the door of the heart, as he did Lydia's, by his powerful and efficacious grace. It should also be proved, that God, in conversion, does command and require men to open their hearts unto him, neither of which can be proved either from this text or from any other in the whole Bible; nor is it in the power of unregenerate men, being dead in trespasses and sins, nor in their will, inclinations, desires, and affections, their *carnal mind* being *enmity against God* and Christ, to open their hearts and let them in. And supposing that these words do represent Christ standing and knocking at the door of men's hearts, by the external ministry of the word, has he not *the key of the house of* David, with which *he opens and no man shuts?* and lets himself in by the power of his grace, without offering any violence to the wills of men, since his people are made *a willing people in the day of his power.* Hence his knocking is not in vain, since to his elect not only sufficient but efficacious grace is given, by which the door of their hearts is opened to him, and others are left inexcusable, who are ready to make such shifts as these; had he knocked, I would have opened; had I heard, I would have believed; had I known, I would have done this and the other thing. But,

2. These words are not spoken to nor of unregenerate sinners, nor have they any reference to the opening of men's hearts in conversion, but are directed to *the angel of the church of the* Laodiceans, and to the members of that church, persons that professed the name of Christ; who, though they were not hot, yet were not cold, and for whom Christ had a regard, though they were in this lukewarm state; and, therefore, takes every proper method to bring them out of it; which was much the same with the church in Cant.

v. 2, *I sleep, but my heart waketh : it is the voice of my beloved that knocketh, saying, Open to me, my sister, my love, my dove, my undefiled—* a place parallel to this text, and which is the only one besides in which Christ is said to knock, and require any to open to him. Now his *standing at the door* may either mean his near approach to judgment, see James v. 8, 9; (this church of Laodicea, being the last of the churches, represents the state of the church in the last times, which will bring on and conclude with the general judgment;) or else his attendance on this church is meant, which shows his continued love, care, condescension, and patience towards it. His *knocking* at the door is not by the ministry of the word, but by some afflictive dispensation of providence, perhaps persecution. This church was in a sleepy, lukewarm, indifferent, secure frame of spirit, as appears from ver. 15—18. Christ will not suffer her to continue so, and, therefore, takes his rod in his hand, stands at her door, and gives some severe knocks and raps to bring her to herself, and out of this indolent, supine, and self-confident state and condition she was in; which sense is confirmed by the preceding verse, *as many as I love, I rebuke and chasten : be zealous, therefore, and repent.* The promise he makes to such who *hear* his *voice,* that is, the *men of wisdom, who hear the rod, and who hath appointed it,* when *the Lord's voice crieth,* to a *city,* or a church, and *open* to him, that is, by the lively exercise of faith and love, and which is owing to his *putting in* his *hand by the hole of the door,* is, that he *will come in to* them, and *sup* with them, and they with him, which may, in general, design communion and fellowship in his house and ordinances, or in particular, *the marriage-supper of the Lamb,* to which they who are *called* are pronounced *blessed.*

PART II

CHAPTER I

OF REPROBATION

THE following sections contain an answer to Dr. Whitby's first chapter concerning the decree of Reprobation, with which he has thought fit to begin his discourse upon the Five Points—a method the Remonstrants[*] formerly were very desirous of taking, though far from being just and accurate, since what is called reprobation is no other than nonelection, or what is opposed to election; wherefore, that ought to be considered in the first place, which, if it cannot be supported, the other must drop in course. But it is easy to observe the design of these men, which is, that by exposing to contempt the

doctrine of reprobation, which is sparingly spoken of in Scripture, and left to be concluded from that of election, and being most odious to carnal minds, they hope to weaken all regards to the doctrine of election, which stands in glaring light, and with full evidence in the word of God. The Doctor pretends to give us the state of the question concerning God's absolute decrees of election and reprobation out of Bishop Davenant's Animadversions on Hord, a book deservedly valuable, and which he would have done well to have employed his learning and abilities in the refutation of, before he had written this discourse. But, instead of giving us the true state of the question, relating to these decrees, out of that book, which he might easily have

* Vide Act. Synod. Dord. Sess. 42, p. 160, &c.

done, he has picked out some passages here and there, the most exceptionable, and made some rhetorical flourishes upon them. I confess I dislike the Bishop's notions of a twofold decree, respecting reprobates, the one eternal and absolute, the other revealed, evangelical, and conditional, and of God's giving sufficient grace or sufficient means of grace to them, and therefore think myself not obliged to defend them. What is said concerning Adam's sin, and the imputation of it, will be considered hereafter. The true state of the question before us, and what ought to be attended to, is this, that as God, of his sovereign good will and pleasure, has, from all eternity, chosen some men unto salvation by Jesus Christ, through sanctification of the Spirit, and belief of the truth, so he has, of his sovereign will and pleasure, from all eternity, passed by others, and determined to leave them to themselves, and deny them that grace which he gives to others, and damn them only for their sin. This author* observes, "That the word, ἀδόκιμος, which we render *reprobate*, hath no relation, in Scripture, to any decree concerning the damnation of men, or withholding from them the means by which they may escape it, but only denotes such actions which will certainly be disapproved by God and man." But then it should also be observed, that in all those places, 2 Tim. iii. 8, Rom. i. 28, Tit. i. 16, Heb. vi. 8, 1 Cor. ix. 27, excepting the last, referred to by this author, the word relates not to the evil actions, but to the persons and internal dispositions of the most profligate and wicked among mankind; so that though there is no express mention of any decree of reprobation concerning them, yet there is a great deal of reason to conclude, from the account given of them, that they were such whom God had never chosen in Christ, but had passed them by, and had determined to leave them to their own heart's lusts, to deny them his grace, and justly damn them for their iniquities. But I proceed to the vindication of those passages of Scripture, in which this writer says, there is nothing relating to this decree, or from which it can reasonably be inferred.

SECTION I

The Lord hath made all things for himself;
yea, even the wicked for the day of evil.—
Prov. xvi. 4.

1. THESE words are not to be understood of God's creating all things out of nothing, or of his production of creatures into being for his own glory, nor of his wise ordering and disposing all things in providence for himself, which are both truths, but not of this text. It is certain that all things that are made, are made by Jehovah, for himself, and not another; not because he had need of them but to declare his greatness, and communicate his goodness, for his will and pleasure, his praise and glory; yet this is not intended here, for the word here used is neither ברא

nor עשה, which are commonly used when creation, and the works of it, are spoken of. It is also most certain, that all things in this world, as they are upheld and preserved in their being by God, so they are governed, influenced, ordered, and disposed of by him, for the good of his creatures, and the glory of his name; yet not this, but the decrees, purposes, and appointments of God, respecting his creatures, are here designed; in which sense the word פעל, here used, is sometimes to be taken, as in Exod. xv. 17: *Thou shalt bring them in, and plant them in the mountain of thine inheritance, in the place, O Lord, which* פעלת, *thou hast appointed for thee to dwell in, in the sanctuary, O Lord, which thy hands have established.* For the tabernacle, or sanctuary, was not yet made. So in Psal. xxxi. 19: *O how great is thy goodness, which thou hast laid up for them that fear thee; which,* פעלת, *thou hast prepared, provided, and appointed, in thine eternal counsel and covenant, for them that trust in thee before the sons of men.* In the same sense the word ποιέω is used in the New Testament, particularly in Mark iii. 14: *And he,* ἐποίησε, *made, or ordained twelve.* And in Heb. iii. 2: *Who was faithful,* τῷ ποιήσαντι, *to him that made, or appointed him.* Now the sense of these words is this: that all things are appointed by God for his own glory; all things, particularly respecting man, concerning his temporal estate, the time of his birth, the place of his abode, his station and condition of life, the various changes of it, prosperous and adverse, death itself, and all the means leading on to it; as well as all things respecting his spiritual and eternal state, the provision and mission of a Saviour, both as to the time of his coming into the world, and of his sufferings and death, with all the circumstances thereof, the conversion of a sinner, time, place, and means, all times of darkness, desertion, and comfort; yea, the final state and portion of all men: all these are fixed and appointed by God, and, in one way or another, make for his glory; yea, even he has appointed *the wicked for the day of evil,* which is mentioned partly to illustrate the general proposition in the text, and partly to obviate an objection, which might be taken from them against all things being made or appointed for his glory. But,

2. It is commonly said, that it is our sentiment, and the sense we give of this text, and what may be inferred from the doctrine of predestination, that God made man to damn him; whereas this is neither our sentiment, nor is it the sense we give of this text, nor is it to be inferred from the doctrine of predestination; for there is a wide difference between God's making man to damn him, and his appointing wicked men to damnation for their wickedness, which is the meaning of this text, and of the doctrine of reprobation we assert. We say, that God made man neither to damn him nor to save him; neither salvation nor damnation were God's ultimate

end in making man, but his own glory, which will be answered one way or another, either in his salvation or damnation.

It is asked,* " What is it that they would infer from these words? Is it that God made men wicked?" To which I answer, no. We know as well as this interrogator that *God made man upright*, and that he has made himself wicked; and abhor, as much as he, the blasphemy of God's being the author of sin, or of his making his creatures wicked. It is one thing for God to make men wicked, another to appoint a wicked man to eternal wrath on the account of his wickedness. The same author goes on to interrogate, " Is it with Dr. Twiss, that all, besides the elect, God hath ordained to bring forth into the world, in their corrupt mass, and to permit them to themselves to go on in their own ways, and so finally to persevere in sin; and lastly, to damn them for their sin, for the manifestation of his justice on them?" This passage of the Doctor's is picked out as a very exceptionable one; though for my part, I think it fitly expresses both the sense of this text and of the doctrine of reprobation, and is to be justified in every part of it. He says, that *God ordained to bring forth all, besides the elect, into the world in their corrupt mass.* And where is the hurt of saying this? Is it not fact, that they are brought into the world in this manner? Nor is it repugnant to the perfections of God to produce, bring into being, and multiply the individuals of human nature, though that nature is vitiated and corrupted with sin, which he may do, and does, without being the author of their wickedness; nor is this injurious to, or any particular hardship on, the non-elect, since the same is true, and is what we, with the Scriptures, affirm of the elect of God themselves. The Doctor proceeds to observe, that God ordained *to permit them to themselves to go on in their own ways, and so finally to persevere in sin.* That God does give up men to *their own hearts' lust*,† as he did the Israelites of old, and suffers whole *nations to walk in their own ways*,‡ as he did the Gentiles formerly for many hundreds of years, is certain; and for God to ordain, or determine, to permit them, can be no more contrary to his perfections than the permission itself; nor does such an appointment infringe the liberty of their wills; nor can it be any injustice in God to suffer them finally to persevere in sin, since they say, *we will walk after our own devices, and we will every one do the imagination of his evil heart.*§ And, whereas the Doctor concludes that God has ordained *to damn them for their sin, for the manifestation of his justice on them:* this fitly expresses the sense of the text and of the doctrine of reprobation, especially that part of it which divines call predamnation. Reprobation may be distinguished into preterition and predamnation. Preterition is God's act of passing by and leaving some, who are called *the rest*, when he chose others to salvation; and is the effect of God's sovereign good will and pleasure, being an act over and above the fall, and without the consideration of it, or of any actual sin or transgression whatever; nor is this unbecoming the moral perfections of God, or doing any injustice to his creatures, since the objects of this act were considered in the pure mass of creatureship, were found in this pure mass, and left in it, God neither putting nor supposing any wickedness in them. Predamnation is God's appointing men to damnation, in consideration and on account of sin; not God's decree, but sin, which interferes between the decree and the execution of it, is the cause of damnation: God damns no man but for sin, nor does he appoint any to damnation but on account of it. Now, if it is not unjust to damn men for sin, it cannot be an unrighteous thing with God to appoint unto damnation for it. These things being considered, the doctrine of reprobation will not appear so horrible and shocking as it is represented to be by our opponents. Our author goes on and observes, " or lastly, they only mean that God, for the glory of his justice, had appointed, that wicked men perishing impenitently in sin, should be obnoxious to his wrath; and then they assert a great truth." But we mean more than this, we mean not only that such persons who are left to persevere in sin, and remain finally impenitent, are obnoxious to the wrath of God, but that they are appointed to wrath; and which we believe to be the sense of this text, and the truth contained in it. Though,

3. It is observed,‖ that the words should be rendered, *the Lord hath made all things to answer to themselves*, or *aptly to refer to one another, even the wicked for the day of evil.* But supposing that the word לְמַעֲנֵהוּ is derived from ענה, to *answer*, it should not be rendered *to answer to themselves* but *to him*, since the affix to it is singular, and not plural, and the meaning will be, that *the Lord has made*, or appointed *all things to answer to himself*, that is, to his own will and pleasure, and to subserve the ends of his own glory. Agreeable to this sense of the phrase the Jewish writers interpret it.¶ R. Sol Jarchi explains it by קילוסו *for his praise.* R. Isaac by לְמִין חפצו ורצונו נשביל, *for his will and pleasure.* R. Jonah by לעין בו רוצה שהוא, *for the thing in which he takes pleasure.* R. David Kimchi thinks it may be rightly explained by בעבורו, *for himself*, or *for his own sake.* All which confirm our sense of it. Nor is the meaning of the words, that God has made the wicked man to be the executioner of evil to others; though this is sometimes the case, and is such a sense of the words, as is no ways subversive of the doctrine of reprobation. But the plain meaning of them is, that God has appointed all things for his own glory, and which he will secure even in the destruction of wicked men, to which for

---

* Whitby, p. 10.
† Psalm lxxxi. 11, 12.   ‡ Acts xiv.
16.   § Jer. xviii. 12.   ‖ Whitby, p.

11, 94; ed. 2. 93.   ¶ Vide R Sol. Hammelec. in loc., and R. David Kimchi, in Sepher Shorash, rad. ענה.   ** Whitby, p. 11,

their sins they are justly reserved ; and this sense of them is confirmed by the Targum, Septuagint, Syriac, and Arabic versions.

SECTION II

Therefore they could not believe, because that Esaias had said again, He hath blinded their eyes, and hardened their hearts ; that they should not see with their eyes, nor understand with their heart, and be converted, and I should heal them.—John xii. 39, 40.

It is said,* that " this text is cited to prove the decree of reprobation, or preterition ; and that the inference made from it, contains this strange and uncomfortable doctrine, viz. That the infidelity of God's own people is to be resolved, not into the perverseness of their wills, or the evil dispositions of their hearts, but into the divine predictions, or into a judicial blindness and obduration, wrought by God upon them ; which renders it, though not naturally, yet, morally impossible for them to believe." But,

1. I do not find that these words are cited by any of our writers to prove the decree of reprobation, or preterition, or any eternal purpose of God to blind the eyes, and harden the hearts of men, by any positive act of his, with a view to hinder their conversion, and that his decree of condemnation might take place. The Contra-Remonstrants,† indeed, make use of them to prove, that the Gospel is preached to many who do not believe, and who cannot believe ; because it is not attended with an internal, powerful operation of divine grace, and that very rightly ; which is exactly agreeable to the words of Isaiah, cited in the preceding verse, *Who hath believed our report ? And to whom hath the arm of the Lord been revealed ?* And, which stand in close connection with these, *Therefore, they could not believe, &c.*

2. It would be strange and uncomfortable doctrine, indeed, should any make an inference from hence, containing this in it, that the infidelity of *God's own people* is owing to divine predictions, or judicial blindness, wrought by God upon them, which renders it morally impossible for them to believe. Seeing God's own people are not spoken of in the text, nor are there any predictions in scripture respecting their final unbelief, nor are they ever given up to judicial blindness and hardness ; but, being ordained unto eternal life, are enabled, by divine grace, to believe in Christ to the saving of their souls, notwithstanding the perverseness of their wills, and the evil disposition of their hearts.

3. It is evident that the words are to be understood of the unbelieving Jews who rejected the Messiah, though they heard his doctrine, and saw his miracles, whereby the predictions of the prophet Isaiah, were fulfilled ; which, though they had no such influence on the wills of these men,‡ as to lay upon them a co-active necessity, or force

them to do or answer to the things foretold, yet were to have, and had, an infallible event or completion ; otherwise, the foreknowledge of God, and the authority of the prophetic writings, could not be maintained : wherefore the Evangelist observes, that *though he* (Christ) *had done so many miracles before them, yet they believed not on him, that the saying of Esaias, the prophet, might be fulfilled, &c.* Also, *Therefore, they could not believe, because that Esaias said again, &c.*

4. It is certain, that the impossibility of their after-believing, is to be resolved into the judicial blindness and hardness of their hearts, to which they were justly left, having contemned both the doctrines and miracles of Christ. It is of no great moment whether the *he*, who is said to blind and harden, be God or Christ, or whether the words be rendered, *it hath blinded, &c.* that is, malice or wickedness hath blinded,§ or be read impersonally, *their eyes are blinded, &c.* Since God, or Christ,blind and harden, not by any positive act, or putting in blindness or hardness, but by leaving and giving men up to the blindness and hardness of their hearts, and denying them grace ; which was the cause of these Jews ; so as never to be *converted*, or turned even by external repentance and reformation, that they might be *healed* in a national way, or be preserved from national ruin. All which is consistent with God's command,‖ and Christ's exhortations to them to believe, which were antecedent to the judicial blindness and hardness of their hearts, and were, with the miracles and doctrines of Christ, aggravations of their unbelief ; and therefore, they might be justly objected to them by the evangelist as their great crime, as it certainly was ; being owing to the perverseness of their wills, and the evil dispositions of their hearts.

SECTION III

And a stone of stumbling, and a rock of offence, even to them that stumble at the word, being disobedient, whereunto also they were appointed.—1 Pet. ii. 8.

These words are spoken of the reprobate Jews, to whom Christ was a *stone of stumbling, and a rock of offence*, in his birth, parentage, and education, in the mean appearance he made in his own person and in his apostles, in his ministry, and the audience that attended it, and the company he kept, in his doctrine, miracles, crucifixion, and death ; who *stumbled at the word* of the Gospel, despised, and rejected it, being left to the prevailing infidelity of their corrupt hearts ; all which was not casual and accidental, but pursuant to a divine purpose and appointment. This passage, in connexion with the words preceding, plainly shows, that as there were some, whom God had appointed and fore-ordained to believe in Christ, on whom he determined to bestow true faith in him, to whom he is *the elect, precious corner*

---

* Whitby, p. 11, 12.   † In Coll. Hag., art iii. and iv. p. 209, 242.   ‡ Whitby, p. 14.   § Ibid. p. 16 ; ed. 2. 15.   ‖ Ibid. p. 12, 14.

stone ; so there were others, whom he determined to leave as *children of disobedience,* in the infidelity and unbelief in which the fall had concluded them ; through which disobedience or infidelity, they stumble at Christ, and his word, and in consequence thereof, justly perish. This also appears from the antithesis in ver. 9, where God's elect are opposed unto, and distinguished from, these persons, *but ye are a chosen generation, a royal priesthood, an holy nation, a peculiar people, &c.* But,

1st. It is said,* "That this scripture, to be sure, cannot signify, that God absolutely ordained the unbelieving Jews, εἰς ἀπείθειαν, *to disobedience ;*" when,

" 1. As yet they were not, and therefore were not disobedient." I reply, this scripture certainly signifies, that these persons were appointed to stumble at Christ and his words through unbelief, which is all one as not to believe in him ; or, to express our sense and meaning, and also the sense and meaning of this text more fully, God absolutely willed the fall of man, which brought all mankind into a state of infidelity ; in which God has determined to leave some, and not give them that grace which can only cure them of their unbelief, whereby they *stumble* at Christ and his Gospel, *being disobedient* to the divine revelation. Now such a determination, or appointment, did not require their present actual existence, only their certain future existence, much less that they should be disobedient, previous to this appointment.

2. It is added,† as another reason against this sense of the text, "That then their future disobedience was purely a compliance with the divine ordinance or will, and so could not deserve the name of disobedience ; because it could not be both a compliance with, and disobedience to the will of God." To which may be replied, that God's will is either secret or revealed, purposing or commanding ; the one is the rule of his own actions, the other of his creatures : now it oftentimes is so, that what accords with the secret and purposing will of God, is a disobedience to his revealed and commanding will. As Dr. Manton‡ observes, "Things that are most against his revealed will, fall under the ordination of his secret will ; and, whilst men break commandments, they fulfil decrees : his revealed will showeth what should be done, his secret will what will be done." So, for instance, it was agreeable to God's secret will, that man, should fall ; yet, eating the forbidden fruit by which he fell, was an act of disobedience to his revealed will : The crucifixion of Christ was according to the determinate counsel and fore-knowledge of God ; and yet, this act of the Jews was a disobedience to the sixth commandment, *Thou shalt not kill.* The kings of the earth, giving their kingdom to the beast, was a fulfilling of the secret will

of God, nay, he put it into their hearts to do it ; and yet, giving the beast that support, power, homage, and worship, they did, were an open violation of the laws of God.

3. It is urged,§ that, according to this sense of the words, "This disobedience could not be objected to them as their crime ; unless compliance with the will of God be so ; and it be a fault to be such as God, by his immutable counsel and decree, hath ordained we should be ; or it should render men criminal and obnoxious to punishment, that they have not made void God's absolute decree, or have done what that made it necessary for them to do." I answer, that God's decrees, as they do not infringe the liberty of man's will, so they do not excuse from sin. The selling of Joseph was according to the purpose and decree of God, who, as he *meant,* so he over-ruled it *for good ;* yet it was an evil in his brethren, and so they meant it ; and, therefore, might be justly objected to them as their crime. The Jews, when they crucified Christ, did no other than what the *hand* and *counsel* of God *determined before to be done ;* and yet, by their own *wicked hands,* they crucified and slew him. God's determinations and decrees about this affair, neither exempted them from being criminals, nor from being obnoxious to punishment.

2dly. The meaning of these words, agreeably to Dr. Hammond's sense of them, is said to be this: ‖ "That the unbelieving Jews, being disobedient to the Gospel so clearly revealed, and by so many miracles and distributions of the Holy Ghost confirmed to them, were appointed, as the punishment of that disobedience, to fall and perish ; for, so the Hebrew word *chasal,* and the Greek προσκόμμα and σκανδάλον, import, namely the ruin and the fall of them who stumble at this stone." But, let it be observed, that the phrase, to *stumble* at Christ, and *the word,* is not expressive of their punishment, but of their sin, *being disobedient.* As, to *stumble at the law,* Mal. ii. 8, is to offend against, break and transgress it ; so to *stumble at the word,* or Gospel, is to blaspheme and contradict it, reject and put it away, as the Jews of old did, *being disobedient,* left and given up to the infidelity and hardness of their hearts. To stumble at the word, and to stumble at Christ, and to be offended in him, or at him, are one and the same thing ; and the latter always signifies a crime, and not punishment, Matt. xi. 6, and xiii. 57, Mark vi. 3, Luke vii. 23. The sin of these persons is expressed by *stumbling and falling :* and their punishment by being *broken ;* Isa. viii. 14, 15, Matt. xxi. 44. So the Hebrew word נשׁל, signifies to stumble and fall ; that is, to sin ; see Prov. xxiv. 17, Hos. xiv. 1, Mal. ii. 8. Hence כב שׁול עינם, *the stumbling-block of their iniquity,* that which is the occasion of sin, Ezek. vii. 19, and xiv. 3, 4, 7. So the Greek words προσκόπτω, προσκόμμα, προσκοπή, Rom. ix. 32,

---

* Whitby, p. 20.   † Ibid. ; Remonstr. in Act. Synod. circ. art. i. p. 208.

‡ On Jude, ver. 4, p. 176.

§ Whitby, p. 20.   ‖ Ibid. p. 21 ; ed. 2. 20. See remonstr. in Act. Synod. circ. art. i. p. 208 ; and Limborch. p. 355.

33, and xiv. 20, 21, 2 Cor. vi. 3, Σκανδαλίζω and σκανδάλον, Matt. xviii. 6—9, Rom. xiv. 13, 21, 1 Cor. viii. 13. And, after all, this sense of the words pleaded for, proves a fore-appointment of some to punishment, as the fruit of disobedience; which is that part of reprobation, commonly called *predamnation,* we contend for.

3dly. It is said,* "The words will fairly bear this sense; *to them that believe,* belongs ἡ τιμὴ, *the honour* (of being built upon this corner-stone into a spiritual house, *but to them that are disobedient* belongs that of Psalm cxviii. 22,) and (also to them he is) *a stone of stumbling, and a rock of offence, even to them that stumble at the word, Εἰς ὃ καὶ ἐτέθησαν, for which also these stones were laid,* or *put,* the corner-stone for the building up of believers, the stone of stumbling for the disobedient to stumble at." But it should be observed, that the corner-stone, and the stone of stumbling, are one and the same stone, and therefore it could not, with propriety, be said of that stone, *for which also* they *were put or laid.* Besides, "the word τιθέναι, as Dr. Hammond observes, is ordinarily used for appointing and ordaining, and being applied to God, doth often signify his decree, or destination; thus John xv. 16, Acts xiii. 47, 1 Thess. v. 9." And here, his decree and appointment concerning reprobates, as appears from the antithesis in ver. 9. Moreover, admitting that Christ is here said to be laid, or put, as a stumbling-stone for the disobedient to stumble at; since he is said κεῖαθαι εἰς πτῶσιν, *to be set,* that is, as the above-mentioned Doctor observes, decreed by God (the same that τίθεαθαι, *to be set* or *ordained* here,) *for the falling of many in Israel,* Luke ii. 34. I say, admitting this, the sense will be much the same, whether we suppose Christ is *set* or *put,* that is, ordained, decreed, and appointed, to be a stumbling-stone for men to stumble at; or, whether they are ordained, appointed, to stumble at him; that is, to despise, refuse, and reject him, through infidelity.

SECTION IV

For there are certain men crept in unawares, who were before of old ordained to this condemnation, ungodly men, turning the grace of our God into lasciviousness, and denying the only Lord God, and our Saviour Jesus Christ.—Jude, ver. 4.

THE apostle, in this text, speaks of some persons, perhaps the followers of Simon Magus, or other immoral *heretics,* who had privily *crept into* houses, and *unawares* into the churches, and, perhaps, into the ministry, and had insinuated themselves into the affections of the people; and yet were *ungodly men, did not* worship God sincerely, and according to his appointments, misinterpreted the gospel of the grace of God, translated it to a wrong use, and abused the design of it, yea, denied both the Father and the Son. Now these persons were *of old,* that is, from all eternity,

as Dr. Manton on the text observes, *before ordained* to just condemnation for their wickedness. These words may be considered then as a proof of reprobation, or of God's appointing some men to damnation before they had a being. In answer to this it is said,†

1. "The verse in the Greek text runs thus: *Some ungodly men, turning the grace of God into lasciviousness, have entered into* (the church) *of whom it was before written, that this should be their sentence or punishment.*" But, to this version of the text may be objected, that besides the transposing of the words, and dropping part of the character of these men, the word πάλαι, *of old,* is entirely neglected. Nor does the verse in the Greek text run thus: περὶ ὧν προγέγραπται τοῦτο τὸ κρῖμα, *of whom this sentence or punishment was before written;* but, οἱ πάγαι προγεγραμμένοι εἰς τοῦτο τὸ κρῖμα, *who were of old before written to this condemnation.*

2. "That this cannot be meant of any divine ordination or appointment of them to eternal damnation before they had a being, is evident; because it cannot be thought without horror, that he, who is the lover of souls, should appoint any, much less the greater part of them, to inevitable destruction before they had a being." But, where does the horror of this doctrine lie? Does it lie in the appointment of men to damnation before they had a being? If there is any divine ordination or appointment to it, it must be before men have a being, even from eternity, since no new appointment, decree, purpose, or ordination is made by God in time. If election is from eternity, reprobation must be so too, since there cannot be one without the other. If some were chosen before the foundation of the world, others must be left, or passed by as early. If some were appointed unto salvation from the beginning, others were appointed unto wrath or *were of old,* מו שוריא, *from the beginning,* as the Syriac version renders the word (compare this with 2 Thess. ii. 13, Prov. viii. 22), *fore-ordained to condemnation.* Or, does the horror of it lie in this, that this appointment is ascribed to *the lover of souls?* Why may it not be thought without horror, that he, who is the lover of souls, should appoint some men to eternal damnation for sin before they had a being, as well as hate Esau before he had done any evil, and yet loved Jacob before he had done any good? Or does it lie here, that God should appoint *the greater part* of men to damnation? But the question before us is not, whether God has appointed the greater or lesser part of mankind to destruction for sin, but whether he has appointed any; and, if he could appoint any, he could appoint many, yea, all mankind; as he did the whole body of apostate angels, without any impeachment of his wisdom, justice, or goodness. But perhaps the horribleness of this doctrine is thought to lie here, that God has appointed men *as creatures, without any consideration of sin,* unto eternal damnation. If this was our doctrine,

---

* Whitby, p. 21; ed. 2. 20.

† Whitby, p. 22, ed. 2. 21.

I should not wonder that it should be thought of with so much horror and detestation; but this is a most vile misrepresentation of it. For, though the Supralapsarians do not premise the consideration of sin to the act of preterition, or God's leaving and passing by some, when he chose others; yet both they, and the Sublapsarians premise the consideration of sin to predamnation, or God's appointing men to destruction. We say, God damns no man but for sin, and that he appointed to damn none but sinners. And cannot this be thought of without horror? Our author himself owns it, as will quickly appear.

3. It is said,* that "the word κρίμα relates not to sin, but punishment, the fruit of sin; so Mark xii. 40, Rom. ii. 3. Now, God ordaineth none to punishment but sinners and ungodly men; and such, by the text, these persons are here styled." To which may be replied, that, though the word κρίμα, in the passages referred to, and in many others, signifies damnation, yet, elsewhere, it relates to things criminal; a sinful blindness and hardness of heart, which God sometimes leaves persons to: so when our Lord says,† εἰς κρίμα, *for judgment I am come into this world, that they which see not might see, and that they which see might be made blind*. Thus, these persons in the text, having gone great lengths in sin, were given up to a reprobate mind to do things not convenient; to neglect and despise the worship of God, abuse the gospel, and deny both the Father and the Son. Now, εἰς τοῦτο τὸ κρίμα, to this judicial blindness and hardness, they were of old before ordained. This is a sense of the words which cannot easily be confuted, and is, indeed, acknowledged by the Remonstrants.‡ But, however, we are willing to allow that κρίμα here relates to punishment, and not sin, as in the parallel place, 2 Pet. ii. 3. And we say, with our author, that God ordains none to punishment but sinners; only we say, that this ordination was from eternity, and this is the doctrine of the text, and which we contend for.

4. It is observed,§ that " these were men of whom it was *before written* or *prophesied*, that they should be condemned for their ungodliness, as by Enoch, ver. 14. And, that this also is the import of the word προεγράφε, Rom. xv. 4, Gal. iii. 1. The writers and interpreters on the Arminian side are pretty generally agreed that these words refer to some prophecy concerning these men, somewhere or other in Scripture, but are not agreed about the particular passage. Some think the apostle‖ has a regard to the parallel place in 2 Pet. ii. 1—3; but if he had this in his view, he would never have said that they were *of old*, a long while ago, before written or prophesied of; since, according to the common calculation, that epistle of Peter's was written in the very same year as this of Jude's. Besides, Peter says, at the time of his writing, that the *judgment* of these men was *of a long time*, that is, had been long ago pronounced, and did not *linger*. Others think,¶ that reference is had to the prediction of Christ, in Matt. xxiv. This is, indeed, carrying the prophecy further off. But then, as no such persons are described there as here, so neither is there any mention of their punishment or condemnation. Others,** as our author supposes, that the apostle respects the prophecy of Enoch; this, indeed, was *of old*. But, though it is true that Enoch prophesied of these persons, yet, as his prophecy was never written, that we know of, and, therefore, these men could not be said to be fore-written of in it; so it is easy to observe, that the apostle speaks of this prophecy as something distinct from these persons being fore-written to condemnation, when he says, ver. 14, and *Enoch also prophesied of these*. Besides, as Vorstius,†† a writer on the other side the question, observes, " It is all one whether we understand it, that these men were of old appointed and designed by God to this condemnation; or, whether this condemnation was of old written concerning them in the Old Testament." Since such a prophecy concerning them must be founded upon an antecedent, divine ordination and appointment. Nor is prophecy the import of the word προεγράφε, especially in Gal. iii. 1, and only regards things, and not persons, in Rom. xv. 4. And here intends, not their being fore-written in any of the books of Scripture, but in the book of God's eternal purposes and decrees.

SECTION V

And all that dwell upon the earth shall worship him; whose names are not written in the book of life of the Lamb, slain from the foundation of the world.—Rev. xiii. 8.

With 2 Cor. iv. 3, 2 Thess. ii. 10—12, 1 Cor. i. 18, Rom. ix. 18.

THE learned‡‡ writer attended to, observes, that Dr. Twiss confesseth that the Scriptures speak fully of election, sparingly of reprobation, in most places; yet, some passages we have, saith he, which give light and evidence to both alike. The passages referred to are, for the one, Acts ii. 47; Matt. xxiv. 24; Acts xiii. 48; Luke x. 20; Heb. xii. 23. For the other, 2 Cor. iv. 3; 2 Thess. ii. 10—12; 1 Cor. i. 18; Rom. ix. 18; Rev. xiii. 8, and xvii. 8. Now, to all these citations, most of which are said§§ to be palpably impertinent, (though whether they are or no, will be seen hereafter) this is the general answer, "That they signify no more than those words of Christ, Mark xvi. 16, Luke xiii. 3—5; and of the Baptist," John iii. 36. The sum of which is, that he that believes

---

* Whitby, p. 22; ed. 2. 21.　　† John ix. 39.　　‡ In Act. Synod. circ. art. i. p. 205.　　§ Whitby, p. 22, 23.
‖ So Grotius, in loc.　　¶ Hammond, in loc.　　** Limborch, p. 354.
†† Perinde est sive intelligas illos jam oli m

fuisse a Deo destinatos sive designatos ad hoc Judicium, sive accipias de illis jam olim in Vet. Test. scriptum esse. Vorst. in loc.
‡‡ Whitby p. 23.
§§ Whitby p. 24; ed. 2. 23.

and repents, shall be saved; and he that does not believe and repent, shall be damned. Which is a considerable mistake; seeing the words of Christ and of the Baptist regard only the revealed will of God, in the external ministry of the word; and the passages cited, the secret will of God, in giving grace to some, and denying it to others. The main thing to be attended to is, how it comes to pass, that some men have faith and repentance, and so are saved; whilst others have neither, and so are damned. Some men have faith and repentance: how come they by them? God freely gives these graces to them, and implants them in them; and why does he do so? Because of his sovereign good pleasure he has, from all eternity, willed and determined to do so; which is a considerable branch of election. On the other hand, some men have neither faith nor repentance; what is the reason of it? Because, being by nature in a state of infidelity and impenitence, God does not give them that grace which only can deliver them from it. And why does he not give them that grace? Because, of his sovereign will and pleasure, he has determined not to give it them; which is a considerable branch of reprobation. To some of these citations our author thinks fit to reply, by saying, that "those that are lost, 2 Cor. iv. 3, are those that believe not, ver. 4. And those who perish, 2 Thess. ii. 10, are those who believe not the truth, ver. 12. And they who perish, 1 Cor. i. 18, are the unbelieving Jews and Gentiles. And they who are hardened, Rom. ix. 18, are *the vessels of wrath fitted for destruction*, by their own wickedness, completed by their infidelity, or want of faith." But still the question returns. How come these persons to want faith, to be unbelievers, not to believe in Christ, or the truth, whilst others do? It is not because they are left to their natural infidelity, and given up to judicial blindness, and hardness of heart? And why are they thus left? Or, why does God deny them that grace which only can cure them of all this? but, because it is his will, and he has determined to deny them it? Now, this is one part of reprobation we contend for. From these this celebrated writer* proceeds to those places, which may seem to require a more particular notice. And,

1st. Begins with the phrase of being *written in the book of life*, Rev. xiii. 8, and xvii. 8. Which,

1. He says, is Jewish, and doth not signify the absolute election of any person to eternal life, but only the present right of the just person to life; and therefore it is called *the book of life written for the just*, Targum on Ezek. xiii. 9. And, *the book of the just*, Targ. Jon. on Exod. xxxii. 32. To which I answer, that the book spoken of in the Scriptures under consideration, is not called *the book of the just*, nor *the book of life written for the just*, but *the book of life for the Lamb*, a phrase never to be met with in Jewish writings. But, admitting an allusion to these

phrases used by the Jews, let it be observed, that just or righteous persons are particular ones: all men are not righteous; only such whom God from all eternity willed to be righteous, through the righteousness of his Son. Now, as many as are written in the book of life God willed to be righteous, through the righteousness of his Son; and, as many as he willed to be righteous, through the righteousness of his Son, he wrote their names in the book of life. Hence the same individual particular persons, who are said to be *written in heaven*,† are called *just men made perfect*, that is, through the righteousness of Christ imputed to them; which gives them not only a *present*, but a future continued right to eternal life, which can never be lost. For, whom God did *predestinate*, them he *called;* and whom he *called*, he *justified*, and whom he *justified*, them he *glorified*.‡

2. It is observed, that, in this book, " The *apostolical institutions (constitutions*, I suppose, it should be,) say, we come to be written τῇ ἡμετερα εὐνοια καὶ σπουδῇ, *by our good affection and industry.*" What these *constitutions* say will not meet with much credit; since, not only they appear to be a spurious work, and not the genuine writings of the apostles, but also, we find nothing in the sacred writings to confirm such an assertion; and, indeed, how is it possible that any should come to be written in this book, through their good affection and industry, when the book was *written from the foundation of the world*, Rev. xvii. 8, and so before men had done either good or evil?

3. It is said, that, "from this book, men, as they may be written in it, when they are converted from vice to virtue, so may they be blotted out, when they backslide from virtue to iniquity, according to Psalm lxix. 28, Rev. xxii. 19, Exod. xxxii. 33." To which I reply, that, as men are not first written in this book when they are converted, since this book was written from the foundation of the world, before men had a being, and consequently before they were converted, so neither may they or can they be blotted out when they backslide; for God not only *heals the backslidings* of his people, and still *loves* them *freely*,§ but he has promised to him that *overcometh*, as all his elect do and shall, that *he will not blot out his name out of the book of life*. Nor do the passages alleged prove that they may or shall be blotted out; not Psalm lxix. 28, which is a petition concerning wicked men, either that they may die, their memory perish, never be mentioned with the righteous, nor appearing among them at the last day; or that they might be excluded from the visible church, the congregation of saints, and appear to be what they really were, none of God's elect; and, supposing *the book of the living* intends the book of election, blotting out of it is no more, as is evident from the text itself, than not writing them in it; nor Rev. xxii. 19, for taking away the man's *part out of the*

---

* Ibid. p. 25; ed. 24.　　† Heb. xii. 23.　　‡ Rom. viii. 30.　　§ Hos. xiv. 4; Rev. iii. 5.

book of life is only taking away that which he seemed to have, and not what he really had, agreeable to Luke viii. 18. And as for Exod. xxxii. 33, it is not there said, *Whosoever hath sinned against me, him will I blot out of the book of life,* as this writer inadvertently cites the words, but *out of the book which I have written,* that is, either out of the book of the law, according to R. Sol. Jarchi; his name shall not be mentioned there; or, of this temporal life, he shall die and not live.

4. "This book is said to be written from the foundation of the world, God having Adam and others, who are styled the sons of God; and not to have a name written in it, is not to be owned as God's sons and faithful servants; when therefore St. John saith, that they *whose names were not in this book of life writ from the foundation of the world, worshipped the beast;* he means they, and they only, did so, who never were by God esteemed, or registered in the number of good Christians." But if this book was written from the foundation of the world, it must be written before these sons of God had a being, and before they knew, or were known by others, that they were the sons of God. And if none but such whom God owns and esteems as his sons were written in it, then none but such who are really so, or such who were predestinated to the adoption of sons, are written in it. And if none but these are written in it, then those whose names are not written in it are such who are passed by and rejected of God, which is what we contend for, and this passage of Scripture is brought to prove.

2dly. "The passage cited from the Thessalonians is said* only to concern the Jews, who rejected the gospel of our Lord and their Messiah, confirmed by the strongest evidence of innumerable miracles; and so believed not the truth at all, or else revolted from it after they had embraced it." Though it rather seems to concern the followers of Antichrist, and the worshippers of the man of sin, when he should be revealed, to whom God would *send strong delusions, that they should believe a lie, and be damned.* But, let it concern who it will, it is certain it respects such persons who would be left of God to their infidelity, and given up to the power of Satan, and to judicial blindness of mind; and are distinguished from the elect of God that should be saved, ver. 13, 14.

3dly. "The passages cited from Rom. ix., it is said, can be nothing to the purpose; that chapter having no regard to God's absolute decrees, concerning the final and external state of mankind in general, or of any particular persons, but his providential dealings in rejecting the Jews, and receiving the Gentiles." But I hope to make it appear, in a subsequent section, that that chapter is designed to illustrate personal election and reprobation. Nor does the apostle's recapitulation, ver. 30, contradict this; since the Jews not attaining to the law of righteousness, was owing to their stumbling at that stumbling-stone to which they were appointed; and the Gentiles attaining to righteousness, was in consequence of their being vessels of mercy, afore prepared to glory; and both to be understood of particular persons. Nor does the apostle's prayer, chap. x. 1, contradict the decree of reprobation concerning the Jews, or his knowledge of it; since this might be the effect of natural affection to them, as his countrymen, and not arise from the exercise of faith and spiritual knowledge.

CHAPTER II

OF ELECTION.

THE following sections contain a reply to Dr. Whitby's exceptions in the third chapter of his Discourse, concerning absolute election, to our arguments for it, taken from some of the more principal passages of Scripture used by us in favour of it, with a particular consideration of Rom. v. 19, and the doctrine of the imputation of Adam's sin, which the Doctor, in the fourth chapter of the said discourse, makes to be the foundation of the decree of election. As I have nothing to object to his stating our sense of predestination, or the absolute election of some particular persons to eternal life, I shall immediately attend to what he has to object to the Scriptures, produced in proof of it.

SECTION I.

But ye are a chosen generation, a royal priesthood, an holy nation, a peculiar people, that ye should shew forth the praises of him, who hath called you out of darkness into his marvellous light.—1 Pet. ii. 9; together with 2 John i. 13; James ii. 5; Matt. xx. 16, and xxiv. 22, 24, 31; Luke xviii. 7; Rom. xi. 5.

IT is said,† "That the election, mentioned in the holy Scriptures, is not that of particular persons, but only of churches and nations; and imports rather their being chosen to the enjoyment of the means of grace, than to a certainty of being saved by those means." For the proof of this, several passages are cited out of the Old Testament, showing what will not be denied by any, and so might have been all spared, that the whole Jewish nation, good and bad, were styled the elect of God: but then, though that whole nation was chosen to external means and privileges, yet there were some particular persons among them who were also chosen to grace itself, and to certain salvation; and, accordingly, in the writings of the Old Testament, mention is made of the election of particular persons, as Moses, Aaron, David, and others, Psal. cvi. 23, and cv. 26, and lxxxix. 3, 19, and iv. 3. And, also, of some among the Gentiles, distinct from the Jews, Isa. xliii. 20, and lxv. 15, 22. And, of the latter, even before they were called by grace. It is, moreover, ob-

---

served,* that "when the word *elect* is, in the New Testament, applied to Christians, it plainly doth include as many as were converted to the Christian faith; for, when it is applied to the Jewish converts, it plainly signifies all that had been converted to the Christian faith." It is certain, that Christians are such as are converted to the Christian faith, and Jewish converts made be such, and those, who are really converted, are the elect of God; but then, they are not elected because they are converted, but they are converted because they are elected; and conversion being a sure and certain fruit of election, becomes the evidence of it. Now, to prove this sense of the word, when applied to Jewish converts,

1st. This passage of the apostle Peter is produced, though it rather seems to regard the Gentiles, as appears not only from the place in Isaiah,† out of which it is taken, where this chosen people are distinguished from the Jews, the posterity of Jacob and Israel; but, also, from the words following the text, *which in time past were not a people, but are now the people of God; which had not obtained mercy, but now have obtained mercy;* being a citation from Hos. i. 23, and applied to the Gentiles by the apostle Paul, in Rom. ix. 25. However, their election was not of them as a nation, or a church, since they were neither, being *strangers scattered throughout Pontus, Galatia, Cappadocia, Asia,* and *Bithynia.* Nor was it barely to means of grace and outward privileges, but both to grace and glory, seeing they are said to be *elect, according to the foreknowledge of God the Father, though sanctification of the Spirit, unto obedience, and sprinkling of the blood of Jesus Christ.‡* And in consequence of this, were regenerated by the grace of God, and were kept by his power, through faith, unto salvation; and so must be men absolutely designed for eternal happiness. But, to this are excepted,§

1. That the apostle "exhorts these elect, in chap. i. 14, and ii. 10, 11, and iv. 2, 3, 15, to avoid offences which are not incident to men elected to salvation, whilst they continue so to be." To which I reply, that such, who are elected to salvation, always continue to be so; nor are there any sins, excepting the sin against the Holy Ghost, which God's elect, before or after conversion, may not be guilty of. And the offences which the apostle here exhorts them to avoid, are such as are incident to men elected to salvation, as the cases of David, Peter, and others, do abundantly declare.

2. "That he affirms the same thing of the whole church of Babylon, chap. v. 13. Now, it was more than he could know, that all the members of that great church were absolutely elected to salvation." What church is meant by the church of Babylon, and how great it was, is not easy to know; and it is equally as difficult to say what an inspired apostle could or could not know. However, without a revelation, though that is no absurdity to

suppose, he might affirm of that church in general, that it was *elected together* with these, as he did affirm, in a judgment of charity, that the churches at Colosse and Thessalonica were the elect of God, though every member of it, in particular, was not elected to salvation, without any prejudice to the doctrine of eternal absolute election, since all the members of this church were under a visible profession of religion, and, no doubt, the far greater part, at least, were true believers in Christ.

3. "That, whereas this epistle is inscribed to the *elect,* the second epistle, sent to the same persons, beginneth thus: *To them who have obtained like precious faith with us;* and speaks of some who had *forsaken the right way;* and prophesies, that *false teachers should make merchandize of some of them.*" Be it so, that the *elect,* and *who have obtained like precious faith with* the apostles, are the same persons, which must be allowed; their having the same faith with them is a strong evidence of their being men absolutely designed for eternal happiness, and not barely chosen to the means of grace, or external privileges; yet, it is not true that the apostle speaks of any of the elect he writes to, that they had *forsaken the right way,* but of some other persons who are distinguished from them; and, though he prophesies that *false teachers should make merchandize of some of them,* his meaning is, that they should be able to draw their money out of their pockets, not that they should destroy the grace of God in their hearts.

4. That "these words are plainly taken from Isaiah xliii. 20, 21. Now, though the whole Jewish nation are styled God's *chosen generation,* and *peculiar people,* it is as sure that they were not all elected to salvation; we then may reasonably conclude, that the same words applied by St. Peter to all these Christian churches, do not imply that all their particular members were elected to salvation, but only, that they were all members of the church of Christ." I answer, that the apostle takes these words out of Isa. xliii. 20, 21, or at least, refers to that place, will be allowed; but then the words of that prophecy do not regard the whole Jewish nation, who though they are styled, yet not there, God's chosen generation and people, but a set of persons among the Gentiles, whom God had chosen, and formed for himself, to show forth his praise; who are distinguished from the Jews, the posterity of Jacob and Israel; opposed to them, ver. 22, *But thou hast not called upon me, O Jacob; but thou hast been weary of me, O Israel.* Besides, these words are not applied to several Christian churches; for the apostle did not write to churches, as such, but to strangers scattered about the world, whether Jews or Gentiles; though, upon the consideration of their being church members, he might, in a judgment of charity, pronounce them *elect.* And whereas it is owned, that the words imply that they were

* Ibid. p. 40; ed. 2. 39.   † Chap. xliii. 20, 21.   ‡ 1 Pet. i. 1—5.   § Whitby, p. 41; ed. 2. 40.

all members of the church of Christ; which, if understood of *the general assembly, and church of the first-born, whose names are written in heaven*, is the same as to be elected to salvation. For, to be a member of this church, and to be an elect person, one absolutely designed for happiness, is the same thing; and that these persons were such is evident, from their being *called out of darkness into marvellous light*.

2dly. Another instance of the word *elect*, when applied to Jewish converts, signifying such as are converted to the Christian faith, is in 2 John i. 13, where we read of the *elect lady*, and her *elect sister*, that is, says our author,[*] the Christian lady and sister. That these were Christian ladies is certain, but that they were Jewish converts to the Christian faith is not so certain. However, it is most certain that these are no instances of the election of nations or churches, but of particular persons, whom the apostle, in a judgment of charity, and from a thorough persuasion of their having received the grace of God, might address under this title and character; though I rather think it is here used as a term of civil honour and respect, than in a religious sense, and so has no concern in this controversy.

3dly. When St. James says, *God has chosen the poor of this world, rich in faith, and heirs* of the kingdom, it is said[‡] his meaning is, that they were called out of the world to the profession of the faith, which, if they lived according to it, would make them heirs of his heavenly kingdom." Now, though the apostle James wrote to the twelve tribes, and so chiefly designs Jewish converts, yet he neither writes to them as a nation, or as a church, seeing they were scattered abroad. Nor can these words be applied to them, or any other, under either of these considerations; since all the individuals of a nation, and all the members of churches, are not *the poor of this world*, but are to be understood of some particular persons, in such circumstances, on whom God, in consequence of their eternal election, bestows the precious grace of faith, which receives the blessing of free justification, by the righteousness of Christ, when they openly become the heirs of glory; for, being *justified by his grace*, they are *made heirs according to the hope of eternal life*.[‡] This, and this only, and not a profession of the faith, no, nor a life according to it, makes them heirs of the heavenly kingdom.

4thly. "When Christ saith,[§] *many are called, but few chosen*, it is said[||] these parables plainly relate to the Jews; and the import of them is, that though many of them were called by Christ and his apostles to faith in him, yet few did or would accept of him as their Saviour, or embrace the faith of Christ; so that here the elect and the believers of the Christian faith are the same persons;" But, though these words may primarily relate to the Jews, yet they are also of the Gentiles to this day, and the plain import of them is, that many of them are externally called, by the preaching of the Gospel, but few are, or appear to be, chosen unto eternal life. Were embracing the faith of Christ, and accepting of him as a Saviour, intended by the words, it should rather have been said, *many are called but few choose*, that is, Christ and salvation by him, as Mary is said[¶] to *choose that good part which shall not be taken away*; and not as it is, *many are called, but few chosen*; which does not express any act of man's, such as accepting Christ, and embracing the faith of him, but God's act, to whom alone, and not man, election is always ascribed in scripture; and, therefore, the elect are called *God's elect*, and *his own elect*. Besides, though election sometimes intends effectual vocation, yet never when calling and election are mentioned together in the same verse, for then they are to be distinguished one from another. Moreover, were true believers here meant, this would not militate against eternal election, since their being believers is an evidence of it; and, after all, the *few chosen* must design particular persons, and not either nations or churches, no, nor mere nominal believers of the Christian faith.

5thly. "When he (Christ) says,[**] that *for the elect's sake those days shall be shortened*, it is said,[††] he styles the faithful, left in the midst of the unbelieving Jews, the elect." So that believers are intended: be it so; then not whole nations, or churches, or communities, are designed, but particular persons; though they seem rather to be such who were unconverted, to be the people among the Jews whom God had *foreknown*, who were a *remnant according to the election of grace*, and therefore should *obtain*, whilst the *rest were blinded*; for whose sake, the days of affliction and trouble in the Jewish nation should be shortened, or there should be some respite given, that so there might be an opportunity of preaching the Gospel, which should become the power of God unto salvation to his chosen people; just as, on the other hand, the day of Christ's second coming is deferred until all the elect are gathered in, God being unwilling that any one of them should *perish*, but that they should *all come to repentance*.

6thly. "When he (Christ) adds, ver. 24, that the false christs and false prophets should do as much as in them lay, by signs and wonders, to deceive the elect; it is said,[††] There also are we to understand the persevering Christians." I reply, that such who are converted, or are true believers, are, and will be, persevering Christians, and such are certainly the elect of God; but then the reason why they are elected is not because they are converted, or are true believers, or are persevering Christians; but, on the contrary, the reason why they are converted, become true be-

---

* Whitby, p. 42; ed. 2. 41.   † Ibid.
‡ Tit. iii. 7.   § Matt. xx. 16.
|| Whitby, p. 42.   ¶ Luke x. 42.
** Matt. xxiv. 22.   †† Whitby. 43;
ed. 2. 42.   ‡‡ Whitby, p. 43; ed. 2. 42.

lievers, and so persevering Christians, is, because they are elected; conversion, faith, and perseverance, being not causes and conditions, but fruits and effects of election.

7thly. "When he saith, ver. 31, that God (it should be the Son of Man) *shall send his angels to gather his elect from the four winds,* it is said, the meaning may be, either that he would send his angels to warn the Christians in all the quarters of Judea, to gather together from the unbelieving Jews, that they might be preserved from ruin; or, that he would send his messengers with the Gospel, to gather together as many as did, or would believe, from among the nations of the earth." But the first of these cannot be the meaning of the words; these elect cannot be the Christians in Judea; since they were to be gathered, not from all the quarters of Judea, but *from the four winds, from one end of the heaven to the other ;* and if any from among the nations of the earth, or Gentiles, are intended by the elect, who, after the destruction of Jerusalem, were to be gathered by Christ's ministers, his *angels,* to himself, with the sound of the Gospel trumpet, God having resolved to *take out of them a people of his name,** when the Jews were rejected and cut off; yet these are not such as did believe the Gospel, or would of themselves believe it, but unconverted persons who were destitute of faith, on whom God, of his free grace, would bestow it as a fruit of his electing love: or else, all the chosen vessels of mercy are meant by the elect, even *the dead in Christ,* who *shall rise first,* when the Lord descends *from heaven with a shout, with the voice of the archangel, and with the trumpet of God,*† even all those who will be gathered together, and placed at his right hand; to whom he will say,‡ *Come, ye blessed of my Father, inherit the kingdom prepared for you from the foundation of the world ;* a character aptly descriptive of persons absolutely chosen to eternal salvation.

8thly. "The *elect,* in Luke xviii. 7, are said,§ to be the whole body of true believers; and it is suggested, that the faith of many of these should fail." Be it so, that the whole body of true believers are intended, this no ways prejudices the doctrine of eternal election; since they are styled elect, not from their faith, but from God's choice of them to everlasting life; whence they are called *his own elect.* Nor does the inquiry in ver. 8, show that the faith of many, or any of these elect, should fail at the coming of the Son of Man; for though, when he comes, the doctrine of faith will be greatly departed from, and the grace of faith will be very rare, and at a low ebb, yet Christ prays for the faith of all his elect, as he did for Peter's, that it *fail not.*

9thly. It is observed,‖ that " *the election according to grace,* mentioned Rom. xi. 5, doth, in like manner, signify the whole body of the Jewish converts, even all that did embrace the Christian faith. A great number of these turned afterwards apostates, and renounced the Christian faith; and St. Paul was afraid that some of these *elect* would afterwards *draw back unto perdition.* From all which, it is extremely evident, that the apostle neither did, nor could speak of this *remnant according to the election of grace,* as persons absolutely elected to salvation." I answer, that though the Jewish converts, such as were true believers, were *the remnant* in being at that time, *according to the election of grace,* before the world began; yet all that bore the name of converts, or externally embraced the Christian faith, were not of that number: nor did any of the remnant turn apostates, renounce the Christian faith, and so come short of heaven; otherwise, how could it be said, *the election hath obtained it?* nor was the apostle Paul afraid that any of these elect should draw back to perdition; but affirms the reverse, *we are not of them that draw back to perdition :*¶ nor do any of the passages, cited from the epistle to the Hebrews, suppose that any of these elect might, or did apostatize, or draw back unto perdition; as has been made to appear in the former part of this work.

SECTION II

And not only this, but when Rebecca also had conceived by one, even by our father Isaac, (for the children being not yet born, neither having done any good or evil, that the purpose of God, according to election, might stand, not of works, but of him that calleth) it was said unto her, The elder shall serve the younger; as it is written, Jacob have I loved, but Esau have I hated.—Rom. ix. 10—13.

With Rom. viii. 33.

THE design of the apostle, in this chapter, is to show, that though the Israelites in general were a chosen people, had peculiar privileges, to whom the promises were made; yet, the word of God was not made void, or took no effect; notwithstanding few of them believed in Christ, the greater part were rejected of God, and the Gentiles shared the blessings of the new covenant; seeing there were then, as there always had been, two sorts among them; the one were *children of the flesh,* the natural descendants of Abraham only; the other also *children of the promise,* who were counted for the spiritual *seed.* To the latter of which the promises were always made good; and these always shared, as they then did, the spiritual blessings of grace; wherefore, the word of God had its designed accomplishment. And, lest this should seem any new, or strange thing, the apostle instances in the immediate offspring of Abraham, Isaac, and Ishmael; the one was born after the Spirit, the other after the flesh; the one was the son of the free, the other of the bond-woman; the one continued in the house, the other was cast out. And to pre-

---

* Acts xv. 14.   † 1 Thess. iv. 16.
‡ Matt. xxv. 34.

§ Whitby, p. 43; ed. 2. 42.
‖ Ibid., p. 43, 44.   ¶ Heb. x. 39.

vent any objection that might be taken from Ishmael's being born, not of the lawful wife, but of the bond-woman, as being the reason of his rejection, the apostle proceeds to mention the case of Jacob and Esau, who not only had the same father, but the same mother, Isaac's lawful wife; these were conceived at once, were in the womb together, were twins; and if any had the preference, Esau by birth had it, being born first; and yet a difference was made between these two by God himself; who said to the mother of them, *The elder shall serve the younger;* which is interpreted of God's loving the one, and hating the other; and this was notified to her, in consequence of an eternal purpose, *before the children were born,* and when they had *done neither good nor evil;* so that it could not be said, that Jacob was loved for his good works, nor Esau hated for his evil ones; wherefore the *purpose of God,* respecting the *election of Jacob,* fully appears to to depend *not of works,* but of the grace *of him that calleth.* From all this we conclude, that the predestination of men, either to life or death, is personal : that the objects of either branch of predestination are alike, or are considered in the same situation or condition, whether in the pure, or corrupt mass, or in both; that God was not influenced or moved, in the election of the one, by their good works, or in the rejection of the other, by their bad ones; that God's decree of election stands firm and immoveable, not upon the foot of works, but of the grace of God; and, that love and hatred are the real springs and source of predestination in its respective branches. But the grand exception to this instance and example of personal election and rejection, is, that these words do not " respect the persons of Jacob and Esau, but their whole nation and posterity; and this is said to be plain,"[*]

1. From the words of God to Rebecca, *Two nations are in thy womb, and two manner of people shall be separated from thy bowels; and the one people shall be stronger than the other people, and the elder shall serve the younger.* To which I reply, that this oracle primarily respects the persons of Jacob and Esau as the roots of their respective offspring; and only, secondarily, their posterity, as branches that should sprout from them; it properly regards their persons, and only, in an improper, figurative, and metonymical sense, their seed; for, in no other sense could two nations, or two manner of people, be in Rebecca's womb, than as there were two persons there, who would be the authors of two nations and people; and, admitting that their respective posterities are in ever so strict and close a sense intended, this can never be understood to the exclusion of their persons; any more than they can be thought to be personally excluded from any concern in the loss or enjoyment of the birthright and blessing;

for, were the posterity of Esau only deprived of the birthright and blessing? Was not he himself personally supplanted with respect to both? Did the posterity of Jacob only enjoy the birthright and the blessing? Did not Jacob himself, in his own person, purchase the birthright, and receive the blessing?

2. This is said[†] to be plain, " from this observation, that, as to the persons of Jacob and Esau, this was never true, that *the elder* did *serve the younger;* but only, as to their posterity, when the Edomites became tributaries to David, 2 Sam. viii. 14." But this observation supposes that this is to be understood of outward temporal servitude; and, indeed, in this sense, it was never true of their persons; so far from being so, that Jacob, as soon as he had got the birthright and the blessing, was obliged to flee from Esau; and when, after many years, he returned, he sends messengers to his brother, in a very submissive manner, charging them, saying, *Thus shall ye say to my lord Esau, Thy servant Jacob saith thus, &c.* And, when he found that his brother was coming to meet him, it threw him into a panic fear, lest he should *smite* him, *and the mother with the children;* he prepares presents for him; and when he came to him, bowed himself to the ground seven times, and so his wives and children all bowed to him; and the language in which he addressed him, while they conversed together, was that of *my lord.*[‡] Now it is not credible, that if this oracle is to be understood of temporal servitude, that it should have no appearance, nor the least shadow of an accomplishment, in their persons, supposing it was to have a greater in their posterity; and, indeed, the completion of it in this sense, in their posterity, is not so exceeding evident. It is certain, that there was a long train of dukes and kings in Esau's posterity before there was any king in Israel.[§] They were in lordly grandeur and splendour, when the children of Israel were oppressed with hard bondage in Egypt. The single instance referred to, when the Edomites became tributaries to David, was near a thousand years after the giving out of this oracle : and this servitude did not continue long; for, in Joram's time, they revolted,[||] and so continued; and it is plain, that, at the time of the Babylonish captivity, the children of Edom were prosperous and triumphant; who said,[¶] concerning Jerusalem, *Raze it, raze it, even to the foundation thereof.* This servitude, therefore is to be understood in a spiritual sense of Esau's exclusion from the favour of God, and the blessings of grace : for these two phrases, *The elder shall serve the younger,* and *Jacob have I loved, but Esau have I hated,* are of the same signification : the one is explanative of the other. When Jacob got the birth-right, and received the blessing, this oracle began to have a visible accomplishment. Esau then appeared not to be the son and heir of promise,

* Whitby p. 45; ed. 2. 44. So Curcellæus' p, 378; Limborch, p. 350.

† Whitby, p. 45; ed. 2. 44.

‡ Gen. xxvii. 43, and xxxii. 3. 4, 11, 13, and xxxiii. 3, 5—8, 13—15.   § Gen. xxxvi. 31.

|| 2 Kings viii. 22.   ¶ Psalm cxxxvii. 7.

who was to abide in the house; and therefore departs, and pitches his dwelling elsewhere; all which showed he had no interest in spiritual adoption—no right to the blessings of the covenant of grace—nor was he an heir of heaven; these belonged to Jacob. Esau was a servant of sin, under the dominion of it, and in bondage to it; whilst Jacob was the Lord's freeman, and, as a prince, had power with God, and with men, and prevailed. Esau was serviceable to Jacob, even in spiritual things, as reprobates are to the elect; for all things are for their sake, and all things work together for their good. Jacob's being obliged to flee from his brother, was for his good; by this providence, he got him a suitable wife, and large substance. His brother's meeting him on his return, which gave him so much pain and uneasiness, issued in his spiritual good; this sent him to the throne of grace, to humble himself before God, acknowledge his mercies and dependence on him, to implore his help, and plead his promises. And thus the oracle was verified in the persons of Jacob and Esau.

3. It is urged,* that "what is here offered, as a proof or confirmation of this, is cited from the prophet Malachi, who prophesied long after Jacob and Esau were personally dead, and speaks expressly of the nation of the Edomites." It is very true, that Malachi prophesied long after Jacob and Esau were dead personally; and it is as true, that what God there says by Malachi so long after they were dead, is only an explanation of what he had said to Rebecca before they were born; as appears from the apostle's citing both passages as of like import, and the one as interpreting the other. It is plain, that the Lord, in the prophecy of Malachi, directs the murmuring Jews to the personal regard he had to Jacob and Esau; and which had continued in numberless instances to their respective posterities, in order to stop their mouths, and reprove their ingratitude; and though he speaks of the nation of the Edomites, and also to the posterity of Israel, yet it is evident that he has a respect to the persons of Jacob and Esau, from whence they sprung, when he says, *was not Esau Jacob's brother?* Now, though an Edomite may be said to be brother to an Israelite, yet Esau is never said, nor can he, with any propriety, be said to be the brother of Jacob's posterity.

4. That the persons, and not the posterity of Jacob and Esau, are here designed, is evident from the personal account that is given of them; for whatever may be said for their taking their rise from one common father, Isaac, or for their being chosen or rejected as nations before they were born, or had done good or evil; yet it cannot be said with any propriety at all, that *Rebecca conceived* their respective posterities *by one, even by our father Isaac.* Moreover, the Scriptural account of these two accords with a personal

rejection of the one, and an election of the other. Esau is represented as a *profane person;* yea, is expressly† said to be ἀπεδοκιμάσθη, *rejected,* that is, from inheriting the blessing. Jacob, on the other hand, is spoken of as a *plain* and upright man; one interested in the covenant of grace, and a chosen vessel of salvation. Besides, this sense of the words only agrees with the scope and design of the apostle, which is to prove, that all were not Israel which were of Israel, and that all the natural seed of Abraham were not the children of God: this he could not better exemplify, than in the persons of Jacob and Esau; for to have instanced in the posterity of Esau, would have been foreign to his purpose. Add to all this, that the apostle continues his discourse, in the following verses, upon the subject of personal election and rejection; he observes, ver. 15, 18, that God *will have mercy on whom he will have mercy, and whom he will, he hardeneth;* which respects persons, and not nations; and instances in Pharaoh, which surely cannot be understood of the posterity, but of the person of Pharaoh; and in ver. 22, 23, speaks of *vessels of wrath fitted to destruction,* and of *vessels of mercy afore prepared for glory;* which design neither nations, nor churches, nor Jewish converts only, but particular persons among Jews and Gentiles; which latter appear to be the people and beloved of God, and vessels of mercy, by their being called by grace. Hence,

5. It does not clearly follow, as is said,‡ that the apostle cannot here discourse of any personal election to eternal life, or of any personal love or hatred with respect to eternal interests; since he manifestly speaks of the persons, and not the posterity of Jacob and Esau: and did he, it would not follow, as is suggested, that according to this opinion, the whole nation of Israel must be elected to eternal life, and the whole posterity of Esau be the objects of God's hatred and reprobation; since the people of Israel in general might be said to be loved and chosen of God, the far greater part of them being so, the line of election running among them as it did for many hundreds of years; and yet some of them be instances of God's displeasure and hatred: and on the other hand, the posterity of Esau in general might be said to be rejected, the far greater part being so, the line of rejection running among them as it did for many hundreds of years; and yet some of them, as Job and his friends, be chosen vessels of mercy. Nor,

6. "Is it certain,§ That the apostle here only speaks of the election of one seed and nation before another, to be accounted and treated by him as the seed of Abraham, or owned for his peculiar people. For nothing is more certain than that the apostle here speaks of the election of some of the same seed, and of the same nation, before others, who were to be accounted and treated as the

---

* Whitby p. 45, ; ed. 2. 44; Limborch, p. 350. † Heb. xii. 17.

‡ Whitby, p. 45 : ed. 2. 44. § Ibid. p. 46 ; ed. 2. 45.

spiritual seed of Abraham; and owned for God's peculiar, special people, before others who were, equally with them, the natural seed of Abraham.

7. The last instance of the sense of the word *elect*, when applied to Jewish converts, is in Rom. viii. 33, *Who shall lay any thing to the charge of God's elect?* And, "here again it is said, that* the elect and true believers are the same." I see no reason why the elect here should be confined to Jewish converts; for though the apostle speaks of himself and others, he is writing to the Romans. And be it so, that the elect design true believers, it is plain they were such who were *predestinated* before they were *called;* and so were the elect of God antecedent to their being true believers, and therefore are not denominated God's elect from their being so; and besides, they were such as were chosen not barely to external means of grace, and outward privileges, but to grace here and glory hereafter, ver. 30, and so were not whole nations, or churches, or communities, but particular persons.

SECTION III

Put on therefore (as the elect of God, holy and beloved) bowels of mercies, &c.—Col. iii. 12. *Together with* 1 Thess. i. 4, 2 Thess. ii. 13, 2 Tim. ii. 10, Tit. i. 1.

OUR author goes on to observe,† " that suitable to this notion of the word election, where it respects the Jewish nation, or the Jewish converts, is the import of it in these epistles, where whole nations, communities, or churches, are styled the elect;" that is, that it means converts to the Christian faith, or true believers. But surely, whole nations are never styled the elect in such a sense; and, indeed, this author does not attempt to propose one instance of it, and only takes notice of churches or communities. And,

1. Observes, that " all the faithful brethren in Colosse, are styled‡ the elect of God;" and the same apostle saith to the whole church of Thessalonica,§ *Knowing your election of God;* and in his second epistle, he saith, *We ought to give thanks for you, that God hath elected you from the beginning to salvation.*|| All which he might say without a special revelation, in a judgment of charity; for, though every individual member of these churches were not chosen to salvation, yet, inasmuch as they were all under a visible profession of religion, and the major part of them were truly believers, he might write to them as such: nor do the cautions, exhortation, care and fear, expressed by him, militate against this their character; since these might be all designed, and be made use of for their perseverance as such in grace unto glory.

2. Another instance is in 2 Tim. ii. 10, where the apostle says, *I endure all things*

for the elect's sake; And we are told¶ that " if we compare this with a parallel place in Col. i. 24, 25, we shall find the elect to be no other than the whole church of Christ, of which he was a minister." But by comparing this text with that in Colossians, it appears that the church of which the apostle was a minister, is no other than the body of Christ; and intends *the general assembly and church of the first-born which are written in heaven,*** and not any particular society, or community of men, under a profession of Christianity; for of such a particular church the apostle was no minister. Nor would this have been agreeable to his character as an apostle, who was not fixed with any particular church, but had the care of all the churches upon him. Besides, the elect here were such who were not yet called by grace, for whose sake the apostle endured, and was willing to endure, reproach and persecution, in preaching the Gospel; that *they also,* as well as such as were already converted, might *obtain that salvation which is in Christ Jesus with eternal glory.*

3. The apostle in Tit. i. 1, styles himself *an apostle according to the faith of God's elect;* which is interpreted††of the faith of Christians in general. But this interpretation will not hold good of nominal, only of real Christians, who become so because they are God's elect, to whom true saving faith in Christ is peculiar; for *all men have not faith;* to the elect only is it given, whilst others believe not in him, *because* they *are not of his sheep.*

SECTION IV

According as he hath chosen us in him before the foundation of the world, that we should be holy, and without blame before him in love.—Eph. i. 4.

THESE words are, indeed, a strong proof of the doctrine of an eternal, personal, and unconditional election of men to grace and glory; yet the whole strength of the doctrine is not placed in them, as is suggested :‡‡ we have other strengthening proofs of the proof of it; though we readily own this to be a very considerable one. This passage of Scripture proves, that the choice of men to holiness and happiness, is an eternal act of God the Father, or what passed before the world began; since it is expressly said, that *he hath chosen us in him,* that is, in Christ, as the head of the elect, *before the foundation of the world;* and not as the author§§ attended to, either through inadvertency, or with design, cites the words, *from the foundation of the world.* For the phrase is not ἀπὸ καταβολῆς κόσμου, as in Rev. xiii. 8, but πρὸ καταβολῆς κόσμου, and is expressive of the eternity of it, agreeable to other scriptures; as 2 Tim. i. 9, 2 Thess. ii. 13, compared with Prov. viii. 22, 23. It also proves, that this choice is of particular persons, *he hath chosen us,* and not

---

* Whitby, p. 45; ed. 2. 44.
† Ibid. p. 45; ed. 2. 44.   ‡ Col. iii. 12.
§ 1 Thess. i. 4. || 2 Thess. ii. 13.

¶ Whitby, p. 47; ed. 2. 46.
** Heb. xii. 23.   †† Whitby, p. 47; ed 2. 46.   ‡‡ Ibid.; ed. 2. 48.   §§ Ibid.

of nations, or churches; seeing the apostle is not writing to, nor speaking of a nation: nor is it very evident that he is writing to a church; for he expresses himself with much caution and distinction, when he inscribes this epistle *to the saints which are at Ephesus, and to the faithful in Christ Jesus.* And it is still less evident, that he is speaking of these same persons, or of them as a church; yea, it is manifest, that he is speaking of himself and others, as partakers of the several blessings of grace mentioned in the context; *who first trusted in Christ,* and were not members of this particular church. These are distinctly spoken of from ver. 3, to ver. 12, inclusive; and then the* apostle addresses himself to the Ephesians in ver. 13, and says, *in whom ye also trusted, after that ye heard the word of truth, the gospel of your salvation.* Besides, admitting that these words are spoken of *the saints* and *faithful* at Ephesus. and of them as a church; they are not said to be chosen as a church, or chosen to be one, but that they *should be holy, and without blame;* who might be called by the apostle *chosen in Christ,* or the elect of God, as the churches of Colosse and Thessalonica are from their visible profession of religion, and from the majority among them of such as were truly so. Wherefore these words still continue a proof of personal election. Add to this, the phrase of being *chosen in Christ,* is sometimes used of a single person, as in Rom. xvi. 13. Once more, this text proves that this eternal election of particular persons to salvation is absolute, unconditional, and irrespective of faith, holiness, good works, and perseverance, as the moving causes or conditions of it; all which are the fruits and effects of electing grace, but not causes and conditions of it; since these are said to be chosen, not because they *were* holy, but that they *should be* so. And supposing that the apostle is here speaking of *the saints and faithful in Christ,* they are not said to be chosen, as such, or because they were such: nor does it follow that they were so antecedent to their election, because they were so when the apostle wrote this epistle, any more than they were so antecedent to their redemption and effectual vocation; since these same persons are said to *have redemption in Christ,* and *the mystery of God's will made known* unto them; which would imply this contradiction, that they were saints before they were called with an holy calling, and faithful before they were believers. And whereas it is said,† that these persons "were not all infallibly predestinated to salvation, but only to the adoption of children," ver. 5. It may be replied that if they were infallibly predestinated to the adoption of children, which adoption does not so much design the bless-

ing itself prepared in divine predestination, or the grace received in effectual vocation, as the inheritance to which the saints are adopted, even the heavenly glory, see Rom. viii. 23, then they were infallibly predestinated to salvation; and what short of salvation can be meant by being *holy, and without blame before him in love?* But that these words are spoken of such as were chosen out of the world to be God's church and people, and not of persons infallibly predestinated to salvation, is thought to be exceeding evident.‡

1. "From the exhortations and cautions given to these persons in this very epistle; such as in chap. iv. 17, and v. 6, and vi. 13. All which are inconsistent with the character of the elect, that is, of persons infallibly predestinated to salvation." I reply, That the exhortations *not to walk as other Gentiles,* and to *take to* themselves the *whole armour of God,* though the former seems rather a testimonial of their pious walk than an exhortation to it; these, I say, are so far from being inconsistent with their character as elect, that nothing could be more pertinent to them who were chosen. to be holy, and which were designed, and doubtless were blessed, as means of their perseverance in grace and holiness. And as for the caution given them, that no man deceive them into the commission of sins there mentioned, with this very good reason, *for because of these things cometh the wrath of God upon the children of disobedience;* nothing could be more proper to give them a just idea of the evil nature of sin, and the resentment of it by God, in order to their avoiding it; and yet no ways prejudice their absolute and infallible election to salvation, nor their faith and hope in it; seeing *the wrath of God cometh* not upon them, but *upon the children of disobedience.*

2. "From the apostle's prediction, Acts xx. 29, 30." But though the apostle prophesies, that after his *departure* either from them, or out of the world, *grievous wolves* should *enter among them,* and *of themselves men* should *arise speaking perverse things;* yet not that any of them who were *chosen* in Christ *before the foundation of the world,* should be such or act in this manner. For these words, as has been already shown, are not spoken of the members of the church at Ephesus; and were they spoken of them, the apostle in his prediction could never design any of *the saints* and *faithful in Christ Jesus,* who then constituted the church at Ephesus, but others that should creep in, and rise up among them in some time to come.

3. "From his advertisement to Timothy, in 2 Tim. i. 15, and ii. 18, and iv. 3, 4; 1 Tim. i. 19, and v. 15, and vi. 21, that some had or should turn away; all which is inconsistent with the character of the elect." I reply

---

* Qui enim præsperasse potuerunt, id est, ante sperasse in Deum quam venisset, nisi Judæi, quibus Christus prænuntiabatur ab initio? Qui ergo prænun tiabatur ille et præsperabatur, atque ideo hoc ad se, id est, ad Judæos refert ut distinctionem faciat, conversus ad natienes; in quo et vos quum audissetis Sermonem veritatis, Evangelium in quo credidistis et signati estis Spiritu promissionis ejus Sancto.—Tertullian adv. Marcion, l. 5, c. 17, p. 607, 608; ed. Paris.

† Whitby, p. 47; ed. 2. 48.

‡ Ibid.

that some of these passages do not seem to have any immediate relation to the members of the church at Ephesus, nor any of them to them who were *chosen in Christ before the foundation of the world;* some of them speak not of men's turning from the faith, but from the apostle slighting and neglecting him when he was in necessity; and others not of what was then done, but what should be hereafter; and though some then present instances of apostacy are mentioned, yet it is also affirmed, that *nevertheless the foundation of God standeth sure, having this seal, the Lord knoweth them that are his.* So that these instances carry in them nothing inconsistent with the character of the elect, that is, of persons infallibly predestinated to salvation, nor prove what they are produced for.

SECTION V

And we know that all things work together for good to them that love God, to them who are the called, κατὰ πρόθεσιν, *according to his purpose; for whom* προέγνω, *he did foreknow, he also* προώρισε, *did predestinate.*— Rom. viii. 28, 29.

THESE three words πρόγνωσις, *the foreknowledge,* πρόθεσις, *the purpose,* and προωρισμὸς, *the foreappointment of God,* are used in the New Testament to express the doctrine of election; which show that the predestination of men to eternal life, according to the foreknowledge and purpose of God, is a special, unchangeable, and eternal act of his grace. Though,

1. It is affirmed,[*] "that none of them relate to particular or individual persons (save only when they are used of our blessed Lord and his sufferings for us), but only to churches and nations in the general." But surely they do not relate to churches and nations in the general, in the text before us; for then it would unavoidably follow, that whole churches and nations in general are conformed to the image of Christ, justified and glorified, seeing these things are said of those whom God foreknows and predestinates; nor do the instances alleged prove the assertion; not Eph. i. 5, 11, where the apostle speaks of some whom God had προορίσας, *predestinated to the adoption of sons,* and who were προορισθέντες κατὰ πρόθεσιν, *predestinated according to the purpose* of God, which passages regard not nations or churches, but particular persons, as has been shown under the foregoing section; nor 1 Pet. i. 2, where some are said to be elect, not κατὰ πρόθεσιν, *according to the purpose,* as Dr. Whitby very wrongly cites the words, but κατὰ πρόγνωσιν, *according to the foreknowledge of God the Father,* which intend particular persons, and not nations or churches; for not to such does the apostle write, but to *strangers scattered throughout Pontus, Galatia, Cappadocia, Asia, and Bithynia;* nor Rom. ix. 11, where the ἡ κατ' ἐκλογὴν τοῦ Θεοῦ πρόθεσις, *purpose of God according to election,* concerns not the

posterity of Jacob and Esau, but the single person of Jacob only, as has been made to appear in a preceding section.

2. It is said,[†] "that this foreknowledge, purpose, or appointment, is only that of calling men to the knowledge of salvation by Christ Jesus." But, if by calling men to the knowledge of salvation by Christ Jesus is only meant, as it seems to be by what follows, a bare external call by the ministry of the gospel; it must be denied that foreknowledge, purpose, and appointment, only regard this; seeing many are *called according to the purpose of God, with an holy calling,* such an one as is powerful, and effectual to their real sanctification, and which is secured to them by God's foreknowledge, purpose, and appointment, though it is something distinct from them, being an act of God's grace in time, whereas the other respects his knowledge and will from all eternity.

3. It is farther said,[‡] that "this calling is by God designed ἐπὶ τοῦτο, that they who are thus *called* might *obtain salvation through sanctification of the Spirit and belief of the truth;* all Christians being chosen to this end, *that they might be holy, and unblameable before God in love.* But hence it cannot reasonably be argued, that this election is no larger than the holiness designed to be produced by it." I reply, that effectual calling by the grace of God, which is the calling according to purpose the Scriptures speak of, is not only designed by God, that such who are thus called might obtain salvation, but is really and infallibly succeeded to such an end; though it would be more proper, and more agreeable to the Scriptures to say, that such *obtain salvation by Jesus Christ,* being *chosen to* it *through sanctification of the Spirit and belief of the truth;* which holiness is not only designed to be produced in consequence of electing grace, but is really produced. Nor is this election larger, nor it does not extend to more persons than holiness; just as many persons are made holy in time as were chosen to be so from eternity: holiness is a certain fruit and effect of election. The instances of God's general goodness, the mission of the Baptist, and the outward ministry of the gospel of grace, not always having a good effect upon men, are not to be put upon a level with the purposes and *counsel* of God, which shall certainly *stand;* for he *will* always *do* his *pleasure.* As to the end of the Messiah's coming, *to save his people from* their sins, that ought not to have been mentioned with the former instances; since that is fully answered, and has had its sure effect and accomplishment.

4. It is observed,§ that "as men were appointed to be called from the beginning, and the gospel is that ἣν προώρισεν, *which God had fore-appointed* to be preached to them for that end, 1 Cor. ii. 7; so by virtue of this purpose and fore-appointment men were in time called by the gospel to faith in Christ, where they are said to be *called according to purpose,*

---

* Whitby, p. 49; ed. 2. 48.   † Ibid p. 49.   § Ibid. p. 51   ed. 2. 50.
50; ed. 2. 49.   ‡ Whitby, p. 50; ed. 2.

Rom. viii. 28, 2 Tim. i. 9. And the purpose of sending Christ to die for the remission of sins, being the ground of this calling, he is said to be given up to death, *according to the foreknowledge of God and his foreappointed counsel*, Acts ii. 23. And *they who slew him* are said to have done only *what his counsel had foreappointed to be done*, Acts iv. 28." Which observations are very just ; but are so far from militating against the doctrine of absolute election, that they establish it ; since, according to them, not only the end but the means, the death of Christ, the preaching of the gospel, and calling men by it, are appointed and fixed, which infallibly succeed to bring about the end, eternal salvation.

SECTION VI.

All that the Father giveth me shall come to me ; and him that cometh to me I will in no wise cast out.—John vi. 37.

THESE words contain three of the most glorious truths of the Gospel, namely, the doctrines of particular election, efficacious grace in conversion, and the final perseverance of the saints.

1st. The doctrine of particular election. The *all*, πᾶν, design not the apostles only, who were given to Christ as such ; for these did not all, in a spiritual manner, come to him, and believe in him, one of them was a devil ; much less every individual of mankind. These are in some sense given to Christ, to subserve some ends of his mediatorial kingdom, and are subject to his power and control ; yet do not come to him, believe in him,* *all men have not faith:* but the whole body of the elect, who, when they were chosen by God the Father, were given, and put into the hands of Christ, and therefore are said to be *chosen in him :*† he was chosen as head, and they as members of him. God made a covenant with him, as the head of the election of grace ; in which he gave his chosen people to him as his seed, his spouse, his sheep, his portion and inheritance, and to be saved by him with an everlasting salvation. This was done before time ; otherwise how could these persons be blessed with all spiritual blessings, and have grace given to them in Christ, before the world began; if their persons had not also been given to Christ, and secured in him? And though Christ here expresses this act of his Father's in the present tense, *all that the Father* δίδωσί, *giveth me*, perhaps to express the continuance and unchangeableness of it ; yet he expresses it in ver. 39, in the past tense, *all that* δέδωλέ, *he hath given me*, and respects an act of God, antecedent to coming to Christ, and believing in him ; which is *the faith of God's elect*, the fruit and effect of electing love ; for *as many as were ordained unto eternal life believed.*‡ Now to this sense of the words the following things are objected.

1. "That§ to be given of the Father, can-

not signify to be absolutely chosen by God to eternal life ; for then the Jews could not be reasonably accused for not coming to Christ, or not believing on him; much less could it be imputed to them as their great crime, that they would *not come to* him, or believe in him; since upon this supposition none could come but whom God had chosen." I answer, There is a difference between coming to Christ, and believing on him as the Messiah, or giving a bare assent to him as such, and coming to him as a Saviour, or believing in him for life and salvation. The Jews might be reasonably accused for not believing on him as the Messiah, *whom the Father had sent ;* since they had such a demonstration of his being so from his character, miracles, and doctrines ; though none but those among them, whom the Father had given to Christ, could believe in him to the saving of their souls. And even not coming to Christ, and believing in him, in this spiritual manner, when he is revealed in the external ministry of the word, as God's way of salvation, is criminal and blameworthy, notwithstanding men's want of both will and power; since this does not arise from any decree of God, but from the corruption of nature through sin : and this being blameworthy, what follows upon it, or is the effect of it, must be so too.

2. " Hence it must follow (it is said) that Christ could not reasonably have invited them to come to him, or called them to believe in him, who were not given him of the Father; since he well knew they could never come."‖ I reply, that Christ, as a preacher of the Gospel, and a minister of the circumcision, might exhort the Jews in general to *labour for*, that is, use the means of obtaining *the meat which endures unto eternal life ;* he might inform them, *that this is the work of God*, which he himself works, as well as commands, that they *believe in him whom he hath sent ;* he might say to them, *My Father giveth you the true bread from heaven*, since he, who is the Bread of life, was come down from heaven, and was among them; and *these things* he might *say unto* them, that they *might be saved*, without any prejudice to the doctrine of particular election, and with a special view to the good of those among them his Father had given to him. And after all, it will not be easily proved, that Christ ever invited any to come in a spiritual way to him, and believe in him savingly, but such as the Father had given him. The words in Matt. xi. 28, are directed, not to unconverted sinners, much less reprobates, but to such who were under a work of the Spirit of God, labouring, and being *heavy laden*, with a sense of sin, and breathing and seeking after spiritual rest.

3. It is further objected,¶ that "were this so, the Jews must have just occasion to complain of Christ and of his doctrine, as being that which revealed to them their eternal and inevitable reprobation, and made it not only

---

* 2 Thess. iii. 3.   † Eph. i. 4.   Limborch, p. 347.   ‖ Whitby, p. 51, 52.
‡ Acts xiii. 48.   § Whitby, p. 51, 52 ;   ¶ Ibid. p. 53 ; ed. 2. 52.

necessary, but even equitable to reject him; because the blessings which he tendered belonged not to them in general, but only to some few, who by the Father should be given to him." It is true, indeed, that the doctrine of Christ was oftentimes very expressive of God's special and distinguishing grace, which raised loud complaints, and even indignation,[*] in the Jews against him, but without any just occasion or reason; since the grace of God is his own, and he may do with it as he pleases, and give it to whom he will. And as for their destruction, it was wholly owing to themselves; nor had they any just occasion, by Christ's doctrine, to complain of any but themselves, who ought to have been received by them as the Messiah; by whom it was necessary and equitable he should be received, and not rejected, even by those who were not given of the Father to him. Though Christ did not offer or tender the blessings of grace to any, much less to them in general; but as a preacher of the Gospel, published the truths of it to all; and as the Mediator of the new covenant, dispensed the blessings of it to those who *were* (not *should be*) given him by the Father.

4. It is observed,[†] that "Christ here gives a reason why they believed not, namely, *Ye have seen, and believed not; because ye are not given to me of my Father.* Now it is reasonable to conceive this reason should agree with all the other reasons assigned of their infidelity; which yet are manifestly founded, not on anything wanting on the part of God, but in themselves." But it should be observed, that Christ is not here giving a reason why some believed not, but rather why others did, and would believe, while some remained unbelievers in him, who saw his miracles; when others, even all those the Father had given to him, should come to him, and believe in him, and so never perish. But admitting that Christ here gives a reason of the infidelity of some; it is such an one in the sense of it contended for, that is agreeable to other reasons of infidelity elsewhere assigned; such as, *Ye therefore hear not, because ye are not of God,*[‡] do not belong to him, are none of his, neither chosen of him, nor born of him: and in another place, *Ye believe not, because ye are not of my sheep,*[§] whom the Father has given me, and made my care and charge.

5. It is said,[‖] that "the true import of this phrase, *To be given of the Father,*" is,

(1.) To be convinced by the miracles which God wrought by Christ, that he was the Messiah; which appears from the description Christ gives of the persons the Father had given him, John xvii. 8, and from a like expression in the book of Deuteronomy. On which I observe, that as the miracles Christ wrought were by the Spirit of God, so the conviction which came by them, was by the same hand. Hence such who denied Jesus to be the Messiah, against such conviction, sinned the sin against the Holy Ghost, which is unpardonable; whence it follows, that since conviction by miracles that Jesus was the Messiah, is not the act of the Father, but the work of the Spirit; therefore to be so convinced, is not the true import of this phrase. And admitting such a conviction to be the act of God the Father; yet this is what is wrought internally in the consciences of men, and not an act towards them, or concerning them, as this of giving them to Christ is. Add to this, that some persons were convinced by miracles, that Jesus was the Messiah, who never came to him in a spiritual saving way, or believed in him to the saving of their souls, though they might give their assent to his being the Messiah; whereas these words declare, that *all that the Father giveth to* Christ *shall come to him,* and never be cast out, or perish. Nor does this sense of the phrase appear from the description of those who were given to Christ in John xvii. 8, which is spoken of Christ's disciples; for though these *saw his miracles, and believed on him,* and knew that he came from God, and was sent by him, yet this was not all: Christ *manifested* his Father's *name,* person and glory, mind and will, his love and grace, to these *men which he gave* him *out of the world;* which donation of them to him was made antecedent to their seeing of his miracles, and believing in him, to the manifestation of his Father's name unto them. The passage referred to in Deuteronomy[¶] is not all to the purpose; since it appears from thence that miracles may be wrought, and yet not be taken notice of, or men may not be convinced by them: which was the case of the Israelites, to whom *the Lord* did *not give an heart to perceive, and eyes to see.* For to read the words with an interrogation, is contrary to the ancient and modern versions; and still more impertinent is this passage alleged to prove this to be the import of the phrase under consideration.

(2.) It is also urged,[**] that such "are said to be given of the Father to Christ, who are so convinced by his miracles of the truth of the promise of eternal life, as to expect to receive it by faith in him, and obedience to his doctrine; and were so affected with it, as to esteem it above all other things; and so were willing to apply themselves to those duties by which this life might be acquired, and to reject and quit those things which might obstruct them in the prosecution of it." This sense of the phrase not only makes eternal life to be acquired by men's duties, contrary to its being both a promise of grace, and a gift by it, but also makes this act of the Father's to consist in a revelation of the promise of eternal life, and in a conviction of the truth of it by the miracles of Christ; when such a revelation and convic-

---

* See Luke iv. 25—28.

† Whitby. p. 53; ed. 2. 52.

‡ John viii. 47.   § Chap. x. 26.

‖ Whitby. p. 54, 55; ed. 2. 53, 54.

¶ Chap. xxix. 3, 4.   ** Whitby. p. 56; ed. 2. 54, 55.

tion of the truth of it by the miracles of Christ; when such a revelation and conviction are to be ascribed not to the Father of Christ, but to *the Spirit of wisdom and revelation in the knowledge* of Christ, whose proper business it is to *convince of sin, of righteousness, and of judgment ;*[*] and so of the truth of the promise, and of their need of enjoyment of eternal life by Christ. And, supposing all this to be done by the Father, yet this regards something internal in the minds and consciences of men; and not an act concerning them, as is the giving of them to Christ; which is no other than interesting him in them, putting them into his hands, and him into the possession of them, making them his care and charge; which was done, when they were chosen in him unto eternal life before the foundation of the world. To this I take leave to add the two following observations; though they do not properly fall under this head of discourse. That,

2ndly. The doctrine of efficacious grace in conversion is strongly asserted in these words; for such who are given in eternal election, and in the everlasting covenant of grace to Christ, *shall* in time *come unto* him, that is, believe in him. Which is not to be ascribed to any power and will in them, but to the power and grace of God; for there is not in them naturally any will, desire, or inclination, to come to Christ for life; they had rather go any where else, than to him for it; for *no man can come to Christ except the Father draw him.*[†] It is not here said, that such who are given to Christ have a *power* to come to him, or *may* come if they will; but they *shall* come, efficacious grace will bring them to Christ as poor perishing sinners, to venture on him for life and salvation.

3rdly. The doctrine of the saints' final perseverance may be established on this text; for such who come to Christ in a spiritual manner, and are brought to believe in him truly and really, he not only receives them kindly, but keeps and preserves them, and will not cast them out. The words are very strongly and emphatically expressed in the original, οὐ μὴ ἐκβάλω ἔξω, *I will not, not,* or *never, never,* we render it *in nowise cast out without,* or cast out of doors. Christ will never cast them out of his affections, nor out of his arms, nor out of that family that is named of him, nor out of or from his church, which is his body, and of which they are members, nor out of a state of justification and salvation; and therefore they shall never perish, but have everlasting life.

SECTION VII

And as many as were ordained unto eternal life believed.—Acts xiii. 48.

THIS act of ordination to eternal life, is no other than God's act of predestination of some

persons to glory, or his eternal choice and appointment of them to life and salvation by Jesus Christ, which the scriptures frequently speak of. Now, seeing that as many as were ordained to eternal life, did in the times of the apostles, and do in all ages, believe in consequence thereof, election must be an act of God's grace, irrespective of faith, is not on account of the foresight of it; faith being not the cause, but a fruit and effect of it; and it must also relate to particular persons only; since all men have not faith, nor will enjoy eternal life; both which are firmly and infallibly secured by this act of grace to all those who are interested in it. To which is objected,

1. That these words speak not of preordination,[‡] much less of divine preordination. The persons spoken of are not said to be προτεταγμένοι *foreordained,* but τεταγμένοι, *ordained ;* and not said to be ordained *by God,* but were such who disposed themselves unto eternal life. To which I reply, that the words are rendered both by the Vulgate Latin, and by Arias Montanus, quotquot erant præordinati, *as many as were preordained.* And it is certain, that they speak of an ordination to what is future, eternal life, and to that antecedent to believing, and why not then before the foundation of the world, agreeable to other scriptures? especially since there was a promise (and therefore why not a purpose?) of eternal life made by God before the world began.[§] And though here is no mention made of God, yet who can ordain to eternal life, or dispose of it but God? *Eternal life is the gift of God through Jesus Christ our Lord.*[||] And could these words be understood, even of an internal disposition in man unto eternal life; who can dispose unto it, any more than of it, but God? For *we are not sufficient of ourselves, to think anything as of ourselves, but our sufficiency is of God.*[¶]

2. It is said,[**] "That these words cannot signify that there is a fixed number of persons absolutely by God ordained to eternal life, is evident from this consideration, that if the reason why these men believed were only this, that they were men ordained to eternal life, the reason why the rest believed not can be this only, that they were not by God ordained to eternal life. And if so, what necessity could there be, *that the word of God should be first preached to them?* as we read ver. 46. Was it only that their damnation might be the greater? This seems to charge the Lover of souls with the greatest cruelty; what could even their most malicious and enraged enemy do more? This is to make God as instrumental to their ruin as the very devil." To which may be replied, that though faith is a fruit of, and what follows upon, electing grace, and therefore is called *the faith of God's elect,* yet election is

---

* Eph. i. 17 ; John xvi. 8.   † John vi. 44.
‡ Remonstr. Coll. Hag. art. i. p. 93 ; and Act. Synod. circa art. i. p. 61 ; Hammond in loc. ; Limborch, p. 342, 739.   § Tit. i. 2.

|| Rom. vi. 23.   ¶ 2 Cor. iii. 5.
** Whitby, p. 57 ; ed. 2. 56, 57.
†† Eph. ii. 8 ; Col. ii. 12 ; Rom. x. 17.

not the immediate cause of it, but the grace and power of God: hence it is said to be *the gift*, and *of the operation of God*,* and comes *by hearing the word*, as an instrumental means. So, likewise, though unbelief follows upon God's denying his grace, which is agreeable to a previous determination, yet neither the denial of his grace, nor his determination to deny it, is the cause of unbelief, but the vitiosity and corruption of nature, and, therefore not to be charged on God's not ordaining them to eternal life, which is no instance either of cruelty or injustice, for then it would have been both cruel and unjust with God to deny and determine to deny his grace to fallen angels. And whereas it is asked, to what purpose was the word of God preached to them; was it for their greater damnation? I answer, that the preaching of the Gospel to men is not to aggravate the damnation of any; for, though the condemnation of men becomes the greater by it, yet this is only accidental to it, or owing to the wickedness of men, but is not the end and design of God in it, which is partly to gather out his elect from among them, and partly to leave the rest inexcusable, who would be apt to say, Had we heard of Christ, we should have embraced him; had the Gospel been preached to us, as unto others, we had believed, even as they.

3. It is observed,† that "the apostle gives this reason why he turned from the Jews to the Gentiles, because the *Jews thrust away the word of God from them, and judged themselves unworthy of everlasting life*, ver. 46. Whereas, according to this supposition, that could be no sufficient reason; for it was only they among the Jews, who were not ordained to eternal life, that refused to believe and obey the word of God; and as many among the Gentiles, who were not thus ordained, must necessarily do the same." I reply, that the reason was a sufficient one; for these Jews, as a body of men, rejected the Gospel; not one gave heed unto it; wherefore the apostles rightly concluded, that God had no more work for them to do among them; that there were no more of his elect to be gathered out from them, and therefore, they turned to the Gentiles, as the Lord had commanded them; expecting and believing that God would take out of them, through their ministry, a people for his name and glory. And it is easy to observe, that this was the rule of their conduct among the Gentiles; for, according as they were directed by the Spirit of God, or were able to make a judgment, whether God had a people to be called by grace or not, they continued, or departed, or turned aside. Thus they *were forbidden by the Holy Ghost*, at a certain time, *to preach the word of God in Asia;* and when *they assayed to go into Bithynia, the Spirit suffered them not; and passing by Mysia, they came down to Troas*,‡ where, by a vision, they were directed to *Macedonia;* from whence they assuredly ga-

thered, that the Lord had called them to preach the Gospel to them, and that some persons were to be converted there, and not in the other places at that time where they were not permitted to go. The apostle Paul, when he went to Corinth, first preached among the Jews; but they opposing themselves, and blaspheming, he turned to the Gentiles, and had this encouragement from the Lord to continue in his ministrations to them, from this consideration,§ that he had *much people* in that city.

4. Whereas the apostle preached the doctrines of remission of sins, and justification to the Jews, and exhorted them to beware, lest what was spoken of in the prophets should come upon them. It is asked,‖ "Could God have determined that these very persons should not believe to life eternal, and yet commission his apostles to tell them these things? Could it be revealed to St. Paul that they could not believe to life eternal, as being not by God ordained to it; and yet would he so passionately exhort them to that faith in Jesus which he well knew, by virtue of this revelation, belonged not to them, nor could they possibly exert?" But who says that God had determined they should not believe, or that it was revealed to St. Paul that they could not believe to life eternal, as being not by God ordained to it? The apostle Paul, with the rest of the apostles, had a commission to preach the gospel to all nations, beginning with the Jews, which, as it was designed to gather in the elect of God among them, so it was faithfully executed by them. They preached these doctrines of grace promiscuously to all, not knowing who were ordained to eternal life and who were not, or who would believe and who would not; the judgment they were able to form in anywise of these things, did not arise from any special or extraordinary revelation, but from the success of their ministry. Thus, from the Jews rejecting the gospel, and thereby judging themselves unworthy of everlasting life, they might justly fear they were left of God, and did not belong to him, and might rightly conclude that many among the Gentiles were ordained to eternal life, from their believing in Christ; and, therefore, in perfect consistence both with the design of God and the nature of their commission, could, and did preach and propose these things to them.

5. It is urged,¶ that "the words will very well admit of this sense, as many as were *disposed for eternal life believed.*" Which sense is pleaded for from the use of the word τεταγμένος, in this very book of the Acts of the Apostles, and in the Son of Sirach, from some passages in Philo the Jew, from Simplicius on Epictetus, and from the opposition in the context between the indisposed Jews and the disposed Gentiles. To which I reply, that the place referred to in this book is no

---

* Eph. ii. 8; Col. ii. 12; Rom. x. 17.   xviii. 10.   ‖ Whitby, p. 58.   ¶ Ibid.
† Whitby, p. 58; ed. 2. 57; Limborch, p.   p. 59; ed. 2. 58; Remonstr. and Limborch, ubi
342.   ‡ Acts xvi. 6—10.   § Chap.   supra.

proof of such a sense of the word; for it is not the same word in the same simple form with this here that is there used, but as in composition with the preposition διὰ; it is not τεταγμένος, but διατεταγμένος; nor does that signify disposition of mind, but determination and foreappointment. The words are these,* *We went before to ship, and sailed unto Assos, there intending to take in Paul, οὕτω γὰρ ἦν διατεταγμένος, for so had he appointed,* not as Dr. Whitby renders it, *for so was he disposed:* the disposition of his mind is expressed by the following phrase, *minding himself to go afoot.* It is plain that it was a determined case, which had been concerted and agreed upon between Paul and his associates, that they should go with the ship to Assos, and he would go afoot thither, where they should take him in; so that this place, instead of making for, so makes against the sense of the word contended for. The Son of Sirach says,† that *the government,* or *principality of a wise man, is* τεταγμένη, which the Vulgate Latin renders *stabilis erit, shall be stable* or *firm.* The reason is, because it is ordained by God; for, as the apostle Paul says,‡ *the powers that be are* τεταγμέναι, *ordained by God,* which is an instance of the use of the word in favour of our sense of it. The passages out of Philo are no proofs of the word signifying an internal disposition of mind, being allusions to the marshalling and ordering of persons in a military form, which is the frequent use of ταττω in Xenophon and other writers. Though Simplicius interprets τεταγμένος ὑπὸ θεοῦ, in Epictetus,§ by προτρεπόμενος ὑπὸ θεοῦ, yet both the one and the other phrase signify the force and power of the fatal decree, ordaining things; which is made use of as an argument with the philosopher, why he should choose and retain them. For O another place, says Epictetus,‖ *Lead me, O Jupiter, and thou fate,* ὅποι ποθ᾽ ὑμῖν εἰμι διατεταγμένος, *whither I am by you appointed, and I will cheerfully follow.* So ὥρα τεταγμένη, is used by him for a *stated hour,*¶ just as ἡμέρα τεταγμένη is by Porphyry,** for a *fixed day,* or *appointed time.*

But, after all, to settle the true sense of the word in the text, it will be proper to inquire in what sense it is used by the historian Luke, in this book of the Acts of the Apostles, where we shall always find it signifies determination and appointment, and not disposition of mind. So in chap. xv. 2, *When therefore Paul and Barnabas had no small dissension and disputation with them,* ἔταξαν, *they determined that Paul and Barnabas, and certain others of them, should go up to Jerusalem.* Again, in chap. xxii. 10, *The Lord said unto me, Arise, and go into Damascus, and there it shall be told thee of all things which,* τέτακται, *are appointed for thee to do.* Once more, in chap. xxviii. 23, *And when* ταξάμενοι αὐτῷ ἡμέραν, *they had appointed him a day, there came many to him.* By these instances we may judge of

the sense and translation of our text. Besides, both the ancient and modern versions agree in favouring the translation and sense we contend for; nor does the opposition in the context favour the other; for the comparison is not between the blaspheming Jews and the believing Gentiles, but between one part of the Gentiles and the other; the one believing, and the other not; the one being ordained unto eternal life, and the other not ordained to it. Add to this, that the phrase of being *disposed to,* or *for eternal life,* is a very unusual, if not a very improper, and an inaccurate one. Men are said to be disposed to a habit or an action, as to vice or virtue; but not to reward or punishment, as to heaven or hell. Nor does it appear that these Gentiles had any good dispositions to eternal life, antecedent to their believing; for, though they are said, in ver. 42, to beseech the apostles to preach the same things to them the next sabbath, yet the words may be rendered more agreeable to the order in which they lie in the original text thus : *They,* that is, the apostles, παρεκάλουν τὰ ἔθνη, *besought the Gentiles, that these words might be preached to them the next sabbath;*†† that is, they entreated them that they would come and hear them again at such a time. And as for their being *glad,* and *glorifying the word of the Lord,* it is not evident that it was before their believing; and suppose it was, this has been found in persons who have had no true, real, inward dispositions to spiritual things, as in many of our Lord's hearers; and, indeed, there are no such dispositions in men previous to faith in Christ, for *whatsoever is not of faith is sin.* Before believing, men are dead in trespasses and sins, given up unto them, live in them, and fulfil the lusts of the flesh, and are insufficient either to think well or do well. Besides, admitting that there are in some persons good dispositions to eternal life, previous to faith in Christ; and that desiring eternal life, and seeking after it, be accounted such; yet these may be, where faith does not follow. The young man in the Gospel had as many dispositions of this sort, perhaps, as ever any had, who were destitute of faith; and yet was so far from believing in Christ, that he went away from him sorrowful. As many, therefore, as are so disposed unto eternal life do not always believe, faith does not always follow such dispositions. And, after all, one would have thought that the Jews themselves, who were externally religious, and were looking for the Messiah, though they did not believe that Jesus was the Christ; and especially the *devout and honourable women,* were more disposed unto eternal life than the ignorant and idolatrous Gentiles; and yet the latter believed, and the former did not. It follows, then, that their faith did not arise from previous dispositions to eternal life, but was the fruit and effect of divine ordination.

---

* Acts xx. 13. † Eccl. x. 1. ‡ Rom. xiii. 1. § Enchirid, c. 29. ‖ C. 77. ¶ C. 35. ** De Styge, c. 285 ; ed Cantabr. †† Vide Lightfoot, vol. ii. p. 692.

6. Another sense which these words are said* to be capable of, is, that *as many as were well disposed, believed unto eternal life*. But it has been already proved, that τεταγμένοι, does not signify *well disposed;* and as for joining the phrase *eternal life,* to the word ἐπίστευσαν, *believed;* that stands at too great a distance to admit of such a construction: and should it be allowed, it would make no considerable alteration in the sense of the text; which would be read thus, *as many as were ordained, believed unto eternal life;* that is, as many as were chosen of God, and appointed by him to obtain salvation by Jesus Christ, believed in him to the saving of their souls. Let the words be placed in construction either way, the sense is the same.

SECTION VIII

For whom he did foreknow, he also did predestinate to be conformed to the image of his Son; that he might be the first-born among many brethren. Moreover, whom he did predestinate, them he also called; and whom he called, them he also justified; and whom he justified, them he also glorified.—Rom. viii. 29, 30.

THE meaning of these words is, that those whom God foreknew, or loved with an everlasting love, he predestinated to conformity to his Son; which conformity begins in grace, and will be finished in glory; and whom he has thus predestinated to grace and glory, he in time calls unto both; and whom he calls by his powerful and efficacious grace, he justifies by the righteousness of his Son, revealed to them by his Spirit, and received by faith; and whom he justifies, he will glorify, with the enjoyment of himself to all eternity. Whence it follows, that those, and none but those who are called, justified, and glorified, are loved by God with an everlasting love, and appointed unto salvation by Christ: and that all those, and none but those who are foreknown, or loved by God with a special love, and are predetermined to grace and glory, shall certainly be called with a holy calling, be completely justified by Christ's righteousness, and at last be eternally glorified. So that these words confirm the doctrine of the eternal predestination, or election of particular persons to salvation. Now to set aside this sense of the words, and the argument upon it in favour of this doctrine, the Arminians† have given us another sense of them, which is this: that those whom God foresaw would be true lovers of him, and devoted to his service, and whom he approved of as persons fit to be received into his favour, he foreappointed to be like to his Son in sufferings; and whom he thus predestinated, he in due time called to suffer; and whom he thus called to suffer, upon their faith and patience under their sufferings, he approved of as sincere and faithful servants; and whom he thus justified or approved of, he gave them a glorious reward of all their sufferings; or he made them glorious under sufferings by the Spirit of glory and of God resting on them; or by giving them his Holy Spirit, to enable them to work the greatest miracles.‡ But,

1. The *foreknowledge* here spoken of, is not of men's works or graces, as the cause and reason of their predestination; since these are fruits and effects of it, and what follow from it; and therefore can never be the causes of it. It is true that God foreknew who would believe and love him, and be devoted to him; he having determined to bestow these graces on them, and ordained or prepared good works for them, that they should walk in them. The text does not say, that those whom God foreknew would be lovers of him, or fit for his kingdom, or devoted for his service, he predestinated; these are additions to it, and neither expressed nor implied in it; it only says, *whom he foreknew;* and which is owned§ "to relate to God's affectionate knowledge of these persons, as his chosen generation, his peculiar people:" words of knowledge being often expressive of affection, Psal. i. 6, Jer. i. 5, 2 Tim. ii. 17, Matt. vii. 23. And it may be justly added, that it relates to God's affectionate knowledge of them from all eternity: since they were so early his chosen generation, and peculiar people, and as early loved by him with an everlasting love; to which, and to which alone, their predestination, or election to eternal life, is owing, and is the true meaning of the phrase here; whom God thus foreknew, or affectionately loved before the world began, them he predetermined, or foreappointed, to everlasting happiness. Hence,

2. The *predestination* of these persons to *be conformed to the image* of Christ, is not a foreappointment of them to be like him in sufferings: for though the saints are appointed unto sufferings, and sufferings or afflictions are appointed for them; and though there is some likeness between Christ the head and the members of his body in suffering; yet this cannot be intended here: since the image of Christ, to which they are predestinated to be conformed, always designs something great and glorious, and not mean and abject; it is *the image of the heavenly,* in opposition to the *image of the earthly;* and is no other than *the glory of the Lord,* into which the saints are *changed from glory to glory, even as by the Spirit of the Lord.*‖ Besides, Christ is never said to be *the first-born* with respect to afflictions, but with respect to pre-eminence, honour, and glory; see Psal. lxxxix. 28, Col. i. 18, Rev. i. 5. This conformity to the image of Christ, to which they are predestinated who are loved by God, seems ra-

---

* Whitby, p. 60; ed. 2. 59.

† Remonstr. in Coll. Hag. art. i. p. 93; Curcellæus, p. 375; Limborch, p. 345, 346. Though Arminius himself owns that these words are to be understood of eternal predestination to grace and glory. Disput. Privat. Thess. xl. p. 309, inter ejus opera, ed. 4°.

‡ Whitby, p. 61, 63—65, 447; ed. 2. 60, 62—64, 435, 436.   § Whitby, p. 448.

‖ 1 Cor. xv. 47; 2 Cor. iii. 18.

ther to be a spiritual likeness to Christ, which is begun in this world upon believers, and will be finished in the other; when they *shall be like him* both in soul and body, as perfectly as they will be capable of; when the great ends of predestinating grace will be fully answered upon them; or rather, particularly, this conformity is to be understood of a likeness to the filiation of Christ, or a likeness to the image of Christ as the Son of God; for though the saints are not in the same class of sonship with Christ, yet their sonship bears some resemblance to his; as he is the Son of God by nature, they are the sons of God by grace; as he is the dear Son of God, they are the dear children of God; as he is the first-born among many brethren, they are the first-born with respect to the angels; and as he has an inheritance, being heir of all things, so have they, being heirs of God, and joint-heirs with Christ; which likeness of sonship will more fully appear hereafter; for though *now are we the sons of God, it doth not yet appear what we shall be: but we know that when he shall appear, we shall be like him; for we shall see him as he is.** This sense of the words is strengthened by a parallel place, Eph. i. 5. *Having predestinated us to the adoption of children by Jesus Christ to himself, according to the good pleasure of his will.* Besides, it is owned,[†] that "according to the received interpretation of the *ancient fathers*, the import of these words is this; that whom God foreknew, he predetermined to render conformable to the image of his Son, that is, to be like him in glory:" or as in another place,[‡] "he predestinated, or foreappointed them to be conformed to the image of his Son, their elder brother; that is, to be *sons of God and joint-heirs with Christ;*" and the § author I am concerned with, after he had considered the text in every light: "conceives the sense of it to be this; those whom he hath so foreknown as to make them *his elect*, and *peculiar people;* for them he hath designed the choicest blessings, even the adoption of sons, and their being co-heirs with Christ." Wherefore,

3. The *calling* here intended, is not of persons to suffering in this life: for though such who are called by grace, are generally an afflicted people, they meet with many afflictions between their call to glory, and the enjoyment of it; yet they are not properly called to them, but to faith and patience under them: which is the meaning of the words of the apostle;‖ *If when ye do well, and suffer for it, ye take it patiently, this is acceptable with God; for even hereunto were ye called,* that is, not so much to sufferings, as to patience under them. And when in other places the saints are said to be called, it is either to grace or glory; thus they are called unto

marvellous light, unto *liberty*, to *the fellowship of his Son Jesus Christ*, to *peace* and holiness, to a *kingdom and glory*, even to *the obtaining of the glory of our Lord Jesus Christ;*¶ and here, in the context, they are said to be** *called according to his purpose;* which is the same with being *called with an holy calling, according to the grace which was given us in Christ before the world began.*†† Besides, all that are called to afflictions, or sufferings, are not justified and glorified; as for instance, the young man in the Gospel, to whom Christ said, *Take up the cross and follow me,* who was *sad at that saying, and went away grieved:* and all such professors, who, *when tribulation or persecution ariseth because of the word, by and by are offended.*‡‡ Add to this, that according to the received interpretation of the ancient fathers, the sense of the phrase is,§§ that "whom God foreappointed to be the sons of God, the method he used to bring them to this adoption was this; to call them to the faith of Christ; or as elsewhere‖‖ expressed, "them also, in due time, he called to the salvation promised and offered in the gospel." And our author himself, at last¶¶ conceives this to be the sense of it: "that in order to this adoption designed for them, it is that he hath chosen them out of the world to be his church, an holy nation, and peculiar people to himself." And therefore,

4. When God is said to have *justified* the persons whom he foreknew, predestinated, and called; the meaning is not, that he *approved* of them as sincere and faithful, on the account of their faith and patience in suffering: for though God does approve of, and is well pleased with the faith and patience of his people under afflictions, yet no instance can be produced of the use of the word in this sense: not James ii. 21, 25, where Abraham and Rahab are said to be *justified by works;* the meaning of which is, not that they were approved of by Christ, or accepted by him on account of their works, but that their faith was evidenced to the world, their cause vindicated, and they cleared by them from all false charges and imputations: nor Matt. xi. 19, where *wisdom* is said to be *justified of her children;* that is, not barely approved of by them, but vindicated, and acquitted from the charge of libertinism: nor Matt. xii. 37, where it is said, *by thy words thou shalt be justified, and by thy words thou shalt be condemned;* since justification stands directly opposite to condemnation, and is used in a forensic sense, as it is throughout this epistle to the Romans, and in this very chapter and context. Besides, according to the above-mentioned received interpretation of the ancient fathers, the sense of the expression is,*** that "whom God in due time

---

* 1 John iii. 2.   † Whitby, p. 63; ed. 2. 62.   ‡ Ibid. p. 448; ed. 2. 436.
§ Ibid. p. 449; ed. 2. 437.
‖ 1 Pet. ii. 20, 21.   ¶ 1 Pet. ii. 9; Gal. v. 13; 1 Cor. i. 9; Rom. i. 7; Col. iii. 15; 1 Thess. ii. 12; 2 Thess. ii. 14.

** Ver. 28.   †† 2 Tim. i. 9.
‡‡ Mark x. 21, 22; Matt. xiii. 21.
§§ Whitby, p. 448; ed. 2. 436.
‖‖ Ibid. p. 63; ed. 2. 62.
¶¶ Ibid. p. 449; ed. 2. 437.
*** Whitby, p. 63; ed. 2. 62.

called, and they believing in Christ upon this call, he justified them from, and remitted all their past sins. And according to our author's* last conception of it, the meaning is, "he hath justified them, or given them a full remission of their sins." Hence,

5. The *glorification* of them is not a making them glorious under sufferings; much less by them the extraordinary gifts of the Spirit to enable them to work miracles. The word is never used in this sense : not in 2 Cor. iii. 8—11, where the Gospel ministration is said to be ἐν δόξη *in glory;* but not on the account of the extraordinary gifts and miracles of the Holy Ghost, but because it is *the ministration of the spirit of righteousness,* and *of life,* in opposition to the law, *the ministration of condemnation and death;* and because it *remains* when the law is *done away;* and is attended with evidence, clearness, and perspicuity, when the legal dispensation had a great deal of darkness and obscurity in it : nor John xvii. 22, where our Lord says, *The glory which thou gavest me, I have given them;* which is not to be understood of the miraculous gifts of the Spirit; since the words are spoken not of the apostles only, but of all them that *should believe* in Christ *through their word,* ver. 20, but rather of the glorious gospel of the blessed God, and the excellent truths and doctrines of it; see ver. 8 : nor Acts iii. 13, where it is said, that *God hath glorified his Son Jesus Christ;* which was done, not by bestowing the extraordinary gifts of the Spirit on him, nor merely by the miracle then wrought, by the raising him from the dead, ver. 15; the thing he prayed for under this expression, John xvii. 1, and firmly believed, John xiii. 31, 32. Moreover, God is never said to glorify his people in this way. It is true, indeed, miracles were wrought, that *the Son of God might be glorified,* John xi. 5. And in this way the Father did *honour* the Son, John viii. 54. And Christ was *glorified of all* on this account, Luke iv. 15. And the Spirit of God now *glorifies* Christ by receiving of his, and showing them to his people, John xvi. 15. But God is never said to glorify them by these gifts. Indeed some of the members of Christ's body are *honoured* with gifts and graces more than others, 1 Cor. xii. 26. And should it be allowed, that extraordinary gifts are intended in this last-cited passage; yet this cannot be the meaning of the word here : since the apostle is speaking not of particular persons, but of all the saints in general, who were the sons and heirs of God, ver. 17; had received the first-fruits of the Spirit, and were waiting for the adoption, ver. 23; all who loved God, and were his called according to his purpose, ver. 28; even all God's elect, ver. 33. Now all these are not glorified in this sense; besides, were this the meaning of the phrase, then none would be predestinated, called, and justified, but such as have the extraordinary gifts of the Spirit : and on the other hand, none would have the extraordinary gifts of the Spirit but such as are predestinated, called, and justified : whereas, it is certain, that many might have, and had in the apostles' days, such gifts, and yet were destitute of the grace of God. It is much more agreeable to the context, and to the analogy of faith, to understand this phrase of eternal glory; since it is what the apostle speaks of in ver. 17, 18, 21, 23, and is what God's elect are predestinated and called unto; and what the righteousness of Christ, by which they are justified, gives them a right and title to; and which they shall certainly enjoy. The main objection† to *this sense* of the phrase is, "That when the apostle speaks of our final justification (glorification it should be) in this chapter, he still speaks of it as a thing future; saying, *We shall be glorified with him,* ver. 17, 18, 21. Whereas here he speaks of it as a thing past; saying, *Whom he hath justified, them he hath also glorified.*" To which may be replied, Not to insist upon the change of tense, the past for the future, which is no unusual thing in scripture; this is strictly true of that part of the body of God's elect, who are already in heaven, called *the family in heaven,* and *the things in heaven;* who *through faith and patience have inherited the promises:*‡ and is in some sense true also of the other part on earth, who are called and justified; since they are made glorious both by the robe of Christ's righteousness put upon them, and by the grace of Christ wrought in them; which makes them *all glorious within,* and is the beginning of eternal glory; for a saving knowledge of God in Christ is *life eternal.* Nor ought this sense of the phrase to be objected to by our opponents; seeing if such may be said to be glorified, who had the gifts of working miracles, much more may they be said to be so, who have the true grace of the Spirit, which is superior to all other gifts. Besides, God's elect may be said to be glorified, because of the certainty of their glorification. It is a kingdom prepared for them from the foundation of the world; which Christ has gone afresh to prepare by his presence and mediation in our nature; which he is in the possession of on the behalf of his people, and which is ascertained to their faith and hope : hence they are said to be *saved by hope,* and *by grace through faith.*§ Add to this, that they are in the same sense glorified in Christ, their representative head; in which they are said to be *raised together,* and *made to sit together in heavenly places* in him.‖

SECTION IX

Nevertheless the foundation of God standeth sure; having this seal, The Lord knoweth them that are his.—2 Tim. ii. 19.

IF the Lord knows them that are his, in distinction from others who are not his, and loves them with a special, peculiar, and ever-

---

* Ibid. p. 449; ed. 2. 437.   † Whitby, p. 64; ed. 2. 63.   ‡ Eph. iii. 15; Coloss. i. 20; Heb. vi. 12.   § Rom. viii. 24; Eph. ii. 8.   ‖ Eph. ii. 6.

lasting love; then there is a select number, whom God has chosen to be his by a firm, immutable, and unalterable act of his grace, which *stands sure* and inviolable. But, the Lord knows them that are his: therefore, in answer to this argument,

1. It is observed,* "That by the foundation of God, we are to understand the doctrine of the resurrection; which is the foundation of the church, Matt. xvi. 18; of our faith and hope, 1 Cor. xv. 19, 1 Thess. iv. 13, 14, styled τὸ θεμέλιον, *the foundation of the doctrine of the resurrection*, Heb. vi. 1, 2; the faithful saying, ver. 11, by denying of which the Christian faith is overturned, ver. 18, to which fundamental doctrine God hath set this seal, for confirmation of it, *The Lord knoweth them that are his;* that is, loveth and approveth of them, so as to reward them at the resurrection." To which may be replied, that it will easily be granted that the doctrine of the future resurrection of the dead is spoken of in the context: nor will it be denied, that it was a fundamental article in the Jewish creed, Heb. vi. 1, 2; or of the Christian faith, 1 Cor. xv. 13, 14, 19. Though it does not seem to be the foundation of the church, Matt. xvi. 18, but the doctrine of Christ's deity and sonship, owned by Peter, or rather the person of Christ himself, whom he confessed: nor does it seem to be intended here; seeing the seal, *The Lord knoweth them that are his*, which regards particular persons, cannot well agree with it; since the resurrection will be both of the just and unjust. And if only the doctrine of the resurrection to eternal life is intended; and the meaning is, that God stands so kindly affected to his people, his sheep, whom he has given to Christ, that though they die, he will raise them up to eternal life; this is so far from militating against, that it rather establishes the doctrine of absolute election, Besides, *the foundation* of God standing sure, here spoken of, is opposed not to the error and heresy of Hymeneus and Philetus; but to the persons of them, and others, who through them apostatized from the faith: so that by *the foundation of God*, is to be understood the church of the living God, *the pillar and ground of truth,†* which holds it forth, supports, and maintains it; even *the general assembly and church of the first-born, which are written in heaven;‡* the whole body of the elect; that *church* which is built upon a *rock*, the immoveable foundation, Jesus Christ, against which *the gates of hell cannot prevail;§* who every one of them are brought in time to possess, and exercise the faith which is||, *the substance of things hoped for*, and will never fail: to these persons this seal is annexed, *the Lord knoweth them that are his;* he knows whom he has chosen, he loves them with a peculiar affection, takes care of them, provides for them, protects them, so as that they shall never perish.

2. It is also observed,¶ "That these words are taken from Numb. xvi. 5, where, as it is declared, that *God knoweth them that are his*, that are separated to his service, and will maintain their cause and calling, against all opposers; so here, that God will own his apostles and ministers, against all those that set up against them." Be it so, that the apostle refers to the place cited; yet as there Moses speaks of persons, whom God had chosen to be priests, whom he would stand by and preserve, whilst the earth swallowed up their opposers, from whose tents the Israelites were bid to depart; so here the apostle speaks of a *chosen generation, a royal priesthood*, who were made *kings and priests:* titles under the gospel-dispensation, not peculiar to ministers, but common to them, with all the saints; who are opposed not only to Hymeneus and Philetus, but to those whose faith was subverted by them; and who should stand, though they fell, being under the special notice and care of God; and are therefore bid to depart from apostates, their doctrines, and practices; *let every one*, not only ministers, but all *that name the name of Christ, depart from iniquity*, as an evidence of their election, and the means of their final perseverance. The simile the apostle uses in ver. 20, 21, of *vessels of gold and silver, and also of wood and of earth, some* being *to honour, and some to dishonour*, is much the same with that he uses in Rom. ix. 22, 23, and manifestly shows that he is speaking of elect persons, in opposition to others. Nor does Theodoret's descant upon these words, mentioned by our author, contradict the doctrine of absolute election, when he says, *God foreknoweth both them that believe, and those who openly fight against the truth.*

SECTION X,

For as by one man's disobedience many were made sinners.—Rom. v. 19.

THE reason why this text comes to be considered in this discourse of election is, because it is said,** that the "foundation of this decree is laid in the sin of Adam, imputed by God's arbitrary will to his posterity." Though this author must needs have known, that the Supralapsarians especially consider the decree of election as antecedent to and irrespective of the fall of Adam; and therefore the sin of Adam, and the imputation of it to his posterity, could not be the foundation of such a decree; which has no other foundation than the sovereign will and pleasure of God. However, I shall consider the objections made to this doctrine.

1st. As to the objections†† made against "Adam's sin being every man's personal sin, and consented to by every man's personal will; because it is said,‡‡ in Adam there was not only the will of one singular man, but the universal will of all mankind, and of

---

* Whitby, p. 67; ed. 2. 66.   † 1 Tim. iii. 15.   ‡ Heb. xii. 23.   § Matt. xvi. 18.
|| Heb. xi. 1.   ¶ Whitby, p. 68; ed. 2. 67.

** Ibid. p. 77; ed. 2. 76. —81; ed. 2. 78, 79.   †† Ibid. p. 79   ‡‡ Davenant's Animadv. on Hord, p. 231.

every singular person," I have no concern with; let such who fall in with these assertions defend them: for I must own, that if Adam's sin is every man's personal sin, then every man must have personally existed in Adam, and personally sinned in him; and then this sin being personal with respect to them, must also be actual; and so the distinction between original and actual sin must drop. Moreover, if this is every man's personal sin, it must be their own; and then they are not made sinners by another, but by their own disobedience; and not by the sin of one, but by the sin of many. Besides, this seems repugnant to the doctrine of the imputation of Adam's sin to his posterity: since, if it is their personal sin, then not theirs by imputation, in the sense we use the word, and which is the doctrine we undertake to defend. But,

2ndly. It is said,* that it "cannot truly be affirmed that we all sinned in Adam, and by his disobedience were made sinners; because his sin and disobedience was, by God's arbitrary will, imputed to us. For,

1. "The Scripture nowhere maketh mention of anything of another's imputed to any man for reward or guilt, but only of some personal thing or action of his own." To which I reply, that the imputation of Adam's sin is not to be placed to the mere arbitrary will of God; but the ground and foundation of it is the law, or covenant of works, made with Adam, and broken by him, as the federal head of his posterity: the constitution and tenor of which was, that what he did as such, either in a way of sin, or righteousness, should be imputed to his posterity. And when we use the word *imputation*, we use it not in a moral sense, as when a man's own personal action, good or bad, is accounted to him: but in a forensic sense, as when the debts of one man are in a legal way transferred, and placed to the account of another. And in this sense, the Scripture makes mention of the things of one imputed to another for guilt, or for obligation to payment or punishment; as when Paul said† to Philemon, concerning Onesimus, *if he hath wronged thee, or oweth thee anything, put that on my account*, τοῦτο ἐμοὶ ἐλλόγει, let that be imputed to me; in this sense God *laid on* Christ, made to meet upon him, and imputed to him, *the iniquity of us all;* and he, by imputation, *was made sin for us:* and on the other hand, God *imputeth* to us his *righteousness, without* any consideration of our *works.‡*

2. It is argued,§ "either this imputation makes the sin of Adam truly ours, or it does not; if it does not, how can we be made sinners by it? if it does, then death came upon us for *our sin;* and so not for *the sin of one*, but for the sin of all." I answer, the imputation of Adam's sin makes it truly ours in the same sense as the imputation of Christ's righteousness makes that truly ours. Now

the imputation of Christ's obedience and righteousness, though it makes it truly ours, gives us an interest in it, so as that we have the benefit of it, and it is styled *the righteousness of the saints;* yet it does not make Christ's obedience our act, nor so ours, but that it is still another's, and distinct from our righteousness, and is in Christ as its proper subject and author, though put upon us, and imputed to us. So the imputation of Adam's sin, though it makes it truly ours, so that we are involved in the guilt and punishment of it through the federal relation he stood in to us; yet it does not make it our act, or so ours, but that it is his act, and is distinct from our actual transgressions, and is only ours by imputation; and so we are made sinners by, and death comes upon us for, not our sin, nor the sin of all, but of one.

3. It is asked,‖ "Whether this imputation made the posterity of Adam sinners, or whether it found them so before? If the latter, it was plainly needless, for they might have been condemned to death without it; if the former, then, since this imputation is the act of God, and not of man, it plainly follows that God must be the author of this sin." I reply, that though this act makes them sinners, yet not inherently, only imputatively; it puts sin upon them, and reckons it to them, but does not put any sin in them. And though this imputation is God's act, it does not follow that therefore he is the author of this sin: the imputation of Christ's righteousness is God's act, yet not he but Christ is the author of that righteousness; so, though the imputation of Adam's sin to his posterity is God's act, yet not God but Adam is the author of the sin. And whereas it is insinuated,¶ that this "imputation must be false, as charging them with sin whom he did not find sinners;" it should be observed, what has been already said, that imputation is to be taken not in a moral but forensic sense; and does not imply any false measures taken, or wrong judgment passed, any more than when the debts of one man are by agreement reckoned to another, who previous to that imputation owed the creditor nothing. And whereas it is further urged,** that "if Adam's sin becomes ours only by imputation, it deserves condemnation only by the same, to which action of God it is to be ascribed; whence, according to this opinion, man's destruction must be of God." It may be replied, that as the placing of one man's debt to another's account by agreement, which is no criminal action, is not that for which the other man is cast into prison and suffers, but the debt itself; so it is not the imputation of Adam's sin, but the sin imputed, for which condemnation and death passed upon men.

4. It is observed,†† that "we are not guilty of any other sin of Adam; therefore we are

---

* Whitby, p. 81; ed. 2. 80.
† Philemon, ver. 18.   ‡ Isa. liii. 6;
2 Cor. v. 21; Rom. iv. 6.   § Whitby,

p. 81; ed. 2. 80.   ‖ Whitby, p. 81;
ed. 2. 80.   ¶ Ibid.   ** Ibid. p.
82; ed. 2. 81.   †† Ibid. p. 81; ed. 2. 80.

not guilty of the first sin of Adam." But this does not follow, the reason for the one and the other not being the same: when Adam committed his first sin, he stood as a federal head to his posterity, which is the true reason of their being involved in it; but upon his commission of this sin, he ceased to stand in this relation, the covenant was broken, and it was hereafter impossible for him to perform sinless obedience, and in that way convey life to his offspring. He ceasing to be their covenant-head, they have no farther concern with him, or what he did afterwards; hence neither his after sins, nor his repentance, nor good works, are imputed to them; and this may be an answer to such queries,* why " should they be charged only with his first, and not with his following transgressions? or, why should his guilt rather be imputed to them than his repentance?" But,

3rdly. The covenant, or "compact made with Adam,† is represented as forged, exceeding cruel, and plainly inconsistent with the justice, wisdom, and goodness of our gracious God; and invented to excuse him from cruelty, in subjecting myriads of men and infants to the most direful and lasting torments, which without this imaginary pact he could not with the least pretence of justice do." That Adam was a covenant-head to his posterity may be proved, which he could not be if there was no covenant subsisting; besides, those words of God to Adam,‡ Of every tree of the garden thou mayest freely eat, but of the tree of the knowledge of good and evil, thou shall not eat of it, for in the day that thou eatest thereof thou shalt surely die, are expressive of a covenant. The threatening of death in a case of disobedience implied and included a promise of life in case of obedience. This being proposed to Adam, and he consenting to it, formally constituted a covenant; in which he was considered not as a private but public person, having all his posterity in his loins. This compact therefore is no forgery; and where is the cruelty of it? since had Adam stood, his posterity had been partakers of his righteousness, and of all the benefits and advantages arising from it. Yes, but then it is said, his righteousness was a defectible one, liable to be lost, either afterwards by himself, or some one of his posterity, which would have put them in the same sad case they are now. But why should it be thought that Adam's righteousness would have been any more defectible than that of the angels? Why may it not as well be concluded, that had Adam stood upon the trial of his obedience, that, he and his posterity would have been secured from after-falling, or been made impeccable as the angels are? And where is the inconsistence of this compact with the justice, wisdom, and goodness of God? Did not God make a covenant with Abraham, and by it obliged his posterity in future ages to the observance of circumcision? Is it

any unusual thing, or an unjust, or an unwise action, for men to make covenants, and bind their children unborn to the performance of them. Has it not been reckoned just both with God and men, that in some cases children should be punished for their parents' sins? Does not God say, that he will visit the iniquities of the fathers upon the children unto the third and fourth generation of them that hate him?§ Does not the treason of a nobleman taint his blood, and involve his posterity, until restored? Is not such a procedure according to the law of nature and nations, and justified by the sense and practice of mankind?

4thly. It is said,‖ that the words of the apostle, by one man's disobedience many were made sinners, must have a metonymical sense; and the meaning is, that they were obnoxious to death for his sin, or that they become sinners by a metonymy of the effect, by suffering the punishment God had threatened to Adam for it. But this is to depart from the proper signification of the phrase; no instance can be produced of the apostle's using it in this sense, either in the context or elsewhere: the word ἁμαρτωλοὶ always signifies persons guilty of a fault, and only obnoxious to death for that fault. This sense of the words is contrary to the apostle's scope and design, which is, to give an account of the original of sin, and how condemnation and death came upon men through Adam's sin, and their being made sinners by it, is contrary to the distinction he all along makes between sin and death, the one being the cause, the other the effect, and is to be disproved by the sense of the opposite part of the text, by the obedience of one shall many be made righteous. The active obedience of Christ is opposed to Adam's act of disobedience; the righteous are opposed to sinners; and a being made righteous by the one, is opposed to a being made sinners by the other. Now, by the rule of opposition, as to be made righteous by Christ's obedience, is to be formally constituted and accounted so for the sake of his obedience and righteousness; and, in consequence of it, such become partakers of freedom from condemnation and death. So to be made sinners by Adam's disobedience, is to be formally constituted and esteemed sinners on the account of it; and, in consequence thereof, become obnoxious to condemnation and death. Nor will the parallel of Christ bearing our sins, and being made sin for us, at all help this sense of the words; since Christ bore our sins, and was made sin for us, not barely by bearing and suffering the punishment of sins, but by the imputation of them to him; in consequence of which imputation he was made a curse, and bore and suffered the punishment due to sin. And, after all, it will not be easy to reconcile this with the justice of God, that men should be obnoxious to death for Adam's sin, and suffer the punishment threatened

---

* Whitby, p. 79; ed. 2. 78.   † Ibid.
p. 83, 84; ed. 2. 82, 83.   ‡ Gen. ii. 15,
17.   § Exod. xx. 5.   ‖ Whitby,
p. 85; ed. 2. 84.

him, when they are no ways chargeable with the guilt of it; what reason can be given, why they should suffer death for that sin of which they are in no sense guilty?

CHAPTER III

OF REDEMPTION

THE following *sections* contain a vindication of some *arguments* taken from passages of Scripture in favour of particular redemption, which Dr. Whitby calls *objections* to the universal scheme, and which he attempts to answer in the first, second, and fifth chapters of his discourse, concerning the extent of Christ's redemption; to which he premises the state of the question, by showing what limitations and restrictions of our Lord's general redemption he cannot admit of, and in what sense they who maintain that doctrine assert it. The distinctions of Christ's dying *sufficiently* for all, but *intentionally* only for the elect, and for all if they will believe and repent, but moreover for the elect, to procure faith and repentance for them, he rejects; and which, for my own part, I can no more admit of than himself. He adds positively, that Christ died equally for all, for Judas as for Peter, though not *absolutely*, but conditionally, or so as that they should be made partakers of the blessings of his salutary passion, upon condition of their faith, repentance, and sincere obedience to the laws of the new covenant; but did not purchase actual pardon or reconciliation for all men, only put all men, by his death, in a capacity of being justified and pardoned upon their conversion and faith. On the other hand, I firmly believe that Christ died for all the elect of God, and them only; that, by his death, he has procured for them actual pardon, reconciliation, and salvation; and, that in consequence of the absolute and unconditional covenant of grace being ratified and confirmed by his blood, faith and repentance are bestowed upon and wrought in these persons, not as conditions but blessings of that covenant; in which way they are brought to the full enjoyment of that salvation Christ has obtained for them. Which is what I undertake to vindicate.

SECTION I

Even as the Son of man came not to be ministered unto, but to minister, and to give his life a ransom for many.—Matt. xx. 28.

THESE words not only express the great blessing of redemption, and the Author of it, *the Son of man*, a character of the Messiah, and the manner of his obtaining it, by giving *his life*, his own life, *a ransom*, a redemption price *for*, in the room and stead of the persons redeemed by him, but also point out the persons ransomed, who are said to be *many*, not *all*, and so may be considered as a proof of particular redemption; since, as our opponents themselves allow,[*] that though "all men certainly are many, yet many are not necessarily all." To which the following things are objected.

1st. That [†] "since what is, in some few places, said of many, is not only in more, but in the same places said of all, it is certain that Christ cannot be said to die for many exclusively of *all*." To which I reply: that we do not say Christ died for many exclusive of *all*, for then he must die for none; but that he died for many exclusive of *some*; nor are the places fewer in which he is said to die for many, than those which say he died for all; nor is it true, that what is in some places said of many, is in the same places said of all. But let us consider the passages themselves. And,

1. Begin with the text under consideration, on which this observation [‡] is made; "that the same Scripture which saith, Christ gave *his life a ransom for many*, says also, that he *gave himself a ransom for all*." This is, indeed, said in the same book of Scripture, but not in the same passage of Scripture; nor is the text referred to, 1 Tim. ii. 6, to be understood of every individual of mankind, but either of some of all sorts, or of the Gentiles as well as Jews, as has been shown in the former part of this work; and in which sense, perhaps, the word *many*, in this text, is to be taken, as Grotius [§] himself upon it observes. Moreover, all those for whom Christ gave his life a ransom, are either ransomed by it, or they are not; that all are not ransomed, or redeemed from sin, the law, Satan, and the second death, is evident, since many live under the power of their sins, and, at last, die in them; and, having sinned against the law, are under it, and the curses of it, and will be punished by it; nor are they delivered from the bondage of Satan, but are *led captive by him at his will*, all their days, and their everlasting *portion is the second death*. Now, if some persons, for whom Christ gave his life a ransom, are not ransomed, then that shocking absurdity, which follows upon the notion of men's justification by their own obedience to the law, follows upon this, namely, that *Christ is dead in vain*, or, that so far he gave his life for a ransom in vain; wherefore it will be rightly concluded, that he did not give his life a ransom for every individual man. Besides, such who are ransomed by Christ, are represented as a *peculiar people*;[||] they are called *the ransomed of the Lord*, to distinguish them from others, and by the name of *Jacob*, which, when mystically or figuratively understood, only designs the church of God. Add to

---

* Whitby, p. 115; ed. 2. 113. So Limborch, p. 325.   † Ibid.   ‡ Ibid.

§ Quanquam πολλοὶ interdum omnes significat, puto tamen hoc verbum δοῦναι, et prepositionem ἀντὶ, cum effectu intelligendum, ideoque agi de credituris in Christum, qui ideo vocentur πολλοὶ, hoc loco et apud Dau. ix. 27, רבים. Ut intelligantur ad eum numerum non Judæi tantum sed et alienigenæ pertinere. Grotius in loc.

|| Tit. ii. 14; Isa. xxxv. 10; Jer. xxxi. 11.

this, that such whom Christ gave his life a ransom for, are described by such characters as cannot agree with every individual of mankind, such as *the church, the children of God, his sheep and people,*[*] unless all mankind can be thought to be the church of God, the sheep of Christ, and his special people.

2. It is further observed,[†] "that he who said, *This is my blood shed for many, for the remission of sins,* said also, for that very reason, *drink ye all of it,* for it was shed *for you, for the remission* of sins." But it should be considered, that the *all* Christ bid to drink of the cup were his immediate disciples and apostles; and, should it be extended to others, it can only design such who are the true disciples of Christ; who only share in the remission of sins, and therefore ought only to drink of the cup. If the blood of Christ was shed for the remission of the sins of all mankind, then all their sins would be remitted, or Christ's blood must be shed in vain; but it is certain, that the sins of all men are not remitted; the sins of many will be brought into judgment, and for them, they will be everlastingly punished. And, therefore, there is reason to believe Christ's blood was not shed for them, since there is such an efficacy in that blood, to *cleanse from all sin;* and God, on the account of it, is *just and faithful to forgive us our sin, and to cleanse us from all unrighteousness.*[‡]

3. "That there is no inconsistence betwixt dying for many and for all, is [§] said to be evident from this consideration, that even in the same chapter the apostle saith, that by one sin of *Adam many* died, Rom. v. 15, and *all* died, ver. 12; *many were made sinners,* ver. 19, *and all sinned,* ver. 12; and that *by the obedience of one shall many be made righteous,* δικαιοι κατασταθήσονται, shall be justified, ver. 19; and that *by the righteousness of one, the free gift came upon all men to justification of life,* ver. 18." To which I answer, that it will be readily allowed, that the many that sinned and died in Adam, and through his offence, are the same with the *all* that sinned and died in him on the account of it, and that these intend all mankind, to whom Adam was a representative head; also it will be granted, that the many who are made righteous by the obedience of Christ, are the same with the *all* on whom the free gift comes to justification of life; but then these regard not all mankind, but such to whom he is a representative head, and who are his spiritual seed and offspring; for if all mankind were made righteous and justified by Christ, they would be all saved and glorified; *whom he justified, them he also glorified,* and none would be condemned; whereas the sentence, *go, ye cursed,* &c., will not only be pronounced, but executed on many.

4. It is also urged,[‖] "that in the same epistle in which it is said, "Christ *bore the sins of many,* it is expressly said, *he tasted death for every man.*" As to the latter expression, it has been made to appear, in the former part of this performance, that it is to be understood not of every individual man, but of the sons, the children, the brethren, the church, and seed of Abraham, spoken of in the context; and as to the former, the *many* cannot be extended to all mankind; since, if Christ bore the sins of them all, they must be put away, finished, made an end of, and never be found more; nor shall they be borne by them in a judicial way; whereas the sins of many go beforehand to judgment, of which they will be convicted, and for which they will be righteously punished. Besides, the persons whose sins Christ bore, being laid on him, are represented as particular and peculiar persons, *the seed* of Christ, and whom he *justifies.*[¶]

2ndly. It is observed,[**] "That as when the kindness designed by Christ's death to all upon the conditions of the Gospel is expressed, it is said Christ died for all; so when the effect and benefit of it is expressed, the word *many* is most proper; for his blood shed procures remission of sins only to penitent believers: and in this sense Christ gave his life a ransom only for many, even for as many as would believe and obey his Gospel." But this is to separate the design and effect of Christ's death, and to assert, that it does not reach its designed effect, which is to render it so far in vain. Besides, this makes the efficacy of his death to depend on the faith, repentance, and obedience of men; and, after all, *many* can only mean some, and not all, since all do not repent, believe, and obey.

SECTION II

And I lay down my life for the sheep.—John x. 15.

THE argument from hence, in favour of the doctrine of particular redemption, is taken from the character of the persons for whom Christ laid down his life, who are his *sheep,* whom he is said to know, and they are said to know him, hear his voice, and follow him; to whom he gives eternal life, so as that they shall never perish: all which is not true of every individual of mankind. In some parallel places they are said to be his *friends,* for whom he laid down his life, John xv. 13, and are distinguished from others; being such who *keep the commandments* of Christ, which all men do not; as having the secrets of Christ communicated to them, which *servants* have not; and as being *chosen* and ordained by Christ to *go and bring forth fruit,* which is not the case of all mankind. And in Eph. v. 25, they are said to be *the church,* for whom Christ gave himself; which must be distinct from the world, and can design no other than *the church of the first-born, whose names are*

---

* Eph. v. 2, 25; John x. 15. and xi. 51, 52; Matt. i. 21.   † Whitby, p. 115; ed. 2. 112.   ‡ 1 John i. 7, 9.
§ Whitby, p. 114, 115; ed. 2. 112.

‖ Ibid. p. 114, 115; ed. 112.   ¶ Isa. liii. 6, 11, 12; 1 Pet. ii. 24.   ** Whitby, p. 116; ed. 2. 113.

written in heaven: and, therefore, since these are the discriminating characters of the persons for whom Christ died, it follows, that he died for some only, and not for every individual of human nature. In answer to this,

1. It is observed,[*] that "in none of these places it is said that Christ died *only* for his *sheep,* for his *friends,* or for his *church ;* and, therefore, none of them say anything in contradiction to our assertion" of general redemption. I reply, this objection is much like what the Papists make against the doctrine of justification by faith. They own the Scriptures say, that we are justified by faith, but not by faith *only.* Now it may with as much propriety be said, that others, besides those *which be of faith, are blessed with faithful Abraham,* because the Scriptures do not say that they which be of faith *only* are blessed with him, or that there are more gods and more mediators than one, because the text does not say, there is *only* one God, and *only* one Mediator ; yea, it might be urged with equal strength, that men may love other women besides their own wives, in the same manner they love them, because it is not said, husbands love your wives *only,* as it may that Christ loved others, and gave himself for others, besides his church ; because it is not said, he loved his church *only,* and gave himself for his church *only.* But, though this restrictive word is not expressed, it is evidently implied ; for, if Christ laid down his life, and gave himself for every individual man, these peculiar and discriminating characters would be utterly unnecessary. And, after all, it is owned by our opponents,[†] that "eventually Christ is the Saviour of his body, and died only for his sheep and friends."

2. The argument is retorted upon thus ;[‡] "He that died for his friends, and for his enemies, for the church of God, and for the unrighteous, that he might bring them to the church of God ; for the sheep that heard his voice, and for the lost ones that did not hearken to his voice, died for all. But Christ died for his friends, &c., therefore he died for all." The fallacy of this argument will easily appear, when it is observed, that they are the same individual persons who are styled the enemies and friends of Christ, the unrighteous, and the church, the lost sheep, and such as hearken to Christ's voice ; being the former as considered in their unregenerate estate, and the latter through the power of his grace upon them.

SECTION III

I pray for them: I pray not for the world, but for them which thou hast given me ; for they are thine.—John xvii. 9.

THE death of Christ, which was the oblation of himself as a sacrifice, and his intercession, are the two principal parts of his priestly office ; and relate to the same persons. Those

for whom he died, for them he *also maketh intercession ;* and for whom he is *the propitiation,* for them he is an *advocate with the Father ;* and for whom he *sanctified,* or sacrificed himself, for them he *prays.*[§] Now, such who have an interest in his prayers, are a special people, opposed to *the world,* and distinguished from them by the peculiar character of being *given* to Christ by the Father ; and therefore those for whom he died, being the same persons, must be a special and peculiar people. It follows then that Christ died not for every individual of mankind, since he does not intercede for every one. But,

1. This is said[‖] "to be contrary both to reason and the Holy Scripture : to reason ; for can it rationally be imagined that he, who was perfect in charity, should be wanting in this highest act of charity ? that the beloved Son of God should charge this upon us as our duty, to pray for our enemies, and he himself neglect it ? Moreover how often doth he say of the Jews, *Ye are of the world ;* and yet says to them, εἰ ἔγνως, *How do I wish that thou hadst known in this thy day the things which do belong to thy peace !* and hanging on the cross, he said, *Father, forgive them, they know not what they do :* thus did he make *intercession for the transgressors.* Now, this prayer implies a possibility of their receiving forgiveness, and that, a disposition in God to grant it ; and consequently a satisfaction provided, such as will be acceptable, if they do their parts towards the obtaining of it." To which I reply, that it is certain Christ was perfect in charity ; nor was he wanting in this highest instance of it, praying for his enemies ; and yet did not pray for every individual man ; and though he charges it on us to pray for our enemies, yet not for every particular person : there are some we are not to pray for, 1 John v. 16. Nor do the instances produced prove, that Christ prayed for all the individuals of human nature. The passage in Luke xix. 42, regards only the Jews, and is no prayer at all, much less for their eternal salvation : since it only concerns their civil and temporal, not their spiritual and eternal peace ; and is only an instance of Christ's human compassion towards a people whose condition was irretrievable by prayer or other ways. His prayer on the cross was heard and answered, being made, not for all his enemies, but for such who were afterwards converted, as three thousand of them were under one sermon ; and their number after that was increased ; and which prayer not only implied a possibility, but a certainty of their receiving forgiveness of sins upon the foot of a satisfaction ; which was acceptable and available, not for anything done by them towards the obtaining of it, it being perfect in itself ; but because of the dignity of Christ's person, and the virtue of his blood and sacrifice. And thus indeed he made *intercession for transgressors.* But then these were no

---

* Whitby, p. 116 ; ed. 2. 114 ; Remonstr. in Coll. Hag. art. ii. p 172 ; Limborch, p. 325.

† Whitby, p. 117 ; ed. 2. 114.

‡ Ibid. p. 119 ; ed. 2. 114.

§ Rom. viii. 34 ; 1 John ii. 1, 2 ; John xvii. 9, 19.   ‖ Whitby, p. 129 ; ed. 2. 126.

other than his own *people*, for whose transgressions he was *stricken, wounded,* and *bruised ;* the *many* whose sins he, *bore,* and whom he *justified,* Isa. liii. 5, 8, 11, 12.

2. It is urged,* that " our Lord says not this absolutely, but only in respect to that very prayer he was then offering up for his apostles ; in which he was asking those things which could agree to them alone." But it is absolutely said, *I pray not for the world ;* nor is this prayer Christ was then offering up, peculiar to the apostles. In the beginning of it he takes notice, that his Father *had given him power over all flesh, that he should give eternal life to as many as he had given him,* ver. 2. Now were the eleven apostles the *many,* and the only ones the Father had given to Christ, and to whom he gives eternal life ? Did Christ only manifest his Father's name, glory, and gospel, to them ? Are they the only persons opposed unto and distinguished from the world ? Yea, does not Christ say of the persons he is praying for, *All mine are thine, and thine are mine,* ver. 10, which manifestly includes and designs the whole election of grace ? And, as if it was observed on purpose to obviate such an objection, he says, ver. 20, *Neither pray I for these alone, but for them also which shall believe on me through their word.* Besides, the things he asks for are such as were not peculiar to them as apostles, but common to them with other saints ; such as preservation from the evil of the world, ver. 11, 15 ; sanctification through the truth, ver. 17, 19 ; perfect union, ver. 21, 23, and eternal glory, ver. 24.

3. It is observed,† that " this very prayer in which he saith, *I pray not for the world,* was made for the sake of the world, and with respect to their saving faith, ver. 21, 23. And out of that affection to the world, and with design that the preaching of the apostle to them might be more effectual for their conversion and salvation." But it should also be observed, that the word *world* is an ambiguous one, and is used in various senses in this prayer ; and in the passages referred to does not intend such who were opposed unto, and distinguished from those who were given by the Father to Christ, as it does in the text under consideration ; but the elect of God in an unconverted state, who should be brought under the ministry of the apostles, and other preachers of the Gospel, to believe on Christ, to own him whom the Father had sent, and to know and partake of that love and favour which God bears to his own people.

SECTION IV

Who is he that condemneth ? It is Christ that died.—Rom. viii. 34.

THE argument from these words, in favour of peculiar, and against universal redemption, stands thus : Those for whom Christ died are God's elect ; and these in virtue of his death are freed from condemnation, and may boldly say, *Who is he that condemneth ?* But God's elect are not all men, or all men are not God's elect ; nor are all men freed from condemnation by the death of Christ ; nor can they all say, *Who is he that condemneth ?* It follows, that Christ died not for all men. That those for whom Christ died are God's elect, is evident from the connexion of the words with the preceding verse : *Who shall lay anything to the charge of God's elect : It is God that justifieth,* that is, his elect ; *Who is he that condemneth ?* that is, the elect of God : *It is Christ that died,* that is, for God's elect. Should it be said,‡ as it is, that by God's elect are meant true believers ; it should be observed, that they are not denominated God's elect from their being true believers, but they become true believers in consequence of their being God's elect. Besides, should this sense of the phrase be admitted of, it will be of no service ; for if, instead of God's elect, we read true believers, the sense of the words will be this ; *Who shall lay anything to the charge* of true believers ? *It is God that justifieth* true believers ? *Who is he that condemneth* true believers ? *It is Christ that died* for true believers. Now all men are not true believers, to whom Christ is precious ; nor have all men that faith which works by love. Moreover, that all for whom Christ died are, by his death, freed from condemnation, and may say, *Who is he that condemneth ?* will abundantly appear from these considerations ; that Christ, by dying, has had the sentence of condemnation they deserved, executed on him, in their room and stead ; sin, the cause of condemnation, is removed by his death, the full pardon of it procured, and a justifying righteousness brought in, with which the law and justice of God, are fully satisfied : and therefore, consistent with the justice of God, the persons for whom Christ died cannot be condemned ; and should any of them be condemned, his death would not be a security from condemnation ; nor would it be a sufficient foundation for the apostle's triumph of faith. Now it is certain that all men are not secured from condemnation ; there is a *world* that will be *condemned,* 1 Cor. xi. 32. Whence it follows, that Christ died not for all men. To this is excepted,§

1. " That this argument supposeth, that Christ died for none who shall hereafter be condemned." Which is very true ; for should any be condemned for whom Christ died, his dying for them must be in vain, and be no security against condemnation : and whereas it is asked, " Must it not hence follow, that none of the unbelieving Jews among whom Christ preached, nor none of the unbelieving world to whom the apostles preached, shall be condemned for not believing in him ? Since they could never be obliged to do so for whom he never died, which is contrary to John iii. 18, Mark xvi.

---

* Whitby, p. 129 ; ed. 2. 126.   † Ibid. p. 130 ; ed. 2. 127 ; Limborch, p. 326.

‡ Whitby, p. 46 ; ed. 2. 45.   § Ibid. p. 151 ; ed. 2. 148.

16." It may be replied, that the Jews and Gentiles to whom Christ is preached, are obliged to believe that Christ is God, the Son of God, the true Messiah, &c., according to the tenor of the revelation made to them; and may be justly condemned for not believing in him as such, even though he died not for them; for that he died for them, is what they are not obliged to believe, that being no part of the revelation made to them; nor will they be condemned for not believing that he died for them, but for their neglect, contempt, and unbelief of him and his Gospel, which is the sense of the passage alleged.

2. It is said,* that "there is no such proposition in the Scripture as this, that *all for whom Christ died may say, who shall condemn them?* but only that the persons there spoken of may say this, who were *the sons and heirs of God,* ver. 14—17; had received *the first-fruits of the Spirit,* ver. 23; *loved God,* ver. 28; and were justified by him; ver. 33." To which I answer, that though this proposition is not expressed in so many words in Scripture, yet it is strongly supported by the passage under consideration; and should it be admitted, that only the persons spoken of in the context may say this, yet it is certain, that all who are partakers of the same grace, and have received the same Spirit, may also say so too; yea, all the elect, even all that Christ died for, may say so sooner or later: for though the elect themselves cannot say this till they have believed, yet as their faith and repentance do not interest them in Christ, nor in his death, nor in the benefits of it; so they do not say so, as is suggested, upon their faith and repentance, but upon the account of Christ's death. Besides, our argument does not barely rest upon the elect, or those for whom Christ died, *saying,* or being able to say this, but upon the doctrine contained in it; that all those for whom Christ died, are by his death secured from condemnation; if therefore, any of the sons and daughters of men shall be condemned, as multitudes will be, we conclude that Christ died not for them.

SECTION V

He that spared not his own Son, but delivered him up for us all, how shall he not with him also freely give us all things?—Rom. viii. 32.

THE *us all,* or *all us,* for whom God has delivered up his Son, are no other than the predestinated, called, justified, and glorified, ver. 30, which cannot be said of every individual of mankind. Moreover, those on whose account God spared not his Son, but delivered him up into the hands of justice and death, in their room and stead, to be a sacrifice and ransom for them, will certainly be spared by him, and be delivered from the wrath to come; it being consistent neither with the justice nor with the love of God, to cast his wrath upon them, or deliver them up to eternal punishment. Now, it is certain,

that some persons are not spared by him, nor do escape eternal damnation: whence it must needs follow, that Christ being not spared: was not on their account; otherwise they would have been spared; and that though he was delivered up to justice, and to death, yet not for them; otherwise they would have escaped everlasting destruction. Besides, to all those for whom God has delivered up his Son, he freely gives all things: but there are thousands in the world to whom God does not give his Son, and all things freely with him; and therefore, it may be strongly concluded, that for these he did not deliver him up. In answer to this it is said,†

1. That this argument, as before, supposes "that Christ died only for those who shall be saved, and so liable to all the absurdities before mentioned; and to these that God could not equitably require all men to repent, nor could he equitably require of them obedience to his laws." To which I reply, that we freely own the assertion, and abide by it, that Christ died only for those who shall be saved; the end of his dying being salvation: if any for whom he died should not be saved, the end of his death would not be answered; and so be in vain with respect to them. As to its being liable to the former absurdities, these have been removed; and as to the additional ones, it is certain that God might have required repentance and obedience of men, if Christ had never died for any, or at all; as has been observed in the former part of this work.‡

2. It is here, as before said,‡ " That there is no such proposition in Scripture as this, *to all those for whom God delivered up his Son, he will give all things:* the Scripture cited respects only *us,* who are the adopted sons of God, &c." I reply, that this Scripture does abundantly confirm the truth of the proposition: for admitting that it only respects the adopted sons of God, to whom God gives the blessings of the new covenant: not because they have performed the conditions of it, as is intimated; for then he could not be said to give them *freely;* yet the Apostle's argument does not proceed upon their being the sons of God, and still less, upon their having fulfilled the conditions of the covenant, but upon God's delivering up his Son for them, and therefore will hold good with respect to all those for whom he has delivered him up, as it did with respect to them. For it may be as strongly concluded, that God will give all things freely to all those for whom he has delivered up his Son, as that he would bestow them on these particular persons: since there is the same reason for the one as for the other. Else there is no force in the Apostle's reasoning, no weight in his argument, nor any real conviction or solid consolation to be received from it; since it might be replied to him, that God might deliver up his Son for persons, and yet not freely give all things with him to them.

---

* Whitby, p. 152; ed. 2. 148, 149.
† Whitby, p. 153; ed. 2. 149.

‡ Sect. xxxii.   § Whitby, p. 154; ed. 2. 150.

SECTION VI

*For if, when we were enemies, we were recon-
ciled to God by the death of his Son, much
more, being reconciled, we shall be saved by
his life.*—Rom v. 10.

THE argument from these words, in favour of
particular, and against universal redemption,
stands thus : such for whom Christ died are
reconciled to God by his death; and such
who are reconciled to God by his death shall
be saved by his life. If therefore Christ
died for all men, and all men are reconciled
to God by his death, then all men shall be
saved by his life. But all will not be saved
by his life ; therefore all men are not reconciled to God by his death, nor did he die for
all men. In answer to which,

1st. It is observed,* that "this argument
supposes that Christ died to reconcile no man
to God who shall not be saved." It is very
true, and we not only suppose but affirm it,
and argue thus : Those for whom Christ died
to reconcile them to God, are either reconciled to him or they are not ; if they are not
reconciled to him, then Christ with respect to
them must die in vain; if they are reconciled
to him, then according to this text they shall
be saved. Whence it necessarily follows, that
he died to reconcile none to God, who shall
not be saved. But then it is said, it must
follow,

1. "That no man can be condemned at the
last day for neglecting that great salvation
tendered to, or purchased for him ; Christ
having neither purchased for or offered to
them any salvation, unless he offered to them
that salvation which he never died to purchase for them." It is certain, that for those
who shall not be saved, salvation was not purchased, nor should it be offered to them, nor
indeed to any. Such for whom salvation is
purchased, are the 'church whom Christ has
purchased with his own blood ; and to these,
this salvation is not offered, but applied. The
Gospel is not an offer, but *the power of God
unto salvation,* to these persons. And as for
others, they will be condemned at the last
day, for their sins and transgressions against
the law of God. And such who have had
the opportunity of hearing the Gospel, and
have neglected, despised, and reproached it,
their condemnation will be thereby aggravated.
But,

2. It is also said, that "it must follow
from hence, that all who are not saved, never
had any Saviour or Redeemer, and so were
never in a capacity to sin against a Saviour ;
nor can their sins be aggravated by this consideration that they are committed against
redeeming love. I reply, that *saviour* and
saved are relative terms, and mutually put
for each other : a Saviour supposes persons
saved, and the saved supposes a Saviour.
Now Christ can be a Saviour to no more than
to them who are saved ; and to such who are
not saved, he is no Saviour ; and yet such

may be capable of sinning against him as a
Saviour, though not as their Saviour ; they
may deny him to be the Saviour, despise, reproach, and neglect him as such, as Jews,
Deists, and others, have done. And though
their sins are not aggravated by this consideration, that they are committed against redeeming love, as having any share in it themselves,
yet may be aggravated by their contempt of
it, as the blessing of others. Moreover,
Christ may be sinned against by these persons
as a Saviour, in a way of providence, though
not in a way of grace ; and their sins may be
aggravated, as being committed against his
providential goodness, if not against his redeeming love. Though strictly, and properly
speaking, sin is not against Christ as a Saviour, but against God as the Lawgiver ; and
not against redeeming love, but a law of
righteousness.

2ndly. It is allowed,† that "the conclusion
of this argument, all that are reconciled to
Christ (God I suppose is meant) shall be
saved, may be true ; but not that all, for
whom Christ died, are reconciled to God." But
if all for whom Christ died are not reconciled to
God, then one principal end of his death, which
was *to make reconciliation for sin,* is not answered; and consequently his death must be so
far in vain. And whereas it is observed, that
" Christ died for them when sinners, unjust,
ungodly, and unbelievers, who cannot be actually reconciled to God, as none can, until
they believe and are justified ; and that reconciliation by the death of Christ, is only by
faith in it ; and that God never sent his Son
to purchase actual reconciliation for any but
conditionally, if, and when they believed." I
reply, that though no man is reconciled to
God's way and method of salvation by Christ,
or has peace in his soul, flowing from a sense
of atonement and justification by the blood of
Christ, until he believes ; which is meant by
the phrase, *much more being reconciled ;* and
regards not any performance of Christ's, but
the work of the Spirit of God upon the soul :
yet this hinders not but that men, whilst sinners, ungodly, and unbelievers, may be reconciled to God by the death of Christ ; that is
to say, that their sins may be expiated, and
fully atoned for ; for faith is not the cause or
condition of this reconciliation ; faith does
not make peace with God, or reconciliation
for sin, but receives the atonement already
made. Nor is it anywhere said, either that
God sent his Son to procure reconciliation, or
that Christ has obtained it on condition of
man's believing. The scheme of reconciliation was drawn by God without any respect
to faith, and was completely obtained by
Christ without any consideration of anything
done, or to be done by us. The consequence
of which is reconciliation of our souls to this
way of peace, by the Spirit of God ; and the
sure and certain effect of this, is everlasting
salvation to all those who are thus reconciled.

---

* Whitby, p. 154; ed. 2. 151.

† Whitby, p. 155; ed. 2. 151, 152.

SECTION VII

Greater love hath no man than this, that a man laid down his life for his friend.—John xv. 13.

THESE words contain an argument in favour of the doctrine of particular redemption, taken from the greatness of Christ's love in laying down his life for men, and may be formed thus: Those for whom Christ died, he loves with the greatest love: but he does not love every individual man with the greatest love; therefore he died not for every individual man. In answer to this argument, it is said,*

1. That it "plainly supposes, that Christ died for none who shall not actually be saved; whence it must follow, that only the elect are, or can be guilty of sinning against the love of God in Christ Jesus." To which may be replied, that we not only suppose but affirm, that Christ died for none who shall not actually be saved; and that for this reason, because Christ must have died in vain for such persons. But God forbid it should be said, that his death was in vain, in any one single instance. Nor are we afraid of the consequence of this affirmation, that only the elect are, or can be guilty of sinning against the love of God in Christ Jesus; since sin is properly against a law, *sin is the transgression of the law.* And though some men may be said to sin against the love of God in Christ, when they sin against God, notwithstanding their enjoyment of it, which is an aggravation of their sin, and in which sense they only can be guilty who do enjoy it; yet others may sin against providential kindness, and indeed against special love, when they despise the gospel, and ministers who publish it, and that itself, because it is discriminating.

2. That† "there is no assertion in the holy Scripture, that *those for whom Christ died, he loved with the greatest love.* Christ only says, that one man shows no greater love to another, than that of laying down his life for his friend. But this he neither did nor could say of the love of the Father, nor of himself: for *God commended his love to us, that while we were yet sinners* Christ died for us; and he died *for the ungodly, the just for the unjust;* and therefore this text is nothing to the purpose." To which I reply, that though this assertion is not expressed in so many words in the holy Scripture, it may be easily proved by it; and is manifestly implied in the words of this text. For when Christ speaks of the love of one man to another, by laying down his life for his people, as the greatest instance of it, he tacitly hints at his own love in laying down his life for him; for in the preceding verses, he is speaking of his *love* to his disciples, which he represents as equal to his Father's love to him, and as a pattern and example of theirs one to another; and in the verses following, applies the cha-

racter of *friends* unto them. And though Christ is said to die for his, *while sinners,* and *for the ungodly* and *unjust;* yet these are the same persons whom he calls *friends,* they being by nature as sinful and wicked as others. Which epithets and characters are made use of, not to express any greater, but the same act of love in dying for them, which is illustrated by their sinfulness and unworthiness.

3. "It is granted,‡ Christ showed the greatest love of benevolence to all for whom he died; but then it is added, that he shows his love of friendship and beneficence only to those that bear a true reciprocal affection to him." Which love of friendship and beneficence, it is said, "depends on our repentance, conversion, faith, and obedience." Now not to take any notice of the distinction of Christ's love, into that of benevolence and beneficence, being a groundless one, when, like himself, it is, *the same yesterday, to-day, and for ever;* Christ's death does not merely express a love of benevolence, or only shows that he wished them well for whom he died, or willed good things for them; but was an act of beneficence, or an actual doing good things for them; since by it he reconciled them to God, brought them near unto him, redeemed them from all iniquity, finished their transgressions, made an end of their sins, and brought in everlasting righteousness for them. Nor does what is called a love of beneficence, depend on our repentance, conversion, faith, and obedience: for though Christ loves them that love him, and grace is upon all them that do so, yet it is not their love that is the cause of his; but on the contrary, they *love him, because he first loved them.* Moreover, were there any foundation for this distinction of the love of Christ, yet his dying for men, which is styled his love of benevolence, is a greater expression of his love than the application of the salutary effects of his death, which is reckoned his love of beneficence; and he that has a share in the former, will certainly enjoy the latter; the apostle argues from the one to the other, as from the greater to the lesser; when he says, *If, when we were enemies, we were reconciled to God by the death of his Son, much more, being reconciled, we shall be saved by his life.*§

CHAPTER IV

OF EFFICACIOUS GRACE

THE celebrated writer‖ chiefly attended to, has filled up above *twenty pages* in stating the question about the grace of God in conversion. The sum of which is, that there are some inward operations of the Spirit vouchsafed in that work; but that these only consist in representing divine truths to our understandings, and bringing them to our remembrance, and thereby raising some ideas in the brain, and making some impressions on it; which he allows to be physical, and irre-

---

* Whitby, p. 156; ed. 2. 152.   † Ibid. ed. 2. 152, 153.   ‡ Whitby, p. 157; ed. 2. 153; Limborch, p. 327.

§ Rom. v. 10.   ‖ Whitby, p. 208—231; ed. 2. 203—225.

sistible in their production, and in which men are wholly passive ; but utterly denies that any supernatural habits are infused, or that any supernatural aid is requisite to the conversion of a sinner besides the forementioned. He oberves that the word *grace* in scripture, always signifies the favour and goodness of God, but never any supernatural or infused habit : contrary to Rom. v. 20, 21, and vi. 14, 2 Cor. viii. 7, and ix. 8, 14, Col. iii. 16, 1 Tim. i. 14, 2 Pet. iii. 18, with many others : yet owns, that the foresaid ideas raised in the brain, according to their nature, use, tendency, and effects, may be called either exciting, or restraining, or preventing, or assisting, or the subsequent grace of God ; and may be either sufficient or efficacious, common or special. My business in the following *Sections* will be to prove, that the work of grace or conversion, is an internal one, wholly owing to the efficacious grace of God, and wrought in the soul by a supernatural, irresistible, and insuperable power, in the production of which man is purely passive ; and to vindicate the passages of scripture made use of in proof of this doctrine, which are objected to.

SECTION I.

And what is the exceeding greatness of his power to us-ward who believe, according to the working of his mighty power, which he wrought in Christ, when he raised him from the dead.—Ephes. i. 19, 20.

SINCE the apostle, in these words, plainly intimates, that the work of grace upon the hearts of believers is to be ascribed not only to the *power* of God, but to the *greatness*, yea, the *exceeding greatness* of his power, and which is represented as equal to that which was put forth in raising Christ from the dead ; we think we have good reason to conclude, that this work is a work of almighty, irresistible, and insuperable power, and in which men, in the first production of it, are purely passive. It is indeed said,[*] that " it must be absurd hence to infer, that the power of God working faith in believers is equal to that which effected the resurrection of our Lord, and that we must be therefore purely passive in the whole work of our conversion." But certain it is, that the power here spoken of is said to be κατὰ τὴν ἐνέργειαν, *according to the working* or *energy of his mighty power, which he wrought in Christ, when he raised him from the dead.* And if the work of faith and conversion is intended, men must be passive under the energetical influence of divine power effecting it, as the body of Christ was, when, by the same power, it was raised to life. But let us attend to the reasons given :

1. It is said,[†] that " this power is not consistent with the persuasions and exhortations used in Scripture to move men to repent, and turn themselves from their iniquity." I reply, that the exhortations to repent and turn from iniquity do not regard the first work of conversion, or the inward work of grace upon the soul, which is here designed, but an outward reformation of life. Besides, supposing the exhortations referred to respect the internal work of faith and conversion, they may be attended with that power from God, who makes use of them, so as to produce such principles of life and grace, in which men are purely passive ; by virtue of which they may become active, and be enabled to answer to such exhortations ; even as the command of Christ to *Lazarus* to *come forth* was attended with such a divine power as produced a principle of life in him, in which he was purely passive ; though by virtue of it he became active, *came forth*, and answered the word of command.

2. This is also said‡ to be inconsistent " with a rational choice." I answer, that no doubt, whilst men are in a state of nature, they are able, without the special and powerful grace of God, to make a rational choice in things natural and civil, but not in things spiritual and eternal. How should they, when they are under the power of sin, influenced by their corrupt and deceitful lusts, and enslaved by Satan ? Such men will always *choose their own ways, for their soul delighteth in their abominations ;* which makes the powerful and efficacious grace of God necessary to enlighten their understandings, inform their judgments, guide their affections, and influence their wills.

3. It is urged§ that if this was the case, " it could not properly be said that they turned, but only that they were turned, to the Lord." To which may be replied, that when the Scriptures speak of the internal work of conversion upon the heart, it is expressed in the passive form, *they were turned*, see Jer. xxxi. 18, 1 Pet. ii. 25. And when they speak of external reformation, or of such a turning to the Lord as is the fruit of faith, then it is expressed in the active form, *they turned to him*, see Acts xi. 21.

4. It is observed,‖ that " this exposition is not agreeable to the words ; for the apostle speaks not of the power exercised on us to render us believers, but of the power which shall be exercised on us who believe already." But nothing is more evident, than that the apostle speaks not of a power which *shall be* exercised on believers, but of a power which *is* exercised upon them, and is continued to be so ; and is the same with that which was put forth when they first trusted in Christ, and must be continued to carry on and perfect the good work. Now, if the exceeding greatness of God's power is necessary to carry on and perfect the work of faith, it must be much more so to produce, plant, and form it at first.

It is asserted,§ that the apostle speaks " not of the power to be exercised on our souls, to raise them from a death in sin to a life of righteousness, but of the power to be

* Whitby, p. 272 ; ed. 2. 266. † Ibid.
‡ Whitby, p. 672 ; ed. 2. 266. § Ibid.
‖ Ibid. ¶ Ibid. Vide Coll. Hag. art. iii. and iv. p. 293, 294 ; Limborch, p. 388.

exercised on our dead bodies, to give them a glorious resurrection to eternal life, as he had done already in the body of our head Christ Jesus." But though the apostle, in order to illustrate that power which is exalted towards them that believe, takes notice of the power which was wrought in Christ when he was raised from the dead; yet he says not one syllable concerning the resurrection of the saints. Moreover, the apostle is speaking not of a power *to be* exercised, but of one that *is* now exercised upon believers; whereas the resurrection of our dead bodies is an act of God's power, which is to be exercised; it is future, yet to come. Besides, this power is limited to believers; whereas the resurrection of the dead will be both of the just and unjust; and the resurrection of the one will be as much an instance of the exceeding greatness of God's power, as the resurrection of the other. Add to this, that at the resurrection the people of God will no longer bear the character of believers, (for faith will be changed into vision,) but that of saints and just men, being in themselves made perfectly so; whereas the subjects of this power are such *who believe.* To conclude, these words stand in connection with chap. ii. 1: *And you hath he quickened, who were dead in trespasses and sins,* which is the plain instance of God's power the apostle had in his view; for all that is said between them, concerning the resurrection, exaltation, and headship of Christ, may be read in a parenthesis, and are only mentioned to illustrate and set forth the exceeding greatness of the power of God in this instance of it.

SECTION II

Therefore if any man be in Christ, he is a new creature—2 Cor. v. 17; *with Gal.* vi. 15; *Eph.* ii. 10, *and* iv. 24.

THE work of grace upon the soul being expressed in these passages by καινὴ κτίσις, *a new creation,* or *creature,* and a being *created in Christ Jesus,* manifestly shows, that it is to be ascribed to the efficacious grace of God, and that man is purely passive in it. But it is observed,[*]

1. " That this metaphor affords no certain proof that wheresoever it is used, the person it respecteth must be purely passive, and have done nothing towards the act styled *creation,* is evident from Isa. xliii. 1, and liv. 16." To which I reply, that if the metaphor elsewhere used affords no certain proof, that the person it respecteth must be purely passive, and have done nothing towards the act styled *creation,* yet, if it does in the instances before us, it is sufficient to our purpose; now nothing appears to the contrary. And, indeed, the other passages referred to are far from making it evident, that the metaphor affords no certain proof of the person's passiveness whom it respecteth; not Isa. xliii. 1, where God is said to have *created Jacob, and formed Israel,*

which is not to be understood literally of the people of the Jews, when God formed them as a nation, or body politic, or when he constituted them to be his church and people, and they entered into covenant to have him for their God; but of the elect of God, whether Jews or Gentiles, as appears from ver. 5—7, 19—21, compared with 1 Pet. ii. 9, 10, and designs this new creation work of grace upon their souls in effectual vocation; by which God *forms* them *for* himself, that they may *show forth* his *praise.* Now, though they are active in showing forth the praise of God, yet are entirely passive in being created and formed for that purpose. So in the other instance, in Isa. liv. 16: *I have created the waster to destroy.* Though the waster is active in destroying, yet he is purely passive in being created, appointed, and raised up to destroy.

2. It is urged,[†] that man is not holy passive in the case before us is " certain, from the nature of faith and godly sorrow, which are men's acts, and not God's, and from God's frequent calls upon the wicked *to turn from their transgressions to the Lord.*" I reply, that when we say that men are passive in the work of grace upon them, we speak not of the exercise of grace, in which, it is allowed, men are active, but of the implantation and production of grace in them. Though men, and not God, believe and repent, yet faith and repentance are the gifts of his grace and the produce of his power. And though they are active in turning to the Lord, yet this is in consequence of their being first turned by him. Besides, God's frequent calls to men to turn themselves, regard not the first work of conversion, but an external reformation of life, as the fruit, effect, and evidence of it.

3. It is further observed,[‡] that "God is, in Scripture, said to create that which he brings into a new and better state, as in Psal. li. 10, Isa. lxv. 17, 19. To this sense the Scripture plainly leads us, when it saith, *If any man be in Christ, he is a new creature.* And all the Greek fathers confirm this exposition, by saying, that this new creation only importeth, μεταβολὴν εἰς τὸ κρεῖττον, *a change for the better.*" Admitting that this is the sense of the word create, in the places cited, and that the sense of the Greek fathers is just, the question before us is not whether this new creation is a change for the better, but, whether this is to be ascribed to the irresistible and efficacious grace of God, in which man is passive, or to the active power of man's free will. But neither the sense of the Greek fathers is just and proper, which seems to imply that man, before this new creation, was in a good state, though this changes him into a better. Whereas this is not an improvement of what he was, or had before, but an infusion of that into him which he had not. Nor does it appear so manifestly to be the sense of the word create, in the places referred to; not in Psal. li. 10,

* Whitby, p. 272; ed. 2. 266.
† Whitby, p. 273; ed. 2. 266.   ‡ Ibid.
p. 273, 274; ed. 2. 267.

Create in me a clean heart, which strongly expresses the sense David had of his fall, of his own inability to help himself, and of his need of so much of divine power to restore him, as is put forth in an act of creation. And from hence it may be rightly concluded, that if a fallen believer, who has the grace of God in him, is not able to create a clean heart in himself, much less able is an unregenerate sinner. Nor in Isa. lxv. 17, where it is said, *Behold, I create a new heaven, and a new earth;* since it follows, and the former shall *not be remembered, nor come into mind.* Nor in ver. 19, *Behold, I create Jerusalem a rejoicing, and her people a joy;* which will be done, not barely by renewing, or bringing into a better state the former individuals, which before constituted Jerusalem, or the church, but by an immediate thorough conversion of multitudes, which shall be added to her; for then *the earth shall be made to bring forth in one day,* and *a nation shall be born at once,* chap. lxvi. 8. Much less in the text before us, seeing it is immediately added, *Old things are passed away; behold, all things are become new.* This new creation is not an improvement, or a mending of the old principles of nature, but an infusion of new ones, and so is properly styled a creation.

SECTION III

Jesus answered, Verily, verily, I say unto thee, Except a man be born of water and of the Spirit, he cannot enter into the kingdom of God.—John iii. 5.

Since the work of grace upon the soul is here expressed by a being *born again,* or *from above;* and since this is ascribed to *water* and *the Spirit,* not baptismal water, which has no regenerating virtue in it, nor is it absolutely necessary to salvation; but either the grace of the Spirit or spirit of grace, compared to water, Ezek. xxxvi. 25, John iv. 14, and vii. 37—39; we conclude, that this is wrought by the omnipotent and unfrustrable grace of God, in which man is as passive as an infant is in its natural generation and birth. In answer to which it is said,[*]

1. That "the falsehood of this argument is evident from this consideration, that this new birth is ascribed to the word and ministers of God, Rom. x. 17, 1 Pet. i. 23, James i. 18, 1 Cor. iv. 15, who work upon us by moral suasion; and since this cannot import, that they produce it by an irresistible action, in which we are purely passive, it will not follow that God, or his good Spirit, doth so convert men, because they are said to be born of God, or of the Spirit." To which I reply, that though faith comes by hearing, and we are said to be begotten by the word of God and truth, as a mean, yet faith is a gift of grace, and *of the operation of God;*[†] which *work of faith,* as it will be fulfilled, so

it is begun and carried on by the power of God, which can never be resisted so as to be overcome. And though ministers are represented as spiritual fathers, yet they are only instruments by whom we believe; and were no more done, than what is the effect of moral suasion through them, the work would never be done at all. Moreover, it does not follow, that because they do not and cannot produce this work by an irresistible action, in which we are passive, that therefore God does not convert men in such a way; since it is certain he makes use of them in such a manner, as that *the excellency of the power may* appear to *be of God, and not of man.*[‡] Besides, we are never said to be born of the word, or of ministers, but by them; whereas we are said to be born of God, and of the Spirit, which is expressive not of bare means, or mere moral suasion, but of the powerful efficiency.

2. It is observed,[§] that this "phrase is used by the Jews concerning their proselytes, they being then said to be *recens nati,* newborn babes; and from them our Lord translates the metaphor to his disciples, renewed after the image of God in true holiness, and sanctified throughout in all their whole man." But the phrase of being *born of water and of the Spirit,* is never used by the Jews concerning their proselytes. It is true, indeed, they have such a saying as this, גר דמי שנולד כקטון שנתגייר, *One that is made a proselyte, is like a child new born:*[‖] but then they used this not in a spiritual but in a civil sense, signifying by it, that such ceased from all natural and civil relations to parents, masters, &c. Such an one might marry his mother, or mother's sister, be no longer under obligation to a master, standing no longer in any relation to them, being as a new-born babe; and might be admitted, in civil cases, as a witness equally with a Jew, with many other things of the like nature.[¶] And admitting that our Lord had reference to the use of this phrase among the Jews, it was to show, that another kind of birth was necessary to the enjoyment of the kingdom of God, that either the Jews, as being the descendants of Abraham, or than the proselytes, by coming over to the Jewish religion, had. Besides, since in the objection it is observed, that this metaphor is translated to such who are renewed after the image of God in true holiness, and sanctified throughout in all their whole man; yea, it is added, that there is such intrinsic change in *the whole spirit, soul, and body,* that they may be said to be much more other men, than Saul, when the Spirit of prophecy came upon him : and seeing it is owned, that this change is wrought within us by the operation of the Holy Spirit, why should it not be ascribed to the unfrustrable and irresistible power and grace of the Spirit, in which men are entirely passive?

---

* Whitby, p. 274, 275; ed. 2. 268.
† Eph. ii. 8; Col. ii. 12; 2 Thess. i. 11.
‡ 2 Cor. iv. 7. § Whitby, p. 275;

ed. 2. 268. ‖ Talm. Jebamot, fol. xxii. 1, xlviii. 2. lxii. 1, and xcvii. 2. ¶ Vide Maimon. Issure Bia, c. xiv. s. 11; and Eduth. c.xiii. s. 2.

SECTION IV

And you hath he quickened, who were dead in trespasses and sins.—Eph. ii. 1; with Colossians ii. 13.

MEN in an unregenerate state, being represented in these passages as *dead in sin*, shows, that whilst they are in such a state, they are as incapable of spiritual motion or action, or of quickening themselves, as a dead man is of natural motion, or action, or of raising himself from the dead. Whence it must needs follow, that the work of conversion is a work of God, and not man, and to be ascribed to *the exceeding greatness of his power;* in which man is passive as a dead body is in its resurrection from the dead. In answer to which,

1st. It is said,* "that the metaphor of being *dead in trespasses and sins,* cannot warrant our saying anything of unregenerate persons, which may properly be affirmed of the dead;" for,

1. "A dead body is void of all sense; whereas the unregenerate man is often under strong convictions, and a deep sense of his present misery." To which I reply, that it is one thing for a man to be under strong convictions, and a deep sense of his present misery, or of the evil and mischief which comes by sin, which sense is purely natural; and another thing to be under real convictions, and a deep sense of the true evil and wickedness that is in sin, which is purely spiritual, and arises from the quickening influences of the Spirit of God.

2. A dead man cannot awake himself out of the sleep of death; but God saith to the spiritually dead man, *Awake, thou that sleepest, arise from the dead, and Christ shall give thee life,* it should have been *light,* Eph. v. 14. I reply, that these words are not spoken to the spiritually dead, but to professors of religion, as abundantly appears from the context; who were fallen into a drowsy, sleepy frame, which was very much owing to their conversation with dead sinners: wherefore the Apostle exhorts them, to rouse themselves from this lethargy, and arise, and depart from their dead companions, and unfruitful works of darkness, when they might expect more light and liveliness in their souls from Christ.

3. "A dead man cannot hear: but to the spiritually dead, God saith, *Hear, and your souls shall live,* Isa. lv. 3." To which may be replied, that there is a twofold hearing of the word; an external one, which regards the outward ministry of it, and an internal one, so as to understand it; the former, men spiritually dead may be capable of, but not of the latter; see John viii. 43, 47. Besides, the persons spoken to in the passage of Scripture cited, were not spiritually dead, but were such as were quickened, who had a principle of spiritual life implanted in them. In con-

sequence of which, they *thirsted* after spiritual things, ver. 1, though greatly distressed under a sense of their spiritual poverty. Wherefore, the Lord encourages them to *hearken* to him, and listen to his covenant grace and promises, that they might *live* comfortably.

4. "It would be absurd to exhort a dead body to turn about and live; whereas God thinks it not incongruous to say to persons spiritually dead, *Turn yourselves, and ye shall live,*" Ezek. xviii. 32, and xxxiii. 11. I reply, that the passages referred to, do not regard such who were spiritually dead; since they concern the whole house of Israel, and every one of them: of whom it cannot be said, that they were dead in trespasses and sins: nor do the exhortations relate to the first work of conversion, but to an external reformation of them as a body politic, that they might peaceably live in their own land, and comfortably enjoy the good things of it.

5. "Good Christians are said to be *dead to sin,* Rom. vi. 2, 11; *to the law,* Gal. ii. 19, *and to the world,* Gal. vi. 14." Now if hence we cannot truly argue, that they cannot sin at all, that they can do nothing relating to the world, or to the law; neither can we argue from the metaphor of being *dead in trespasses and sins,* that we can do nothing in obedience to the calls of God, or compliance with the motions of his word and Spirit. To which I reply, that the meaning of the phrases in the passages mentioned is, that believers are freed from the damning power of sin, and from the curse and condemnation of the law, and are delivered from this present evil world. Now, whereas we can truly argue from hence, that believers are so dead to sin, the law, and the world, and these to them, as that they cannot condemn, damn, or destroy them; so we can truly argue from the metaphor, of being dead in trespasses and sins, that men can do nothing spiritually good, until God powerfully calls them by his grace, and they feel the quickening influences and motions of his Spirit.

2ndly. In answer to the argument from these Scriptures, it is observed,† that "both the places cited concern only the Gentile world; and so we cannot argue from those words, which do so certainly relate to the worst of Heathens, that this must be the natural state of all men: or, that the same power is requisite to convert the unregenerate Christian, and the worst of Heathens." I reply, that these persons spoken of were Heathens, is readily granted; but that they were the worst of Heathens is not so manifest, though, probably, they were as bad as any. However, I cannot but take notice of *the unregenerate Christian,* as a mere paradox, a contradiction in terms; since no man can be truly a Christian but he that is regenerated by the Spirit of Christ. But, passing these things, let it be observed, that the same character of being *dead* in a moral or spiritual

---

* Whitby, p. 276; ed. 2. 269.

† Whitby, p. 276, 277; ed. 2. 270.

sense, is given to unregenerate Jews, which is here given to the unconverted Gentiles, Matt. viii. 22, John v. 25. For that they were Jews, and not Gentiles, our Lord speaks to and of in the places referred to, is evident from this consideration, that as yet the Gospel was not sent to the Gentiles; nor were there any among them as yet who heard his voice or followed him. Nothing is more certain and true than this, that he, or *she, that liveth in pleasure,* whether Jew or Gentile, are *dead* while they *live.* Besides, the apostle says the very same things, in the same words, of himself, who was a Jew, and a devout one, and of others, while unconverted, as he does of these worst of Heathens, Ephes. ii. 4, 5. So that we may truly argue, and safely conclude, that this must be the natural state of all men; and that the same power is requisite to convert an unregenerate Jew, yea, an unregenerate man living where Christianity is professed, and the worst of Heathens; since the same characters belong to them.

SECTION V

But the natural man receiveth not the things of the Spirit of God: for they are foolishness unto him: neither can he know them, because they are spiritually discerned.— 1 Cor. ii. 14.

THE *natural man* is not barely the sensual man, who is abandoned and given up wholly to his carnal lust and pleasures; since he is not the only person who is ignorant of spiritual things; which sense of the phrase the Arminians* were formerly fond of, though they have now quitted it; but rather the man of reason, who is merely ψυχικος, has nothing but a soul, or bare reason in him, destitute of the grace of God; which is the case of every man in a natural state. Now this man, whilst he is such, and by the mere light of nature, *cannot know* the things of the Spirit of God. The utmost knowledge he can have of the doctrines of the Gospel, here intended, is merely notional and speculative, not spiritual and experimental. The reason is, *because they are spiritually discerned,* that is, tried and judged in a spiritual way. Nor can he *receive* them, so as to love and approve of them; because *they are foolishness unto him,* absurd and ridiculous. Wherefore, a divine operation of grace upon his understanding, affections, and will, is absolutely necessary, in order to his spiritual knowledge, affectionate reception of, and hearty subjection to, the Gospel of Christ; and without this he will never understand it spiritually, nor receive and embrace it cordially. But to this are excepted,

1. That† "the natural man here is not barely the unregenerate man; but the wise man, and disputer of the world, who will admit of nothing but what he can see proved by reason; and so receives not things revealed by the Spirit." I reply, admitting

this sense of the phrase, it follows, that if an unregenerate wise man, one of the greatest abilities, and most refined parts, in whom reason is sublimated, and wound up to its highest pitch it can well be, in unsanctified nature, cannot know and receive spiritual things; then an unregenerate foolish man, or one of meaner abilities, and of a lower rank and size, can never, as such, understand and embrace them. The apostle has pitched upon an instance which must necessarily conclude all men that are unregenerate, in a state of ignorance of spiritual things, and in an incapacity of knowing them, without the special illuminating grace of the Spirit.

2. That‡ "the apostle speaks not of the inability of a Heathen to understand the meaning of any revelation discovered unto him: for how, then, it is asked, is it discovered to him? but of the necessity of a supernatural revelation, that the hidden wisdom of God might be made known to the world." In answer, a Heathen, whether a philosopher, or a man of a more ordinary size, may be capable of understanding the literal, grammatical meaning of a revelation made to him, even of the external revelation God has made to the world; as that the import of it is, among other things, that Jesus is the Messiah, was born of a virgin, suffered, died, and rose again, and thereby procured salvation for men; and yet, have no spiritual sense and apprehension of these things, any relish for them, gust of them, or faith in them; all which he will remain a stranger to, unless accompanied with a special, internal revelation, and application of them to him by the Spirit of God. The necessity of which, and not of an external, supernatural revelation, the apostle here demonstrates; for the latter, the natural man, whether among Jews or Greeks, had; otherwise, it could not with any propriety be said, that he *receiveth* not, or rejects these things, and accounts them *foolishness;* which were in consequence of an external, supernatural revelation made in the ministry of the apostles, who *preached Christ crucified, to the Jews a stumbling-block, and to the Greeks foolishness;*§ it being with respect to them unattended with *the demonstration of the Spirit and of power.*

SECTION VI

*Not that we are sufficient of ourselves to think anything as of ourselves; but our sufficiency is of God.—*2 Cor. iii. 5.

THE argument from hence, proving the insufficiency of man's free will, and the necessity of the grace of God to the doing of that which is spiritually good, stands thus: If men are insufficient of themselves to, or cannot by the strength of free will, think anything that is spiritually good, much less can they will, and still less perform, that which is so. But,

1. It is said,‖ that this argument, "if it

---

* Remonstr. Act. Synod. circ. art. iv. p. 159; Curcellæus, p. 38; Limborch, p. 28, 382.
† Whitby, p. 177; ed. 2. 270.

‡ Ibid. p. 277, 278; ed. 2. 271.
§ 1 Cor. i. 23, and ii. 4. ‖ Whitby, p. 278; ed. 2. 271.

proves anything, it proves too much; namely, that we are not sufficient of ourselves, λογίσασθαί τι, *to think anything* at all, whether it be good or bad." I reply, that neither the words of the apostle, nor our argument upon them, prove so much; nor the words of the apostle; since by τι, *anything*, he means either any good thing, or any evil thing, or any thing that is neither good nor evil; not any evil thing, for *the imagination of the thoughts of man's heart is only evil continually ;** nor any thing that is neither good nor evil; for men are capable of themselves of thinking of things natural and civil, which, in a moral sense, are neither good nor evil. It remains, then, that he means any good thing which respects God, and Christ, and faith in them; as when our Lord says, *Without me ye can do nothing ;†* his meaning is not, that we can do no natural or civil action of life, or no evil action, without him, but no good one. Nor does our argument, on these words of the apostle, prove so much; since it is limited to things which are spiritually good. Moreover, the λογίσασθαι, here used, does not signify barely to think, but to think with judgment and affection, see Phil. iv. 8, which no man, with respect to spiritual things, is capable of without the grace of God.

2. It is urged,‡ that "the words relate to the apostles, and to them alone, and are a declaration of their own insufficiency to carry on the great work of conversion of the world to the Christian faith by their own strength and wisdom, without the illuminations and powerful operations of the Holy Ghost." To which I answer, that the apostle is indeed speaking of the ministry of the Gospel by him and others, and of the success of it, and of their trust and confidence through Christ concerning it, ver. 3, 4; yet in these words he speaks in general terms; *Not that we are sufficient of ourselves, to think anything as of ourselves*, either with respect to the work of the ministry, or the conversion of souls, or our trust in God, or anything else that is of a spiritual nature; *but our sufficiency*, for every spiritual work, is of God. And then he proceeds to take notice particularly of their fitness for the ministry they had of God. *Who also hath made us able ministers of the New Testament.* Whereas, if the words in the *fifth verse* relate particularly to the sufficiency the apostles had from God for the work of the ministry, he must be guilty of a very great tautology in the *sixth verse ;* for the sense of both must be this; *We are not sufficient* for the work of the ministry *of ourselves, but our sufficiency* for it *is of God ;* ὃς καὶ, *who also hath made us sufficient ministers of the New Testament.* Besides, if the apostles were not sufficient of themselves to *think*, study, or collect anything together, fit for the ministry of the Gospel, and so as to be useful to the good of souls, much less must a natural man be able to think any spiritual good thing, and still

less be able to do anything towards his regeneration, or in the real work of faith and conversion, which is entirely owing to the efficacious grace of God.

SECTION VII

For without me, ye can do nothing.—John xv. 5.

THAT men in an unregenerate state are capable of performing natural and civil actions, and such as have the appearance of moral good, will be allowed; but that they are able to do that which is spiritually good, or any good thing in a spiritual manner, must be denied; for even believers themselves are not able to do anything of this kind of themselves, or without Christ, and the Spirit and grace of Christ, as is sufficiently evident from these words. But,

1. It is objected,§ that "these words of Christ are spoken expressly to those who were abiding in Christ, and truly believed already." Be it so; if such were not able of themselves to do anything that is spiritually good, much less able are they who have no abiding in Christ, or true faith in him.

2. It is said,‖ that these words being spoken to the twelve apostles, "signify, that without the gifts and powerful assistance of the Holy Spirit, who belonged only to them that abode in Christ, they could do nothing to convert the world." I reply, though these words are spoken to the apostles, yet not to them only; for our Lord's words throughout the context are so expressed, as that may be applied to any other persons under a profession of faith; much less are they spoken to them as apostles, but as in union with Christ, believers in him, professing faith in him, as branches in him the vine, deriving all their grace, life, liveliness, and fruitfulness, from him, by which they performed every spiritual action; all which are far from being peculiar to them as apostles. Moreover, this sense of the words makes Christ to stand for the gifts and assistance of the Spirit; whereas the phrase *without me*, signifies *separate*, or *apart from* him, that is, from his person and grace, and not the gifts and assistance of his Spirit. Besides, it is not true that the Holy Spirit, with respect to his gifts and assistance, qualifying for and succeeding in the work of the ministry, only belonged to them that abode in Christ; since many may, and have had the Spirit in this sense, as Judas, who never had any real being or abiding in Christ.

3. It is observed¶ from Gataker, "that χωρὶς ἐμοῦ, *without me*, is the same as χαριθέντες ἀπ' ἐμοῦ, *being separated from me*, ye can do nothing; which, if we extend to all true Christians, only signifies, that "without abiding in the faith, they cannot be faithful in the faith; and without their continuing united to Christ by the Spirit, they cannot bring forth the fruits of the Spirit." It is

---

* Gen. vi. 5.   † John xv. 5.
‡ Whitby, ibid.; Remonstr. Act. Synod, circ.
art. iv. p. 168; Limborch, p. 383.

§ Whitby, p. 279; ed. 2. 272.   ‖ Ibid.
¶ Ibid.

certain, that men without abiding in the faith, can never be faithful in it; and without continuing united to Christ, cannot bring forth the fruits of the Spirit; though all that are truly in the faith shall abide in it, and such as are really united to Christ, shall continue so, and bring forth fruit. But then, if these cannot bring forth fruit without abiding in the faith, and continuing united to Christ, how should such bring forth fruit who never were in the faith, nor in Christ? Gataker's observation, and which is also Piscator's, is a very good one; and the sense of the words it confirms is this; that could the apostles, or any other believers, be supposed to be, or could possibly be separated from Christ, they would not be able to do anything that is truly and spiritually good. And if so, how should such who are χωρὶς Χριστοῦ, *without Christ*, Ephes. ii. 12, as all unregenerate persons are, be capable of doing anything of that nature? It is true, they may be able to attend to the hearing of the word, by which faith comes, may ask, seek, and knock for the good Spirit, may consider of the ways of God, and turn their feet to his testimonies; but unless they are renewed by the Holy Ghost, are created in Christ Jesus, and have faith in him, they will not be able to do these, nor anything else in a spiritual manner. The Remonstrants themselves own,* "that man in a sinful state, cannot of himself think, will, or do that which is truly good, and that it is necessary that he should be regenerated, and renewed of God in Christ by his Holy Spirit, in the understanding, affection, and will, and in all his powers, that he may be able rightly to understand, meditate, will, and perform that which is truly good; as it is written, *Without me ye can do nothing.*"

SECTION VIII

No man can come to me, except the Father which hath sent me draw him: and. I will raise him up at the last day.—John vi. 44.

1. THIS passage of Scripture is no inconsiderate proof of the doctrine of the powerful and efficacious grace of God in the work of faith and conversion. To *come* to Christ, is to believe in him. This is not to be attributed to the free will and power of man, but is owing to the Father's *drawing*; which is to be understood not of moral suasion, but of the internal and powerful influence of his grace. This act of drawing, is an act of power, even almighty power; as appears from its being something distinct from and superior to both doctrines and miracles. The Capernaites had heard the doctrine of Christ, which was taught with authority, and had seen his miracles, which were full proofs of his being the Messiah; and yet believed not, but continued murmuring at his person and parentage. This gave occasion to Christ to observe to them, that something more than these was necessary to their coming to him,

or savingly believing in him, even the powerful and efficacious grace of the Father in drawing. Besides, if this act of drawing was only an act of moral suasion, and not of almighty power, then a lesser action is ascribed to the Father who sent Christ, than is to Christ himself; though he is here spoken of as Mediator; since he takes to himself the power of raising such up at the last day who come unto him, which must be allowed to be an act of omnipotence; when moral suasion is what belongs to every ordinary minister of the word. Add to this, if it be considered what men, in conversion, are drawn off *from* and *to*, from their beloved lusts and darling righteousness, to look unto and rely upon Christ alone for salvation; from what was before so very agreeable, to that which, previous to this work on their souls, was so very disagreeable; to what else can this be ascribed, but to unfrustrable and insuperable grace? But then, though this act of drawing is an act of power, yet not of force: God, in drawing of unwilling, makes *willing in the day of his power;* he enlightens the understanding, bends the will, gives a heart of flesh, sweetly allures by the power of his grace, and engages the soul to come to Christ, and give up itself unto him; he draws *with the cords of a man, with the bands of love.*† Drawing, though it supposes power, yet not always co-action, or violence. Music draws the ear, love the heart, and pleasure the mind, *trahit sua quemque voluptas.*‡ The Jews have a saying,§ that the proselytes in the days of the Messiah shall be גרים גרורים כולם, *all of them proselytes drawn*, that is, such as shall freely and voluntarily become proselytes.

2. In answer to this sense of the word,‖ it is said, "that to be drawn of God, cannot import our being moved by any inward and irresistible impressions to believe in Christ; for then no man could come to Christ without this irresistible impression; and then no other person could be blame-worthy for not believing on him, because they could not do it without that powerful attraction which God was not pleased to afford them; nor could it be praiseworthy to believe in him, because they only did so when they could not choose but do it, as being moved in so doing by a force they were not able to resist." To which I reply, that if by an irresistible impression, is meant such an internal influence of the grace of God upon the soul, which, though opposed, cannot be resisted so as to be overcome, and rendered ineffectual, we affirm, agreeable to these words of Christ, that without this no man can come to him; yet, notwithstanding this, persons may be blame-worthy, as the Jews were, for not believing on him as the Messiah; though without this powerful attraction they could not come to him, and believe in him to the saving of their souls. Besides, though the ability of coming to Christ in a spiritual man-

---

* In Remonstrantia, p. 9. † Hos. xi. 4.
‡ Virgil. § In Talmud, Avoda Zara, fol. 24, vol. i. ‖ Whitby, p. 280; ed 2. 273.

ner is owing to the powerful grace of God in drawing; yet the disability of coming to Christ does not arise from a defect, or want of that powerful attraction, but from the corruption and vitiosity of nature, which being blame-worthy, what springs from it must be so likewise. Moreover, we readily allow, that it is not praise-worthy in men to come to Christ, and believe in him, but that all the praise is due to God, and to his efficacious grace, by which they are what they are in conversion; since faith is the gift of God, and of his sole operation: nor could any come to Christ, unless *it were given unto him of the Father;* and therefore he ought to have all the praise and glory.

3. Whereas it is affirmed,* that " to be drawn of God can only signify,

(1.) " To be persuaded and prevailed upon to come to Christ, by the consideration of the mighty works which God had done to justify that he was the true Messiah; to which Christ appeals as divine testimonies of him, and by which the unbelieving Jews became inexcusable." I answer, it is true, that miracles were proofs of his Messiahship, and which left the Jews, who rejected him, without excuse; but then these works, properly speaking, were done by Christ himself, and the conviction of his being the Messiah from them, and the persuasion to come to him, and believe on him, on the account of them, were from the Spirit; and neither of them the acts of the Father, and so not intended by this act of drawing. Besides, multitudes of souls, both under the Old and New Testament, before, and since the coming of Christ, have been enabled to come to him for life and salvation, who never were persuaded and prevailed upon so to do, by the consideration of miracles. And many who did see the miracles of Christ, did not, in a spiritual manner, come to him, and believe in him. Wherefore our Lord ascribes faith in him to a superior power, to the unfrustrable influences of divine grace, which are here signified by the Father's drawing. Or,

(2.) It is said,† to be drawn by the Father signifies " to be moved by the great promise of eternal life confirmed by these miracles to do it; for where there is a firm belief, and lively sense of that inestimable blessing, it must strongly engage to come to Christ, from whom it is only to be expected." To which I answer, eternal life is, indeed, only to be expected from Christ; and when there is a firm belief and lively sense of it, as in him, and to be had from him, persons will be strongly engaged to go to him for it: but then, what is it that gives that firm belief, and fixes that lively sense of this blessing, so as strongly to engage to come to Christ for it, but the powerful and efficacious grace of God? The bare external revelation of the promise, though confirmed by miracles, will not do it. Instructions by the ministry of the word are not sufficient, unless accompanied with *the demonstration of the Spirit, and of power.* The following words are not a proof of it, *It is written in the prophets, And they shall be all taught of God; every man therefore that hath heard, and hath learned of the Father, cometh unto me :‡* which do intend mere external instructions, or objective teachings, for multitudes are in that way instructed who never come to Christ; but special teachings, such as are attended with the energy of divine grace, with the laws and doctrines of Christ put into the inward part, and written on the heart. Add to all this, our Lord himself explains what he means by the Father's drawing, ver. 65, where he says, *No man can come unto me, except it were given unto him of my Father;* which is more than affording means and motives, it is giving faith itself. What is said to answer to the argument from Matt. vii. 18, and Rom. viii. 7, will be considered hereafter in the next chapter.

SECTION IX

Then hath God also to the Gentiles granted repentance unto life.—Acts xi. 18; with Ephes. ii. 8.

THESE scriptures prove that faith and repentance are the gifts of God, and owing to the powerful operation of his grace. Now.

1. To confront this, it is said,§ " What God commands we must do; and therefore must be active in it : but *God commands all men every where to repent,* Acts xvii. 30, *and to believe in the name of Christ,* 1 John iii. 23, therefore we must be active in the works of faith and repentance." To which I reply, that though what God commands is the rule of man's duty, yet it is not the measure of his strength. It is no good arguing from God's commands, to man's power in his present state. God requires men to keep the whole law; it does not follow from thence, that they are able to do it. So, though it is *his commandment, that we should believe in his Son Jesus Christ, and repent;* yet it is certain, that faith is *not of ourselves,* it is a *gift* of grace, and *of the operation of God;* and the same may be said of repentance. Moreover, though believers are active in the exercise of the graces of faith and repentance; for it is the convinced sinner, and not God or Christ, or the Spirit, who repents and believes; yet in both men are purely passive in the first production and implantation of them in their hearts. But we are told, ‖ that by this way of arguing, the Jews must have been purely passive in all their hardness of heart, Ahab's false prophets in lying, the enemies of God's church in all the evils they do to her, and in the blasphemies they utter against him; because God is said,¶ to *give* a spirit of slumbering, a lying spirit, power to take peace from the earth, and a mouth

---

* Whitby, p. 280; ed. 2. 273.   † Ibid.;
ed. 2. 274.   ‡ Ver. 45.
§ Whitby, p. 283; ed. 2. 276.

‖ Ibid.   ¶ Rom. xi. 8; 1 Kings xxii.
23; Rev. vi. 4, 8, and xiii. 5, 7.

speaking blasphemies. To which I answer, that these judicial acts of God, and as such the persons to whom they relate, were indeed passive in them, these being purely God's acts, and not man's; and yet the Jews were active in hardening their own hearts, Ahab's prophets in following the suggestions of the lying spirit, and the enemies of God's church in using their power to make war with the saints, and in opening their mouths in blasphemy against him.

2. This is laid down * "as a general and rule, *that where God is said to give any thing, the exercise of that faculty is still supposed which he hath given us already;* and God is only said to give it by giving those faculties by which we are enabled to obtain it, and the means and motives which are sufficient to excite those faculties to the performance of their proper actions. Thus it is always with respect to natural and spiritual gifts; for thus God *giveth riches and wisdom.* Thus the Jews say, that God hath *given repentance* to the Gentiles, when, by Peter's preaching to them peace through Jesus Christ, and promising remission of sins upon their repentance, they repented, and believed in Christ. So faith is said to be the gift of God; because the objects of it are only by divine revelation made known, and are only confirmed, and made credible by the testimony God hath given to them." But though the Gentiles repented, and believed in Christ, upon Peter's preaching peace and pardon to them through him; yet it was not through the strength of their natural faculties, or barely through means and motives, exciting their faculties to the performance of these actions, but through the power of the Holy Ghost; for *while Peter yet spake these words, the Holy Ghost fell on all them that heard the word;†* who produced in them these graces of faith and repentance, and assisted them in the exercise of them on their proper objects. Besides, if God may be said to give faith and repentance to men, when he only gives the means of them, and motives to them, he may be said equally to give faith and repentance to men, who do not believe and repent; which is a contradiction in terms, provided they have the same means and motives as those who do. And so Chorazin, Bethsaida, and Capernaum, may be said to have faith and repentance given them; because they had the means of them, and motives to them; the doctrines of Christ were preached unto them, and his mighty works done among them; though our Lord upbraids them with their impenitence and unbelief. So, when faith is said to be the gift of God, if no more is meant by it, than that the objects of it are made known, confirmed, and rendered credible by a divine revelation; then all those may be said to have it given to them, to whom the objects of it are so made known and confirmed. Whereas there are multitudes, who through the external revelation of the word, know that Christ is the object of faith, and yet have no true faith in him. Therefore more is meant than this, even the donation of the grace itself; for *it is given* to men *to believe,* even actually to exercise faith. To which is required, besides the confirming evidence of revelation, the power and grace of God; *for no man can come* to Christ, that is, believe on him, *except the Father draw him.* Nor is it always true, with respect to natural gifts, that God gives riches and wisdom to men, when he gives them faculties, means, and motives of getting wealth and wisdom, see Eccles. ix. 11. When he does give riches and wisdom, he gives more than barely faculties, means, and motives to get them; he gives riches and wisdom themselves: so when he gives faith and repentance, it is not merely natural faculties capable of them, or the bare means of them, or motives inducing to them, but the things themselves.

SECTION X

Whose heart the Lord opened, that she attended unto the things that were spoken of Paul. —Acts xvi. 14.

THE heart of man is naturally shut up against God and Christ, and every thing that is spiritually good; and nothing less than divine power can open it, nor any other but *he that have the key of the house of David, that openeth, and no man shutteth; and shutteth, and no man openeth;‡* which proves that conversion is God's work, and wrought by the power of his grace. In answer to which,

1. It is owned,§ that "God inclined Lydia to do this; but the only question is said to be, whether he did it by any extraordinary and irresistible influence? This it seems reasonable to deny." But, why should it seem reasonable to deny it? Surely, that action which overcomes resistance, and takes out of the way every thing that obstructs, must needs have an irresistible influence. Now, such is this action of opening a poor sinner's heart; it overcomes the opposition within, and removes that which shut, and kept the heart shut to every thing that is spiritually good, and, therefore, must be done by an irresistible influence. Our author proceeds, and reasons thus: "Either she alone was ἀξία, prepared, disposed, and fitted to receive this influence, and then she had done something already towards her conversion; or if it were absolutely necessary that she might believe, and yet she alone, though no more fitted or prepared for it than the rest, received it; the other auditors for want of this extraordinary influence, must lie under a necessity of not believing; and so it could not be blame-worthy in them, that they did not believe." I reply, whether Lydia was the only person or no converted, at this time, is not certain, no mention is made of any other; and that she was fitted and disposed to receive this influence does not appear, no not from her being σεβομένη τὸν Θεόν, *one that worshipped God;* for in

---

* Whitby, p. 283—285; ed. 2. 276—278.
† Acts x. 44.

‡ Rev. iii. 7.   § Whitby, p. 285; ed. 2. 278.

Antioch there were many of these σεβομένων γυναῖκων, *devout and honourable women*, who were so far from being fitted and disposed to believe, that they *raised a persecution against Paul and Barnabas, and expelled them out of their coasts.** And had she been fitted, prepared, and disposed to receive this influence, it does not follow that she had done something towards her conversion, since this might be, and yet no conversion; and, besides, this disposition might be of God, and not of herself. On the other hand it is urged, if she was no more fitted for it than others, and yet received it, the rest, for want of it, must lie under a necessity of not believing, and so could not be blamed for their unbelief. But it should be observed, that though such is the condition of man by the fall, that he cannot believe in Christ, without the powerful influence of divine grace, which God is not obliged to communicate; yet, it is not the withholding of that influence, or denying that grace, which lays him under a necessity of not believing, but it is the corruption of his nature that lays and holds him in the chains of unbelief; and, therefore, his unbelief is not to be imputed to the want of this powerful influence, which God is not obliged to give, but to the vitiosity and wickedness of his heart, on which account he is justly blame-worthy.

2. It is alleged,† that "to *open the heart*, and *to open the ear*, are Scripture phrases of like import; for the effect of both is the same, namely, the rendering the person willing and inclined to do the thing. Now this God sometimes does by his afflicting hand, and sometimes by the preaching of the word; so that they, who have their hearts affected with, and inclined by it to what is good, may be said properly enough to have their hearts opened by it." To which I reply, that both the opening of the ear and of the heart are God's acts, and not man's: and, though God sometimes does these things by afflictions, and by the preaching of the word, as moral instruments, yet neither the one nor the other will ever produce them, without the mighty power of his Spirit and grace accompanying them: and, whereas it is said, that such who have their hearts affected with the word, and inclined by it to that which is good, may be said to have their hearts opened by it. But who, or what is it that gives and produces this affection and inclination? All that hear it are not affected with it, and inclined by it: to what else can this be ascribed, but to the powerful and efficacious grace of God?

3. It is observed,‡ that "God is here said to *open the heart of Lydia*, not to believe, but only προσέχειν, *to attend to the things spoken of Paul;* that is, to weigh and seriously consider of the greatness of the blessings promised to believers, namely, remission of sins and eternal life; and that attention produced faith in her." I reply, that it is true, that

faith comes by hearing, and attending to what is heard; but it is neither hearing nor attention that produces faith, but the grace and power of God: hence it is said to be *the work of God, and of the operation of God.*§ And, if such an act of God's grace and power, as the opening of the heart, is necessary to a proper, profitable, and useful attention to the word, and to a serious consideration of the blessings of it; how much more necessary must it be to the work of conversion, to true saving faith in Christ?

SECTION XI

Turn thou me, and I shall be turned; for thou art the Lord my God.—Jer. xxxi. 18; *with* Deut. xxx. 6.

SINCE God promises to *circumcise the heart,* and Ephraim here, being under afflictive providences, which had not such an effect upon him as to turn him heartily and effectually to the Lord, prays that he would take the work into his own hands more immediately, believing that then he should be thoroughly converted; we conclude, that the circumcision and conversion of the heart are the works of God in us, in which we are passive; that they are wrought by his powerful grace, without which all means are insufficient to produce them. Now,

1. In answer to such texts as these, in general, this is laid down as a most certain rule:‖ "that when God doth require us to do what he himself doth promise, and hath made it our duty to perform, his promise is only to perform what is requisite, on his part, towards the work." But this author should have informed us what that is which is requisite on God's part, and what that is which is man's duty to perform, towards the work of conversion. Whereas nothing is more certain, than that God does both require of us to do, and he himself promises to do, the whole work of conversion; which he does not by persuasion, or laying before us inducements to it, as is suggested, but by unfrustrable influence. And yet his command to do it does not imply that we are gods, or have equal power with him, as is intimated; nor does praying to him for the performance of what he requires of us, and he has promised, suppose a desire to be excused from obeying his commands. The commands of God show his authority, and man's duty; the promises of God discover his grace and power, and are a relief to man's weakness, which no way lessen his obligation to duty.

2. It is observed,¶ that "the same God, who promiseth to circumcise the hearts of his people, requires them to circumcise their own hearts, Deut. x. 16, Jer. iv. 5. And it is suggested, that the promise is conditional, namely, if they would call to mind the blessings and curses he had pronounced, ver. 1, and turn to the Lord, ver. 2, and that it is made to all their seed, to nations, and not

---

* Acts xiii. 50.   † Whitby, p. 285, 286; ed. 2. 279.   ‡ Ibid.   § John vi. 22;

Coloss. ii. 12.   ‖ Whitby, p. 286, 287; ed. 279, 280.   ¶ Ibid. p. 217; ed. 2. 280.

particular persons." I reply, that the passages referred to have been considered in the former part* of this performance; and as to the conditions mentioned, if they are conditions, they are not conditions of the circumcision of the hearts of God's people, but of turning‧ their captivity. And though this promise is made to their seed, as well as to themselves, yet not to *all* their seed, much less to nations. Besides, it particularly regards the time of the Jews' conversion, when all the elect of God among them shall be saved.

3. It is said,† that "seeing God so frequently requires of the same persons, that they should turn themselves from their transgressions, promising life to the penitent, and threatening those that would not with death; and seeing he complains so oft‧of his own people, and of that very Ephraim which made this prayer, that they would not turn to him; it must be absurd to urge this prayer to excuse men from a duty required by God under such dreadful penalties." To which may be returned: that the duty required by God, in the places referred to, does not design internal conversion, but external reformation; which latter, men may be capable of effecting, though not of the former. Though admitting internal conversion is meant, God's requiring it does not suppose man's ability to perform it, but his need of it; and is done with a view to bring him to a sense of his state, and that he may apply to God for it, as Ephraim did. Nor does such a prayer for conversion excuse men from obligation to turn to the Lord, or any duty respecting the outward walk and conversation; so far from it, that converting grace, when obtained, puts men into a capacity, and engages them to *live soberly, righteously, and godly in this world.* And whereas it is added, "that by comparing this prayer with the preceding chapter, in which God promises so oft to turn their captivity, it appears this is only a prayer that God would bring them out of that‧thraldom, like that of the Psalmist, Psal. cxxvi. 4." Let it be observed, that this is a sense which the Jews themselves, who are ready to explain scriptures this way whenever they have the least opportunity, do not give into. The Targum paraphrases the words thus, לפולחנך אתיבנא, *turn us to thy worship.* Kimchi observes, that it is as if it was said קבלני בתשובה, *receive me by repentance.* Besides, it is plain, that what Ephraim here prayed for, he quickly had, as appears from ver. 19, upon which followed true repentance; and being a dear son, and pleasant child to God, ver. 20, he comforts him by assuring him that he would have mercy on him; and as an evidence of it, bids him *turn again to his cities,* which indeed designs the turning of his captivity: but then this is manifestly distinguished from the turning Ephraim prayed for, and which he enjoyed before he had this encouragement to turn to his cities.

4. The Remonstrants‡ formerly paraphrased the words thus: "As thou hast chastised

Ephraim, O Lord, so chastise me; for though I am in part chastised, yet chastise me more and more:" and they farther suggest, "that they do not intend first conversion; since he being converted prays." In which may be observed, that this sense of the text introduces another person, speaking to the Lord, besides Ephraim, contrary to the express words, and plain reading of them: nor is the word שוב, here translated *turn,* ever used for affliction or chastisement in all the word of God, though sometimes for deliverance from it: nor is there any command, or example of men's praying for affliction; for though they sometimes pray, that afflictions may be sanctified, and that they may be supported under or delivered from them, yet never, that they may be brought upon them, or increased. And as to what is intimated, that the text is not to be understood of first conversion, being the prayer of a converted man; it may be replied, that it does not appear that Ephraim (for no other person can be meant) was then converted, at least in his own apprehensions, but afterwards, see ver. 19. Moreover, Ephraim is to be understood not of a single person, but of a body of men; many of whom, and it may be the greatest part, were not converted: nor is his praying a sufficient evidence of his conversion; since a natural man is capable of praying, and of praying for conversion, under some awakenings of conscience. But be it so, that Ephraim was converted, and that he prayed not for the first work of conversion, but for the farther progress and carrying of it on, or for a renewal of it after backslidings; yet if this could not be done by himself, but required the grace and power of God; much less can the first work of conversion be wrought by a graceless creature; and much more must that work require the powerful and efficacious grace of God.

SECTION XII

But this shall be the covenant that I will make with the house of Israel; After those days, saith the Lord, I will put my law in their inward parts, and write it in their hearts.—Jer. xxxi. 33.

THESE phrases of *putting,* and *writing* the law of God *in the inward parts* of the heart, do not mean barely a making known the nature of the moral law, as to the spirituality and perfection of it, or the glory and excellency of the gospel, its truths and ordinances; but a creating in the soul a real and hearty affection for these things, and a subjecting of it to them by the power of divine grace; and indeed, are expressive of an internal work of the powerful grace of God upon the soul, in which man is as passive as a vessel is, in which any thing is put; or as paper and parchment on which any thing is written. Now, to this the following things are objected.

1st. That "these promises are made ex-

---

pressly to the whole house of Israel, to all with whom the *old covenant* was made, and whom God *brought out of Egypt,* and would bring again *out of captivity;* and therefore can be no covenant made with the elect of the house of Israel and Judah; because then the whole nation of the Jews must have been elected and converted; and because it is made with those who *kept not his former covenant;* whereas the elect always persist, say these men, in their covenant with God; this therefore can be no new covenant with them.''* To which I reply, that these promises are not made to the same individual persons, not to all, nor to any, with whom the old covenant was made, whom God brought out of Egypt, and whose carcasses fell in the wilderness, but their posterity; for it is expressly said in ver. 32, that this new covenant is *not according to the covenant that God made with their fathers in the day* he *took them by the hand to bring them out of the land of Egypt.* And though they are made to the house of Israel, yet they are not said to be made to the *whole* house of Israel, and to *all* the children of Israel and Judah; and therefore might be made to the elect of the house of Israel. Whence it does not follow, that the whole nation of the Jews must have been elected and converted; nor was it made with those who kept not the former covenant; nor do we say that the elect always persist in *their* covenant with God; for we know that the covenants, vows, and promises they make, are often broken; but we say, that they always abide in God's covenant with them, and are always his people, and he their God; and which notwithstanding is a new covenant to them, especially under the gospel-dispensation, to which these promises refer, being under a new mode of administration, and always new in perpetual force and vigour. Besides, the house of Israel, and the house of Judah, may be taken literally or figuratively; if literally, this prophecy concerning them was accomplished in the times of Christ and his apostles, who first preached the gospel, and made known the new covenant of grace to the Jews; many of whom were converted under it, the gospel *being the power of God unto salvation, to the Jew first, and also to the Greek:*† they may be taken figuratively, and design the elect of God, whether among Jews or Gentiles; for as there was an *Israel after the flesh,* so there was one after the Spirit: even *the whole Israel of God,* the chosen vessels of salvation, to whom the new covenant and all the blessings of it peculiarly belong.

2dly. It is said,‡ that "these words. *I will put my law in their inward parts, and write it in their hearts,* import two things:

1. "That he would clearly make known his will to them, so that they need not be at much pains to find it out, as in Deut. xxx. 11—14, Rom. x. 8, and ii. 14." To which I answer, that though these words import a

clear and plain discovery of God's will, yet that is not all; for there may be and is a clear and plain revelation of God's will externally made in the scriptures, and by the ministry of the word to some persons, in whose hearts nothing is internally put or written: whence it follows that putting and writing the law of God in the heart, is something more, and what is distinct from, a bare making known the will of God, though never so clear and plain; and must intend an internal operation and application of God's grace. Moreover, where the knowledge of God, of his grace, mind and will, is spiritual, experimental, and saving, that follows upon, and is the fruit and effect of the putting and writing the law in the heart, as appears from the following verse; and is owned by the author of this exception. Once more, when the Gospel, which is the grand revelation of God's will, has a place in the hearts of any, it is owing to the powerful and efficacious grace of God that accompanies it, opens the heart, and lets it in; where it is not only clearly known, but affectionately received, experimentally felt, and truly believed.

2. "An§ inculcating them on the soul by the Holy Spirit, so as that they may be still fresh upon the memory; so Deut. vi. 6, and xi. 18, Prov. iii. 1, 3. Whence it follows, that these promises cannot be so understood, as if God by them engaged to do the whole work, which he hath engaged us so expressly to perform." To which I reply, that the persons spoken to in the cited passages were not unconverted persons, but such who had been under the first work of conversion: and the phrases of laying up and writing the laws of God in their hearts intend more than a bare remembrance of them, even a strong affection for them, and close attachment to them; so *the sin of Judah* is said‖ to be *graven upon the table of the heart,* which does not intend their consciousness of it, and the keeping of it in their memory; but on the contrary, stupidity, insensibility of it, indolence about it, and a stiff tenacious adherence to it, as well as affection for it. And should these phrases intend no more here, can it be supposed, that there should ever be an affection for the law of God, or a close adherence to the Gospel of Christ, in such whose *carnal minds* were *enmity to God,* and not *subject to the law of God, nor could* they be, without the powerful operation of God's mighty grace? Since then these words import, besides a clear knowledge of the law and Gospel, and an imprinting the eternal truths of both in the mind, a hearty affection for them, which issues in a professed subjection to them; this must be owing, not to the power and will of man, but to the unfrustrable and insuperable grace of God. And this objector owns, that the inculcating them on the soul must be purely passive. The passage in Jer. xxxii. 49, will be considered under the head of the saints' perseverance.

---

* Whitby, p. 288, 289; ed. 2. 281, 282.   ed. 2. 282.   Ibid. p. 290; ed. 2. 282.
† Rom. i. 16.   ‡ Whhitby, p. 289;   ‖ Jer. xvii. 1.

SECTION XIII.

A new heart also will I give you, and a new spirit will I put within you; and I will take away the stony heart out of your flesh, and I will give you a heart of flesh.—Ezek. xxxvi. 26.

THESE words, with those chap. xi. 19, 20, prove that conversion is the work of God, and not of man; that man is passive in and cannot contribute to his regeneration and renovation, his heart being like a stone, hard and inflexible, on which no impressions are made until this hardness is removed; which man is incapable of, and is done by God, when he gives *a heart of flesh*, a soft and sensible one, or *a new heart*, and *a new spirit*, in which are new principles, affections, and resolutions; and which can be ascribed to nothing less than the omnipotent and unfrustrable grace of God. Now it is said,* that the arguments, taken from both these places, have two of the general faults which render all arguments of this nature null. As,

1st. "That they speak of all the whole house of Israel, chap. xi. 15, and xxxvi. 21, 22, to all that were *gathered out of all countries, and brought to their own land*, ver. 24, and so belong not to the elect only." But it should be observed, that all the whole house of Israel, and every individual thereof, were not gathered out of all countries, upon the return of the Jews from the Babylonish captivity, which seems to be here designed; nor are the whole house of Israel here spoken of, neither is it here promised, nor in Ezek. xi. 19, to the whole house of Israel, that God would give to them all a new heart, and a new spirit, only to some who are distinguished from them, ver. 21, *whose heart walked after the heart of their detestable things, and their abominations:* and therefore the Lord threatens to *recompense their ways upon their own heads.* It remains then, that these promises were made to and fulfilled in the spiritual Israel, the elect of God among them, the people whom he foreknew. Farther,

1. It is said,† if it "respects their return from the Babylonish captivity, it must be conditional, the books of Ezra and Nehemiah, and especially the complaints of the prophet Malachi, showing that they were never fulfilled in many of them, and from Ezek. xi. 21." To which I answer, that these promises were not made to all the people of Israel, as has been observed; therefore there needed no condition to be either understood or expressed either in this or in the parallel text, to suit them to these people and times; for, though the people was wicked who returned from captivity, yet there was not only an external reformation made among them, but an inward sense of things was given to a large number of them, as appeared at the reading of the law to them by Ezra. And it may be observed, that the people was never so addicted to idolatry after their return from their captivity as before; so that the promises in this and the preceding verse had a considerable accomplishment at this time.

2. Moreover, it is also objected,‡ that "according to this exposition it must follow, that not one good man came out of the captivity, not one of them with a new or a clean heart; but all of them with a *heart of stone*, which was to be taken away." I reply as before, that these promises were not made to them all; and therefore the consequence does not follow. Besides, some good men might, as no doubt did, come out of the captivity; though the majority might be wicked, who stood in need of the things promised. Moreover, good men stand daily in need of being *renewed in the spirit of* their *minds*, and often of having *clean hearts created, and right spirits renewed in* them.

3. It is also suggested,§ that this promise "relates to the conversion of the Jewish nation yet to come, and to them alone; and therefore all Christians may as well expect to be exempted from *famine*, ver. 30, and to have *increase of corn*, ver. 27, and their waste *places and fenced cities built*, ver. 33, 35, as the other blessings promised here." To which I answer, that though the temporal blessings here promised were peculiar to the Jews, yet the spiritual ones are such as all real Christians not only may expect, but have; and therefore, admitting that the words refer to the time of the conversion of the Jews, inasmuch as Gentile believers are made partakers of the same spiritual blessings and promises, are called in the same hope of their calling, and saved by the same grace of the Lord Jesus, as the Jews will be; there is all the reason imaginable to conclude, that they are regenerated and converted by the same grace and power; God not making use of two different methods of conversion, one among the Jews, and another among the Gentiles.

2dly. It is observed,‖ that "God doth expressly command these persons, by the same prophet, *to make themselves a new heart and a new spirit*, chap. xviii. 31, which assures us that something was required, on their parts, towards the completion of this promise." But these cannot be the same persons whom God, by the prophet, commands to make them a new heart, to whom he here promises to give one, if this promise relates, as it is said to do, to the conversion of the Jewish nation yet to come; seeing the persons God commands to make themselves a new heart were the house of Israel, then in being of Ezekiel's time; the meaning of which exhortation, and its consistence with man's passiveness, and the efficacious and unfrustrable grace of God in conversion, have been shown in the first part of this work.¶

---

* Ibid. p. 292; ed. 2. 284.
† Ibid.   ‡ Ibid.   § Ibid.

‖ Whitby, p. 292, 293; ed. 2. 285.
¶ Sect. **xxi**.

SECTION XIV

For it is God which worketh in you, both to will and to do of his good pleasure.—Phil. ii. 13; *with Heb.* xii. 21.

FROM these passages it appears, that the work of grace is the work of God only, which he produces by an irresistible and insuperable power, according to his sovereign will and pleasure; that there is no good thing in us, but what he works in us; and no good thing done by us, but what is owing to his efficacious grace; the will and power to do any thing spiritually good are both from him, for man, in his fallen state, has neither of himself. Now, "that God doth this is not denied: the question is, whether he doth it by a physical operation, unfrustrable by the will of man, or by internal suasion, or inducements to prevail upon us thus to will and do; and that he doth this only in this latter sense is said,* to be evident,

"1. From ver. 12, where we are commanded to *work out our own salvation,* in which we cannot be purely passive; nor is it a reason, that God works in us both to will and to do, why we should, but rather why we should not will, or work at all; if both is and will be irresistibly performed without us. We are also bid to do this *with fear and trembling;* but surely, if God unfrustrably works in us both to will and to do, there can be no possibility of miscarrying, and so no ground for fear and trembling. Besides, the Philippians were exhorted to do this *much more in St. Paul's absence than in his presence.* The only reason of which is, that he being present, stirred them up by his counsels and exhortations to do what was according to the mind of God, to which they in his absence were immediately excited by the suggestions of the Holy Spirit." To all which I reply, that the salvation the apostle exhorts the Philippians to work out, was not the spiritual and eternal salvation of their souls in general, nor the work of conversion in particular, which was already wrought in them; but the duties of religion, or things which accompany salvation, as has been shown in the former† part of this work; in which they might be active, though in the good work of grace upon their souls they had been passive. Nor could any thing be a greater encouragement to them, to be active in the discharge of duty, than this; that God had laid in them principles of action, had wrought in them *both to will and to do.* The *fear and trembling,* with which they were to do these things, is not a slavish fear lest the work of grace should miscarry, but a reverence of the Divine Being, and humility of soul, which become believers in the performance of every religious action. And as for their obeying, *much more in St. Paul's absence than in his presence,* this is no part of the exhortation, but is prefaced to it

by way of commendation, in order to animate and excite them to it with more diligence and cheerfulness. After all, if God works in us not by an unfrustrable operation, but by an operation frustrable by the will of man, how does he *work in us both to will and to do of his good pleasure?*

2. It is observed‡ that the word ἐνεργεῖ doth not require this sense is evident; "because in Scripture it occurs very often, when it must be understood not of a physical, but only of a moral operation, as in Eph. ii. 2; 2 Thess. ii. 7, 9, 11; Heb. iv. 12; 1 Thess. ii. 13; Gal. v. 6; Philemon 6; Rom. vii. 5." I answer, that this word always signifies a powerful and efficacious operation, agreeable to the nature of the person or thing which is said to work; so Satan and Antichrist are said to *work,* Eph. ii. 2, 2 Thess. ii. 7, 9, and that effectually, *with all power and lying wonders;* so *the word of God is powerful, and works effectually in them that believe,* Heb. iv. 12, 1 Thess. ii. 13, when it comes *not in word only, but also in power, and in the Holy Ghost;* or when it is clothed with a divine power, though the former of these texts seems rather to be understood of Christ, the essential Word, than of the written word. So *faith* is said to *work by love,* Gal. v. 6, and *the communication* of it, and not charity, to be *effectual,* Philemon 6, when by the secret power of the Spirit it is influenced, and drawn forth into exercise, and shows itself by love and good works. So *the motions of sin,* in the hearts of unregenerate men, *work* powerfully, effectually, and without control, *to bring forth fruit unto death,* Rom. vii. 5. And, where this word is made use of to express any action of God's, it always signifies such an operation as is not to be frustrated, or made void, see Eph. i. 11, and iii. 20, Phil. iii. 21, Col. i. 29, and that it has this signification in the text before us is evident, both from the general sense of the word, and the nature of the work. Add to this, in the King's manuscript§ the words are read ὁ ἐνεργῶν ὁ γυνάμει ἐν ὑμῖν, *who worketh by his power in you;* therefore, not by moral suasion, but by the mighty power of his grace.

3. It is said,‖ "that both these places speak of men already believing, and converted; and therefore must be impertinently alleged to prove men must be purely passive in the work of conversion." But admitting this, which will be readily done, the allegation of them is not impertinent; since, if persons already believing and converted, are not able either to will or to do any thing spiritually good of themselves, much less able must unconverted persons be. And if so much is required to work in them both to will and to do, how much more is requisite in the regeneration and conversion of a dead sinner? And if the saints are so passive under the exertions of that power which enables them to act, insomuch that they do not

---

* Whitby, p. 294.   † Sect. xliii.
‡ Whitby, p. 295; ed. 2. 286. 287.
§ See Grotius and Hammond, in loc.

‖ Whitby, ibid.; Curcell. p. 410; Limborch, p. 387.

and cannot act until it is put forth, much more must they be passive in the first production of the work of grace upon their souls.

SECTION XV

For who maketh thee to differ from another? And what hast thou, that thou didst not receive? Now if thou didst receive it, why dost thou glory as if thou hadst not received it?—1 Cor. iv. 7.

NOT man's free will, care, industry, and diligence, but efficacious grace makes the difference in conversion; as abundantly appears, when two men, equally enjoying the same means, and are equally called in an external way, and the one is converted, and the other not: for who is it, then, that puts the difference? Not man, but God. Now,

1. It is excepted,* "that the apostle manifestly speaks here of those extraordinary gifts of the Spirit, the gifts of tongues and prophecy, &c., which being infused without human industry, and conferred on Christians without any such co-operation of their faculties as is required to the exercise of any Christian duty or moral virtue, it cannot with like reason be inquired of these duties, as it may be of those gifts, *Who made thee to differ from another* in them? Nor can it from them be duly inferred, that no man doth any thing to make himself differ from another in any virtue or pious disposition, to which men are stirred up by powerful motives, and praised by God for doing what others neglected to do; as in the case of the *Bereans*, the *elder* and the *younger* son, the *publicans* and *harlots*, compared with the *scribes* and *pharisees*, the penitent *publican* and the proud *pharisee*." To which may be replied, that there is not the least syllable said by the apostle, either in the text or context, of the gift of tongues, or of any other extraordinary gift of the Spirit; nor is he speaking to ministers, or of any gift of theirs, by which they were distinguished from other men, or from one another; but to private Christians, the members of the church at Corinth, who were striving about and boasting of their ministers, and crying up one to a neglect and contempt of another: one valued himself upon his being converted under such a man's ministry, and being baptized by him; another under another man's ministry, and being baptized by him, and of the good judgment each of them had formed, and the choice they had made of their respective ministers; wherefore, the apostle † exhorts them not to *think of men above that which is written, that no one of* them *be puffed up for one against another,* that is, for one minister against another; *for,* adds he, *who maketh thee to differ?* Some of you have been converted under this, and some under that man's ministry; but these men have been only instruments in your conversion; it is God, who, by his grace, has made the difference between

you and others; and if you have enjoyed any blessing under their respective ministrations, you have received it from God; and, therefore, should not glory either in yourselves or in them, but in God, who has distinguished you by his favours. Now, since the apostle speaks not to ministers, but to the body of the people, it does not appear that he manifestly speaks of the extraordinary gifts of the Spirit: for were they *all workers of miracles?*‡ Had they *all the gifts of healing?* Or could they *all speak with tongues,* or *all interpret?* Besides, suppose the apostle does here speak of extraordinary gifts; since true saving grace in conversion is preferable in its nature and use to them all, and God is allowed to make a difference by the one, why not by the other? Shall we allow him to make a difference in and by the lesser instance of his favours, and not in the greater? Moreover, the apostle does not expressly instance in any one particular thing, but in general inquires, *Who maketh thee to differ?* in any thing, in any one instance whatever: *What hast thou that thou didst not receive?* nothing at all; and therefore holds good, and is equally true of the difference made in conversion, and of the blessings then bestowed, as of any thing else. As to Christian duties, or moral virtues, in the exercise of which men distinguish themselves from one another, that is not the point in question. The question is not, whether men may make themselves to differ from others in the performance of these things, but, whether one man, by the power of his free will, can make himself to differ from another in conversion; this difference, we affirm, is owing to the efficacious grace of God. Besides, the performance even of these things, in a spiritual manner, is not owing to the power of men's free will, or barely to the exciting grace of God, or to men's being stirred up to them by motives, but to the powerful grace of God enabling them so to act. What was it else but this grace, which so powerfully operated in the Bereans, as that they received the word readily, and searched the Scriptures with so much diligence, which remarkably distinguished them from the Thessalonians? Was it not the grace of God which enabled the *elder* son to repent and go and work in his father's vineyard, when the second or *younger* son was left to his own free will, and the bare resolutions of nature? To whom can it be ascribed, but to him who has *the key of David, who opens and no man shuts, and shuts and no man opens,* that *publicans and harlots* should *go into the kingdom of God* before the self-willed *scribes and pharisees?* And it was nothing less than the powerful grace of God which wrought in the heart of the penitent *publican,* and made him so; which gave him the sense he had of himself, and of his need of mercy through a mediator, which rendered him more acceptable to God than the proud *pharisee.*

2. "To the question, when two are equally

---

* Whitby, p. 296; ed. 2. 288; Remonstr. in Coll. Hag. art. ii. & iv. p. 316; Limborch, p. 389.

† Verse 6.   ‡ 1 Cor. xii. 29, 30.

called and one converted, *Who is it that puts the difference?* it is said,* the answer, grounded on God's own righteous judgment, will be this: that man puts the difference, and not God only, because God judges not his own acts, but the acts of men." I reply, that this is a very improper answer to the question; which is not when two men are before the judge, the one is condemned, and the other acquitted, *who puts the difference?* But when two men are equally called by the external ministry of the word, the one is converted and the other not, *who makes the difference?* The methods God takes in conversion, and which he will take in the last judgment, are very different, as the things themselves are; in the former, he proceeds according to his justice. Men will be judged according to their works, but none are saved, or called, or converted by them, or according to them; in conversion he makes a difference, in the future judgment he will find one, and act according to it. Men will be considered, in that awful day, not barely as converted or unconverted persons, but as righteous or sinners; none will be condemned because God did not convert them or call them by his grace, but because they sinned against his law. On the other hand, the saints will be acquitted as righteous persons, through the righteousness of Christ, which gives them a title to heaven, and for which regenerating and converting grace makes them meet.

SECTION XVI

For by grace are ye saved through faith; and that not of yourselves, it is the gift of God; not of works, lest any man should boast.—Ephes. ii. 8, 9; with 1 Cor. i. 29.

THE arguments in favour of the efficacious grace of God in conversion, from these passages of scripture, are as follow,

1st. Faith, through which men are saved, and which is so considerable a part of the work of grace that the whole is denominated from it; *the work of faith is not of ourselves*, it does not spring from nature, nor is it produced in us by our own power, but is entirely *the gift of God's* grace, which he implants in us, enables us to exercise, supports and increases, and perfects, or fulfils with power. To which is excepted, that "Faith is not here called the gift of God,† but salvation by grace through faith." I reply, admitting that the apostle does not so immediately refer to faith in particular, but to salvation in general, as the gift of God; yet, since this salvation is wholly of grace, and not of works, is through faith, not as a work, having any casual influence, but as a mean of God's appointing, it cannot stand excluded from being a gift of God; nor is this the only place in which it is so called, see John vi. 65, Phil. i. 29.

2dly. If salvation is wholly of grace, and

not of works, then conversion, which is a considerable branch of salvation, is also of grace, and not of works; and consequently there is no room for boasting; whereas, if conversion were the work of man's power and free will, and not the work of God's powerful and efficacious grace, he would have whereof to boast. In answer to which,

1. It is said,‡ that the phrase, *Ye are saved by grace*, "cannot mean that they are actually saved, but only that they were called to a state of salvation, enjoyed the means, and were put into the way of salvation by grace." But, why not actually saved? Since salvation was not only in God's purpose appointed for them, and was actually wrought out and obtained for them by Christ, but was also brought home, and really applied to their souls by the Spirit of God; so that they were now *saved according to the mercy* of God, *by the washing of regeneration, and the renewing of the Holy Ghost.*§ Besides, if all such may be said to be *saved by grace*, who are externally called, or enjoy the means, the gospel of the grace of God; then unbelievers, as well as believers, such who put away the word of God from them, as well as they that receive it, such to whom it is the savour of death, as well as those to whom it is the savour of life, may be said to be saved by grace.

2. It is affirmed,‖ that "though actual salvation depends upon good works, or sincere obedience, and though faith is the condition of justification, and good works of salvation, yet is all boasting utterly excluded; because the revelation, which contains the matters and motives of faith, and the miracles which engage to it, is the free gift of God; and because the good works we do, proceed not from ourselves, but are the fruits of faith, and performed in the strength of God. It is of his preventing and exciting grace that we will, and of his assisting grace that we are enabled to perform that will: and it is still of grace that any of these things, which deserve nothing from God, find acceptance with him." I am very glad to observe, that all these things, last-mentioned, are owned to arise from the grace of God; which is far from agreeing with the scheme our author contends for throughout this performance of his, and contradicts the notion of salvation depending on good works; which notion is against the express letter of the text before us, as well as thwarts many other passages of Scripture; see Rom. iii. 20, 28; 2 Tim. i. 9; Tit. iii. 5. Moreover, if actual salvation depends on good works, man has something to boast of; *boasting* is not *excluded by the law*, or doctrine *of works*, that is, by the doctrine of salvation by works; *if Abraham*, or any other man, *were justified by works, he hath whereof to glory*, Rom. iii. 27, and iv. 2.

3. It is observed,¶ "that the Scripture

* Whitby, p. 297; ed. 2. 289.
† Remonstr. in Coll. Hag. art. iii. & iv. p. 306; Curcell. p. 465.   ‡ Whitby, p. 210, 297;
ed. 2. 204, 290.   § Tit. iii. 5.
‖ Whitby, p. 298; ed. 2. 290.
¶ Ibid. p. 299; ed. 2, 392.

plainly grants that there is καύχημα, or *matter or glorying*, in things done by the assistance of the grace of God, as in 1 Cor. ix. 15 ; 2 Cor. xi. 10, and i. 12 ; Gal. vi. 4." I reply, that the words καύχημα, and καυχαομαι, are used by the apostle Paul,* and do not signify an ascribing anything to one's self, as proud boasters do ; but a satisfaction, pleasure, and exultation of mind, as in the places referred to. The two first of which, 1 Cor. ix. 15, 2 Cor. xi. 10, respect his preaching of the gospel, and not barely that, but the preaching of it without charge ; which upon reflection, for many reasons, gave him an inward pleasure and satisfaction, and at the same time he declared, that *though* he *preached the gospel*, he *had nothing to glory of.* The next passage cited from 2 Cor. i. 12, regards the agreeable life and *conversation* of the apostle, and other ministers *in the world ;* which he attributes, *not to fleshly wisdom*, then there would be room for glorying ; but to *the grace of God*, which was matter of *rejoicing*, though not of vain boasting. The last of these scriptures, Gal. vi. 4, regards also the external conversion of the saints ; which, when agreeable to the gospel of Christ, yields a pleasing reflection within a man's self ; so that he has no need to look out to others, to borrow any glory from them, by comparing himself with them, as the proud Pharisee did, when he said, *God I thank thee that I am not as other men are, extortioners, unjust, adulterers, or even as this publican.*

3rdly. God has so contrived the business of our salvation, that *no flesh should glory in his sight.* Now if salvation, in any part of it, is to be ascribed to man, if conversion is not entirely God's work, but man co-operates with him in the production of grace, then the whole glory of that work is not due to God. But,

1. This is thought † to be "sufficiently accounted for by observing, that the principle, by which man co-operates with him in this work, is derived from him ; and all the motives which excite this principle to act, arise purely from God's preventing and exciting grace." I confess, this is owning a great deal, but not enough : for this principle is not barely *derived* from God, but *implanted* by him ; in which man is purely passive, and does not nor can he co-operate with him in the production of it. Moreover, though the motives which excite this principle to act are from the Lord, yet they must be attended with the powerful grace of God, or they will never excite the principle to act. Besides, though man is an agent, and acts for God, and his glory, under the influence of grace, in consequence of a principle of it wrought in him, yet he is no agent in the forming of that principle ; were he, though an under one, part of the glory of it would belong to him ; wherefore if God is chief

agent, yet, if not a sole one in this work, the whole glory of it is not due to him.

2. It is observed,‡ that "our Lord, and his apostles, often commend the good actions of men ; and Christ will at last say to the righteous man, *Well done, thou good and faithful servant.*" But then it should be observed, that these praises and commendations do not regard the work of grace and conversion, but the fruits of it in the lives and conversations of the saints ; which though God, of his great grace and goodness, is pleased to praise, commend, and signify his acceptance of, yet, these persons are taught by the same grace to own, that when they have done all they can, they are but *unprofitable servants ;* and that it is *by the grace of God* they are what they are, and do what they do.§ And when Christ at the last day shall speak of their good works, and say to them,‖ *I was an hungred, and ye gave me meat, I was thirsty, and ye gave me drink*, &c., they will reply, as having forgotten them, putting no trust in them, or ascribing the glory of them to themselves, *When saw we thee an hungred, and fed thee ; or thirsty, and gave thee drink ?* &c.

CHAPTER V.

OF THE CORRUPTION OF HUMAN NATURE, AND THE IMPOTENCE OF THE WILL OF MAN TO THAT WHICH IS SPIRITUALLY GOOD

THE learned writer,¶ whose performance I am now considering, affirms, "that the doctrine which teacheth that man, by the fall, hath contracted such a disability to what is good, that without the special grace of God he can do nothing that is truly good, and is fallen under such a servitude to sin, as renders it necessary for him to be still doing evil, has no foundation in the holy Scriptures." And, whereas "it is very reasonable to expect both plain and frequent testimonies of the holy Scriptures, saying, that man is, by the fall of Adam, become utterly unable to do anything that is good, or anything that God requires of him in an acceptable manner ; yea, that by reason of the fall alone, his faculties are so horribly perverted, that he can do only what is evil, and cannot but do evil ; the whole Scripture hath not one saying of this nature." The falsehood of which will appear in the following sections ; where I shall endeavour to make it evident, that such is the corruption of human nature, derived from Adam, and such man's disability, contracted by it, that without the special grace of God he can do nothing spiritually good, and only that which is evil ; and that from those very passages of Scripture, this author singles out, and objects to as proofs of it.

---

* Vide Beza, in Gal. vi. 14.
† Whitby, p. 300 ; ed. 2. 292.   ‡ Ibid. p. 301 ; ed. 2. 294.   § Luke xvii. 10 ;

1 Cor. xv. 10.   ‖ Matt. xxv. 35, 37.
¶ Whitby, p. 323, 325 ; ed. 2. 315, 317.

SECTION I

*Who can bring a clean thing out of an un-
clean?   Not one.*—Job xiv. 4.

ABEN EZRA observes, that the sense of these
words is the same with Psal. li. 5, and
the meaning of them is, who can bring one
that is pure, כחובין מן גבר דאסתאב, *from a man
defiled with sins?* as the Targum paraphrases
them; none but God can do this; of which
there never was but one instance, the man
Christ Jesus, who not descending from Adam
by ordinary generation, was not polluted with
sin.   Now Job makes mention of the corruption of nature, as the source of all the
sorrows and frailty of man in general, ver. 1,
2, and as matter of humiliation to himself,
and as a reason why he could not bear the
strict judgment of God, but must humbly
plead for his grace and mercy, ver. 3.   But,
against this sense of the words,

1. It is objected,* that they are obscure,
and interpreters disagree about the meaning
of them; and therefore can be no solid proof
of the point in question.   But, perhaps, the
obscurity is not so much in the words as in
the interpreters, who give either false or improper senses of them.   Some understand
them of the impurity of matter, out of which
the body of man was formed at first; whereas, neither that matter, nor the body of man
formed out of it, was impure.   Others, of
the vileness of man, when compared with
God, as in chap. iv. 17—19, and xv. 14, 16,
and xxv. 4, 5.   When neither here, in the
places cited, is any mention of a comparative
uncleanness of men with God, but of the
angels, the heavens, the moon and stars;
from whence a real impurity in man is argued,
who therefore must be abominable in the
sight of God.   Others think Job refers to
the impurity of men's actions; and that his
meaning is, that nothing is to be expected
from a polluted man, but what savours of
the corruption of his nature.   This is a truth,
but not the truth of the text; yet not subversive of it, it rather confirms it.

2. It is urged,† that Job here speaks not
of a moral but physical uncleanness; such as
diseases, filthy ulcers, &c., arising from the
infirmity and corruptibility of nature; and
that his meaning is, it was enough that he
was attended with common infirmities, without being pressed with greater and extraordinary ones.   But, are all men attended with
diseases?   Yea, are all so, who are born of
distempered parents?   Are all born with
filthy ulcers?   Was Job brought into the
world with his boils upon him?   If it should
be said, though this is not the case of all
men, yet there is the common infirmity of
nature, the spring of all these disorders, in
all men.   It is true, indeed, that man, in his
fallen state, is subject to these things? but
from whence does this infirmity of nature

arise, but from the corruption and vitiosity
of it?

3. It is said,‡ that the meaning of this
Scripture is, "that from parents, obnoxious
to sin, will spring forth children; that when
they come to discern between good and evil,
will be obnoxious to sin also."   I answer,
that parents and their children are not only
obnoxious to sin, but are really sinners; and
be it so, that they are only obnoxious to sin,
from whence does this obnoxiousness arise?
It must be either from example, or from depravity; not from the former, since men are
obnoxious to, and capable of committing sins
they never saw committed; wherefore, this
must spring from the corruption of nature.

SECTION II.

*Behold, I was shapen in iniquity, and in sin
did my mother conceive me.*—Psalm li. 5;
with Psalm lviii. 3; Isa. xlviii. 8.

DAVID, having committed some very great
sins, and being made sensible of them, inge-
niously confesses them, and mourns over the
depravity of his nature, the fountain of them;
which he mentions not as an extenuation, but
as an aggravation, of his iniquities, since he
had been so early and so long a sinful creature.   The sin and iniquity he speaks of he
does not call *his* sin, and *his* iniquity, though
it was so, being in his nature, but *sin* and *iniquity*, being common to him with all mankind, and which attended his conception and
formation in the womb, before he was born,
and so before he had committed any actual
transgression; and, therefore, cannot design
any thing else but the original corruption of
his nature.   Now, to this sense of the words
many things are objected.

1. It is observed§, from Clemens of Alexandria, Chrysostom, and Theodoret, that
" David speaks this of his mother Eve, and
of our first parents, whose posterity were begotten after they had sinned."   I reply, David,
indeed, might well enough call Eve his mother, since *she is the mother of all living;* but
could not, with any propriety, say that she
conceived him: this could only be said of his
immediate parent, not of his next grandmo-
ther, much less of Eve, at the distance of
three thousand years.   It is also certainly
true of our first parents, that their posterity
were begotten after they had sinned.   But
then it will follow, that if they were begotten
not before, but after they had sinned, they
must be begotten, not in the image of God, in
which man was created, and was now lost by
sin, but in the sinful and corrupt image of
Adam; which was the case not only of Cain,
but of Seth, and of all others who have since
descended from him by ordinary generation,
among whom David was one.

2. It is objected,‖ that David here speaks
not of his own, but of his mother's sin, and
a very broad¶ intimation is given, that this
was the sin of adultery; and, indeed, if he

---

* Curcellæus, p. 140.   † Episcop. Instit.
Theol. l. 5, c. 2, p. 406, 407; Limborch, p. 192.
‡ Whitby, p. 326; ed. 2. 317.

§ Whitby, p. 326; ed. 2. 318.
‖ Limborch, p. 192.
¶ Sicut ergo cum dicimus, aliquem natum esse

was conceived in a sin of his mother's, what else could it be? This shows, that these men are grievously pinched with this text, and miserably put to their shifts, to betake themselves to such an interpretation, at the expense of the character of an innocent person, of whom there is not the least suggestion of this kind in the sacred writings; but on the contrary, she is represented as a religious person. David valued himself upon his being related to her, and pleads, that he might be regarded by the Lord for her sake.* Moreover, had this been the case, David must have been excluded from entrance into the congregation of the Lord; for there was a standing law† in Israel, which forbade a bastard to enter there until the tenth generation; whereas it is certain, that David often *went into the house of God with company*, where he enjoyed much spiritual pleasure and delight.‡ Once more, it is beside David's scope and design to expose the sins of others, much less his own parents, whilst he is confessing and lamenting his own; and to what purpose should he mention theirs, especially if he himself was not affected by them, and did not derive corrupt nature from them? To say no more, the particle ב, *in*, relates not to his mother, but to himself; it is not said, *my mother in sin*, that is, being in sin, or through sin, *conceived me*; but, *my mother conceived me in sin*, that is, as soon as I was conceived in the womb, and the mass of human nature was shaped and quickened; or as soon as soul and body were united together, sin was in me, and I was in sin, or became a sinful creature.

Some, who do not run this length, yet say, that the sin and iniquity in which David was conceived and shapen, was the sinfulness of his parents, in the acts of begetting and conceiving him, though in lawful wedlock. But this cannot be true; since the propagation of the human species, by natural generation, is a principle of nature implanted by God himself, and therefore cannot be sinful; and is agreeable to the first law of nature, given to man in a state of innocence, *be fruitful and multiply*. Marriage was instituted by God in paradise, and in all ages has been *honourable in all, when the bed is undefiled*. Besides, one of the words here used, חוללתי, translated *shapen*, is of the passive form, and designs something in which both David and his parents were entirely passive, and means no other than that amazing and surprising act of formation he so much admires in Psal. cxxxix. 13—16.

Others§ interpret these words of his mother's conceiving him *in profluviis*, which

usually produced σῶμα οὐ καθαρὸν καὶ εὐκρατον, *a body impure, ill tempered, and subject to evil passions*. The Jews and Isidore are referred to for this sense of them, though the former, as far as I have been able to observe, say nothing of it. R. Sol. Jarchi, R. David Kimchi, R. Aben Ezra, and R. Abendana,‖ understand the words of יצר הרע, the corruption of nature in man as soon as he is born. And as for Isidore,¶ both elder and younger understand these words of original sin, in which David and all men are involved. However, nothing of this nature can be concluded from the sacred Scriptures concerning David, but rather the reverse; since he is taken notice of, as no other man is excepting Moses, for his being *comely, ruddy, of a beautiful countenance*, and *goodly to look to*;** and so far from having an unclean body of an ill temperament, or subject to bad qualities.

3. It is observed,†† that David here makes no mention of Adam, and goes no higher than his mother, and, therefore, what he says makes nothing for original sin. In answer to which, it will be sufficient to say, that inasmuch as natural generation is the channel in which the corruption of nature is derived, David, in speaking of it, and his particular concern in it, had no need to take notice of any other than his immediate parents, through whom it was conveyed to him; for God *hath made of one blood all nations of men*.‡‡ This blood being tainted in the fountain of it, the first man, must be so in its streams; and so all are corrupted that partake of it.

4. It is further urged,§§ that David is speaking here only of himself, and not of all mankind: he does not say that all men, but that he was *shapen in iniquity*, and *conceived in sin*; and, therefore, can be no proof of the original corruption of the whole human nature. To which may be replied, that what is here said of David is true of all men; since *every imagination of the thoughts of* men's hearts, both in the old and in the new world, is evil ‖‖ from their infancy; and that not only *the wicked are estranged from the womb*,¶¶ but the elect of God are, *by nature, children of wrath, even as others*;*** which suppose them to be guilty and polluted as others; and, how should it be otherwise? for *that which is born of the flesh is flesh*.††† Besides, the argument from David to other men is very strong; for, if he who was so famous for his early religion and piety, *a man after God's own heart*, raised up by him to *fulfil all* his *will*, from whose seed sprang *unto Israel a Saviour Jesus*;‡‡‡ if he was *shapen in iniquity*, and *conceived in sin*, is it not reasonable to conclude, that this is the

---

in adulterio, non ipsum, sed ejus parentes accusamus: Ita quando David, se in iniquitate formatum, et matrem suam se calefecisse in peccato fatetur, non aliud quam patris et matris peccatum intellexit. Curcellæus, p. 140.
  * Psalm lxxxvi. 16, and cxvi. 16.
  † Deut. xxiii. 2.   ‡ Psalm xlii. 4, and lv. 14, and cxxii. 1, and lxiii. 1, 2, and lxxxiv. 1, 10.   § Vide Whitby, p. 326; ed. 2. 318.

  ‖ In loc.   ¶ Pelusiota, ep. l. 1, ep. 100; Hispalensis de different. spiritual, p. 187.
  ** 1 Sam. xvi. 12, 18.   †† Limborch, p. 192; Curcellæus, p. 140.
  ‡‡ Acts xvii. 26.   §§ Curcellæus and Limborch, ibid.   ‖‖ Gen. vi. 5, and viii. 21.   ¶¶ Psalm lviii. 3.
  *** Eph. ii. 3.   ††† John iii. 3.
  ‡‡‡ Acts xiii. 22, 23.

case of others? Who can stand up, and exempt himself from such a conception and birth, and say, he was not shapen and conceived in this manner?

5. If all this will not do to set aside the sense of the text we plead for, we are told * that the words are an hyperbole, of the like kind with Job xxxi. 18, Psalm xxii. 10, 11, and lxxi. 6, and lviii. 3, Isa. xlviii. 8, and mean no more than that he had not only sinned now, but very often from his childhood. To which may be answered, that to say that being *shaped in iniquity, and conceived in sin,* means no more than a frequency of sinning from the youth upwards, is to contradict the express letter of the text; nor should we depart from the literal sense of words, and put a figurative one upon them, unless there is an absolute necessity, of which there can be none here, unless it be to serve a turn. The places referred to are no hyperboles. The words in Psal. xxii. 9, 10, are not the words of David, but of Christ, who, through the care of Divine Providence, and powerful operation of the Holy Ghost, was preserved from the original taint of sin. Job xxxi. 18, Psal. lxxi. 5, 6, ought not to be any more accounted hyperbolical expressions than those which say, that Jeremy was *sanctified before he came out of the womb;* and that John the Baptist was *filled with the Holy Ghost from his mother's womb.* † But, admitting that the last-mentioned texts are aggravations of Job's pity and compassion, and of David's trust and confidence, it does not follow, that the words under consideration are hyperbolical exaggerations of sin, since the Psalmist is here making a sincere and hearty confession of sin, in which it is not usual with saints to hyperbolize, that is, either to make their sins lesser or greater than they are; and, indeed, the sinfulness of nature cannot well be hyperbolized; *for the heart is deceitful above all things, and desperately wicked: who can know it?*‡

6. To confirm this hyperbolical sense of the text, the words of the Pharisees to the blind man are produced, *thou wast altogether born in sins, and dost thou teach us?* On which it is observed, that had they a regard to original sin, they could not have justly objected this to him, since he might have recriminated them with it. To which I answer, it is very true, no doubt they were both born in sin alike; but then these words are no hyperbole, but express the real sentiments of these Pharisees, who had either given in to the Pythagorean notion of the transmigration of souls, and supposed that this man's soul had sinned greatly in another body before, and therefore was grievously punished in this; or at least, they imagined that none were born in sin, but such who had some marks of deformity upon them, as blindness, lameness, and the like; but I hope we are not bound to believe the same things,

nor should any expression or doctrine of theirs be urged to disprove any truth of the Gospel.

As for Psal. lviii. 3, it is true of all men, that they are *estranged from the womb* from all righteousness, and *alienated from God, and the life of God,* being *dead in trespasses and sins;* and therefore it is no strange thing that *they go astray* מבטן, *from the belly;* since they are devoid of the principles of real justice and truth: and hence, as soon as they are capable of speaking, they go about *speaking lies.* Now, to what can such early impieties be ascribed, but to the corruption of nature? To the same purpose are the words in Isaiah xlviii. 8, *and wast called a transgressor from the womb;* in which the corruption of nature is represented as the spring and fountain of all that treachery, stubbornness, hypocrisy, and idolatry, the people of Israel are charged with in the context. It is objected § that this passage implies something not common to all, but peculiar to the people of Israel, but surely if the people of Israel, who were an *holy people to the Lord,* and *chosen* by him *to be a special people unto himself, above all people on the face of the earth,* || were called *transgressors from the womb,* much more may others be so called. It is further alleged, that this does not regard their natural birth, but their coming out of Egypt, when they were formed into a civil state, and in a figurative sense was their *birth;* from which time they discovered a proneness to impiety and idolatry. Be it so that this is the sense of the passage, to what can this impiety and idolatry be ascribed, when they were a people indulged with so many peculiar and special favours by God, but to the abominable corruption originally seated in their natures? As to what is usually ¶ objected to this and the preceding scripture, that they cannot be understood of original sin; because these holy men, David and Isaiah, must object to, and upbraid these wicked men with that which they themselves were guilty of; I need only observe, that the words under consideration, are not the words of Isaiah, but of God himself, who in his eternal prescience foreknew the original and actual transgressions of these people; which he observes both to prove his own Deity, and point out to them the fountain of all their iniquities. As to the preceding passage, David might, with great propriety, take notice of the original corruption of the wicked, of which he was so sensible himself, and acknowledged in as strong, or stronger terms than here used: since his design is to expose the internal wickedness of some who appeared outwardly righteous, and made great pretensions to holiness, justice and truth, when, in their hearts, they wrought wickedness, which sprang from the original depravity of their natures, as appears from the connexion of the words with the two foregoing verses.

---

* Curcellæus and Limborch, ibid.; Grotius in loc. † Jer. i. 5; Luke i. 15.
‡ Jer. xvii. 9.   § Whitby, p. 327; ed.

2. 318. || Deut. vii. 6.
¶ Episcopius, Curcellæus, Limborch, ubi supra.

SECTION III.

And God saw that the wickedness of man was great in the earth ; and that every imagination of the thoughts of his heart was only evil continually.—GEN. vi. 5.

THIS text represents not only the *heart* of man in general to be *evil*, but the *thoughts* of his heart ; not only these, but the *imagination* יצר, the *substratum* of thought, the very first motion to it, and the formation of it ; yea, *every* imagination, or formation, and that *only* so, nothing good in it, nay *always*, היום כל, every day ; and so is a considerable proof of the general and original corruption of human nature : to which the following things are objected.

1st. That these * words regard not all mankind, but only the antediluvian world : and not every one of them, since Noah is excepted as a *just* and *perfect man ;* nor are they spoken of any sin common to all men, as original sin is supposed to be, but of some gross sins committed by the worst of men, who had corrupted themselves by a long course of continual impiety. To which I reply, that the former part of the text, *and God saw that the wickedness of man was great in the earth,* has a special regard to the flagitious crimes of the men of that generation, which brought down the judgment of God upon them in an universal deluge ; but the latter part of the text, *and that every imagination of the thoughts of his heart was only evil continually,* respects the fountain and spring of all their wickedness, which is the corruption of nature, common to them with all men that were before them, or have since risen up after them. The words are expressed in very general terms : it is not said, *every imagination of the thoughts of the heart* of these men, or the men of this generation, *is only evil continually ;* but *every imagination of the thoughts of men's hearts* is so. Noah's being a *just and perfect man,* was owing to the free favour of God ; for it is said, that he *found grace in the eyes of the Lord,* and to the *righteousness* of Christ, of which he was a *preacher ;* otherwise, *by nature* he was as corrupt, as much a child of *wrath of others ;* no thanks to his nature that he was just and perfect, but to the distinguishing grace of God he was made a partaker of. Moreover, what is here expressed, is elsewhere said of all men without any exception. It is to me very probable, that the Psalmist has reference to this very passage before us in Psalm xiv. 2, 3, which the apostle Paul, in Rom. iii. 9—12, without any restriction or limitation, applies to all men, Jews and Gentiles. Add to this, that the very same thing, in almost the same words, is said in Gen. viii. 21, of man after the flood, as is here said of him before it ; yea, when there was only Noah and his family in being. But, on this last cited text, two things are observed.

1. That the words † should not be translated, *I will not again curse the ground any more for man's sake, for,* but, *although,* or *for this,* or *upon this account, that the imagination of man's heart is evil from his youth:* And it is said, that the usual way of reading that text, carries in it this absurdity, that the same reason which moved God to destroy the world before, now moves him to spare it. But let it be observed, that the reading pleaded for, is contrary to the common sense of the particle כי, as these men themselves own, to the Targums of Onkelos, and Jonathan Ben Uzziel, who render it by ארום and ארי, to the versions of the Septuagint, Syriac, Arabic, Samaritan, and Vulgate Latin, and to many modern ones, which translate the particle *for,* and not *though:* nor is there any absurdity in the common reading ; for as the phrase, in the other text, accounts for the justice of God, and his proceedings against the men of the other world, this here represents the inconvenience of the continuance, or frequency of such proceedings ; since he must be always destroying the world, and the inhabitants of it, and consequently could have no church abiding ; nor would there be any society of men subsisting, *for the imagination of man's heart is evil from his youth.* Besides, should the reading contended for be admitted, for it will be owned that the particle may be sometimes so rendered, nothing will be got by it ; should the words be read, *I will not again curse the ground for man's sake, though the imagination of man's heart is evil from his youth,* or *for this,* or *upon this account, that the imagination of his heart is evil from his youth ;* either reading both expresses and implies, that the imagination of man's heart is evil from his youth, which is the only thing for which we produce it.

2. It is objected,‡ that " the word מנעריו, doth not signify *from their birth,* but only *from their youth ;* for he speaks of *the imaginations of their hearts,* and so only of the time when they are able to entertain and prosecute the thoughts of their evil hearts ; nor doth this phrase, it is said, signify an original, but only a long-contracted custom, an habitual course of doing what is either good, or evil, or indifferent." To which I reply, that the Lord here speaks not of what man did, but what was *the imagination* of his *heart,* the *substratum* of his thoughts, and which is antecedent to the entertainment and prosecution of them, that this was evil מנעריו ; which Onkelos renders by מוזעירות, *from his infancy ;* and agrees with the derivation of the word from נער, which signifies § to *shake out ;* and with the sense of the ancient, and some of the modern Jews,‖ who say that the

---

* Curcellæus, p. 139; Limborch, p. 191; Whitby, p. 327 ; ed. 2. 319.

† Curcellæus, Limborch, and Whitby, ubi supra.   ‡ Whitby, p. 328 ; ed. 2. 320.

§ Vide Buxtorf and Schindler in Lexicis.

‖ R. Joden, in Bereshit Rabba, fol. 30, 1 ; Talmud Sanhed. fol. 91, 2 ; R. Sol. Jarchi, in Gen. viii. 21, and R. Aben Ezra, in Psalm li. 5.

יצר הרע, *the evil figment*, or corruption of nature, is in man from the time of his formation in the womb ; or from his birth, as soon as משנוצר *he is shook out of his mother's bowels.* Moreover, some of the texts brought to disprove this sense of the phrase serve to confirm it ; particularly Job xxxi. 18, Psal. lxxi. 5, 6, where *from my youth,* and *from my mother's womb,* are mentioned as terms synonymous. Add to this, that such an interpretation well agrees with other scriptures ; where men ļare represented as *shapen in iniquity, and conceived in sin, and as transgressors from the womb.** But to return to the consideration of what is further objected to our sense of the particular passage under consideration.

2ndly. It is said,† that " the wickedness the text speaks of was voluntary, and was the moving cause of God's destroying the world by the flood ; which cannot be said of original corruption, since that being always the same, would always have been a reason why he should do so ; and besides, if the corruption of nature is here intended, in vain did God invite men to repentance by the ministry of Noah, and wait for it one hundred and twenty years ; since, without the almighty power of God, they could no more conquer this, than they could change their sex, or raise a dead man to life." In answer to which, let it be observed, that though the *wickedness* spoken of in the former part of the text designs personal, actual, and voluntary transgressions ; yet *the evil imagination,* in the latter part of it, intends the corruption of nature, which is the fountain of actual transgressions ; nor is this doing any violence to the text, or separating what the Scripture has joined together ; but distinguishing between the cause and the effect, the fountain and its streams, the tree and its fruit. Nor do I see any reason why original sin, and the corruption of nature, may not be thought, with actual transgressions, to be the cause of the flood ; since all actual transgressions flow from thence ; and especially, since infants, who *sinned not after the similitude of Adam's transgression,* suffered in the universal deluge ; which cannot be accounted for, but by supposing original sin, or the corruption of nature, in them. Nor is it any sufficient objection to its being a cause of this calamity, that it had always been, and so must always have been, a reason for it ; seeing God might defer such a strict and severe observance of it ; partly until his elect in this interval were gathered in ; partly to show his patience, forbearance, and long-suffering, until iniquity was fully ripe, and this corruption had broken out, and showed itself to such a degree, that God must be, beyond all dispute, justified in his sharpest resentments against it. Nor was *the long-suffering of God,* which *waited in the days of Noah,* in vain : since, though such was the rooted corruption of human nature, that none can con-

quer it without the unfrustrable grace of God ; yet these men, under the advantages they had, might have attained to an external repentance and reformation ; which would have secured them from temporal destruction, and therefore were left inexcusable. Besides, God might, by these means, bring some of his elect to true repentance, whom he would not have perish, and whom he might take to himself, before the general calamity ; as well as he saved Noah and his family in the midst of it.

SECTION IV

That which is born of the flesh is flesh.—John iii. 6.

THESE words are expressed by Christ to show that men, by their natural birth, are carnal, and stand in need of regeneration, in order to entrance into the kingdom of God ; and the meaning of them is, that that which is born in a natural way, is not only corporeal, but corrupt and sinful ; so the word flesh is often used, see Gen. vi. 3, Rom. viii. 1, 5—8, Gal. v. 17, 19. Hence man in his natural estate, can do nothing but what is carnal and sinful ; and is wholly incapable of doing that which is spiritually good, until he is born of the Spirit. To which are excepted,

1. That ‡ this " exposition renders it impossible for a man to do any thing toward his own conversion ; and so renders all God's commands of it, exhortations to it, promises of pardon for it, threats of death if neglected, and complaints against those who would not do it, vain and absurd." To which I answer, that it is, indeed, impossible, considering the state of men, and the nature of regeneration and conversion, that he should be able to do any thing more towards it, than to make use of means ; such as prayer, hearing the word, &c., in which God oftentimes is pleased to effect it, by the mighty power of his Spirit and grace. And as for commands and exhortations to regeneration, or promises of pardon to such who regenerate themselves, or threats of death to those who neglect it, or complaints against those who would not do it, I know of none in the whole word of God ; what is referred to, only regards an external reformation of life and manners, and not regeneration, or the first work of conversion.

2. It is said,§ " that to be *born of the flesh,* here only signifies, that natural generation, by which a man is born into the world, of the will of the flesh ; and that this is the plain meaning of our Lord, that besides that natural birth, by which we receive only our flesh and body from our parents, there is need of a spiritual birth, to fit us for the kingdom of God." I reply, it will be allowed, that our Lord is speaking of natural generation by which a man is born into the world ; though how that should be of the will of the

---

* Psalm li. 5 ; Isa. xlviii. 8.
† Curcellæus and Limborch, in locis supra

citatis.   ‡ Whitby, p. 329, 281 ; ed. 2.
274.   § Ibid. p. 330 ; ed. 2. 321.

flesh, if flesh stands only for body, is not very intelligible: but then he speaks of men's being born into the world as corrupt and sinful, which appears from the opposite part of the text, *that which is born of the Spirit is spirit*, that is, that which is born of the Spirit of God is spiritual, as the new creature is; for by *spirit*, is not meant the soul, as is, when it is opposed to flesh, signifying the body, but that which is spiritual; and flesh being opposed to it, must signify that which is corrupt and sinful, as the nature of man is by his first birth: and therefore according to the plain meaning of our Lord, he must stand in need of a spiritual birth to fit him for the kingdom of God. And if man is not corrupt and sinful, what need would there be of regeneration? and since this is his case, though he does not lie under any force, or co-active necessity to do only that which is evil, to which his will is entirely free; yet he is in an utter incapacity to regenerate himself.

SECTION V

For I know that in me (that is, in my flesh) dwelleth no good thing; for to will is present with me, but how to perform that which is good, I find not. For the good that I would, I do not: but the evil which I would not, that I do.—Rom. vii. 18, 19.

FROM these words the following things may be fairly concluded, namely, If no good thing dwells in a regenerate man, that is, in his flesh, much less in an unregenerate one, who is wholly flesh, carnal, and corrupt; and if in a renewed man, where there is a will, there is not a power to do that which is spiritually good, much less is an unrenewed man to do that which is so, who has neither power nor will; and if such is the strength of corrupt nature in one that is born again, as often to hinder him from doing that good he would, and to put him on doing that evil he would not, how much greater must its strength be in unsanctified persons? These conclusions will appear to be just, if it is but allowed, that the apostle is here speaking of himself, and of himself as regenerate. But to this, the following things are excepted.

1st. "The scope of the place;[*] which is to show the necessity of the abrogation of the law, from the inefficiency of it to deliver men from sin; since it rather increased it; to prove which, an unregenerate person, in whom sin reigns, was the most proper instance the apostle could pitch upon." But to this may be replied, that though the apostle, in the beginning of the chapter, is speaking of the abrogation of the law to believers by the body of Christ, yet, nearer the discourse in controversy, his obvious scope and design is to show the spirituality and perfection of the law; that it was holy, just, and good, and that it was owing to the weakness of man that it was not fulfilled. This he could not better illustrate and exemplify than in a regenerate person; for if such an one does not come up to the spirituality of the law, and is not able to keep it perfectly, it cannot be thought that an unregenerate man should.

2ndly. The coherence of the words;[†] It is observed, "that the apostle speaks of an unregenerate man from ver. 7 to the 14th, and therefore, why should it be thought that he discontinues his discourse concerning him?" In answer to this it should be observed, that the apostle, even within the limited period, is not speaking of a man in a pure, natural estate, but of himself, under great convictions of sin, under the powerful work of the law upon his conscience, showing him the exceeding sinfulness of sin. Besides, the apostle changes the *tense*; for whereas, within the mentioned compass, he speaks in the *past tense*; from ver. 14, to the end of the chapter, he uses the *present tense*. And therefore supposing, that in the former part of the chapter, he considers himself as unregenerate; there is good reason to conclude, he does not continue his discourse of himself as such, or of any unregenerate man. And whereas it is urged,[‡] that he says in ver. 9, *I was alive without the law once*, or *I lived without the law once*; which it is observed cannot be true of him in his own person, seeing he was born a Jew, and brought up under the law all his days: it may be replied, that though he never lived without the letter of the law, yet without the knowledge of the spirituality and perfection of it; or that he was *alive*, that is, in a fair way for heaven and eternal life, in his own apprehensions, before the law came with power, and entered into his conscience; but then *sin*, which lay before as dead, *revived*, and he *died* to all his hopes of obtaining life by his obedience to it.

3rdly. The most considerable objection is taken from the description and character of the person spoken of; as,

1. "He is said[§] to be *carnal*, ver. 14, whereas regenerate ones have *crucified the flesh with the lusts*, and are *debtors, not to the flesh to live after the flesh*, Gal. v. 24, Rom. viii. 12." I answer, though regenerate persons have crucified the flesh, and are not debtors to it to live after it, yet from some considerations may be denominated carnal; as partly from their first birth, and the corruption of nature they bring into the world with them; partly from the continuance of the flesh, in which *dwells no good thing* and with which they *serve the law of sin*; and partly from *the lusts of the flesh*, which remain in them, and war against them; and on account of which the Corinthians, though *babes in Christ*, and so regenerate ones, are styled and treated as *carnal*. Add to this, that the apostle here says of himself, *I am carnal*, in comparison of *the law*, which was *spiritual*. And, indeed, when compared with this, the holiest man in the world must

---

* Vorstius, in loc.; Limborch, p. 458, 459.
† Ibid.   ‡ Vorstius and Hammond in loc.   § Vorstius and Limborch, ibid.

be reckoned carnal; for if the holy angels, when compared with the Divine Being, are chargeable with folly, much more must the saints, in this state of imperfection, be accounted carnal in comparison of the spiritual law of God, which is a transcript of the divine nature.

2. "He is said* to be *sold under sin*, ver. 14, which is a character of the greatest sinners; as of Ahab, 1 Kings xxi. 20, and others, Isaiah l. 1, and even of revolters from the true religion, 1 Mac. i. 16, and signifies, that he was a servant and slave to sin; whereas regenerate persons are *free from sin*, and become *the servants of righteousness*." I reply, that though the person spoken of is said to be *sold under sin*, yet not to *sell himself to work wickedness*, as Ahab and others did; between these there is a wide difference; in the one, man is passive, in the other, active; the one is against his will, the other with it. So, though the apostle was sold under sin, it was not his own act, and was against his will, as a renewed man; with his *flesh* he *served the law of sin*, but with his *mind the law of God;* which proves, that he speaks of himself as regenerate: for his character as unregenerate was, that he was *serving*, that is, readily, cheerfully, and willingly, *divers lusts and pleasures*. Besides, the apostle is to be understood of his other *I*, which was *carnal*, of the flesh, or old man, which was under sin; and not of the new man, which is not *under the law* of sin, *but under grace*, as a reigning, governing principle.

3. "He is said *not to do the good he would, but the evil which he would not*, ver. 16,† whereas it is said of regenerate persons, that they *work out their salvation with fear and trembling*, God working in them *both to will and to do of his good pleasure;* that they *walk in newness of life*, and *after the Spirit, and not after the flesh*, Phil. ii. 12, 13; Rom. vi. 4, and viii. 1." To which I reply, that though regenerate ones do that which is good, yet not always, *there is not a just man on earth, that doth good and sinneth not;‡* nor does God always work in them to will and to do, but when he pleases, *of his own good pleasure*. Besides, the good this person did not, he willed it, he desired it; whereas a carnal man wills, desires, and savours the things of the flesh, and them only, and not the things of the Spirit; and also hated the evil he did; whereas an unregenerate man chooses his own ways, and his soul delights in his abominations: so that this character proves the person to be a regenerate, and not an unregenerate man.

4. "It is said of this person, that *sin dwelleth in him*, ver 17, 20,§ but regenerate ones are *dead to sin* and *alive to God*, and the Spirit of Christ, and Christ himself dwells in them, Rom. vi. 11, and viii. 11, Gal. ii. 20." To this may be replied, that though the saints are dead to sin, being justified from it by the righteousness of Christ, and freed from the dominion of it by the power of divine grace, yet they are not delivered from the being of it; sin is in them, dwells in them, lives in them, though they do not live in sin, and sometimes very strongly works in them; all which is no contradiction to the inhabitation of Christ, and his Spirit in them. These dwell under the same roof with sin, but not in the same apartment; sin dwells in the flesh, in the old man, in the unrenewed self, in which dwells no good thing; Christ and the Spirit dwell in the new man, in the new heart, in the renewed self. Moreover, the saints in all ages have found, and have complained of sin dwelling in them, as Job, David, Solomon, the church in Isaiah's time, and the beloved disciple John.‖ This character therefore agrees with a regenerate man.

5. "This person affirms of himself that *no good thing dwelt* in him, ver. 18, whereas there are many good things dwell in regenerate ones." This is very true, there are many good things in the saints; as the good work of grace and the good word of God, the good Spirit of Christ, and Christ himself, yea, God the Father dwells in them, and makes his abode with them. But then let it be observed, how cautiously and with what limitation the apostle expresses himself: *In me, that is in my flesh, dwells no good thing*. Now had he spoken of himself as unregenerate, or in the person of an unregenerate man, he had no need to have used this restrictive clause; for who knows not, that in an unregenerate man dwells no good thing?

6. "This man is said to *will* but not to *perform that which is good*, ver. 18, whereas¶ regenerate men are *the workmanship of God, created in Christ Jesus, unto good works*, and God *works in them both to will and to do*." What has been said in answer to the third objection may be sufficient to remove this; for though the saints do that which is good, yet not always, nor does God always work in them to do, when they have a will to do that which is good. Besides, in unregenerate persons, there is no will present with them to that which is good; they desire not the knowledge of God's ways; their carnal minds are enmity against God, and are not subject to the law of God; nor can they be subject to it, without the grace of God.

7. "This person complains that he was a *captive of the law of sin*, ver. 23, whereas** regenerate persons are *freed from the law of sin and death*, Rom. vii. 2." But though they are freed from condemnation by sin, which is what is meant in the place referred to, as appears from the context, and from the dominion of sin, yet not from the being of it, nor altogether from the power of it; for it sometimes brings into captivity, though

---

* Whitby, p. 332; ed. 2. 323; Vorstius and Limborch, Ibid.   † Vorstius and Limborch, Ibid.   ‡ Eccles. vii. 20.   § Limborch, Ibid.   ‖ Job ix. 20;   Psalm xxxviii. 3, 4; Prov. xx. 9; Isa. xiv. 6; 1 John i. 8.   ¶ Limborch, ibid.   ** Vorstius and Limborch, ibid.

even then it has not the dominion; a man may be taken prisoner, and carried captive, and yet remain a subject of his lawful prince; so the saints may be brought into captivity to the law of sin, and yet not be under the dominion of it, but continue under the reign of grace, and in the kingdom of God's dear Son.

8. " This same person bitterly complains of a *body of death*, and desires to be delivered from it; which shows* that he was detained by it, and under it." I reply, that the desire of deliverance from the body of death shows that it was distressing, uneasy, and uncomfortable to him, but not that it had the dominion over him; he was delivered from condemnation by it, and from the government of it, and was very desirous of being freed from the very being of it, which was so great a clog and incumbrance to him; and this none but a regenerate person truly desires, as none but such an one knows from whence a deliverance of this kind comes, which proves the person speaking to be a renewed man, since he adds, *Thanks be to God through Jesus Christ our Lord.*

9. " The apostle† elsewhere speaks of himself in a different manner, as one that walked worthy of the Gospel, to be imitated by others, and who was able to do all things through the grace of God, 1 Cor. xi. 1; Phil. iii. 17, and iv. 13." But then this does not contradict what he here says in this chapter, which perfectly agrees with other passages of his, in which he owns his sinfulness and weakness, and ascribes all he did to the grace of God, see 1 Tim. i. 15; 2 Cor. xii. 10; 1 Cor. xv. 10. It is evident, from all his epistles, that this great man God lived under a continual sense of the corruption of his nature, his own unworthiness and inability.

10. " Origen, Chrysostom, Theodoret, and others, interpret‡ these words of men under the thraldom and dominion of sin, through a long use and custom." This interpretation of the words was indeed first given by Origen, was greedily catched at by Pelagius, revived by Socinus and his followers, and some popish writers, and at last adopted by the Arminians. But Methodius,§ a martyr, whose judgment Dr. Whitby seems fond of, first in the words of one Procius, and then in his own, delivers the sense of them agreeable to ours, understanding them of a regenerate man. Wherefore what Vorstius affirms is false, that all the ancients before Austin interpreted these words of unregenerate men. I shall now,

4thly. Subjoin some arguments, proving that this part of the chapter, from ver. 14 to the end of it, is spoken by the apostle of himself, and of himself as regenerate.

1. The apostle all along speaks of himself in the first person: *That which I do I allow not; what I hate that I do; I know that in me, that is in my flesh, dwelleth no good thing; I delight in the law of God; I find a law in*

my members; yea, says he, *With the mind I myself, αὐτὸς ἐγὼ, serve the law of God*; which can never be understood in a figurative sense as personating another; nor do the passages usually alleged prove such a way of speaking common, as 1 Cor. vi. 12, and x. 23, and xiii. 1—3; Gal. ii. 18, 20.

2. When he speaks of his unregenerate state, and the first convictions of sin, he speaks of them as things past: *When we were in the flesh; I had not known sin, but by the law; Sin taking occasion by the law wrought in me all manner of concupiscence, deceived me, and by it slew me; I was alive without the law once*, &c. But from ver. 14 to the end of the chapter, he speaks in the present tense, of what he then was, and found: *I am carnal, I do what I would not, I consent to the law that it is good, I delight in the law of God*, &c.

2. The several things which are said of this person, cannot agree with the apostle, nor with any other, but as regenerate; such only *hate evil, delight in the law of God*, and *serve* it with their *mind*.

3. The distinction of *flesh* and *spirit*, the inward and outward man, is not applicable to any other but a regenerate man; for the spirit, and inward man, is not the soul, opposed to the body, but the spiritual man, the new man, the hidden man of the heart, the truth of grace, in opposition to the flesh, the old man, or corrupt nature. Now only the latter, and not the former, is to be found in an unregenerate man.

5. The struggle between flesh and spirit, between *the law in the members* and *the law of the mind*, proves that these words can belong to no other than a regenerate person; with which agrees Gal. v. 17. Only in *the Shulamite‖* true believers are to be seen, *as it were the company of two companies*, flesh and spirit, sin and grace, warring against each other.

6. The thanksgiving for deliverance from sin through Christ, towards the close of the chapter, can only come from a believer; none but a regenerate man knows any thing of the nature of it, from whence it is, and can only be thankful for it.

SECTION VI

Because the carnal mind is enmity against God; for it is not subject to the law of God, neither indeed can be; so then, they that are in the flesh cannot please God.—Rom. viii. 7, 8.

THE *carnal mind*, or τὸ φρόνημα τῆς σαρκὸς, which may be rendered the *wisdom of the flesh*, signifies the wisest and best part of man, the soul, with all its powers and faculties; and this being carnal is a strong proof of the wretched corruption of human nature. Besides, this carnal mind is not only an enemy to, but *enmity* itself *against* that *God* who made it, upholds it in life, and loads it with benefits; and therefore is not *subject to the*

---

* Vorstius, ibid. † Limborch, ibid.
‡ Whitby, p. 332; ed. 2. 323.

§ Apud Epiphan. hæres. 64. ‖ Cant. vi. 13.

law of God, which is holy, just, and good; nor indeed can it be, considering its state and circumstances, without the powerful and efficacious grace of God; wherefore the apostle's conclusion is exceeding just, *so then they that are in the flesh*, that is, in an unregenerate state, and are wholly carnal and corrupt, *cannot please* God; that is, do those things which are pleasing to him. To which is objected,

1. That "this text [*] with the preceding one, were abused by the ancient *heretics*, to prove that the flesh, or body of man, is, by nature, evil; and they that are in the body of flesh, cannot be subject to the law, or please God." But what is this to us, who by *the flesh* in both places, understand not the body, to which wisdom does not belong, and in which men may please God, and be subject to his law, but the corrupt nature of man, or men, in an unregenerate estate; who, whilst such, are enemies to God, unsubjected to his law, and cannot please him?

2. It is owned,[†] that "the apostle doth indeed say, that they who thus mind carnal things, while they continue so to do, cannot please God, or live in subjection to his laws; but does not say, that they cannot be made good; for by his frequent exhortations to these carnal men, to *crucify* and *mortify the flesh*, to *put off the old man with his deeds*, joined with threats and promises, plainly shows, that men may cease to live according to the flesh, and may obtain that assistance of the Spirit by which they shall mortify the deeds of the flesh, and live after the Spirit." Upon which I observe, that all that are after the flesh, or in an unrenewed state, mind carnal things; and since it is allowed, that while they continue so to do, as they will, so long as they remain unconverted, they cannot please God; the words prove what we produce them for, namely, the corruption of man's nature, and his disability to do that which is spiritually good. But it is observed, that the apostle does not say such cannot be made good: nor do we say so, but we affirm, that they cannot make themselves good, and that they cannot be made good but by the grace of God; and that until they are made so, they cannot do that which is spiritually good, no more than an evil tree can bring forth good fruit. And as for the exhortations to *crucify* and *mortify the flesh*, and to *put off the old man*, the passages in Rom. viii. 13. Gal. v. 24, referred to, are not properly exhortations; and neither they, nor the other, belong to carnal men, but to believers in Christ, who were Christ's and had the spirit of Christ already; and were *debtors, not to the flesh, to live after the flesh*, but to the Spirit, to live after the Spirit; and therefore fall short of proving that carnal men may make themselves good, or of themselves cease to live after the flesh.

CHAPTER VI.

OF PERSEVERANCE

I NOW proceed to consider Dr. Whitby's discourse on the perseverance of the saints. His first chapter is taken up in premising that which is granted on both sides, for the better stating of the *question* between us. For his own side he grants, that they, who are preserved to salvation, are so preserved *by the power of God through faith;* that God has engaged his faithfulness, that all, who do not wickedly depart from him, shall never be forced from him by the power of any adversaries; and that God has promised perseverance in the ways of righteousness to the end, to those who constantly and conscientiously use the means prescribed by him for that end: but utterly denies, that God has promised to keep them by his power from making shipwreck of faith, and from falling into those sins he cautions them to avoid; or to interpose his power unfrustrably to engage all true believers to use the means prescribed by him. He goes on to observe, that the assertors of the doctrine of the saints' final perseverance hold, that the foundation of it is the absolute election of persons to salvation, and to the means which shall unfrustrably conclude in it; that they grant that it is not from the strength, steadiness, and immutability of the new nature, renewed mind, will, and affections, but purely from the promise of God, that true believers cannot fall away; and that though they cannot fall totally and finally, yet may fall into horrid sins; such as may at present unfit them for heaven, require a renewal of grace, and by the guilt of which they stand condemned till they are renewed by faith and repentance. I own, that election is a foundation of the saints' final perseverance, but it is not the only thing on which it is founded; nor does this show the inconsistency of two of our arguments for perseverance, taken from the prayers of the saints, and the intercession of Christ, as is intimated; since the saints may pray, as Christ did, John xvii. 1, 5, for that which God has absolutely decreed, from all eternity, shall come to pass. And though we grant that it is from the promise, yet not *purely* from the promise of God, that true believers cannot fall away; for though we own that the new creature is imperfect, yet affirm that such is the nature, strength, and firmness of true grace, that it can never perish. Wherefore our arguments, taken from the nature of faith, conversion, and the new birth, sufficiently prove the doctrine we plead for. Moreover, though we allow that true believers may fall into gross sins, which may require a renewed exercise of faith and repentance, yet that they shall not deprive them either of meetness or right to heaven; nor do they ever stand condemned before God for them. The doctor's second

---

[*] Whitby, p. 282, 333; ed. 2. 324.

[†] Ibid. p. 333, 334; ed. 2. 275, 325.

chapter contains arguments from scripture against the doctrine of the saints' final perseverance, which have been considered in the former part of this work. His third and fourth chapters are an answer to those texts produced on our side in favour of the doctrine: the vindication of which texts is attempted, in the following Sections.

SECTION I.

Having loved his own which were in the world, he loved them unto the end.—John xiii. 1.

THESE words are expressive of the unchangeable and everlasting love of Christ to his people; who are *his own* by choice, by his Father's gift, and his own purchase. Now such shall certainly persevere to the end, and be eternally saved; for *who shall separate from the love of Christ?* But to this, the following things are objected.

1. That " Christ speaks not of them, whom he had chosen to eternal life, but of them only, whom he had chosen to be his apostles."* To which I reply that though Christ speaks of his apostles, yet not of them all; *I speak not of you all,* says he, *I know whom I have chosen:* and of whom he does speak, he does not speak of them as chosen to be apostles, but as men chosen to eternal life; which was not the case of them all, nor were they all *his own* in this special sense; one of them was a *devil,* and *the son of perdition.* Nor does he speak only of these. Were none *his own* but the apostles? Had he no propriety in any but *them?* Certainly he had: and if he loved his apostles unto the end, why may he not be thought to love all to the end, who are equally his own, and equally loved by him as they were?

2. That Christ's loving them to the end, only signifies " the affection he showed to them, by washing their feet when he was to leave them."† To which may be replied, that this was not so much an instance of affection to them, as of humility and meekness; and was designed as an instruction and example to them, how they should behave to each other; and at most was an instance only of his love to them, and what Judas had a share in with the rest of the apostles; and not to be compared with some other instances of his love, and which were nearer the end of his life, as particularly his shedding his blood for them on the cross. Now there is no comparison between washing the feet of his disciples with water, and washing us from our sins in his own blood.

3. That he here speaks " not of his love of them to the end of their lives, but of his own life on earth."‡ Christ's love is not allowed to continue to the end of their lives, for that would prove their final perseverance; but the end of his life, as if his love ended with his life: whereas Christ still expresses his love to his people, by appearing in the presence of God, acting as an advocate, and interceding with the Father, and preparing mansions in his Father's house for them. It is much, that the love of Christ to his own is not confined, by the writers of this cast, to supper time, or to the end of the supper; since it immediately follows, *and supper being ended,* which would scarce be a more jejune sense of the words than what is given. Why may not τέλος be understood of the end of their lives, as in Matt. xxiv. 13? or of the end of the world, ver. 6, 14? or of the end of all things, as in 1 Pet. iv. 7? Besides, εἰς τέλος may be rendered *continually,* as it is in Luke xviii. 5, or *for ever,* in which sense it is used by the Septuagint in Psal. ix. 6, 18, and xliv. 23, where it answers to לנצח, which signifies *for ever:* and agreeably the words may be read, *Having loved his own which were in the world, he loved them for ever,* as they are rendered by the Ethiopic version. And then the sense of them is, that those who are Christ's, are loved by him with an everlasting love; and therefore shall not perish, but have eternal life.

SECTION II.

While I was with them in the world, I kept them in thy name: those that thou gavest me, I have kept: and none of them is lost, but the son of perdition: that the scripture might be fulfilled.—John xvii. 12.

THE argument formed from this text, in favour of the saints' final perseverance, stands thus: If those who are given to Christ are so kept by him, from the evil that is in their own hearts, and in the world, as that they shall not be eternally lost; then they must and shall persevere unto the end. But those that are given to Christ, are so kept, &c., therefore, &c. To which is answered,§

1. " That this passage was spoken only of the twelve apostles, as is evident from the whole context; and so there is no reason to extend it to all true believers." What has been said under the preceding Section, is a sufficient reply to this: for though it is evident from the context, that Christ is speaking primarily, and more immediately of the apostles, yet not of them only, nor of them as apostles, but as members of him, given unto him, and believers in him, and so preserved by him. And if the preservation of them was secured to them, by being so, why may not the preservation of all other true believers be equally as sure and certain?

2. It is said,‖ that " the very next chapter shows that this was spoken of their preservation from temporal death; Christ requesting that his disciples might be permitted to go away when he was apprehended, that this saying of his might be fulfilled, John xviii. 8, 9." I reply, that though the very next chapter shows that these words of Christ were fulfilled in the temporal preservation of the disciples; yet it does not fol-

---

* Whitby, p. 437; ed. 2. 426. Hag. art. v. p. 91. § Whitby, p. 438;
† Ibid. ‡ Ibid., and remonstr. Coll. ed. 2. 426. ‖ Ibid.

low, that this was all, or that it was the principal thing designed by them; for Christ
prays the Father that he would keep them
as he had done.   Now the rest of the petitions are of a spiritual kind; such as sanctification through the truth, perfect union and
eternal glorification : wherefore, it is reasonable to suppose, that this was of the same
nature also.   Besides, if this was spoken of
preservation from temporal death, the sense
of the words must be this : *those that thou
gavest me, I have kept* from a temporal death,
and none of them is lost by a temporal death;
but the son of perdition, he is lost by a temporal death :   which last was not true; for
Judas was yet alive, he had not at this time
betrayed him; and it was not until after the
condemnation of Christ that he went and
hanged himself.   Add to this, that as Christ
had kept his disciples, so he prays that his
Father would keep them, ver. 11, 15.   Now,
if he prayed for their preservation from temporal death, he was not heard; for every one
of them died a violent death, suffered martyrdom, though they were all in a spiritual
sense preserved to the kingdom and glory of
God, as all true believers will be.

3. It is observed,* that this passage,
taken in " our sense, is rather an argument
that some of them, who were given by God
to Christ, may perish; because it is affirmed,
that one of them, who was thus given to
Christ, did so."   To which I answer, that
though Judas, the son of perdition, was given
to Christ, and chosen by him as an apostle,
yet he was not given to him by a special act
of the Father's grace, nor chosen in him, or
by him, and united to him, as a member of
him, as the rest of the apostles and all the
elect of God are.   *I speak not of you all,*
says he,† *I know whom I have chosen,* that is,
to eternal life; for, otherwise, he had chosen
Judas as an apostle equally with the rest :‡
*have I not chosen you twelve, and one of you is
a devil ?*   And from all the accounts that are
given of him, it does not appear that he ever
received the true grace of God ; and therefore
his perdition, to which he was appointed,
which is the reason of his being called *the
son of perdition,* is no instance of the apostacy
of a real saint, or true believer, or of one
who, in a way of special grace, was given by
the Father to Christ. Moreover εἰ μή, which
is rightly rendered by our translators *but,* is
not exceptive, but adversative,§ and does not
imply, that Judas was one of those that were
given to Christ, and that his perdition is an
exception to the preservation of them all ;
but the sense of the text is, *None of those
that thou gavest me is lost ; but the son of
perdition* is lost, he having never been given
to me as an object of thy love, only as an
apostle, and, therefore, is left to that perdition to which he was appointed; whereby the
Scripture, that speaks of his destruction, will
be fulfilled.

SECTION III

*For the gifts and calling of God are without
repentance.*—Rom. xi. 29.

THE *gifts of God,* such as justification, pardon of sin, adoption, sanctification, and eternal life, flow from his immutable decree of
election, as appears from the preceding verse.
The *calling* here spoken of, is that internal,
effectual calling, with which God's elect are
called *according to the purpose and grace of
God.*   Now, since the purpose of God to
bestow the gifts of his grace stands firm and
sure, and these *gifts,* when bestowed in *calling,* are *without repentance,* and will never be
taken away, the final perseverance of these
called ones must be certain.   And though
the apostle is only speaking of the elect of
God among the Jews, the argument holds
equally good of all others, who have, or for
whom God has designed, the same gifts and
calling.   But to this is excepted,‖ that,

This " passage is evidently spoken of those
Jews who were then hardened, given up to a
spiritual slumber, *broken off from their own
olive-tree,* and in that state of infidelity in
which they have continued almost one thousand seven hundred years; and only intimates, that God will, in his good time, receive them again into his favour."   But
nothing is more evident, than that the apostle
is speaking of the Jews in the latter day, and
of God's eternal purposes and promises of
grace concerning them ; which shall be accomplished when the fulness of the Gentiles
is come in, towards whom he had gracious
designs, for whom he had gifts in reserve,
and whom he would call by his grace, in such
a manner, as that neither his gifts nor his
calling should be repented of, and so *all
Israel* should be *saved ;* and not of that present generation, much less of those Jews who
were then hardened, given up to a spiritual
slumber, and broken off; for these were *the
rest* that were *blinded,* and are distinguished
from *the election* that then *obtained,* and who
never were called, nor had any spiritual gifts
or saving blessings of grace bestowed on
them.

The arguments from the three last scriptures are said to need very little answer, as
being wholly alien from the purpose, and
very impertinent ; but, whether they are so
or no, the reader must judge.   Our author
proceeds to consider the arguments which
seem to have a greater force in them, taken
either from those scriptures which seem
plainly, or by just consequence, to assert this
doctrine, or else to promise this perseverance
of the saints; the vindication of which will
be attended to.

SECTION IV.

*For there shall arise false Christs, and false
prophets, and shall shew great signs and*

---

* Whitby, p. 438; ed. 2. 426.

† John xiii. 18.   ‡ Ibid. vi. 70.   § As in
many places. See Gal. i. 7.; Rev. xxi. 27.

‖ Whitby, p. 438; ed. 2. 426; Remonstr.
Coll. Hag. art. v. p. 85, 86;

wonders; insomuch that (if it were possible) they shall deceive the very elect.— Matt. xxiv. 24.

1st. THE argument from hence, in favour of the perseverance of the saints, very much depends on their being *the elect* of God, the impossibility of their deception being placed to this their character; which designs particular persons absolutely, and from eternity, chosen to everlasting life, who therefore cannot be so deceived as to be lost for ever, since their election is an eternal act, and therefore cannot be made void by a temporal one: it passed before the persons had *done either good or evil;* wherefore, as no good thing done by them was the cause of it, so no evil thing can annul or frustrate it; which strongly concludes the sure and certain salvation of all who are interested in it.

But it is said* that by the elect we are to understand the choicest believers, or the persevering Christians. To which I reply, that it is certain that such who are truly converted, or are true believers, are persevering Christians, and such without dispute are the elect: but then the reason why they are, and are called the elect, is not because they are converted, are true believers, and persevering Christians; but, on the contrary, the reason why they are converted, become true believers, and so persevering Christians, is because they are elected. Conversion, faith, and perseverance, are not the causes or conditions, but fruits and effects of election: hence faith is styled *the faith of God's elect;†* and it is also said, that *as many as were ordained unto eternal life believed;* wherefore such cannot be finally deceived. Besides, to talk of the final seduction of a persevering Christian is a contradiction in terms: such an interpretation of the phrase must be absurd and impertinent; for who knows not, that a persevering Christian cannot be finally and totally deceived?

2ndly. When we say, that the elect of God cannot be deceived, we allow that they may be, and are deceived before conversion. This is one part of their character, whilst unregenerate,‡ *foolish, disobedient, deceived,* &c., yea, that they may be, and oftentimes are, deceived after conversion; but then this is in part only, and not totally; in some lesser, and not in the greater matters of faith; not so as to let go their hold of Christ, the head, and quit the doctrine of salvation by him, or fall into what the apostle calls§ *damnable heresies.* They may be seduced from the simplicity of the gospel, but not finally; for they shall be recovered *out of the snare of the Devil,* and not be left to perish in such deceivings. To this are excepted,

1. That Christ‖ solemnly exhorts his disciples to use the greatest caution that they be not deceived; and, in the same chapter, to watch and pray, lest the hour of temptation should come suddenly on them; which, surely, he would not do, if he knew that they could not be deceived. To which I reply, that inasmuch as they were liable to a partial seduction, and for a time, though not to a total and final one, there was good reason why these exhortations should be given and taken. Besides, such cautions might be useful to quicken their diligence to search and read the Scriptures, and by them try the spirits, whether they were of God or no, and by their *fruits,* their doctrines, discover impostors, and avoid them. Hence these cautions should not be improved into arguments against the final perseverance of the saints, seeing they may be considered as means of it.

2. That ¶ Christ here declares, that by reason of the extreme affliction of these times, *many should be offended, and their love wax cold.* But it should be observed, that supposing true believers are intended, love in them may wax cold when it is not lost, which was the case of the church at Ephesus; and so is no proof of the saints falling from grace. Besides, the *many* that shall be *deceived, offended,* and fall off from the doctrine of faith are not the same persons with, but distinguished from, the elect, who cannot be deceived.

3rdly. When we say, that it is *impossible* that the elect of God should be deceived, we mean not that it is impossible they should, considered in themselves, or if left to themselves, being, generally speaking, *the foolish things of this world;* or if left to that *old Serpent, the Devil and Satan, which deceiveth the whole world;* or to false teachers, who *lie in wait to deceive:*** but we say it is impossible, considering the purposes and promises of God, the provisions of his grace, the security they have in the hands of Christ, and their preservation by the mighty power of God: and upon this account we judge, that their final and total deception is here represented as impossible.

But to this is excepted,†† that the phrase εἰ ογυνάτον, *if it were possible,* denotes only a great difficulty in the performance of an act possible, so Acts xx. 16, Rom. xii. 18, Matt. xxvi. 39, and also that it does not import what the event would be, but the vehemency of the endeavours of seducers, who would do the utmost they could to seduce Christians: and should it respect the event, it is only with relation to the means here mentioned, being such as should prevail to seduce even Christians, were it possible for impostors, by lying signs and wonders, to deceive them who are invested with a power of working greater signs and wonders. To which I reply, the instances to prove that this phrase only denotes great difficulty, and not an ab-

---

* Whitby, p. 43; ed. 2. 42; Remonstr. Coll. Hag. art. i. p. 85; art. v. p. 83; Limborch, p. 723.   † Tit. i. 1; Acts xiii. 48.   ‡ Tit. iii. 3.   § 2 Pet. ii. 1.   ‖ Whitby, p. 439; ed. 2. 427; Remonstr. Coll. Hag, art. v. p. 82; Limborch, p. 723.   ¶ Whitby, p. 440; ed. 2. 428; Remonstr. and Limborch, ibid.   ** 1 Cor. i. 27; Rev. xii. 10; Eph. iv. 14.   †† Whitby, p. 440, 441; ed. 2. 429; Remonstr. and Limborch, ibid.

solute impossibility, are insufficient. The words of the apostle Paul, in Acts xx. 16, are conjectural; he knew not whether it was possible or no, that he could be at Jerusalem before Pentecost; of which sort, surely, the words of Christ here cannot be thought to be. The same apostle's exhortation in Rom. xii. 18, supposes, that which is matter of fact, that it is impossible to live peaceably with some men; and what followed upon our Lord's petition in Matt. xxvi. 39, shows, that it was impossible that the cup should pass from him, considering the purpose of God, his covenant with him, and the salvation of his people. Moreover, should this phrase only import the vehemency of the endeavours of seducers, and not respect the event only with relation to the means here mentioned, *great signs, and wonders,* it follows, that if, notwithstanding the vehement endeavours of seducers, and the utmost they can do to deceive the saints; if, notwithstanding their showing *great signs and wonders,* they are not able to prevail over them, being invested with a power superior to them; it may be concluded and pronounced, that it is impossible they should be deceived either by them, or by any other, or by any other means; since these are the most effectual of any, being according to *the working of Satan, with all power, and signs, and lying wonders, and with all deceivableness of unrighteousness in them that perish:* but says, the apostle, in the same place,* *we are bound to give thanks always to God for you, brethren, beloved of the Lord, because God hath from the beginning chosen you to salvation;* which is the saints' grand security from a final and total deception, either by Satan or any of his emissaries.

SECTION V

And this is the Father's will, which hath sent me, that of all which he hath given me, I should lose nothing; but should raise it up again at the last day. And this is the will of him that sent me, that every one which seeth the Son, and believeth on him, may have everlasting life; and I will raise him up at the last day.—John vi. 39, 40.

THE persons here spoken of, are such as were given by the Father to Christ in eternal election, and in the everlasting covenant of grace, and who in time are enabled to believe on him for life and salvation; concerning whom the will of God is, that Christ should lose none of them, nor anything that belongs to them, neither their souls nor their bodies, no, not the least dust, but that *he should raise it up again,* and that these should also have everlasting life; which is the will of the Father of Christ, as well as of their Father, and therefore will be strictly regarded. Besides, this is the will of God, and not man, which cannot be resisted, so as to be frustrated; and is eternal, and therefore cannot

be made void by any temporal act; and consequently, these words furnish out a considerable argument in proof of the saints' final perseverance. To which is excepted,

1st. That "they treat not of the loss of believers by a defection from the faith, but of their perdition by death; wherefore Christ promises, that he would raise them from death to a salutary life."† Be it so, that these words speak not of the saints' preservation from an apostacy from the faith, but of their resurrection at the last day; yet, since their resurrection will be the resurrection of life, or will be unto eternal life, they must persevere to the end, and die in the Lord, in order to enjoy such a resurrection. If, therefore, it is the will of God, that all those whom he has given to Christ, and who see the Son, and believe on him, should be raised unto eternal life, their perseverance in grace is out of question; and after the resurrection, they will be out of any danger of apostacy; for being raised, they will be caught up with living saints to meet the Lord, and shall be *for ever* with him.

2ndly. It is said,‡ that "promises and declarations of the like nature with these which engage that God will give eternal life to the believer, are only to be understood of such a faith as doth endure to the end, and belong only to such as continue in the faith: and then it is demonstratively evident, that perseverance is included in them; and therefore cannot be proved from them, without begging the question." To which I reply, that all true faith does endure to the end; it is an *incorruptible seed* of grace; part of that *living water,* which *springs up into everlasting life; is the gift of God;* whose *gifts and calling are without repentance; of the operation of God,* which he begins and performs *with power;* Christ is *the author and finisher* of it, and his powerful and prevalent intercession secures it from ever failing: hence those who have it, shall continue in it; and therefore their perseverance is certain. And if perseverance is insured to true faith, and is included in these promises of eternal life to true believers, to them only do such promises belong; for such who fall away were never true believers: then it is demonstratively evident, that it is to be proved from them, and that without begging the question. But to this it is objected,

1. That such who fall away,§ " are expressly styled true believers, as others are." But the places where they are so expressly styled cannot be named; the instances alleged from Matt. xviii. 6, 14; Luke viii. 13; Rom. xiv. 14, 15, 20; 1 Cor. viii. 11; John iv. 39, 42; Acts viii. 10, and xxi. 20, are insufficient proofs of it. Some of the persons instanced in, though they may be allowed to be true believers; yet it does not appear, from what is said of them, that they totally and finally fell away; such as the *little ones*

---

* 2 Thess. ii. 9, 10, 13.   † Remonstr.   441, 442; ed. 2. 430.
Coll. Hag. art. v. p. 91.   ‡ Whitby, p.   § Ibid. p. 442; ed.
                                2. 431.

that believed in Christ, Matt. xviii. 6, and the *weak brother* in Rom. xiv., and 1 Cor. viii. Since what is said of their being offended and perishing, is not to be understood of eternal destruction, but of their being slighted and rejected, and their minds grieved, consciences wounded, and their spiritual peace broken in upon and interrupted; as has been shown in the former part of this work :* nor does it appear that the Samaritans, who believed in Christ, all fell off from him to Simon Magus; since those who truly believed might be dead, and safe in heaven, before his infatuation began and spread in Samaria: besides, it is not very evident that they were true believers in Christ; they might give their assent to him, as the Messiah and Saviour of the world, without having true saving faith in him for themselves: nor does it appear that many of those myriads of Jews that believed, afterwards fell away. The epistle to the Hebrews is no proof of it. And if any of them did, it will not be easily proved that they were true believers. And it is certain that those represented by the stony ground, in Luke viii. 13, who *believed for a while*, and then fell away, had not the true grace of God; since it is expressly said of them, that they had *no root in* them.

2. It is observed,[†] "that this faith, that is, of such who fall away, as to its kind, is true; is evident from this consideration, that Christ and his apostles require such persons not to change it, but only to continue in it; not to believe with a faith true and real as to kind, but to be steadfast in the faith they had already." But the passages produced do not prove that Christ and his apostles spoke to such persons; not the passage in John viii. 31, where our Lord says to the Jews *that believed on him, If ye continue in my word, then ye are my disciples indeed;* that is, you will appear to be really so, and will be made free by the truth; and consequently, it will be evident, that you are sons who shall abide in the house for ever, and never be cast out: nor the passage in Acts xiv. 22, where Paul and Barnabas exhort the believers, *to continue in the faith;* in which they do not give the least intimation, or supposition, that any of them should fall away, but, on the contrary, that *through much tribulation,* they should *enter into the kingdom of God;* and in order to their preservation to it, *commended them to the Lord, on whom they believed.*

3. It is said,[‡] that "this answer thwarts those numerous texts of scripture, which suspend the benefits promised to believers on their continuance in the faith." To which I answer, that the numerous scriptures referred to, which are Colos. i. 23; 1 Tim. ii. 15; Heb. iii. 6, 14; 1 John ii. 24; Rom. xi. 22, do not represent continuance in the faith as a precarious and uncertain thing; or suppose, that true believers may fall away finally and totally; nor do they suspend the benefits promised to believers, on the continuance of their faith, as a condition of their enjoying them; but represent continuance in the faith, as the evidence of their partaking of some of them already, and as a pledge and assurance of their enjoying the rest hereafter.

4. It is further objected,[§] that if this be the case, "all exhortations to steadfastness in the faith are enervated; and all declarations that we must be faithful to death, and endure to the end, are needless." To which I reply, that exhortations of this kind are not hereby enervated, nor are such declarations needless; since these may be, and are, made use of by the Spirit of God, for the increase of faith, and steadfastness in it; and so be the means of the saint's final perseverance. And whereas it is said,[||] that the only distinction between a living and dead faith is, that the one is attended with, the other is without good works; and that the only difference between a temporary and saving faith, is this, that the one continues, and the other does not: it may be replied, that though good works are an evidence of a living faith, yet the life of faith does not consist in works, but in special acts of it on its proper object, Christ; and a temporary faith is only an assent to the truth of some propositions concerning Christ; but is not as saving faith, a going out unto him, depending on him, and believing in him, for the salvation of the soul.

SECTION VI

God hath not cast away his people which he foreknew.—Rom. xi. 2.

THOUGH the number of God's people, in some ages of the world, is very small, as it was among the Israelites at the time of the apostle's writing this epistle, yet God has not, nor will he cast away, or cast off his people, whom he has foreknown; he may hide his face from them, afflict them in a fatherly way, and not immediately arise for their help; yet he will not cast them out of his affections, nor from his sight, nor out of the hands of his Son, nor out of the covenant of his grace, nor out of his family, or so as that they shall perish eternally: so far from it, that he takes the utmost delight and pleasure in them, gives them the greatest nearness to himself, lays them in his bosom, embraces them in his arms, keeps them as the apple of his eye, holds them by his right hand, and preserves them by his power unto salvation: the reasons of which are, his everlasting love unto them, his unchangeable purposes and promises concerning them, and because they are his jewels, his portion and inheritance: wherefore their final perseverance is certain. But to the argument from hence, it is objected.[¶]

"That this text cannot relate to any foreknowledge God hath of his elect from all eternity, but only to his foreknowledge and choice of the Jewish nation, before any other nations of the world; and only signifies, that God had not entirely cast off his people, Israel." To which I reply,

1. That it is most reasonable to conclude, that the word προέγνω is used in the same sense here, as it is elsewhere in this epistle; particularly in Rom. viii. 29, 30, where God's foreknowledge is spoken of as antecedent to predestination, vocation, justification, and glorification: and so must relate to God's foreknowledge of his elect from all eternity, and not of the Jewish nation; since all of them are not predestinated, called, justified, and glorified.

2. Though the people of Israel were *chosen to be a peculiar people above all people*,* and were *known before all the families of the earth:* yet they were not all a *foreknown* people in the special sense; and which is the apostle's sense of the phrase; *all were not Israel that were of Israel*.† Among that chosen and known people there were a special foreknown people, a *remnant, according to the election of grace ;*‡ who were *the election* that *obtained*, when *the rest were blinded.* And these are the people God had not cast away; for as for the bulk, and body, and majority of that people, God had, or was about to cast them away, as is sufficiently evident from this chapter. And the apostle's single instance of himself, and could he have instanced in seven thousand more, as in the times of Elias, would have been an insufficient proof of God's not having cast away the bulk and body of that people; but is a full and pertinent one, of God's not having cast away his special and foreknown people among them.

3. Though this text relates to the elect of God among the Jews, yet, inasmuch as the same characters belong to the elect of God among others, as that they are his special *people*, whom he has *foreknown*, being *elect, according to the foreknowledge of God the Father;*§ it is equally true of them, as of the elect among the Jews, that God has not, nor will he, cast any of them away.

The sense of the words in Rom. viii. 30, and the argument upon them, have been already considered and vindicated, under the head of ELECTION.

SECTION VII.

For I am persuaded, that neither death, nor life, nor angels, nor principalities, nor powers,' nor things present, nor things to come, nor height, nor depth, nor any other creature, shall be able to separate us from the love of God, which is in Christ Jesus our Lord.— Rom. viii. 38, 39.

IF *neither death*, in any view of it, *nor life* under any consideration whatever, *nor angels*, good or bad, *nor principalities, nor powers,* civil magistrates, ever so potent, tyrannical, fierce and cruel, *nor things present, nor things to come*, whether good or evil, *nor height, nor depth*, anything in heaven, earth or hell, *nor any other creature*, any person, or thing, within the compass of created beings, *shall be able to separate from the love* with which God loves his people; since it is the *love of God*, and not man; the love of him who changes not, and is besides *in Christ Jesus our Lord ;* then those who are interested in it cannot perish, or fail of glory; for it is impossible that any should perish, and yet continue the objects of God's love. Now,

1. It is owned,‖ that these words respect not "the love with which we love God, but his affection towards us; and that the apostle only intimates, that such persons continuing in the love of God, shall be preserved by him from the temptations here mentioned; and so supported by his grace and Spirit as to be able to bear them." And if so, since all such who have interest in the love of God, shall continue in it, what should hinder their final perseverance? And whereas it is observed,¶ that " he does not say, the love of no Christian shall *wax cold*, Matt. xxiv. 12, that none of them shall *lose his first love*, Rev. ii. 4. And were there no cause to fear this, it is asked, why doth Christ exhort his disciples to *abide in his love*, John xv. 9, and his apostles exhort others to *keep themselves in the love of God*, Jude 21, and to *look diligently* to it, that they *fall not from the grace and* favour *of God*, Heb. xii. 15, and to *continue in the grace of God*, Acts xiii. 43?" I answer, that the love even of true believers may *wax cold*, and yet not cease, nor the love of God cease towards them; nor does the scripture anywhere say, that any of them has lost, or may *lose*, but only have *left* their *first love;* nor do the exhortations of Christ and his apostles, to *abide in his love, and keep themselves in the love of God*, suppose this, but are made use of as means to prevent it : and as for the two last passages referred to, they are not to be understood, either of the love of the saints to God, or of his love and favour to them, but of the doctrine of grace.

2. It is farther observed,** " that the apostle does not say, that nothing can separate true believers from the love of God, or Christ ; but only declares his persuasion, that nothing would do it, or that they had no cause to fear these things, or to be shaken from their steadfastness, in expectation of those inestimable blessings God had promised to, and Christ had purchased for them, by any of " these tribulations." But, if this persuasion of the apostle's was a well-grounded one; and if there was no just cause of fearing these things; then it is certain, that nothing can separate true believers from the love of God. And besides, since " they have good ground to hope, that all the evils they shall bear shall conduce to their good, that Christ will still be ready to support them under them by his power, and to help their infirmities by his Spirit, and at last give them the glory prepared for the sons of God;" not only the apostle might well persuade

---

* Deut. vii. 6; Amos iii. 2.   † Rom. ix. 6.
‡ Rom. xi 5, 7.   § 1 Pet. i. 2.   ‖ Whitby, p. 457; ed. 2. 438; Remonstr. Coll. Hag. art.
v. p. 108; Limborch, p. 724.   ¶ Whitby, p. 458.   ** Whitby, p. 458.

himself, but they also may well persuade themselves, that nothing shall ever be able to separate them from this love of God : nor do the fears the apostle elsewhere expresses, of their being shaken and tempted, so as that his *labour* would be *in vain*, and the arguments and motives he offers to prevent this effect of temptations, contradict this persuasion : nor was this persuasion of his concerning them, that they would persevere, and continue steadfast in the love of God, to which they had so great inducements ; but that nothing should separate them from the affection of God towards them ; which sense this author himself before acknowledged ; though he now* thinks fit to contradict himself.

SECTION VIII

In whom, after that ye believed, ye were sealed with that Holy Spirit of promise : which is the earnest of our inheritance, until the redemption of the purchased possession, unto the praise of his glory.—Ephes. i. 13, 14. *See also* Ephes. iv. 30, 2 Cor. i. 21, 22.

THE argument from these passages of scripture, proving the saints' final perseverance, may be thus formed : if true believers are *sealed*, certified and assured, by the Spirit of God, that they are the sons and heirs of God, and shall enjoy the heavenly *inheritance* : and if the same Spirit is the *earnest* and pledge of it, and that *until the redemption of the purchased possession*, or until *the day of redemption ;* that is, until all those who are *the possession* of Christ, or his peculiar people, whom he has *purchased* with his blood, are *redeemed* from their mortality and corruption, which will be done in the resurrection morn, and not before ; I say, if the Spirit of God does thus seal believers, and is, and continues to be an earnest of their future glory, until this time ; then they shall certainly and finally persevere. But the Spirit of God does do, and is all this to them, unto this time ; therefore, they shall certainly and finally persevere. In answer to this it is said,†

1st. " That these metaphors neither do, nor can signify that they, who have once the Spirit, can ever lose him, or cause him to depart from them, is evident from these considerations ;

1. " That they who have been *the temples of God*, by virtue of his Spirit dwelling in them, may so corrupt this temple as to be themselves destroyed, as is demonstrable from 1 Cor. iii. 16, 17, and that they, whose bodies are *the members of Christ*, and who are *one spirit with him*, may make these bodies *the members of an harlot ;* and so cease to be the members of Christ, 1 Cor. vi. 15." I reply that these metaphors both can, and do signify that they, who have once the Spirit, can never wholly lose him, or cause him finally and totally to depart from them ; for otherwise he would not be a *sealer* of them, nor an *earnest* of their *inheritance* to them,

until the day of redemption : nor do the words of the apostle, in 1 Cor. iii. 16, 17, demonstrate that they, who have been the temples of God, may so corrupt this temple as to be themselves destroyed ; but only that such, who attempt to corrupt or defile the temple and church of God, by bringing in among them *damnable heresies*, shall be destroyed by God ; and not they who are the temples of God : nor do the words, in 1 Cor. vi. 15, prove that they, whose bodies are the members of Christ, may make them the members of an harlot. The apostle only puts the question, *Know ye not that your bodies are the members of Christ ? Shall I then take the members of Christ, and make them the members of an harlot ?* Which he answers with a *God forbid.* And his design is to show how unbecoming the sin of fornication is to such, whose bodies are the members of Christ, and temples of the Holy Ghost ; but does not in the least insinuate that such, who were truly so, might cease to be the members of Christ, or cause the Holy Spirit entirely to depart from them.

2. This is also said‡ to be " farther evident from the apostle's fears, that Satan might so far have tempted his *Thessalonians,* as to render *all his labour vain among them ;* whom yet he acknowledges, had *received the word with joy of the Holy Ghost*, and were *the elect of God.*" But it should be observed, that the apostle's fears were not, lest, through Satan's temptations, they might so fall away as to cause the Holy Spirit wholly to depart from them ; but lest Satan, through false teachers, should so stagger their faith, that they should in any respect give way to erroneous principles and practices ; and thereby not *all* his labour, but that part of it should be *in vain*, which he had bestowed upon them in establishing them in the truths of the gospel.

3. This is said§ to be still farther evident " from the exhortations in these epistles, directed to those men, who are said to have this seal and earnest of the Holy Spirit ; as to the Corinthians 2 Cor. vi. 1 ; xi. 3, and xii. 20, 21, and to the Ephesians, chap. v. 3, 6, and iii. 13, and vi. 13." To which may be replied, that these exhortations, which regard the saints continuing in the doctrines of the gospel, avoiding sin, and withstanding temptations, though they imply danger to the saints, as considered in themselves, as of falling from some degree of steadfastness in the faith, and into sin, and of fainting in the evil day ; yet do not suppose that they may, or shall fall finally and totally, or so as that the Holy Spirit would wholly withdraw from them ; though they might so fall and faint as to *grieve* him, to do which would be unkind and ungenerous ; since he is the *sealer* of their persons, and *the earnest* of their *inheritance.* Besides, these exhortations are to be considered as means, being designed, and doubtless as such

---

* Ibid. p. 459.　　　† Whitby, p. 459 ; ed. 2. 439.　　‡ Ibid. p. 460 ; ed. 2. 440.

§ Ibid. p. 460, 461 ; ed. 2. 441, 442 ; Remen tr. Coll. Hag. art. v. p. 54.

were blessed, for the final perseverance of God's sealed ones.

2ndly. In answer to the argument above, it is observed,* that "the expressions are designed only to inform us that the Holy Spirit, vouchsafed to Christ's church and members, gave them a just assurance of the truth of the Christian faith; and consequently of the farther blessings promised to his faithful persevering servants in the world to come. Whence it is evident, that they who had these first fruits of the Spirit, had thereupon an argument to satisfy them of the future blessings promised to them. And hence they, by his Spirit, are said to have the *earnest* of their future inheritance, and to be *sealed up to the day of redemption.*" But let it be observed, that the Holy Spirit, vouchsafed to Christ's church and members, does not only give a just assurance of the truth of the Christian faith, as a doctrine; but also assures believers of the truth of the grace of faith, and of all other graces in them, and of their right to glory, and certain enjoyment of it. Moreover, if the Spirit, thus vouchsafed, gives a just assurance of farther blessings promised by Christ; and if such, who have these first fruits of the Spirit, have thereupon an argument to satisfy them of these blessings; then they may, with faith and patience, wait for *the redemption of the body:* and be assured that when *this earthly tabernacle is dissolved,* they *have a building of God, an house not made with hands, eternal in the heavens;* and that *the Lord will deliver them from every evil work, and preserve them unto his heavenly kingdom.*† The argument from 2 Tim. ii. 19, is vindicated, under the head of Election,‡ whither the reader is referred.

SECTION IX

Who are kept by the power of God, through faith unto salvation, ready to be revealed in the last time.—1 Pet. i. 5.

THESE words, in connection with the preceding verses, show that such as are *elect according to the foreknowledge of God the Father,* and are *begotten again unto* a *lively hope* of an *incorruptible inheritance,* are *kept φρουρουμένους,* as in a garrison, *by,* or *in the power of God,* safe and secure from a final and total falling away, *through* the grace of *faith unto* consummate *salvation,* to be enjoyed for ever in heaven. In answer to which, it is said.§

1. "That this place only proves that all, who are preserved to salvation, are so kept by the power of God; but not that all believers are so kept." I reply, we do not say, that all believers are so kept; since there are some who are nominal believers, have no true grace, believe but for a time, and fall away; but then we say, that all true believers are so kept; otherwise the words of our Lord, Mark xvi. 16, would not be true, nor the will of his Father, John vi. 40, be fulfilled; for how should every one that believes be saved, unless they are preserved unto salvation? And if those who are preserved unto salvation, are kept by the power of God unto it, as is owned; it follows, that since every true believer will be saved, and in order to it be preserved unto salvation, then every one of them is, and will be, kept by the power of God unto it.

2. It is farther said,‖ that this place "proves only that they are kept through faith; that is, if they continue in the faith, and hold the beginning of their confidence steadfast unto the end." But it should be observed, that there is no *if* in the text; faith is not represented as a condition, but as a means of preservation, engaged by the power of God, for that is as much secured by the power of God as salvation itself, or preservation to it. Besides, such a sense of the words is no other than this, that these persons are kept by the power of God, if, or so long as, they keep themselves; which, as it greatly depreciates the power of God, and ascribes too much to the creature, so it is in itself exceeding trifling. Add to this, that if this faith, through which believers are kept to salvation, will render them victorious over the world, enable them to resist the temptations of the devil, to prefer afflictions before the pleasures of sin, and even to suffer death, not accepting deliverance, in expectation of a better resurrection; and, lastly, engage the power of God in their preservation, and so cause them *out of weakness to be strong,* all which is owned by our author; this, surely, proves that they shall certainly continue in the faith, and so be preserved safe unto the kingdom and glory of God.

SECTION X.

They went out from us, but they were not of us; for if they had been of us, they would, no doubt, have continued with us. But they went out, that they might be made manifest, that they were not all of us.—1 John ii. 19.

THE meaning of these words is, that there were some persons in the apostle John's time, who had made a profession of religion, were members of the church, and some of them, perhaps, preachers; and yet departed from the faith they professed, withdrew themselves from the church or churches, to which they belonged, and set up separate assemblies of their own. These, the apostle says, *were not of us;* that is, they were not regenerated by the grace of God, and so apparently were not of the number of God's chosen ones; for had they been born again of the incorruptible seed, had they had that anointing which abides, and from which persons are truly denominated Christians; as they would have appeared to have been chosen, so they would have *continued* in the faith, and have remained with the churches

---

* Whitby, p. 462; ed. 2. 442.
† Rom. viii. 23; 2 Cor. v. 1; 2 Tim. iv. 18.
‡ Sect. ix.   § Whitby, p. 463.

‖ Ibid. p. 463, 464; ed. 2. 443, 444; Remonstr. Coll. Hag. art. v. p. 93.

of Christ, and not have fallen into such errors and heresies, into which it is impossible that God's elect, or true believers, should ever fall. But the defection of these persons was permitted by God, that *they might be made manifest*, that they had never received the grace of God in truth. It follows, therefore, that as such who so fall were never true believers, so such who are true believers, shall never totally and finally fall away. To which is answered,*

1. "That these words, *they were not of us*, cannot signify they were not of the number of the elect; but only they were not of the church in general, and of the mind of the apostles, and the church that adhered to them." But surely the apostle would never deny that these persons were of the church, and of the same mind with it, at least in profession, antecedent to their going out; for had they not been in communion with the church, they could not be properly said to go out of it; and if they had not been of the same mind and faith and profession, they could not be said to depart from it. The reason this author gives, as an evidence of their not being of the church, "that from them they went out, and with them they might have remained," is a reason invincibly proving that they were of them, as a church, otherwise they could not have went out from them; with whom they not only *might* but *would* have remained, had their hearts been right with God. And whereas it is farther observed, that "they could not go out from the elect only, who are not visible, nor could they have remained with them, who were never of them;" it may be replied, that though they were never of them as elect, yet they were of them as a church, become visible by a profession of faith; and therefore could, as they did, go out from them as such; though had they been true believers in Christ, they would have appeared to have been elect likewise, and would have continued and remained with them both as elect and as a church. It is moreover added,† that "their going out from them for a season, was no certain argument that they were not of the elect; since it is confessed, that they may fall totally, though not finally." Who they are that have made this confession, I shall not inquire; for my own part, I affirm that God's elect, or true believers in Christ, cannot totally fall, that is, wholly and entirely lose the grace of God bestowed on them, or wrought in them. However, the going out of these persons was in such a manner, that it was a certain argument that they were not of the elect; since they became *antichrists*, ver. 18, the forerunners of the man of sin, avowed enemies to Christ, who denied him to be the *Christ*, ver. 22, or that he was come in the flesh, chap. iv. 3, and therefore said to be of the world, and not of God, ver. 4—6.

2. It is said,‡ that "the true sense of the words seems plainly to be this: these antichrists, or deceivers, went out from the apostles and churches of Judea, Acts xv. 1, 24, to preach destructive doctrines to the Gentiles, which both the church of Judea, and the apostles assembled for that purpose, flatly disowned and censured; by which it sufficiently appeared, that all the preachers of these doctrines were not of them." But this sense of the words confines them to preachers only; whereas, though many of these antichrists might be preachers, yet not all; whoever denied the Father and the Son, or that Christ was come in the flesh, was an antichrist, whether he was in a public or private capacity. Besides, not the true and faithful ministers of the word, but private believers, are opposed to these persons in the following verse, *But ye have an unction from the Holy One*, &c. This sense of the words also makes the *us* to be the apostles, and churches of Judea; whereas, when the apostle John wrote this epistle, the rest of the apostles were all dead; and he speaks of these antichrists as men that were, in that last time, risen up among them, and went out from them; and, therefore, could not, with any propriety, say that they went out from the apostles. Besides, whenever this pronoun *us* is used elsewhere, in this epistle, it is never restrained to the apostles; but the apostle John in it includes, with himself, all true believers. Nor is there any reason to conclude, that he had in view the church of Judea, and a case in which that was concerned near forty years ago, but rather the churches of Asia, among whom he was, and particularly the church at Ephesus, where he is generally thought to have resided. Now the apostle Paul, many years before this, had told§ the elders of the church, that after his departure, not only *grievous wolves* should *enter in* among them, but also *of their own selves* should *men arise, speaking perverse things, to draw away disciples after them:* and the apostle John lived to see these predictions fulfilled. Add to all this, that this sense of the words makes their going out to be merely local and corporal.—Now to go out from the apostles, in this sense, was not criminal; the persons that went down from Judea to Antioch, Acts xv. 1, 24, are not blamed for going thither, nor for going out from the apostles thither, but for *troubling* the disciples *with words* to *the subverting of their souls.* Nor was a corporal departure from the apostles any evidence of not being of the same mind with them, for they often departed one from another, and yet continued of the same mind and faith. The departure here spoken of was of men from the true church of Christ, both in doctrine and in affection; and that not of preachers only, but of others who were only nominal Christians, and was so understood by the ancient fathers, particularly Tertullian‖ and Cyprian.¶

* Whitby, p. 463, 464; ed. 2. 443, 444.
† Ibid. p. 465; ed. 2. 445.   ‡ Ibid.; Remoustr. Coll. Hag. art. v. p. 96.   § Acts xx. 29, 30.   ‖ De Prescript. Hæret. p. 231.
¶ Epist. lv. p. 116. and lxxvi. p. 208. De Unitate Ecclesiæ, p 256

SECTION XI

Whosoever is born of God doth not commit sin ; for his seed remaineth in him ; and he cannot sin, because he is born of God.—1 John iii. 9.

HE that is *born of God* is one that is regenerated by the Spirit and grace of God ; and that *which is born of the Spirit is spirit,* or spiritual ; it is a *new man,* a *new creature,* which neither does, nor can commit sin ; though it is as yet imperfect, there is no impurity in it, no bias, tendency, or inclination to sin, but all the reverse ; it is born of an *incorruptible seed* which *remains,* it is a principle of grace which is of God, and can never be lost. Hence it follows, that regenerate persons cannot cease to be so. In answer to this, it is said,*

1. " That these words cannot be intended to signify that he who is *born of the Spirit* and the *word,* can never fall from that state is evident ; partly, because he hath been proved already that the Holy Spirit may depart and quit his habitation ; and so he who was once born of the Spirit may cease to be so ; and partly, because men may not continue in the word, nor the word abide in them, nor they in Christ, and may lose their interest in God, and the things which they had wrought, as is clearly intimated by these exhortations, 1 John ii. 24, 27, 28 ; 2 John 8, 9." But it has been also already proved that the Holy Spirit does not finally and totally depart from true believers. Nor is it possible that he that is once born of the Spirit can cease to be so ; a man can be but once regenerated ; and he that is once born again cannot be again unborn. Nor do the exhortations referred to intimate that regenerate persons may not abide in the word, or that in them, or they not in Christ, or that they may lose their interest in God ; but are so many encouragements to the performance of duty, as a means of their final perseverance.

2. It is argued† that " as those words of Christ, Matt. vii. 18, and those of the apostle, Rom. viii. 7, do not prove that a corrupt tree cannot cease to be corrupt, and become good ; or that the carnal mind cannot cease to be so, and become spiritual, so neither do these words prove that he who is born of God cannot cease to be so." But it should be observed, that as the words of Christ and the apostle referred to, prove that a corrupt and carnal man cannot become good and spiritual without the powerful and efficacious grace of God, which can only make him so ; so these words prove that a regenerate man cannot cease to be one, or in such sense sin as to be lost and perish ; for this reason, because there is a principle of mighty grace in him, which overcomes the world, the flesh, and the devil.

Again, it is urged,‡ that " as these words

in Matt. xii. 34, John vii. 7, and xii. 39, and xiv. 17, do not signify an impossibility that it should be otherwise, but only their present indisposition to the contrary, and the aversation of their minds from those things which it is said they cannot do : so those words do not import any impossibility that they should do so, but only that they have at present that frame of spirit, which renders them strongly averse from sin, and indisposed to yield to any temptations to commit it." But it is easy to observe, that the apostle does not conclude the regenerate man's not sinning, or not being able to sin, from any present precarious frame of spirit ; but from his constitution, as being *born of God,* and from *the seed of God,* a principle of grace remaining and abiding in him.

3. It is said,§ that " the interpretation which many of the ancient *fathers* give us of these words, are a demonstration that they believed not the doctrine of the *saints' perseverance ;* for they expound the words thus ; *He that is born of God sinneth not, neither can sin,* quamdiu renatus est, *whilst he is born of God ;* because he ceaseth to be a child of God when he sins." Whether the ancient fathers believed the doctrine of the saints' perseverance, or not, will be considered (God willing) in an after part of this work. Who the many of the ancient fathers are, that give this interpretation of the words, we are not told : not Ignatius, nor Clemens of Romê, nor of Alexandria, nor Irenæus, nor Justin Martyr, nor Cyprian. Tertullian comes the nearest to it, when he says.‖ Hæc non admittet omnino qui natus a Deo fuerit, non futurus Dei filius si admiserit ; *He that is born of God, will not at all commit these things,* speaking of some grievous sins ; *should he commit them he would not be a child of God.* His meaning I take to be this ; should any one that professes to be born of God, commit such and such things, it would be evident that he was not a child of God : but he adds afterwards, *We know that every one that is born of God, sinneth not ;* scilicet, delictum quod ad mortem est, *namely, the sin unto death.*

SECTION XII

For the mountains shall depart, and the hills be removed ; but my kindness shall not depart from thee, neither shall the covenant of my peace be removed, saith the Lord, that hath mercy on thee.—Isaiah liv. 10.

THESE words contain an irresistible argument in favour of the saints' final perseverance ; proving that they cannot fall from the grace of God, or ever be deprived of an interest in the covenant of peace, and the blessings of it. In which, the unalterableness of God's love to his people, and the immoveableness of his covenant with them, are illustrated and confirmed, by the departure and removing of mountains and hills ; when neither of these shall depart, nor be removed. Wherefore if

---

* Whitby, r. 166 : ed. 2. 446.   † Ibid. p. 467, ed. 2 4:7.   ‡ Ibid.   § Whitby, p. 467 ; ed. 2. 448.   ‖ De Pudicitia, c. xix. p. 741 ; ed. Paris.

the kindness of God to them never will depart from them, notwithstanding their fall in Adam, the depravity of their natures, their many actual sins before conversion, their frequent backslidings after; and though he hides his face from them as to sensible communion, and chides and chastises them in the course of his providence; if this is the case, I say, as it certainly is, then it is impossible that persons, thus held and embraced in the arms of everlasting love, should ever totally and finally fall away, so as to be lost and perish eternally. Moreover, if the covenant of peace is an immoveable one, as there is the highest reason to believe it is; since God has not only said, but swore to it, that he *will not break it nor alter the thing that is gone out of his lips;* seeing it is made with Christ, with whom it shall *stand fast:* then the persons interested in it cannot fail of grace here, and glory hereafter, which are blessings secured for them in it. But, in answer to these arguments,

1. It is said,* "that it is exceeding evident that this place, with some others, hereafter to be considered, speaks of nations in the general, and not of a few private persons among them." To which I reply; that it is exceeding evident that the persons spoken to, which are no other than the church of Christ, are spoken to in the singular number, as appears from the words *thou* and *thee* used almost in every verse in the chapter; which is not very suitable to the nations in general. Besides, the relations that Jehovah stands in to these persons are such in which he does not stand to the nations in general; for, though he is the *maker* of them all, and the *God of the whole earth;* yet he is only a *husband* and a *redeemer* of particular persons, ver. 5. Likewise, the expressions of God's love and kindness, ver. 7—10, are too strong to be applied to the nations in general; as well as the promises of glory and happiness, ver. 11, 12, and particularly, that *all her children* should *be taught of the Lord, and great* should *be the peace* of them, ver. 13. Add to this, that these persons are distinguished from the nations in general, ver. 3, and from those that should gather and rise up against them, ver. 15—17. And the whole prophecy, concerning them, concludes thus; *this is the heritage of the servants of the Lord, and their righteousness is of me, saith the Lord:* which words contain in them both characters and privileges which do not belong to the nations in general.

2. It is further objected,† that the prophet here speaks of the time of the Jews' general conversion to the faith; as is evident from ver. 11, 12, compared with Rev. xxi. But it unhappily falls out for this objector, that the prophet is speaking of the conversion of the Gentiles, and not of the Jews; as appears from ver. 1—3, compared with Gal. iv. 27, in which he predicts, that the instances of

conversion among the Gentiles, at the first preaching of the Gospel to them, would be far more numerous than what had been among the Jews. And it is evident from ver. 11, 12, compared with Rev. xxi. that he is there speaking of a very glorious state of the church among the Gentiles in the latter day; when their *fulness* shall *come in,* and *the nations of them that are saved shall walk in the light* of that glorious state, and *the kings of the earth shall bring the glory and honour of the nations to it.*‡ And it is also very evident, that the prophet is speaking, in ver. 12, of the time when the *earth,* not the land of Judea, but the Gentile world, shall be full of the *knowledge of the Lord, as the waters cover the sea.*§ But supposing that the time of the Jews' conversion is here referred to, and the converted Jews are the only persons intended; how does this militate against the saints' final perseverance? Since these converted Jews will appear to have a share in that *kindness* which shall never *depart* from them, and to be interested in that *covenant* which shall never be *removed.* And it should be observed, that this exception destroys the former; for if the Jews, and their conversion are spoken of, then not the nations in general.

3. It is farther urged,‖ that "the promise of a *covenant of peace* that should not fail, was made under a condition, as the words in chap. lv. 3, show." To which I answer, that the phrases of inclining the ear, and hearkening to the Lord, mentioned in the place referred to, were not the conditions of God's making, that is, making known, and confirming his covenant to them; but the promises of making good, and applying the blessings of the covenant, is used as an encouragement to incline the ear to hearken to him. Besides, were this covenant of peace a conditional one, depending on any thing to be performed by man, it would not be better than the old covenant; whereas the covenant of grace and peace, is represented as a *new* and a *better* one, *established upon better promises,*¶ which are absolute and unconditional. Add to this, that the covenant here spoken of, is represented to be such a one, ver. 9, as was made with Noah. Now the covenant made with Noah was without any condition required on the part of man, as appears from Gen. ix. 11.

SECTION XIII.

As for me, this is my covenant with them saith the Lord, My Spirit that is upon thee, and my words which I have put in thy mouth, shall not depart out of thy mouth, or out of the mouth of thy seed, nor out of the mouth of thy seed's seed, saith the Lord, from henceforth, and for ever.—Isaiah lix. 21.

THESE words are to be understood of the

* Whitby p. 469, ed. 2. 449.   † Ibid. p. 471; ed. 2. 450.   ‡ Rev. xxi. 19, 23, 24.   § Isa. xi. 9.   ‖ Whitby, p. 472; ed. 2. 452; Remonstr. Col. Hag. art. v. p. 72.   ¶ Heb. viii. 6—8.

church of Christ under the New Testament dispensation, and of all true believers, which are the *seed* of the church, and her *seed's seed* in successive ages ; being *born in* her, *nursed up* at her *side*, and are her *children* in a spiritual sense ; among whom the Spirit and the Word, two grand blessings of the covenant of grace, shall always remain, and never depart from them ; and so contain a very considerable argument, not only of the continuance of the church of Christ in all ages, and of his Spirit and gospel in it, but of the final perseverance of particular saints. For, if the Spirit of the Lord shall not finally and totally depart from such, in whom he is as a spirit of regeneration, sanctification, faith, adoption, &c., though his grace in them is not always in exercise, and he may, for a time, withdraw his sensible presence and gracious influence, then the saints shall finally persevere, and cannot perish ; for it is impossible they should ever perish with him in them, who is "the well of living water springing up unto eternal life :" the abiding *seed* in them, who is "greater than he that is in the world ;" and will "perform the good work of grace begun in them, until the day of Christ." Moreover, if the gospel, though it may depart from a nation, as it did from the Jews, and has done for others, and from visible, particular congregated churches such as the seven churches of Asia, and out of the mouths of formal professors, who may drop, deny, and blaspheme it ; shall never depaat out of the mouths of such who have received it in the love of it, and in whose hearts it works effectually, then they shall finally persevere ; since this "gospel is the power of God unto salvation" to them, and the "engrafted word able to save" them. But, in answer to this, it is urged,

1. That the words are a conditional promise,[*] being made with such who *turn from transgression*, ver. 20, and on the account of their so doing ; and no longer binding, than that is continued. To which may be replied, that there is not the least appearance of a condition in the words, or in the preceding *verse* referred to : it is not said, *If they turn away from transgression* then *my spirit and my words shall not depart from* them. Their turning away from transgression is mentioned not as the cause, or condition of God's covenant with them, and of these articles in it ; but only as descriptive of the persons interested therein. Besides, as the words are cited by the apostle Paul in Rom. xi. 27, they contain an absolute promise of what the Redeemer would do for them when he came, and not what they should do themselves.

2. It is observed,[†] "that something external, and peculiar to the Israelites, is here promised." To which I reply ; whatever may be said for *the words* of the Lord being in their *mouths*, as something external ; it is certain that the *Spirit* of the Lord being *upon*, or *in* them (for ‫על‬, is put for ‫ב‬, as Kimchi ex-

plains the words) designs nothing external, nor the gifts of the Spirit, either ordinary, or extraordinary; but the internal operations of his grace, in which sense the phrase is used in Isaiah xliv. 3, 4. Moreover, though the Jews, under the Old Testament dispensation had many external things peculiar to themselves, in which they had the advantage of the Gentiles ; yet, under the New Testament dispensation, there is no difference made between believing Jews, and believing Gentiles; see Gal. iii. 28; Coloss. iii. 11. Besides, these promises were not made to the Israelites or Jews, literally considered ; but to the church of Christ, and true believers in him, figuratively signified by Zion and Jacob.

3. It is added,[‡] "that these promises regard a particular time from which they commenced, *from henceforth, and for ever ;* and particular persons, who are distinctly and emphatically, and by a climax, mentioned; *from thy mouth, and the mouth of thy seed, and of thy seed's seed.* Whereas the promise of perseverance, according to our notions of it, must belong equally to all the elect in all ages, before, as well as after, these promises were made." To which I answer, that the covenant here spoken of regards the new covenant, or the administration of that covenant of grace, under the gospel dispensation, which was to take place from the coming of the Redeemer, ver. 20, the date intended, nor was there any need to include more ; nor could more be included in these promises than the saints under the gospel dispensation. And the reason why the church, her seed, and seed's seed, are so distinctly mentioned, may be to remove all doubts and scruples from the minds of believers, in all the periods of that dispensation, and the more strongly to confirm them in the belief of these things.

4. It is said,[§] "that the apostle Paul plainly refers these words to the time of the Jews' conversion to the faith; who, when brought home to Christ, should never fall from him." Be it so, that they do more particularly belong to that time, than any other: this sense of them is far from militating against the saints' final perseverance ; since it strongly proves that the Jews, when converted, shall not finally and totally fall away; which is not a blessing peculiar to them, but what they will have in common with Gentile believers.

5. It is urged,[||] that "if these promises belong to the elect, the seed of the elect, and their seed's seed, must be elected also; whereas it is certain, from experience, that the seed of the elect are often very wicked; and therefore not elect, but reprobates." It must be owned, that there would be a good deal of force in this objection, were the words to be understood of believers, and their natural seed and offspring, as such ; and therefore such who understand the words in this sense, would do well to consider how they betray the doctrine of perseverance into the

---

* Remonstr. Coll. Hag. art. v. p. 72.
† Ibid. p. 73.   ‡ Ibid.
§ Whitby, p. 471 ; ed. 2. 450.
|| Ibid. p. 470 : ed. 2. 450.

hands of our opponents. But when it is observed, that these words respect not *the children of the flesh*, or the natural seed of believers, but *the children of the promise*, who *are counted for the seed*,* there will appear no weight in the objection.

SECTION XIV

And I will betroth thee unto me for ever ; yea, I will betroth thee unto me in righteousness, and in judgment, and in loving-kindness, and in mercies. I will even betroth thee unto me in faithfulness, and thou shalt know the Lord.—Hos. ii. 19, 20.

THE certain and final perseverance of the elect, appears very evident from this passage of scripture. For, if the Lord Jesus Christ does, by an act of his free grace, *betroth* his people to himself; and that *in righteousness*, in the wedding garment of his own righteousness; and also *in judgment*, which may intend the powerful protection of them from all insults and injuries; and likewise *in loving-kindness*, and *in mercies*, which he has shown in dying for them, in nourishing and cherishing of them, and in sympathizing with them, as well as in *faithfulness*, which he will never suffer to fail; and all this *for ever ;* so that this marriage relation shall never cease; I say if Christ has thus closely and eternally joined and united his people to himself, it is not possible they should ever be separated from him; or so fall from his grace as to be eternally lost. But to this, the following things are objected.

1. That these words † are spoken "of them, who *came out of the land of Egypt*, who had *burnt incense to Baalam*, and whose *feast days* were *new moons and sabbaths*, and so cannot concern the elect only, or their final perseverance." To which I reply, that it is very evident, that though these words are spoken of the Israelites, yet not of the same individual persons who came out of Egypt, or who had burnt incense to Balaam; but regard other persons and times, even the times when the ceremonial law was to be abolished, and the *new moons, sabbaths*, and *solemn feasts*, made to cease, ver. 11, when the land of Judea with its *vines* and *fig-trees*, shall be destroyed, ver. 12, and which are distinguished from the days of the youth of this people, as a body politic, when they came out of the land of Egypt, ver. 15, and so concern the elect of God among that people, who being *allured* into the *wilderness* of the *Gentile* world, ver. 14, were met with, and converted under the ministry of the apostles, and so openly betrothed unto the Lord Jesus Christ : and was a pledge of what will be more largely done at the time of their general conversion; when it shall be said, *the marriage of the Lamb is come*. Besides, these words regard not only the elect of God among the Jews, but among the Gentiles also, as appears from Rom. ix. 23—26.

2. It is objected,‡ that "if these spiritual promises respect the elect, then the temporal ones must do so likewise; and then they must abound *with corn, and wine and oil*, ver. 22, which yet were never looked upon as promises made to the elect, much less as things peculiarly belonging to them." But why these should not be looked upon as promises made to the elect, I see not : does not God take care of his own elect in temporal things ? which, though not peculiar to them, yet are given to them in a peculiar manner, being blessings indeed to them, whilst they are curses to others. Besides, nothing is more evident than that oftentimes, in the writings of the Old Testament, temporal blessings are spoken of, as figurative of spiritual ones.

3. It is moreover observed,§ " that the promise here made to Israel, is only made to her *returning to her first husband*, ver. 7," and is not an absolute, but a conditional one. But whoever reads it with any care, will easily see that it is expressed in the most absolute and unconditional terms ; no less than three times, to express the certainty of the thing, does the Lord say, *I will betroth thee unto me*, and adds, *and thou shalt know the Lord ;* that is, believe in him, own, acknowledge, love, honour, and obey him, as thy lord and husband. He does not say, if thou wilt own and acknowledge me, love, honour and obey me, or return to me, and remain inviolably chaste and faithful to me, then I will betroth thee to myself ; nor is there any connection between these words and ver. 7. And was there any between them ; yet even they are delivered in very absolute terms thus, she shall say under strong convictions of mind, and impressions made by powerful and efficacious grace, *I will go and return to my husband, for then was it better with me than now.*

SECTION XV

And I will make an everlasting covenant with them, that I will not turn away from them to do them good ; but I will put my fear in their hearts, that they shall not depart from me.—Jer. xxxii. 40.

IF the *covenant* God makes with his people is an *everlasting* one, interest in it indissoluble, the grace of it always sufficient, its blessings irreversible, its promises sure, and the mediator of it always the same, than which nothing is more certain ; if God, the maker of this covenant, *will not turn away* his love and affections from them, but *will do* them all *the good* he has either purposed or promised, and if he *puts* his *fear in their hearts*, so as that *they shall not depart* totally from him ; their final perseverance must be abundantly secured. Now, in answer to this it is said,

1. That "these‖ promises are made expressly to the whole house of Israel, and to all the children of Israel and Judah; and

* Rom. ix. 7.   † Whitby, p. 469; ed. 2. 449.   ‡ Ibid. p. 470; ed. 2. 449, 450. § Ibid. p 472; ed. 2. 452.

‖ Whitby, p. 288, 469; ed. 2. 281, 449; Remons'r. Coll. Hag. art. v. p. 69; Limborch, p. 722.

therefore cannot concern the elect only, or their final perseverance." I reply, that Israel and Judah were typical of God's elect, under the gospel dispensation; and supposing that they are literally intended, it is enough to secure the faithfulness of God in these promises, that they were made good to his elect among them. The apostle has taught us to answer such an objection in this manner, when he says,* " Not as though the word of God hath taken none effect, for they are not all Israel, which are of Israel; God hath not cast away his people which he foreknew; the election hath obtained it, and the rest were blinded." Besides, the words *all* and *whole*, are neither in the text, nor context; and were they, yet, if these promises regard the time of the Jews' conversion as this author pleads for, when *all Israel shall be saved*, and so appear to be elected, these must needs concern the elect only, and their final perseverance.

2. It is objected,† that " these promises are for 'the good of their children after them,' who therefore must be elected also; whereas it is certain from experience, that the seed of the elect are often very wicked persons." To which may be replied, that God does not here promise to *make an everlasting covenant* with their children, nor that he *will not turn away from* their children *to do them good*, nor that he will *put his fear in the hearts* of their children that they *shall not depart from* him; only that he " will give them one heart, and one way, that they may fear him for ever, for the good of them and of their children after them;" which is true, since the religious conduct of parents towards their children, the religious examples set them, and the religious education given them, may be in many instances for their good, even though many of them may prove wicked, and without supposing them all to be elected.

3. It is excepted,‡ that " if these spiritual promises respect the elect, then the promises of temporal blessings being made to the same persons, must respect them also; and so they must all abide safely in the land of Canaan and buy there fields for money." In answer to which, it is easy to observe, that very frequently in the prophecies of Isaiah and Jeremiah, especially when God promises temporal blessings, and particularly deliverance from captivity to the people of the Jews in general, he takes the opportunity to make mention of some spiritual blessings which were peculiar to his elect among them, and who in common shared the temporal blessings with them; which spiritual ones are the same, his elect in all ages, and in all nations, partake of. Besides the temporal blessings promised to the Jews were, in many instances, figurative of spiritual ones, which God's elect among the Gentiles, as well as Jews in the times of the

gospel, were to enjoy; who though they are not blessed with the temporal blessings promised to Abraham, and his natural seed, yet are " blessed with faithful Abraham," and his spiritual seed, with all spiritual blessings.

4. The promises here made are said§ to be conditional; whereas there is not the least indication of a condition in any of them, but are expressed in the strongest and most absolute manner imaginable. *I will* make an everlasting covenant with them, *I will* not turn away from them, *I will* put my fear in their hearts, that they *shall* not depart from me: as are also the passages referred to, to be joined with these promises, though without any reason, as Jer. xxiv. 7, and iii. 19, Isa. lv. 3. The text in Jer. xii. 16, the only conditional one mentioned, regards not the people of Israel, but their evil neighbours, as is evident both from the text and context.

5. It is urged,‖ that "the promise is not an absolute promise, that they should fear him always; but only an indication, that his kind providences should be such towards them as should lay upon them the highest obligations to continue stedfast in his fear: *le* and *lebalti* being often used, not to signify the certainty of the event, but the design and purpose of God in affording the means; so Deut. x. 13, and xvii. 19, 20, and iv. 10, John xvi. 1, Ezek. xi. 19, 20." But, if this is not an absolute promise, *I will put my fear in their hearts*, what can be called so? And surely, God's putting his fear in their hearts, is more than by kind providences to lay upon them the highest obligations to continue stedfast in his fear, or barely affording means thereof; but must intend an internal, special, powerful operation, and implantation of his grace in their hearts. Nor does the word here used, signify only God's design, and not the certainty of the event. The text should not be read *that they may not depart*, but that *they shall not depart from me*. The Hebrew particle לבלתי, lebilti, not lebalti, signifies the certainty of the event, as well as design; see Lev. xxvi. 15, Deut. iv. 21, Ezek. xx. 15, nor is it used, but in one of the passages referred to by the learned objector; and it is very odd that John xvi. 1, should stand among the instances of the sense of a Hebrew particle. Besides, admitting that it signifies here the design and purpose of God, this is not to be separated from the event, which is certain by it; since his *counsel shall stand*, and he *will do all* his *pleasure*.

6. Whereas it is further objected,¶ that "this text only contains a promise, that when the Jewish nation shall be converted at the close of the world, they should never fall off any more from being his people, as they had done before." This is so far from militating against the doctrine of the saints' final perseverance, that it serves to confirm it; since,

* Rom. ix. 6, and xi. 1, 2, 7.   † Whitby, p. 470; ed. 2. 450.   ‡ Ibid.
§ Whitby, p. 290, 291, 470; ed. 2. 283, 452.

‖ Ibid. p. 472, 473; ed. 2. 452; Remon. p. 70.   ¶ Whitby, p. 291, 471; ed. 2. 284, 451.

when the Jews shall be converted, they shall not fall away, but "all Israel shall be saved;" so all God's elect, being converted, whether among Jews or Gentiles, shall certainly persevere to the end, and be saved; seeing they are converted by the same grace, and kept by the same power, as the Jews then will be. The Remonstrants* own, that this promise regards the Gentiles under the New Testament.

SECTION XVI

And I will pray the Father, and he shall give you another Comforter, that he may abide with you for ever.—John xiv. 16, with John iv. 14, and vi. 35.

THE other Comforter Christ prays to his Father for, is no other than the *Spirit of truth*, ver. 17, which is the *Holy Ghost*, ver. 26, who, when he once takes up his residence in the hearts of any, never departs, but *abides* for ever; otherwise, this prayer of Christ would not be answered. Whence it follows that true believers, who are the temples of the Holy Spirit, shall certainly persevere to the end, and not be eternally destroyed. In answer to this,

1. It is affirmed,† "that the Holy Spirit may entirely depart from them, in whom he once inhabited." This is said, but not proved: the graces of the Spirit may be very low as to the exercise of them, believers may be without the comforts and gracious influences of the Spirit; they may so vex and grieve him, as that he may leave them, for a while, without his sensible presence; and yet not entirely depart from them who *know him*, and have had an experience of his powerful operation on them; *for he dwelleth with* them, *and shall be in* them, and that for ever.

2. It is urged,‡ that this "promise is only made on condition that they continue so to *love* Christ as to *keep his commandments*. To which I reply: that this promise is entirely absolute, nor is there the least intimation of a condition in it: Christ says not, if ye love me so as to keep my commandments, *I will pray the Father;* or, if ye do keep my commandments, the Father will *give you another Comforter;* or, if ye do whatsoever I enjoin you, then the Spirit shall *abide with you for ever;* but he says, *I will pray, he shall give, that he may abide.* Besides, the giving of the Spirit to the Lord's people, is antecedent to their keeping of the commands of Christ, and in order to *cause* them *to walk in* his *statutes*, and to *keep* his *judgments, and do them.*§

3. It is said,‖ that this promise "seems only to concern Christ's apostles, with whom he was then corporally present; or to concern only the Spirit's presence with his church in general, not in the heart of every Christian; for so Christ himself abode not with them." I answer; admitting that it concerns the apostles only, it will be allowed, it is to be hoped, that it secured their perseverance: and why may not the perseverance of others

be as certain, who *have been all made to drink into one spirit,*¶ have received the *same spirit of faith,* and have been *baptized into one* and the same *body?* Though if this promise only concerned the apostles, why should it be said, *that he may abide with you for ever?* It seems rather to concern a succession of men, of believers unto the end of the world; see Isa. lix. 21. Moreover, should it be thought that it rather concerns the presence of the Spirit with the church of Christ in general; the Spirit dwells there, by dwelling in the hearts of particular believers; where also *Christ dwells by faith,* and with whom he makes his abode: it is in the hearts of particular saints, that the Spirit of the Lord is *a well of water springing up into everlasting life;* which must certainly secure their final perseverance: for he is *a well of water,* to supply all their wants, and satisfy their thirst, and as such abides for ever, and can never be expelled; otherwise, it could not be said to be *springing up into everlasting life,* nor be *the earnest* of their future *inheritance,*** though this text now mentioned, John iv. 14, together with John vi. 35, *He that cometh to me shall never hunger, and he that believeth in me shall never thirst,* it is said, may be understood of Christ's doctrine; and the meaning be, "he that cometh to learn my doctrine, and believeth it when he hath learnt it, shall need no further teaching in order to his future happiness; because the observance of what he hath learned from me already will bring him to eternal life." Now, besides the falsehood of the last sentence, which attributes eternal life to what they have learnt, being contrary to the grace of God, and the righteousness of Christ, which only bring persons to it; let it be observed, that sensible sinners come to Christ, not barely to learn his doctrine; but they come to him as *the bread of* life, for food for their souls, for righteousness and eternal life, for grace here, and glory hereafter. Besides, they first learn the doctrine of eternal life and salvation, and him, in some measure, before they come to him for it: *Every man that hath heard and learnt of the Father, cometh unto me;* and such shall be preserved and nourished unto everlasting life.

SECTION XVII

And I give unto them eternal life, and they shall never perish; neither shall any pluck them out of my hand.—John x. 28.

THESE words are spoken of the *sheep* of Christ who *hear* his *voice* and *follow* him, true believers; whose final perseverance, and everlasting safety, are here strongly asserted: for if Christ *gives* them *eternal life,* they can never be hurt of the second death; if he says *they shall never perish,* who dare say they may or shall? And, if none *can pluck* them *out of his hands,* they must be safe, and shall be saved with an everlasting salvation. But,

* In Coll. Hag. art. v. p. 69. † Whitby, p. 474; ed. 2. 453. ‡ Ibid.; ed. 2. 454; Remonstr. Coll. Hag. art. v. p. 77. § Ezek. xxxvi. 27. ‖ Whitby, p. 474; ed. 2. 454; Remonstr. Coll. Hag. ibid. ¶ 1 Cor. xii. 13; 2 Cor. iv. 13. ** Whitby, p. 474, 475.

1. It is said,[*] that "the frequent cautions and exhortations directed in the scripture to Christ's sheep, not to fall from grace, but continue steadfast in the faith, are certain demonstrations that they may do so." To which I reply, that there is not one single caution, or exhortation, much less frequent ones, directed in the scripture to Christ's sheep not to fall from grace; they are, indeed, directed to take heed lest they fall; but not lest they fall from grace: they may fall into many sins, snares and temptations, which make such cautions necessary; and yet not fall from grace. Where any intimations are given of the danger any are in of falling from, or failing of the grace of God, as in Gal. v. 4, Heb. xii. 15, these are to be understood, not of the grace and favour of God in his own heart towards them, nor of his grace implanted in them; but of the doctrine of grace they had made a profession of. And, though there are exhortations directed in scripture to the saints to continue steadfast in the faith; yet these, at most, only suppose, that they are in danger of falling, or that they may fall from some degree of steadfastness in it; and which they may be left to, without falling finally and totally from the grace of God. Besides, such exhortations are designed to make and keep them steadfast and immoveable in it, and are made use of, and blessed by the Spirit of God, as means of their final perseverance; and therefore are not in vain, nor should they be improved into arguments against it.

2. It is urged,[†] as a direct anwer to this text, "that Christ here only promises his sheep should never perish through any defect on his part, or by the force of any plucking them by violence out of his hands: not but by the allurements of the world, the flesh and the devil, they may choose to go from him, though they are not snatched out of his hands." To which I reply, that the promise here made, that Christ's sheep *shall never perish*, is absolute and full, not depending on any thing to be performed on the part of the sheep; the fulfilment of it wholly and entirely lying on Christ. If therefore they shall never perish through any defect on his part, they shall never perish at all; since he is both able and willing to keep them from falling, and has a power to give, as well as to promise, eternal life to them. Moreover, if Christ's sheep cannot be plucked out of his hands by the force and violence of all their adversaries, then they shall never perish; and this the particle καὶ, which, as the learned writer attended to observes, is here illative, shows *they shall never perish*; *for none shall pluck them out of my hands.* Now, if these sheep may perish and come short of eternal life, then the illation, the consequence, is not just, proper and pertinent, and is to be denied; since it may be objected, that they may be lost by some means or other, though they cannot, by force and power, be snatched out of Christ's hands. But Christ says *they shall never perish*, and gives this as the reason of it. Besides, as

the world, the flesh and the devil, cannot, by open force and power, pull Christ's sheep out of his hands; so neither can they, by secret allurements, snares and temptations, draw them from thence, see 1 Cor. x. 13. Add to this, that it is not only contrary to the will of the Father who has committed these sheep to the care of Christ, but also to the love and affection which Christ has expressed towards them particularly by laying down his life for them; and even to his office as the great shepherd of them, to suffer any of them to be lost in any way whatever; for it is his work and business, as such, not only to protect his sheep from the open rapine and violence of their enemies; but also to preserve them from secret snares, and to restore them, even when they, either of themselves or through temptation, wander and go astray: and this he does as the good shepherd; he seeks that which was lost, and brings again that which was either driven, or which went away; and so not one of them shall perish, but have everlasting life.

3. It is farther observed,[‡] that "this text seems only to speak of such sheep, who have already persevered; and so is not a promise of perseverance, but of the reward of it, eternal felicity, which shall be incapable of interruption." But this is not to be gathered, as is said, from the former verse, where Christ describes his sheep as such who *hear* his *voice*, and *follow* him; which represents them as then hearing his voice, and at that time following him: but not as having hearkened to his voice, and having followed him to the end: and therefore he may be reasonably supposed to promise that they should hear his voice, and follow him still unto the end; since he adds, *I give unto them eternal life*; the promise of it, a right unto it, that grace which makes meet for it, and is connected with it, pledges, and foretastes of it; and therefore, *they shall never perish*, but everlastingly enjoy it. Besides, if these words speak only of such who have already persevered, it speaks not of living saints who now hear Christ's voice and follow him in this militant state, but of the saints that are dead; for none can be said to have already persevered to the end, but such as are dead. And the saints, as soon as they die, are in heaven, enjoying eternal life, in no fear or danger, no not in their own apprehensions of perishing, or of being plucked out of Christ's hands; and so stand in no need of such promises to support faith, or to comfort them under trials from the world, the flesh and the devil, which no more attend them; and as these words, in this sense of them, are needless to the saints above, so they must be useless to those below; since, notwithstanding what is said in them, Christ's sheep, whilst in this state, may be plucked out of his hands, even by force and violence, as well as drawn from him by deceits and allurements; and so perish eternally, and never enjoy everlasting life.

SECTION XVIII.

Who shall also confirm you to the end, that ye be blameless in the day of our Lord Jesus Christ. God is faithful, by whom ye were called unto the fellowship of his Son Jesus Christ our Lord.—1 Cor. i. 8, 9.

With 1 Cor. x. 13; Phil. i. 6; 1 Thess. v. 23, 24; 2 Thess. iii. 3.

THE argument from these passages of scripture, in favour of the doctrine of the saints' final perseverance, stands thus: If God's fidelity be engaged to *confirm them unblameable to the end*, whom he hath called to the communion of his Son; if his faithfulness will not *suffer* them *to be tempted above what they are able to bear*, but *will make a way to escape;* if St. Paul had ground of confidence, that "he, who had begun the good work in his Philippians, would perform it until the day of Jesus Christ; if it be part of God's fidelity to sanctify them wholly, and to preserve their whole spirit, soul and body, blameless, unto the coming of our Lord Jesus Christ whom he hath called; then must they persevere to the end, but all these are the express assertions of the holy scriptures; therefore, now,

1st. For a general answer to all these texts, it is proposed * to consideration, " that God in scripture is often said to do a thing, when he does that which hath a proper tendency to the effect, and is sufficient to procure it, and hath done all that was requisite on his part in order to it; so that if the effect be not wrought in us, it is by reason of some defect in us, or some neglect of doing that which he hath given us sufficient means and motives to perform." Of which divers instances are produced out of Ezek. xxiv. 13; Jer. xiii. 11; Isa. xlviii. 17, 18, and xliii. 21—23; Jer. li. 9; Rom. i. 20, 21, and ii. 3, 4; 2 Cor. v. 19, 20; Tit. ii. 11, 12; Acts ii. 47: 1 Cor. i. 18. To which I reply, that this rule can only hold good in moral cases, in which God only acts as a moral agent; but not in such which require a divine operation and almighty power, and solely belong to him to begin, carry on and finish, all which he promises absolutely to perform, which is the case before us. Besides, the instances produced are very impertinent. When God is said to *have purged Jerusalem*, and she was *not purged*, it does not signify what he had done sufficient for her purgation; but what he had commanded to be done, and was not done. When he is said to *have caused the whole house of Israel to cleave unto him, as the girdle cleaves to the loins of a man;* it is expressive, not of what he had done, which proved ineffectual; but of the temporal good things he had bestowed on that people; which showed them to be a people near unto him, and which he mentions to expose their base ingratitude, who, notwithstanding, would not hearken to him. When he is said to *teach Israel to profit*, and *lead him in the way he should go*, though he *hearkened* not *to his commandments*, it is to be

understood of those moral instructions, and civil laws given to them, as a nation, which, had they hearkened to, would have issued in their temporal peace and prosperity. The *people* the Lord had *formed* for himself, are not the same with Jacob and Israel, of whom he complains that they were *weary* of him; but the Gentiles, whom he had determined to call, and did call by his grace, that they might *show forth his praise:* see 1 Pet. ii. 9, 10. As for what is said of Babylon, *we would have healed Babylon, and she is not healed;* they are not the words of God; but either of the Israelites or of some others concerned for her temporal welfare. The heathens had not only the means to know God imparted to them by his providence, but they did know him as the God of nature, though they did not glorify him as such; and therefore were given up to judicial blindness. The *goodness of God*, indeed, has a tendency to *lead* persons *to repentance;* and one would think, if any means or motives would do it, this would; and yet such is the hardness of men's hearts, that they will still remain impenitent, unless God exerts his powerful and efficacious grace. When *God was in Christ reconciling the world to himself, not imputing their trespasses unto them*, he actually reconciled them to himself, and forgave their iniquities; nor is this contradicted by the exhortation of the apostle, *Be ye reconciled to God;* since that is spoken to believers, and regards their peaceable submission to the dispensations of providence, and to the order and ordinances, discipline and laws of Christ, in his house. The gospel of the grace of God is called *saving grace*, not because it teacheth us to do that which, if we conscientiously perform, we shall be saved; but because it brings the good news of complete salvation by Jesus Christ. The converted Jews are, indeed, styled δι σωζόμενοι, *the saved;* but then it can never be proved, to the end of the world, that any one of them, whom the Lord then added to the church, and are said to be *such as should be saved*, ever fell away so as to be lost and perish. Nor are all the members of the church at Corinth styled *the saved*, much less those who repented not of their sins and iniquities, but all those, and only those, who were *called* by grace, whether Jews or Gentiles, ver. 24. But,

2ndly. Our author proceeds to a a particular answer to the texts alleged; and,

1. To words cited from 1 Cor. i. 8, 9, and observes,† that " these cannot contain a promise of perseverance made to the elect only among the Corinthians; because,

(1.) " The apostle plainly speaks to the whole body of the church at Corinth." Be it so, inasmuch as the whole body of this Church, and the several members of it, were under a visible profession of Christianity, and were considered as *sanctified in Christ Jesus, and called to be saints*, and so looked upon as the elect of God; upon this supposition, which is no uncharitable one, the apostle might affirm, with the greatest assurance,

---

* Whitby, p. 477, 478; ed. 2. 456, 457.

* Whitby, p. 478, 479; ed. 2. 458.

that God would *confirm* them *to the end blameless.* Moreover, though this epistle was in general directed *to the church of God, which is at Corinth,* yet the apostle had a particular regard to such among them, who were truly *sanctified in Christ,* and really *called to be saints ;* and not only them, but *all that in every place,* as well as at Corinth, *call upon the name of Jesus Christ our Lord, both theirs and ours,* ver. 2. Besides, those whom the apostle says, *God is faithful to confirm to the end,* are such whom he had *called,* not externally, or to some outward privileges, but *unto the fellowship of his Son Jesus Christ.*

(2.) " Because he speaks not only of their not falling away finally, but of their being preserved unblameable ; whereas it is certain that the elect are not always so preserved." I observe, that it is allowed that the apostle speaks of these persons not falling away finally, which is the thing we contend for ; and also of their being preserved blameless, which it is suggested cannot be said of the elect, because they are not always so preserved. Which, if understood of them in themselves, and in this life, it will be readily granted, that they are not all of them, nor any of them, always so preserved ; but then they are all of them always so preserved in Christ, and will appear so *in the day of our Lord Jesus ;* for they are *chosen in him,* that they *should be holy, and without blame before him in love.**

(3.) The sense of these words, according to the ancients is said to be this ; " God is faithful, who hath promised to them that obey the Gospel, υιοθεσίαν, *the adoption ;* that is, *the redemption of the body,* or that they shall be partakers of that kingdom and glory to which he hath called them." But the phrase, *to them that obey the Gospel,* is neither in the text, nor context : and supposing it had been in either, or should it be thought to be implied, those that truly obey the Gospel are called by grace, and such are the elect of God : if therefore God is faithful, who has promised them *the adoption,* to which they are *predestinated, according to the good pleasure of his will ;†* or, that they shall be partakers of the kingdom and glory to which he has called them ; then they must persevere to the end.

(4.) These words are said to be " well expounded by Grotius, thus : *He will do,* quod suarum est partium, *all that is requisite on his part,* to render you unblameable to the end ; so that you shall not fail of being so through any want of divine grace requisite to that end, or any unfaithfulness on his part to his promise." To which I reply : that Scripture is not of private interpretation ; nor are we bound down to the sense given of Scripture, either by ancient or modern interpreters. That these words are not well expounded by Grotius, appears from this consideration, that God's faithfulness is engaged to confirm to the end unblameable, not in part,

but in whole ; the work is wholly his, what he has promised to do, and will faithfully perform. And therefore, if the saints shall not fail of being so, through any want of divine grace requisite to that end, whose *grace is sufficient ‡* for it ; or through any unfaithfulness to his promise, who, though *we believe not, yet abides faithful ;§* it is certain that they shall be confirmed to the end, and be preserved blameless, or in other words, finally persevere. The text in Coloss. i. 22, 23, is not conditional, but descriptive of the persons who shall be presented unblameable, and unreprovable in the sight of God.

2. To the words in 1 Cor. x. 13, it is answered, ||

(1.) " That these words ought not to be restrained to the elect ; for the preceding ones are spoken to the whole church at Corinth." What has been said to a like objection to the sense of the foregoing text, may be a sufficient reply to this.

(2.) It is said, " this text must be impertinently alleged ; because it only contains a promise of ability sufficient to resist temptations, if men will use it ; but doth not contain an engagement that this strength shall be effectual, or certainly informed to the end." But these words do not contain a promise of sufficient ability to *resist* temptations, but of sufficient strength to *bear* them ; which strength God put into his people, and does not leave it barely to their use, but makes his *strength perfect in their weakness.¶* Besides, these words do not contain *only* a promise of this, but also that God *will make a way to escape,* that they *may be able to bear* them.

(3.) This author says, " I have showed, when I discoursed of the cautions given to believers, that in the words immediately preceding and following, there is a plain indication that they, who truly think they stand, may fall, as did the Jews there mentioned, and might be guilty of idolatry ; which he (the apostle) himself declares to be a sin exclusive from the kingdom of Christ, 1 Cor. vi. 9." And I have also showed, in answer to it, that there is not, in those words, a plain indication that they, who truly think they stand, may fall ; but that such, who *seem* to themselves and others to stand, may fall : and that, supposing them spoken to true believers, such exhortations may be useful to them, to preserve them from partial falls to which they are subject, and be blessed to them as means of their final perseverance.

3. To the words cited from Philippians i. 6, it is answered,**

(1.) " That it is evident the apostle speaks not out of any opinion of the election of any, much less of all the Philippians to eternal life, or of the certainty of their perseverance to the end ; for why then doth he exhort them as he does in chap. ii. 12, 16, and iv. 1 ?" I answer, that these exhortations are so far from militating against either their election of God, or perseverance to the end, that they

---

* Ephes. i. 4.   † Ibid. 5.   ‡ 2 Cor. xii. 8.
§ 2 Tim. ii. 13. || Whitby, p. 479, 480 ;
ed. 2. 459.   ¶ Cor. xii. 8.
** Whitby, p. 480 ; ed. 2. 459, 460.

express the fruits and effects of those things, through which men are chosen unto salvation; and which, as has been before observed, are made use of, and blessed as the means of the saints' final perseverance.

(2.) It is affirmed,* that " he (the apostle) speaks this from a judgment of charity; because, says he, *it is just or fit for me to conceive thus of you,* by reason of that great affection you have for me, and your patience under the like sufferings." I reply, that the apostle does, indeed, speak from a judgment of charity in ver. 7, when he says, *Even as it is meet for me to think this of you all;* where the word *all* is used, which is not in ver. 6, and seems to be carefully omitted by our author in his citation of ver. 7. Now the apostle, from a judgment of charity, did say this of them all; but with the strongest confidence of them in whom the good work was begun. A judgment of charity is precarious and uncertain; but the persuasion of the apostle was sure and firm, and which he expresses with a view to encourage a like persuasion of their own salvation in the hearts of those he writes to; which surely must be more than a judgment of charity concerning themselves, and their own state and condition. Besides, a judgment of charity proceeds upon external signs; whereas the apostle's confidence and firm persuasion was grounded, not on their affection to him, or patience under sufferings, but upon the nature of the good work of grace begun in them, and upon the promise and power of God to perform it; and was greatly encouraged by their continuance in an inward, spiritual *fellowship in the gospel from the first day until now,* ver. 5.

4. It is said,† that "those words, 1 Thess. v. ver. 23, 24, and for the same reason the words cited from 2 Thess. iii. 3, do only signify that he (God) will not be wanting, on his part, towards sanctifying and preserving them blameless unto the end; for if the fidelity of God required he should do this without their care and industry, or should work in them certainly and absolutely that care, and the apostle believed this; how could he fear, lest these Thessalonians should be so overcome by Satan's temptations, as that *his labour with them might have been in vain?*" To which I reply, that the care and industry of God's people, in the use of means, are very proper and requisite, and what the grace of God wrought in their souls will put them upon: nor are they set aside, or rendered useless, by the promise and faithfulness of God in keeping them; but rather made more necessary and useful thereby. But then it should be observed, that God's fidelity is engaged to *sanctify* them *wholly,* and to *preserve* their *whole spirit, soul, and body, blameless;* so that the work is entirely his own; and that *until the coming of Christ;* after which there will be no danger nor fear of apostacy; whence it must needs follow, that the saints shall certainly persevere to the end; nor do the fears expressed by the apostle, concerning the Thessalonians, contradict it; since these fears do not concern their eternal salvation; but lest, through the afflictions that attended the gospel, their faith should be in any measure weakened though not dropped; or lest they should be any way corrupted from the simplicity of the Gospel; and so his labour, in instructing and establishing them in gospel truths, be so far in vain.

PART III

CHAPTER I

OF REPROBATION

THE decree of reprobation is said ‡ to be " contrary both to the nature and will of God, to his perfections, attributes, and glory." It must be allowed, that the nature and will of God, and not the nature and fitness of things, as some say, are the rule and measure of the divine conduct. God cannot do any thing contrary to his nature and the perfections of it; as for instance: he cannot do any thing contrary to his justice and holiness, for he is *without iniquity;* nor to his truth and faithfulness, for he cannot lie; nor indeed, to any other perfection of his nature, for he *cannot deny himself.* If therefore the decree of reprobation is contrary to the nature and perfections of God, it ought to be rejected as against the will of God; for the nature and will of God never

contradict each other; and yet it is certain, that reprobation is according to the will of God; *Whom he will, he hardeneth.*§ And, *what if God, willing to show his wrath, and make his power known,* &c. Besides, his *making* or appointing *the wicked for the day of evil,*‖ is *for himself,* for his own glory, as well as his making or appointing all other things: so that reprobation, or appointing the wicked to destruction, as it is not contrary to the will of God, so neither to the perfections of his nature, and the glory of them. But let us attend to what is offered in proof of this assertion, that the decree of reprobation is plainly contrary to the nature and will of God. And,

I. It is observed,¶ that " God doth immutably and unchangeably, and from the necessary perfection of his own nature, require that we should love, fear, and obey him.— That he cannot but be desirous that all men

---

* Ibid.; Remonstr. Col. Hag. Art. v. p. 80.

† Whitby, p. 481; ed. 2. 460.

‡ Whitby, p. 27; Remonstr. Act. Synod. circ.

art. i. p. 241, &c.; Curcellæus, p. 366; Limborch, p. 334.   § Rom. ix. 18, 22.   ‖ Prov. xvi. 4.

¶ Whitby, p. 27, 28.

should imitate his moral and imitable perfections of holiness, justice, truth, goodness, and mercy, all which is agreeable to the light of nature and revelation; and therefore he cannot have decreed, that the greatest part of men should be for ever left under an incapacity of loving, and fearing, and obeying him; and seeing he must earnestly desire that all men should be holy, righteous, kind, and merciful, he cannot have ordained they should be otherwise, for want of any thing on his part to make them so; much less can he command them under the penalty of his severe displeasure, so to be, and yet leave them under an incapacity of being so." To which I reply :

1. It will be granted, that God requires all men, and it is their indispensable duty, to love him with all their heart, soul, and strength, to fear him always, and keep his commandments; and that he desires that all men should imitate him in his moral perfections; all which the heathen sages were, in some measure acquainted with by the light of nature; and which God has more clearly discovered as his will to his people, under the various revelations he has made: but then none of these things contradict the decree of reprobation; for they only express God's will of command, and show what is man's duty to do; and which, if done, would be grateful and well-pleasing to God, and approved of by him, but not his will, determining what shall be done. Now could it be proved, that God has willed, that is determined that all men should love, fear, and obey him, all men would do so; for, *who hath resisted his will?* This, indeed, would contradict a decree of reprobation; then a decree to reject or punish any part of mankind could never be supposed. But for God to require all men to love, fear, and obey him, and to signify that these things are approved of by him, are no contradictions to any decree of his, to leave some men to themselves, to the freedom of their own wills, or to any determination of his, to punish them who do not love, fear, and obey him.

2. It is certain, that all men, in a state of nature, are in an incapacity to love, fear, and obey God; *the carnal mind* is so far from loving, that it *is enmity against God;* there is neither any fear of God in the heart or before the eyes of an unregenerate man; nor is he *subject to the law of God,* or obedient to it; *neither, indeed, can he be,* without the grace of God.* Now this incapacity arises from sin, and the corruption of nature; and therefore, as it no way lessens men's obligations to love, fear, and obey God, nor weakens his authority to require these things, so it is not to be ascribed to the decree of reprobation. Could it be thought that such a decree puts men into an incapacity to love, fear and obey God; it would be apparently contrary to his moral perfections, and unworthy of him. But reprobation does not, in

any view of it, render men incapable of these things; for, consider the objects of preterition either as fallen or unfallen creatures; if as unfallen, it finds and leaves them so, without putting them in an incapacity, or supposing them in an incapacity to love, fear, and obey God; and therefore neither finds nor leaves them in such an incapacity; if as fallen creatures, it finds them in this incapacity; and seeing this is owing to themselves, it cannot be contrary to his moral perfections to leave them in it, or to determine to leave them in it.

3. Let it be observed, that it is the grace of God only that can remove this incapacity, or make men incapable of loving, fearing, and obeying him. "We love God, because he first loved us;" love is a fruit of the Spirit, and the produce of his grace. An *heart* to *fear* the Lord, is a part of the new covenant; in which covenant God has also promised to put his Spirit within his people, to cause them to walk in his statutes, and *keep his judgments, and do them.*† Now the grace of God is his own, and he may do what he will with it, bestow it on whom he pleases, and withhold it from whom he thinks fit, without any impeachment of his moral perfections; wherefore to leave men without his grace, and in an incapacity of loving, fearing, and obeying him, and to determine to do so, even though he determines and approves of these things, cannot be contrary to the perfections of his nature. For,

4. It is not to be doubted of, that God requires the very devils to love, fear, and obey him; they are under obligation to these things, and it is their sin that they do not do them; and should they be done by them would be approved of by God : and yet they are not only in an incapacity to do them, but are all of them, and that for ever, left in this incapacity. Now if it will comport with the moral perfections of God, to leave the whole body of apostate angels, for ever, in an incapacity of loving, fearing, and obeying him; though he requires these things of them, and they would be grateful to him if done, it cannot be contrary to the perfections of his nature, to leave, and to determine to leave, even the greatest part of mankind, and that for ever, in such an incapacity.

5. It is a misrepresentation of the decree of reprobation, that God has ordained that men should not be holy, righteous, kind, and merciful, for want of anything on his part requisite to make them so. Since, though by this decree God has determined to deny them his grace to make them so, yet he has not by it ordained that they should be unholy, unrighteous, unkind, and unmerciful; only has determined to leave them to themselves, and the freedom of their own wills, which issues in their being so, wherefore their being so, is not to be ascribed to the denial of his grace, much less to his decree to deny it, but to their own wickedness; nor is his command, even

* Rom. viii. 7. and iii. 17.
† 1 John iv. 19; Gal. v. 22; Jer. xxxii. 39, 40; Ezek. xxxvi. 27.

under the penalty of his severe displeasure, that they be holy, righteous, kind, and merciful, inconsistent with his leaving them, or his determining to leave them in an incapacity of being so ; since, as has been shown, that incapacity is from themselves.

II. The decree of reprobation is represented * as "contrary to the mercy of God, and as charging him with cruelty and want of compassion to the greatest part of mankind." The mercy of God is either general or special. The general mercy of God reaches to all his creatures ; *his tender mercies are over all his works.*† From a share in this, the decree of reprobation does not exclude any man ; reprobates may have a larger share of providential mercies and goodness than others ; wherefore the decree of reprobation is not contrary to the mercy of God in general. The special mercy of God, as it is guided by the sovereign will of God ; for *he hath mercy on whom he will have mercy, and whom he will, he hardeneth ;*‡ so it is, indeed, limited to the elect, who are styled *vessels of mercy*, in distinction from the non-elect, who are called *vessels of wrath.* This mercy, which lies in pardoning sin, in regenerating men's hearts, in their final perseverance and complete salvation, the decree of reprobation denies to the objects of it ; with such a mercy dispensing these blessings of grace to all men, the decree of reprobation cannot stand, we freely own : but then it does not appear to us that there is any such mercy in God, dispensing, pardoning, regenerating, and persevering grace, to all men, for there are some, that *he that made them will not have mercy on them, and he that formed them will show them no favour ;*§ could it be proved that there is such a mercy in God, preparing for and giving the special blessings of grace to all men, the decree of reprobation must at once be exploded. But though this decree is opposite to any such mercy in God towards those who are included in it, yet it is no ways contrary to the mercy of God shown to the elect ; wherefore we cannot but conclude, that our doctrine represents God as merciful, yea, more merciful than that which is opposite to it ; since, according to our doctrine, God, of his abundant grace and mercy, has determined to give pardoning, regenerating, and persevering grace, to a certain number of men, whereby they shall be infallibly saved, when he denies it to others ; whereas, according to the contrary scheme, God has not absolutely chosen one single person to salvation ; but his choice proceeds upon their faith, repentance, and perseverance ; which also are left to the power and will of man ; so that at most, the salvation of every man is precarious and uncertain, nay, I will venture to say, entirely impossible.

I proceed to consider the particular instances of the cruelty and unmercifulness of the decree of reprobation.

1. The Supralapsarian scheme is greatly found fault with ; and it is asked,‖ "What can be supposed more cruelly of God, than that he should, of his mere will and pleasure, appoint men *nondum consideratos ut condendos*, not yet considered as to be created, much less as sinners, to the everlasting torments of hell ?" "I observe, that this learned writer greatly mistakes the Supralapsarian scheme : which considers the objects of election and reprobation as men either already created, but not fallen, or to be created, and in the pure mass of creatureship, but not as men not yet considered, whether they should be created or no. Besides, he confounds, as these men usually do, the decree of negative with positive reprobation, or the decree of preterition with that of damnation ; whereas the Supralapsarians, though they think men were not considered as sinners in the act of preterition, or passing by some, when others were chosen ; yet they always suppose men to be considered as sinners in the decree of damnation, and that God appointed none but sinners, and no man but for sin, to everlasting torments ; and where is the cruelty of this doctrine ?

2. The Sublapsarians are represented¶ as thinking unworthily of God ; "who, knowing that all the lapsed sons of Adam were equally the objects of his pity and compassion, equally capable of his mercy, and equally his offspring, and so no more unworthy of it than the rest, believe that his decrees of governing and disposing of them are wholly founded on such an absolute will, as no rational or wise man acts by ; so that he determines of the everlasting fate of the souls he daily doth create, after the fall of Adam, without respect to any good or evil done by them, and so without respect to any reason why he puts this difference, or any condition on their parts ; and yet afterwards, in all his revelations, made in order to the regulating of their lives, suspends their everlasting state upon conditions." I reply, that all the lapsed sons of Adam are equally the offspring of God, as men, and equally capable of his mercy, as being miserable ; and equally unworthy of it, as having sinned against him ; and therefore the reason why he shows mercy to one, and not to another, can be no other than his sovereign will and pleasure ; who *hath mercy on whom he will have mercy, and whom he will he hardeneth.* But then it is intimated, that "this is to believe, that God's decrees of governing and disposing of men, (by which I suppose is meant, his decrees of showing mercy to some, and withholding it from others,) are wholly founded on such an absolute will, as no rational or wise man acts by." But it should be observed, that neither the mercy nor the will of God are to be compared with the mercy and will of man. The mercy of God is not to be considered, *quoad affectum*, as an affection moved by the misery of a creature, as it is in man, but *quoad offec-*

---

* Remonstr. Act. Synod. circ. art. i. p. 242 ; Curcellæus, p. 370 ; Limborch, p. 339.

† Psalm cxlv. 9. ‡ Rom. ix. 18.

§ Isa. xxvii. 11.

‖ Limborch, p. 339.

¶ Whitby, p. 29, 32 ; ed. 2. 28, 32.

tum, as an effect guided by the sovereign will of God, to whatsoever object he thinks fit; nor is the will of God to be judged of by the will of man, since he does *according to his will in heaven and in earth*, and is accountable to none of his creatures; there is a βάθος, a *depth in the riches of his wisdom and knowledge*, that is unfathomable, *his judgments are unsearchable, and his ways past finding out.** Besides, wise and rational men, whose wills are the most absolute, as kings and princes, when their subjects have rebelled against them, and have fallen into their hands, have thought it most advisable to show both their clemency and justice, by pardoning some, and not others, who were equally their subjects, equally objects of their pity and compassion, equally capable of mercy, and no more unworthy of it than the rest; so that such a method is justified by the conduct of the wisest and most rational men. But the most cruel part seems to be thought to lie in "determining the everlasting fate of the souls he daily doth create after the fall of Adam, without respect to any good or evil done by them." By *determining the everlasting fate of souls*, I apprehend is meant, God's appointing them either to salvation or damnation. Now, God's appointment of men to salvation, that is, to eternal glory, is not without respect to any good thing done by them, but with respect to their faith, repentance, and perseverance: for God chooses to *salvation through sanctification of the Spirit, and belief of the truth;* though not with respect to these, as causes of his decree, but as means unto the end, or as graces which he prepares, determines to bestow, and does bestow upon them, in order to bring them to glory: so that their everlasting fate is not determined without respect to any good done by them, nor without any reason on the part of God, though without conditions on their parts. So the determining the everlasting fate of souls, or the appointing of them to damnation, is not without respect to evil done by them: though this is to be considered, not as the cause of God's decree, which is his own sovereign pleasure, but as the cause or reason of the thing decreed: so that this is not without reason on the part of God, nor without cause on their parts. And hence the entrance of each of these persons upon their everlasting state, so determined, though not the determination of it, is suspended until these several things take place. And where is the injustice or unmercifulness of such a procedure? But, perhaps the cruelty lies here, that "God determines of the everlasting fate of the souls he daily doth create after the fall of Adam;" the meaning of which is, either that God has determined the everlasting fate of souls, and appointed them to damnation after the fall of Adam, which is what we deny; since no decree or determination of God is temporal, but eternal: or that God has appointed men to damnation

for the sin of Adam, in consideration of his fall, and their concern in it: a doctrine, by no means to be rejected, since *death hath passed upon all men: for that*, or *in him*, that is, Adam, *all have sinned;*† *and by the offence of one, judgment came upon all men to condemnation;* it can never be unworthy of God, or contrary either to his justice or mercy, to determine the everlasting fate of men, considered as fallen in Adam, by resolving to punish some and spare others. Though none, as I know of, affirm, that God has appointed such who live to riper years, to damnation purely for the sin of Adam, but for their own actual transgressions; and as for such who die in infancy, God's determinations about them are a secret to us; and if they perish, it is for, and in the corruption of nature in which they are born. Or the meaning is, that "it must be a piece of cruelty in God, daily to create souls after the fall of Adam, whose everlasting fate was before determined, without any respect to good or evil, done by them." Now, though God's decree or determination concerning the final state of man, was before they had done either good or evil, nor was good or evil the cause of his decree; yet neither salvation nor damnation were decreed without respect to good or evil, as has been shown; and, therefore, it could not be unworthy of God to bring creatures into being, whose everlasting fate he had before determined, no, not after the fall of Adam; since the souls he has since created, and daily does create, are not made sinful by him, nor are they created by him for misery, but for his own glory.

3. This decree is represented as unworthy of the God of love and mercy,‡ since it "leaves men incapable of salvation; and then God not only bids them *save themselves*, invites, encourages, sends messengers to entreat them to be reconciled, knowing he doth all this in vain, when he does no more; and then eternally torments them for neglecting that salvation; though he knows they never can do otherwise, without that grace which he hath absolutely purposed for ever to deny to, or withhold from them." I answer: negative reprobation, or the act of preterition, in the Supralapsarian way, neither finds nor leaves men incapable of salvation; but as it finds so it leaves them, in the pure, unfallen, and uncorrupted mass. The decree of damnation finds and leaves men sinners; yet not the decree, but final impenitence and infidelity, leave them incapable of salvation; for the gospel declaration is indefinitely made,§ *Whosoever believeth shall be saved:* but though the Gospel is preached or published to all men, yet God no where bids all men to save themselves; nor does he anywhere invite, encourage, or, by his messengers, entreat all men to *be reconciled to him.* Peter,‖ indeed, exhorted and encouraged the three thousand converts to *save* themselves from that *untoward generation*, among whom

---

* Dan. iv. 3⁵; Job xxxiii. 13; Rom. xi. 33.
† Rom. v. 12, 18.   ‡ Whitby, p. 29.

§ Mark xvi. 16.   ‖ Acts ii. 40.

they lived, by separating from them, and professing the name of Christ: and the apostle Paul entreated* the members of the church at Corinth, to *be reconciled to God;* neither of which were ever thought to be placed under any absolute decree of reprobation. And though no man, without the grace of God, can savingly and cordially embrace the Gospel, and that salvation which it publishes; which grace God is not obliged to give, and which he may determine to deny to and withhold from men, without any impeachment of his perfections; yet it is not the denial of his grace, nor his purpose to deny and withhold it, that is the cause of their neglecting and despising the Gospel of salvation, but their own iniquity, for which they are justly punished. Besides, though this is an aggravation of *condemnation,*† that the light of the Gospel, and the good news of salvation by Christ, are *come into the world, and men love the darkness* of sin, error, and infidelity, *rather than* these; yet God does not eternally torment them merely for the contempt of the Gospel and their unbelief, but for their many sins and transgressions against his law.

4. It is observed,‡ "that sorely he thinks more worthily of the God of love and mercy, who looks upon him as an universal lover of the souls of men, who therefore *would have all men to be saved,* and *gives them all things necessary unto life and godliness;* draws them to him *with the cords of a man, the cords of love,* and by the most alluring promises, and by the strivings of his holy Spirit; swears to them, that *he would not they should perish;* warns them of, and conjures them to avoid the things which tend to their eternal ruin; directs them to the means by which they may certainly escape it; *rejoiceth more at the conversion of one sinner, that at the righteousness of ninety-nine persons who need no repentance:* and when all the methods of his grace are lost upon them, breaks forth into compassionate and melting wishes, that they had *known the things which belong to their eternal peace!*" But it unhappily falls out for this author, that not one part of this pathetic harangue can be applied to all the individuals of mankind, as it should, to prove that the God of mercy and love is an universal lover of the souls of men, respecting their everlasting salvation. It is not the determining will of God, that every individual of human nature should be saved: for then every one of them would be saved; besides, whom he wills should be saved, he wills that they should *come to the knowledge of the truth:*§ whereas, to multitudes, he does not so much as afford the means of knowledge. Nor does he give to all men *all things necessary to life and godliness,* only to those whom he calls to glory and virtue, to whom are *given exceeding great and precious promises,* and who are made *partakers of the divine nature.*‖ Nothing is more untrue, than that God draws all men with *the cords of love;* for as none can come to Christ, and believe in him, but whom the Father draws, so all that he draws in this manner come to him, and are saved by him. The persons he swears he *would not that they should perish,* or die, but live, were not all mankind, but the house of Israel, and respects not their eternal but temporal ruin; as the compassionate, melting wishes of Christ, regard not the eternal, but temporal peace of Jerusalem. To conclude: where is the mercifulness of this universal scheme, and how unworthy is it of the God of love, that after all the kind things spoken of to men, all the methods of his grace should be lost upon them, be it even through their own wickedness; when it lay in the power of his hands, had it been in his heart, notwithstanding all their wickedness, to have made them effectual?

III. The decree of reprobation is objected to as "irreconcileable with the wisdom of God:" this, if it can be fairly made out, must remove any such decree from God; for nothing unbecoming that glorious perfection of Deity ought to be ascribed to him. Though it should be observed, that we finite, short-sighted creatures, who are of yesterday, and know nothing, comparatively speaking, are very improper judges of what does or does not become the wisdom of God to do. But,

1. We are desired¶ to "consider, whether he conceives more truly and honourably of God, who thinks he chooses his favourites without reason, and rewards them without any qualifications but those he irresistibly works in them; or he who looks upon him as one who dealeth with all men, not according to his, but their own works, as they are willing and obedient, as they render themselves fit objects of his love, and rewards them as they use duly, or receive his grace in vain, as they improve the talents he has given them, or hide them in a napkin?" Now, not to take any notice of the impertinency of what is submitted to consideration—the former part of it respecting the decree of election, and not reprobation; and the latter, God's rewarding of men according to their own works—let it be observed, that though God chooses his favourites, without respect to any thing in them, or done by them, as the reason of such a choice, yet not without a reason in himself, which is his own sovereign will and pleasure. And shall we deny that to the King of kings, which is allowed to every earthly prince, to choose his own favourites as he pleases? Should it be said, that no wise prince would choose and reward men unworthy of his favours, or unqualified for his service: it ought to be considered, that in the case before us, none of all the human race are worthy to be the favourites of God, or qualified for his service; none of them are willing and obedient, or willing to be obedient, until they are made so, *in the day of the power* of his grace upon them;

* 2 Cor. v. 20.   † John iii. 19.   Pet. i. 3, 4.   ¶ Whitby, p. 30; ed. 2. 29.
‡ Whitby, p. 29, 30.   § 1 Tim. ii. 4.   ‖ 2

none can render themselves fit objects of his love, or duly use and improve even the common gifts and mercies of life, without his grace: since then, if he chooses any of them to be his favourites, and he must give them the necessary qualifications for usefulness, service, and ends of his own glory, his wisdom is most highly displayed in fixing upon the most unworthy and unpromising in themselves, in this *the foolishness of God is wiser than men: for ye see your calling, brethren, how that not many wise men after the flesh; not many mighty, not many noble, are called; but God hath chosen the foolish things of the world to confound the wise; and God hath chosen the weak things of the earth to confound the things which are mighty; and base things of the world, and things which are despised, hath God chosen; yea, and things which are not, to bring to nought things that are, that no flesh should glory in his presence.**

2. It is asked,† " doth it become the wisdom of God to use, or to appoint these means, for the effecting what he would have done which he knows to be no means, because no ways sufficient to produce the assigned end, and to withhold, yea, to decree to withhold that which alone could make them so?" I reply, that what God would have done, that is, whatever is his determining will, shall be done, is done either with or without means; if with means, he not only appoints and uses them, but makes them every way sufficient to produce the designed end; nor does he withhold, nor decree to withhold, that which alone can make them so; should he, it would highly reflect on his wisdom indeed. Now could it be proved that God, in this sense, would have all men converted, regenerated, be brought to repentance unto life, and everlastingly saved; and that he has appointed, and uses means for the effecting of all this, and yet withholds, and has decreed to withhold that which alone can make these means sufficient; as there would be an apparent contradiction in his will, his purposes, and decrees, and actions, so it would be a most gross impeachment of his wisdom. But then we utterly deny that God has willed converting and regenerating grace, evangelical repentance, and everlasting salvation, to every individual of mankind; or that he has appointed, or uses means for the effecting of these in all men; and therefore, as it is no contradiction to his eternal purposes, nor to his methods of acting in time, to withhold, and to decree to withhold from, or to deny his grace to some men, so it can be no reflection upon his wisdom to do so. It is true, indeed, it is his will of command, that all men should repent, and turn from the evil of their ways; but this is more properly expressive of what is man's duty, than of what is the will of God; or in other words, this shows what God has made it man's duty to do, and not what he himself has willed shall be done. Now God has appointed means, and he uses

them, and makes them sufficient to acquaint men that he has made such and such things their duty; whereby they are left inexcusable, though he does not give them grace to repent and turn, which he is not obliged to.

3. It is said,‡ that " this decree cannot be reconciled to the divine wisdom, because it introduces God expecting what he never would have done, and which cannot be done, the conversion of the reprobates; and enjoining, under a promise of eternal life, what he himself will do, and which, unless he does it, cannot be done, namely, faith and obedience in the elect." It is strange! that the decree of reprobation should have anything to do with the elect, or introduce God enjoining them faith and obedience: though for God to enjoin his elect these things, under a promise of eternal life, when they cannot be done without his grace, is no ways alien from his wisdom; since hereby he secures his own authority to command, shows his people their weakness, and magnifies the riches of his grace. But it is stranger still! that the decree of reprobation should introduce God expecting the conversion of the reprobates, when one part of the decree is to deny them that grace by which their infidelity and impenitence can only be removed, and they be savingly converted. Nor do the Scriptures anywhere represent God looking for or expecting any such thing in them.

IV. The decree of reprobation is thought greatly to affect the truth and sincerity of God in his declarations, calls, commiserations, promises, and offers of grace to men. And,

1. It is asked,§ " Whether he represents God honourably, who believes that God, by his revealed will, hath declared, he *would have all men to be saved*; and yet by an antecedent secret will, would have the greatest part of them to perish?" I answer; that we do not believe, nor do the Scriptures teach us to believe, that God by his revealed will hath declared, that he would have all the individuals of mankind saved; for then all of them would be saved; whereas they are not, neither will they be all saved. The Scriptures, which are God's revealed will, declare Judas to be *the son of perdition;* and antichrist *the man of sin,* goes by the same name; *whom the Lord shall consume with the spirit of his mouth, and shall destroy by the brightness of his coming;* yea, that there are some that *should believe a lie, that they all might be damned;* and that God is *willing to show his wrath* upon *the vessels of wrath fitted to destruction.*‖ Wherefore it is no contradiction to the revealed will of God, and so no ways opposes his truth; nor is it any dishonourable representation of him, to believe, that by his secret will he has determined that some should perish; and it should be observed, that we do not believe that God has determined that any one should perish but for sin; or that he has secretly willed that any should perish, whether they believe and repent or not: therefore his secret will

---

* 1 Cor. i. 25—29.   † Whitby, p. 31.
‡ Limborch, r 339.   § Whitby, p. 30.
‖ John xvii. 12; 2 Thess. ii. 4, 11, 12; Rom. ix. 22.

does not in the least contradict his revealed one, that *whosoever believeth shall not perish, but have everlasting life.** I observe, that the emphasis is laid upon *the greatest part* of mankind being willed to perish by the secret will of God : how many, and who they are, God has willed should perish, we know not : but supposing there was but one man, whom God, by an antecedent, secret will, had determined should perish, would not this be thought to be a contradiction to his revealed will, and a dishonourable representation of God ? Could the truth and sincerity of God be supported, notwithstanding this instance? If they could, why may it not be thought that he has, by his secret will, determined that two, or two hundred, or two thousand, or many millions, yea, even the greatest part of men should perish in and for their sins, without any impeachment of his truth and sincerity.

2. It is further asked,† "whether he represents God honourable, who believes that he hath imposed a law on men, which he requires them to obey, on penalty of his eternal displeasure ; though he knows they cannot do it without his irresistible grace, and yet is absolutely resolved to withhold his grace from them, and then to punish them eternally for what they could not do without it ; and after all inquires, *why will ye die?* &c. or he that believes it more agreeable to the truth and sincerity of the divine nature, to deal plainly with his creatures, and mean what he says?" I reply ; that it can be no dishonourable representation of God, to believe that he has imposed a law upon men, who are his creatures, and over whom he has a sovereign dominion, or that he requires them to obey it on penalty of his eternal displeasure, since it is holy, just, and good, and every way agreeable to his nature and perfections ; and especially when it is considered, that when his law was imposed on man, as it was agreeable to his nature, make, and condition, so he was sufficiently furnished with abilities to obey and keep it ; and though man has, by the fall, lost his power to obey, God has not lost his authority to require obedience, and which he does require ; though he knows man cannot perform it without grace from him, which he is not obliged to give ; and in all this he deals plainly with his creatures, and means what he says. But perhaps the insincerity is thought to lie here: that after God had absolutely resolved to withhold, and had withheld that grace, without which they could not yield obedience to his law, he inquires what was wanting on his part to enable them to do it. But no such inquiries are made by God ; the passages referred to regard not the spiritual and eternal state of all mankind, only the civil and political state of the Jews ; towards the welfare and prosperity of which civil state nothing had been wanting on the part of God.

3. It is also asked,‡ "does it become his (God's) sincerity, to seem so earnest in his calls to them (men) to repent, and turn themselves from their transgressions, and live ; when he himself hath passed that act of preterition on them, which renders it impossible for them to repent, or turn from the evil of their ways, and therefore impossible that they should live ?" I answer, that whenever God calls men to repent, he not only *seems* to be, but he really *is* serious, and in good earnest ; but then the calls referred to in Ezekiel,§ respect not internal conversion, and evangelical repentance, but a national repentance, and an external reformation of manners, as has been shown in the *first part* of this performance ; of which reprobates·are capable, and by which they may be preserved from temporal calamities, as the Ninevites were. And it will be difficult to prove, that God anywhere calls and invites all mankind, and particularly such who are not eventually saved, to spiritual and evangelical repentance ; for, whom he thus calls, to them he gives repentance and remission of sin. Besides, it is not the act of preterition, but the corruption of nature, which makes this repentance impossible ; and therefore, supposing the corruption of nature, and no act of preterition and reprobation, repentance and conversion would be impossible without the grace of God : hence the same charge of insincerity, and want of seriousness in the calls of God to repentance and conversion, would remain, supposing no act of preterition, where the grace of God is not given.

4. The decree of reprobation is thought to be‖ " inconsistent with the sincerity of God, in his ardent wishes, vehement desires, and passionate concern for the welfare of men ; such as are expressed in Deut. v. 29, and xxxii. 29 ; Psalm lxxxi. 13, 14 ; Ezek. xviii. 30—32." But, as has been made to appear in another part of this work, these things are only to be ascribed to God, after the manner of men, in a figurative, and improper sense : and, at most, only show what would be agreeable to him if done, but not what is his determining will should be done. Besides, they relate only to the people of Israel, and respect not their spiritual and eternal, but civil and temporal welfare. Whereas, if anything is done to purpose on this head, in order to disprove the decree of reprobation, it ought to be proved that God has ardently wished for, vehemently desired, and has shown a passionate concern for the spiritual and eternal welfare of every individual of human nature, even of those who are not eventually saved.

5. It is argued,¶ that "if God promises pardon and salvation for the non-elect, on a condition which his own act of preterition hath rendered impossible for them to perform, how can a God of truth and sincerity be said to promise seriously, and in good earnest ?"

---

* John iii. 16.   † Whitby, p. 30.
‡ Ibid. p. 33, 75, 233 ; ed. 2. 32, 74, 227, 228.   § Ch. xviii. 30—32.

‖ See Whitby, p. 33, 34, 222, 236 ; ed. 2. 32, 33, 217, 230 ; Curcellæus, p. 370.
¶ Whitby, p. 243 ; ed. 2. 237.

I reply, that the promise of pardon is not made to any, no not to the elect, upon a condition to be performed by them; it is an absolute unconditional one, and runs thus;[*] *I will be merciful to their unrighteousness, and their sins and their iniquities will I remember no more:* and though this promise is made to faith, yet not as a condition of it, but as descriptive of the persons who enjoy it, and as the hand by which they receive it. And, it is so far from being made upon a condition to the non-elect, that it is not made to them at all, the promise of pardon being a new covenant one, reaches to no more than to those who are in that covenant, and they are only the elect of God, and much less upon a condition rendered impossible by the act of preterition; since not that, but the corruption of nature, renders faith, repentance, conversion, or whatever else of a spiritual kind that may be thought to be the condition, impossible without the powerful grace of God.

6. It is intimated,[†] that, "supposing an absolute decree of reprobation, the tenders of the gospel to reprobates must be false and hypocritical; and the offers of grace are not made in good earnest, and with sincerity." But it should first be proved, that there are any offers of grace at all, made to any, whether elect, or non-elect. The gospel is not tendered to the elect, but is *the power of God unto salvation* to them. The grace of God is bestowed upon them, applied to them, and wrought in them, but not offered. And as for the non-elect, grace is neither offered to them, nor bestowed on them, and therefore there can be no falsehood or hypocrisy, dissimulation or guile, nothing ludicrous or delusory in the divine conduct towards them, or anything which disproves God's act of preterition or reprobation.

V. The decree of reprobation is thought [‡] to be "repugnant to the holiness of God;" since it is said,

1. "It makes God the author of sin, according to the doctrine both of the Supralapsarians and the Sublapsarians; seeing the former affirm, that God, before he decreed to make man, decreed his destruction; and that he might justly inflict it, decreed, that man should fall into sin, as a means of bringing the reprobate to appointed ruin, and the latter, though they do not assert that God decreed sin as a means of attaining his own end, yet say that Adam fell into sin necessarily, by the decree of God, from whence all after sins, and the corruption of all mankind, necessarily follow; and both agree that God imputes that sin of Adam's to all his posterity: and from that imputation follows a necessity of sinning; and therefore God, by this imputation of his, is the cause of all the sins which follow it." I reply, this author seems to mistake the doctrine both of the Supralapsarians and Sublapsarians. The Supralapsarians distinguish the decrees of God into the decree of the *end*, and the de-

cree of the *means;* the former respects not man's salvation, or damnation, but the glory of God as the end; the latter, with respect to the elect, includes the decree of creation, the permission of sin, redemption by Christ, the giving of grace, perseverance in it, and eternal salvation, as one complete mean to bring about the glory of God in a way of mercy tempered with justice; with respect to the reprobate, it includes the decree of creation, the permission of sin, dereliction in it, damnation for it, as one entire complete mean for the bringing about of God's glory in a way of vindictive justice. Now let it be observed, that though God decreed man's destruction before his creation, yet he decreed to damn no man but for sin; and though he has willed, or decreed, that sin should come to pass, or that man should fall into sin; yet he wills this not by effecting, but by permitting it; and therefore is not the author of it. Besides, it is not sin, but the permission of sin, that is the mean, in order to the end; which end is not man's destruction, but God's glory; the permission of sin is, with other things, the means of God's glory, but not of man's destruction; for permission of sin stands in the same place in the decree of the means, with respect to the reprobate, as it does in the decree of the means, with respect to the elect. As therefore the permission of sin, is not the means of the salvation of the elect, so it is not the means of the damnation of the reprobate; but, as with respect to the elect, it is, together with their salvation, means of, and is requisite to, the manifestation of God's glory, in a way of mercy mixed with justice; so it is, together with the damnation of the reprobates, the means of, and requisite to, the display of his glory, in a way of wrath and justice; and therefore permission of sin no more supposes, or proves God to be the author of sin in the reprobates than in the elect. And though the Sublapsarians hold, that Adam's fall was according to the decree of God; yet they do not say, that Adam fell into sin *necessarily* by that decree, or that he was laid under a force, or necessity of sinning by it, or that his sinning followed upon it, as the effect follows the cause: for though God's decree made his fall infallibly necessary, as to the event, yet not by way of efficiency, or by force and compulsion on the will; it put nothing in him, or at all infringed the liberty of his will. And though both Supra and Sublapsarians agree in saying, and that very rightly, that God imputes the first sin of Adam to all his posterity; yet not from that act of imputation, but from the corruption of nature derived from Adam, follows the necessity of sinning in his posterity: which necessity of sinning is perfectly agreeable to the natural liberty of the will; wherefore the corrupt heart and will of man, and not God, by this imputation of his, is the cause of all the sins that are committed.

2. It is observed [§] that "no man can

* Heb. viii. 12.   † Whitby, p. 341, 343; ed. 2. 382, 334; Limborch, p. 337; Curcellæus, p. 370.   ‡ Limborch, p. 334; Curcellæus, p. 366, 367.   § Whitby, p. 74; ed. 2. 73.

think that man hath a true love for holiness, who will do nothing that is in his power to make others so, as far as he is able, and it is fit for him to do it." And it is asked; "Can then that God, whose love to holiness, doth infinitely transcend the love which the most holy man bears to it, and who commands us to *be holy as he is holy*, have passed a decree from all eternity, which renders the want of holiness in most men an infrustrable event?" I reply, the holiness of God and man are not to be compared; the love of God to holiness, infinitely transcends the love of the most holy man to it; nor is there any proportion between the power of the one and of the other to make men holy. A sinful creature can neither make himself nor others holy; and could he, God does not lie under the same laws and obligations to act to the uttermost of his power and ability in such things as man does. Certain it is, he could, if he would, make all men perfectly holy, as the angels in heaven, but it is evident he does not; and yet this is no impeachment of his holiness. It is enough that he made man upright and holy, who, by sinning against him, has lost the uprightness and holiness of his nature, which God is not obliged to restore unto him. Now, if it is not contrary to the holiness of God to leave men, as he does many, destitute of holiness, in a want of it, it cannot be contrary to his holiness, to decree to leave them in such a case. Besides, it is not any decree, passed from eternity, that renders the want of holiness an infrustrable event: but the corruption of nature, through sin, has rendered it so, without the grace of God. And, whereas, it is suggested, as if there was a contradiction between the decree of reprobation, which leaves men in a want of holiness, and God's command to men, that they should *be holy as he is holy*. It may be replied, that the words* referred to, are not a command to all men to be holy, but an exhortation to the Israel of God, to such who were called, by the grace of God, to be holy and unblameable, to which they were chosen in Christ, before the foundation of the world; but admitting they are a command to all men to be holy, God's command only expresses what is his will should be man's duty, not what he has determined shall be done. It may be every man's duty to be holy, and yet God may resolve not to give his grace to some persons to make them holy, without which they cannot be so. Hence it follows, that between God's command of holiness to all men, and his decree to leave some in the want of holiness, is no contradiction; nor is such a decree repugnant to the holiness of his nature, nor to his love of it.

VI. The decree of reprobation is represented† as "incompatible with the justice of God, for these reasons.

1. "Because, by this decree, God reprobates men, considered as innocent, and appoints innocent persons to eternal destruction, according to the Supralapsarian scheme, or such whom, of his mere will and pleasure, he was about to make nocent, having deserved no such thing, according to the Sublapsarian scheme." Another writer‡ observes, "this obvious exception lies against the equity of his proceedings with the sons of men, that most of the sons of Adam lie under death eternal by his peremptory decree, for the sin of their forefather, committed long before they had a being, and so before they were in a capacity of any personal offence." I answer, the Supralapsarians distinguish reprobation into negative and positive; negative reprobation is non-election, or preterition, a passing by of some, when others were chosen; the objects of this decree, are men considered as not yet created, and so neither wicked nor righteous. Positive reprobation is the decree of damnation, or that which appoints men to everlasting ruin, to which it appoints no man but for sin. It is therefore a most injurious representation of the Supralapsarians, that they assert that God has reprobated, that is, appointed innocent persons to eternal destruction; when they, over and over, say, as may easily be observed in the writings of that famous Supralapsarian, Dr. Twiss, that God has not decreed to damn any man, but for sin: and that the decree of reprobation is of no moment, or reason of nature, before, and without the consideration of sin. Now, if it is not incompatible with the justice of God, to damn men for sin, it can be no ways incompatible with his justice, to decree to damn men for sin. The Sublapsarians are equally abused, when they are represented as holding, that God reprobates such, whom, of his mere will and pleasure, *redditurus erat nocentes*, he was about to make nocent, having deserved no such thing: whereas they neither say that God of innocent creatures, makes nocent, or sinful ones, and then reprobates them; though with the scriptures, that *God made man upright; but they have sought out many inventions,*§ sinful ones; whereby they have lost their uprightness and innocency, and so justly deserve the displeasure of God: nor that the objects of reprobation are such, who are to be made nocent or sinful, either through themselves or any others, when it is well known that these divines always consider the objects of reprobation as men already created and corrupted. But let the objects of the decree of reprobation be considered either in the pure, or in the corrupt mass; that decree puts nothing in them, it leaves them as it finds them, and therefore does them no injustice. Nor is it any obvious exception against the equity of God's proceedings with the sons of men, that most of the sons of Adam lie, yea, if even all of them had laid under death eternal, by his peremptory decree, for the sin of their forefather; if the wages of sin is death eternal, and all

---

* 1 Pet. i. 16.   † Curcellæus, p. 367; Limborch, p. 334.   ‡ Whitby, p. 32.   § Eccl. vii. 29.

the sons of Adam, were concerned in that sin, as the Scriptures declare; for *in him all have sinned;* and by his *offence judgment came upon all men to condemnation.** Though none as I know of, say, that any of the sons of Adam, who live to riper years, are laid under eternal death only for the sin of Adam, but for their numerous actual sins and transgressions, and for their final impenitence and unbelief. And as for infants dying in infancy, their case is a secret to us; yet inasmuch as they come into the world *children of wrath,* should they go out as such, is there any unrighteousness in God?

2. This decree is said† to be "contrary to the justice of God; because by it God is made to require faith and obedience of persons from whom he has either taken away strength to perform, or to whom he has absolutely decreed not to give it; which makes it impossible for them to believe and obey: and no man is bound to do that which is impossible." I reply, that the rule, which is so frequent in the mouths and writings of our opponents, *Nemo obligatur ad impossibile,* no man is bound to that which is impossible, in many cases will not hold good; a debtor may be in such a case as that it is impossible to pay his creditor, and yet he is obliged to it. It is impossible for man in his present sinful state, to keep the whole law of God, and yet he is obliged to it. It will be owned, by those who are on the other side of the question, that a man, by a long train of sinning, or by a continued course of vicious practices, may be so habituated to sin, as that it is as impossible for him to do good, as it is for the Ethiopian to change his skin, or the leopard his spots; yet it will not follow that he is obliged any longer to do that which is good. It is man's duty to believe the word of the Lord, and obey his will, though he has not a power, yea, even though God has decreed to withhold that grace without which he cannot believe and obey. So it was Pharaoh's duty to believe and obey the Lord, and let Israel go; though God had determined to harden his heart, that he should not let them go. However there are many things which may be believed and done by reprobates, and therefore they may be justly required to believe and obey; it is true, they are not able to believe in Christ to the saving of their souls, or to perform spiritual and evangelical obedience, but then it will be difficult to prove that God requires these things of them, and should that appear, yet the impossibility of doing them, arises from the corruption of their hearts, being destitute of the grace of God, and not from the decree of reprobation, which though it denies them that grace and strength, without which they cannot believe and obey in this sense, yet it takes none from them, and therefore does them no injustice.

From the whole it appears, that the decree of reprobation is not contrary to the nature and perfections of God, or unworthy of him; and therefore, since it has the testimony of divine revelation, ought to be believed by us. But we are told,‡ that "infinite are the demonstrations which might be produced against this tremendous decree, which our author, at present, waves, intending in the next section, containing arguments against an absolute election, to confute both these decrees together:" whither I shall next follow him.

CHAPTER II

OF ELECTION AND REPROBATION

Dr. WHITBY, in the *fourth chapter* of his *discourse concerning election,* proposes arguments against the doctrine of an absolute election to salvation, and consequently to the means which shall inevitably, and unfrustrably produce it, and to confute the doctrine of absolute reprobation; they are as follow:

Argument I. "He § who would have all men, to whom the Gospel is vouchsafed, sincerely to believe in Christ, to come to repentance, and yield sincere obedience to his will revealed to them; hath not prepared this saving grace only for some few Christians, leaving the rest under a necessity of perishing for the want of it; for to all such persons he hath promised, that they shall not perish. Now, that God seriously wills, that all to whom the gospel is vouchsafed, should repent, believe, and yield sincere obedience to his laws, is evident from the Scriptures: frequently and expressly declaring the doing of these things to be the doing of the will of God, and the neglecting of them to be the neglecting and even rejecting the will of God; from God's calling them to faith, repentance, and obedience, from his sending his apostles and messengers to invite them to them, and from his compassionate declarations, and enquiries concerning them." To which I answer;

1. That this argument, supposing it never so strong in favour of the persons included in it, namely all, to whom the gospel is vouchsafed, is too much limited and restrained, to militate against the doctrines of absolute election and reprobation; seeing there have been, and are, multitudes of men and women, to whom the gospel has not been, and is not vouchsafed. God formerly *shewed his word to Jacob, his statutes and his judgments unto Israel; he hath not dealt so with any nation: and as for his judgments, they have not known them;*‖ for many hundreds of years God *suffered all* other *nations to walk in their own ways.*¶ The gospel has been taken away from the Jews, and carried among the Gentiles; yet in no age has it been vouchsafed to all nations at once, much less to all the individuals of mankind in all nations: no, nor to all the individuals in a nation where it has been, or is preached; the greatest part have generally been without it. Now

---

* Rom. v. 12, 18.

† Curcellæus, p. 308; Limborch, p. 336.

‡ Whitby, p. 35; ed. 2. 34.   § Ibid. p. 70;

ed. 2, 69.   ‖ Psal. cxlvii. 19, 20.

¶ Acts xiv. 16.

admitting that it is the will of God, that all men to whom the gospel is vouchsafed should believe, repent, and obey, nay, supposing that they should all of them actually believe, repent, and obey, which is more than is in the argument; this would not be sufficient to set aside the doctrines of absolute election and reprobation; since these persons, enjoying the gospel, the means of grace, and obtaining grace itself, should rather appear to be owing to an eternal secret will and purpose in God, or to an absolute decree of election, preparing this grace, and providing these means for them, in order to bring them to salvation; whilst others have neither means nor grace, being denied them by an act of preterition or reprobation. If any thing is done to purpose, it should be proved, that God has vouchsafed the gospel to all men; that he has given to all men sufficient means of grace, and has put them all into a capacity of obtaining the blessings of grace and glory.

2. This argument proceeds upon God's will of command, which does not thwart his will of purpose. These two wills, though they differ, are not contradictory; the purpose of God is from eternity: his command is in time; the one is within himself, the other put forth from himself; the one is always fulfilled, the other seldom; the one cannot be resisted, the other may; the will of command only signifies, what is the pleasure of God should be the duty of man, or what he *should* do, but not what he *shall* do. Now admitting that it is God's will of command, that not only all to whom the Gospel is vouchsafed, but even all mankind, should repent, believe, and obey; it does not follow, that it is the determining will of God to give grace to all men to repent, believe, and obey; nor does it contradict such a will in God, determining to give grace to some, to enable them to repent, believe, and obey, and to deny it to others. Could it be proved, that either God has willed to give this grace to all men, or that there is no such will in God to give it to some, and deny it to others, the controversy would be shut up, and we should have no more to say.

3. What is said for the illustration and confirmation of this argument, is founded upon passages of scripture which are not to the purpose; some of them belong only to the Jews, and not all mankind, nor even to all to whom the Gospel is vouchsafed, and are either exhortations to a national repentance, and outward reformation of manners, as Ezek. xviii. 30, Acts iii. 19; or are compassionate enquiries, and vehement desires concerning their civil and temporal welfare, as Deut. v. 29, Psal. lxxxi. 13, Isa. v. 4, Ezek. xviii. 31, and xxiv. 13, Luke xiii. 34, some of them contain exhortations to persons already converted and called by grace; as 2 Cor. v. 20, Phil. ii. 12, 2 Pet. i. 10, as has been made evident in the *first part* of this work; where also the text so much insisted

on, 1 Tim. ii. 4, is proved to intend only some, and not all the individuals of human nature. Others of them are expressions, declarations and invitations of grace, delivered out in indefinite terms, for the encouragement and relief of sensible sinners, to believe in Christ for life and salvation; as John iii. 16, Prov. ix. 6, Rev. xxii. 17, and those which are most for the purpose, as 1 John iii. 23, Acts xvii. 30, only declare God's will of command, or what he has made man's duty, but not his intentions, purposes, counsels and decrees concerning what man shall do, or he will bestow upon him; and so in no wise contradict the doctrines of absolute election and reprobation.

Argument II. "This decree* is absolutely false in the foundation of it, that being laid in the sin of Adam, imputed by God's arbitrary will to his posterity." To which I reply, not to take notice that this argument has not the form, and scarce the appearance of one; it is not very easy to determine what decree the author means, whether the decree of election, or of reprobation. If the decree of election is intended, the imputation of Adam's sin to his posterity is not the foundation of that, either according to the Supra or Sublapsarian scheme. The Sublapsarians, indeed, suppose the objects of election to be men considered as fallen; but the Supralapsarians suppose them considered as unfallen, not yet made, in the pure mass of creatureship; yet both, with the scriptures, make the foundation of this decree to be the sovereign will and pleasure of God. If the decree of reprobation is designed, this, according to the Sublapsarians, finds and leaves men sinners, and, as such, appoints them to damnation; and according to the Supralapsarians, it finds and leaves men unfallen, but appoints no man to damnation but for sin; yet both agree, that sin, either actual or imputed, is the foundation or cause of the decree, which can only be the will of God; but of damnation, the thing decreed. It might, with much more propriety, be said that the imputation of Adam's sin is founded on that decree, than that the decree is founded on that imputation. Hence it follows, that whereas neither the decree of election, nor the decree of reprobation, are founded upon the imputation of Adam's sin, to his posterity; they neither stand nor fall by it. Moreover, though the sin of Adam is imputed to his posterity, yet not merely by the arbitrary will of God. It is true, it is the will of God that it should be imputed to them, but then it is imputed to them, not in a way of mere pleasure, but in a way of justice; for if *all sinned in him* it is but just that *judgment should come upon all men to condemnation:* if it was the sin of our nature, and all human nature was corrupted and defiled with it, it is but a righteous thing that the guilt of it should be charged upon all. The several things which are proposed for the strengthening of this argument, and objected to the doctrine of the imputation of Adam's sin to his posterity, have been replied to in the *second part* of this performance, to which I refer the reader.

Argument III. "This* decree is false both in the parts and the end of it. The parts of it are these; that God hath, from all eternity, elected a certain number of persons to salvation; and in order to the accomplishing of it, has decreed to afford them that grace which shall infallibly, and unfrustrably bring them to it; and that he hath left the rest under an absolute decree of reprobation or preterition, infallibly to fail of eternal life; of which there can be no other cause but God's own free-will; for predestination being an immanent act, cannot be dependent on any foreseen acts of man's will. The end is the manifestation of his grace and mercy in the salvation of the one, and of his justice and sovereignty in the damnation of the other." Now,

I. It is said,† "the falsehood of these decrees, touching the absolute election of some persons to salvation, is sufficiently argued in the *fifth discourse*, from God's command to all Christians, to make their calling and election sure; from his exhortations and cautions directed to them; and from the threats denounced against them." But how these things militate against an absolute election of some persons to salvation, is not easy to discern; since the command, as it is called, to make election sure, supposes an election of some, or it could not be made sure; and the making of it sure, respects not the thing itself, but the evidence of it to others, by an agreeable conversation. Besides, it is given, not to all men, but to Christians; and admitting it respects all Christians, for though all that bear that name, are not really and truly so, yet inasmuch as they are, and whilst they are under a profession, in a judgment of charity, they are to be esteemed the elect of God, and may be exhorted in this manner. But then all Christians are not all men, and all men are not Christians, in the largest and most extensive sense; wherefore this hinders not, but that there may be an absolute election of some certain persons to eternal salvation. And as for the exhortation to continuance in the faith, cautions about falling away, and threats against such that draw back, unless it can be proved from hence, that any good Christians, who have been really and truly so, any true believers, have totally and finally fallen away, the doctrine of absolute, particular election, cannot be disproved by them. In the *first part* of this performance, I have given the sense of the passages referred to, answered the objections taken from them, and have shown that they are so far from militating against the saints' final perseverance, that they are designed and used by the Spirit of God, as the means of it; and therefore cannot contradict the choice of some persons to eternal life.

2. It is further observed,‡ that "as these decrees respect those that are supposed to lie under an absolute decree of reprobation, the falsehood of them hath been fully proved in the *second discourse;* from God's serious and earnest invitations of them to repentance; from his vehement desires of their reformation and obedience: from his declarations, that he had done for them what was sufficient to produce it; from his promises to excite them to it; from his threats to deter them from their evil ways, and from the manifold declarations afforded in Scripture, that he doth not look upon wicked men as under an utter disability of being reformed by his judgments or mercies, or of hearkening to his calls and invitations, to return and live."

I reply; that these calls, desires, declarations, promises and threats, do not respect all men, only the people of Israel; and not their spiritual and eternal, only their civil welfare, as a body politic; and could they be thought to all mankind, even to such who are not eventually saved, it would not disprove the decree of reprobation; since they only regard external repentance, outward reformation and obedience, which we readily own, wicked men may be capable of, by the judgments or mercies of God; and which are not only agreeable to God, but are for their good, even for the good of reprobates, *quo mitius puniantur,* that their punishment may be the milder.

3. It is urged,§ that "such a decree as this, being a secret of God's counsel, no man can know that God has made it, but from the express and clear revelation of the holy Scriptures; and so no person can have any reason to assert it on any other account. Now the Scripture hath said nothing of the decree of election, and that it is absolute, and without respect to man's faith, repentance, or perseverance; nor has it one syllable to prove, that the object of this election is a certain number of singular persons, or that God hath absolutely ordained one single person to faith, repentance, and perseverance to the end." I answer; that the decree of election is a secret of God's counsel, and that no man can know that God has made it, but from the revelation of the holy Scripture, and so can have no reason to assert it on any other account, is readily granted; and we desire to bring it to no other test or standard, being well assured, that the Scripture has said a great deal concerning it; and we are willing that it should be tried by it, whether election is conditional or absolute, respective or irrespective to man's faith, repentance, and perseverance; and whether it has for its object, churches and nations, or a certain number of singular persons. I have shown in the *second part* of this work, that the Scriptures often speak of this decree, and that as absolute and unconditional; and, as of a certain number of persons, whom the Lord knows to be his, who are the little flock and sheep of Christ, the Father has given to him; not as Judas was, to be his

---

* Ibid. p. 76; ed. 2. 85.
† Whitby, p. 87; ed. 2. 86.

‡ Ibid. p. 88; ed. 2. 87.
§ Whitby, p. 88, 89; ed. 2. 87, 88.

apostle, but to be saved by him with an everlasting salvation. When we say that this decree is irrespective of faith, or holiness, or perseverance in grace, we do not mean that God, in this decree, had no respect to these things; for we know, that whom he hath chosen, they *are chosen by him through sanctification of the Spirit, and belief of the truth;*[*] and that God saves none, and has determined to save none of riper years but such who believe, and persevere to the end: so that this decree perfectly agrees with the express declarations of Scripture in Mark xvi. 16, and others of the like kind. But we say, and mean, that God, in this decree, did not consider these things as to be performed by the will of man, and as motives inducing him to make such a decree, but as what he determined to bestow upon them, as means of salvation. And as for God's ordaining single persons to faith, repentance, and perseverance to the end, we say, with the Scriptures, that men are *ordained to eternal life;*[†] which cannot be understood of churches or nations, but of single persons; and that he has determined to give them grace to repent, believe, and persevere to the end, that they may enjoy that eternal life, which he has ordained them to.

4. But it is objected,[‡] that "to say that election, or predestination, being an immanent, eternal act of God's understanding, or rather of his will, can have no dependence on, or respect to, any act of man's will, by way of motive, or condition, is to say things contrary to Scripture, and to common sense: for, did not God decree from all eternity, to pardon the penitent, justify him that believes in Jesus, save the obedient, glorify them that suffer for Christ, judge all men according to their works, offer to man a new covenant of grace, promising pardon and salvation to him, upon condition of his faith, repentance, and sincere obedience; and that he that believeth in his Son should have everlasting life: and must not those immanent, eternal acts, have respect to the temporal acts of men?" I answer; that since election, or predestination, is an immanent act of God, it must be within himself, and therefore, nothing without him can be the cause or condition of it, or motive to it: and seeing it is an eternal one, not any thing done in time, can have any influence upon it; and inasmuch as it is an act of his will rather than of his understanding, it cannot depend upon, or be moved by any act of man's will, without making the will of God dependent on the will of the creature, and the first mover of it. It is true, indeed, that God did, from all eternity, decree to pardon the penitent, justify the believer, save the obedient, glorify such who suffer for Christ, judge men according to their works; and did, from all eternity, really make a covenant of grace with Christ, on the behalf of the elect; but did not decree to offer to man a new

covenant of grace, nor make one promising pardon and salvation to them, upon condition of their faith, repentance, and sincere obedience, but upon condition of the perfect obedience and sufferings of Christ; and has also declared in the gospel, that he that believes in his Son, shall have eternal life: but then, as repentance is not the cause of pardon, nor faith of justification, nor obedience of salvation, nor sufferings for, and with Christ, of glorification; so when God, from all eternity, did decree to pardon, justify, save, and glorify, these persons, he had no respect to these things by way of motive or condition; he did not decree to pardon, justify, save, and glorify, upon a foresight of these things, as arising from the will of man: but having resolved to pardon, justify, save, and glorify these men, he determines to give them, of his own will and pleasure, the grace by which they should become penitent believers, obedient and cheerful sufferers for, and with Christ. So that faith, repentance, obedience, and the like, cannot be considered as conditions of, or motives to the decrees of God, since they spring from the grace which God, in these decrees of his, has determined to bestow upon the persons he bears such a good will unto. If sin, as is suggested, is the inducement to God, from all eternity, to decree to cast *some* men out of his favour, it must have been an inducement to cast *all* men out of his favour, since all have sinned, and are equally unworthy of it; and if those actions, wrought by the assistance of his grace in some, are inducements to him, to decree to reward them with eternal life, how comes it to pass, that such actions are not wrought by the assistance of his grace, in all men? It remains, that nothing can be the cause of these immanent and eternal decrees of God, but his own will and pleasure.

5. Whereas we say that God's ultimate end in these decrees is his own glory, the manifestation of the glory of his grace and mercy, together with his justice by the one, and the manifestation of the glory of his vindictive wrath and justice by the other; our author § takes some pains to show that "the end for which he decrees any thing concerning us is not, and cannot be, any advantage or good he expects to reap from it; he being from all eternity past as completely happy as he can be to eternity to come; and therefore what other end, he asks, can he be supposed to aim at in these things, but our good?" I reply, that it will be freely owned that God is completely happy, nor can any thing in time or to eternity be added to his happiness and glory; yet his great design in all his ways and works is the manifestation of his glory to his creatures; *for of him, and through him, and to him, are all things, to whom be glory for ever. Amen.*[‖] Which may be concluded, without entertaining such vain imaginations and conceits, as if his view was to "gain esteem or a good word from

---

* 2 Thess. ii. 13. † Acts xiii. 48,
‡ Whitby, p. 90, 91; ed. 2. 89, 90

§ Whitby, p. 92; ed. 2. 91.
‖ Rom. xi. 36.

such wild creatures as we are; or as if he was concerned, whether we approve or disapprove of his proceedings; or as if he can be tickled with applause, and aim at reputation from us in his glorious design." Moreover, though the good of the elect, even their eternal salvation, is a subordinate end in the decree of election, yet what good can be designed for the reprobates in the decree of reprobation, even according to our author's own scheme of it, is not easy to discern; for he says,* " He, that is God, from his justice, hath decreed from all eternity to cast some men out of his favour; the inducement to it is that sin, which hath rendered them unworthy of it, and rendered it inconsistent with his holiness and justice to admit them 'to it." But it is certain from the Scriptures, which only can give us an account of these decrees, that God's design in the one is the declaration of his wrath and justice; and in the other, of his grace and mercy; for not to take notice of Prov. xvi. 4, the sense of which passage, and the argument upon it, have been vindicated in the *second part* of this work, the Scripture saith unto Pharaoh, *Even for this same purpose have I raised thee up, that I might show my power in thee, and that my name might be declared throughout all the earth.* And a little after, *What if God, willing to show his wrath, and make his power known, endured with much long-suffering the vessels of wrath fitted to destruction; and that he might make known the riches of his glory on the vessels of mercy, afore prepared unto glory?*† Add to this that well known place ‡ of scripture, *Having predestinated us to the adoption of children, by Jesus Christ, to himself, according to the good pleasure of his will, to the praise of the glory of his grace.* This writer suggests,§ that "if it is for the glory of his grace to decree to save some, it must be more for the glory of it to decree to save more; and most of all, to decree to save all, and to prepare saving grace for all, and not restrain it to a few." To which I reply, that had God decreed to save all men, and had prepared saving grace for all men, then all men would be saved; what should hinder? But I do not find that the opposite scheme provides for this any more than ours, and therefore no more magnifies the glory of God's grace and mercy than ours does, if so much; since it provides not for a certain but an uncertain precarious salvation. Besides, if God had decreed to save all men, and had prepared saving grace for all men, here would indeed have been a display of the glory of his grace and mercy; but where would have been the declaration of his wrath and justice? Especially, the glory of God's sovereignty more appears by these distinct decrees, than if no such distinction had been made; for hence it is evident, that *he will have mercy on whom he will have mercy, and whom he will he hardeneth.*‖

6. The other black part of this decree is said ¶ to be " still more horrible in its immediate consequences; for it makes God to create innumerable souls, after the fall of Adam, to be inevitably damned without the least compassion for them, or will to afford them means sufficient to exempt them from that dreadful doom; and in prosecution of this end, having created them pure and innocent, it makes him to put them into bodies, that so they may be made or deemed the offspring of Adam ; and, by being so, may be made the fit objects of eternal wrath." I answer; that innumerable souls are made since the fall of Adam, and are put into, or united to, human bodies, are things generally agreed upon; but how these souls are united to human bodies, and how they become polluted with sin, and so fit objects of God's wrath, and, indeed, whether they are, by immediate creation, or *ex traduce,* or both, cannot be so easily determined : however, that God created souls to be inevitably damned, and put them into bodies, that they might be fit objects of his eternal wrath, are things we abhor and detest ; and are no consequences of, nor can they be fairly deduced from the decree of reprobation; which, whether it considers creatures fallen or unfallen, leaves them as he finds them, and puts nothing in them ; nor is creation the means of damnation, nor damnation the end of creation : God made no man to damn him ; but he made him 'for himself, for his own glory.

To conclude ; this author himself owns a decree of God from all eternity, to cast *some* men out of his favour, induced to it by sin; and another decree, to reward *some* of them with eternal life, or the enjoyment of himself, induced to it by those actions wrought in them by the assistance of his grace ; and, according to this scheme, salvation and damnation are as inevitable, as they are according to ours; since God's foreknowledge of sin and damnation, of grace and salvation, is as infallible as his decree to damn or save ; and the absurdities, which are supposed to follow upon our scheme, must follow upon this : for God foreknew that these men would sin and continue in it ; whereby he would be induced, nay, on the account of which, he decreed to cast them out of his favour ; and yet he creates them, permits them to sin, when he could have hindered it, and to many of them he does not give the outward means of grace, and to none of them the assistance of his grace, by which those actions are performed, which induce him to reward others with eternal life, when it is equally in his power to assist them as others; and in a word, denies them that grace which would cure them of their impenitence and unbelief, as it does in others to whom it is given; but suffers them to continue in sin, when he could have restrained them from it, and delivered them out of it; the consequence

---

* Whitby, p. 91 ; ed. 2. 90.

† Rom. ix. 17, 22, 23.   ‡ Eph. i. 5, 6.

§ Whitby, p. 95 ; ed. 2. 94.   ‖ Rom. ix. 18.

Whitby, p. 95 ; ed. 2. 94.

of which is, their everlasting ruin and destruction.

CHAPTER III

OF REDEMPTION

I PROPOSE in this chapter to consider the arguments from reason, for and against the universality of Christ's redemption; and such as are said * plainly to offer themselves to confirm this doctrine, are these:

I. "If God intended not the death of Christ for the saving of any but the elect, then he never intended the salvation to any to whom the gospel is revealed, but the elect; and then he never designed any salvation for the greatest part of men, to whom the gospel was or is revealed, on any condition whatsoever; for since *there is no other name under heaven given by which we can be saved;* salvation could not be intended for them on any condition whatsoever, to whom the benefit of Christ's death was not intended." To which I answer; that God never intended the death of Christ for the saving of any but the elect, is evident from this consideration, that none are saved but the elect; no one will say, that any are saved who are not the elect of God. This author himself will allow, that such who repent and believe, and are persevering Christians, are the elect, and such are all those that are saved. Now if God intended to save any besides the elect, his intentions are frustrated, and he disappointed; things which cannot be said of, and ascribed to the Divine Being. Besides, what is God's intending to save any by the death of Christ, but the very act of election itself? It is no other than an appointing to salvation by our Lord Jesus Christ. Wherefore to talk of God's intending the death of Christ for the saving of any, or intending to save any by the death of Christ, besides the elect, is a contradiction in terms. Nor is the gospel revealed internally to any but the elect, even to *those to whom God would make known what is the riches of the glory of this mystery among the Gentiles, which is Christ in you, the hope of glory.* To these only *it is given to know the mysteries of the kingdom;* to others, they are hid in parables; for, *if our gospel be hid, it is hid to them that are lost.*† Hence it follows not, that God never designed any salvation for the greatest part of men, to whom the Gospel was or is revealed; since he has designed salvation for all, and every one of those to whom the gospel was, or is thus internally revealed, and they shall all of them enjoy it. It is true that the gospel is externally revealed, or the outward ministry of it is vouchsafed to more than to the elect; but then the outward ministration of it, in an indefinite manner, is only designed and blessed for the effectual vocation of the elect; but what means this restraining clause, *to whom the gospel was, or is revealed?* For if

God intended the death of Christ for the saving of any besides the elect, he intended it either for the saving of all and every one besides them, or only for the saving of some; if he intended it for the saving of all besides them, why is not the gospel revealed unto all men? Strange! that God should intend the death of Christ for the saving of all men, and yet not afford the knowledge, no, nor the means of the knowledge of salvation by his death, or of the saving benefits of it to all men! If he intended it only for the saving of some besides the elect, even of those to whom the gospel was, or is revealed, the weakness and inconclusiveness of this argument, for the universality of redemption, are easily discerned; who does not see, that it must be exceeding weak to argue from God's intention to save *some* by the death of Christ, for an *universal* redemption by it? nothing is more certain than that salvation could not be intended for any, to whom the benefit of Christ's death was not intended; since salvation is the benefit of Christ's death, and which is not intended for any persons conditionally, it being absolutely designed for the elect, absolutely wrought out for them, and absolutely applied unto them; nor is such a special intention of Christ's death, for the saving of the elect only, contrary to the love of God to the world, or to his mercy and goodness to the sons of men; the passages referred to being either impertinent, or misunderstood and misapplied, as has been shown in the *first part* of this performance, to which I refer the reader.

II. It is further urged,‡ that "hence it must follow, that Christ never died with an intention to save them whom he doth not actually save and deliver from the wrath to come." I answer, it is very true; for if he had died with an intention to save them whom he doth not actually save, not only his designs must be defeated, and his intentions frustrated, but his death be so far in vain. Moreover, their being not actually saved, must arise either from an incapacity in him to save them, and a superior power in other men, or devils, or both, to obstruct his methods and designs; which can never be thought of him, who is *the Almighty;* or from a change of his intentions and purposes, which can by no means agree with him who is *Jesus, the same yesterday, to-day, and for ever.* The passages opposed to this either regard the elect of God only, whether among Jews or Gentiles, or else have no concern with redemption, either general or particular, the thing in controversy between us, as has been made to appear in that part of this work just now referred to.

III. It is said,§ "Hence it must follow, that none of those, to whom God never intended salvation by Christ, or who shall not be actually saved by him, are bound to believe in him." I reply: the consequence is

* Whitby, p. 158; ed. 2. 154.
† Col. i. 27, Matt. xiii. 11; 2 Cor. iv. 3.
‡ Whitby, p. 161; ed. 2. 157.

§ . Whitby, p. 152; ed. 2. 136; Remoustr. Act. Synod. circ. art. ii. p. 337; Curcellæus, p. 360; Limborch, p. 322.

very just; none are bound to believe in Christ, but such to whom a revelation of him is made; and according to the revelation is the faith they are obliged to. Such who have no revelation of him, as the heathens, are not bound to believe in him in any sense; and, indeed, *how shall they believe in him, of whom they have not heard? and how shall they hear without a preacher?* Such who have only an external revelation of him by the ministry of the word, are obliged to believe no more than is included in that revelation, as that Jesus is the Son of God, the Messiah, who died and rose again, and is the Saviour of sinners, &c., but not that he died for them, or that he is their Saviour. It is true, the ministers of the Gospel, though they ought not to offer and tender salvation to any, for which they have no commission, yet they may preach the gospel of salvation to all men, and declare, that *whosoever believes shall be saved;* for this they are commissioned to do: *Go ye into all the world, and preach the gospel to every creature: he that believeth and is baptised, shall be saved.*† But then this preaching of the gospel to all indefinitely, no ways contradicts the particular redemption and special salvation of the elect only; it being designed, and blessed, for the effectual gathering of them to Christ; and does become *the power of God* to their *salvation*, and to theirs only.

IV. It is also said,‡ "Hence it clearly follows, that no man can be condemned hereafter for final impenitency and unbelief, seeing he transgresseth no law of God by his unbelief; for, surely God commandeth no man to believe in Christ for salvation, for whom he never intended salvation by Christ; or to repent for salvation, whom he intended not to save by Christ." I answer; why repentance unto salvation, or final impenitency, should be brought into this argument, I see not; since God might have required repentance of men, and have justly condemned them for final impenitence, supposing Christ had never died at all, or for any at all; and as for final unbelief, none, who have not enjoyed a revelation of Christ, as the Pagans, will be condemned for not believing in him, but for their sins against the law and light of nature; and as for such who have enjoyed the external revelation of the gospel, and yet have remained finally unbelievers, as the Jews and others, they will be condemned, not for not believing that Christ died for them, or that he was their Saviour; but they will be condemned, and die in their sins, for their not believing that he was God, the Son of God, the Messiah and Saviour of the world, and for the contempt of his gospel, and for their transgressions of the law of God.

V. This author goes on to observe,§ that "hence it will follow, that neither the elect, nor non-elect, can rationally be exhorted to believe; nor they who are not elected, because Christ died not for them; nor the elect, for he that knows himself to be one of that number, hath believed and repented already; if he do not know this, he cannot know that Christ died for him, and so he cannot know it is his duty to believe in him for salvation." I reply, that ministers, in exhorting men to believe in Christ, do not, and cannot consider them as elect or non elect, but as sinners, standing in need of Christ, and salvation by him; and that either as sensible, or as insensible of their state and condition; not as insensible of it; for I do not find that any such are exhorted to believe in Christ for salvation; but as sensible of it, as the jailor was, who *trembling said, Sirs, what must I do to be saved?* When the apostle exhorted him, saying, *Believe in the Lord Jesus Christ, and thou shalt be saved.*‖ Besides, such who have believed already, and do know that Christ has died for them, and that they are of the number of God's elect, may be rationally exhorted to walk on in Christ, as they have received him, and to go on believing to the saving of their souls.

VI. It is further observed,¶ "that hence it must follow, that God hath not vouchsafed sufficient means of salvation to all to whom the gospel is revealed, which is said to be contrary to the whole tenor of the gospel: and it is argued, that if men have not sufficient means to be saved by the covenant of grace, then have they only means given them to increase their condemnation, which is contrary to the mercy of God; and that all men, under the gospel, have not means sufficient to repent and believe, so as that they may be saved, vouchsafed by God, then he must still withhold something from them, without which they cannot repent and believe to salvation; upon which these absurdities will follow, that God condemns them to destruction for that which is no sin; and then must every impenitent and unbelieving person have a just excuse, and a sufficient plea, why he should not be punished and condemned for his infidelity and unbelief." To all which I reply, that there is no pardon, justification, peace with God, deliverance from wrath to come; in short, no salvation but by Christ; that no means of salvation are sufficient without the grace of God; that all men are so far from having an interest in the death of Christ, and salvation by him, that there have been, and are, multitudes that know nothing of either, and are so far from having sufficient means of salvation, that they have none at all; and could it be allowed, that sufficient means of salvation are vouchsafed to all to whom the gospel is revealed, who are but a few, comparatively speaking, this would not prove universal redemption, or that Christ died for all men; since, in all ages, God has given his word

* Rom. x. 14.

† Mark xvi. 15, 16.   ‡ Whitby, p. 163; ed. 2. 159; Remonstr. Act. Synod. circ. art. ii. p. 369; Curcellæus, p. 361; Limborch, p. 324.

§ Whitby, p. 164; ed. 2. 160.
‖ Acts xvi. 30, 31.   ¶ Whitby, p. 164; ed. 2. 160.

and ordinances but to a few, and has suffered whole nations to walk in their own ways. And, indeed, all to whom the gospel is only externally revealed, have not sufficient means of salvation; for, besides an interest in Christ and his death, the sanctification of the Spirit, and belief of the truth, or regenerating grace, and faith in Christ, are requisite means of salvation, which all who enjoy the outward ministry of the gospel are not possessed of: nor is this contrary, but perfectly agreeable, to the whole tenor of the gospel; for, though *the gospel is the power of God to salvation,** it is only *to them that believe*, which all men do not who are under the external ministry of the word. *The word of grace, which is able to build us up, and give us an inheritance among them that are sanctified,*† is not the written but the essential word, Christ Jesus, who is *full of grace and truth*. *The grace of God which bringeth salvation*, that is, the doctrine of the grace of God, the gospel, which brings the good tidings of salvation, hath indeed, *appeared to all men :*‡ but then it does not *teach* all men to whom it appears, only *us* that believe, *that, denying ungodliness and worldly lusts, we should live soberly, righteously, and godly.* The *Scriptures are* also *able to make men wise unto salvation ;* § but then it is *through faith which is in Christ Jesus,* and when they are accompanied with the Spirit of God, which first inspired them. Many of the signs and miracles which Christ did, are written,‖ *that men might believe that Jesus is the Christ, the Son of God, and that, believing,* they *might have life through his name ;* but then these signs, when either seen, or heard, or read of, were not, nor are they sufficient to bring persons to believe in him, and so to have life through him, without the powerful grace of God ; for *no man can come to* Christ, or believe in him, *unless the Father draw him,* notwithstanding all his doctrines and miracles. But it is further urged, that "if men have not sufficient means to be saved by the covenant of grace, then have they only means given them to increase their condemnation."¶

I reply : that by the covenant of grace, not only provision is made of sufficient means of salvation, but of salvation itself, even of all grace and glory ; but then this provision is made only for those who are interested in it, and they are only the elect of God. Though, I suppose, this author, by the covenant of grace, means no other than the gospel or gospel dispensation. Now this, though it is not a sufficient means of salvation, without the grace of God ; and though the rejection and contempt of it is an aggravation of men's condemnation, yet is far from being given on purpose to increase their condemnation : which is wholly owing to their own wickedness : and therefore the giving of it can be no ways contrary to the mercy and goodness of God, or any unnatural action in him. It is added,** that "if all men, under

the gospel, have not means sufficient to repent and believe, so as they may be saved, vouchsafed by God, then must he withhold something from them, without which they cannot repent and believe to salvation ; namely, special grace, an irresistible impulse, a divine energy, or an almighty power." But what has this kind of reasoning to do with the doctrine of general or particular redemption, the controversy before us, when it rather belongs to the doctrine of sufficient and efficacious grace ; and besides, is wholly confined to persons living under the gospel ? whereas it should be proved, that God has vouchsafed to all men, whether under, or not under the gospel, sufficient means to repent and believe, so as they may be saved : to make things comport, in any tolerable manner, with the notion of universal redemption. And supposing that sufficient means are not given to all men in either situation, as it is certain they are not given to all men even under the gospel, what follows upon it ? Why, that "God withholds from them special grace, an irresistible impulse, and a divine energy." And is he obliged to give special grace to all under the gospel ministry ? or throw in an irresistible impulse upon them ? or put forth a divine energy, or an almighty power, to enable them to repent and believe ? These things depend upon his sovereign will and pleasure. But then we are told,†† " that if the want of all, or any of these things, be the reason why so many, who live under the gospel dispensation, do not believe and repent to salvation, and, upon this account, continue in their impenitence and unbelief, great absurdities will follow." But who says that the want of these things is the reason or cause of men's unbelief and impenitence, and of their continuance in them, than the sun, and the withdrawing of its light, is the cause and reason of darkness. It is true, that it is only the grace of God that can cure men of their impenitence and unbelief ; but then it is not the want of it that is the cause or reason of either, but the vitiosity and corruption of their hearts ; wherefore no great absurdities can follow. But what are these supposed ones ? One is, "that God condemns them to destruction for that which is no sin ;" as if unbelief and impenitence were not sins, because they can only be cured by the grace of God, without which no man can truly repent and believe ; and because God is pleased to withhold this grace from, and not bestow it upon some men, therefore he cannot condemn for these things as sins ; whereas, it should be observed, that God does not condemn men for the want of that grace which he does not think fit to bestow upon them, without which they cannot repent and believe, so as to be saved ; but for the impenitence and unbelief he finds in them, and which he is not obliged to cure them of. According to this author's reasoning, because man cannot be subject to the law, without

---

* Rom. i. 16.   † Acts. xx. 32.   ‖ John xx. 30, 31.   ¶ Whitby, p. 166;
‡ Tit. ii. 11.   § 2 Tim. iii. 15.   ed. 2. 162.   ** Ibid.   †† Ibid.

the power and grace of God, it can be no sin in him to remain unsubjected to it: for then it must be the sin of man, not to be God: and if he punish him for not being subject to the law, he must punish him for not being equal in power with God himself. Such reasonings need no confutation, they carry their own in them. The other absurdity is,* that "then must every impenitent and unbelieving person, have a just excuse, and a sufficient plea, why he should not be punished or condemned, for his infidelity and unbelief. And such another plea is put into the mouths of these persons as was used by the officers of the Jews, to Pharaoh; *There is no straw given to us, and thou sayest to us, make bricks;* no special grace, no divine energy afforded us, and thou sayest to us, Do that which can no more be done without it, than men can make bricks without straw; and *thy servants are beaten, but the fault is in him* who denies us straw, and yet requires bricks; yea, who requires that faith, and that repentance, which he never would afford us sufficient means to perform." This is a bold charge, an insolent way of treating the Almighty, to compare him with Pharaoh's officers, and say the fault is in him who requires faith and repentance, and affords no special grace, no divine energy to perform. Moreover the case is not parallel; the impotence of the Israelites to make bricks, arose from straw being denied them, and withheld from them, which they formerly had; but the impotence of men to believe and repent, does not arise from special grace and a divine energy being denied or withheld from them, which they never had: but from the corruption and vitiosity of their nature, their enmity to God, alienation from him, through the ignorance that is in them, because of the blindness or hardness of their hearts. Besides, God never calls persons to evangelical repentance, or requires them to believe in Christ to the saving of their souls, but he gives that special grace, and puts forth that divine energy which enables them to believe and repent. God does not require all men to believe in Christ, and where he does, it is according to the revelation he makes of him. He does not require the heathens, who are without an external revelation of Christ, to believe in him at all; and those who only have the outward ministry of the word, unattended with the special illuminations of the Spirit of God, are obliged to believe no further than that external revelation they enjoy, reaches; as that Jesus is the Son of God, the Messiah, &c., not to believe these things is the sin of all that are under the gospel dispensation, as it was of the Jews; who though they saw his miracles, and heard his doctrines, yet, through the corruption and prejudices of their minds, did not believe him to be the Messiah, and therefore died in their sins; nor had they a just excuse, or sufficient plea, why they should not be pun-

ished or condemned, for their infidelity and unbelief respecting the Messiah, even though they could not come to him, or believe in him to the saving of their souls, without the special grace of God; they were not condemned for the want of that they had not, and which was not bestowed upon them; but for that which was really in them, the sin of unbelief; nor were they, nor are any, condemned for not believing that Christ died for them, but for the transgressions of the law of God, and the disbelief or contempt of his gospel. And as for those, who besides the external, have also an internal revelation of Christ, as they are called to the exercise of evangelical repentance, and to faith in Christ, as their Saviour and Redeemer, who loved them, and gave himself for them; they have that grace bestowed upon them, and that power put forth in them, which enables them to believe and repent. I make no use of a reply commonly made on our side the question, "that we all had sufficient strength to believe, in our first parent Adam, which we have lost by our fall in him; and though we have thus lost our power to believe, yet God has not lost his authority to require it, and may deal with us as if we had it still;" since, according to the scheme I proceed upon, that, as is the revelation God makes to the sons of men, such is the faith he requires of them, there is no need of it. However, I cannot consider it as such a lamentable weak pretence, and so sure a sign of a desperate cause, as our author,† from Dr. Claget, represents it to be; for, that Adam, in a state of innocence, had a power of believing in Christ, and did believe in him as the second Person in the Trinity, as the Son of God, cannot well be denied; since with the other two Persons, he was his creator and preserver; the knowledge of which cannot well be thought to be withheld from him. And his not believing in him as the Mediator, Saviour, and Redeemer, did not arise from any defect of power in him, but from the state, condition, and situation in which he was, and from the nature of the revelation made unto him; for no doubt, Adam had a power to believe every word of God, any revelation that was, or might be made unto him. Now all mankind were in him, in such sense, as Levi was in the loins of Abraham, and paid tithes in him long before he was born; yea, they were in Adam as their federal and representative head, and so had representatively the power he had, which when they sinned in him, and fell with him, in his first transgression, they lost; hence followed a depravation of nature, an enmity to God, an opposition to his will, and an impotence to all that is spiritually good, which is the root and source of infidelity; but though men have lost the power of believing, and are shut up in unbelief, God may justly require them to give credit to, and believe, whatever revelation he is pleased to make. As for those

---

* Ibid. p. 167; ed. 2 163.

† Whitby, p. 168; ed. 2. 164.

texts of Scripture,* I know of none, that exhort and command all men, all the individuals of human nature, to repent, and believe in Christ for salvation; they can only, at most, concern such persons who are under the gospel dispensation; and, in general, only regard an external repentance and reformation, and an historical faith in, or assent to, Jesus as the Messiah. Our blessed Saviour's† marvelling at the unbelief of his countrymen, and at the faith of the centurion, is to be understood of him as man, and no way contradicts men's disability to believe: he marvelled at the unbelief of his countrymen, that they should be offended at him, and reject him as the Messiah, on account of the meanness of his parentage and education, when they had such large means, by his ministry and miracles, to convince them that he was the Messiah; whom they might have believed in, and received as such, though they lay under a disability of coming to him, or believing in him to the saving of their souls, without the special grace of God: he marvelled at the faith of the centurion, that he, who had such small means, and such little knowledge of him, yet should so strongly believe in him: which greatly argued the mighty power of God in him, and is what our Lord designed those about him should take notice of to the glory of God. The instances ‡ from Scripture of Christ's upbraiding persons for their impenitence and unbelief, respect himself as the Messiah, and not assenting to him as such, and not repenting of their rejection of him, when they had such plain proofs, demonstrations, and examples; and are far from disproving man's disability to repent and believe in a spiritual manner. The parables of the marriage-supper, and the talents, are foreign to the purpose; the design of the one being to show that men may be externally called, by the ministry of the word, and not be chosen; and have neither the grace of God, nor the righteousness of Christ; and so will, at the last day, be speechless, and have nothing to say why they should not be condemned for their many actual sins and transgressions, from which, the grace of God, and the righteousness of Christ, could only save them; though they could not obtain, procure, and merit either of these by their own deservings, since, as they were destitute of them, so they were unconcerned about them, made no application for them; but, perhaps, slighted and contemned them. The design of the other, is to show the nature and use of external gifts for the ministry, which men may have, and use, and improve, as they ought, and as they have power to do, even though destitute of the grace of God. But these instances, as they do not properly belong to this branch of the argument, so most, if not all of them, have been considered in the first Part of this performance, which the reader may consult.

VII. It is said,§ that "that which doth render this doctrine (of particular redemption) most worthy to be rejected by all who truly love their God and Saviour, is this consideration, that it unworthily reflects upon our good and gracious God, our blessed Lord and merciful High Priest, who is, in Scripture often said, but, by this doctrine is denied to be, *the Saviour of the world;* for it, in effect, declares he who is, in Scripture, styled *Love,* hath from eternity, hated the greatest portion of mankind; represents him as having no bowels of compassion, no drop of mercy, no inclination to do good to the generality of his most noble creatures; and renders the God of truth and sincerity, full guile, deceit, and insincerity, dissimulation, and hypocrisy." To all which I reply,

1. As to what is said, that "this doctrine unworthily reflects on our blessed Lord and merciful High Priest, who is, in Scripture, often said, but by this doctrine is denied to be, *the Saviour of the world;*" I observe, that Christ is not often, only twice, in Scripture said to be *the Saviour of the world,* John iv. 42; 1 John iv. 14; nor is he denied to be so by the doctrine of particular redemption; though, according to that doctrine, this phrase is to be understood in a limited and restrained sense; as it appears it should be, from those Scriptures in which he is oftener said to be *our Saviour,* the *Saviour of Israel,* and *the Saviour of the body,* the church. He is, indeed, a *merciful* High Priest, but it should be observed, that he is also a *faithful* one, *in things pertaining to God, to make reconciliation for the sins of the people;* but if he has not taken care of *things pertaining to God,* so as to make full atonement for the sins of his people, that justice may have no more to require, and they be entirely free from any further demand of his, and not liable to future punishment, I cannot see how he can be either a merciful or a faithful High Priest. And it deserves consideration, whether that doctrine does not most unworthily reflect upon our blessed Lord and merciful High Priest; which represents him not as procuring, by his death, an actual pardon and reconciliation for any, only a conditional one for all; not as obtaining certain salvation for any of the sons of men, only as putting them into a salvable state, or into a capacity of being pardoned, reconciled, and saved, through conditions of their own performing, and as dying in vain for multitudes, whom he came into the world to save.

2. As to the love and mercy of God, these are to be considered, not *quoad affectus,* as affections, or passions, in him; which are to be moved, raised, and influenced, by anything out of himself, as the misery or goodness of an object; so to think of God, is to conceive most unworthily of him, to *take him to be altogether such an one as ourselves,* and savours rankly of Atheism, and scarcely de-

---

* Whitby, p. 169; ed. 2. 165.   † Ibid. p. 172; ed. 2. 168.   ‡ Ibid. p. 173; ed. 2. 169.   § Whitby, p. 176, 177, 179; ed. 2. 171, 172, 175.

serves any other name; but they are to be considered *quoad affectus*, as to their effects; which are guided by the sovereign will of God, to whatsoever objects he pleases, for he *will have mercy on whom he will have mercy.* Add to this consideration, that the love, grace, and mercy of God, and the glory of them, lie not in the numbers to which they extend, but in the freeness of them, or in the liberal manner in which they are communicated to objects altogether undeserving of them, for that of Austin will always hold good, Gratia non est gratia, nisi omnino gratuita, *Grace is not grace, unless it is altogether free.* Besides if the glory of God's love, grace, and mercy, is more advanced by the redemption of all men, according to this way of reasoning, it would be still more advanced by the salvation of all men, and most of all, by the salvation of all the devils, as well as all men; and therefore. if God does not save all men, and all the devils, when it is in his power to do it, it must be a reflection upon his love, grace and mercy, and upon him, as the *Lover of souls and Father of spirits.* And indeed, what is said by our author,[*] in favour of general, and against particular redemption, upon this head, may be argued in favour of the redemption and salvation of devils, in opposition to a restraint of it to the sons of men; as, 1st. that God, by sending his Son to be the Saviour of the world, or in giving him up to the death, had no other primary end, than the glorifying himself in the salvation of men; had he therefore designed his death for the salvation of *all the devils,* upon conditions possible to be performed by them, he must have glorified himself more than by restraining the design of it only to the salvation of *men.* 2ndly. That the death of Christ was a sufficient sacrifice for the sins of *all the devils,* and so might have procured a conditional pardon for *all them,* as well as for *all men,* had God been pleased to give him up to the death for *them* all. 3rdly. That it could be no ways more dishonourable to God, or more inconsistent with his justice, wisdom, hatred of sin, or any other of his attributes, to have designed Christ's death for the salvation of *all the devils,* than to intend it only for the salvation of *men.* 4thly. That the *devils,* who are supposed to be excluded from any benefit by Christ's death, were as much the offspring of *the Father of spirits,* and every whit as miserable, and as much wanting an interest in our Lord's salutary passion, as *men,* who are supposed to be the objects of the pardon and salvation purchased by our Saviour's blood; can it be then consistent with the grace, goodness, and mercy of the divine nature, and of the lover of souls, and the relation which this *Father of spirits* beareth to them, to consign the death of Christ only to *men,* and to suffer *a large number of his creatures,* which were equally his offspring and as miserable, and so in the

same need of pardon and salvation with *men,* to remain inevitably miserable, only for want of God's designing the same sacrifice for the procuring mercy to them as well as others?"

If this reasoning is closely attended to, the patrons of universal redemption, as well as we, must fly to the sovereignty and prerogative of God over his creatures, in showing and denying mercy to whom he pleases; which is never to be mentioned and compared with that absolute power, prerogative, and sovereignty, exercised by Grecian or Roman governors, or any other princes over their subjects.

But to proceed: Where is the love, grace, mercy, and goodness of God, in sending Christ to die only to procure the possibility of salvation for all men, and leave it precarious and uncertain whether any are saved at all? What kind of love and mercy is that which sends Christ to die for men, and then leaves them to deny that Lord who is supposed to have bought them, and to aggravate their guilt by sinning against him? It must have been much better for them if he had never been sent, or had never died for them, or had never bought them. What sort of love is that which gives Christ to die for men, and yet withholds the gospel of salvation from them, and does not send down the Spirit of God into their hearts, to reveal and apply salvation to them, purchased by Christ? How easily might the several things, objected by our author,[†] be retorted upon this scheme, to show that God, according to it, must hate the greatest portion of his creatures, and have no mercy, bowels of compassion, or any inclination to do good unto the generality of them; might it not be said, with equal force, that if God himself saith, *Jacob have I loved, and Esau have I hated,* only because he *laid the mountains and heritage of Esau waste;*[‡] is there not greater reason to say he hated all those souls whom he has *suffered to walk in their own ways;*[§] whose *times of ignorance he has winked at, or overlooked;* and, notwithstanding all his seeming love in sending Christ to die for them, he "does not so much as give them an external revelation of him, the outward means of grace, the ministry of the word?" If he is said‖ to *hate his brother in his heart,* who suffers him to go on in his sin without reproof, must not he hate those souls much more who, "though he has given his Son for them, does not so much as send his Spirit to them to reprove them of sin, of righteousness, and of judgment?"¶ Our Lord makes it the particular case of Judas,** that *it had been better for him he had not been born;* whereas this doctrine makes it the case, "even of multitudes redeemed by Christ, who, notwithstanding their redemption by Christ, are left to perish in the horrible pit, in the mire and clay of an unregenerate state." Now can we imagine, that that God who will

---

* Whitby, p. 177, 178; ed. 2. 173, 174.
† Whitby, p. 176, 177; ed. 2. 172, 173.
‡ Mal. i. 2, 3.   § Acts xiv. 18, and xvii. 30,   ‖ Lev. xix. 17.   ¶ John xvi. 8.   ** Matt. xxvi. 24.

require the blood of souls from every watch-man, who doth not warn the sinner to turn from his iniquities, that he die not, should himself leave them to perish in it, "and not warn, even multitudes of his redeemed ones, of their sin and danger?" So that what he doth threaten to him only,[*] *who being often reproved hardeneth his heart*, should be the state and case of many for whom Christ has died, namely, *to be destroyed without remedy*. And is not this to represent our God and Saviour more uncompassionate to the souls "redeemed by Christ; who seeing them in their blood, does not say unto them, live; *or*, dead in trespasses and sins, does not quicken them,[†] when it is in his power to do it;" than were that priest and Levite to their brother's body, who seeing him ready to perish by his wounds,[‡] passed unconcerned by another way? And when the apostle inquires, *If any man see his brother in need, and shutteth up his bowels of compassion from him, how dwelleth the love of God in him?*[§] Would not this doctrine teach them to reply, even as it dwells in God himself, towards "a con-siderable number of those his Son died for; who seeing them in extreme need, in a state of sin and misery, yet shuts up his bowels of compassion from them; withholds the out-ward means, the ministry of the word, from them; does not give them the least know-ledge of his Son, the Saviour of the world, nor the least measure of the grace of the blessed Spirit?" In a word, the love, grace, mercy, and goodness of God, are more mag-nified and displayed in the doctrine of parti-cular redemption, which provides for the sure and certain salvation of some men, for their actual participation of grace here, and glory hereafter, than by the doctrine of universal redemption; which provides for the possi-bility of the salvation of all men, leaving it to the mutable will of man, and to conditions to be performed by the creature, which makes it precarious and uncertain whether any will be saved or no.

3. As to the charge of guile, deceit, and insincerity, which the doctrine of particular redemption is thought to fix upon the Divine Being; this proceeds upon a mistaken sense of several passages of Scripture, which con-tain declarations, calls, and exhortations of God to men, and expostulations with them, and ardent wishes concerning them; all which either only regard civil and temporal, and not spiritual and eternal things; or do not belong to all mankind, or are not directed to any who are not eventfully saved; as has been made appear in the *first Part* of this performance, where the Scriptures referred to are particularly considered under distinct sections.

VIII. It is urged,[||] that "this doctrine of particular redemption is visibly destructive of almost all the acts of piety and virtue; as prayer, thanksgiving, loving the Lord with all our hearts and souls: when, on the other hand, the doctrine of general redemption layeth the greatest obligations on us to fear the Lord, and to serve him; gives him the glory of his free love, rich goodness, great mercy and compassion to the sons of men, far above the contrary doctrine; instructs us how to imitate the goodness, mercy, and compassion of God, administers just ground of comfort to the greatest sinner, and gives life and energy to all the exhortations to him, to return and live." And,

1. It is observed,[¶] that "all prayer is the duty of all Christians, to be performed in every place, and at all times, for all Christians, and all men; and that in faith, and in the name of Jesus, for pardon." And it is asked, "How can we have access to God in our prayers for pardon, or for any other spiritual blessings, for all men, through the blood of Jesus, if he did not shed his blood for all?" I answer; that all prayer is the duty of all Christians, is certain; and that this is to be made for all Christians, for *all saints*, is as certain; yea, even for our *enemies*, as well as for our *friends*; but that we are to pray for all the individuals of human nature, that have been, are, or shall be in the world, is not so certain; since then we must pray for the dead as well as the living, for the saints in heaven, and the damned in hell, and for them that are not yet born, as for those that are; and yet so we should pray to answer to the extent of the redemption pleaded for. The apostle, indeed, exhorts[**] *that supplications, prayers, and intercessions, be made for all men;* that is, for men of all sorts, ranks, and degrees; particularly *for kings, and for all that are in authority*, and chiefly respecting the civil affairs of govern-ment, that kings may act for the glory of God, and the welfare of their subjects; and that the latter, especially such who are Christians, *may lead a quiet and peaceable life, in all godliness and honesty.* The scripture gives us no warrant anywhere to pray for the pardon and salvation of all men, collectively; to do so, would be to act contrary to divine revelation; which represents to us, that the sins of all men will not be pardoned, and that all men will not be saved. And if a man prays for the pardon and salvation of any particular person or persons, for whom he is more especially concerned, it should be always with submission to the will of God, who *will have mercy on whom he will have mercy;* for no man can pray in faith, and with confidence, but for such things as are agreeable to the revealed will of God. There is, indeed, great encouragement for a man to go to God through Christ, and pray for the discovery of pardon, and application of salvation, to him-self and others, upon the scheme of particular redemption: since *the blood* of Christ was *shed for many, for the remission of sins:* and therefore, why not for their sins? and he

---

* Prov. xxix. 1.   † Ezek. xvi. 6; Eph.
ii. 5.   ‡ Luke x. 31, 32.   § 1 John
iii. 17. || Whitby, p. 182, &c.; ed. 2. 177,

&c.   ¶ Ibid. p. 182; ed. 2. 177.
** 1 Tim. ii. 1.

came to *save the chief of sinners*, and, there-fore, why not them? But, upon the scheme of general redemption, a man has no encou-ragement to pray for pardon and salvation, either for himself or others; since, according to that scheme,* Christ, by his death, has not procured actual pardon, reconciliation, or salvation; only obtained a new covenant, in which these things are promised, on con-ditions to be performed by men; so that all a man has to do, is to perform these condi-tions, and then he may claim his interest in pardon and salvation, and consequently has no need to pray for them. When these things are considered, it will be easy to judge which scheme is likely to damp devotion, or to be destructive of fervent prayer.

2. It is further observed,† that "it is the duty of all Christians to *give thanks always to God, in the name of our Lord Jesus Christ*, &c., and this we are to do for all men; and that opinion which obstructs this gratitude, must be repugnant to Scripture and reason." I reply; that it is beyond dispute, the duty of all Christians, to give thanks to God in the name of Christ, for all things which they have received, enjoy, and are made partakers of; and particularly for God's sending his Son to die for them, and for their redemption by him: and though he is not an universal Saviour, yet the greater part of Christians, that is, believers, by the scheme of particular redemption, are so far from being disobliged, and incapacitated, as is suggested, reasonably to thank or to praise him for anything that he hath suffered and done; that they are all, and every one of them, laid under the great-est obligations, and put into the best capa-city of gratitude and thankfulness, on the account thereof; for these grounds of thanks-giving respect all Christians, all believers in Christ, who have any degree of faith and hope in him, though they may not be fully assured of their salvation by him. But then, that it is their duty to give thanks for all men, and for redeeming grace, and other spiritual blessings, which they have not re-ceived, do not enjoy, are not made partakers of, does not at all appear. *Giving of thanks is*, indeed, *to be made for all men*, on the account of civil and temporal blessings they enjoy, and because of that use and service they are of to others; though this cannot be extended to every individual, as to a perse-cuting tyrant, or an infamous heretic. Add to this, that the form of thanksgiving and praise, used by the saints on the score of re-demption, which is referred to in the margin by the learned Doctor, but not transcribed, runs thus: *Thou art worthy to take the book, and to open the seals thereof; for thou wast slain, and hast redeemed us to God by thy blood, out of every kindred, and tongue, and people, and nation ;‡* not every kindred, every tongue, every people, and every nation.

3. It is said,§ that "the great duty

required from the Jew and Gentile is, to *love the Lord with all our hearts;* but if he in-tended no such kindness to the greatest part of mankind (as the sending of his Son to be their Saviour,) what motive can they have to love him, who never had any love to their souls? Surely they cannot be obliged to love him for that redemption which never was intended for them, or for that grace which will not be vouchsafed to them." To which may be replied; that it is the duty of all men to love the Lord, as they are the creatures of his make, the care of his providence, and supplied by him with the blessings of life; and, so long as they are, the obligation to love him continues, and would have continued, had there been no redemption at all by Christ. It is true, redemption by Christ lays a fresh obligation on those who are interested in it, to love the Lord; and, indeed, those who have no interest in that special blessing of grace, have reason to love the Lord upon the account of it; since it is owing to Christ's engagement to redeem his own people, that the rest are continued in their being, and supplied with the blessings of providence, which were forfeited by sin. Besides, though such cannot be obliged to love the Lord for that redemption which never was intended for them, nor for that grace which will not be vouchsafed to them; yet, all to whom the gospel revelation comes, are obliged to love the Lord on the account of redemption by Christ; since all who see their need of it, and are desirous of interest in it, have no reason to conclude otherwise, than that Christ died for them, and has redeemed them by his blood.

4. It is urged,‖ "that the doctrine of general redemption layeth the greatest obli-gations on us to fear and serve the Lord." But why may not the doctrine of particular redemption be thought to lay as great obli-gations on us to do the same? For if *God* thus *first loved us*, when we did not love him, and *sent his Son to be the propitiation for our sins*, and not the sins of others; surely we stand bound to show our love to him by that obedience, which is the only test of our sin-cere affection; and if Christ has bought us, and not others, with *the price of his own precious blood*, we ought to *glorify him with our souls and bodies, which are his:* and especially, this doctrine may be thought to lay as great obligations on us, to fear and serve the Lord, since it teaches us, that *Christ gave himself for us, that he might redeem us from all iniquity, and purify unto himself a peculiar people, zealous of good works ;¶* yea, this doctrine may be thought to lay greater obligations on us than the other, to fear and serve the Lord; since, ac-cording to the scheme of general redemption, no actual pardon, reconciliation, and salva-tion, were procured by the death of Christ; only by it men were put into a capacity, and

* See Whitby, p. 109, 110; ed. 2. 106, 107.
† Ibid. p. 184; ed. 2. 179, 180.
‡ Rev. v. 9. § Whitby, p. 185; ed. 2.
181. ‖ Whitby, p. 186; ed. 2. 181.
¶ Tit. ii. 14.

there was a possibility of their enjoying these things on certain conditions to be performed by them; whereas the doctrine of particular redemption assures the salvation of all, who have interest in it; which every one has reason to conclude, who is sensible of sin, of his need of Christ, and salvation by him.

5. It is said,* that the doctrine of universal redemption tends highly to the promotion of God's glory; it gives him the glory of his free love, rich goodness, great mercy, and compassion to the sons of men, far above the contrary doctrine." But how does it promote the glory of God, when, notwithstanding this redemption by Christ, it is possible not one soul may be saved; and they that are saved, must *save themselves* by performing the conditions of the new covenant, which is all that Christ has obtained by his death? And where does the glory of his free love, rich goodness, great mercy, and compassion to the sons of men appear; when, notwithstanding his sending his Son to be their Saviour, he does not so much as give, to multitudes of them, any knowledge of him, or means of knowing him; and where the external revelation of the gospel does come, to multitudes, he does not give his Spirit to make known and apply salvation by Christ to them? And if, as it is said, "to redeem any, doth magnify his goodness; to redeem many, doth increase it; to redeem all, doth advance it to the highest pitch;" it would follow, that not only to redeem all mankind, but redeem all the devils, would tend most highly to magnify the goodness of God; but the glory of God's grace, mercy, and goodness, lies not so much in the *numbers* to which they are extended, as in the *freeness* of them; as I have observed under the preceding head of argument; where I have also shown, that the love, grace, mercy, and goodness of God, are more magnified by the doctrine of particular redemption, than by that of general redemption. The instance of a king's redeeming one hundred of his subjects, when he found five thousand of them in thraldom, upon a declaration he would be gracious to them all; and which is therefore represented as delusory and insincere, inhuman and unmerciful, is foreign to the purpose; since God has no where declared, that he would show himself gracious to *all* the individuals of mankind; but, on the contrary, that he *will be gracious* to whom *he will be gracious;* nor has he any where declared, that he is *not willing any of them should perish.*

6. It is observed,† that "this doctrine of general redemption doth best instruct us how to imitate the goodness, mercy, and compassion of our God, even by being kind and merciful unto all, and ready to procure, as much as in us lies, the welfare of all men, Matt. v. 44, 45, Luke vi. 35, 36, 1 Thess.

iii. 12, and iv. 9, Eph. iv. 32, Matt. xviii. 35." But, without this doctrine, we are sufficiently instructed, even by the providential goodness of God to all his creatures, to which the passages in Matt. v. 44, 45, Luke vi. 6—35, 36, refer, to imitate the goodness, mercy, and compassion of God, by being kind and merciful to all men. Nor do we need this doctrine to teach us to love all men, as men and fellow-creatures, nor to love one another as Christians, or believers in Christ; since all that are *born again, are taught of God* in regeneration, to *love as brethren,* all that are regenerated by the grace of God, which is the meaning of 1 Thess. iv. 9. Such who have received, or expect to receive, forgiveness from God, ought to forgive one another, every man his brother's trespasses; but then the rule of this proceeding is not, nor is it necessary that it should be, *even as God, for Christ's sake, has forgiven* all men, which the argument in favour of general redemption requires, but *even as God for Christ's sake, hath forgiven you,* Eph. iv. 32.

It is said,‡ "that it is not a sufficient answer to the argument to say, that God is kind in temporals; for this is indeed no kindness, if all these temporal enjoyments, without grace and interest in Christ, which is denied them, can only be abused to the aggravation of their guilt and punishment; and that it is thinking unworthily of God, that he should take such care of human bodies, and make no provision for their souls." I reply, that it must be kindness in God, to bestow temporal blessings upon the sons of men, seeing they are altogether undeserving of them, which should engage them to seek and serve him; and it is owing to the wickedness of men, that they are abused by them; for without the grace of God, and interest in Christ, temporal enjoyments may be so used as not to be abused; nor does it become us to say, what is worthy or unworthy of God, respecting the communications of his providential goodness of special grace, since they depend entirely on his will and pleasure. Though it is an awful consideration, that God should bestow upon some of the sons of men such a large share of temporal blessings, and withhold from them his special grace; and, on the other hand, make such large provisions of grace for his dear children, and yet suffer many of them to be in strait circumstances, and without the conveniences of life: what shall we say to these things, but what the apostle does? *O the depth of the riches both of the wisdom and knowledge of God! How unsearchable are his judgments, and his ways past finding out!*§

7. It is thought,‖ that "the doctrine of general redemption administers most comfort to sinners, under the terror of God's threats and convictions of conscience." I answer, it must be matter of comfort to distressed minds, that *Christ came to seek that which*

---

* Whitby, p. 86; ed. 2. 82.
† Whitby, p. 187; ed. 2. 183.
‡ Ibid. p. 188, 189; ed. 2. 184.

§ Rom. xi. 33. ‖ Whitby, p. 190; ed. 2. 185.

was lost, to save *the chief of sinners*; that *whosoever comes to him, he will in no wise cast out*; *and whosoever believes in him, shall not perish, but have everlasting life*. All which perfectly agree with the doctrine of particular redemption, and which administers better ground of comfort to distressed minds than the other doctrine does, since it secures both grace and glory to those who are interested in it. Whereas the other leaves the salvation of every man very precarious and uncertain, and, at most, barely possible, if it can be said to be so, when it depends upon conditions to be performed by themselves; what comfort can that doctrine yield to a distressed mind, which tells the man, that *Christ died for all men, and has redeemed all men by his blood*, and so *himself* among the rest; and yet he may be damned for all this, and be in no better or safer state than Cain or Judas? Whereas the doctrine of particular redemption ascertains the salvation of some, and all that believe in Christ have reason to conclude their interest in it, and take comfort from it, believing that they shall have, in consequence of it, every blessing of grace here, and eternal life hereafter; so that penitent believers may take as much, yea, more comfort from this doctrine than the other. Could our opponents, upon their general scheme, ascertain salvation to all men, they would have some room and reason to talk upon this head.

8. It is said,* "that this doctrine (of general redemption) gives life and energy to all our exhortations to the sinner, to return and live; whereas, the contrary persuasion robs them of their strength and virtue." I reply; for my own part, I know of no exhortations to dead sinners, to return and live, in a spiritual manner. Those referred to in Ezex. xviii., I have often observed, respect civil and temporal, and not spiritual and eternal things; we may, and should indeed, encourage and exhort sensible sinners to believe in Christ, and testify their repentance, by bringing forth fruits meet for the same; and to such exhortations the doctrine of particular redemption gives life and energy, and cannot rob them of any strength and virtue; since it ascertains complete salvation, continuance in grace here, and glory hereafter, to all that repent and believe: whereas the other doctrine does not; for, according to that, persons may repent and believe, and yet finally and totally fall away, and at last be damned. Let any unprejudiced person judge which doctrine gives most life and energy to these exhortations, or robs them of their strength and virtue: and, with respect to men in general, I see not why, upon our scheme, we may not as briskly put the question, *How shall we escape, if we neglect so great salvation?* and, as boldly inquire, why *despisest thou the riches of his goodness and forbearance, and long-suffering; not knowing that the goodness of God leadeth thee to repentance?* The learned writer attended to,

proceeds† to remove an objection or two lying in his way; as,

(1.) "That after all our quarrelling about this affair, we seem both, at last, to say the same thing; the one, that Christ will save none but the elect; the other, that he will only save those who perform the conditions of the new covenant: now these are the same men both for number and quality. And the actual salvation of men being not enlarged by their doctrine, it seems not to be much more worthy of God, or to represent him more a lover of souls, or more concerned for their welfare than the other." To this he answers, that "though the persons saved be eventually the same, yet the doctrine is by no means the same, nor is the honour of God as much consulted, or his love to souls as much demonstrated by the one as by the other." To which I reply; that the doctrine is by no means the same, is certain; and as for the absurdities which this author thinks the doctrine of particular redemption is clogged with; as, that no salvation ever was by God designed for some persons; and as if they are damned for unbelief, must be damned for what they neither could do, nor were, by any law of God, obliged to do; and because they want sufficient means, on God's part, to render their salvation possible; and that this doctrine represents the God of truth and sincerity full of guile, deceit, dissimulation, and hypocrisy, and is visibly destructive of all the acts of piety and virtue. All this has been replied to before. I shall only observe, that by the doctrine of particular redemption, the honour of God is more consulted, and his love to souls is more demonstrated, than by that of general redemption; for according to the former, all the gracious purposes and designs of God, respecting the salvation of men, are fully accomplished; his justice is fully satisfied by the obedience and sufferings of his Son; his grace and mercy are wonderfully displayed, and all his people are certainly saved with an everlasting salvation; whereas, according to the latter, the gracious purposes and designs of God, respecting the salvation of men, are, with regard to a large, if not the largest number of them, entirely frustrated; his justice does not appear to be satisfied with the sacrifice of his Son for their sins; nor are his grace and mercy displayed in the application of salvation to them; this doctrine not providing for the sure and certain salvation of any, but leaving it upon a precarious bottom, to be procured upon conditions of men's own performing; so that if it is obtained, it is rather to be ascribed to the free will of man, than to the free grace of God; and if so, how is the honour of God consulted by this doctrine? And that the love of God is more demonstrated by the doctrine of particular, than by that of general redemption, has been shown in the consideration of the preceding argument.

(2.) The other ‡ objection is, "that God is no debtor to any man; he was at perfect freedom, whether he would show mercy to any, or make provision for the salvation of the smallest number, and so he could not be termed unmerciful, had he made no provision for the salvation of all." To this he answers, that "God is no debtor to any man; but yet, he is most certainly obliged, by the perfection of his own nature, to act suitably to his attributes." It is very true; but let it be shown, and proved, if it can be, that God is showing mercy to some men, and not to all, in making provision for the salvation of some, and not for all, in sending his Son to die for some, and not all, and so in saving of some, and not all, when he could, in justice have damned all mankind for sin, acts unsuitably to any of his attributes. The main of this author's reasoning in his answer to this objection, belongs to the doctrine of efficacious grace; and therefore must be thought to be impertinent, and does not require an answer here, but must be referred to its proper place. From the whole,

(3.) The two corollaries, or inferences, namely, that "there is no absolute decree of reprobation excluding from saving mercy;" and that "there is no absolute decree of election of a certain number of particular persons to salvation," do not necessarily follow, as it is said:* but, on the contrary, that whereas there is a redemption of particular persons, by the blood of Christ, whose everlasting salvation is procured and secured thereby; so there is an election of particular persons in Christ, who shall certainly enjoy all the grace and glory to which they are chosen. The harangue this author makes upon this, proceeds upon some passages of Scripture, which either have no manner of relation to this controversy, or are misunderstood, and misapplied, as I think has been sufficiently shown in the *first Part* of this work.

I now proceed to consider the answers of this learned writer to our arguments, and what he calls objections, made from rational accounts, against the doctrine of general redemption, contained in the seventh chapter of his discourse upon this subject. And,

1. The first argument, or objection, he takes notice of, is, that " it is not reasonable to believe, that Christ should die in vain, with respect to any: whereas, if he had died for all, he must have died in vain, with respect to the greatest part of mankind." Which is said with a great deal of reason; for if Christ died for all men, and some, or many of them perish, then he must die in vain, with respect to these persons. But that a matter of so much moment and importance, as the death of Christ, whereby the purposes of God, the promises of the covenant, and the salvation of men, were to be accomplished; in which the wisdom, love, and grace of God are so much displayed; his holiness and justice, truth and faithfulness, so much concerned, should, in any respect, be thought to be in vain, is an unreasonable

conclusion. In answer to this it is said,† "that all those acts of divine grace, whose effect depends upon the will of man, or which are offered to him upon conditions which he may perform or not, are, through man's wickedness, too often done and offered in vain; as that imports their being done and offered without any benefit man receiveth by them." And then instances are produced, of the law and ordinances of God, his fatherly corrections, the gospel, and the ministry of it by Christ and his apostles, being often in vain. But what are all these things to the purpose? Does it follow, that because corrections are sometimes in vain, and the external ministry of the word and ordinances have been in vain, that therefore the death of Christ may be, in any respect, in vain? Does the effect of it depend upon the will of man, or is it ever offered upon conditions to men? To suggest any thing of this kind, must be injurious to, and highly reflect upon the sufferings and death of Christ. This learned writer affirms,‡ that "to say indeed Christ died to no purpose, or to no good end, is a great absurdity; but to say, he died in vain, eventually, for them who will not repent or believe in him, is none at all." But surely to die in vain for any, is to die to no purpose, or to no good end with respect to them; and therefore, if to die to no purpose, or to no good end, is a great absurdity, to die in vain must be so too; for to what purpose or good end can Christ die for those, for whom he died in vain? Besides, the apostle represents Christ's dying in vain as a great absurdity, when he says,§ *If righteousness came by the law, then Christ is dead in vain.* And with equal strength of argument it may be said, if men can be saved without the death of Christ, or any are not saved for whom Christ died, then is he dead in vain with respect to them.

II. Another argument or objection against general redemption is, "that a general will that all men should be saved carries some marks of imperfection in it, as representing God wishing somewhat which he could not accomplish; whereas infinite perfection can wish nothing but what it can execute; and if it be fit for him to wish it, it must be fit for him to execute it." The answer to it is,‖ that "this objection advances a metaphysical nicety against the clearest revelations of the Holy Scripture, Psalm lxxxi. 12, 13; Isa. xlviii. 18; Deut. xxxii. 29; Isa. v. 4, 5; Matt. xxiii. 37; Luke xix. 42." I reply, it will be allowed that God sometimes wishes that to be done by others which he himself does not think fit to execute; but then wishing is to be ascribed to him only in a figurative and improper sense, and is only expressive of what, if done, would be grateful and well pleasing to him, but not of what is his proper will and determination should be done, in which sense the passages referred to are to be understood; and be-

---

* Whitby, p. 196; ed. 2. 191.   † Ibid. p. 199; ed. 2. 194.   ‡ Whitby, p. 200; ed. 2. 195.   § Gal. ii. 21.   ‖ Whitby, p. 201; ed. 2. 196.

sides, they regard not the spiritual and eternal salvation of all mankind, only the civil and temporal welfare of the Jewish nation, as has been shown in the *first Part* of this performance, and so are not apposite and pertinent to the case before us. It should be proved that there is in God a general will that all men should be saved, or that he anywhere wishes for and desires the salvation of all the individuals of mankind. For God to will or wish the salvation of all men, and intend the death of Christ for that purpose, and yet not save all men, is inconsistent with the perfection of his nature and the immutability of his counsel. Nor is this argument, that God wills not what he sees not fit to execute, attended with those dreadful consequences as are suggested,* as "that God is not willing any should obey his will who doth not obey it; and that he is not unwilling any one should sin whom he restrains not from it; and that he is not willing any one should repent who doth not repent." Since God's commanding and approving will is one thing, and his determining will another, in the former sense God wills what he does not see fit to execute; it is what he commands and approves of, that men should obey his will, abstain from sin, and repent of it, when he does not see fit to give them grace to enable them to do these things; but God never wills, that is determines, any thing but he sees fit to execute, and does execute, it. Besides, it is one thing for God to will and wish, that is, command and approve, what is entirely man's duty to do, though he does not see fit to give him grace to execute it, which he is not obliged to do; and another thing to will and wish the salvation of all men, which entirely depends upon himself, and which, if he did wish, he would surely see fit to execute.

III. Another argument taken notice of is, that "if Christ died for all men, and all are not saved, the wisdom of God must be defective and imperfect; for, to fall short of what a man intends, argues a deficiency in point of wisdom." The meaning of which is, that if God intended the death of Christ for the salvation of all men, and all are not saved, his intentions being frustrated, there must be a deficiency of wisdom in the case, which is by no means to be ascribed to the all-wise Being; it should therefore seem rather, that God never intended the death of Christ for the salvation of all men. To this it is answered,† that, "if this be so, then every prince, parent, master, neighbour, or schoolmaster, who cannot make their subjects, children, servants, friends, or scholars, as good as they intended they should be, must be deficient in wisdom." To which may be replied; that, "the instances are very impertinent, since it is not in the power of a prince, a parent, a master, a neighbour, a schoolmaster, to make those with whom they are concerned as good as they would have them to be; and so it is no impeachment of

their wisdom, that their good intentions do not succeed, when they have taken wise and proper methods, but their ill success must be ascribed to the evil dispositions of the persons related to them. Whereas God is able to save as many as he pleases; salvation does not depend upon the dispositions and inclinations of men, but lies entirely in the breast, and depends upon the will and pleasure of God." Now, if God intended the death of Christ for the salvation of all men, and all men are not saved, either the means he has pitched upon are not sufficient to answer the end, or he has changed his mind and altered his intentions, either of which would imply deficiency of wisdom in him. Should it be said, that God intended the death of Christ for the salvation of all men, upon certain conditions to be performed by them, and that it is the non-performance of these conditions which is the reason why some are not saved. Now, not to observe that this greatly reflects upon the death of Christ, as though it was insufficient and ineffectual to the salvation of men, without some performances of theirs, I argue thus; God foreknew either that these conditions would be performed, or that they would not be performed; if he foreknew they would be performed, and yet are not performed, he must be defective in his knowledge; if he foreknew they would not be performed, where is his wisdom in appointing the death of his Son, and intending that for the salvation of all men, when he knew that multitudes would not perform the conditions on which their salvation depended? Moreover, it is further observed,‡ that "if a God, perfect in wisdom, can intend nothing but what he actually doth compass and perform, it plainly follows that he intended not, by his prohibition of sin, that any person should avoid or abstain from it, who doth not actually do so; or by his exhortations to repentance, holiness, obedience, that any person should repent, be holy, or obedient, who is not actually so." I reply, that whatever God intends, resolves, and determines upon, he always actually compasses and performs; so when he intends, that is, resolves, that men shall avoid and abstain from sin, repent, be holy, and obedient, his intentions are never frustrated; men do actually avoid and abstain from sin, repent of it, become holy and obedient. But his bare prohibitions of sin, and exhortations to repentance, holiness, and obedience, are not expressive of his intentions, resolutions, and determinations, of what shall be avoided or done, but declare his will of command what should be avoided or done; and which, if avoided or done, would be agreeable and well-pleasing to him; and this, indeed, is not always, yea very rarely, accomplished; and therefore he may justly blame and punish for those things which are contrary to his revealed will, though he, in his secret intentions and purposes, has determined not to give them that grace to enable them to avoid

---

* Ibid.   † Whitby, p. 202; ed. 2. 197.   ‡ Whitby, p. 202; ed. 2. 197.

sin, repent of it, be holy and obedient, which he is no ways obliged to give.

IV. A fourth objection or argument against universal redemption is, " If Christ died for all men, and all men are not saved, then is not God omnipotent, since he could not apply to them that benefit which he was willing should be procured for them." For that the benefit of redemption is not applied to some persons must arise either from want of power or from want of will in God; not from want of will, for it would be exceeding strange that he should be willing it should be procured for them, and not be willing it should be applied to them; and if from want of power, then he is not omnipotent. But it is suggested,* that it is owing to "a want of will, and a perverseness or evil disposition in others obstructing his kind influences on, or intentions towards them, and that it cannot be applied because of their unbelief." The consequence of which is, that he is not omnipotent; for can he be omnipotent whose influences can be obstructed by the perverseness of a creature's will? Cannot an omnipotent Being remove that unbelief which stands in the way of the application of the benefit of Christ's death? And if he can do it, and will not, it follows, that though it is his will the benefit of redemption should be procured for all men, yet it is not his will that it should be applied to them; and then where is the love and kindness of God so much boasted of in the universal scheme? That God wills, that is, commands and approves many things which he does not effect, is certain, and no way impeaches his omnipotence; wherefore the instances alleged in the *second* answer to this argument being of this kind, are impertinent; but that he should intend to bestow any benefit or blessing upon any persons, and not bestow it upon them, or not make them partakers of it, must arise either from a change of mind, which is inconsistent with the perfection of his nature, or from want of power to give it, which is contrary to his omnipotence.

V. Another argument or objection, and which is said to be but the first, in other words, is, "That if Christ died for all men, and all men come not to be saved, then the great love of God in giving his Son to men, is useless and unprofitable; for to what purpose, or of what use is the love of God and the gift of his Son to men, if he doth not withal give them faith in his Son?" And indeed, what kind of love can that be thought to be in God, which gives his Son to die for men, and by his death to procure redemption for them, but does not give his Spirit to apply, nor faith to receive this benefit, without which it must be useless, and of no service to them? It should seem rather, that *if God has not spared his own Son, but has delivered him to death* for all the individuals of human nature, that he should *with him also freely give them all* things, his Spirit and faith, and every other grace, and at last glory; and if he does not, it will be more rational to conclude, that he has not delivered up his Son to death for all mankind. The answer to this is,† "As if all God's acts of grace and favour to men which are not effectual, through men's perverseness of their wills, to obtain his gracious purposes, must be in vain and fruitless on his part, if he also giveth not the grace which will make them effectual to his ends." Why, really I think, that both the gracious purposes of God are made void, and his acts of grace and favour vain and fruitless, if they become ineffectual, through the perverseness and stubbornness of men's wills, to those ends for which they were made; and particularly, that the act of God's grace and favour, in giving his Son to die for the salvation of men, is vain and fruitless, if they are not saved by his death. The providential goodness of God, the external ministry of the word, God's prohibitions of, and revelation of wrath from heaven against sin; his commands and gracious calls to the sons of men, instanced in, though they are oftentimes ineffectual with respect to man, yet always answer the ends God has designed by them; and besides, are not to be put upon a level with the gift of his Son. What though providential goodness, the external ministry of the word, &c., are fruitless and ineffectual; does it follow, that the death of Christ, which is of so much consequence and importance, and which depends not upon the will of men, but of God, should be so in any respect? And should it be so, it must be asked again, of what use is the love of God, in the gift and mission of his Son?

VI. The favourers of particular, and who oppose general redemption, are introduced arguing in this manner: "no man wittingly pays a price of redemption for a captive, which he certainly knows this miserable man will never be the better for; Christ therefore paid no price of redemption for any man who will never be the better for it. And indeed no wise man would do so, and therefore it must be unreasonable to conclude, that the only wise God and our Saviour should act in this manner." To show the absurdity of this objection, the dispensations of God, from the beginning of the world, are taken notice of ;‡ as, the striving of the Spirit of God with the old world, and allowing them space to repent; the sending of the prophets with promises and threats to the Jewish nation, and the ministry of Christ and his embassadors, when God knew that men would be never the better for either of them. I reply; that some, though not all, were the better for these dispensations of providence, and the rest left *without excuse;* and it is easy to observe the wisdom of God, his long-suffering and forbearance to them; whereas for Christ to pay a price for the redemption of men, and the justice of God to accept of that price, and yet men be never

* Ibid. p. 203; ed. 2. 198.
† Whitby, p. 205; ed. 2. 200.

‡ Whitby, p. 206; ed. 2. 201.

the better for it, one must be at an eternal loss to account for the divine wisdom in such a procedure. Besides, the offer of the things instanced in, according to this author, depended on the will of man; whereas the price of man's redemption, the acceptance of it, and the consequences attending it, or the effects of it, wholly depend on the will of God, and the covenant transactions between the Father and the Son. To say,* "this objection or argument is built upon a false supposition, namely, that Christ paid no such price for them that perish, as for them that will be saved;" is a mere *petitio principii*, a begging of the question; it is the very thing in dispute. And though, under the old law, the same sacrifice was offered to make atonement for a single person, and for the whole nation of the Jews, it does not follow, that the sacrifice of Christ was offered to make atonement for the whole world; for though those sacrifices were typical of Christ's sacrifice, yet the people for whom they were offered, were not typical of the whole world, but only of God's elect, the true and spiritual Israel. Remission of sins is indeed received, but not obtained by faith; not that, but the grace of God, gives an interest in Christ's atonement. The reason why one man has the remission of sins, and faith to receive it, is, because the blood of Christ was shed to obtain it for him; and the reason why another man has not the remission of sins, nor faith given him to receive it, is, because the blood of Christ is not shed for him, nor any atonement made by that blood on his account.

Thus having vindicated the arguments in favour of particular, and against general redemption, taken from rational accounts, from the exceptions of Dr. Whitby, I shall proceed to observe some others which he has omitted, and have been taken notice of by the famous Limborch; and are as follow.

VII. Another argument against general, and for particular redemption, is formed thus: "If grace and remission of sins is procured for all men by the death of Christ, it is necessary that the word of grace and redemption should be preached to all and each, at all and every time, that so by faith they may be made partakers of this reconciliation; or otherwise Christ died in vain for many, to whom this revelation never comes; which is very absurd. But the word of reconciliation is not preached to all and each, at all and every time; for before the coming of Christ, God excluded the Gentiles from the knowledge of his law, Psalm cxlvii. 19, 20, Acts xiv. 16. Nor did he suffer the apostles at a certain time to preach the gospel in Asia, Acts xvi. 6. And now the Indians and other nations are yet destitute of the knowledge of the gospel." The more general answer to this is,† "that when Christ is said to die for all men, so as that they may obtain salvation through the benefit of his death, respect is chiefly had to them to whom the gospel is preached; that, according to the

intention and command of God, it ought to be preached to all men; that there has never been an age, from the fall of Adam to the present time, which has been entirely destitute of it; and that the reason why it is at any time removed from a people, is their own fault; they having either neglected or despised it, or held it in unrighteousness." I reply; to say, that respect is chiefly had in this argument to those to whom the Gospel is preached, is not only to alter the state of the question, but, in a good measure, to give up the cause; for the question before us is, not whether Christ died for all to whom the Gospel is preached; but whether he died for all the individuals of mankind; and if he died only or chiefly for those to whom the Gospel is preached, then he died not for all mankind; since the Gospel is not, and never was preached to every man. It is indeed the will and command of God now, that it should be preached to every creature; but this was not always his will and pleasure: it is of a late date, and belongs only to the times of the Gospel. It is true, there never was an age entirely destitute of it; but then, the revelation was made to some particular persons, and those but few, or to a particular nation to the exclusion of others, excepting a few particular persons only among them. There never was an age since the creation of the world to the present time, in which the Gospel was preached to all nations, and to all the individuals of them, nor is it now; there are multitudes that know nothing at all of it. It has been indeed preached where it is not now, and its removal has been owing to men's neglect, contempt, or abuse of it; but why should their posterity be deprived of it? Surely, if God had a people among them, and Christ had died for them, he would have sent his Gospel, age after age, to make known their Saviour to them, and the benefits of his death, that they, through faith in him, might enjoy them. To this a more special answer is ‡ returned; "that the people who are now destitute of the knowledge of Christ, either have been before called to believe in him by the Gospel; but, through their own wickedness and infidelity, are deprived of it; or the Gospel was never sent to them: if the former, the answer is easy, that God once vouchsafed the favour to them, and willed that they should propagate it to posterity; but if negligent, the fault is not in God, who is to be considered as having called their posterity virtually by them; but in men's neglecting their duty. As for those to whom the Gospel was never preached, as the Indians, it is certain, that God has now abolished all distinction among people, and wills that the Gospel should be preached to all nations, and to all and each man among all nations, without any difference, for their conversion; and that those who are converted might instruct others, which is all one as if he virtually called them. But if men are negligent, or the people to whom they come

---

* Ibid. p. 207; ed. 2. 202.   † Limborch, p. 307.   ‡ Ibid. p. 328.

stubborn, and by force drive away the preachers, and reject the truth; the fault is not in God, but men. It is granted, that it may be that God may never expressly send ministers of the word to some men, and yet he never denies the communication of his grace, unless it be for men's demerits." To which may be replied; that some persons, to whom the gospel has been vouchsafed, have been deprived of it through their own wickedness and infidelity, will not be denied; but that the salvation of any for whom Christ died, should depend upon the will and conduct of other men, or that the means of the knowledge of Christ, of the benefits of his death, and salvation by him, should be withheld from such for whom Christ died, through the negligence, ingratitude, or unbelief of others, is neither consistent with the perfections nor providence of God. Besides, if it was his will, where the gospel has been sent, that it should be propagated to posterity, this will of his is either an imperfect velleity, a faint wish, which is not to be ascribed to God, or his proper will, and this would have been fulfilled; *for who hath resisted his will?* Nor can God be thought to have virtually called the posterity of those men to whom his gospel has been sent, who have neither received it themselves, nor is it transmitted to them. Can the present inhabitants of Ephesus, Smyrna, and other places in Asia, where the gospel was once preached, be said to be virtually called by God, by the means of their ancestors, who in process of time, either neglected or despised the gospel, or held it in unrighteousness? As to what is said respecting the Indians, or such to whom the gospel was never sent, the former part of the reasoning upon it is very impertinent; seeing it supposes, not only that it is the will of God that the gospel should be preached to them; which, if it was, it doubtless would be preached to them; but that it has been sent unto them, and rejected by them. It is owned that God may never send the ministers of his gospel to some men; but why does he not? Is it because they are more unworthy of it than those to whom they are sent? This is not said, what should be the reason of this inequality and difference, that God sends his gospel to some, and not others; gives his grace to the more unworthy? The learned writer, attended to, is obliged to own, that no reason can be assigned by us; that it depends on the mere will and pleasure of God, and is to be referred to the secret treasures of divine wisdom, unsearchable by us.

VIII. The next argument is, that " if Christ died for all men, it follows, that he died for Cain, the Sodomites, Pharaoh, Judas, &c., as well as for Abel, Lot, Abraham, David, Peter, &c., yea, for the impenitent, and even for those who were already dead in their impenitence, before he himself died." To this it is answered,* as before, that " special regard is had to those who live after

Christ died, and to whom the Gospel is preached, that though those who died in their impenitence before the death of Christ, could receive no benefit by it; yet Christ is truly said to die for them, since, had they seriously converted themselves to God, as they might by the grace of God, they would have found remission of sins in the blood of Christ hereafter to be shed; even as those did who repented and died in piety before the death of Christ. That the case of Judas is single, and is no exception to the universality of Christ's death; though there is no need to except him, for Christ may be rightly said to die for him, and he might have been a partaker of the benefit of Christ's death, and that on a twofold account. First, inasmuch as by grace communicated to him, because of the death of Christ, a little after to be endured, he might have abstained from the great sin of betraying him. And secondly, had he repented, he would have obtained pardon of God for it." I reply, as before, that the controversy between us, is not whether Christ died for those who lived before or after his death, but whether he died for all the sons and daughters of Adam, whether they lived before or after his death? And if he died only or chiefly for those who lived after his death, and to whom the Gospel is preached, then not for all men; since the far greater part of mankind lived before his death, and to whom the Gospel was never preached. With what view, upon what consideration or account soever, could Christ be said to die for those that were already dead in their impenitence? Had he died for them, grace would have been communicated to them on the account of his death hereafter to have been endured, as the author says in the case of Judas; and so they would have repented and been converted, as well as have received remission of sins in his blood hereafter to be shed. But inasmuch as they neither had grace to repent, nor forgiveness of sins, by virtue of the future death of Christ, as others had, it is most reasonable to conclude, he never died for them; for to what purpose should he or could he die for them that were already damned? As to the case of Judas, though single, it must be an exception to Christ's dying for every individual man; though I think the cases of Cain, the Sodomites, Pharaoh, such who have sinned the sin against the Holy Ghost, antichrist, the man of sin, &c., are much alike exceptions to it. What grace Judas had communicated to him on the account of Christ's death, a little after to be endured, by which he might have abstained from the sin of betraying of him, I do not understand, when his betraying of him was to be the means of his death: and as for his repentance, this writer himself owns, that God justly deprived him of the power of repenting, and so the death of Christ was of no advantage to him.

IX. Another argument against universal redemption, stands thus: " If they can

---

* Limborch, p. 329.

perish, and some of them do perish, for whom Christ died, then their sins are twice punished: once in Christ, who died for them, and again in themselves undergoing the punishment of everlasting fire:" which is contrary to the justice of God, which will never inflict punishment and require satisfaction twice for the same offence, and must greatly reflect upon the satisfaction and atonement of Christ as insufficient. The answer to this* is, " that Christ was not properly punished for men, nor did he properly translate the punishment of sin from sinners to himself, that their sins might be punished in him." But surely, if Christ did not translate to himself and bear the punishment of our sins, how could he be said to be *made sin and a curse for us*, to have *the chastisement of our peace upon him*, to be *wounded, bruised, and die for our sins*, to be *stricken and cut off* in a judicial way *for the transgressions of* his *people ?*† And if he was, and underwent all this for all mankind, their sins must have been punished in him; and therefore it would not be consistent with the justice of God to send any of them into everlasting fire, when Christ bore what was equivalent to it in their room and stead.

X. " If Christ died for all men, then also for infants dying in their infancy; but this the Remonstrants do not believe; since they affirm, that infants are born without original sin, and are not guilty of eternal condemnation; and therefore, according to them, need no Redeemer:" and, indeed, if they have neither original nor actual sin, and so not liable to condemnation and death, what should they be redeemed from? The answer is,‡ " Not from sin, but from an hereditary death they derived from Adam." But how comes death to be hereditary to them, or how come they to derive it from Adam, if they are not involved in his sin and guilt? Besides, they are not redeemed by Christ from this hereditary corporeal death: *Death reigned from Adam to Moses*, and so it has ever since, *even over them that had not sinned after the similitude of Adam's transgression.*§ Should it be said, they will be redeemed from it in the resurrection; so will all the wicked, who will have no share in eternal life, and so no proof of their redemption by Christ; should it be urged, that they will not only be redeemed from this death, but also translated into the possession of eternal life, through the death of Christ; this must be in consequence of their redemption from sin, the cause of this death, by virtue of Christ's righteousness wrought out for them, which justifies from sin, and gives a title to eternal life. The case is this, either infants dying in infancy are sinners, or they are not; if they are, they must be so by virtue and in consequence of original sin, which the Arminians deny; if they are not sinners, they stand in no need of a Saviour, they are not the objects of redemp-

tion, Christ died not for them; and if not for them, then not for all mankind.

XI. The last argument is, " If Christ died for all men, even for them that can and do perish, then no consolation nor certainty of salvation can be had from the death of Christ, even by those that believe he died for them, seeing, notwithstanding he has died for them, they may perish: but this is absurd, and contrary to Rom. viii. 34, where believers conclude, from the death of Christ, that they cannot come into condemnation." The consequence of this argument is denied.‖ But how is it possible, that there should be any solid comfort or real certainty of salvation from the death of Christ, when, notwithstanding complete redemption is obtained by it, the benefit of it enjoyed, sin really forgiven in Christ, and the remission of it truly applied, yet persons may fall from the enjoyment of those benefits through sin and unbelief, and eternally perish? So that the benefit of Christ's death, and continuance in the enjoyment of it, depend on the will of man, and certain conditions to be performed by him; whence if any comfort or assurance of salvation arise, which must be very low and precarious, they must arise, not from the death of Christ, but from the performances of men: whereas, on the other hand, the doctrine of particular redemption secures grace here, and glory hereafter, to all the subjects of it; so that those who believe in Christ, may take solid comfort from his death, that they shall never enter into condemnation, but shall be for ever with him; and may be strongly assured of this, that maugre all the opposition of sin, Satan, and the world, they shall be saved with an everlasting salvation by him.

CHAPTER IV,
OF EFFICACIOUS GRACE.

DR. WHITBY, in the second chapter of his *Discourse of sufficient and effectual, common and efficacious grace*,¶ proposes arguments to overthrow the doctrine of irresistible or unfrustrable grace, as necessary in the conversion of a sinner; and begins with some general considerations, which he thinks sufficient to cause any man to distrust, if not entirely reject it; as, that the defenders of it grant, what is inconsistent with it, " That preventing grace is given irresistibly and universally to men, and is never taken away by God from any man, unless he first, of his own accord, rejects it; that there are certain inward workings and effects wrought by the word and Spirit of God, preceding conversion and regeneration, in the hearts of persons not yet justified; which God ceaseth not to promote and carry on toward conversion, till he be forsaken of them by their voluntary negligence, and his grace be repelled by them; that God doth very seri-

---

* Limborch, p. 329.   † 2 Cor. v. 21; Gal. iii. 13; Isa. liii. 5, 6; 1 Cor. xv. 3; Isa. liii. 8.   ‡ Limborch, p. 330.   § Rom. v. 14.   ‖ Limborch, p. 330.   ¶ Whitby, p. 231—233; ed. 2. 226, 227.

ously and in earnest call all those to faith and repentance, and conversion, in whom, by his word and Spirit, he works a knowledge of the divine will, a sense of sin, a dread of punishment, some hopes of pardon; and yet, that all these men, excepting the elect, are not converted, through a defectiveness in the grace of God to do it, or for want of means sufficient for their conversion, and because God never intended by these means salvation to any but the elect." Who these *defenders* are that make these concessions I am not concerned to know, the inconsistency of them with the doctrine of efficacious grace, will be readily owned; how can grace be said to be given universally to men, when multitudes of men have not so much as the means of it? or be said to be given irresistibly, when man of his own accord, may reject it? And though some certain effects may follow upon hearing the word—as, awakening of the natural conscience, fear of a future judgment, and trembling of the spirits in some persons—as in Felix, who never were or will be converted; yet these things are not promoted and carried on by God, nor were ever designed to be promoted and carried on by him towards conversion, or in order to do it: had they been wrought or designed for that purpose, man's forsaking the Lord by voluntary negligence, or repelling his grace, could never frustrate his designs, or cause him to cease promoting the carrying on his own work until he has brought it to perfection. Nor is it true, that God calls all those to faith and repentance, and conversion, who have a knowledge of the divine will, a sense of sin, a dread of punishment, and some hopes of pardon: for the devils have all these but the last, whom he never calls to faith and repentance, and the latter, as well as the former, some men may have, and yet be never called by the grace of God; indeed, all those to whom God, by his Spirit and word, gives a spiritual knowledge of his will, a real thorough sense of the evil nature of sin, as well as of the punishment that comes by it, and a good hope through grace, of pardon through the blood of Christ, he not only calls seriously and in earnest to faith and repentance, but he bestows these gifts of his grace upon them. But I proceed to the consideration of the arguments which, it is said, evidently seem to confute the doctrine of irresistible and unfrustrable grace in conversion. The *first four* arguments, with the *eighth* and *ninth*, are founded upon passages of Scripture, which have been considered in the *first Part* of this work, to which the reader is referred; the rest shall be attended to, and are as follow.

I. "If such a divine unfrustrable operation is necessary to the conversion of a sinner, then the word *read* or *preached* can be no instrument of their conversion, without this divine and unfrustrable impulse, because that only acts by moral suasion."[*] I answer: it is very true that the word read or preached is not, nor can it be an instrument of conversion, without the powerful and efficacious grace of God; and it is abundantly evident, that it is read and preached to multitudes on whom it has no effect, and to whom it is of no use and service. Some persons are, indeed, *begotten with the word of truth, and through the gospel;* and are *born again of incorruptible seed by the word of God;*[†] but then all this is by and through it, not as it comes *in word only*, or as it acts by moral suasion, or as it is a mere moral instrument, but as it comes *in power and in the Holy Ghost*, or *with the demonstration of the Spirit and of power.*[‡] The Spirit of God is the efficient cause of regeneration and conversion, the word is only a means which he makes use of when he pleases; for though he, generally speaking, works upon men by and under the means, yet not always; the work of grace upon the soul is not such an effect as doth entirely depend upon these two causes, so that, without the concurrence of them both, it will not be produced: wherefore the argument will not hold, that "he that hath it always in his power to resist, that is, to hinder the operation of the one upon him, must also frustrate the other, and consequently hinder the effect." For though the word, unattended with the Spirit and power of God, may be resisted, so as to be of no effect, yet neither the operations of the Spirit, nor the word, as attended with them, can be resisted, so as either of them should be ineffectual. And though the work of grace is wrought by an irresistible and unfrustrable operation, and the word without it is insufficient to produce it, yet it is not unnecessary; for *it pleases God, by the foolishness of preaching, to save them that believe;*[§] whereby he *confounds the wisdom of the world;* and, by making use of weak means, he magnifies his own grace and power; he puts *the treasure* of the gospel *in earthen vessels, that the excellency of the power* ‖ in conversion *may appear to be of God*, of his operation, and not of man's moral suasion.

II. It is said,¶ "Hence it must also follow, that no motive can be offered sufficient to induce the person who believes this doctrine, to enter upon a change of life, or a religious conversation, till he feel this irresistible impulse come upon him." I reply: that internal conversion, and an external change of life, regeneration, and a religious conversation, are different things. Though no man can be regenerated and converted without the powerful and efficacious grace of God, yet they may, without that grace, enter upon an outward change of life, and a religious conversation with and before men, though no motive can be offered sufficient to induce any person, whether he believes or does not believe this doctrine, to regener-

---

* Whitby, p. 255; ed. 2. 249.   † James i. 18; 1 Cor. iv. 15; 1 Pet. i. 23.   ‡ 1 Thess. i. 5; 1 Cor. ii. 4.   § 1 Cor. i. 21.   ‖ 2 Cor. iv. 7.   ¶ Whitby, p. 259; ed. 2. 252.

ate and convert himself; which does not lie in his own power, but is entirely owing to an unfrustrable operation of grace; yet many motives may be offered, sufficient, without an irresistible impulse of grace, to induce him to an external reformation and amendment of life, and a religious conversation. Though it must be owned, that a change of life, and a religious conversation, when genuine, are the fruits and effects of regeneration and conversion; nor do men truly and rightly enter upon them, nor are these. established upon the best principles, until they are regenerated and converted by the Spirit and grace of God.

III. It is further urged,* that "if man be purely passive in the whole work of his conversion, and it can only be wrought in him by an irresistible act of God upon him, then can nothing be required as a preparation, or a pre-requisite to conversion." I answer: for my own part, I must confess, I know of no works preparatory to conversion. Works are either good or evil; evil works cannot be thought to be preparatory to it; and good works, which are strictly and properly so, spring from a principle of grace implanted in regeneration, and so follow upon it, and are not preparatory to it. And, indeed, what things preparatory to conversion can be thought to be in a natural man, that neither knows or receives the things of the Spirit of God? or in a carnal heart, which only minds the things of the flesh? or in a dead man, in order to be made alive? There is no middle state between a regenerate and an unregenerate one; what preparatory works were there in a persecuting, blasphemous, injurious Saul? 1 Tim. i. 13, or in those mentioned by the apostle? 1 Cor. vi. 9—11. There are some things which sometimes precede conversion, and which the Spirit of God makes use of for that purpose, such as reading, hearing the word, &c., but then he does not always make use of these for conversion, nor does it always follow upon them. God's exhortations to men to consider and turn unto the Lord, are said to demonstrate that this consideration is a pre-requisite to conversion: what exhortations are referred to, I know not; the Scriptures, whch speak of men's considering and turning from their evil ways, regard that consideration which is requisite to an outward reformation of life, the fruit of regeneration, and internal conversion, and so not preparatory to it; and, indeed, there is want of spiritual consideration and attention in every man, until God opens his heart, by his powerful grace, as he did Lydia's, to *attend to the things which are spoken,* or which regard his spiritual and eternal welfare. The parable of the seed sown, instanced in, shows, that the hearts of unregenerate men are unfit and unprepared to receive the word, and therefore it becomes unfruitful to them; and that it is only fruitful where it is received *in an honest and good heart,* made so by the Spirit and grace of God in regeneration; whence it follows, that regeneration is rather a preparation for the right hearing of the word than the hearing of the word is a preparation for regeneration. *Faith,* indeed, often *comes by hearing, and hearing by the word of God,*† when that is attended with the Spirit and power; and therefore it is no wonder, that the *Devil comes and endeavours to take away the word out of men's hearts,* their minds and memories, by diverting them to other objects, lest *they should believe and be saved* ;‡ since he knows not who will believe and be saved, nor to whom the word will be made effectual, and to whom it will not; nay, even where it is attended with an unfrustrable assistance, he will endeavour to hinder men's believing to salvation, though he knows his attempts are in vain; which at once discovers both his folly and his malice.

IV. It is said,§ that "the opinion (of God, working upon men and converting them in a way of moral suasion) tendeth much more to the glory of God, than doth the contrary opinion:" and it is urged,

1. That the wisdom of God is most glorified by that opinion which supposeth he acts with man in all his precepts, exhortations, invitations, promises and threats, suitably to those faculties he has given." I reply, according to our opinion God does not act unsuitably to the rational powers and faculties he has given, when he clothes his word with omnipotence, makes it *the power of God unto salvation,* and attends it with an unfrustrable operation upon the understanding, will, and affections; since no coactive force or violence is offered to them, the understanding is wonderfully enlightened, the will is sweetly drawn, and the affections delightfully engaged and moved, without any injury, yea with an advantage, to these natural faculties; and therefore can be no imputation upon the divine wisdom; nor does our opinion suppose, that God "uses and appoints means for the recovery of mankind, which he knows cannot in the least degree be serviceable to that end;" but on the contrary, that whatever means he uses and appoints, he makes them powerful and effectual to the ends and purposes, for which he appoints and uses them, and does not leave them to the uncertain, precarious, and impotent will of man, so that our opinion is so far from impeaching and depreciating the wisdom of God, that it magnifies and exalts it; nor, according to our hypothesis, as is suggested, might he as well send ministers to preach to stones, and persuade them to be converted into men, because his omnipotency can produce such a change in them. There is no doubt, but that God could convert stones into men, and make them his children; but he has no where signified that he would do this upon men's preaching to them; whereas he has not only signified it as his will, that the gospel should be preached *to every creature,* but that it shall be *the power of God* in the conversion of many souls, both among Jews and Gentiles;

---

* Ibid.   † Rom. x. 17.   ‡ Luke viii. 12.   § Whitby, p. 264; ed. 2. 257.

wherefore there is not the same reason for sending his ministers, and for their preaching to the one as to the other, though equal power is necessary for the conversion of the one as of the other. Not that unregenerate men are altogether like stocks and stones; for though they cannot contribute anything to their regeneration or new birth, yet they are capable subjects of having the grace of God implanted in them, which stocks and stones are not; but nevertheless, if God did not make bare his holy arm, and exert his mighty power in the conversion of sinners, ministers would preach with as much success to stones as to men; and consequently the wisdom of God, according to our scheme, is greatly displayed, in accompanying the word preached with a divine energy, and an unfrustrable operation; so that all his gracious designs towards his people are effectually answered, and not leaving it to the bare force of moral suasion.

2. It is observed,* that "whereas according to our doctrine (of moral suasion) the truth and faithfulness of God, and the sincerity of his dealings with men is unquestionable; according to the other doctrine (of efficacious grace (God seems to promise pardon and salvation to all men sincerely, and yet in truth, intends it only to some few persons whom he designs to convert by an irresistible power." To which may be replied, that whenever God promises, he not only seems to promise sincerely, but he really does promise sincerely, and is as good as his word; he will never suffer his truth and faithfulness to fail. But then, according to the doctrine of efficacious and irresistible grace in conversion, God neither seems to promise, nor has he promised pardon and salvation to all men: his promise in Christ runs thus, *To him give all the prophets witness, that through his name, whosoever believeth in him, shall receive remission of sins;*† and to all these is it given by Christ, who *is exalted to be a Prince and a Saviour, for to give repentance, and forgiveness of sins,*‡ not to all men, but to Israel; how then does this doctrine detract from the sincerity, truth, and faithfulness of God? And, on the other hand, according to the contrary doctrine of moral suasion, these things do not appear so unquestionable as is pretended; for if God has promised to any of the sons of men, to *put his law in their inward parts, and write it in their hearts,* to *give them new hearts and new spirits,* to *take away the stony heart out of their flesh, and give them hearts of flesh,* and to put his *spirit within them, to cause them to walk in his statutes and keep his judgments, and do them;* and yet leaves all this to be brought about by the mere force of moral suasion, and power of man's free will, and does not exert that powerful and unfrustrable grace without which he knows none of these things can be done; where is his sincerity, truth, and faithfulness in his promises?

3. It is also said,§ that "whereas the justice of God shines evidently from the doctrine which asserts that God doth only punish men for wilful sins, which it was in their power to avoid; it never can be glorified by that doctrine which supposes, that he punisheth men with the extremest and most lasting torments, for not accepting those offers of grace tendered by the gospel, which it was not possible for them to comply with or embrace, without that farther grace which he purposed absolutely to deny them." I reply, for my own part, I do not think that any man will be punished for not accepting offered grace, he could not comply with or embrace, for want of further grace, because I do not believe that grace was ever offered to them; but then they will be punished for their wilful contempt and neglect of the gospel preached unto them; and for their manifold transgressions of the righteous law of God, made known unto them; and surely this doctrine can never be derogatory to the glory of God's justice.

4. It is asked,‖ "Is it not for God's glory, that the praise of what good we do should be ascribed to his grace, and the shame of our evil doings should rest upon ourselves? But what reason can there be for this, unless we suppose it possible for the wicked to have been converted, or have ceased to do evil?" And let me ask, in my turn, which doctrine, that of free will or of free grace, does most ascribe the praise of either what good is in us, or is done by us, to the glory of God's grace? Not the former, surely, but the latter; and if so, the glory of God's grace is more magnified by the one than by the other. And as this doctrine ascribes the praise of all the good that is done by men to the efficacious grace of God, which makes for his glory; so it leaves the shame of evil doings to rest upon the authors of them, who are not partakers of the grace of God; even though it is not in their power to convert themselves, or cease to do evil; since this is owing to the vitiosity and corruption of their nature, of which they have reason to be ashamed; from whence all their evil doings spring, which being voluntarily committed, are their faults, though conversion-work transcends all the power of man to perform. Our author thinks, that if this be the case, their evil actions may be their misfortunes; but how they should be their faults, it is not easy to conceive; whereas let conversion be by moral suasion, or by omnipotent power, it makes no alteration in the nature of evil actions; they are voluntary transgressions of God's law, and as such, faults in men, as well as misfortunes to them, whether men are turned from them to God by the force of moral suasion, and the power of man's free will, or by the mighty power of God's grace.

I now proceed to mention some arguments in favour of efficacious and irresistible grace

---

* Whitby, p. 264; ed. 2. 257.
† Acts x. 43.   ‡ Chap. v. 31.

§ Whitby, p. 265; ed. 2. 258, 259.
‖ Ibid.

in conversion, and consider the exceptions to them. And,

I. If the grace by which we are converted, does not work with that efficacy, that it cannot but obtain the effect, but the co-operation of free-will is required, then grace is not the beginning of every good thing, but the free will of man, yea, the efficacy of grace is made to depend upon the will of man; and so the good work of faith and conversion, from whence all other good things spring, must be ascribed rather to the will of man, than to the grace of God; whereas *every good and every perfect gift comes from above*, from the grace of God, as the spring and source of it, and not from below, as it must, if it comes from the will of man; for to say, as is said,* that when equal grace is conferred on two persons, and the one believes, and the other does not, that the reason is, because the one receives it by the right use of free-will, excited by the grace of God, and the other rejects it by the wicked abuse of free-will, and fresh obstinacy against the grace of God; what is this but to make the free will of man the chief cause of believing? when nothing is more certain than that faith is the sole gift of God, and the operation of his power.

II. If God, in the conversion of man, does not make use of that efficacious operation which determines man, but it is in his power to embrace or refuse the grace of God, or to do any thing towards his conversion, which another neglecting to do, is not converted, then he makes himself *to differ*, and has matter and occasion of boasting. The exceptions to this argument have been considered in the *second part* of this performance, whither the reader is referred.

III. If such determining grace, or such a powerful operation of it, is not requisite to men's conversion, and is not put forth in it, then God does not bestow any more singular special grace on them who are converted, than he does on them who are not converted; and so no more grace was given to Peter than to Judas, to Paul than to Pilate; whence it follows, that he that believes has no more reason to give thanks to God, than he that does not believe. In the reply to this, it is owned,† that God, in the ordinary vocation of men, does not give to one more grace than to another, or any special singular grace which he denies to another; but gives equal and sufficient grace to all to obey the call, provided by more grace is meant the species of grace, but not the same degree. But if the same degree of grace is not given to one as to another, how does it appear that God gives equal grace to all, and what is sufficient for them to obey the divine call? or that the greater degree of grace is not attended with such an efficacious operation and irresistible power pleaded for by us? Moreover, it is said to be no absurdity, that he who does not believe has equal reason to give thanks to God as he who does believe, if we respect the

first offer of grace. But surely, according to this writer's own scheme, it can never be thought that he, who, though he has the same kind of grace bestowed upon him, yet not the same degree of grace, and so does not operate in the same way, nor produce the same effect in him as it does in others, can ever have the same reason to give thanks to God, as such have who have a greater degree of it, and in whom it is productive of true faith and real conversion.

IV. Such is the method of Divine Providence, that second causes should so depend upon God, in their beings and operations, that they cannot determine themselves to any act; but it is requisite that they be fore-ordained from eternity, and in time be pre-determined by God, not only to the act itself, but to the mode of it. The answer to this is,‡ that if this was admitted, a fatal and an inevitable necessity of all things and events, negative and positive, and of actions, good and bad, would be introduced, and God must be the only cause of all the sins and iniquities committed in the whole world. To which may be replied, that the dependence of second causes upon God, in their beings and operations, and the preordination and predetermination of them to their acts, do indeed introduce a necessity of the event, that is, that such and such things shall be done, and in the manner appointed by God; but do not introduce a coactive necessity or force on the will of man; neither God's purposes in eternity, nor his pre-determinations in time, infringe the liberty of man's will, nor make God the author or cause of any one sin, as appears from the instances of the selling of Joseph by his brethren, and the crucifixion of Christ by the Jews.

V. The opinion which makes the grace of God resistible, leaves it uncertain whether any one will be converted by it or not; for, if God did not work with an irresistible operation of grace upon the hearts of men in conversion, it was possible that not one soul would have been converted. To this it is answered,§ "that it leaves it as uncertain, whether any one will be converted or not." I reply; since this irresistible grace finds all men unconverted, and considering the irresistibility of it, and the state and condition of man, that he is dead in sin, in enmity against God, his heart hard, and his will obstinate and perverse, it is not so uncertain whether any one will be left by it unconverted, as that whether any one will be converted by it. It is moreover said, that‖ "a man may, notwithstanding this opinion, be infallibly certain, otherwise, that many will be found true converts at the last, because he knows that many have already died in the fear of God, and in the faith of Christ; and because the holy Scriptures do assure us, that *some shall arise to everlasting life*, and receive *the end of their faith in the salvation of their souls.*" This is very true, and yet,

* Limborch, p. 388.   † Ibid. p. 390.   ed. 2, 295.   ‖ Ibid. p. 303.
‡ Limborch, p. 390.   § Whitby, p. 302;

according to this opinion, it was possible that not one of these might have been converted, because they might have resisted the grace of God, and made it of none effect. Besides, such who will be found true converts at last, who die in the fear of God, and in the faith of Christ, who shall arise again to everlasting life, and receive the end of their faith, the salvation of their souls, are such who are regenerated and converted by the efficacious and irresistible grace of God, and are kept by the power of God, through faith unto salvation. It is further observed,[*] that " to say that it is barely possible, in the nature of the thing, that none may be converted, hath no inconvenience in it, because it tends not to hinder any man's endeavours after his conversion." I reply; supposing it does not, yet it has these inconveniences in it, that if it is possible that none may be converted, then it is possible that God's choice of persons to eternal life may be made void, and all his counsels and purposes concerning his elect frustrated. It is possible, that the purchase and redemption by Christ may become of no effect, and he *not see the travail of his soul, and be satisfied,* though it is promised to him; and it is possible, that the Spirit and grace of God may have none of the glory which arises from the conversion of a sinner, as well as that the salvation of every man must be very precarious and uncertain.

CHAPTER V

OF THE FREEDOM OF THE WILL OF MAN

I HAVE considered the nature of the power and liberty of man's will in the *first part*[†] of this work, where I have shown, that the liberty of it does not consist in an indifference or indetermination to either good or evil; that the will of man is free from coaction or force, but not from an obligation to the will of God; the powerful influence of whose grace it stands in need of, to move and act in any thing that is spiritually good, without any infringement of the natural liberty of it; for the opposition we make is not to the natural, but moral liberty of the will, which is lost by the fall. And though we cannot allow that man has either will or power to act in things spiritually good, as conversion, faith, repentance, and the like, yet we readily grant, that he has a power and liberty of performing the natural and civil actions of life, and the external parts of religion: hence all the instances produced by Dr. Whitby, to prove the liberty of the will as opposite not only to coaction, but necessity, are to no purpose; since they relate to such cases as are allowed to be within the compass of the natural power and will of man;[‡] such as choosing and retaining virginity, a power of eating and drinking, giving of alms, and the external ministration of the gospel. I have likewise considered, in the same per-

formance, the several passages of Scripture which are thought to contain arguments in favour of man's free will and power in conversion,[§] taken from the calls, invitations, commands, and exhortations of God to it, as is supposed. In the *second part* of this work I have endeavoured to vindicate such passages of Scripture objected to, which represent the depravity and corruption of human nature, and the disability of man to that which is spiritually good; what remains now, is to consider the arguments taken from reason, to prove the liberty of the will from necessity, that it cannot consist with a determination to one, namely, either good or evil; and that it does not lie under a disability of choosing and doing that which is spiritually good. And,

I. It is said,[||] "that the freedom of the will, in this state of trial and temptation, cannot consist with a determination to one; namely, on the one hand, in a determination to good only, by the efficacy of divine grace; seeing this puts man out of a state of trial, and makes him equal to the state of angels; nor with the contrary determination to evil only; for then man, in this state of trial, must be reduced to the condition of the devil and of damned spirits." And it is more than once urged,[¶] "that the doctrine which teacheth that man is so utterly disabled by the fall of Adam, that, without the efficacious grace, which God vouchsafes only to some few who are the objects of his election to salvation, he hath no power to do what is spiritually good, or to avoid what is spiritually evil, must be destructive of the liberty belonging to man, in a state of trial, probation, and proficiency." This seems to be the principal argument, and on which the greatest stress is laid, since it is so often repeated and referred to. In my *first Part*,[**] I have considered this case, whether man is now in such a state of trial and probation as is contended for; where I have shown, by several arguments, that man is not in such a state; and have given an answer to those which are brought in favour of it; and therefore am not concerned to reconcile the doctrine of man's disability to do that which is spiritually good, to the liberty of man in such a state; or what becomes of this imaginary state, and the liberty of man in it. But though man is not in such a state, and his will is biassed and determined, either by the efficacy of divine grace, to that which is good, or through the corruption of nature, to that which is evil: yet he is not, by the one, made equal to the state of angels; nor by the other, reduced to the condition of the devil and of damned spirits: for though regenerated persons, when and while they are under the divine impulse, or powerful operation of grace, are biassed and determined to that which is spiritually good, as the angels are, without any violation of the natural liberty

* Whitby p. 303.   † Sect. 5.
‡ Whitby, p. 338, 339; ed. 2. 329, 330.
§ See Whitby, p. 344, 345; ed. 2. 335, 386.

|| Whitby, p. 309, 310; ed. 2. 301, 302.
¶ Ibid. p. 314, 319; ed. 2. 306, 311.
** Sect. iv.

of their wills; yet they are not in an equal state with them, for they are still liable to sin, and their obedience is imperfect; neither of which can be said of angels. Besides, at the same time, there is a principle of corruption in them, sin, that dwells in them, the old man, which is as much biassed and determined to that which is evil, as the new creature, or the new man, is biassed and determined to that which is good. And as for unregenerate men, whose hearts are *fully set in them to do evil*, though their hearts and inclinations may be as bad as the devils and damned spirits, yet they are not reduced to the same condition with them; for, besides their not being in a state of punishment, and being in the enjoyment of many mercies, and in a capacity of attending to the external ordinances, and duties of religion, there is a possibility of their having the grace of God implanted in them.

II. Another argument against this disability of man is thus formed;* "That which disables any man from choosing what is spiritually good, or refusing what is thus evil, and therefore must be destructive to his soul and spirit, must also take away his liberty to choose what is spiritually good, and to refuse what is spiritually evil." I reply; It is certain that what disables man from choosing what is spiritually good, or refusing what is thus evil, must take away his liberty to choose and refuse them: nor do we say, that man thus disabled, has still a freedom in reference to these actions, nor a power of doing otherwise; we deny both; these are the things in controversy between us. We allow that man has a faculty and power of willing and doing things natural, but not a power and faculty of willing and doing things spiritual; we own that this disability is destructive to his soul and spirit; if by being destructive, is meant being injurious to the well-being of it, to its spiritual and eternal welfare, unless the grace of God takes place; but if by it is meant, that it is destructive to the natural powers and faculties of the soul and spirit, this must be denied; for though the moral liberty of the will is lost by sin, yet the natural liberty of it remains. Now, the moral liberty of the will is not essential to it, and therefore may be taken away without the destruction of it. I doubt not, but it will be allowed, that the liberty to choose what is spiritually good, and refuse what is spiritually evil, is the same liberty which is pleaded for in man's supposed state of trial and probation; and yet this learned writer freely owns,† that this is not essential to man, as man; and consequently may be taken away, without the destruction of the soul, or spirit, or will of man: he owns, that it is no perfection of human nature, yea, that it is an imperfection, and that it will, with our other imperfections, *be done away*. So that the doctrine of man's disability to that which is

spiritually good, is not destructive of any of the natural faculties of the soul or spirit, nor of the will, nor of the natural liberty of it.

III. It is further urged,‡ that "the doctrine of man's disability, by the fall of Adam, to do what is spiritually good, is inconsistent with the new covenant of grace, established in the blood of Jesus, and tendered to all to whom the gospel is vouchsafed." Some men, indeed, plead for offers of Christ, and tenders of the gospel; but the offer or tender of the new covenant, is what I never met with in other writers. If this covenant is tendered, upon the conditions of faith and repentance, to all to whom the gospel is vouchsafed, how can it be said to be *established* in the blood of Jesus? It must be very precarious and uncertain, until the conditions of it are fulfilled by those to whom it is tendered. The doctrine of man's disability to do what is spiritually good, may seem inconsistent with the covenant of grace, to such who have no other notions of it, than that it is a conditional one; that faith, repentance, and obedience, are the conditions of it; and that these are in the power of man to perform; but not to those who believe, and think they have good reason to believe, that the covenant of grace is made with Christ, as the head and representative of the elect, and with them in him, and with them only; and that, with respect to them, it is entirely absolute and unconditional, to whom grace is promised in it, to enable them to believe, repent, and obey. The covenant of grace supposes the disability of man to do that which is spiritually good, and therefore provides for it; for God promises in this covenant to *put his law in the inward parts, and write it in the hearts* of his people: yea, to *put* his *Spirit within* them, and *cause* them *to walk in his statutes;* and says, they *shall keep* his *judgments, and do them.*§

IV. It is argued,|| that "if the will of man is determined to one, namely, to that which is good, by the grace of God; or to that which is evil, through the disability contracted by the fall; this must take away the freedom of men's actions: since then, there is no place for election and deliberation; it being certain, that the liberty of man must be deliberative, if it doth choose, there being no election without deliberation." To which I reply; Supposing choice necessary to free actions, a determination of the will to some one thing, is not contrary to choice, for the human will of Christ, and the will of angels and glorified saints, are determined only to that which is good; and yet they both choose and do that good freely. And again, all that is done freely, is not done with deliberation and consultation; a man that falls into water, and is in danger of being drowned, spying something he can lay hold on to save himself, does not stay to consult and deliberate what he had best to do; but immediately, without

* Whitby, p. 313; ed. 2. 305.   † Ibid. p. 307, 308; ed. 2. 299, 300.   ‡ Ibid. r. 316; ed. 2. 308.   § Jer. xxxi. 33; Ezek. xxxvi. 27.

|| Whitby, p. 310, 312, 355; ed. 2. 302, 304, 346.   ¶ Ibid. p. 308, 310; ed. 300, 302.

any deliberation or consultation, lays hold upon it; and yet this he does freely. Besides, neither the disability of man, nor the efficacious influences of grace, at all hinder the freedom of human actions. A wicked man, who is under the strongest bias, power, and dominion of his lusts, acts freely in his fulfilling of them; as does also a good man, in doing what is spiritually good; and never more so, than when he is under the most powerful influences of divine grace.

V. It is observed,* that "the freedom of man's will, pleaded for, is absolutely requisite, to render our actions worthy of praise or dispraise: and that a determination to one, leaves no room for either of these." I reply; As to good men, they are not solicitous about the praise of their actions, being very willing to give the praise and glory of them to the grace of God, by which they are what they are, and do what they do; though I see not why these should not be praiseworthy; and the more, for being done in a dependance on the grace of God, and under the influences, and by the assistance of it. The good actions of angels and glorified saints are praiseworthy; they are commended for doing the commandments of the Lord, for their constant and perfect obedience to his will; hence our Lord taught his disciples to pray, that the will of God might be done on earth, as it is done in heaven; and yet the wills of these celestial inhabitants are only determined to what is divine, spiritual, and heavenly. And as to the actions of wicked men, notwithstanding their disability to do that which is spiritually good, they are worthy of dispraise; for if bad fruit may be dispraised which comes from a corrupt tree, that brings it forth by a physical necessity, a necessity of nature, much more must the actions of wicked men be worthy of dispraise, who voluntarily choose their own ways, and delight themselves in their abominations. The actions of apostate angels deserve dispraise, and they have been rebuked for them by the Lord himself: and yet their wills are determined only to that which is evil.

VI. It is said,† that " the freedom pleaded for, is such, as is absolutely requisite, to render our persons worthy of rewards or punishments;" and that "without such a power and liberty to choose or refuse what is spiritually good,‡ men are no more rewardable for choosing it than the blessed angels, and as little liable to punishment for not doing what is spiritually good, as the devils and damned spirits;" or, as it is elsewhere§ expressed, " then must all future recompenses be discarded, it being sensibly unjust to punish any man for doing that which it never was in his power to avoid; and as unreasonable to reward him for the action which cannot be praiseworthy." I have already observed, that actions to which men are directed, influenced, and determined by the grace of God, are commendable and praiseworthy; as the services of angels and glorified saints, and so are rewardable by the grace of God, though not through any merit or desert in them; for as the saints have all they have through the grace of God, and do all they do, that is well done, by the assistance of it, so they expect no other reward but what is according to it. And as to wicked men, they are justly liable to punishment for their wicked actions, since these are committed by them against the law of God, voluntarily, with a full will, desire, delight, and affection, without any force upon them : though they are influenced and determined to them by the corruption of their nature; which corruption of nature is so far from excusing them from condemnation and punishment, that it is an aggravation of it : even as the devils are not only liable to punishment for their former transgressions, but to greater degrees thereof, by their daily repeated sins; though their wills, through the malice and wickedness of their natures, are only determined to sin.

VII. The learned writer‖ attended to, argues from what he had more largely insisted on elsewhere, to show, that " God acts suitably to our faculties, by the illumination of our understanding, and by persuading the will by moral causes; and from his having demonstrated the falsehood of that supposition, that though God has laid no necessity upon man to do evil by his own decrees, yet man lies under a necessity of doing evil since the fall, by reason of the disability he hath contracted by it, to do any thing which is truly good; and from his having showed, that though the evil habits, added to our natural corruption, do render it exceeding difficult, they do not render it impossible for them to do what is good and acceptable in the sight of God." I reply; If no more light were put into the understanding of man, or communicated to him, but what is done by moral causes, he would never be capable of knowing and receiving the things of the Spirit of God; and if the will of man were no otherwise wrought upon than by moral suasion, it would never be subject to the law of God, or gospel of Christ. Nor has this author demonstrated the falsehood of the hypothesis, that though God has laid no necessity upon men to sin, by his decrees, yet such is the disability of man, contracted by the fall, that he cannot but sin; for God's decrees do not all infringe the liberty of the will, as the case of Joseph's being sold by his brethren, and the crucifixion of Christ, do abundantly declare; and that such is the state of man since the fall, such the corruption and impotency of his nature, that he cannot do that which is spiritually good, and is fully set and wholly bent upon that which is evil, both Scripture and all experience sufficiently testify. I observe, this author allows of the natural corruption of man, which he elsewhere seems unwilling to own;

---

* Ibid. p. 308, 310; ed. 2. 300, 302.
† Whitby, p. 308; ed. 2. 300.   ‡ Ibid. p.
320; ed. 2. 311, 312.   § Ibid. 15.
‖ Ibid. p. 353; ed. 2. 344.

and that evil habits added to it, render it exceeding difficult, though not impossible, to do that which is good: whereas the prophet represents* it as impossible for persons *to do good*, that *are accustomed to do evil*, as it is *for the Ethiopian to change his skin, or the leopard his spots.*

VIII. The same† author argues from the received notion of the word, that "that only is said to be free for us to do, which it is in our power to do; which may be done otherwise than it is done, and about which there is ground for consultation and deliberation." I reply: that these rules will hold good about the natural and civil actions of life, which, it is allowed, are in the power of man to do, are controllable by his will, upon consultation and deliberation; and as to outward acts of religion, there are many things in the power of man, which may be done otherwise than they are, upon consultation and deliberation. But as to spiritual things, they are not in the power of man, and yet they may be done freely, under the influence and by the assistance of the grace of God; and if no actions can be free, but what may be done otherwise than they are, then the actions of the holy angels and glorified saints, of Christ as man, yea, of God himself, cannot be free. And as to evil actions, committed by wicked men, they are done by them freely; even though they are such slaves to sin, so overcome by it, and so much under the power of it, that they cannot do otherwise but sin; and that oftentimes, without consultation or deliberation, the corruption of their natures strongly inclining and pushing them on unto it.

IX. This author goes on‡ to argue from Le Blanc, that " all the actions which proceed freely from us, may be subject to a command, and by the law of God or man may be enjoined or forbidden; but this cannot agree to those acts, circa quos voluntas immutabiliter se habet, in which the will is so immutably determined, that it never can or could do otherwise." To which may be replied; that the actions of the holy angels and glorified saints are subject to a command, and are done in obedience to the will of God, and which proceed from them freely, though their wills are immutably determined, that they never can do otherwise. On the other hand, the evil actions of devils are forbidden by the law of God, and proceed from them freely, though their wills are immutably determined, that they never can do otherwise. And if so, why may not, on the one hand, the good actions of saints, done in obedience to the law of God, proceed freely from them, though their wills are influenced and determined by the grace of God to them? And, on the other hand, why may not the actions of wicked men, forbidden by the law of God, proceed freely from them, though their wills are influenced and determined to them

through the corruption of their nature? This writer§ further observes, " that if this be the case of lapsed man, his sin cannot proceed freely from him, and so cannot reasonably be forbidden; and that those laws are certainly unjust, which prohibit that under a penalty, which a man cannot possibly shun, or require that which cannot possibly be done:" or, as he elsewhere‖ expresses it, " to make laws for lapsed man, impossible to be performed by him, is unsuitable to the divine wisdom; to punish him for not doing what he could not do; or performing what he could not avoid, is unsuitable to the divine justice: and to excite them to their duties by motives, which he knows cannot work upon them, is unsuitable to the sincerity of God." I answer: that when God first made and gave laws to man, he was in a capacity to obey them; they were not impossible to be performed by him, he was not then in his lapsed estate; and therefore it was not unsuitable to the divine wisdom to make and give out the laws he did; nor is it now unsuitable to it to continue them; which is necessary to support his own authority, though man has lost his power to obey. Man's present impossibility to fulfil the law of God, does not arise from the nature of that law, nor from his original constitution, but from that vitiosity and corruption which he has contracted by sin: wherefore, it is not unsuitable to divine justice to punish for that which man cannot do, or cannot avoid: any more than it is unjust in a creditor to demand his just debts, and punish for the same, though the debtor is not in a capacity to pay. Nor is it unsuitable to the sincerity of God, nor in vain, that he makes use of motives, as promises and threatenings, to excite men to duty, which he knows cannot work upon them without his powerful grace; since by these he more fully points out the duty of man, admonishes him of it, expresses more largely the vile nature and dreadful consequences of sin, leaves the impenitent inexcusable, and, by the power of his grace accompanying these means, brings his own people effectually to himself.

X. Another argument to prove freedom from necessity, is thus¶ formed: "If wicked men be not necessitated to do the evil that they do, or to neglect the good they do neglect, then have they freedom from necessity, in both these cases; and if they be thus necessitated, then neither their sins of omission nor of commission could deserve that name." It is elsewhere said,** " that the notion concerning the consistence of liberty with necessity, and a determination to one, is destructive of the nature of vice and virtue:" and if this be true,†† " then vice and virtue must be empty names." I reply: As to the first of these, the definition of sin is not to be taken from the power of man, or from what he can or cannot do, but from the law

---

* Jer. xii. 23.   † Whitby, p. 354; ed. 2. 345.
‡ Ibid. p. 356; ed. 2. 347.
§ Whitby, p. 356, ed. 2. 347.   ‖ Ibid.

p. 315; ed. 2. 307.   ¶ Ibid. p. 357; ed. 2. 348.
** Whitby, p. 322; ed. 2. 314.
†† Ibid. 15.

of God; for *sin is a transgression of the law ;* and that action which is voluntarily committed against the law of God, is blameworthy, and deserves the name of sin or vice, and so is punishable; though the will may be influenced and determined to it by the corruption of nature; for sin is no less sinful, because man has so corrupted his way, and implicated himself in sinning, that he cannot do otherwise. The devils can do nothing else but sin; and yet, surely, their actions deserve the name of vice. As to the actions of good men, performed under the influences of the grace of God, it is certain, that they are called* virtues in Scripture, and are truly and properly so; it is strange, that the grace of God, which influences, determines, and enables men to perform an action better, should destroy the goodness of it, and take away both his name and nature. The good actions of the holy angels may be called virtues, though their wills are influenced and determined by the grace of God to these, and these only.

XI. It is affirmed,† "that there is a plain agreement betwixt the doctrine of Mr. Hobbes and of us (Calvinists) concerning this matter, as to the great concernments of religion." Be it so; if it be truth we agree in, it is never the worse for being held and maintained by a man otherwise of corrupt principles. Truth is truth, let it drop from what mouth or pen soever; nay, if delivered by the devil himself, it ought to be assented to as such; but perhaps, upon an examination of this matter, it will not appear, that there is such a plain agreement between our sentiments and those of this gentleman. For,

1. The question between Mr Hobbes and Bishop Bramhall, as drawn up by the latter, and allowed by the former, was plainly this ;‡ " whether all agents and all events, natural, civil, moral (for we speak not now of the conversion of a sinner, that concerns not this question), be predetermined extrinsically and inevitably, without their own concurrence in the determination; so as all actions and events, which either are or shall be, cannot but be, nor can be otherwise, after any other manner, or in any other place, time, number, measure, order, nor to any other end, than they are, and all this in respect of the supreme cause, or a concourse of extrinsical causes determining them to one." So that the conversion of a sinner did not concern the question between them; whereas this is the main thing between us and the Arminians, " whether the conversion of a sinner is to be ascribed to the efficacy of the grace of God, or to the power of man's free will."

2. The dispute between Mr. Hobbes and his antagonist, was not about the power of the will, or of man to do this or that thing, but about the natural liberty of his will. Mr. Hobbes allows,§ that " man is free to do what he will ;" but denies that " he is free to will ;" and therefore declares, that whatever is alleged to prove that a man hath liberty to do what he will, is impertinent to the question ;‖ and complains of the bishop, who " would fraudulently insinuate, says he, that it is my opinion, that a man is not free to do if he will, and to abstain if he will; whereas, from the beginning, I have often declared, that it is none of my opinion, and that my opinion is only this, that he is not free to will, or which is all one, he is not master of his future will ;" which he elsewhere explains thus :¶ " Put the case, a man has a will to-day to do a certain action to-morrow, is he sure to have the same will to-morrow, when he is to do it? Is he free to-day to choose to-morrow's will? this is that now in question." Hence it appears, that though he denies the natural liberty of the will, or that the will has a liberty of itself to will, but supposes it is necessitated by preceding causes : yet he affirms, that man has a power of doing whatsoever he will: in which he agrees not with us, but with the Arminians ; as is more fully manifest from what he observes concerning the covenant made with man, *Do this, and thou shalt live.* It is plain, says he,** that if a man do this he shall live; and he may do this if he will : in this the bishop and I disagree not. This, therefore, is not the question; but " whether the will to do this, or not to do this, be in a man's own election ;" whereas, on the other hand, we believe that man has no power to do anything that is spiritually good, and that if he had a will to keep the law of God, he is not able to do it ; we affirm with the apostle,†† that *though to will is present with* us, *but how to perform that which is good* we *find not.*

3. The learned author himself, I attend to, has such an observation as this :‡‡ " It is no great difference," says he, " betwixt the opinion of these men and that of Mr. Hobbes, that the one destroys the liberty of all our actions, and theirs only destroys our liberty in spiritual and moral actions." This observation implies that there is a *difference,* though it supposes *no great difference,* between our opinion and that of Mr. Hobbes. The difference must appear considerable to every one that observes, that as the case is here stated, the one *only* destroys our liberty in spiritual and moral actions, the other destroys the liberty of *all* our actions. We say, that " the moral liberty of the will is only lost by the fall, but that the natural liberty of it continues, and is even preserved in all those actions, in which man appears to be a slave to his sinful lusts and pleasures." We suppose that man has a liberty of will in things of a natural and civil, but

---

* Phil. iv. 8; 2 Pet. i. 3, 5.

† Whitby, p. 359; ed. 2. 350.   ‡ The questions concerning Liberty, Necessity, and Chance, clearly stated and debated, p 3. 34. Ed. 1655.   § The questions concerning Liberty,

Necessity, and Chance, clearly stated and debated, p. 4.   ‖ Ibid. p. 143.   ¶ Ibid. p. 310.   ** Ibid. p. 191.   †† Rom. vii. 18.   ‡‡ Whitby, p. 362; ed. 2. 354.

not in things of a moral and spiritual kind.

4. Our opinion is, that "the will of man is moved and determined by the special influence of the grace of God, to that which is spiritually good; as it is moved and determined, whilst the man is in a natural estate, by the influence of corrupt nature, to that which is evil." Mr. Hobbes will not allow, that the will is determined by special influence from the first cause: "that senseless word *influence*," says he,[*] "I never used;" nor will he allow, that the will is *moved* at all; and still less, by any thing *infused*: whereas we suppose, that grace is infused into the soul: and by this the will is moved and determined to that which is spiritually good;" his words are these ;[†] "and because nothing can move, that is not itself moved, it is untruly said, that either the will, or anything else, is moved by itself, by the understanding, by the sensitive passions, or by acts or habits, or that acts or habits are *infused* by God; for *infusion* is motion, and nothing is moved but bodies."

5. The necessity we contend for, that the will of man lies under, is only a necessity of obligation to the will of God, and a necessity of immutability and infallibility with respect to the decrees of God, which have their necessary, unchangeable, and certain event, and a necessity of influence by the power of the grace of God, to that which is spiritually good; and by the strength and prevalence of corruption, to that which is evil; all which is consistent with the natural liberty of the will; but then we say, it is free, not only from a necessity of coaction or force, but also from a physical necessity of nature; such as that by which the sun, moon, and stars, move in their course, fire burns, light things ascend upwards, and heavy bodies move downwards; whereas Mr. Hobbes affirms,[‡] that "every man is moved to desire that which is good to him, and to avoid that which is evil to him, especially the greatest of natural evils, death; and that by a certain necessity of nature, no less than that by which a stone is moved downwards." And elsewhere he expresses himself thus :[§] "My meaning is, that the election I shall have of anything hereafter, is now as necessary, as that the fire that now is, and continueth, shall burn any combustible matter thrown into it hereafter; or, to use his (the bishop's) own terms, the will hath no more power to suspend its willing, than the burning of the fire to suspend its burning; or rather, more properly, the man hath no more power to suspend his will, than the fire to suspend its burning."

6. Mr. Hobbe's opinion makes God the cause of all sinful actions, as well as good; and this is not only a consequence deduced from his principles by his opposers, but is what is allowed by himself, though he will not admit that it follows, that God is the author of them. "Author," he says,[∥] "is he which owneth an action, or giveth a warrant to it : do I say," adds he, "that any man hath in the Scripture (which is all the warrant we have from God for any action whatsoever) a warrant to commit theft, murder, or any other sin? Does the opinion of necessity infer that there is such a warrant in the Scripture? Perhaps he (the bishop) will say, no; but that this opinion makes him the cause of sin. But does not the bishop think him the cause of all actions? and are not sins of commission actions? Is murder no action? and does not God him say, *Non est malum in civitate quod ego non feci?* And was not murder one of these evils? Whether it were or not I say no more, but that God is the cause (not the author) of all actions and motions; whether sin be the action or the defect, or the irregularity, I mean not to dispute." But in another place,[¶] he will by no means admit of the distinction between the action, and the sinfulness or irregularity of it.

Now, though our opinion is often charged with making God the author of sin, yet we are far from admitting such a charge to be just, and one way of clearing ourselves from such an imputation, we take, is by using the distinction of an action, and the ataxy, disorder, or irregularity of it, which Mr. Hobbes disallows of. And so far are we from making God the cause of sin, that we allow sin to have no efficient, but only a deficient cause, though Mr. Hobbes is of opinion,[**] "that the distinction of causes into *efficient* and *deficient*, is *bohu*, and signifies nothing." All these things being considered, it will not appear that there is such a plain and manifest agreement between the doctrine of Mr. Hobbes and us concerning this matter, as to the great concernments of religion, as is undertaken to be shown. But supposing there is a plain agreement between him and us in this *single* point, of the consistence of liberty with necessity, why should it be cast upon us in a way of reproach? when it is notorious, that in *many* things there is a plain and manifest agreement between him and the Socinians and Arminians; for, not now to give instances of his agreement with the former, about the doctrine of the Trinity,[††] the person,[‡‡] and offices of Christ, and his satisfaction,[§§] the doctrine of justification,[∥∥] the immortality of the soul,[¶¶] its state after death, and the eternity of the future tor-

---

* The questions concerning Liberty, Necessity, and Chance, clearly stated and debated, p. 190, 231.   † Ibid. p. 246.   ‡ Fertur enim unus quisque, &c.—Hobbes de Cive, c. 1, sect. 7. p. 11, Ed. Amsterd. 1657.   § The questions concerning Liberty, Necessity, and Chance, clearly stated and debated, p. 232.   ∥ Ibid. p. 175.   ¶ Ibid, p. 89. See also his Leviathan, c. 46,

p. 322. Ed. Amsterd. 1670.   ** Ibid, p. 175.   †† Leviathan, c. 16, p. 81; c. 46, p. 317; Append. ad. Lev. c. 1, p. 333, 339, 342, 346.
‡‡ Ibid. c. 46, p. 317; Append. c. 1, p. 339.
§§ Ibid. c. 38, p. 217; c. 41, p. 226, 227.
∥∥ Ibid. c. 43, p. 287; de Civ. c. 18, p. 12.
¶¶ Ibid. c. 38, p. 211; c. 44, 295; Append. c. 3, p. 363.

ments of the wicked :* I shall just hint some few things in which he agrees with the latter ; by which it will appear that if any reproach attends an agreement of sentiments with him, it will fall upon them, and not upon us. And,

1. We say that all men are, as David was, *shapen in iniquity, and conceived in sin ;* that they are evil from their birth, and are *by nature children of wrath.* But Mr. Hobbes says,† "that men are by nature evil, cannot be granted without impiety ; and though from their birth they may have desire, fear and anger ; yet they are not to be reckoned evil on the account of these, since the affections of the mind, which flow from the animal nature, are not evil ; but the actions which arise from them are sometimes so, when they are noxious and contrary to duty. Infants, unless you give them all that they desire, weep and are angry, and even beat their parents, and this they have from nature ; and yet they are without fault : nor are they evil : first, because they cannot hurt ; and next, because, wanting the use of reason, they are free from all duty." In this the Arminians agree with him, who, one and all, deny the doctrine of original sin : it would be needless to refer to authorities in proof of this.

2. We say that every imagination of the thought of the heart is evil ; that the first thought and desire of sin, or inclination and motion to it, is sinful. "But," says Mr. Hobbes,‡ "their opinion, who say the first motions of the mind are sins, seems to me to be too severe, both to themselves and others." He denies "that the affections of the mind are evil," or "that the passions of men are sins." And do not the Arminians agree with him, when they say,§ "that concupiscence, and the first motions of it, are no sins ; and that it was not forbidden to Adam in his state of innocence ?"

3. We say, that men have no good thing in them, but what is put into them by the grace of God ; that they cannot think a good thought of themselves ; and that everything of this nature comes from God. But Mr. Hobbes says,‖ that "the schools, not knowing the nature of the imagination and

sense, teach what they have learnt ; some, that the imaginations arise from themselves, that is, without a cause ; others, that, for the most part, they arise from the will ; and that good thoughts are inspired into men by God, and evil ones by the devil ; or that good thoughts are infused into men by God, and evil ones by the devil." This he represents as a great mistake, and arising from gross ignorance, that good thoughts are infused by God ; and what else do the Arminians say, when they affirm,¶ "that man, before regeneration, has a power of willing that which is good ; and that the will of man is flexible to that which is good, without the grace of God ; and observe,** that when the apostle says, *not that we are sufficient to think anything as of ourselves,* that he does not say that they were not sufficient to think any *good* thing of themselves ; intimating that men are sufficient of themselves to think that which is good."

4. We affirm, that the understanding of man is so darkened by sin, that, without the illumination of the Spirit of God, he cannot understand the mind of God in the Scriptures. On the other hand, Mr. Hobbes†† intimates, that "men, without a supernatural revelation or inspiration, which he calls enthusiasm, may, by mere natural reason, know what God says, and understand the Scriptures, as much as is necessary to know our duty to God and man." And do not the Arminians teach the same, that the mind and will of God may be easily known from the sole reading of the Scriptures, without any illumination of the Holy Ghost ; for, say‡‡ they, "a sense superinfused, would be the sense of the Holy Ghost, and not of the Scripture ; and that men endued with common sense and judgment may understand the meaning of them ; and that there is a natural power, common to all that are endued with reason, to attain unto it."

5. We say, that faith is the gift of God, and does not proceed from natural causes, and that all grace is implanted in us, and infused into us by the Spirit of God. Mr. Hobbes rejects everything of this kind ; and says,§§ "that these phrases, *infused virtue, inspired virtue,* are insignificant, mere sounds,

---

* Ibid. c. 38, p. 210, 211 ; c. 44, p. 295, 300, 301.   † Objectum porro a nonnullis est, quod omnes homines non modo malos, sed etiam (quod concedi sine impietate non potest) natura malos esse, &c.—Hobbes Præfat. in lib. de Cive.   ‡ Sententia igitur eorum qui motus animi primos peccata esse aiunt, tum aliis tum sibimet ipsis nimirum severa mihi videtur.—Leviathan, c. 27. p. 138. Affectiones animi mali non sunt ipsi.—Præfat. 1. de Cive. Passiones hominum peccata non sunt.—Leviathan, c. 13, p. 65.   § Concupiscentia in primo statu Adamo vetita non est, ac proinde peccatum non fuit.—Episcop. disp. 20, thes. 16. Primos concupiscentiæ, motus quibus assensum non præbat voluntas, dicunt quidem esse peccata, sed Scriptura ita de illis non judicat.—Curcellæus de Pecc. Orig. s. 35, 36. Vid Institut. Rel. Christ. l. 4, c. 16, s. 9.
‖ Est aute n hoc opus scholarum —nescientes

enim imaginationis et sentionis naturam, &c.—Leviathan, c. 2. p. 8.   ¶ Voluntas hominis post lapsum, ante regenerationem retinuit libertatem seu facultatem liberam sive bonum sive malum volendi.—Remonstr. sex colloc. Hag. p. 250. An tu negas liberum arbitrium esse flexibile in utrumque partem, addo et sine gratia ? flexibile enim est natura sua.—Armin. contr. Perkins, p. 604.   ** Vide Act. Synod. circ. art. iv. p. 168.   †† Ex quibus scripturis per interpretationem rectam, &c.—Leviathan, c. 32, p. 176, & c. 33, p. 176.   ‡‡ Sensus ille superinfusus non erit sensus verborum Scripturæ, sed sensus Spiritus Dei, &c.—Remonstr. Apolog. pro Confess. c. 1, p. 34. Ib. Confessio, c. 1, s. 14, p. 6. Vide Episcop. disp. 3, thess. 1, 2.   §§ Verba hæc *infusa virtus, inflata virtus,* nomina sunt insignificantia.—Leviathan, c. 4, p. 19. Nihil neque *fusile* sit, neque *spirbile,* præter corpus.—

and are equally as false as, that a foursquare is round; and that it is giving the name of body to an accident, to say that faith is infused or inspired, when nothing is fusible or spirable but a body." He reckons* it among the diseases of a body politic, as a seditious opinion, and what makes men apostates from natural reason, "that faith and holiness cannot be acquired by study and reason, but are supernaturally inspired or infused ;" and roundly† asserts, that "though faith and holiness are scarce, yet not miracles; and that they proceed from education, discipline, correction, and other natural causes." And elsewhere‡ he says, "that God disposeth men to piety, justice, mercy, truth, faith, and every kind of virtue, moral and intellectual, by doctrine, example, and other natural and frequent methods." And though he is obliged to own,§ that "faith is the gift of God, which he works in different persons, and in different ways, as seems good unto him, and is what he gives and denies to whom he pleases; yet," he says, "when he gives it, he gives it by teachers : and therefore the immediate cause of faith is hearing; as in a school, where many are taught, some are proficients, some not, the difference is not always from the master. All good things, indeed, come from God; but most commonly by natural means; therefore we must not rashly give credit to them, who, in their doctrines, pretend to a supernatural gift; for their doctrine is first to be examined by the church. Though elsewhere, when it serves his purpose, he thinks fit to contradict himself, and asserts,‖ that faith is an act of the mind, not commanded, but wrought by God; which, when, and to whom he will, he gives or denies." And moreover says,¶ that "the hearts of all men are in the hands of God, who works in men both to do and to will; and without his free grace, no man hath inclination to good, or repentance for sin." And do not the Arminians agree with this man in his other expressions ? since they deny** the infusion of habits, before any act of faith, or that any grace is infused into the will, or that the internal principle of faith is a habit infused by God, or that faith is called the gift of God, in respect of any actual infusion of it into our hearts; and affirm,†† that no other grace is necessary to draw forth an

act of faith, than that which is of a moral nature, or that which uses the word as an instrument to produce faith; which word of the gospel is the sole and ordinary means of conversion, without the concurrence of any internal, efficacious, and irresistible act of the Holy Ghost.

6. We say, that that faith which is commonly called *justifying* faith, or that by which we *believe to the saving of our souls*, is not a general assent to the person and offices of Christ, and to the truths and doctrines of the gospel; but is that grace by which a soul goes out of itself to Christ, and relies upon him for pardon, righteousness, life, and salvation; by which it appropriates Christ to itself, and is a holy and humble persuasion and confidence of interest in him, and in the blessings of grace procured by him. But Mr. Hobbes‡‡ says, that "the only article of faith which the Scriptures make necessary to salvation is, that Jesus is the Christ." And not much different from this, is the definition of faith given by the Arminians, who say,§§ that "justifying faith is that by which we believe in Christ as the Saviour of them who believe in general;" or, "that it is a fiducial assent to the gospel, by which a man is persuaded that all that is in it is true, and by which he trusts and acquiesces in God through Christ."

7. We affirm, that we are only justified by the righteousness of Christ imputed to us, and not by faith or works, as the matter of our justification before God; that faith is that grace by which we receive the righteousness of Christ, as a justifying one, by which we have the sense and perception of our justification, and enjoy the peace and comfort which flow from it; and that good works, springing from faith, are declarative of it before men. But Mr. Hobbes says,‖‖ that "both faith and obedience justify, God accepting the will for the deed; that obedience justifies, because it makes righteous, in the same manner as temperance makes a man temperate, prudence makes a man prudent, and chastity makes a man chaste, namely essentially : faith justifies in the same sense as a judge is said to justify, who absolves by a sentence which actually saves; in this acceptation of justification, faith alone justifies ; in the other, obedience alone."

Ib. c. 5. p. 22.   * Fidem et sanctitatem acquiri studio et ratione non posse, sed supernaturaliter inspiratas vel infusas esse, sed seditiosaopinio. L. de Cive, c. 12, s. 6 ; & Leviathan, c. 29, p. 152.

† Fides sit sanctitas etsi raræ, &c.—Ib. p. 153.

‡ Homines enim ad pietatem, &c.—Ib. c. 36, p. 200.   § Est enim fides donum Dei,—Sed tatem quando dat, per doctores dat, et proinde causa fidei immediata est auditus, &c.—Leviathan, c. 43, p. 282, 283.   ‖ Credere enim animi actus est, non adeo jussus sed factus quem quando et quibus vult, Deus dat negatque.—Ib. c. 26, p. 136.   ¶ Sine cujus gratia libera nemo habet neque inclinationem ad bonum neque resipiscentiam a malo.—Ib. c. 44, p. 300.

** Corvin. ad. Walachr. p. 67 ; Grevinchov. contr. Ames. p. 327 ; Remonstr. in Coll. Hag.

art. iii. & iv. p. 308.   †† Acta Synod. circ. art. iv. p. 62. Ib. p. 128.   ‡‡ Unicus articulus fidei quem ad salutem æternam necessarium faciunt Scripturæ sacræ, hic est, quod Jesus est Christus.—Leviathan, c. 43, p. 28 ; l. de Cive, c. 18, s. 6.   §§ Fides justificans est qua creditur in Jesum Christum tanquam in salvatorem credentium universe, Armin. Artic. perpend. de fide art. vi. est autem fides in Christum assensus fiducialis evangelio adhibitus, &c.—Episcop. disp. 14, thess. 3.   ‖‖ Fides et obedientia utraque justificent, sed in diversa significatione *Justificare*. Leviathan, c. 43, p. 287, 288. Justificat ergo obedientia, quia facit justum eo modo, quo temperantia fecit temperatum, &c., justificat ergo fides eo sensu quo justificare dicitur Judex, qui absolvit, &c. L. de Cive, c. 18, s. 12.

And how near does this come to the sentiments of the Arminians?* who say "that
faith only, although it is not alone without
works, is imputed for righteousness; and by
this alone we are justified before God, ab-
solved from sin, and reckoned, pronounced,
and declared righteous by him?" and, that
"this, by the free acceptation of God in
Christ, is reckoned for the whole righteousness of the law, which we are bound to perform;" and "that faith is properly to be
taken for the habit, without that obedience
which is to be yielded to the gospel; and by
that we are properly, though freely, justified
and saved by God."

Now, not to take any notice of the agreement of these men with Mr. Hobbes, about
the extent of Christ's death and the nature
of his sacrifice,† the power of man to do
what he will, before observed, and the easy
performance of the laws of nature,‡ when
these things are seriously considered, the
charge of Hobbism or Hobbesianism, will fall
upon them, and not upon us.

XII. It is said,§ "that our opinion differs
very little, and in things only of little moment, from the stoical fate; and lies obnoxious to the same absurdities which the philosophers and Christians did object against
it." To which I reply:

1. That of all the sects of the ancient
philosophers, the stoics come nearest to the
Christian religion, has been observed‖ by
many; and that not only with respect to
their strict regard to moral virtue, but also
on the account of principles and doctrines;
insomuch that Jerome affirms,¶ "that in
most things they agree with us. They assert
the unity of the divine Being, the creation of
the world by the Λογος, or Word, the doctrine of Providence, and the conflagration of
the universe." And it is not to be wondered
at, that they should have any knowledge of
these things, since Zeno, the founder of their
sect, was a Phenician, as was also Antipater
of Sidon; and others of them were of Syrian
extract, as Diogenes Babylonius, and Posi-
donius, who, doubtless conversed with and
received most of their doctrines from their
neighbours, the Jews.** And certain it is,
that several of the first Christian writers
were either of this sect, or much inclined to
it, and greatly favoured it; as Pantænus,
Clemens Alexandrinus, Tertullian, Arnobius,

and others.†† It is an observation of Lip-
sins,‡‡ that "Divine Providence, before it
would spread the first light of wisdom among
us, by sending Wisdom itself, that is, the
Son of God, thought good to send first such
as these, meaning the stoics, and their writings, to light up the sparks thereof, and
drive away some of the Cimmerian darkness
of vice and error." And should it appear, that
we agree with them in the doctrine of God's
decrees, I know no other consequence that
will follow upon it but this, that our doctrine
is consonant to the light of nature, and far
from being repugnant to the natural reason
of mankind. It is indeed, not very easy, to
settle their true sense and meaning of fate,
since they do not seem to agree one with
another, nor to write consistently with themselves; did they, we should not be ashamed
to own an agreement with them. And it
must be allowed, that there are some things
said by them which have an affinity with
some tenets of ours; as,

(1.) When they say that "fate is God
himself, to whom all things are subject, and
by whom they are all determined, ordered,
and directed as he pleases. This is mentioned by Laertius,§§ as one of the positions
of Zeno, the author of this sect, that "there
is one God, who is called the mind, fate,
Jupiter, and by many other names." And,
says Seneca,‖‖ who was one of the best writers among them, "If you call him (God)
fate, you will not be mistaken, since fate is
nothing else but an implicated series of
causes, and he is the first cause of all on
which the rest depend." And a little after,¶¶
"If you call him nature, fate, fortune, they
are all the names of the same God, using his
power in a different way." Panætius, the
stoic, also expressly asserts fate to be God;***
with whom agrees Phurnutus, another of the
same sect, who says,††† that Jupiter is called
fate, because of the invisible distribution or
ordination of things which befal every man
in this life." Now, setting aside the language in which these things are expressed,
there is nothing but what is agreeable to
our sentiments, namely, that God is he who
has fixed and determined all things in their
own order, place and time, according to his
good will and pleasure; and that God's decree is God himself decreeing: and therefore
we also agree with them when,

* Hæc mea sententia est, fidem eamque solum
quanquam sola sine operibus non est, ad justitiam
imputari, &c. Armin. ad Hippol. inter ejus
Opera, p. 772. Hæc per gratuitam acceptilation-
em Dei in Christo habeatur pro omni legis justitia,
quam nos præstare tenebamur. Bert. Discept.
Epist contr. Lubbert. p. 6. Fidem proprie ac-
cipiendam esse pro habitu, &c. Ib. p. 81.

† Vide Leviathan, c. 38, p. 217, &c., 41; p.
226, 227.   ‡ Vide L. de Civ. c. 3, s. 30.
§ Whitby, p. 359; ed. 2. 350.
‖ Vide Gataker, Præloq. ad Marc. Antonin.
¶ Stoici qui nostro dogmati in plerisque con-
cordant. Hieron. in Esaiam, c. 11, p. 22, L.
** Vide Gale's court of the Gentiles, par. 2, b.
4, c. 3, s. 1, 5, 8.   †† Vide Lips. Manuduct.

ad Stoic. Phil. l. 1, diss. 17, p. 100, 101.
‡‡ Divina providentia priusquam lucem sapientiæ plenam, &c. Lips. ib. diss. 16, p. 91.
§§ Εν τε ειναι θεοι, και νουν, και ειμαρμενην,
και δια, πολλαις τε ετεραις ονομασιαις προσονο-
μαζεσθαι.—Laert. in vit. Zen. l. 7.
‖‖ Hunc eundemque et fatum si dixeris, non
mentieris, &c. Seneca de Beneficiis, l. 4, c. 7.
¶¶ Si hunc naturam vocas, fatum, fortunam,
&c. Ib. c. 8. Vide Nat. Quest. l. 2, c. 45.
*** Vide Gale's Court of the Gentiles, par. 2,
b. 4, c. 3, s. 12.   ††† O Ζευς δε εστι και
η μοιρα, δια το μη ορωμενη διανεμησις ειναι των
επιβαλλομενων εκαστω.—Phurnutus de Natura
Deorum, p. 19. Vide Chrysippum apud Ciceron.
de Nat. Deorum, l. 1.

(2.) They represent fate as no other than the will, purpose, and decree of God. This Homer calls* "the counsel, or good will and pleasure of God; and Seneca,† "a divine law, and an eternal law;" which is no other than the eternal will of God, and so agreeable to the derivation of the word,‡ *fatum a fando*. Servius says,§ that "fate is the voice of Jupiter." To this nothing can be excepted, but the use of the word fate, as has been owned by many Christian writers: "what else is fate," says Minutius Felix,‖ "but what God says of every one of us?" And so the great Augustin allows the thing, though he denies¶ the name; "human governments are entirely constituted by Divine Providence," says he; "which if therefore any one will ascribe to fate, because he calls the will or power of God by that name, let him hold his opinion, but correct his language." And when the Pelagians charged the doctrine of grace, as maintained by him, with being the same with the stoical fate,** he replies. "Under the name of grace we do not assert fate, because we say, that the grace of God is not anteceded by any merits of men; but if any please to call the will of the omnipotent God by the name of fate, we shun indeed the use of new profane words, but do not love to contend about them." So our Bradwardine, who was a second Austin, says,†† concerning the stoics: "They spoke of fate according to the efficacy of the divine will, wherefore they were free from all real, though perhaps not from verbal, error; for the word fate is suspected with catholics though the thing itself is right."

(3.) We agree with them when they assert, that "all things that happen‡‡ are determined by God from the beginning or from eternity;§§ and that they happen very justly,‖‖ and always for the best;"¶¶ and therefore advise men to give themselves up willingly to fate, or patiently and quietly to submit to the will of God:*** all which entirely agrees with many passages of Scripture,††† and with the practices of the best of men, both among Jews and Christians,‡‡‡ and of our Lord and Master Jesus Christ himself.§§§

(4.) Some of them were very careful to preserve the natural liberty of the will of man, as we are. Chrysippus, one of the principal among them,‖‖‖ was of opinion, that "the mind was free from the necessity of motion," which, in this case, he disapproved of; and though it was his sentiment, that nothing happened without preceding causes, yet, that he might escape necessity, and retain fate, he distinguished causes; some of which, he said, were *perfectæ et principales;* others, *adjuvantes et proximæ;* and, therefore, when he asserted, that "all things were by fate from preceding causes, his meaning was, that they were so, not by the former, but the latter sort of causes." And says Seneca,¶¶¶ men know not what they may will, but in the very moment in which they will; for to will, or nill, is not entirely decreed to any man. Indeed, they seem to be jealous of the liberty of the will, and fear, where no fear or cause of fear was, as if liberty could not consist with any kind of necessity; and, therefore, Austin blames them when he says,**** "Hence it appears, that that necessity is not to be feared; by fearing which, the stoics have laboured so to distinguish the causes of things, as to withdraw some from, and put others under necessity; and among those which they would not have to be under necessity, they place our wills, lest they should not be free, if put under necessity:" and goes on to prove, that the will may be subject to some sort of necessity, without any disadvantage to it; so that in this he, with whom we agree in some respect, exceeded the stoics themselves.

(5.) It must be allowed, that much the same objections were made against the stoical destiny, as are made against the decree of election; and met with like success, and were refuted in much the same manner. As our opponents argue, that if a man is chosen to salvation, he need not be concerned about the means; whether he has them, and uses them, or not, he shall certainly be saved: but if he is not chosen to it, let him be never so careful and concerned about means, he shall not be saved. So the opposers of the stoics argued against them thus: "If it is

---

* — Διος οτ᾽ ετελειετοβουλη.—Homer. Iliad. 1, lin. 5.   † Seneca cur Bon. vir. Mal. Fiant. c. 5.   Ib. de Benef. l. 6, c. 23, & Ep. 76.

‡ Fatum autem dicunt, quicquid Dii fantur, quidquid Jupiter fatur; a fando ignitur fatum dicunt, id est a loquendo.—Isidor. Hispal. Origin. l. 8. c. 11, p. 72.   § Vox enim Jovis fatum est.—Servius in Virgil. Æneid. l. 10.

‖ Quid enim aliud est fatum, quam quod de unoquoque nostrum Deus fatus est?—Min. Felix. Octavius, p. 39.   ¶ Aug. de Civ. Dei, &c., l. 5, c. 1; vide ib. c. 8, 9.   ** Nec sub nomine gratiæ fatum asserimus, &c.—Aug. contr. duas Epist. Pelag. l. 1,.c. 5.   †† Ipsi enim loquebantur de fato secundum efficaciam voluntatis divinæ, &c.—Bradwardin, de Causa Dei, l. 1, c. 28, p. 267.   ‡‡ Αφης παντα τα γινομενα συμμηρονεται.—M. Antonin. l. 8, s. 23.

§§ Απ᾽ αρχης σοι συγκαθειμαρτο και συνε-κλωθετο παν το συμβαινον.—Ib. l. 4, 6, s. 26.

Εξ αιωνος προκατεσκευαζετο.—Ib. l. 10. s. 5.

‖‖ Παν το συμβαινον, δικαιως συμβαινει.—Ib. l. 4. s. 10.   ¶¶ Οι θεοι, καλως εβουλευσαντο. Ib. l. 6, s. 44.   Μονον φιλειν το εαυτω συμβαινον και συγκλωδομενον, τι γαρ αρμοδιωτερον.—Ib. l. 7, s. 57.   *** Vide Epict. Enchirid. c. 38, 77—79; et Arrian. l. 2, c. 17, et l. 3, c. 26; Antonin. l. 3, s. 16, et l. 4, s. 34, et l. 10, s. 28; et Seneca, ep. 107.   ††† Acts xv. 17, 18; Psalm cxlv. 17; Rom. viii. 28; Jam. iv. 15; Psalm xlvi. 10.   ‡‡‡ 1 Sam. iii. 18; Job i. 21; Psalm xxxix. 9; Acts xxi. 14,

§§§ Luke xxii. 42.   ‖‖‖ Chrysippus—applicat se ad eos portius, qui necessitate motus animos liberatos volunt, &c.—Cicero de Fato.

¶¶¶ Nesciunt ergo homines quid velint, nisi illo momento quo volunt, in totum nulli velle aut nolle decretum est.—Seneca, ep. 20.

**** Unde nec illa necessitas formidanda est, &c. August. de Civ. Dei. l. 5. c. 10.

thy fate that thou shalt recover of this disease, thou shalt recover whether thou makest use of a physician or not ; but if thy fate is, that thou shalt not recover, whether thou usest a physician or not, thou shalt not recover. This argument, in Cicero, is represented agreeable to the philosophers, as αργος λογος, *ignava ratio, iners genus interrogationis,* an idle way of reasoning. Cicero observes, that if there was any thing in this argument, it would hold equally good if fate was never mentioned : his words are these : "You may change, and not use the word fate, and yet hold the same opinion, in this manner : If this was true from eternity, that thou shalt recover of this disease, thou shalt recover, whether thou usest a physician or not ; but if this was false from eternity, that thou shalt recover of this disease, whether thou usest a physician or not, thou shalt not recover." And then proceeds to show in what manner Chrysippus, the stoic, answered and refuted this argument, by distinguishing things into *simplicia et copulata ;* which are illustrated by the instances of Œdipus being begotten by Laius, and Milo's wrestling in the Olympic games ; where he shows, that it is a mistake to suppose that it was destined that Laius should beget Œdipus, whether he had carnal knowledge of a woman or not ; or that Milo should wrestle, whether he had an adversary to wrestle with or not ; for these things, he observes, are *confatalia,* equally included in fate : to which Cicero assents, and says, that in this way all captious arguments of this kind are refuted ; and, upon the whole, Carneades himself, a violent opposer of the stoics, disapproved of this kind of reasoning, and thought the argument was too inconsiderately concluded, and therefore pressed Chrysippus in another way, and left off calumny.* In like manner we say, that "the means, sanctification of the Spirit, and belief of the truth, or faith, holiness, &c., are, to use Chrysippus's phrase, *confatalia,* equally with the end included in the decree of election, as they are left out of the decree of reprobation ;" and therefore pronounce it a captious and idle way of talking, to say, that if a man is elected to salvation, he shall be saved, whether he is sanctified or no, or whether he believes or no ; and if he is not elected, he shall not be saved, let him be never so much concerned for faith and holiness. Again, it was objected to the stoics, that they made God the author of sin, and particularly by Plutarch † to Chrysippus, that, according to him, "there was no intemperance or fraud but what Jupiter was the author of :" and by others,‡ to the same stoic, "that if all things were moved and

governed by fate, and could by no means be avoided, then the sins and transgressions of men were not to be ascribed to their own wills, but to a certain necessity which arises from fate, and is the governess of all things, by which that must needs be which shall be ; and therefore the punishment of transgressions is unrighteously fixed by laws, if men do not willingly commit sin, but are drawn to it by fate." To this Chrysippus answers, and the substance of his answers is this, "that though all things are connected with fate, yet the dispositions of our minds are only subject to it, agreeable to the property and quality of them : for if they are first wholesomely and profitably formed by nature, they more inoffensively and tractably get over all that force which extrinsically comes upon them by fate ; but if they are rough, ignorant, and uncultivated, and not assisted by the help of wholesome arts, though they may be moved by little or no force of fatal disadvantage, yet, through their own badness and voluntary impetus, fall into daily sins and mistakes." This he exemplifies by the rolling of a stone down-hill ; the man that pushes it gives it its first motion, but not its volubility ; and its continuing to move downwards does not arise from him that first moved it, but from its own volubility. So, says he, the necessity of fate moves the kinds and principles of causes ; but it is our own will that moderates, governs, and directs the counsels, determinations, and actions of our minds ; and therefore § denies, "that such vile and wicked men are to be heard or borne with, who, when they are in fault, and convicted of a crime, fly to the necessity of fate, as to an asylum, and say, that what they have wickedly done is not to be ascribed to their own rashness, but to fate." And then some lines in Homer‖ are mentioned, in which Jupiter is introduced complaining that men accused the gods of being the author of their evils, when their sorrows arose from their own wickedness. Now, from hence it appears, whatever mistakes there may be thought to be in this way of reasoning, they did not believe that God was the author of sin, or that the sins of men were to be ascribed to fate, but to the pravity of their wills ; and that whatever distant concern fate had in these things, yet it did not excuse the wickedness of the actions of men, nor exempt them from punishment.

This may be further illustrated by the instance of Zeno and his servant. Zeno caught his servant playing the thief, and beat him for it. The fellow, agreeable to his master's doctrine, as he thought, and in vindication of himself, says, that "he was destined by

* Nec nos impedict illa ignava ratio quæ dicitur. Appellatur enim quidam a philosophis αργος λογος, cui sic pareamus, nihil est omnino, quod agamus in vita. Sic enim interrogant, si fatum tibi est, ex hoc morbo convalescere, sive medicum adhibueris, sive non convalesces, &c.—Cicero de Fato. † Vide Lips. Physiolog. Stoic. l. 1. diss. 14. ‡ Si Chrysippus, inquiunt, fato

putat omnia moveri et regi, peccata quoque hominum et delicta non sustentanda neque concienda sunt ipsis voluntatibusque eorum, sed necessitati cuidam et instantiæ. &c.—Aul. Gell., Noct Attic. l. 6, c. 2. § Propterea negat oportere ferri audirique homines aut nequam, &c. Ib. vid. etiam Ciceronem de Fato.
‖ Homer, Odyss. 1, lin. 22, 24.

fate to steal." "Yes," replied Zeno, "and to be beaten too."[*] When it is objected to us, that we make God the author of sin, we deny it, and clear ourselves, by distinguishing between the action and the disorder of it; for though God is concerned in all motion and action, for *in him we live, move, and have our being;* and he is the first cause and mover of all things : yet the ataxy, disorder, and iniquity of any action, arise from ourselves, and our own corrupt wills and affections; and whatever concern we suppose the decrees of God have about sin, yet they do not excuse the wickedness of men, or exempt them from proper punishment : the same degree which permits sin, provides for the punishment of it.

(6.) How far soever the stoics carried their doctrine of fate or destiny, it is certain they never thought it had a tendency to looseness of life; nor does it appear to have had any such influence upon them; for, of all the sects of the philosophers, none were more addicted both to the love and practice of moral virtue, than this sect. The Manual of Epictetus, his Commentaries, digested by Arrianus, the writings of Seneca, and of the emperor Mark Antonine, do abundantly declare their strict regard to the worship of God, and the doing of justice among men. This made Josephus say,[†] that the sect of the Pharisees, which was the strictest sect among the Jews for morality and external holiness, was very much like to that of the stoics. It is, indeed, said[‡] of Tiberius Nero, that he was more negligent of God and religion, being fully persuaded that all things were done by fate; but then the historian observes, that he was addicted to the mathematics; so that the fate he gave into was not the stoical fate, as asserted by the best writers of that sect, but the mathematical fate, which depended upon the influence of the stars. Now, of these things, in which we agree with them we are not ashamed; and what advantage our opponents are able to make of all this, I see not. But others of this sect, or the same writers, by either contradicting themselves, or one another, or as they have been understood by others, very greatly differ from us in their doctrine of fate or destiny, as when,

(1.) And as far as they agree with the Chaldeans and astrologers, who placed fate in the position and influence of the stars. The wiser sort of them, indeed, rejected the dreams and folies of judiciary astrology,[§] and were far from making fate wholly to consist in these things; and yet it seems as though

they were more or less included by them in their series and connexion of causes, which they make fate to be; however, it is certain that the vulgar sort had no other notion of fate than this, which made Austin ‖ say, that "when men hear fate spoken of according to the usual custom of speech, they understand nothing else but the influence of the position of the stars, such as it is when a man is born or conceived." Now between this notion of fate, and our doctrine concerning God's decrees, there is no manner of agreement. We deny any such influence of the stars which work by a necessity of nature upon the wills and actions of men; and therefore, when this was objected to the doctrine of grace, taught by the above writer, he answers,¶ "They that assert fate," says he, "contend, that not only actions and events, but that our wills depend upon the position of the stars, at the time that a man is conceived or born, which they call constellations; but the grace of God not only exceeds all the stars, and all the heavens, but even all the angels. Moreover, the assertors of fate, ascribe both the good and evil things of men unto it; but God prosecutes the sinful demerits of men with their due reward, and gives good things with a merciful will, through undeserved grace; doing both, not according to the then present consort of the stars, but according to the high and eternal counsel of his severity and goodness; wherefore, we see, that neither belong to fate."

(2.) When they make fate to be something distinct from the divine Being, something without him, and by which he himself is bound and governed, and which he cannot obstruct nor alter, such laws being put in the nature of things, that he cannot change. Seneca says,** "The same necessity binds both God and man, the irrevocable course equally carries things divine as human. The Maker and Governor of all things himself has, indeed, ordained the fates; yet follows them, and always obeys, having once commanded." It is said,†† that "it is not lawful for him to alter the connexion, or turn the course of causes, or go contrary to the laws which he has fixed, and by which he himself is bound; yea, that it is impossible‡‡ for him to avoid the destined fate." So Jupiter is introduced in Homer,§§ complaining that he could not deliver his son Sarpedon from death, which was appointed by fate for him. But we say, that God's decree is within himself, and that whatever is in God, is God; and that his decree is nothing else but himself decreeing, which flows from his

* Ειμαρτο μοι κλεψαι, και δαρηναι, εφα.—Laert. l. 7, in Vita Zeno.   † Η φαρισαιων αιρεσις παραπλησιος εστι τη παρ' Ελλησι στοικη λεγομηνη. Joseph, in vita sua.   ‡ Circa Deos et religiones negligentior, quippe addictus mathematicæ, persuasionisque plenus cuncta fato agi. Sueton. Tiber. Nero, c. 69.   § Vide Cicer. de Divinatione, l. 2:   ‖ August. de Civ. Dei, l. 5, c. 1.   ¶ Fatum quippe qui affirmant, de siderum positione, &c. August. contr. duas

epist. Pelag. l. 2, c. 6.   ** Eadem necessitas et Deos alligat, &c. Seneca de Provid. c. 5.   †† Non illa Deo vertisse licet. Quæ nexa suis currunt causis. Seneca. Œdipus, act. v. chorus. Finxit in æternum causas, &c. Lucan. Pharsal. l. 2, c. 9, &c.   ‡‡ Την πεπρωμενην μοιρην αδυνατα εστι αποφυγεειν και θεω. Herodot. l. 1, c. 91.   §§ Homer, Iliad. v. 16, l. 433, 434. Hoc sentit Homeros cum querenum Jovem inducit, quod Sarpedonem filium a morte contra, fatum eripere non posset. Cicero de Divin. l. 2.

sovereign free good will and pleasure; and that whatsoever he does in heaven or in earth, he does freely, and as he pleases; and can, and does, when he thinks fit, interrupt, stop, or change the natural order and course of things; he can make the sun to stand still, stop the course of waters, and make them to stand up as a wall, hinder the burning of fire, open rivers in high places, and fountains in the midst of the valleys, make the wilderness a pool of water, and dry land springs of water. If indeed, they meant no more, than that God is immutable in his purposes, unalterable in his decrees, and will, *stare decreto*, stand by his decree, and never repent, *primi consilii*, of his first counsel and thoughts, as Seneca * says; we are of the same mind with them: but otherwise, as Lactantius † observes, "If such is the power of the destinies, that they can do more than all the celestial beings, than even the Lord and Governor himself, why may not they be rather said to rule, whose laws and statutes necessity obliges all the gods to obey?"

(3.) When they make fate to be a series of causes, whose connexion is natural, or which are in their own nature fitly and unalterably joined and connected together; for according to Chrysippus,‡ "fate is a natural order or connexion of all things from eternity, one following upon another, such being the complication of them, that it is entirely unalterable;" whereas we say, that all second causes are governed, directed, and disposed of by the will of God, and entirely depend upon his free good will and pleasure; and that, when he pleases, he can break the chain and connexion, and can act without them, besides them, and above them. The sentiments of the stoics in this respect, seem to have the nearest affinity with those of a certain generation of men who have lately risen up among us, who talk of *the nature and fitness of things*, by which God himself is bound, to which he conforms, and according to which he acts: though one would think, if this was the case, the *nature* and *fitness* of things should rather be called God, than he whom they call so.

(4.) When they assert, as Chrysippus does in the above definition, that fate is a series of all causes and things from everlasting; whereas, though we believe that whatsoever comes to pass, was known and determined by God from all eternity, and comes to pass in the way and manner, with, without, or besides

second causes, just as he pleases; yet neither the things, nor their causes, nor the series of them, were from eternity, but arise and proceed in time, according to the eternal will of God.

(5.) When they seem to say, that all causes act naturally, and by their own natural strength produce their effects necessarily,§ and so destroy all contingency in any sense: whereas we suppose, that as there are some causes which act naturally and necessarily, others are free, and produce their effects freely; others are contingent, and produce their effects contingently, in respect of themselves, though with respect to the decree of God they act necessarily.

(6.) When they intimate that the will of man may be forced, though this is sometimes strongly denied by them;‖ and, indeed, they talk much of free will, and say,¶ "A wise man does nothing unwillingly, and escapes necessity; but then it is, because he wills what she would otherwise force him to." And even in that famous wish or prayer of the stoic Cleanthes,** so often mentioned by themselves and others, where, though he desires that fate and Jupiter would lead him to what he was ordained; yet observes, that "if he did not follow, whether he would or no, he must: for," says he, "the fates lead him that is willing, and draw him that will not, that is, by force, whether he will or no." Now we deny that the will of man, though it is in the hand of the Lord, and is influenced and determined by his grace to that which is good, has any violence offered to it, or is forced and compelled unto it. But, supposing there was a greater likeness between our sentiments and those of the stoics concerning fate, why should it be thought so reproachful in us to agree with that sect of philosophers, when it is notorious, that in many things the Pelagians and Arminians agree with them? as will appear from the following hints. As,

(1.) When they†† affirm it to be a mistake, that sin is born with us, or we in sin, or that it comes into the world with us; and say, that nature allures us to no vice; that we are born whole and free; that man is by nature led to that which is convenient and proper for him;‡‡ that nature has laid the foundation, and implanted seeds of virtue in man; that all are born unto it,§§ and that if we look within, there is a fountain of good, which would continually spring up, if we

---

* Nec unquam primi consilii Deos pœnitet. Seneca de Benef. l. 6. c. 23.   † Si parcarum tanta vis est, &c.   Lactant. de Fals. Relig. l. 1, c. 11.   ‡ Ειμαρμενην φυσικην συνταξευτων ωλον εξ αιδιον, &c. Chrysipp apud A. Gell. Noct. Attic. l. 6, c. 2.   § Quid fles? quid optas? perdis operam. *Desine fata Deum flecti sperare precando.* Rata et fixa sunt atque magna et æterna necessitate ducuntur. Senec. epist. 77.

‖ Vide Arrian. Epictet. l 1, c. 6, 17, 19, & l. 2, c. 2, 15, 17, 23, & l. 3, c. 26.

¶ Nihil invitus facit sapiens, necessitatem effugit, quia vult quod ipsa coactura est. Senec.

ep. 54.   ** Αγε δε με ω ζευ, και συ η πεπρωμερη, &c. Quod sic reddidit, Senec. ep. 107
Duc me parens, celsique dominator poli,
Quocunque placuit, nulla parendi mora est,
Adsum inpiger: fac nolle, comitator gemens,
Ducunt volentem fata, nolentem trahunt,
Malusque patiar, quod pati licuit boni.
†† Erras enim si existimas nobiscum vitia nasci, supervenerunt, ingesta sunt, &c. Senec. ep. 94.   ‡‡ Εγω γαρ πεφυκα προς το εμοι συμφερον. Arrian. Epict. l. 1, c. 22.
§§ Omnibus natura dedit, fundamenta semenque virtutem, &c. Senec cp. 73 & 90.

would but dig.* And do not the Pelagians and Arminians agree with them in these things, when they cry up the purity of human nature, and deny original sin? But, on the other hand, we, with the Scriptures, say,† that men are *shapen in iniquity, and conceived in sin;* and that *in us,* that is, in our *flesh, dwells no good thing; and that there is none righteous, no, not one,* of themselves.

(2.) When they talk of their οϱθος λογος, *recta ratio,* right reason, and ascribe so much to it as they do. They say,‡ it is the nature of God, and the same in man as in God;§ only with this difference, that it is in him consummate, in them consummable;‖ that to follow it, is the same as to follow God himself;¶ that it is implanted in nature to live according to it;** and that this completes man's happiness, yea, that this alone perfects a man, and alone makes him happy.†† And do not the Pelagians and Arminians likewise extol it, as the rule of all doctrine and practice, and the measure of happiness?

(3.) When they speak so much concerning τα εφ' ημιν,‡‡ the things that are in our power, and the free will of man. They say,§§ it is in a man's power to be sincere, grave, patient, without love of pleasure; to be content with one's state and condition, to want but little; to be meek, free, without luxury, serious, and sublime; to avoid our own wickedness; yea, to be wholly without any; to live well, to do no other but what God approves of, and cheerfully receive what he appoints. They affirm,‖‖ that both good and evil are in the power of man's will; that if he desires any good thing, he may have it from himself; and that such is the nature of his will, that God himself cannot conquer it; yea, they are bold to say, that God can do no more than a good man; and that there is something in which a wise man exceeds him; since he is wise, not of himself, but by the indulgence of nature. And in this Cicero himself seems to agree with them, when he says,¶¶ "No man ever looked upon himself obliged to God for virtue, and that very rightly; we are justly praised for virtue and rightly glory in it, which could not be, if we esteemed it a gift of God, and not of our-

selves. Did ever any man give thanks to God, that he was a good man? But that he was rich, or honoured, or in health and in safety?" It is easy to observe, how near all this comes to the Pelagian and Arminian tenets; only these philosophers are, perhaps, somewhat more bold and free in expressing themselves than the Pelagians and Arminians are, though many of them have used great liberty of speech.

(4.) When they represent it as possible for a man to live without sin, and arrive to perfection. They say,*** that wise men are without sin, and cannot fall into it. Epictetus††† used to say, that "if a man had but these two words at heart, and took care to observe and obey them, he should be, for the most part, impeccable, and live a most quiet life: the words were, *bear* and *forbear.*" And, said another‡‡‡ of them, "It is now in my power, that there should not be any iniquity or lust, or any perturbation at all in this soul of mine." Zeno, the founder of the sect, in a letter to king Antigonus, tells him,§§§ "that a good genius, with moderate exercise, and by the help of a candid preceptor, might easily attain to perfection of virtue." Now this entirely agrees with the notion of the Pelagians concerning impeccability and perfection, which they supposed persons might easily arrive to by the mere strength and power of nature, as appears from the writings of Augustin and Jerome; the latter of these observes,‖‖‖ that the Pelagians "embraced the poisons of all heretics; which, says he, flow from the fountain of the philosophers, and especially of Pythagoras and Zeno, the prince of the stoics; who assert, that by meditation, and the daily exercise of virtue, sin may be so extirpated out of the minds of men, that no root nor fibre of it may remain."

(5.) When they intimate that virtue may be lost. They are not all of them, indeed, agreed in this point. Chrysippus¶¶¶ was of opinion, that virtue might be lost. Cleanthes differed from him, and affirmed it could not be lost, but remained firm and constant. Seneca**** seems to be of his mind, when he asserts, that virtue is natural, cannot be unlearned; being once received, never departs:

---

* Antonin. l. 7. s. 59.   † Psalm li. 5 Rom. vii. 18, and iii. 10.   ‡ Τις ουν ουσια Ͽεου ;—νους, επιστημη, λογος οϱος.—Arrian. Epict. l. 2, c. 8.   § Εστιν ο οϱϿος λογος, δια παντων τρεχομενος, ο αυτος, εν τω δι.—Laert. in Zeno, l. 7.   ‖ Ratio vero diis hominibusque communis, hæc in illis consummata est, in nobis consummabilis.—Senec. ep. 92.

¶ ΠροσεϿι επι τελευταιον, το επεσϿαι τω λογω, και Ͽεω.—Antonin. l. 12, s. 31.

** Το κατα λογον, ζην οϱϿως γινεϿαι τοις κατα φυσιν—Laert. in Zeno, l. 7.   †† Quid in homini proprium? Ratio. Hæc recta et consummata felicitatem hominis implevit, &c. Senec. ep. 76. Vide Epict. Enchirid. c. 1, 2.

‡‡ Antonin. l. 5, s. 5, & l. 7, s. 71, & l. 8, s. 29, & l. 11, s. 16, & l. 12, s. 11.

§§ Arrian. Epict. l. 1, c. 25. Vide l. 4. c. 10. Ib. c. 22, & c. 1.   ‖‖ Solebat Sextius

dicere, Jovem plus non posse quam bonum virum. Senec. s. 73. Est aliquid quo sapiens antecedat Deum. ille Naturæ beneficio, non suo, sapiens est, Ib. ep. 53.   ¶¶ Cicero de Natura Deor. l. 3. prope finem.   *** Ετι και αναμαρτητους, το απιριπτωσεις ειναι αμαρτηματι. Laert. l. 7, in vita Zeno.   ††† Verba hæc duo dicebat, ανεχου και απεχου. A. Gellius, Noct. Attic. l. 17, c. 19.   ‡‡‡ Νυν επ' εμοι εστιν, &c. Antonin. l. 8. s. 29.   §§§ Φυσις δε ευγενης μετριαν ασκησιν προσλαβουσα επι τε, &c. Laert. l. 7, in Zeno.   ‖‖‖ Omnium hæreticorum venena complecti, &c. Hieron. adv. Pelag. tom. ii. p. 83, M.   ¶¶¶ Και μεν την αρετην Χρυσιππος, αποβλητην, ΚλεανϿης οτε, αναποβλητον. Laert. l. 7. in Zeno.   **** Sed eo majore animo ad emendationem nostri debemus accedere, quod semel traditi boni perpetua possessio est, &c. Senec. ep. 50.

the preservation of it is easy, and is a perpetual possession. But others of them incline to the opinion of Chrysippus, and suggest,* that modesty, meekness, integrity, &c. may be entirely destroyed. Upon the whole, it is certain, that there is a very great affinity between Pelagianism and the stoic philosophy; and it is more than probable, that the former took its rise from the latter. There is one expression of Seneca's, which is the very life and soul of Pelagianism; he says,† "There is one good thing, which is the cause and security of a blessed life, and that is, to trust to one's self." Pantænus and Clemens of Alexandria were both addicted to the stoic philosophy, which led the latter especially to say many things which seem to favour free will. Origen greedily sucked it in, in the school of Alexandria, where the Christian religion received its first taint, or began to be corrupted; and this paved the way for the reception of the positions of Pelagius, when he published them in the world.

XIII. And lastly, it is objected,‡ "that our notions of liberty are contrary to the sense, and repugnant to the common reason of mankind, as will be evident by the rules laid down by them, who were guided only by the light of nature." To which I answer, our case is very hard indeed, for if we seem to agree with the stoics, who were governed only by the light of nature, we are reproached with holding a stoical fate, and charged with the absurdities of it. If we differ from them, we are cried out against as maintaining notions contrary to the sense and repugnant to the common reason of mankind; for, I observe, that the authors this writer refers to, by whom the rules were laid down he produces, were all, excepting Aristotle, of the stoic sect, or inclined to it. And as for the rules themselves; as, "that a lawgiver must act absurdly to command what is impossible; that vice and virtue are in our own power, and are voluntary, otherwise not worthy of praise or dispraise, reward or punishment; that it is no fault not to do that which we have no power to do; that what is natural to all men, cannot be evil; and that there can be no deliberation or consultation about things which are not in our power;" I say, as to these rules laid down, and which are objected to us, I have already considered them, and replied to them, so far as they concern the argument before us. What now remains is only to subjoin some arguments, proving that liberty does not consist in an indifference to good and evil; and that it is consistent with some kind of necessity, and a determination to one, and a vindication of them.

I. God is a most free agent, and liberty in him is in its utmost perfection, and yet does not lie in an indifference to good and evil; he has no freedom to that which is evil; he cannot commit iniquity, he cannot lie, or deny himself; his will is determined only to that which is good; he can do no other; he is the author of all good, and of that only; and what he does, he does freely, and yet necessarily. It is said,§ that "this argument is vain, since he is in no state of trial, nor can he be tempted to do evil." I reply, neither is man in a state of trial, as has been before shown; he may be, indeed, and is tempted to do evil; and there is a propensity in his nature, nay, he is only determined to it before a principle of grace is wrought in him; which shows that the liberty of his will lies in a determination to one. Moreover, since God cannot be tempted to evil, nor is it possible that he should ever commit it, it follows, that true liberty does not consist in an indifference to good and evil.

II. The human nature of Christ, or the man Christ Jesus, who, as he was born without sin, and lived without it all his days on earth; so was impeccable, could not sin. He lay under some kind of necessity, from the purpose of God, the command of God, the covenant between God and him, as well as from the purity of his nature, to fulfil all righteousness; and yet he did it most freely and voluntarily: which proves that the liberty of man's will, in its greatest perfection, which is so in the man Christ Jesus, does not lie in equilibrio, in an indifference to good and evil, but is consistent with some kind of necessity, and with a determination to that which is good only. The objection to the former argument can have no force here, for though Christ was not in a state of trial, as men in common are not; yet he was liable to be tempted, and was tempted to evil, though he had no inclination to it, nor was it possible that he should be prevailed upon to commit it.

III. The good angels, holy and elect, who are confirmed in the state in which they are, and by the confirming grace of God are become impeccable, cannot sin, or fall from that happy state; yet perform their whole obedience to God, do his will and work cheerfully and willingly. The freedom of their wills is not lost, nor in the least curtailed by their impeccability, confirmed state, and determination to take that which is only good. To say, "There was a time when they were not confirmed in goodness, as now they are, and have lost that liberty ad utrumvis, they then had," ‖ is more that can be proved; since, for aught we know, they might be confirmed in goodness from the original of their creation; and the reason why they fell not when others of the same species of creatures did, might be because they were thus confirmed, and the rest left to the weakness and mutability of creatures. I have, indeed, in the first part of this work, allowed the good angels to have been in a state of probation, antecedent to their confirmation, which I am

---

* Vide Arrian. Epict. l. 1, c. 28, & 2, 10, & 4, 9.　† Unum bonum est, quod beatæ vitæ causa et firmamentum est, sibi fidere. Senec. ep. 31.　‡ Whitby, p. 334; ed. 2, 325.

§ Whitby, p. 308; ed. 2. 300.

‖ Whitby, p. 308; ed. 2. 300.

now tempted to retract; but since we know so little of angels, I choose to be in suspense about it. When it is urged,* that being thus confirmed, they are not in a state of trial; it must be replied, as before, nor is man. When it is said,† that they are not under any temptation to do evil, it is saying more than can be made good. But, suppose it true, as it is certain, that there is no propensity in them to sin, nor can they by any temptation be induced to it, it serves but to confirm what is contended for, that liberty does not consist in an indifference to good and evil. When it is further asserted,‡ that their actions are not now rewardable, it is nothing to the purpose, since this no ways affects the liberty of their actions; though I see not why their actions, which are taken notice of with commendation, may not be rewarded now by the grace of God.

IV. The devils and damned spirits have no inclination to, nor capacity of doing that which is good, but are wholly determined to that which is evil, and yet do all they do freely and voluntarily. It is true, they are not in a state of trial: no more are men. But to say,§ they are not subject to any farther punishment for the evil they do, is not consistent with the justice of God, and the dreadful expectation of the devils themselves, who are not as yet in full torment.

V. The liberty of the will of man, in every state he has been, is, or shall be in, lies not in an indifference to good and evil. In his state of innocence, as he was made after the image, and in the likeness of God, so the bias of his soul was only to that which is good, which he performed willingly, in obedience to the will of God. In his fallen state, he is averse to all that is spiritually good, and is a slave to his sinful lusts and pleasures, is wholly set upon them, and given up to them; and yet serves and obeys them with the utmost willingness and freedom. In his regenerate state, there is, indeed, an inclination both to good and evil; but this arises from two different principles in the regenerate man. The new man, or principle of grace, is inclined, bent, and determined to that which is good only; and yet freely serves *the law of God*. The old man, or corrupt nature, is inclined, bent, and determined to that which is evil only; and yet freely serves *the law of sin*. In the state of glorification, the saints will be impeccable, cannot sin, can only do that which is good; and yet what they do, or will do, is and will be done with the utmost freedom and liberty of their wills, whence it follows, that the liberty of man's will does not lie in an indifference or indetermination to good or evil; but is consistent both with some kind of necessity, and a determination to one.

VI. If liberty is not consistent with necessity in any sense, then it is not consistent with the decrees of God, nor even with the foreknowledge of God, from whence must follow some kind of necessity, not, indeed, a necessity of coaction or force upon the will of man, but of event; for if there is not a necessity of the things coming to pass, which are foreknown and decreed by God, then his foreknowledge is uncertain, and is but mere supposition and conjecture, and his decrees must be frustrable and precarious. It is said,‖ this "was of old the chief argument of the fatalists, espoused of late by Mr. Hobbes, and is still made the refuge of the predestinarians." Be it so; if the fatalists and Mr. Hobbes meant no more by necessity than we do, namely, a necessity of the immutability and unfrustrableness of God's foreknowledge and decrees, and not of coaction or force upon the will of man; we have no reason to be ashamed of the argument they made use of; and, instead of making it a refuge, or mere shift, shall think ourselves obliged to defend it, and abide by it.

CHAPTER VI

OF THE PERSEVERANCE OF THE SAINTS

I NOW proceed to consider the arguments taken from reason, against the doctrine of the saints' perseverance; to which will be added, those that proceed upon rational accounts, in favour of it; with a vindication of such as are excepted to. I shall begin with the arguments or objections against it. And,

I. It is objected,¶ that "this doctrine gives a great encouragement to those, who have once gotten an opinion that they are the children of God, to indulge themselves in the like iniquities (that is, such as Lot, David, Solomon, and Peter committed,) as being never able to *separate them from the love of God.*" To which may be replied, that though the sins committed by the persons mentioned, were of such a nature, that those who do the like, and die without repentance for them, and faith in the blood and sacrifice of Christ, *have no inheritance in the kingdom of God and Christ;* to which the law of Moses threatened death, without admission of any atonement by sacrifice, and the severest of God's judgments; yet the persons of these men being high in the favour of God, remained so, when these sins of theirs were abominable in his sight, displeasing to him, and resented by him. He *visited their transgression with a rod, and their iniquity with stripes; nevertheless* his *loving-kindness* he did *not utterly, not at all, take* from them, *nor suffer* his *faithfulness to fail.*** These instances of the falls of good men are not recorded to encourage men in sin, but to caution against it, and to set forth the free, unchangeable, and everlasting love of God, in pardoning and accepting his people, notwithstanding their aggravated transgressions, and so to encourage souls distressed with sin. What use such persons may make of this doctrine, to indulge themselves in sin, who

---

* Ibid.   † Ibid.   ‡ Ibid.   § Ibid.
‖ Whitby, p. 371; ed. 2. 362.

¶ Ibid, p. 487; ed. 2. 466.
** Psalm lxxxix. 32, 33.

have only gotten an *opinion* that they are the children of God, I know not; however, I am sure, that those who are the children of God by *faith*, or who have reason to believe, and do believe that they are so, or who have received the spirit of adoption, witnessing their sonship to them, under the influence of that Spirit, neither can nor will make any such use of it. Nothing has a greater tendency to promote holiness of heart and life, than the absolute promises of God, respecting grace and glory, the assurance of adoption, the certainty of perseverance to the end, and the sure enjoyment of eternal life: *and every man that hath this hope in him, purifieth himself, even as he is pure.** The force of the prohibitions of sin, of exhortations to avoid it, and of cautions to resist and flee from temptations to commit it, is not abated by this doctrine of the saints' perseverance; seeing these things are made use of by the Spirit of God with great energy and power, as means in order to the thing itself. How preposterous and irrational must it be in a man who thinks himself to be a child of God, and believes he shall persevere to the end, from this consideration to endulge himself in all manner of sin, as if resolving that he will persevere no longer!

II. It is said,† that "this doctrine lessens the force of all the motives offered in the Scripture, to engage us to persevere in righteousness and goodness, and *to have our fruit unto holiness, that the end may be eternal life.*" I answer; the doctrine of the perseverance of the saints, and the absolute promises of God concerning their everlasting safety and happiness, are so far from lessening the force of Scripture motives to righteousness, that they are made use of in Scripture to encourage the saints to the practice of them, and to engage them to continue in them. The apostles did not judge it irrational to argue from them to this purpose; nor did they think that hope and fear were excluded by them, when they reason after this manner: *Having therefore these promises, dearly beloved, let us cleanse ourselves from all filthiness of the flesh and spirit, perfecting holiness in the fear of God.‡* Should it be asked what promises these were; they were such as these: *I will dwell in them, and walk in them; and I will be their God, and they shall be my people; and I will be a father unto you, and ye shall be my sons and daughters, saith the Lord Almighty.§* So the apostle Peter, having asserted that the elect of God, and such as are begotten again through abundant mercy, are *kept by the power of God through faith unto salvation,* proceeds to exhort them to *gird up the loins of their mind, to be sober, and hope to the end;* and to *pass the time of their sojourning here in fear;* ‖ not once imagining that the force of these exhortations was lessened or weakened by the doctrine he had before advanced; or that this left no room for

hope and fear, and the proper exercise of them.

III. It is urged,¶ that "it seems not well consistent with the truth, righteousness, and holiness of God, to give an absolute promise of his favour, and the fruition of himself for ever, to any creature, though he fall into the sins forementioned." For God to give an absolute promise of his favour, and the fruition of himself for ever, can never be inconsistent with his truth, righteousness, and holiness. The seeming inconsistency lies in his giving such assurance to any of his creatures, though they fall into sin. That God has given an assurance of his everlasting favour and loving-kindness to his children, though they fall into sin, is certain. *If his children,* says he, *forsake my law, and walk not in my judgments, if they break my statutes, and keep not my commandments, then will I visit their transgressions with the rod, and their iniquity with stripes; nevertheless, my loving-kindness I will not take from him, nor suffer my faithfulness to fail. My covenant will I not break, nor alter the thing that is gone out of my lips.*** Though he sometimes chides his people in a providential way, and hides his face from them on account of their sins, yet *with everlasting kindness will* he *have mercy* on them. *The mountains shall depart, and the hills be removed, but* his *kindness shall not depart from* them, *neither shall the covenant of* his *peace be removed.*†† Nothing shall ever be *able to separate from the love of God which is in Christ Jesus our Lord.*‡‡ Nor is this at all inconsistent with the truth, righteousness, and holiness of God, since the same covenant which gives this assurance, and contains these absolute promises, not only provides fatherly chastisements for sin, but a full and complete Saviour from it; who, by the sacrifice of himself, has made such an entire satisfaction for it, that the purity and holiness of God, in the abhorrence of sin, the truth of his threatenings against it, and his strict justice and righteousness in the punishment of it, are perfectly reconciled to the everlasting standing of these persons in the love and favour of God. As for the promises and declarations of the Old and New Testament concerning this point, they have been taken notice of in the *two former parts* of this work; and what was the sense of the ancient writers upon this head, will be considered in another. I shall only add a few arguments in favour of this doctrine. And,

I. It seems not agreeable to the perfections and attributes of God, that he should take any into his love and favour, show grace and mercy to them, send his Son to die for them, and his Spirit to begin a good work in them, if any of them should fall short of eternal glory and happiness. It would be contrary to his immutability, should he cease to love those whom he once loved, withhold his grace from them, and show no more mercy to

---

* 1 John iii. 2, 3.   † Whitby, p. 488; ed. 2. 467.   ‡ 2 Cor. vii. 1.   § 2 Cor. vi. 16, 18. ‖ 1 Pet. i. 2, 3, 5, 13, 17.   ¶ Whitby, p. 488; ed. 2. 467.   ** Psal. lxxxix. 29–34. †† Isa. liv. 8, 10.   ‡‡ Rom viii. 38, 39.

them, let it be on what account soever: it would be contrary to his justice, to take satisfaction at the hands of his Son for their sins, and yet punish them eternally for them; and it would greatly reflect upon both his wisdom and power, to begin a work of grace upon the souls of any he does not go through with, and which does not spring up unto, and issue in eternal life.

II. That the saints should not persevere to the end, is not consistent with the purposes and counsels of God, which are absolute, unchangeable, and unfrustrable; for if God has chosen and appointed any unto salvation, and these should miscarry of it upon any account, he must be disappointed of his end; which disappointment must arise either from want of foresight of those things which obstruct the attaining of the end, or from want of power to accomplish it; neither of which is to be once thought of him, whose understanding is infinite, and who is the Lord God Almighty.

III. The defectibility, or total and final apostacy of the saints, is contrary to the promises of God, which are absolute, unconditional, and all yea, and amen, in Christ Jesus; for if God has promised, as he certainly has, that he will put his fear into the hearts of his people, that they shall not depart from him, that they shall hold on their way, be preserved blameless to the coming of the Lord, and be eternally saved; and yet some of them at last eternally perish; the reason must be, either because he could not, or because he would not fulfil his promises: to say he could not fulfil his promises, is to impeach his wisdom in making them, and his omnipotence in not being able to keep them; to say he would not make them good, is to reflect upon his truth and faithfulness.

IV. The glory of Father, Son, and Spirit, is greatly concerned in the final perseverance of the saints. Should any of them come short of eternal happiness, the glory of the Father in election, the Son in redemption, and of the Spirit in sanctification, would be entirely lost; for the purpose of God, according to election, would not stand; the price of Christ's blood would be paid and the purchase by it made in vain, and the work of grace upon the soul come to nothing; and consequently, Jehovah must be frustrated of his grand and ultimate end in choosing, redeeming, and sanctifying persons, even his own glory, which is not reasonable to suppose.

V. That the saints may totally and finally fall away from grace, is obstructive of the peace and comfort of believers, impairs their humble confidence in God, and fills them with continual fear and dread of falling from their happy state. To this last argument, many things are excepted; as,

1. In general,* that "the doctrine of the saints' apostacy truly teacheth, with the holy Scriptures, that a well-grounded peace

is the *fruit of righteousness;* that all true peace and comfort arise from the testimony of an upright conscience: that then only have we ground of confidence with God, when *our heart doth not condemn us* of wilfully departing from him; that we ought *to work out our salvation with fear and trembling, and to pass the time of our sojourning here in fear;* and that *happy is the man that feareth always,* with the fear of caution, which renders him more watchful against sin." To which I reply, that a well-grounded peace is, indeed, the fruit of righteousness; but not of our own, which is polluted and imperfect, but of Christ's; for, *being justified by faith* in his righteousness, which for ever secures from all condemnation, *we have peace with God through our Lord Jesus Christ.*† True peace and comfort do not arise from the testimony of conscience, which, being thought to be upright, speaks a false peace; but from the blood of Christ, by which *the heart* * is *sprinkled from an evil conscience,* and though *then have we confidence towards God when our hearts do not condemn us;* yet our confidence in him does not arise from the non-condemnation of our hearts, but from the freedom from condemnation which we apprehend we have through the blood, righteousness, and sacrifice of the Son of God. The fear which the Scriptures referred to speak of, is not a fear and dread of falling from a state of grace, and into hell-fire and everlasting damnation; but a holy, filial, reverential fear of the Divine Majesty, which is consistent with an humble dependence upon him, strong confidence in him, full assurance of his favour, and of final perseverance in grace.

2. It is objected§ more particularly, that "a doctrine is not therefore true, because it is comfortable, if it be liable to just exceptions on other accounts; for very comfortable was the doctrine of the rabbins to the Jews; of Simon Magus, and the Valentinians, to their followers; and of Antinomians and other Solifidians to men of carnal minds; but very opposite to and destructive of *the doctrine which is according to godliness.*" I reply, As to the doctrine of the Jewish rabbins, Simon Magus, and the Valentinians, I have nothing to say in the defence of; but as to those who are reproachfully called Antinomians and Solifidians, who, with the apostle, assert,‖ that *a man is justified by faith without the deeds of the law;* I know of no doctrines they hold which are opposite to and destructive of that which is *according to godliness.* However, let it be observed, that our argument does not proceed upon the comfortableness of the doctrine we plead for, but upon the uncomfortableness of the opposite to it; for though a doctrine may not be true, which is seemingly comfortable to a carnal mind; yet that doctrine is certainly not true, which is really uncomfortable to a sanctified heart, or which manifestly breaks in upon the true peace and comfort

* Whitby, p. 482; ed. 2. 461. † Rom. v. 1. ‡ Heb. x. 22. § Whitby, p. 483; ed. 2. 462. ‖ Rom. iii. 28.

of a believer, as the doctrine of the saints' falling away from grace evidently does.

3. It is said,* that "a possibility of falling into a very great evil, though it be such an one into which I see daily others fall, and to which I may be óbnoxious, creates no trouble or anxiety to any man, provided he knows he cannot fall into it, unless he will and chooseth so to do : and unless he acts contrary to all the rules of reason and discretion, and the strongest motives and sufficient means vouchsafed to avoid it." I answer: that if the evil is of such a nature, as threatens at once an entire deprivation of the grace of God, and a total and final apostacy from him, of which there is a possibility of a man's falling into, which he sees others fall into, and he himself is obnoxious to; it must needs create great trouble and anxiety in one sensible of the weakness of human nature, the strength of temptation, and the insufficiency of moral suasion ; if his preservation from it depends upon his own fickle and mutable will, and the power of it, and his conformity to the rules of reason and discretion, under the influence of that ; notwithstanding all the motives and means vouchsafed to avoid it; whereas, on the other hand, though there is a possibility of falling into such an evil, through the corruption of nature, and the temptation of Satan ; yet if preservation from it is secured by the power of God, which is promised to be engaged, and is engaged for that purpose, it creates no trouble and anxiety ; though it puts a man upon the diligent use of those means, which, by the will of God, are signified to him, and which the power of God makes use of to that end.

4. It is observed, that this doctrine of the impossibility of saints falling finally from grace, cannot be truly comfortable, for two signal reasons.†

(1.) "Because though it seems comfortable to a man, who thinks himself a good Christian, to believe he ever shall continue so ; yet the reverse of this doctrine is as uncomfortable, namely, that he who does not so continue to the end, let him have been never so fruitful in the works of righteousness, or in the labour of love, or in religious duties, or in a zeal for God and goodness, was never better than an hypocrite." To which may be replied, it is certain that such who have made a profession of religion, and drop it, and do not continue to the end, appear to be hypocrites, formal professors, and such who never received the grace of God in truth ; yet it will not be easy to prove that ever any, fruitful in the works of righteousness, which I think a man cannot be without the grace of God, did not continue to the end, or ever proved an hypocrite ; nor has such an one who acts from an internal principle of grace, any reason to doubt either of his sincerity or of his continuance in the way of righteousness ; for though he cannot prove the truth of his faith by better works than an hypocrite may do in show, yet he is conscious to himself of inward principles of love to God, and regard to his glory, from whence he acts which an hypocrite is an utter stranger to. It is, indeed, uncomfortable for a man to doubt either of his sincerity, or of his continuance in the way of righteousness, and a true believer may be left to doubt of both, and yet his final perseverance be certain ; which does not depend upon his frames, but the power of God, the consideration of which may yield him relief and comfort, when the contrary doctrine must be distressing.

(2.) "Let men hold what doctrines they please, yet, as it is with them who question providence and a future judgment, their impious persuasions cannot remove their fears, arising from the dictates of a natural conscience ; so neither can men's theological persuasions remove the fears and doubtings, which do as naturally arise from the dictates of a conscience "enlightened by the word of God." We are obliged to this writer, for the kind and good-natured comparison he makes between us and the disputers of providence and a future judgment; between their impious persuasions concerning these things, and our theological ones, as he calls them, about the doctrine of perseverance ; and between their fears arising from the dictates of a natural conscience, and those of others, arising from the dictates of an enlightened one. Though it should be observed, that the doubts and fears of believers concerning falling from grace, do not arise from the dictates of a conscience enlightened by the word, but rather from a conscience darkened by sin, and loaded with the guilt of it, upon which a wrong judgment is formed of their state and condition.· A believer may fall into sin, and conscience may pronounce him guilty of it, and condemn him for it, whereby his peace may be broken, and his comfort lost ; which are restored, not by sincere repentance, removing the guilt, as is intimated ; but by application of the blood of Christ, which speaks peace, yields comfort, and encourages confidence in God, notwithstanding all the condemnations of his heart and conscience. It is in this way he only desires to have peace and comfort ; nor does the word of God deny it him this way, but gives it and receives it, though his heart cannot afford it, but suggests the contrary ; *for if our heart condemn us ; God is greater than our heart, and knows all things.*‡ And though a believer may lose the comfort of the divine favour, when his interest in it remains firm and inviolable : yet his loss of comfort does not necessarily cut off his assurance of being a child of God, and of his perseverance to the end ; nor has he any reason, upon every fall into sin and condemnation of conscience for it, to suspect his fall from grace, and the truth of his sincerity ; nor does this doctrine of perseverance make men less care-

* Whitby, p. 483, 484 ; ed. 2. 462, 463.
† Whitby, p. 483, 484 ; ed. 2. 462, 463.
‡ 1 John iii. 20.

ful, but more so, to avoid all wilful violations of the law; nor less speedy, but more so, in their application to the blood of Christ, for pardon and cleansing, in the exercise of faith and repentance, and in the performance of every religious duty; since these are means of their holding out and persevering to the end.

CHAPTER VII

OF THE PRESCIENCE AND PROVIDENCE OF GOD

In the controversy between the Calvinists and Arminians, concerning the decrees of election and reprobation, the freedom of man's will, and the speciality of God's grace, it is observed by the former, that many of the arguments of the latter seem as strongly to conclude against God's foreknowledge of future contingencies, as against his absolute decrees; that what is said in favour of the freedom of men's wills, and against the determination of them by a divine influence, weakens the providence of God; and that the case of the heathens being left without a revelation, cannot well be reconciled to the doctrines of universal grace and general redemption. The learned writer attended to, proposes, in his *sixth Discourse*, and answer to these three objections, which he easily saw lay against the doctrines he had asserted in his former discourses, and the arguments by which he endeavoured to confirm them, which I shall consider and reply to in this and the following chapter. And,

I. It must be, and is generally allowed, that God had, from eternity, a prescience or foreknowledge of all future events; of all future contingencies, even of the free actions of men's wills; of every thing that should be done in time, to the end of the world, and to all eternity. He foreknew what all men would do, or would not do; who would believe and repent, and who would not; and who would perish, and who would be eternally saved: which foreknowledge is not conjectural, uncertain, and precarious, but is real, certain, and infallible; whence it must follow, that whatsoever arguments are advanced upon the attributes of God, his wisdom, justice, holiness, truth, sincerity, goodness, and mercy, or upon the methods and dealings of God with the sons of men, against the absolute decrees of God, are as much opposed unto, and lie as strongly against, the foreknowledge of God; since that as much requires the certainty, and secures the infallibility, of the event, as his absolute decrees do; otherwise his foreknowledge would not be knowledge, but conjecture. The answer to this is,[*]

1. "That though this argument be offered in favour of the decrees of absolute election and reprobation, yet doth it plainly overthrow them, or render them superfluous; for be it, that these decrees were made from eternity; yet seeing that God's foreknowledge of the events of all men was also from eternity, must he not know what was the condition of all men when he made these decrees? And what need then would there be of a decree for that event, which was infallible by virtue of his foreknowledge, without that decree?" To which I reply, that the foreknowledge of God is so far from overthrowing or rendering superfluous the decrees of God, that the decrees of God are the foundation of his foreknowledge of future events; for he foresees and foreknows all things that come to pass in himself, in his own will, and the decrees of it. The reason why God decrees this or the other thing, is not because he foreknew they would be, whether he decreed them or not; but he foreknew they would be, because he decreed they should be. God foreknows all things possible in his own power, and all things future in his own will, and the determinations of it; he willed things, and then knew what he willed; though there is neither first nor last in God, yet we are obliged to consider one thing after another. God's decrees are not to be conceived of without his knowledge, nor his knowledge without his decrees; wherefore it follows, that God's foreknowledge does not avert or render his decrees superfluous, nor do his decrees destroy his foreknowledge, or render that insignificant; of the two, the latter might rather be supposed, though it ought not by any means, since God's foreknowledge of future events necessarily arises from himself, his will, and the decrees of it, and are strictly, closely, and inseparably connected with them.

2. It is said,[†] that "this argument is obnoxious to these dreadful consequences, that it plainly renders God the author of sin; and prescience thus stated must be attended with a fatal necessity." To which may be replied, that the foreknowledge of God can never reasonably be thought to make him the author of sin, when even the decrees of God, respecting sinful actions, from whence his foreknowledge of sin arises, and upon which it is founded, do not make him so. God determined the selling of Joseph into Egypt, the betraying of Christ by Judas, and the crucifixion of him by the Jews, and yet was the author of neither of them. Nay, should it be allowed what is suggested,[‡] that "to say God only doth foresee things future, because he hath decreed they should be so, is to say God moves and predetermines the wills of men to those things which are evil;" though I think the difference is very wide between God's decrees of future events, within himself from eternity, and his motions and predeterminations of the wills of men to any actions in time. But supposing such motions and determinations of the wills of men to that which is evil, since he moved David to number the people, and put it into the hearts of the kings of the earth *to fulfil his will, and to agree to give their kingdom to the beast;*[§] even these do not make God the author of sin; for the divine predetermination, motion, and providential concourse respecting men, do not at

* Whitby, p. 491; ed. 2. 407.
† Ibid. p. 492; ed. 2. 470, 471.
‡ Whitby, p. 492; ed. 2. 470, 471.
§ 2 Sam. xxiv. 1; Rev. xvii. 17.

all alter the liberty of the will; men, under them, feel no power or force upon them: they freely will, and voluntarily do what they do; of which not God, but they, are the authors. If, therefore, neither the predeterminations of the wills of men in time, nor the decrees of God from eternity, make him the author of sin, much less his foreknowledge. God foreknew that Adam would fall, as Christ did that Judas would betray him, for he told him of it beforehand; and yet God was no more the author of sin and fall of Adam, than Christ was of betraying by Judas; nor did either Adam or Judas feel any force or constraint from this foreknowledge, obliging them to sin; nor do they ever complain of it, or impute their sin and fall unto it. Prescience, thus stated, introduces no fatal necessity: it is, indeed, attended with a necessity of infallibility respecting the event; but not with a coactive necessity upon the wills of men, which are left hereby entirely free, and so they find themselves in the commission of every action; neither the decree of God, nor his foreknowledge, necessitate men, or oblige and compel them to do¹ the things decreed and foreknown; nevertheless, whatever is decreed and foreknown by God, is certainly, infallibly, and immutably brought to pass, according to his will.

3. It is urged,* "that if there were any strength in this argument, it would prove that we should not deny the liberty supposed in all the arguments used against these decrees, but rather, prescience itself; for if those two things were really inconsistent, and one of them must be denied, the introducing an absolute necessity of all our actions, which evidently destroys all religion and morality, would tend more, of the two, to the dishonour of God, than the denying him a foreknowledge." It is easy to observe, that this author was rather disposed to deny the foreknowledge of God, than to part with his favourite notion concerning the liberty of man's will lying in an indifference to good and evil, and as opposed to any sort of necessity. Socinians, upon this principle, have come into a denial of it; and the Arminians have shown a good inclination to it. Their champion, John Goodwin,† has roundly declared, that "there is no foreknowledge, properly so called, in God." This has been always the way of these men, that, if their notions would not comport with the being and perfections of God, they will shape God and his perfections agreeable to their notions. Though it may be a considerable difficulty to reconcile the prescience of God and the liberty of man's will, yet there is no need to deny either of them: not the natural liberty of the will; this would be to destroy the will itself, which liberty is no ways infringed either by the foreknowledge or decrees of God, though the moral liberty of the will, since the fall, without the grace of God, must

be denied; nor the prescience of God, which introduces no such necessity of our actions, which destroys religion and morality, or tends to the dishonour of God, since it puts no coactive necessity upon us, but leaves us free to the commission of our actions; for to deny this perfection of God, would be to deny God himself; and, one should think, if either of these must be denied, it would be more eligible to deny man what may be thought to belong to him, than to deny that which so evidently belongs to God.

4. It is observed,‡ "that if these decretalists may take sanctuary in the foreknowledge God hath of things future, the Hobbists and the fatalists may do the same; that the Hobbists do found their doctrine of necessity upon the ninth chapter to the Romans, and the fatalists upon the certainty of divine prescience and predictions; and that it was the fear of this, that the liberty of man's will could not be preserved, which made the Greeks embrace this impious doctrine, that God did not foreknow things future and contingent: whereas it is said from Le Blanc, that the truest resolution of this difficulty is, that prescience is not the cause that things are future; but their being future, is the cause they are foreseen." I reply; that if the sentiments of the Hobbists and fatalists were the same with those who are called decretalists, they might justly take, what this author styles, sanctuary in the foreknowledge of God; or, in other words, rightly make use of it in favour of their principles. But it has already been made to appear, that the opinions of these men do not agree with our doctrines concerning the decrees of God, and the liberty of man's will; nor have the same countenance from the prescience of God that ours have. Though Mr. Hobbs makes use of some passages in the ninth chapter to the Romans, it is to prove what cannot be proved by them, and which we deny, namely, "that God, the will and decrees of God, necessitate men to sin." So far as the *stoical* fate can be thought to agree with our doctrine concerning the decrees of God, they might rightly improve the doctrine of prescience in favour of it. Cicero denied the prescience of God, which the stoics, doubtless, had some notion of: though it does not appear, from the passage referred to in him, that they founded their doctrine of fate upon the certainty of it; but rather, as abundantly appears from their writings, upon the fixed and unalterable nature of things. Cicero is arguing against the definition his brother Quinctus had given of divination, that it was rerum fortuitarum presensio, a foresight or pre-apprehension of fortuitous events, after this manner:§ "Nothing, says he, is so contrary to reason and constancy, as fortune; that to me, it does not seem even to belong to God, to know what shall be by chance and fortune; for if he knows certainly, it will come to

---

* Whitby, p. 493; ed. 2. 471, 472.
† Redemption Redeemed, c. 3, s. 2, p. 29.
‡ Whitby, p. 493—495; ed. 2. 472—474.

§ Nihil est enim tam contrarium rationi et constatiæ, quam fortuna, &c. Cicero de Divinat. l. 2.

pass, and if it will certainly come to pass, there is no such thing as fortune; but there is fortune, therefore there is no foresight of fortuitous events; or if you deny that there is fortune, and say that all things which are, or shall be, were from all eternity fatally determined; change the definition of divination, which you said is a foresight of fortuitous events; for if nothing can be done, nothing happen, nothing come to pass, but was certain from all eternity should be in the fixed time, what fortune can there be? which being removed, what room is there for divination? which is said by you to be a foresight of fortuitous events." The Greeks, it seems, upon the same principle on which the Socinians and others since have proceeded, fearing lest the liberty of man's will could not be preserved, embraced this impious opinion, "that God did not foreknow things future and contingent;" whereas it is said with Origen, it must be owned, "not that God's prescience is the cause of things future, but that their being future is the cause of God's prescience, that they will be." And this, saith Le Blanc, is the truest resolution of this difficulty, "that prescience is not the cause that things are future; but their being future is the cause they are foreseen." Which, so far, is very right; but then what is it that gives these things their futurity? Nothing less than the will of God, and his decrees, from whence the foreknowledge of them arises. For, as it is the power of God that gives possibility to things possible, it is the will of God that gives futurity to things that shall be. Nothing that is in time can give futurity to things in eternity: for the futurity of things was from all eternity, or all things which are or shall be in time, were future from all eternity; which futurity could arise from nothing else but the will and decrees of God, which of things possible made them future. Now whatsoever God has determined shall come to pass, he certainly foreknows will come to pass; wherefore it is as absolutely necessary that whatsoever God foreknows will be, should be, as it is that what he has decreed shall come to pass, should. Hence it follows, that whatever arguments lie against the absolute decrees of God, lie against the prescience of God and the certainty of it.

5. It is further* observed, that "God's prescience hath no influence at all upon our actions." It is true, it has no casual influence upon the actions of men, nor lays any coactive necessity upon them to perform them, nor at all impairs the freedom of them; no more do the decrees of God. There is no need of the plain reasoning of Mr. Hobbes, or the more nice and subtile argumentation of Mr Baxter, to prove this. But then, though neither the foreknowledge of God, nor the decrees of God, have any casual influence upon the actions of men, nor do they lay any compulsive necessity

upon men, nor in the least impair the freedom of their actions; yet the latter are the cause of the futurity of such and such actions, and the reason of God's foreknowledge of them as future, and both lay a necessity of infallibility upon them with respect to the event; that is to say, make it necessary that the things determined and foreknown, should certainly come to pass, though every thing in its own way; necessary actions, necessarily; free actions, freely; and contingent ones, contingently; yet all certainly. Neither the decrees of God, nor the foreknowledge of God, put anything in men; nor is there that signal difference between them, as is suggested:† a difference there is between them, the one belonging to his understanding, the other to his will; and so the one can be no more deceived, than the other can be frustrated: but not as is intimated; the decrees of God are no more active and powerful, and lay no more a necessity on our actions, than his foreknowledge. The decrees of God, indeed, include both end and means; and God sees both in the determinations of his will. In the decree of election, God determines to give both grace and glory to the objects of it, and it is a preparation of both for them; but puts neither in them, or them into the possession of either of them; and God, in his infinite knowledge, sees the preparation of both in the determinations of his will, and foresees that both will be certainly bestowed upon them. In the decree of reprobation, God determines to deny both grace and glory to the objects of it; but then this decree is not active, or it does not put anything in man to render him deficient or sinful of necessity, but leaves him as it finds him; and God, in his infinite knowledge, sees this denial of both to them in the determinations of his will, and foresees and foreknows that neither of them will be bestowed upon them. Thus the decrees of God and his foreknowledge go hand in hand together, and exactly agree with each other.

6. It is said,‡ "that God's knowledge reaches not only τα μελλοντα, to *future contingencies;* but also τα δυνατα, *future possibilities;* namely, he knows that such things may be, though they never will be; that I might will and do, what I neither do nor will; and abstain from that I do not abstain from; and that I will this, when I might will the contrary." I reply; *future possibilities* I do not understand: whatsoever is *possible,* may be, and it may not be; but what is *future,* shall be, and so not barely possible, but certain. A future possibility seems to be a contradiction, as is the instance of one of these future possibilities, namely, "that he (God) knows that such things may be, though they never be?" For, how can he know they may be, though they never will be? when, if they never will be, he must know they never will be, and therefore cannot know that they may be. He knows whatever is possible for

* Whitby, p. 495; ed. 2. 474.
† Whitby. p. 496; ed. 2. 475.

‡ Ibid. p. 497; ed. 2. 476,

himself to do, that is, he knows what his power can do, as well as what his will determines to do, or shall be done : the former is called *possible*, the latter *future ;* and God's knowledge reaches to both : but then, every thing that is possible, is not future ; all that God knows might be accomplished by his power, he has not determined that it shall be : and whatsoever is future, ceases to be barely possible. God also knows what is possible for man to do, that he might will and do this, and abstain from that, when he does neither ; that is, he knows that he has a power to will, do, and abstain. These future possibilities, as they are called, which men may do, and may not do, are no other than future contingencies : which are so not with respect to God, but with respect to men ; for it cannot be said of God, that he knows that so it *may* be, that man may will or do this, or abstain from that, which he knows he never will do or abstain from ; or that so it may be, that he may not do what he knows he will do : for then those puzzling inquiries must be made, how can God certainly know I will do, what he sees I may not do ? or how can that be certainly known, which neither in itself, nor in its causes, hath any certain being, but may as well not be, or not be done, as be, or be done ?" Which brings this author,

7. To observe,* " that this argument only opposeth a great difficulty, arising from a mode of knowledge in God, of which we have no idea, against all the plain declarations of his revealed will, produced in great abundance, against the imaginary decrees which men have imposed upon God without just ground." To which I reply : that the mode of knowledge in God is such indeed, that we can have no adequate idea of, nor have we of God himself, of the modus of his being, subsistence, or any of his perfections ; but then the thing itself is certain, that God has a foreknowledge of future contingencies, as is evident from the word of God, which ascribes it to him : from the many predictions of contingent events in it ; from the infinite perfection of God, his complete happiness, and the immutability and infinity of his understanding ; and therefore we may be allowed to advance an argument upon it in this controversy, though we do not use it, and are far from using it, against the plain declarations of God's revealed will. In the *first Part* of this work, I have shown, that there are no declarations of God's revealed will against the decrees of election and reprobation, which are called imaginary ones ; and in the *second Part* of it, that there are many declarations and testimonies of Scripture in favour of them : so that they are not what men have imposed upon God, nor do they depend on a single argument founded upon the foreknowledge of God.

II. That the world is made by the power, and governed by the providence of God, none but Atheists and Epicures will deny. Now much of the providence of God lies in the government of men, in moving of their wills, and ordering of their actions, to bring about his great designs and his own glory. For, as he has made all things for himself, for his own glory, so he orders and disposes all things to answer to that end. *The Lord looketh from heaven, he beholdeth all the sons of men, from the place of his habitation, he looketh upon all the inhabitants of the earth, he fashioneth their hearts alike, he considereth all their works.*† And as he has made and fashioned the hearts of all men, it is as certain that the hearts of all men are under his government ; he can move, influence, and determine them to this and the other action at his pleasure, without offering any violence to them ; for not only *the king's heart,* but every other man's, *is in the hand of the Lord, as the rivers of water : he turneth it whithersoever he will.*‡ God has not made a creature that he cannot govern, or possessed man of a will that is independent of his own. If man was in such sense a free agent, or lord paramount of his own will, or had such an ἀυτεξουσιον, such a power over himself, as not to admit any divine motion, influence, or predetermination of his will, a very considerable branch of providence is lost, and God is shut out from having any concern in the most considerable affairs and events of this lower world ; or as the learned writer attended to has stated our objection,§ " this doctrine must weaken the providence of God ; for if he doth not order and effectually move the wills of men, he cannot compass the designs of providence." To which several answers are returned : as,

1. That‖ " this objection will receive the shorter answer, because it falls into this great absurdity," that " it makes God as much the author of all the evil, as of all the good that is done in the world." To which may be replied ; that the providence of God has for its object evil actions as well as good, or God's providential concourse attends sinful actions, though not as such, as well as good ; and that God orders and moves the wills of men to each, must be allowed ; since he moved David to number the people, and put it into the hearts of the kings " of the earth to fulfil his will, and give their kingdoms to the beast." But then this does not make him as much the author of all the evil as of all the good that is done in the world ; for God, when he moves and influences the wills of men to that which is good, puts his own grace and goodness into them, or stirs up and excites what he had put there before ; and not only his providential concourse attends and assists in the performance of the action as natural, but his grace is concerned in the goodness of it, and attends and assists in the performance of it as a good one ; *for it is God that worketh in us both to will and to do of his good pleasure ;* whereas when he moves the wills of men to evil actions, he puts no

* Whitby, p. 498 ; ed. 2. 477.
† Psalm xxxiii. 13, 15. ‡ Prov. xxi. 1.
§ Whitby, p 505 ; ed. 2. 483. ‖ Ibid. ; ed. 2. 484.

sinfulness into them, only leaves them to the sinfulness he finds, and moves the natural faculty of the will to these actions, not as sinful, but as natural; and his providential concourse only attends and assists in the performance of the action as natural, and is no ways concerned in the vitiosity of it: whence it follows, that since God puts no sinfulness in men, nor moves them to sinful actions as such, nor does his providential concourse assist in the performance of them as such, he cannot be at all, in any sense, the author of sin; as has been fully made to appear by that learned and excellent writer Theophilus Gale, in his *Court of the Gentiles*, Part 4, Book 3, *Of divine Predetermination;* which is well worth the reader's consulting.

2. The more particular answer is,* that "these things seem only necessary to accomplish all the designs of providence; that God hath a perfect prospect of the events of all actions, as well of those which proceed from the free-will of man, as of those w ich issue from natural causes;—that he hath infinite wisdom to direct these actions to their proper ends;—that he hath power to restrain from the execution of those purposes which would thwart the designs of his providence,—without laying any force or necessity upon the wills of men." To which I reply; that the things mentioned are necessary to accomplish the designs of providence will be allowed, but not that they are *only* so; for the perfect prospect or foresight which God has of all actions and their events, arises from the determinations of his will that they shall be; wherefore it is not proper that they should be left, nor are they left, to depend upon the will of man, whether they shall be, or shall not be. Hence it is necessary, that as God has the hearts of all men in his hands, and can turn them as he pleases, he should move, influence, and predetermine the wills of men to such and such actions; and that the concourse of his providence should attend the performance of them, which he has willed shall be, in order to accomplish his designs; which motions, influences, and predeterminations of God, may be, and are, without laying any compulsive necessity or force upon the wills of men, with respect either to good or evil actions. David, though moved to it, freely numbered the people; and the kings of the earth, though it was put into their hearts to give, yet did voluntarily give their kingdoms to the beast; so all good actions which men are moved and influenced to, and assisted in, by the grace of God, are yet freely and voluntarily performed.

3. It is said,† "though this argument from providence doth not concern us (the Arminians) in the least; yet it seems evidently to overthrow the contrary doctrine: for, what answer can they return to these inquiries?"

(1.) "Is it consistent with the justice of providence to wrap up all men's fate in that of Adam's?" I reply, it highly concerns all that have a regard to the doctrine of providence, that it is not in the least curtailed or weakened in any part or branch of it; which it seems to be, by exempting the actions which spring from the free will of man, from divine influx and predetermination; nor are we in any pain lest our doctrine should be overthrown by it; nor are we at a loss to return an answer to the enquiries made, and to this in the *first* place. For by the fate of all men, is either meant their state of happiness or misery in the other world to all eternity; and then it must be replied, that all men's fate is not wrapt up in Adam's; some being saved, as it is reasonable to suppose Adam is; and others lost, when he is not; or, by the fate of all men, is meant their passing under a sentence of condemnation in Adam, whereby they became liable to everlasting punishment. This can never be inconsistent with the justice of providence, that such who sinned in Adam should die in him. If it was consistent with the justice of providence, that if Adam had continued righteous, he having all human nature in him, his posterity would have partook of all the blessings and privileges arising from his continuance in such a state, it cannot be inconsistent with it, that all mankind being in him, both as their common root and parent, and as their federal head and representative, and so sinning in him, should be involved in all the miseries and consequences of his fall. If it was consistent with the justice of providence, to *visit the iniquities of the fathers upon the children, to the third and fourth generation of them that hate* the Lord; it cannot be inconsistent with it to visit the sin of Adam upon all his posterity, their *carnal minds being enmity against God.* As for Adam's repentance being made ours, as his sin is, and we be restored by it to the grace and favour of God, as we became the objects of his wrath by his sin; there is this reason lies against it, the justice of God; which was so far from admitting Adam's repentance to be satisfactory on the account of his posterity, that it would not admit of it as such upon his own account; wherefore God reveals his Son, and the satisfaction to law and justice he had provided in him, *the seed of the woman,* that *should bruise the serpent's head.*

(2.) "Is‡ it not one great part of providence, to give men laws for the direction of their actions, prescribing what he would have men do, and leave undone; and that under a promise of reward to the obedient, and a declaration, that he will certainly and severely punish the wilful and impenitent offender? Now, do not they destroy both the justice and wisdom of this providence, who introduce God, after the fall, giving laws positive and negative for the direction of his (man's) actions, with threats of the severest and most lasting punishments, if he neglect to do what is required, and to avoid what is forbidden; and that after his own decree of

---

withholding from him the assistance absolutely necessary to his doing the good required, or avoiding the forbidden evil?" I answer, that it is one great part of the wise and just providence of God, to give men laws for the direction of their actions, prescribing what he would have done, and left undone, is readily granted. Now, inasmuch as all laws, which are of a moral nature, and serve for the direction of human actions in things moral, were given to, and written upon the heart of man before his fall, when he had sufficient strength and power to keep them; the wisdom and justice of providence cannot in the least be injured, much less destroyed, by the continuance of them after the fall; though man has lost his power to obey them, and cannot obey them without the assistance of divine grace, which is absolutely necessary to his doing anything that is truly good; and though God withholds, having decreed to withhold that assistance of grace from some men, which he is not obliged to give; God's withholding, and his decree to withhold that assistance, being neither of them the cause of man's disability, but his own vitiosity: since the continuance of them is necessary to keep up the authority of the lawgiver, to assert his dominion over man, to declare his will, to show the vile nature of sin, and what satisfaction is requisite for it; to discover the impotency of man, without the grace of God; for the direction of such who have it in their walk and conversation; for the restraint of others under the influence of common providence; and for the declaration of his displeasure and indignation against sin, and his strict justice in punishing of it.

(3.) " It is consistent * with the justice of providence, to aggravate the sins of reprobates on this account, that they *knew their Lord's will, and did it not:* provided that knowledge rendered them no more able to do it than the most ignorant of men; or, to make it such an aggravation of the sins of Christians, that they are committed against greater light, and stronger motives to perform their duty, than ever was vouchsafed to the heathen world; if, after this, they of them who lie under God's decree of preterition, are as unable to perform that duty as the worst of heathens?" To this may be replied, that though the knowledge of the will of God does not give men power and ability to do it; yet it puts men in a better situation, and in a better capacity of doing it, than men wholly ignorant of it are; and it may be more reasonably expected, that such should be disposed to do it, be desirous of it, and implore that assistance which is necessary to it; and therefore, when, on the contrary, such persons *hate* the very *knowledge* they have, and *choose not the fear of the Lord,* but say, *depart from us, we desire not the knowledge of thy ways;* it can never be inconsistent with the justice of providence to aggra-

vate the sins of these men on this account. So the sins of men who enjoy the Gospel revelation, being committed against greater light and stronger motives to perform their duty, than ever were vouchsafed to the heathen world, must be an aggravation of them, notwithstanding their inability to perform it; since that inability does not arise from the decree of preterition, but from their own wickedness; though that any of them, who are truly Christians, lie under God's decree of preterition, or are as unable to perform their duty as the worst of heathens, is never said by any, and must be denied.

(4.) " Is it suitable † to the holiness of providence, or to that purity which is essential to the divine nature, and makes it necessary for him to bear a strong affection to, and to be highly pleased with, the holiness of all that are thus like unto him: and to reward them for it with the enjoyments of himself; notwithstanding, absolutely to decree not to afford, to the greatest part of them to whom he hath given his holy commandments, that aid which he sees absolutely necessary to enable them to be holy, and without which they lie under an absolute incapacity of being holy?" I answer, that holiness is essential to the divine nature, whence he necessarily bears a strong affection to, and is highly pleased with, the holiness of all that are like him, whom he blesses with the enjoyment of himself, is certain; but then, this is no contradiction to any decree of his not to afford his grace, which he is not obliged to give. Certain it is, that he could make all men holy if he would; and it is as certain, that he leaves some destitute of that grace which is absolutely necessary to enable them to be holy, and without which they cannot be so; now, if it is not unsuitable to the holiness of providence, to leave men destitute of that grace, which only can make them holy, it cannot be unsuitable to the holiness of providence to decree to leave them so.

(5.) " Is it reconcileable‡ to the goodness of providence, or to the kindness, philanthropy, the mercy, and compassion of our gracious God, in all his providential dispensations, so highly magnified in holy Scripture, to deal with men according to the tenor of these doctrines?" I reply, that the doctrines of absolute election and reprobation, which are here referred to, are entirely reconcileable to the goodness, kindness, mercy, and compassion of God, which abundantly appear in his saving, and determining to save, some of the sinful race of mankind, when he could, in strict justice, have damned them all, as he has the whole body of apostate angels; but since this has been largely considered in this *Part* already, under the head of *Reprobation,* I shall add no more; especially, since nothing new is offered in this inquiry.

(6.) " Doth it comport§ with the wisdom of providence, to promise or to threaten upon

---

* Whitby, p. 507, 508; ed. 2. 486.
† Ibid.

‡ Whitby, p. 510; ed. 2. 487.
§ Ibid. p. 509; ed. 2. 488.

impossible conditions, an impossible condition being, in true construction, none at all? how much less will it comport with the same wisdom, to tender the covenant of grace to all mankind, to whom the gospel is vouchsafed, upon conditions which the most part of them, before that covenant was established, were utterly unable to perform; and who, by God's decree of preterition, were inevitably left under that disability?" I answer that the covenant of works, which, I suppose, is referred to in the former part of this question, by what follows in the latter part of it, being made with man in his state of innocence, did not promise life, and threaten with death, upon an impossible condition, but upon one that was possible, and which man was then capable of performing; and therefore no ways incompatible with the wisdom of providence. And though man, by breaking this covenant, has lost his power of fulfilling the condition of it, perfect obedience; yet it entirely comports with the wisdom of providence, that he should be subject to the penalty of it, from which he can have no relief, but by the provision made in the covenant of grace; which covenant of grace is not a conditional one, as is suggested; nor is it tendered to any, much less to all mankind, to whom the gospel is vouchsafed, or to any left by God's decree of preterition, under the disability of the fall; but is a covenant made with Christ on the behalf of God's elect; is established in him, on better promises than conditional ones, depending on the power and will of man, being absolute and sure to all seed.

(7.) "On the other hand,* can it accord with the same wisdom of providence, to threaten the severest judgments to them, *if they repented not*, or if *they turned away from their righteousness*, or *fell away from their own steadfastness*, or *endured not to the end ;* whom he had absolutely decreed to give repentance to; and, *by continuance in well-doing*, to preserve them to a blessed immortality; or to caution them not to do so, or to inquire whether temptations had not prevailed upon them so to do, or bid them fear lest they should do so." I answer; that the threatenings, cautions, and exhortations referred to, will appear to accord perfectly with the wisdom of providence, when it is considered, that they are made to societies and bodies of men under a profession of religion, some of which were real, others nominal professors; some true believers, others hypocrites, men destitute of the grace of God; and, perhaps, with a particular view to the latter, were these things given out, to whom God had never decreed to give repentance and perseverance. Besides, allowing that these threats, cautions, and exhortations are made to such to whom he had decreed to give repentance and perseverance, they are to be considered as means leading on, and blessed, in order to the enjoyment

of what God had determined to give; and, therefore, it must accord with the wisdom of providence to make use of them.

(8.) "It is suitable† to the sincerity of his providential dispensations, of which his dealings with men, by his revealed will towards them, make so great a part, to move them to the performance of their duty only by motives, which he knows cannot work upon them, without that farther aid he, from eternity, hath determined to deny them?" I reply; that if, by performance of duty, is meant that men should convert themselves, repent of sin, and believe in Christ, to the saving of their souls, it will not be easy to prove that God makes use of any motives to move any persons to do these things of themselves; and still more difficult to prove, that he makes use of any to induce such persons thereunto to whom he does not give that grace which only can enable them to do them. If by performance of duty, is meant moral obedience to the law of God, this is every man's duty, whether he has any motives to it or not; and if God makes use of any motives to induce unto it, which, without his grace, do not, and cannot, work upon them, the insufficiency of them does not arise from any thing in the motives themselves, nor from the denial of God's grace, nor from his determination to deny it, but from the perverseness and wickedness of men's hearts; wherefore, it is not unsuitable to the sincerity of providence, to make use of such motives, though they do not, and he knows they cannot, influence without his grace, which he is not obliged to give, and which he has determined to deny; since thereby, the perverseness and wickedness of men are more fully discovered, and they left inexcusable. Besides, the instances referred to regard not all mankind, but the people of Israel, and God's dealings with them, not in relation to their spiritual and eternal welfare, but their civil and temporal estate, as a body politic, as has been shown in the *first Part* of this work.

(9.) "It is suitable‡ to the same wisdom and sincerity, to move such persons by promises, to repent and believe; and to require them, *having such promises*, to cleanse *themselves from all filthiness of flesh and spirit, perfecting holiness in the fear of God ?* What wit of man can show, how God can be serious in calling such men to faith and repentance, much less in his concern that they might do so, or in his trouble that they have not done so; and yet be serious and in good earnest in his antecedent decree to deny them that aid, without which they never can believe or repent?" To which may be replied, that God is serious in calling men to faith and repentance, and as serious in his decrees either to give or deny that grace, without which none can ever believe or repent, is certain; and it must be owned, it would appear unsuitable to his wisdom and sincerity,

---

* Ibid. p. 511; ed. 2. 489.

† Whitby, p. 511; ed. 2. 489.

‡ Ibid. p. 512; ed. 2. 490.

should he move such persons by promises, and call such to faith and repentance, to whom, by an antecedent decree, he had determined to deny that grace, without which they could never believe and repent: but, then, it remains to be proved, which I think, can never be proved, that God calls any persons, and moves them by promises to believe in Christ, to the saving of their souls, or to evangelical repentance, to whom he does not give grace to believe and repent, or such who are not eventually saved.

CHAPTER VIII

OF THE STATE AND CASE OF THE HEATHENS

IN favour of the doctrines of absolute election and reprobation, particular redemption, and special grace in conversion, we observe, that, for many ages, God suffered the heathen world to walk in their own ways, leaving them without a revelation of his mind and will, without the gospel, and means of grace; and which has been, and still is, the case of multitudes to this day. This it cannot reasonably be thought he would have done, had it been according to the counsel of his will that all the individuals of mankind should be saved, and come to the knowledge of the truth; or had Christ died for and redeemed them all; or was it the will of God to bestow on all men sufficient grace, whereby they may be saved. Nor can it be thought that God deals more severely with men, according to the above doctrines, than he seems to have done with the heathen world in this respect: particularly, in favour of God's decrees, it is observed, that if God conveys his gospel to, and bestows the means of grace on some people, and not on others, when the one are no more worthy of it than the other, and so must arise from his free grace, sovereign pleasure, and the counsel of his will; why may not the decree of the end of bestowing salvation on some, and not on others, as well as the decree of the means of sending the gospel to some, and not to others, be thought to be equally free, absolute, and sovereign? And seeing it is in fact certain, that the greatest part of mankind have been always left destitute of the means of grace, we need not wonder why that God, who freely communicates the knowledge of himself by the gospel to some nations, denying it to others, should hold the same method with individuals that he doth with whole bodies: for the rejecting of whole nations by the lump, for so many ages, is much more unaccountable than the selecting of a few to be infallibly conducted to salvation, and leaving others in that state of disability in which they shall inevitably fail of it. Now to this it is replied:*

I. "That this objection doth by no means answer the chief arguments produced against these decrees, which are all taken from the inconsistency of them with the truth and sincerity of God's declarations, with his commands to repent, his exhortations and desires that they would, threats of ruin to them that do not, and with all the promises, motives, and encouragements to induce them into it." I observe, that this writer himself seems to be convinced, that this objection answers *some*, though not the *chief*, arguments produced against the absolute decrees of God. And as for those which are taken from the supposed inconsistency of them with the truth and sincerity of God, in his declarations, they have been replied to already, in this *Part*, under the article of *Reprobation*, to which the reader is referred, where it is made to appear, that there is no inconsistency between these decrees and the truth and sincerity of God in his declarations. It is much we should be called upon to show the like inconsistency, as is here pretended, between God's declarations touching the heathen world, and his dealings with them, when it is agreed, on both sides, he has made no declarations of his mind and will to them. This author goes on, and allows,† that there is a greater depth in the divine providence, and in his dispensations towards the sons of men, than we can fathom by our shallow reason; but then, it must be insolence in us to say, that God does not act, in the ordering of affairs in the world, according to the measures of true goodness, because we, who cannot dive into the reasons of his dispensations, cannot discern the footsteps of that goodness in all his various transactions towards men. To which I heartily agree; and it would have been well if this author, and others of the same cast with him, had carefully attended to such an observation, and contented themselves with such a view of things; which must have stopped their mouths from calumnating the goodness of God, on a supposition of his absolute decrees of election and reprobation. It is further observed,‡ "that what God hath plainly and frequently revealed concerning his goodness, ought firmly to be owned and believed, although we are not able to discern how the transactions of God in the world comport with our imperfect knowledge and weak notions of immense and boundless goodness." All very right. To which is added,§ that "seeing the revelations of this nature (of divine goodness) are so clear and copious, have we not reason to believe them, notwithstanding those little scruples which, from our fond ideas and imperfect notions of divine goodness, we do make against them?" But, pray, what are these plain and frequent, clear and copious, revelations of divine goodness? and what the things that are not so clearly revealed? why, we are told, that to apply these things to our subject,

1. "We know from Scripture, how dreadful for quality, how endless for duration, will be the punishment of every Christian who fails of the salvation tendered; but we know so little of the future state of heathens, that

---

* Whitby, p. 515; ed. 2. 493.
† Ibid. p. 516, 517; ed. 2. 494, 495.
‡ Ibid. p. 517; ed. 2. 495.
§ Ibid. p. 519; ed. 2. 496.

we are uncertain both as to the measure and duration of their punishment." Now not to take notice, that salvation is not tendered, and that a Christian, or one that truly deserves that name, cannot fail of it, or be liable to endless punishment; it is strange, that the dreadful punishment of any, and the endless duration of it, should be mentioned among the plain and frequent, clear and copious revelations of divine goodness, when it belongs to the plain and frequent, clear and copious revelations of divine goodness. Besides, though we know so little of the future state of heathens from the Scripture, yet we are not altogether at an uncertainty about either the measure or duration of their punishment; for as to the former, we are told,[*] that *it shall be more tolerable for Tyre and Sidon*, for the inhabitants of these places, who had not the advantage of Christ's ministry and miracles, *at the day of judgment, than for the* inhabitants of *Chorazin and Bethsaida*, who were favoured with them; and it is reasonable to conclude, that this will hold good of all men, without a divine revelation; and as to the latter, it is certain, when our Lord shall descend from heaven, he will *take vengeance on them that know not God*, the Gentiles, *and that obey not the gospel of our Lord Jesus Christ;* meaning such who have enjoyed, but have neglected and despised the means of grace; *who*, one as well as another, *shall be punished with everlasting destruction from the presence of the Lord, and the glory of his power.*[†] Moreover, whereas it is suggested, that Providence may put the heathens into a better state before their final doom, since God *overlooked the times of* their former *ignorance*,[‡] there being the like reason for his still overlooking them; it should be observed, that God's overlooking the times of heathen ignorance, was not an instance of his kindness and goodness, but of his disregard unto them: the meaning is, that he looked over them, took no notice of them, made no revelation to them, but left them in their blindness and ignorance, without giving them any helps, or sending them any persons to instruct and teach them.

2. It is said,[§] "We know that God hath made a tender of the covenant of grace, upon conditions of faith and repentance, to all that live under the Gospel dispensation; and that these decrees of absolute reprobation, and of denying the help necessary to the performing these conditions, are inconsistent with that tender: whereas we know of no such tender made to the heathen world; but rather, that they are still *strangers to the covenant of promise*," Eph. ii. 12. I answer; We know, indeed, from the Scriptures, that God has made a covenant of grace, which is a considerable instance of his divine philanthropy and goodness; but then, this covenant of grace is neither made with, nor tendered to all that live under the Gospel dispensation; it is only made with God's elect in Christ,

and that not upon conditions of faith and repentance; for these are blessings of grace secured for them in this covenant. Hence the decrees of absolute reprobation, and of denying the aid of grace to some persons, are not at all inconsistent with this covenant, and the promulgation of it in the Gospel. We also know of no such covenant made with, nor of any tender of it, nor of any publication of it to the heathen world; but rather, that all that are destitute of revelation, are *strangers to the covenant of promise*, Ephes. ii. 12, which passage likewise acquaints us, that such as are *without* the knowledge of *Christ*, and *God* in Christ, are *without hope;* and that such who live and die so, have no good ground of hope of eternal life and salvation; which plainly points out the state and case of the heathens, and leaves us at no great uncertainty about it: wherefore, we freely own, what is further alleged,[||] that,

3. "We know not any promises God hath made to them;" and we know as little of any promises, or tenders of promises, God has made to the reprobate part of mankind, either with or without conditions, or upon possible or impossible ones: as also, that,

4. "We know[¶] from Scripture that the heathens, who never had Christ preached to them, are not bound to believe in him." This is readily granted; and to it may be added, that they will not be condemned and punished for their unbelief, but for their sins committed against the law and light of nature. And though "we know from the same Scripture, that this is the command of God to all that have heard of Christ, *that they believe in the Son of God;*" yet we know that the faith enjoined and required is proportionate to the revelation that is made of Christ; for no man is bound to believe more than what is revealed. If evidence is given of Christ's being the Son of God, the Messiah and Saviour of the world, as was to the Jews, credit should be ·given thereunto; which the Jews should and could have given, though they could not believe unto salvation, without superior power and grace: if Christ is represented to any persons as a proper object of faith, trust, and confidence; it becomes such persons to believe in him, and rely upon him; and such are, by the grace of God, enabled so to do. If the Spirit of God reveals to a man his particular interest in the death of Christ, or that Christ died for him in particular, he ought to believe it. All which perfectly accords with the doctrine of particular redemption, and is no ways inconsistent with God's decrees of giving the necessary aid of his grace to some, to enable them to believe unto salvation, and of denying it to others.

5. It is added,[**] "We know that God sent his *prophets* and *messengers*, *apostles* and *evangelists*, to move the Jews unto repentance, and those Gentiles to whom the gospel was offered, to embrace it; and that under

* Matt. xi. 21, 22.   † 2 Thes. i. 8, 9.
‡ Acts xvii. 30.   § Whitby, p. 519; ed. 2.

497. || Whitby, p. 519: ed. 2. 497.
¶ Ibid. p. 520; ed. 2. 498.   ** Ibid.

both these dispensations, he established an order of men to call all men indifferently to repentance; but we know not that any thing was done towards those heathens to whom the Gospel never hath been preached, nor ever any messenger or prophet sent." Be it so, as it will be allowed, that proper persons were sent to move the Jews to repentance, and the Gentiles to embrace the Gospel, who were blessed to the conversion of God's elect, which lay among them both; and that nothing of this was ever done to the heathens, to whom the Gospel was never preached; for, indeed, how should any thing of this kind be done to them, this being their case? yet this is not at all inconsistent with God's decrees of election and reprobation, since it will be difficult, if not impossible, to prove that God ever called any person to evangelical repentance, to whom he has not given the grace of repentance; or that he calls all men indifferently to repentance, or any to whom he denies the grace of repentance. Though, admitting he does externally call such persons to repentance, this may be done to expose the vile nature of sin, declare man's duty, and leave him inexcusable, though he denies him, and has determined to deny him, grace to enable him to repent, which he is not obliged to give; all which is consistent with the truth, sincerity, and design of the call.

II. A *second* answer to this argument of ours is,* that "that this objection supposeth it to be the same thing to be without a gospel revelation, and to be without any means of grace at all; which supposition seems plainly contrary to the declaration of the holy Scripture, touching the heathen world." For,

1. As God plainly saith, even in respect to their justification, that *he is the God not of the Jews only, but also of the Gentiles,* Rom. iii. 29, and that *he is the same Lord, who is rich unto all that call upon him,* Rom. x. 12; so has he also, by St. Peter, taught, that *he is no respecter of persons; but that in every nation he that feareth God, and worketh righteousness, is accepted of him,* Acts x. 34, 35. "Whence it appears, that some of all nations, owning the true God, not only might, but actually did *fear God, and work righteousness;* and that God accepts men only because they do so: whence it follows, that those heathens who have at any time attained to the knowledge of the true God, may, in that state, perform those righteous actions which shall be acceptable in his sight." To which I reply; that unless the law and light of nature, by which men may have some knowledge of a divine Being, though they know not who he is, and of the difference between good and evil, and unless the motives from providential goodness to serve and glorify God can be thought to be means of grace, the heathen must be without any, who are destitute of the gospel revelation; and then to be without a gospel revelation, and without any means of grace at all, must

be the same thing; seeing the gospel revelation, the word, and ordinances, are the common and ordinary means of grace. It will not be denied, that God may make use of extraordinary means;† send an angel from heaven to acquaint men with the way of salvation by Jesus Christ, or by some other secret method, unknown to us; yet from the possibility of things to the certainty of them, we cannot argue: and though we would be far from judging of and determining the final state of such who are destitute of revelation; yet, according to the Scripture account of them, we cannot but conclude, that as such, and while such, they are without the means of grace, *being without Christ, aliens from the commonwealth of Israel, and strangers from the covenants of promise, having no hope, and without God in the world.* Nor do the Scriptures alleged prove that they have the means of grace, as will appear from a particular consideration of them. Not Rom. iii. 29, God was, indeed, equally the God of the Gentiles as of the Jews, as the God of nature and providence, being the common creator and preserver of them, and provider for them; but not as the God of grace, or in point of special grace and peculiar privileges, or before the gospel dispensation took place. Now, indeed, the middle wall of partition between Jew and Gentile is broken down; the gospel has been sent and preached to one as to another; and some of both have been brought to believe in Christ; and so God is the God of one as of the other, and stands no more distinguished by the God of *Israel.* And to this the apostle has respect in the place before us, when he puts the question, *Is he the God of the Jews only? is he not also of the Gentiles?* Which he answers in the affirmative, *Yes, of the Gentiles also.* The argument proving this, follows; *seeing it is one God which shall justify the circumcision by faith, and the uncircumcision through faith.* Whence it is manifest, that the apostle is not speaking of the justification of heathens, by their obedience to the law and light of nature, nor of them as heathens, or of God being their God, considered as such; but of their justification by faith in Christ; and so of them as believers, and of God being their God as such, equally with the believing Jews. Could it be proved, that God justifies the heathens by their obedience to the law and light of nature, as he justifies others by faith in the blood and righteousness of Christ, it would be much to the purpose; but since this text gives no such intimation, but the contrary, it must be impertinent to the present argument. Nor Rom. x. 12. There is, indeed, *no difference between the Jew and Greek,* under the Gospel dispensation, *for the same Lord over all,* who has made them, and has a sovereign dominion over them, *is rich,* in the distributions of his grace *unto all that call upon him,* be they Jews or Gentiles. And, for their encouragement, it is observed, ver.

---

* Whitby, p. 521, 522; ed. 2. 499, 500.

† Vide Curcellæus, p. 389; Limborch, p. 563.

13, that *whosoever shall call upon the name of the Lord shall be saved.* But then it is added, ver. 14, *How then shall they call on him in whom they have not believed? and how shall they believe in him of whom they have not heard? and how shall they hear without a preacher?* Which manifestly shows, that though the Lord plenteously distributes the riches of his grace to all that call upon him, without distinction of nations; yet to them only that call upon him aright, that is, in faith; of which faith the preaching and hearing the word are the ordinary means; *Faith cometh by hearing, and hearing by the word of God,* ver. 17.

Now the Gentiles being without these means, and so destitute of faith, cannot rightly call upon God, there being no true invocation of him without faith in him; it follows, that they are not only without the means of grace, whilst this is their case, but even without any hope or likelihood of enjoying the blessings of grace; since these, in the text, are limited to them that call upon the Lord, and that call upon him in faith. Nor Acts x. 34, 35. The character given of Cornelius is, indeed, very great, and no doubt, very just; when he is said to be *a devout man, and one that feareth God with all his house, which gave much alms to the people, and prayed to God alway,* ver. 2. Whose prayers and alms were greatly taken notice of, approved and accepted of God; for the angel said unto him, *Thy prayers and thine alms are come up for a memorial before God,* ver. 4; that is, they were grateful to him, and were remembered by him. But then, it is not so evident, that he was now in a state of heathenism, destitute of divine revelation, of that particularly which was made to the Jews, or destitute of faith in the Messiah, especially as to come, or in a state of unregeneracy. He was, indeed, of heathen extract; was now a Roman soldier, and his falling down at Peter's feet, and worshipping of him, ver. 25, may look like acting the part of an idolatrous heathen; when it was no other than an instance of civil respect, which Peter would not receive, lest the standers-by, or those that came with him, should think more was designed by it. It is moreover said, that Peter should *tell* him *words whereby he and all his house should be saved,* chap. xi. 14. Which may seem to intimate, as if he and his family were not in a state of salvation; which sense, though it would prove that heathens may do many things which are materially good, though they have not all the circumstances of a good action; yet, so far as they are good, may be taken notice of and regarded by God; so that on the account of them they may be saved from temporal ruin, as the Ninevites, upon their repentance, were; and enjoy temporal good, and their future punishment be lessened: but then, this sense would prove what is quite beside and contrary to the scheme of our author, namely, that persons in a state of heathenism, though they may be very devout and religious in their way, and do a great many good things; yet are not in a state of salvation. But I am inclined to think, that the meaning of them is this, that whereas Cornelius and his family were seeking after, and were very desirous of knowing the way of salvation, of which they had some knowledge from the writings of the Old Testament, upon Peter's coming to them, they should be more clearly led into it, and become thoroughly acquainted with the promised Messiah, by whom alone they could be saved; for that Cornelius and his family were *proselytes of the gate,* this writer himself owns;* since the same titles which belonged to the *proselytes of the gate* are given to them. It is evident that Cornelius attended to and complied with the rituals of the Jews, as appears from his observing the same hour of prayer with them, the *ninth hour,* ver. 30, compared with chap. iii. 1, and from his being *of good report among all the nation of the Jews,* ver. 22. He, no doubt, read the prophecies of the Old Testament, attended the synagogues of the Jews, believed in the Messiah to come;† so that his faith was of the same kind with the saints before the coming of Christ, and in this faith he did all the good works he did, which became acceptable to God through Christ; *for without faith it is impossible to please him.‡* And now *God is no respecter of persons,* he makes no difference between nation and nation, *but in every nation,* whether they be Jews or Gentiles, *he that feareth him,* which includes the whole of religion internal and external, and so faith in Christ, and from such a principle worketh *righteousness, is accepted with him;* though let it be observed, that notwithstanding God accepts of such who fear him, and work righteousness, without any regard to their being circumcised or uncircumcised, to their being of this or the other nation; yet their fear of him and working of righteousness, are not the ground of their acceptance; but are to be considered as descriptive of the persons who are accepted in Christ; for there is no acceptance of persons or services but in Christ the beloved. From the whole, it does not appear that heathens, as such, and while in that state, may and actually do fear God, in the true sense of that phrase, as it imports the whole of internal and external religion; to both which, in the truth of them, they are utter strangers, and consequently cannot, and do not *work righteousness,* or what deserves that name, or what springs from the principles of the fear of God, and

---

* Whitby, ibid. So Hammond in Acts x. 2.

† Falluntur enim vehementer, qui Cornelium arbitrantur, vera fide non fuisse præditum, quum εὐσεβὴς, et Deo tam gratas fuisse ipsius preces aperte dicatur. Hoc autem ipsi deerat ut cum venisse crederet, cui tanquam venturo credebat, licet carne incircumcisus.—Beza in Act. x. 4; vide etiam in ver. 35; & Piscator in Act. x. 4.

‡ Heb. xi. 6.

faith in him: and hence it follows not, that heathens may, in that state, perform those righteous actions which are acceptable in the sight of God; since what they perform, is not done in faith, nor directed to the glory of God; and especially in such sense, as that for the sake, and upon the account of them, their persons should be accepted, and they be everlastingly saved by him. For if the works of true believers, which spring from love, are done in faith, in obedience to the will of God, and with a view to his glory, cannot, and do not render their persons acceptable to God, nor procure their salvation, how should it be thought that the actions of heathens should do all this, were they even ten thousand times more and better than they are?

2. It is said * that "this (that the heathens are not without any means of grace at all) may be gathered from these words of St. Paul, *God, who in times past suffered all nations to walk in their own ways, nevertheless left not himself without witness, in that he did good, and gave us rain from heaven, and fruitful seasons, &c.* Acts xiv. 16, 17." I reply; that God's giving of rain and fruitful seasons to the heathens, and filling them with food and gladness, were indeed testimonies of his providence and goodness; in which respect he *left not himself without witness:* but then, though these were instances of providential goodness, yet not means of grace. It is true, that the works of creation were means of men's knowing that there is a God, and that he is to be worshipped; *so that* the heathens were *without excuse, because that when they knew God, they glorified him not as God, neither were thankful, but became vain in their imaginations, and their foolish heart was darkened:†* but then, these were not sufficient means of knowing who this God was, and in what manner he was to be worshipped. So that frequent instances of rain and fruitful seasons, and the daily supplies of food for the bodies of men, are proofs a divine Being, who is kind and good, and of a divine Providence, and lay men under obligation to be thankful, and to seek after God, and serve him; but are not means of grace, or of eternal life and salvation; for these very persons, to whom God gave rain and fruitful seasons, whose hearts he filled with food and gladness, he *suffered to walk in their own ways;* which unavoidably lead to ruin and destruction. What means of grace could these men have, who were thus entirely left of God, to do that which was right in their own eyes; though he did not leave himself without witness? How blind, ignorant, and superstitious were they, that, when they saw what the apostle Paul had done, cried out, *The gods are come down to us in the likeness of men?* and brought out their oxen and garlands, and would have done sacrifice; from which the apostle scarce restrained them by these say-

ings of his. What means of grace could these be supposed to have? when, as this author himself observes,‡ God "so far permitted this, as that he sent them no prophet to instruct them better, and gave them no positive revelation of his will, no written instructions of the way in which he would be worshipped, as he had done unto the Jews."

3. The same, it is observed, may be gathered§ "from those words of the same apostle; *God, that made the world, and all things in it—made all nations of one blood, and hath determined the times before appointed* (that is, the fixed seasons of the year,) *and the bounds of their habitations, that they might seek the Lord, if haply they might feel after him, and find him,* Acts xvii. 24, 26, 27. Whence we learn, that God made the world with this design, that men, by contemplation of the power, wisdom, and goodness, visible in the creation of it, might seek after the the author of it, and seeking, *find* him. That to *seek after God, in the Scripture-phrase,* is so to seek him out, that we may give him that worship which is due to him; and, to find him, is to obtain his grace and favour. That sinners cannot thus hope to seek or find God, unless they can expect to find him merciful in the pardon of those sins they confess and forsake, all which must depend on this foundation, that God is the maker of heaven and earth, and all that is therein; whence it follows, that men guided only by the light of nature, may so acceptably seek God, as to find him gracious and merciful towards them." To which may be replied, that the making of the world, and all things in it, with the suitable provisions for all creatures, is a glorious display of the power, wisdom, and goodness of God; and it will be allowed, that men, by the light of nature, may, as those Athenians might to whom the apostle speaks, so seek after God, and find that there is one, and such an one as *dwells not in temples made with hands, neither is worshipped with men's hands, as though he needed any thing; seeing he giveth to all life, and breath, and all things,* ver. 24, 25; which was sufficient to convince them of the gross idolatry they were guilty of; and that they ought not to think, as they did, that *the Godhead is like unto gold, or silver, or stone, graven by art, or man's device,* ver. 29. But then, it must be denied, that the heathens did, or could, by the light of nature, seek God acceptably, or so as to find him gracious and merciful unto them; for he is only sought acceptably, and found gracious and merciful, in Christ Jesus our Lord. And though propitiatory sacrifices did very early, and long, and generally, obtain among them; yet, as these were not taught them by the light of nature, but were either some broken, mangled traditions, which originally sprang from divine revelation, or satanical imitations of that kind of worship God had appointed; so they were performed in such a manner, as

---

* Whitby, p. 523; ed. 2. 500.   † Rom.
i. 20, 21.   ‡ Whitby, p. 523; ed. 2. 501.

§ Ibid. p. 524—526; ed. 2. 502—504.

abundantly declared the wretched barbarity, ignorance, and stupidity of the worshippers; nor was God ever acceptably sought in them, or even found to be propitious, gracious, and merciful through them. Besides, let it further be observed, that though the passage before us shows, that it is possible for men, by a contemplation of the power, wisdom, and goodness of God, visible in his works of creation and providence, so to seek after him and find him, as to know that there is a God who has made all these; to be convinced of the vanity and falsehood of all other gods, and to see the folly, wickedness, and weakness of idolatrous worship; yet, at the same time, it very strongly intimates to us, how dim and obscure the light of nature is; since those who have nothing else to direct them but that, are like persons in the dark, who *feel** and grope about after God, whom they cannot see; and after all their search and groping, there is only an *haply*, a peradventure, a maybe, that they find him. Add to this, that the times of heathenism are called in ver. 30, *times of ignorance which God winked at*, ὑπεριδών,† overlooked, disregarded, took no notice of, and gave them no means of spiritual light and knowledge. In short, these words, at most, only declare what is the end of man's creation, which is, to seek the Lord and glorify him; and not what man can do, or the heathens have done, by the mere light of nature; and are far from being a proof of their having any means of grace.

4. It is said,‡ that " this may be proved from those words, Heb. xi. 6, *He that cometh to God must believe that he is, and that he is a rewarder of them that diligently seek him.*" Where observe, that *to come to God*, is to serve him, throughout the tenor of the Scripture, and more especially in this epistle, where it signifies to come to his throne of grace by prayer, by the oblation of sacrifices, or by the performance of any other duty; yea, from the context it appears, that it is εὐαρεστῆσαι, *to do that which is pleasing* to him. That all men may so seek God, as to do what is well-pleasing to him, if they diligently endeavour so to do. That if they do so, they shall be rewarded by him. That the heathens may have grounds sufficient to believe, that they shall be rewarded for serving him diligently, according to the light which God had given them. The inference is, "that heathens may have faith in God, even that faith which is *the expectation of things hoped for*, and may encourage them to seek him diligently." I answer, It is strange that this passage of Scripture should be a proof of heathens having the means of grace, or of their being capable of seeking and serving God acceptably, and of their having faith in God, even that faith which in ver. 1 is said to be *the substance of things hoped for, the evidence of things not seen;* when the

apostle is only speaking of such a faith, as is founded upon the word of God, and of such persons only who were favoured with a divine revelation; of the patriarchs before and after the flood, the forefathers of the Jews; various instances of whose faith he produces, partly to prove the above definition of faith, and partly for the imitation, example, and encouragement of the Hebrews, to whom he writes; men who also enjoyed the oracles of God, had plenty of the means of grace, and were blessed with a gospel revelation. Besides, let it be observed, that since to come to God, as this author explains it from the context, is *to do that which is pleasing* to him; and since it appears from the former part of this text, that *without faith it is impossible*, εὐαρεστῆσαι, *to do that which is well-pleasing to God;* and from the words themselves, that believing is absolutely requisite to coming to him; not only that he exists, but that he is, in Christ, a God gracious and merciful, and *a rewarder*, in a way of grace, *of all them that diligently seek him* in his Son, in whom only he is to be so found. And since heathens are without any knowledge of him or faith in him, as such; for, *how shall they believe in him of whom they have not heard? and how shall they hear without a preacher?*§ It follows, that this passage of Scripture proves the reverse of what it is brought for; namely, that it is impossible for heathens to come to God aright, to serve him acceptably; or to do what is well-pleasing to him, because they are destitute of faith; and *whatsoever is not of faith, is sin.*‖ Moreover, there is no such thing as coming to God through Christ, he is the only way of access to God, for Jews and Gentiles; *for through him we both,¶* Jew and Gentile, *have an access by one Spirit unto the Father.* But since the heathens, destitute of divine revelation are *without Christ*, and the knowledge of him, as the way to the Father, they must be *without hope*, and *without God in the world,*** and know not how to come to him, nor can they come to him aright; nor indeed, are they capable of seeking and finding him as the God of grace, or as a God gracious and merciful: since he is only to be sought and found as such in Christ Jesus our Lord. It is true, indeed, that they may and should, by the light of nature, seek after God; and they may find him, as the God of nature, and should glorify him as such, yea, they may do many things materially good, which, though they may not be thoroughly well-pleasing to God; the circumstances of a good work being wanting in them, and also being without a Mediator to render them acceptable to God; yet may be so far approved of by him, as to avert temporal judgments from them, and to lessen their future punishment; so that the heathen world, according to our sentiments of them, is not, as is suggested,

---

* Ψηλαφάω, metaphorice, etiam accipitur pro perscrutari, sumpta translatione, a cœcis qui palpando viam quærunt, ut apud Polybium.—Scapula. Vide Hammond in loc.   † Vide Hammond in

‡ Whitby, p. 526, 527; ed. 2. 504, 505.
§ Rom. x. 14.   ‖ Rom. xiv. 23.   ¶ Eph. ii. 18.   ** Ver. 12.
loc.

exempted from all obligations to seek God, or deprived of any motive to do what appears, by the light of nature, to be the will of God. From the whole, it follows not that heathens may have *that* faith in God *which is the substance of things hoped for, and the evidence of things not seen;* for how should they who are *strangers from the covenant of promise* hope, look for, and expect those things of which they have no revelation, no promise, on which to ground their faith, hope, and expectations?

5. It is moreover said,* that "this may be further evident from those words: *The wrath of God is revealed from heaven against all ungodliness and unrighteousness of men, who hold the truth in unrighteousness.*"† Where observe, that the apostle is speaking of the heathen world, of ·the Gentiles, ver. 16, 23, 35. That this wrath of God was revealed from heaven *against* their *ungodliness,* that is, their impiety, in robbing God of his honour, and giving it to them which by nature were no gods; and in being ungrateful to him who was the author of their blessings; and against their *unrighteousness,* that is, the violation of the laws of justice, charity, and mercy, towards one another. That they did this against sufficient evidence and manifestation of the truth discovered to them, *holding the truth in unrighteousness.* That the great reason of *the wrath of God revealed against them,* was this, that they thus sinned against the knowledge and conscience of their duty. The inference is, "that all the acts of ungodliness and unrighteousness here mentioned (as things too commonly practised in the heathen world), were done against sufficient light and conviction, that they did these things against the natural light of their own consciences, and the knowledge of that duty which was due from them both to God and man." I reply; It is not so evident, that the apostle is speaking, either in the text or context, especially in ver. 16, of the heathen world, destitute of a divine revelation, where the apostle says, *I am not ashamed of the gospel of Christ, for it is the power of God unto salvation, to the Jew first, and also to the Greek.* In which words he intimates, that not only the gospel was now preached to Gentiles, as well as Jews, but that it was *the power of God,* or the power of God had accompanied it, to the conversion of some among the Gentiles, as well as of some among the Jews; and since *therein is the righteousness of God revealed from faith to faith,* he signifies that it became all such who were blessed with this revelation, who embraced this gospel, and made a profession of it, to live by faith; *as it is written, The just shall live by faith;* which faith is productive of good works; for otherwise *faith without works is dead:* wherefore, such who live wicked and ungodly lives, notwithstanding their profession of the gospel, may expect the vengeance of God; *for,* even under the gospel dispensation, *the wrath of God is revealed from heaven* in various awful instances

and examples, *against all ungodliness and unrighteousness of men;* sins against the first and second table of the law, which are no more countenanced under the evangelical than under the legal economy; and especially against the ungodliness and unrighteousness of such *who hold the truth* ἐν ἀδικίᾳ, *with unrighteousness;* that is, who hold and profess the word of truth, the gospel of our salvation, and yet live unrighteously in their conversations, or hinder the spreading of it by their ungodly lives. In this view of things, the words have no reference to the heathen world, as such; but to persons, whether Jews or Gentiles, enjoying the gospel revelation. It is true, the following part of the context seems to regard the Gentiles, as only having the light of nature, and their abuse of it: though Dr. Hammond understands the whole text of judaizing Christians, of the *Gnostics;* and indeed, the whole account well enough agrees with them, who not only had, in common with the Gentiles, the advantages of the light of nature, the works of creation and providence, to lead them to the knowledge of God, whereby they were left without excuse; but even boasted of superior knowledge to other Christians, from whence they had the name of *Gnostics;* and yet these men, who *professed themselves to be wise, became fools,* ran into the idolatry of the heathens, partook with them in their idol feasts, and particularly worshipped the images of Simon Magus and Helena, and were guilty of all the obscenities, impurities, unnatural lusts, and horrible wickedness, mentioned to the end of the chapter; the last words of which may be more properly true of them than of the heathen world: *who knowing the judgment of God, that they which commit such things are worthy of death, not only do the same, but have pleasure in them that do them.* But admitting that the heathen world, as such, is here spoken of, it will only prove what will be readily granted, that the heathens, by the visible works of creation, may know that there is a God, and the invisible perfections of Deity; that he, who is the Creator of all things, ought to be worshipped and adored, and not the creature; that they ought to acknowledge him as the author of their being and mercies; to glorify him on the account of them, and to be thankful to him for them; and should they do otherwise, are inexcusable, sins they must act against the natural light of their own consciences. But how does this prove them to have any means of grace, or means of obtaining eternal life and salvation? So far from it, that it proves, that men being left to the light of nature, even such as are of the highest form, *profess themselves* to be the σοφοὶ, the *wise* men of the world, sink into the greatest blindness and stupidity, fall into the grossest idolatries, become guilty of the vilest ingratitude, and commit the most abominable and unnatural iniquities that were ever heard of.

---

* Whitby, p. 527, 528, 530, ed. 2. 505—508.   † Rom. i. 18.

6. It is further urged,* that "this also seemeth evident from what the apostle hath declared touching the Gentiles, who had not the law, to wit, that God would judge them *according to their works*, Rom. ii. 6. And when the apostle adds, that *the Gentiles, which knew not the law of Moses, did by nature*, that is, by virtue of the law of nature, written in their hearts, *the things contained in the moral law;* he must insinuate, that they had the natural principles of good and evil discovered to them, by their own reason and discretion." To which may be replied; that what the apostle hath declared touching the Gentiles, that God would judge them according to their works, is not to be understood of his justification and acceptance of them on the account of their works, or of his rewarding them with eternal glory and happiness for the sake of them; for, *by the deeds of the law*, whether of nature, or of Moses, *there shall no flesh be justified in his sight;*† but of the righteous condemnation of them, according to their evil works, which, by the light of nature, they knew to be so, and ought to have avoided, as he himself explains it, ver. 12, *As many as have sinned without law, shall also perish without law;* which, surely, can never be thought to be a proof of their having means of grace; but rather the contrary. Indeed, it is true, that they did, by the mere light of nature, know the difference between good and evil in many cases; and, by the mere strength of nature did many things which had the appearance of moral goodness; but then, as their knowledge was very imperfect, and their strength but weakness, there were many things which should have been done, were left undone, and multitudes of sins are committed against the direct law and light of nature: so that they were far from being hereby in a state of justification and acceptance with God, and which occasioned great turmoils of conscience, and restlessness and disquietude of their thoughts within them; all which is largely expressed by the apostle, ver. 14, 15.

III. Having considered the arguments from Scripture in favour of the heathens having means of grace, we now proceed to consider such as are taken from reason. And,

1. It is observed,‡ that " it seemeth evident from reason, that if God should be worshipped, served, and obeyed by his rational creatures, he must have given them sufficient knowledge of that Being whom they are to serve, worship, and obey, and of those laws which he requires them to obey; and also must have given them abilities to do them, as far as he requires this to their acceptance, and motives sufficient to induce them thus to serve and to obey him." I answer; that whereas there is a God, and this God is to be served and obeyed, so he *has not left himself without witness* to the very heathens; he has given to them means of knowing his being and perfections. The things that are made are sufficient proofs of his eternal power and godhead; so that in this respect they are without excuse; nor are they altogether without the knowledge of those laws he requires them to obey; for though they are strangers to the instituted worship and positive laws of revealed religion, for the neglect of which they will not be condemned; yet not to the laws of natural religion: for though they have no written law in their hands to guide and direct them; yet they have the work of the law written on their hearts, to which their conscience bears witness, and their thoughts accuse or excuse, as they do good or evil works; and no doubt but they are able to do more than they do, in a way of natural obedience to these laws; nor are they without motives from the providential goodness of God, to induce them to a regard to them. We do not say the heathens want the means of knowing the natural duties owing to God and man; and so are far from destroying natural religion, or absolving the heathens from obligations to perform it; we say, indeed, that neither they, nor any others, without the grace of God, can *love the Lord their God with all their heart, and their neighbour as themselves*, which are the main parts of the law. But then it does not follow from hence, that these are no duties of natural religion, or that God does not require them, or that men are not under obligation to them, because through their own vitiosity they have lost their power to obey them as they ought. We also say, that those actions of the heathens which are materially good, are yet formally evil, because they are not done out of love to God as the principle, and to God's glory as the end; and indeed how should they do any thing out of love to God, and with a view to his glory, when they know him not? For though they have means of knowing the being and perfections of God, yet they know not who the true God is; but being left to the mere light of nature, fix upon that which is not God, to be so; and consequently can have no true love to the only true God, nor true faith in him, nor a true regard to his glory. And we say the same of the works and actions of all men in a state of nature, before conversion, who are destitute of love to God, and faith in Christ: and so says *the church* of which this author was a member, in her thirteenth article, " Works done before the grace of Christ, and the inspiration of his Spirit, are not pleasant to God, forasmuch as they spring not of faith in Jesus Christ, neither do they make men meet to receive grace, or (as the school-authors say) deserve grace of congruity; yea, rather, for that they are not done as God hath willed and commanded them to be done, we doubt not but that they have the nature of sin." But, after all, supposing that the heathens have sufficient means of knowing God, and the duties of natural religion, and that they do know God,

---

* Whitby, p. 530, 531; ed. 2. 508, 509.
† Rom. iii. 2.   ‡ Whitby, p. 531, 532;
ed. 2. 509, 510.   § Tit. iii. 5, 6.

and do perform the duties of natural religion, are these the means of grace, life, and salvation; when *it is not by works of righteousness*, works done according to a righteous law, and from a principle of grace and holiness, which we Christians, believers in Christ, have done after conversion, in the faith of Christ, from love to God, and a view to his glory, that we are saved; but *according to the mercy of God, by the washing of regeneration, and the renewing of the Holy Ghost, which he shed on us abundantly, through Jesus Christ our Saviour?*[*] To say no more, the argument may easily be retorted thus: It seemeth evident from reason, that if God had willed that all the individuals of human nature, and among the rest the heathens, should be saved through our Lord Jesus Christ, by whom alone we hope to be saved, there being no other way of salvation that we know of; I say, it seemeth evident from reason, that God would have given these persons the means of salvation, the means of knowing Christ, and salvation by him, and the knowledge of these things itself.

2. It is further argued,[†] " If God hath given to all men immortal souls, it seemeth plainly hence to follow, that he had put them some way in a capacity of being happy after death, and hath not left them under an inevitable necessity of being always miserable. For since, according to our Saviour's words, *it had been better for such men that they had not been born;* and, according to right reason, it is better not to be, than to be miserable; and seeing all such men must be subject to a necessity of being miserable, only by being born into the world, that is, by God's own action in giving them life, and infusing a spiritual soul into them; it follows, that either we must deny the immortality of the souls of these heathens, or allow, that they are placed by Divine Providence in a capacity of avoiding being ever miserable." I reply; That God hath given to all men, and so to the heathens, immortal souls, is certain; but from hence it follows not, that he has put, or is obliged to put them some way in a capacity of being ever happy; seeing he makes the angels immortal and immaterial spirits, those that fell from him, as well as those that stand; but he has not, nor is he obliged to put the former any way in a capacity of being ever happy; since they became sinful, and so miserable of themselves, and not by any act of his. So the heathens, to whom God has given immortal souls, of themselves, through their own sin, became miserable, or subject to misery, and not by being born into the world, or by God's own action of giving them life, and infusing an immortal soul into them: God's act of giving them being and life, and infusing an immortal soul into them, is a blessing; it is their own iniquity that subjects them to misery, or makes them miserable, and it can be no unrighteous thing with God to leave them so; nor is it more eligible not to be,

than to be so; our Lord does not say, *it had been better for such men, that they had not been born;* but *it had been good for that man, Judas, if he had not been born.*[‡] And this, as some think, was said according to the judgment of men, and as Judas himself would hereafter judge, and is designed to express the woefulness of his state and condition; though it is not said, *it had been good for him if he had not been,* but *if he had not been born;* that is, if he had been an abortive, had died in his mother's womb. It is not according to right reason, but according to an erroneous judgment, that "it is better not to be, than to be miserable;" for *to be* is something, and something good, though attended with misery; but, *not to be,* is nothing; and *non entis nulla affectio,* can have neither goodness nor bitterness, nor can be properly eligible or desirable. The reasoning, which follows, from the goodness of God in temporal things, to his concern for men's spiritual welfare, and from the law of nature and light of reason, implanted in them, hath been elsewhere considered.

3. It is urged,[§] that "it cannot be consistent with divine equity and goodness, to make that a condition of any man's happiness, which he cannot know to be his duty, or knowing, cannot do. Hence it is evident, that the knowledge of any revelation made to Jew or Christian, cannot be necessary to the happiness of heathens in general, much less the practice of any purely Christian duty; and therefore faith in Jesus Christ cannot be necessary to the salvation of as many of them as have never heard of him." I answer; that the heathens will not be condemned and punished for their ignorance of that revelation which was never vouchsafed to them, nor for the non-performance of and purely Christian duty, such as baptism any the Lord's supper; nor for not believing id Christ, of whom they have never heard, onln for those sins which they have committed against the law and light of nature; but inasmuch as they are without any true knowledge of the way of atonement for sin, and without any revelation from God of the method of salvation from it, they must be considered as destitute of the means of grace, and as far from true happiness and felicity.

4. When this author says,[||] " This I think certain, that God will only judge men at the last for sinning against the means he hath vouchsafed them to know, and to perform their duty, and only by that law which he hath given them. Hence it must follow, that those heathens to whom the law of nature only hath been given, can be judged only for the violations of that law."[↕] This will be readily allowed as agreeable to what the apostle says,[¶] *As many as have sinned without law, shall also perish without law.* But then, this observation is no proof of their having any means of grace; this leaves them without any, and discovers the equity and justice of God in their condemnation.

---

* Tit. iii. 5, 6.   † Whitby, p. 534; ed. 2. 512.   ‡ Matt. xxvi. 24.   § Whitby, p. 536; cd. 2. 514. || Ibid. p. 537; ed. 2. 514, 515.   ¶ Rom. ii. 12.

5. It is further observed,* that "God having laid down this method in the dispensation of his gifts, that *he who is faithful in the least* talent, shall have a suitable *reward;* and that *to him that hath,* so as to improve what he enjoys, *shall more be given,* and *vice versa;* we may hence rationally conclude, that he who diligently endeavours to do good, according to that light he hath received, shall find some tokens of the favour of God; and that if any farther aid be requisite to enable the heathens acceptably to perform their duty, the divine goodness will impart that also to them, by those secret dispensations of his providence which we are not acquainted with." To which may be replied; that the parable of the talents referred to, does not relate either to the gifts of nature, or of special grace; but to ministerial gifts, or such as qualify men for the preaching of the gospel, as has been shown in the *first Part*† of this work; and therefore cannot be of any service in the argument before us. What secret methods God may make use of to impart his grace to heathens, to afford them the aid that is requisite to perform their duty acceptably; to communicate his mercy to them, and apply the meritorious performances of Christ; are, indeed, secrets to us; and *secret things belong to the Lord our God, but those things which are revealed, belong to us and to our children.*‡ It is only according to the revelation God has made we are able to judge of things, and beyond that we cannot go; and according to that revelation, it appears that *Christ is the way, the truth, and the life;*§ the true way to eternal life; that *no man can come to the Father but by him;* that *there is salvation in no other;* that *there is none other name under heaven given among men,* Jews or Gentiles, *whereby we must be saved;*|| that the heathens, destitute of revelation, *know not God;*¶ are *without Christ, strangers to the covenants of promise, without hope and God in the world;*** and consequently, according to all the views of things we are capable of taking from hence, must be without any means of grace and salvation.

6. And lastly, it is said,†† that "we may reasonably conclude, God will deal with them, both with respect to the acceptation and reward of their good, and his displeasure against and punishment of their evil actions, according to the measures of their ignorance and knowledge, the abilities, motives, and inducements afforded to them to do or to avoid them; and that in these particulars. That their good actions, done upon less convictions, aids, and motives, may be more acceptable to God, than the like actions done by Christians, upon much stronger evidence, and better aids, and more powerful inducements to the same actions, according to John xx. 29, Luke vii. 9, Matt. xv. 28. That the heathens may expect a reward upon performance of less duty, according to Luke xii. 48. That God should be more ready to pardon and pass by their transgressions, because there must be in them the more of ignorance, and so the less of contempt, and so the more of that which renders them excusable, and the less of that which aggravates transgression. That God should be more patient and long-suffering towards them before he punisheth, because the less the light is they enjoy, the less is their offence against it. It is also reasonable to conceive, that God may be more gentle in the punishment of their iniquities, according to our Lord's own aphorism, Luke xii. 47." I answer; It cannot well be thought that the actions of heathens, which want the circumstances of a good work, such as love to God, faith in him, a view to his glory, and which have only the appearance of goodness in them, should, upon any consideration whatever, be more acceptable to God, than the actions of Christians done by the assistance of grace, in faith, from pure love to God, and with a single eye to his glory, and which are attended with, and are presented before God, through the sweet incense of Christ's mediation. There must be as much difference between these actions, in point of acceptance, as between the most fragrant flower in the garden, and the most stinking herb of the field. The words of our Lord, John xx. 29, do not compare Christians and heathens together, but Christians and Christians, and commend such who believe on Christ, without the sight of his person and miracles, before such who believed on him upon the sight of them. The centurion, Luke vii. 9, and the Syro-Phœnician woman, Matt. xv. 28, though they were of heathen extract, were not to be reckoned pure heathens, since they conversed among the Jews, and probably were Jewish proselytes, especially the former, and had heard of the Messiah, and were now, moreover, blessed with a gospel revelation, enjoyed the ministry, and saw the miracles of Christ; and, therefore, their actions, and the instances of their faith, are not pertinent to the present argument. The saying of Socrates this author mentions supposes a plurality of gods; and the expressions of Epictetus breathe out the pride and vanity, the affectation and stupidity, of a stoic. Nor have the heathens reason to expect a reward upon performance of less duty; for they have no reason to expect a reward, especially of eternal life, upon the performance of any duty, be it more or less, since the reward must be either of debt or of grace; if of debt, the expectation must be founded upon the performance of the duty itself, and the strict proportion between the duty and the reward; but between eternal life, and the best performances of men, there is no proportion at all, and consequently there is no reward due unto them, and there-

---

* Whitby, p. 539; ed. 2. 516.

† Sect. xxvi.   ‡ Deut. xxix. 29.

§ John xiv. 6. || Acts iv. 12.

¶ 1 Thess. iv. 5.   ** Eph. ii. 12.

†† Whitby, p. 540, &c.; ed. 2. 517, &c.

fore no just expectation can arise from hence; if it is of grace, and the expectation is founded on divine goodness, there must be some notification of it, a promise of eternal life must be given: but the heathens are *strangers to the covenants of promise ;** they have no such promise, and are incapable of having any, without a revelation, as this author himself observes ;† and therefore can have no well-grounded expectation of the reward of eternal life, upon the performance of any duty whatever; but are, as the apostle says,‡ *without hope, that is, of eternal life, which God, that cannot lie, promised before the world began.§* The words of our Lord, in Luke xii. 28, can be no foundation of expectation of reward to heathens, upon performance of less duty, since they know nothing of them; and did they, could be none at all, since they speak not of any reward to be given to men upon performance of more or less duty, only of what is required of men to whom much is committed.

To proceed: though the heathens have more of ignorance, and less of contempt, in their transgressions, than others who enjoy the light of the gospel, and so as their sins are not so aggravated, their punishment will not be so great, but that they may *reasonably expect*, that God should be more ready to pardon and pass by their transgressions, because of their ignorance, when they are not sensible of it, is not easy to be conceived of. Again, though the less the light is men enjoy, the less is their offence against it, and God may be more patient and long-suffering towards them before he punisheth; but that the heathens may expect he will be so on this account, is not very evident. There have been instances, indeed, of God's patience and long-suffering towards them; but that of God's waiting upon the old world, in the days of Noah, who was a preacher of righteousness to them, cannot well be thought to be an instance of God's forbearance of heathens, of men destitute of a divine revelation. It must be owned it is reasonable to conceive, that God may be more gentle and mild in the punishment of the iniquities of heathens, not only from Luke xii. 47, but from the express declaration of Christ,‖ that *it will be more tolerable for Tyre and Sidon, and for the land of Sodom, in the day of judgment, than for Chorazin, Bethsaida, and Capernaum, wherein most of his mighty works were done;* which brings me to the consideration of these words, and the inference said to be made from them. As to the sense and meaning of them, that has been considered already in the *first Part*¶ of this work, to which the reader is referred. The inference said** to be made from them is this, namely, "Hence it appears, that the means of salvation are not always applied to them, whom God foresaw would use them better." By whom this inference is made, I cannot

find, and am jealous, that it is not fairly represented as it was drawn; since these words, according to our sense of them, are not to be understood of God's prescience or foresight of what was certainly come to pass, if such means were vouchsafed; but of a probability and likelihood, according to a human view and judgment of things, that the miracles of Christ would have been more regarded by, and would have had a greater influence upon, the inhabitants of Tyre, Sidon, and Sodom, had they been wrought among them, than on the inhabitants of those cities where they were performed: however, this, I think, may be fairly inferred from them, that God vouchsafes the means of grace sometimes to persons who are not only unworthy of them, but to whom they are of none effect; when he denies them to others, who are no more unworthy of them, and who, in all probability, would show a greater regard unto them. Now, as his withholding them from the one, and giving them to the other, must spring alone from his sovereign pleasure, it shows, that it is not his will that every individual of human nature should be saved, and come to the knowledge of the truth, and therefore must lie strongly against the universal scheme. It is, moreover, said,†† that "in favour of these false interpretations, we add, that it would be an act of cruelty in God to have denied them those means, which he foresaw would have produced in them repentance unto salvation." Now it should be observed, that this is said not in favour of our interpretations, which this author says are false, but upon the false hypothesis‡‡ of our opponents. We do not say, that God foresaw that those means which he denied them would, had he granted them, have produced in them repentance unto salvation, or that God is cruel, when he denies the means of grace to some, and gives them to others; but this we say, and ask, upon the hypothesis of the Arminians, "that if God foresaw those means would have produced in them repentance unto salvation, was it not cruel in him to deny them those means?" This, I find, has been said, and asked by the Contra-Remonstrants, which, perhaps, our author refers to: their words are these ;§§ "If this ought to be so taken, that God must be supposed to have certainly foreknown that these Tyrians would have truly and really converted themselves, if the mighty works had been wrought among them, may it not be gathered from hence, that God is cruel and unmerciful, that he should withhold from such, and would not give unto them, the means necessary to that conversion, who would certainly have converted themselves?" But how can this agree with their (the Remonstrants') opinion, who, in favour of it, produce those words of the apostle, 1 Tim. ii. 4, *who will have all men to be saved, and come to the knowledge of the*

---

* Eph. ii. 12.   † Whitby, p. 538; ed. 2. 515.   ‡ Eph. ii. 12.   § Tit. i. 2.
‖ Matt. xi. 20—24.   ¶ Sect. xxiv.

** Whitby, p. 545; ed. 2. 523.
†† Whitby, p. 547; ed. 2. 524.   ‡‡ Vide Camero in loc.   §§ Col. Hag. art. iii. & iv. p. 241.

truth; especially when they say, that by the word *all,* every individual man, without exception, is to be understood? How could God will to save the Tyrians, from whom he withheld the means necessary to conversion, nor would he give them? From whence it is manifest, that the Arminians ought not to be so forward with their charges of cruelty and unmercifulness against our scheme, on the account either of God's decrees before time, or of the methods of his grace in time, when their own scheme is not free from them. Upon the whole, it appears, that God gives and denies his grace, affords and withholds the means of it, as he himself pleases; and as multitudes in all ages have been without the latter, there is much reason to believe they have been destitute of the former. I conclude, by observing what the church of England, in her eighteenth article, says, which our author was obliged to subscribe and swear to: "They also are to be had accursed that presume to say, that every man shall be saved by the law or sect which he professeth, so that he be diligent to frame his life according to that law and light of nature; for holy Scripture doth set out unto us only the name of Jesus Christ, whereby men must be saved."

The testimonies of the ancient writers in favour of the heathens, cited by this author, and their judgment of their case, will be considered in the *fourth* and *last Part* of this work; in which will be given the sense of the said writers before Austin, upon the points of election, redemption, efficacious grace, free will, and the final perseverance of the saints.

PART IV

INTRODUCTION

SINCE those doctrines which are commonly called Calvinistical are charged with *novelty,* and are represented as running directly contrary to the whole stream of antiquity, and the sentiments of the ancient fathers, and as entirely unknown to the Christian church before the time of Austin; when, on the other hand, the doctrines of the *universal scheme* are said to be confirmed by the concurrent suffrage of all antiquity, and the express and frequent declarations of the ancient fathers;[*] it is necessary that this affair should be inquired into and examined, whether it is matter of fact or no. And this will be the subject of this Fourth Part. But, before we enter upon it, let the following things be observed:

1. That the writings of the best of men, of the most early antiquity, and of the greatest learning and piety, cannot be admitted by us as the rule and standard of our faith. These, with us, are only the Scriptures of the Old and New Testament: to these we appeal, and by these only can we be determined. If therefore the oracles of God are on our side; if we have the concurrent suffrage and the frequent and express declarations of the holy prophets, of Christ and his apostles, we have the best and earliest antiquity for us, and are free, and far enough from the charge of novelty. It is of no great moment with us, what such who lived nearest to the times of the apostles say, unless what they say agrees with *their* words and doctrines. It would indeed be matter of concern to us, should no footsteps, no traces of the doctrines we contend for, appear in the works of the first Christian writers, and would oblige us to lament their early departure from the faith once delivered to the saints. And, indeed,

2. It is easy to observe, and he must be a stranger to antiquity and church history that does not know, how very early after the apostles' days, corruptions, both in doctrine and practice, were brought into the Christian church. For not to take notice of the heretics of those times, and the heresies broached by them, than which, never were more absurd notions, or more horrid and blasphemous doctrines maintained, which made Polycarp,[†] a disciple of the apostle John, frequently say, "Good God, to what times hast thou reserved me!" The purest writers of the first ages were not free from considerable mistakes and blemishes, and deviations from the word of God, and doctrines of the apostles; which having been taken notice of by many learned men, I forbear to repeat. Indeed we have scarce any thing remaining of what was written in the *first century,* and very little of what was written in the *second.* And besides, the writings of these and after-times have been so interpolated, and so many spurious pieces have been ascribed to the writers of those ages, that it has been difficult to know their true and real sentiments. Since the reformation, learned men have taken much pains to separate the spurious and interpolated, from their genuine works.

3. Though it will be readily owned, that the first Christian writers were men of great sobriety and simplicity, of exemplary lives and conversations, and who suffered much and bravely for the sake of the Christian religion, the verity of which they were thoroughly persuaded of; yet they do not appear to have very clear and distinct notions of the doctrines of it, at least are not very happy

---

[*] Whitby's Discourse, &c., p. 96, 198, 345. 489; ed. 2. 95, 193, 336, 468.

[†] Irenæi Epist. ad. Florin. apud Euseb. Eccl. Hist. l. 5, c. 20, p. 188.

in expressing their sentiments of them; for as many of them were men of considerable erudition in Gentile philosophy, they had a better faculty at demolishing the Pagan scheme, than in stating, explaining, and defending the Christian faith.

4. Whereas the times in which these men lived, may be truly called the infancy or youth of the Christian church, and which, as it grows older, may be thought to grow in spiritual light and knowledge, as it certainly will more so before the end of the world; so these writers with more propriety may be called the young men, than the fathers of the church: and, without any detraction from their real worth and value, they were but *children*, in comparison of some of our European divines, since the reformation. And indeed there is a good deal of reason why these should have a better understanding of the Scriptures, and be more acquainted with the doctrines of the gospel; since, besides the advantage of the writings before them, they also had better helps of understanding the Bible in its original languages: for most of the Latin writers knew nothing of the Greek tongue, neither Greek nor Latin writers understood the Hebrew; but a very few indeed. And above all, they had a larger measure of the spirit of wisdom and revelation in the knowledge of Christ: for, setting aside the apostolic age itself, which was favoured with an extraordinary measure of the gifts and graces of the Spirit, or the bringing forth and establishing the Christian religion in the world; there has been no age since, that has been blessed with so much spiritual and evangelical light as the times since the reformation; and it is to be hoped that it will increase yet more and more; though it must be owned, that of late a veil has been drawing over it, which God in his own time, will remove.

5. It may be further observed, that the pens of the first Christian writers were chiefly employed against Jews and Pagans, and such heretics who opposed the doctrine of the Trinity; and who either denied the proper deity or real humanity of Christ; and therefore it is not to be expected that they should treat of the doctrines now in debate among us, any otherwise than *per transitum*, or by the bye. Besides, the doctrines of grace had never been disputed, or made the subject of controversy: Satan as yet had not done playing his first game, which was to depreciate some one or other of the divine persons in the Trinity, which lasted three or four hundred years; and then he brought on a second, and that was to cry up the power of man, in opposition to the grace of God. Now since nothing of this kind was moved in the times of those early writers, it is not to be wondered at that they should write sparingly on such subjects; or, as Austin says,[*] should speak *securius*, "more securely," or should speak as Jerom[†] observes

of the writers before Arius, *innocenter et minus caute*, "innocently and less cautiously." His words are these; "You will say," writing to Ruffinus, "how is it that there are some things faulty in their books? If I should answer, that I do not know the reasons of those faults, I will not immediately judge them to be heretics; for it may be that they have simply erred, or wrote with another meaning; or their writings have been corrupted by little and little, by unskilful librarians; or verily before Arius, as a meridian devil, was born in Alexandria; they spoke some things 'innocently, and less cautiously,' which could not avoid the calumny of perverse men." And, for the same reason, it is no marvel, if, before the Pelagian controversy was moved, they dropped some things which were not so agreeable to the doctrines of special grace, or even to their own sentiments concerning them; since they had never been put upon the more strict examination and defence of these things, and so wrote without guard. This made Austin say,[‡] in answer to Prosper and Hilary, who moved to have the sense of former writers concerning predestination and grace, in order to stop the mouths of some cavillers; "What need is there to search into their works, who before this heresy arose, were under no necessity of troubling themselves to solve this difficult question; which without doubt they would have done, had they been obliged to answer to such things. Hence it is, that what they thought of the grace of God, they have briefly and transiently touched upon in some places of their writings, but dwelt on those things in which they disputed against other enemies of the church."

6. It is worthy of notice, and what serves greatly to show the general sense of the Christian church concerning these doctrines, that when Pelagius first broached his notions concerning grace and free will, they were looked upon as new and unheard of, and were condemned by several councils; by[§] one at Diospolis in Palestine, at which were fourteen bishops; by two at Carthage, in the last of which were sixty-seven bishops; and by another at Milevis in Africa, which consisted of sixty bishops. And in the first of these Pelagius recanted, and was obliged to subscribe the condemnation of his tenets, or else he had been anathematized. So that Austin was far from being the only person that rose up and opposed him. And indeed Pelagius for some time had very few, that either did or dared openly to espouse his notions. And as for Austin, he was so far from being alone in his sentiments, that it was well "known that not only the Roman and African churches, but all the sons of promise in all parts of the world, agreed with his doctrine, as in the whole of faith, so in the confession of grace;" as Prosper observes.||

I have only further to observe, that the

* Contr. Julian. l. 1, c. 2. † Adv. Ruffin.
Apol. 1, fol. 73, N tom. 2. ‡ De Prædest.
Sanct. l. 1, c. 14. § Vide Voss. Pelag. Hist.
l. 1, c. 40—43. || Epist. ad. Ruffin. p. 304.

testimonies produced in the following work, are taken from the writers before Austin. I have made no use of him, nor of Prosper and Fulgentius, his two boatswains, as Dr. Whitby * very wittily, no doubt, as he thought, calls them: nor have I taken any citations upon trust from others; but what is here presented to the reader, is the fruit of my own reading, care, and diligence. I say not this in an ostentatious way, but that the reader may more safely depend upon them. To all which I only add, that I have not attempted an *elegant* translation of these testimonies, but have as much as possible pursued a *literal* one, lest I should be thought to impose my own sense upon an author. Great allowance must be made those writers, on account of the age in which they lived, and the style in which they wrote: nor can it be expected they should write with exactness and accuracy, or express themselves as moderns do, upon points which had never been the subject of controversy. I do not pretend to reconcile all their different expressions, which may seem contradictions to themselves and to truth: what I propose, and have in view, is to make it appear that the Arminians have no great reason to boast of antiquity on their side; and I hope, on the perusal of the following sheet, sit will be allowed that this point is gained.

CHAPTER I

OF PREDESTINATION.

THAT the doctrine of absolute election and reprobation bears a contradiction to the sentiments of the ancient fathers, Dr. Whitby says,† is so evident, that Calvin, Beza, and many other patrons of it do partly confess it; and therefore he shall content himself with three or four demonstrations of this truth. As to the confessions of Calvin and Beza, the former only observes,‡ that the doctrine of election and reprobation, according to God's foreknowledge, has had *magnos authores,* "great authors," or abettors, in all ages; and the latter,§ that Origen led most of the Greek and Latin writers into that gross error, that the foresight of works is the cause of election. But these confessions, as they are called, are so far from granting that the doctrine of absolute election and reprobation contradicts the sentiments of all the ancient fathers, that they plainly suppose that *some* were for it. As for his three or four demonstrations, they are taken from several passages of the ancients, respecting the power of man's free will; from their exposition of the 8th and 9th chapters of the Epistle to the Romans, which will be considered hereafter, and from the testimonies of Vossius and Prosper. The words of Vossius, but not as the Doctor has rendered them, are these:‖ " The Greek fathers always, and those of the Latin fathers who lived before Austin,

are wont to say, that they were predestinated unto life, whom God foresaw would live piously and rightly; or as others say, whom he foresaw would believe and persevere." The Doctor ought to have transcribed what Vossius adds, which serves to explain their sense: "which," says he, "they so interpret, that predestination to glory may be said to be made according to prescience of faith and perseverance;" but they did not mean the prescience of those things which man would do from the strength of nature, but what he would do from the strength of grace, both preventing and subsequent. So that the consent of antiquity nothing helps the Pelagians, or Semipelagians, for they *both* believed that the cause of predestination is given on the part of man, according to all effects. But the Catholics owned that the first grace is bestowed freely, and not of merit. Wherefore neither did they think, that on the part of man is given "any cause of predestination unto preventing grace: yea, it is very probable that all, or most of them, when they make faith prior to election, yet do not consider faith as the cause of election properly so called; as if God, moved with the worthiness of faith, chose some to holiness and life." From whence it appears, that though they held predestination to glory, according to God's prescience of faith and perseverance, which prescience of faith and perseverance proceeds from God's absolute decree to give them both, in which sense none deny it; yet they make predestination to grace to be absolute, without any cause or condition on man's part; for otherwise grace must be given according to man's merits, which was the doctrine of Pelagius, condemned by the ancients, and something in man must be the cause of the divine will; whereas, as Aquinas¶ observes, " no man was ever of so unsound a judgment, as to say that merits are the cause of divine predestination with respect to the act of God predestinating." What is alleged from Prosper, is out of an epistle of his to Austin,** in which he observes to him, "that many of the servants of Christ, at Marseilles, thought that what Austin had wrote against the Pelagians, concerning the calling of the elect according to God's purpose, was contrary to the opinion of the fathers, and sense of the church; and that they defend their obstinacy by antiquity, affirming that what are brought out of the epistle of the apostle Paul to the Romans, to prove divine grace preventing the merits of the elect, were never so understood as they are now, by any ecclesiastical men. "This objection, how it may be removed," says he, " we pray that you would show, patiently bearing with our folly; namely, that they (the Massilians, and not Prosper, as the Doctor translates it, which spoils the ingenuous confession of Prosper the Doctor boasts of) having again perused

---

* Preface, p. 6; ed. 2. p. 3.   † Discourse, &c., p. 96; ed. 2. 95. Postscript, p. 557; ed. 2. 534.   ‡ Instit. l. 3, c. 22, s. 1.   § In Rom.

xi. 35.   ‖ Hist Pelag. l. 6, thes. 8, p. 538, 539.
¶ Sum. pur. 1, iu. 23, art. 5, concl. p. 77.
** Pages 879, 881, 886.

the opinions of almost all those that went before, concerting this matter, their judgment is found to be one and the same, by which they embraced the purpose and predestination of God according to prescience." The sum of which is, that some Frenchmen of Marseilles cavilled at Austin's doctrine, and pleaded antiquity on their side; having, as they said, perused *almost all*, not *all*, that went before them, and which they own did not please them. Austin's answer to this is cited already. And certain it is, that as his doctrines were then generally esteemed, except by these few Frenchmen, so he verily thought that the writers before him were of the same mind with him; for which purpose he cites* particularly Cyprian, Nazianzen, and Ambrose. But what was the sense of these, and other writers before him concerning this point, will be seen in the following *Sections*.

SECTION I

CLEMENS ROMANUS, A. D. 69

CLEMENT of Rome, lived in the times of the apostles, and is, by Clement of Alexandria,† called an apostle. He is thought by some‡ to be the same Clement the apostle Paul speaks of, in Phil. iv. 3, as one of his *fellow-labourers*. He wrote an epistle in the name of the church at Rome to the church at Corinth, about§ the year 69, which is the earliest piece of antiquity next to the writings of the apostles extant, being written when some of them were living, even before the apostle John wrote his Epistles, and the book of the Revelation, and while the temple at Jerusalem was yet standing. In this epistle are several things relating to the doctrine of election, and which greatly serve to confirm it. For,

1. Agreeable to the apostolic doctrine, that God *worketh all things after the council of his own will*,‖ that his purposes shall stand, and that whatsoever he has determined shall come to pass, Clement affirms, that¶ "when he wills, and as he wills, he does all things;" και ουδεν μη παρελθη των δεδογματωμενων υπ' αυτου, and that "none of those things which are decreed by him, shall pass away," or be unaccomplished: which shows his sense of the dependency of all things upon the will of God, and of the immutability of his decrees in general.

2. He not only frequently makes mention of persons under the character of *the elect of God*, but also intimates, that there is a certain, special, and peculiar number of them fixed by him. Speaking of the schism and sedition in the church at Corinth, he represents it** as what was "very unbecoming, and should be far from τοις εκλεκτοις του Θεου, the elect of God." And elsewhere†† having cited Psalm xviii. 26, he says, "Let us there-

fore join ourselves to the innocent and righteous, for εισιν ουτοι εκλεκτοι του Θεου, they are the elect of God;" that is, they appear to be so, these are characters descriptive of them. And in another place,‡‡ enlarging in commendation of the grace of love, he says, "Love knows no schism, is not seditious; love does all things in harmony; παντες οι εκλεκτοι του Θεου, all the elect of God are made perfect in love:" which agrees with what the apostle says of them, that they are chosen to be *holy and without blame before him in love*.‖‖ Moreover, Clement observes,‡ to the praise of the members of the church of Corinth, to whom he writes, that formerly their "contention was night and day for the whole brotherhood, that τον αριθμον των εκλεκτων αυτου, the number of his elect might be saved, with mercy and a good conscience." And elsewhere¶¶ he says, that "God chose the Lord Jesus Christ, and us by him, εις λαον περιουσιον, for a peculiar people."

3. Whereas the apostle Paul, writing to the Ephesians, says; *Blessed be the God and Father of our Lord Jesus Christ, who hath blessed us with all spiritual blessings, in heavenly places, in Christ; according as he hath chosen us in him before the foundation of the world*,*** we conclude from hence, that from all eternity there was a preparation of spiritual blessings made; and agreeably, Clement, our apostolical writer, has these words; "Let us therefore consider,††† brethren, out of what matter we are made; who and what we were when we came into the world, as out of the grave and darkness itself; who, having made and formed us, brought us into his world προετοιμασας τας ευεργεσιας αυτου πριν ημας γενηθηναι, having first prepared his good things for us, before we were born."

4. This very ancient writer plainly intimates, that the special and spiritual blessings of grace are peculiar to the elect of God; and that it is the stable and unalterable will of God, that his chosen ones should partake of them: particularly repentance, and remission of sins: for having mentioned those words in Psalm xxxii. 1, 2, *Blessed is he whose transgression is forgiven, whose sin is covered; Blessed is the man unto whom the Lord imputeth not iniquity, and in whose spirit there is no guile;* he observes,‡‡‡ that this blessedness comes upon, or belongs unto, τους εκλελεγμενους υπο του Θεου, those that are chosen of God by Jesus Christ our Lord." And in another place,§§§ having taken notice of some general instances, declarations, and exhortations, encouraging men to repentance, suggests, that God's design herein, was to bring to repentance such as were interested in his love; his words are these; "Therefore He (that is, God), being desirous that παντας τους αγαπητας αυτου, all his beloved ones should partake of repentance, confirmed it by

---

* De Perseverantia, c. 19.   † Stromat. l. 4, p. 516.   ‡ Euseb. Eccl. Hist. l. 3, c. 15; Hieron. Catalog. Script. Eccl. s. 25.
§ Fabricii Bibl. Græc. l. 4, c. 5, p. 175.
‖ Eph i. 11   ¶ Epist. ad Corinth. i. p. 64.

** Epist. ad Corinth. i. p. 2.   †† Ibid. p. 104.
‡‡ Epist. ad Corinth. i. p. 64.   §§ Eph. i. 4.
‖‖ Ibid. p. 6.   ¶¶ Ibid. p. 130.
*** Eph. i. 3, 4.   ††† Epist. ad Corinth. i. p. 88.   ‡‡‡ Ibid. p. 114.   §§§ Ibid. p. 20.

his almighty will." That is, *God, not willing*, as the apostle Peter says,* *that any of his beloved ones should perish, but that all of them should come to repentance*, fixed it by an unchangeable decree, that they should come to repentance ; and therefore makes use of the above declarations and exhortations as means to bring them to it.

5. As the Scriptures always ascribe the act of election to God, and not men, and represent it as made *in* Christ, and *by* or *through* him ;† that he was first chosen as a head, and the elect as members in him ; so Clement speaks‡ of God as he οεκλεξαμενος τον Κυριον Ιεσουν Χριστον και ημας δι αυτον, who hath chosen the Lord Jesus Christ, and us by him ;" and of the elect as chosen υπω του Θεου δια Ιεσου Χριστου του Κυριου ημων, of God through Jesus Christ our Lord ;" and exhorts men§ to come to God in holiness of soul, lifting up pure and undefiled hands unto him, loving our mild and merciful Father, ημας εκλογης μερος εποιησεν εαυτω, " who hath made us a part of the election for himself."

SECTION II.

IGNATIUS. A. D. 110.

IGNATIUS was made bishop of Antioch, A. D. 71, according to Alsted,‖ and suffered martyrdom according to some,¶ in the eleventh year of Trajan, and according to others,** in the nineteenth year of that Emperor, A. D. 116. There are several epistles written by him still extant ; among which is an Epistle to the Ephesians, and is thus inscribed :†† " Ignatius, who is also Theophorus, To the blessed in the greatness of God the Father and fulness ; τη προωρισμενη προ αιωνων to the *predestinated before ages*, that is, before the world began ; always to be a glory, abiding, immoveable, united and chosen in the true passion by the will of God the Father, and Jesus Christ our God ; to the church, worthily blessed, which is in Ephesus of Asia, much joy in Christ Jesus, and in the unblemished grace." In which, besides the doctrines of Christ's Deity, and the saints perseverance, may be observed that of eternal predestination to grace and glory. In his epistle to the Magnesians,‡‡ he speaks of two sorts of persons, signified by " two pieces of money ; the one belongs to God, and the other to the world ; which have each their own characters upon them, and every one shall go εις τον ιδιον τοπον, to his own place ;" which Barnabas, the companion of the apostle Paul, calls, in his epistle,§§ ωρισμενον τοπον, " the appointed place ;" for as wicked men, such as Judas, go to their own place, which is no other than hell-fire, prepared for the devil and his angels ; so good men go to their own place, appointed by God

for them, which is the kingdom prepared for them from the foundation of the world, and which Polycarp, bishop of Smyrna, and disciple of the apostle John, calls‖‖ τον οφειλομενον αυτοις τοπον, " the place that is due unto them, not by works, but of grace." And here it may be proper to insert a passage out of an epistle¶¶ which the church of Smyrna, of which Polycarp was bishop, and to whom Ignatius wrote one of his epistles, declaring, that when " the executioner sheathed his sword in Polycarp, such a quantity of blood came out as quenched the fire ; and the whole multitude wondered that there was such a difference μεταξυ των τε απιστων και των εκλεκτων, between the infidels and the elect."

SECTION III.

JUSTIN. A. D. 150.

JUSTIN, called the Martyr, to distinguish him from others of the same name, was a native of Samaria ; he was born A. D. 89, was brought up a philosopher, afterwards became a Christian, and suffered martyrdom in the third year of M. Aurelius Antonius, and L. Verus, A. D. 163.*** Several of his writings continue to this day, in which may be observed :

1. That he ascribes to God an eternal and universal prescience of future events ; upon which proceed depredictions in the sacred writings. He asserts that God foreknew who would be good or bad, who would repent and believe, and who not, and who will be saved or damned ; all which, as it perfectly agrees with the word of God, so with our sentiments. Justin no where says, that God foreknew that any would be good, repent, and believe of themselves, without his grace, by the mere strength of nature ; and that he chose any to glory and happiness upon such a foresight of their good works, repentance, and faith : much less that he chose them to grace upon a prescience of these things ; and, indeed, no man in his senses would say, that God chose man to faith upon a foresight of faith ; but lest what this author has said should be thought to militate against us, we will produce the several passages. Addressing himself††† to Trypho the Jew, he thus speaks : " None of you, as I think, will dare to say, *oti me kai prognostes ton ginesthai mellonton en kai estino Theos, kai ta axia ekasto proetoimazon*, that God was not, and is not, foreknowing of what shall be done, or afore prepares not things fitting for every one." And elsewhere,‡‡‡ *alethesteroi oi apo ton ethnon kai pistoteroi proeginoskonto*, " the more true and faithful among the Gentiles, were foreknown ;" that is, it was foreknown by God, that many of them would be so. Hence the prophets, under the inspiration of the Holy Ghost, foretold, that they would

---

* 2 Pet. iii. 9.   † Eph. i. 4, 5.   ‡ Epist. ad Corinth. p. 130, 114.   § Ibid. p. 66.
‖ Thesaur. Chronol. Chron. 43, p. 450.
¶ Hieron. Catalog. Script. Eccl. s. 26.
** Vide Fabricii Bibl. Græc. l. 5, c. 1, p. 39.
†† Ignat. Epist. p. 16.   ‡‡ Ibid. p. 32.

§§ Part ii. s. 1, p. 248.   ‖‖ Epist. ad Phil. apud Euseb. Eccl. Hist. l. 3, c. 36, p. 108.
¶¶ Apud. ib. l. 4, c. 15, p. 134.
*** Vide Fabricii Bibl. Græc. l. 5, c. 1, p. 51. 52.   ††† Dialog. cum Tryph. p. 234.
‡‡‡ Apolog. pro Christian. 2, p. 88, 89.

believe in Christ, when " the Jews and Samaritans, who had the word delivered them from God by the prophets, and were always expecting the Messiah, knew him not when he came; πλην ολιγων τινων, excepting some few, whom the holy prophetic Spirit, by Isaiah, προειπε σωθησεσθαι, foretold should be saved; who, personating them, said, *Except the Lord had left us a seed, we had been as Sodom and Gomorrah.*" He has, indeed, this observation,* and it is a very good one, " that when we assert that what is foretold by the prophets shall be done, we do not say, that it shall be done by the necessity of fate, *alla prognostou tou Theou outos ton mellonton upo panton anthropon prachthesesthai,* but that God foreknows things future, that shall be done *by all men.*" So having cited Isa. xxxiii. 18,† he says, " that the people who were foreknown to believe in him (Christ) *oti laos o eis auton pisteuein proegnosmenos,* should meditate the fear of the Lord, was also foreknown, the very words of the prophecy declare." And in another place,‡ says he, " I am able to show, that all the things appointed by Moses were types, symbols, and declarations of what should be done to Christ; *kai ton eis auton pisteuein proegnosmenon,* and of them that were foreknown to believe in him : and likewise of those things that were to be done by Christ." And elsewhere,§ speaking of the punishment of devils and wicked men, which is at present deferred by God for the sake of men, gives this as the reason of it : *proginoskei gar tinas en me tanoias sothesesthai mellontas, kai tinas medepo isos gennethentas ;* " for he foreknew that some would be saved through repentance ; and, perhaps, some not yet born :" for at first he made mankind intelligent, and able to choose the truth, and to do well ; so that all " men are left without excuse by God."

2. Justin asserts, that God not only foreknows that some will be saved, and others damned, but that he has afore prepared salvation for some persons, and punishment for others. Speaking‖ of the sufferings of Christians for the sake of Christ, he has these words ; which, says he, we bear, that we may not " with our voice deny Christ, by whom we are called εις σωτηριαν την προητοιμασμενην παρα του Πατρος ημων, unto the salvation which is before prepared by our Father." And in another place,¶ treating of Christ as the *Angel of the great counsel,* according to the Septuagint version of Isa. ix. 6, he thus speaks : " The great things, εθεβουλευτό ο Πατηρ, which the Father hath in his counsel appointed for all men," that are or shall be well-pleasing to him, and likewise those that depart from his will, whether angels or men, he only (Christ) hath most clearly taught, Matt. viii. 11, 12, and vii. 22, 23 ; and in other words, when he will condemn the unworthy that shall not be saved, he will say to them, " *Go ye into outer darkness, which*

the *Father hath prepared for Satan and his angels.*" He elsewhere,** indeed well observes, " that it is not the fault of God, οι προγινωσκομενοι και γενησομενοι αδικοι, that those who are foreknown, and shall be unrighteous, whether angels or men, that they are wicked ; but it is through their own fault that every one is such as he appears to be." And a little further, he adds, " Wherefore if the word of God intimates beforehand that some angels and men shall be punished, because that *proeginosken autous ometabletous γenesomenous ponerous,* he foreknew that they would be immutably wicked ;" it has foretold these things, but not that God has made them such ; seeing, if they repent, all, βουλομενοι, that are *willing* to obtain the mercy of God may. To which we heartily agree. We say that God makes no man wicked, but he makes himself so ; that neither the foreknowledge of God, nor his decrees, necessitate men to sin ; and that God damns no man, nor has he decreed to damn any but for sin ; and that whoever is truly desirous of the grace and mercy of God, may obtain it through Christ.

3. This ancient and valuable Christian writer not only speaks of the people of God under the title and appelation of *the elect,* as he does at the close of an epistle ††of his to some persons for whom he prays, that "the Lord of glory, who exists for ever, would give to them all to enjoy honour and rest μετα των εκλεκτων, with the elect ;" but he also speaks of them as a special people, selected out of every nation, and as a fixed number to be completed. In one place, disputing with Trypho the Jew, he has these words :‡‡ " God, out of all nations, took your nation to himself, a nation unprofitable, disobedient, and unfaithful ; thereby pointing out τους απο παντος γενους αιρουμενους, those that are chosen out of every nation to obey his will, by Christ, whom also he calls Jacob, and names Israel." And addressing himself to the same Jew, he says,§§ " In all these discourses I have brought all my proofs out of your holy and prophetic writings, hoping that some of you may be found *ek tou kata charin ten apo tou Kuriou sabaoth perileieiphthentos eis ten aionion soterian,* of the number which through the grace that comes from the Lord of Sabaoth, is left or reserved to everlasting salvation." And in another treatise of his he observes,‖‖ that " God introduced Christ into heaven after his resurrection from the dead, and detains him there until he has smitten his enemies the devils, *kai suntelesthe o arithmos ton proegnosthenon auto aga non ginomenon kai enareton,* and the number of them that are foreknown by him to be good and virtuous is completed ; δι οις, for whose sake he has not yet made the determined consummation." Which perfectly agrees with the doctrine of the apostle Peter, and gives light into the sense of his words in

2 Pet. iii. 9, where the same reason is given for the deferring of Christ's coming to judgment.

There is but one passage out of Justin produced by Dr. Whitby* in opposition to the doctrine of absolute election, and that properly belongs to the article of *free will*, under which it will be considered.

SECTION IV.
MINUTIUS FELIX. A. D. 170

MINUTIUS FELIX was a famous counsellor at Rome ; according to Monsier Daille,† he was contemporary with Fronto the orator, who lived in the times of Antoninus Pius, which emperor died A. D. 161, and, following him, I have placed him in the year as above ; though by others he is commonly put at the beginning of the third century. He wrote a dialogue between Cæcilius a heathen, and Octavius a Christian, which is entitled Octavius, and is still in being. In this dialogue Cæcilius the heathen objects to the Christians, thus,‡ *Nam quicquid agimus, ut alii fato, ita vos Deo addicitis; sic sectæ vestræ non spontaneos cupere sed electos. Igitur iniquam judicem fingitis, qui sortem in hominibus puniat, non voluntatem;* that is, "Whatsoever we do, as others ascribe it to *fate*, so you to *God;* and so men desire your sect not of their own accord, but as *elect;* wherefore you suppose an *unjust* judge, who punishes in men *lot* or fortune, and not the will." To this Octavius replies,§ *Nec de fato quisquam aut solatium captet aut excuset eventum. Sit fortis (sortis,* Ed. Oxon. 1662) *fortunæ, mens tamen libera est et ideo actus hominis, non dignitas judicatur. Quid enim aliud est fatum, quam quod de unoquoque Deus fatus est? Qui cum possit præscire materiam, pro meritis et qualitatibus singulorum etiam fata determinat, ita in nobis non genitura plectitur, sed ingenii natura punitur;* that is, "No man may either take any comfort from fate, or excuse an event; for let it be of lot or fortune, yet the mind is free, and therefore the act and not the worth of the man is judged of. For what else is fate, but what God says of every one of us? Who, since he can foreknow matter, even determines the fates according to the merits and qualities of every one; so that not our nativity (that is, as depending on the position of the stars) but our natural disposition is punished." From whence I observe,

1. That there was a doctrine held by the Christians in those times, which seemed to have some affinity with, and to bear some likeness to, the stoical fate, or Cæcilius could not have thus objected with any face; nor does this objection appear to be altogether groundless, as many of his certainly were, since Octavius, in his reply, does not deny the doctrine of fate rightly understood, though he would not have men shelter themselves under it, and excuse their actions on the account of it; nay, he does not reject

the use of that word, but explains it in a Christian sense, saying, "What is fate, but what God says, or determines, concerning every one of us?" Now no doctrine, but that of predestination, as held by such who are called Calvinists, can be thought to bear any likeness to the doctrine of fate, or be liable to the like objections; wherefore it is reasonable to conclude, that the same doctrine was generally taught and received by the Christians then as it is by them that hold it now, since the same charge is brought against it.

2. That the saints in those times went under the name of *the elect;* and that it was a current opinion among them, that men were converted to the Christian religion, and were brought into fellowship and society with the Christians, not by the power of their own free will, but in consequence of electing grace; and therefore Cæcilius upbraids them as coveting the Christian sect, and joining themselves to it, *non spontaneos,* "not of their own accord," *sed electos,* "but being the elect."

3. What farther confirms this, that the doctrine of predestination was then received among the Christians, is, that Cæcilius goes on to charge the Christian hypothesis with making God unjust; since he must punish men not for what they voluntarily do, but for what they cannot help, for that which is allotted and determined for them to do; which contains the whole strength of what is now objected to the doctrine of absolute reprobation, and what it was of old charged with, even in the apostles' times, *What shall we say then? Is there unrighteousness with God?*‖

4. The latter part of Octavius's reply is indeed produced by the Arminians, as militating against the absolute decrees of God; but without any just reason, since there is nothing in it that is inconsistent with them. We readily own that God can and does foreknow whatever is or shall be; and that according to the qualities of men, he determines their fates, the issues of things, their salvation or damnation, for we say, that "God decreed to damn no man but for sin; and that he appointed none to salvation but through sanctification of the Spirit and belief of the truth;" or in other words, that God foreknowing the faith and repentance of his elect, because he had determined to give them to them, he appoints them to salvation, through them as means; and foreknowing the sin, final impenitence, and unbelief of the rest, he appoints them to damnation; though these things are to be considered not as causes of predestination, *quoad actum volentis,* with respect to the will of God; but *quoad res volitas,* with respect to the things willed. Dr. Twisse, who well understood this controversy, and was an able defender of the absolute decrees of God, agrees with every

---

* Disc. on the Five Points, p. 96 ; ed. 2. 95.
† Apol. part 4, p. 756.   ‡ Min. Felix. Octav. p. 363, ad Calcem Arnobii, p. 11, ed.

Oxon. 1662.   § Min. Felix. Octav. p. 397. Ed. Elmenhorst. p. 39 ; ed. Oxon.   ‖ Rom. ix. 14.

thing that Octavius here says: "As to that of Minutius Felix," says he,¶ "we deny that God doth *sortem in hominibus punire, non voluntatem.* We do not say, *genitura plectitur;* we say, that in every one who is punished by God, *igenii natura punitur;* we confess, that *fatum illud est, quod de unoquoque Deus fatus est;* and that *promeritis et singulorum qualitatibus etiam fata determinat.*"

SECTION V

IRENÆUS. A. D. 180.

IRENÆUS was a disciple of Polycarp, and an auditor of Papais, who were both disciples of the apostle John; he was first a presbyter under Pothinus, bishop of Lyons, in France, and when he died, who suffered martyrdom* about A. D. 178, he succeeded him as bishop of that place, and became a martyr about † A. D. 198. He wrote *five* books against the heresies of the Valentinians and Gnostics, which remain to this day; from whence may be gathered his sense concerning the decrees of God. And,

1. It is evident, that he believed that all things are predetermined by God, and are overruled by him for the good of his church and people; yea, that even the fall of man is used to their advantage; for he says,‡ that God has shown the greatness of his mind in the apostacy of man, for man is taught by it;" as the prophet says, "Thy backslidings shall reform thee." *Prefiniente Deo omnia ad hominis perfectionem.* "God predetermining all things for the perfection of man, and for the bringing about and manifestation of his dispositions, that goodness may be shown, and righteousness perfected, and the church be conformed to the image of his Son, and at length become a perfect man, and by such things be made ripe to see God, and enjoy him."

2. He asserts a preparation of happiness for some, and of punishment for others, upon the prescience or foreknowledge of God; his words are these :§ *Deus autem omnia præsciens utrisque aptas præparavit habitationes, &c.* "God foreknowing all things, has prepared for both suitable habitations;" for them who seek after the light of incorruptibility, and run unto it, *he bountifully gives* that light which they desire; but for others that despise it, and turn themselves from it, and avoid it, and as it were blinding their own selves, he hath prepared darkness fitting for such who are against the light, and for those who shun being subject to it, he has "provided proper punishment." It is true, he puts this upon the prescience of God, foreknowing the different characters and actions of men; and therefore Vossius,‖ and Dr. Whitby,¶ from him, have produced this passage, with others, to prove, that the fathers

before Austin held, that God predestinated men to live from a prescience that they would live piously; but I think it may very well be understood, in a sense entirely consistent with the doctrine of predestination, as maintained by us; for we readily own, that God foreknew who would live piously, and seek after the light of life, because he determined to give them that grace which should enable them so to do, and therefore prepared mansions of light and glory for them; and, to use Irenæus's own phrase, *benigne donans,* of his own grace and goodness liberally and bountifully gives that light unto them which they desire, and he has prepared for them. On the other hand, he foreknew who would despise and shun the light, and blind themselves yet more and more; because he determined to leave them to themselves, to their native blindness, darkness, and ignorance, which they love; and accordingly prepared regions of darkness, as a proper punishment for them. For,

3. He speaks of a certain number of persons chosen to eternal life, and of God's giving up others to, and leaving them in their unbelief, in much such language as we usually do. Treating of the doctrine of the resurrection, he has these words,** "God is not so poor and indigent as not to give to every body its own soul as its proper form. Hence *plerothentos tou arithmou ou autos par auto proorise, pantes oi engrapheetes eis zoen anastesontai,* having completed the number which he before determined with himself, all those who are written, or ordained unto life, shall rise again, having their own, bodies, souls, and spirits, in which they pleased God; but those who are deserving of punishment shall go into it, having also their own souls and bodies in which they departed from the grace of God." And in another place,†† having cited several passages of Scripture which respect the blinding and hardening of the heart of Pharaoh, and others, such as Isa. vi. 9, 10, 2 Cor. iv. 4, Rom. i. 28, 2 Thess. ii. 11, 12, which are commonly made use of in handling the doctrine of reprobation, he thus descants upon them, "If therefore now, as many as God knows, will not believe, since he foreknows all things, *tradidit eos infidelitati eorum,* he hath given them up to their infidelity, "and turns his face from them," *relinquens eos in tenebris,* "leaving them in the darkness which they have chosen for themselves;" is it to be wondered at, that he then "gave up Pharaoh, who would never believe, with them that were with him, to their own infidelity?" And elsewhere‡‡ having mentioned the words in Romans ix. 10—12, so frequently urged in this controversy, he has this observation upon them, "from hence it is manifest, that not only the prophecies of the patriarchs, but the birth of

---

* Riches of God's Grace, against Hord. part 1, p. 54.   † Vide Fabricii Bibl. Græc. l. 5, c. 1, p. 66.   ‡ Vide Dallæi. Apol. par. 4. p. 759.   § Irenæus adv. Hæres. l. 4, c. 72, p. 419.   ‖ Irenæus adv. Hæres. l. 4, c. 76, p. 423.

¶ Hist. Pelag. l. 6 ; Thess. 8, p. 542.   ** Discourse on the Five Points, p. 101 ; ed. 2. 100.   †† L. 2, c. 62, inter Fragment. Græc. ad. calcem.   ‡‡ L. 4, c. 48, p. 389.   §§ L. 4, c. 38, p. 376.

Rebecca, was a prophecy of two people, one greater, the other less; one in bondage, the other free; of one and the same father; one and the same God is ours and theirs, who understands things hidden; *qui scit omnia antequam fiant*, 'who knows all things before they come to pass,' and therefore hath said, *Jocob have I loved, and Esau have I hated.*"

4. Eternal predestination, or predestination before time, before men have a being, was not unknown to this ancient writer; for in one place he says,* "being predestinated indeed *according to the knowledge of the Father; ut essemus qui nondum eramus*, that we might be, who as yet were not, made, or were the beginning of his creation." And not to take any further notice than barely to mention his reading the text in Romans i. 1, *Predestinated to the Gospel of God ;†* and which after him is so rendered by Origen, Chrysostom, and Theophylact, who understand it not of the vocation of Paul to the apostleship, but of his eternal election, and the pre-ordination of him of old, before he was born.

5. He plainly hints at the stability and immoveableness of the decree of election, when he calls it, *turris electionis*, "the tower of election;" for why should he call it a *tower*, but because it is impregnable and immoveable, because "*the purpose of God, according to election, is that foundation which stands sure, not of works, but of him that calleth?*" For having taken notice of some passages of the prophets, he thus says,‡ "These things the prophets declaring required the fruit of righteousness, but the people not believing, at last he sent his own Son, our Lord Jesus Christ: whom, when the wicked husbandmen had killed, they cast out of the vineyard; wherefore the Lord God hath delivered it to other husbandmen, who render him the fruits in their seasons; not now walled about, but spread throughout the whole world; *turre electionis exaltata ubique et speciosa*, "the tower of election being every where exalted and glorious." That is, if I understand him right, the election obtained every where, or electing grace took place, not in Judea only, as heretofore, but in all the nations of the world; for it follows, "every where the church is famous, every where a winepress is dug, and every where there are some that receive the Spirit."

There are two passages cited from Irenæus by Dr. Whitby,§ as militating against the doctrines of absolute election and reprobation, but both of them respect the doctrine of free will; and it must be owned, that there are some things dropped by this writer, which, upon first reading them, seem to favour that doctrine, and will be considered in their proper place.

SECTION VI
CLEMENS ALEXANDRINUS. A. D. 190

CLEMENT of Alexandria, of an heathen philosopher became a Christian, was a presbyter of the church at Alexandria, and, after Pantænus, was master of the school in that place.‖ Several of his works are still extant, some of which were written a little after the death of Commodus the emperor, which, according to Clement¶ himself, was A. D. 194, but according to the vulgar æra, A. D. 192,** in which,

1. He clearly asserts the doctrine of election in many places, for he not only speaks of the people of God, under the character of *elect ;* as when from a book called *Pastor*, the author of which was Hermas, and thought to be the same the apostle Paul makes mention of Romans xvi. 14, he says,†† "that virtue which holds the church together is faith, by which οι εκλεκτοι του Θεου, "the elect of God are saved." And in another place,‡‡ "the generation of them that seek him is, το γενος το εκλεκτόν, "the elect nation." And elsewhere,§§ "not the place, but το αθροισμα των εκλεκτων, "the congregation of the elect, I call the church." I say, he not only speaks often after this manner, but of them as a special, distinct number, predestinated and chosen of God, whom it is his will to save; accordingly he says,‖‖ "as his will is his work, and this is called the world, so his will is the salvation of men, και τουτο εκκλησια κεκλεται, "and this is called the church." And again,¶¶ "If they also had known the truth, they would have all leaped into the way, *ekloge de ouk an en*, "and there would have been no election." And in another place,*** "It is not convenient that all should understand, that is, the meaning of the scriptures, lest taking the things which are wholesomely said by the Holy Spirit, otherwise, they should prove hurtful; wherefore *tois eklektois ton anthropon*, "to those that are chosen from among men," and to them that are through faith admitted to knowledge, the holy mysteries of the prophecies which are preserved are hid in parables." And elsewhere,††† "according to the fitness which every one has, He, that is, God, distributes his benefits both to the Greeks and to the Barbarians; *kai tois ek touton proorismenois*, "and to them who are predestinated from among them, and are in his own time called, faithful, and elect."

2. It is evident that Clement held, that the predestination of men to everlasting life was from eternity, or before the world began, as appears from the following passages; having cited Jeremiah i. 5, 7, *Do not say, I am a child ; before I formed thee in the belly, I knew thee, &c.*, his note upon it is,‡‡‡ "this

---

* L. 5, c. 1, p. 432.   † L. 3, c. 18, p. 276.
‡ L. 4, c. 70, p. 412.   § Discourse on the Five Points, p. 96 ; ed. 2. 95.   ‖ Hieron. Catal. Script. Eccl. s. 48.   ¶ Stromat. l. 1, p. 340.   ** Vide Dallæi Apolog. part 4, p. 760.   †† Stromat. l. 2, p. 384.   ‡‡ Ibid.

l. 7, p. 733.   §§ Ibid. p. 715.   ‖‖ Pædagog. l. 1, c. 6, p. 93.   ¶¶ Stromat. l. 4, p. 505.   *** Ibid. l. 6, p. 677.
††† Ibid. l. 7, p. 702, 703.
‡‡‡ Pædadog. l. 1, c. 7, p. 111.

prophecy intimates unto us, *tous pro kataboles kosmou eis pistin egnosmenous Theo,* "that those who before the foundation of the world are known by God unto faith; that is, are appointed by him to faith, are now babes, because of the will of God lately fulfilled, as we are new-born unto vocation and salvation." Yea, he says, that the Christians were before the world was; for speaking of several nations who boasted of antiquity, he observes,* that "none of them was before this world; but *pro de tes tou kosmou kataboles emeis,* "verily we were before the foundation of the world, who, that we ought to be, were first born in God;" we are the rational formations of God the Word, *di on archaizomen,* "by whom we have antiquity; for the Word was *in the beginning;*" which must be meant of their being chosen in Christ from everlasting. And in another place,† "It is not becoming, that a friend of God, *on proorisen o Theos pro kataboles kosmou eis ten akran egkatalegenai uiothesian,* "whom God has predestinated before the foundation of the world, to be put into the high adoption of children, should fall into pleasures or fears, and be unemployed in repressing the passions." And elsewhere,‡ "what voice should he expect, who according to his purpose knows, *ton eklekton kai pro tes geneseos,* the elect even before his birth, and that which shall be, as though it was?" To which I shall add one passage more, where he says,§ that "such are gathered together by one Lord *tous ede katatetagmenous, ous proorisen o Theos dikaious esomenou pro kataboles kosmou egnokos,* who are already ordained, whom God hath predestinated, knowing before the foundation of the world that they would be righteous." This passage is indeed referred to by Dr. Whitby,‖ in favour of a conditional, and against absolute predestination; but Clement might very well say, agreeable to the absolute scheme, that God predestinated men to glory, knowing they would be righteous; because he ordained them to be righteous, and determined to make them so. He does not say, that he foreknew that they would be righteous of themselves, and therefore predestinated them to happiness, which only would serve the conditional scheme. Besides, neither he, nor any of the ancients, ever said, that God foreknowing men would be righteous, predestinated them to be so; but foreknowing they would be righteous, because he determined they should be, he predestinated them to happiness.

There are two or three more passages of this writer referred to by Dr. Whitby,¶ as opposing the doctrine of absolute election and reprobation, which, as has been before observed concerning some others, from Justin and Irenæus, more properly belong to the doctrine of free will; and if Clement has said some things which look that way, it need not be much wondered at, since both he and his master Pantænus had been addicted to the stoic philosophy; which they might find some difficulty to get clear of, and so might be mixed by them with the Christian scheme, as it is plain it too much was in the school of Alexandria.

SECTION VII

TERTULLIAN. A. D. 200

TERTULLIAN was by birth an African, of the city of Carthage, his father was a Proconsular Centurion; he flourished in the times of Severus, and Antoninus Caracalla, about the beginning of the third century. He was a presbyter of the church, and one of the first of the Latin writers among the Christians. He wrote much, and many of his works remain to this day,** in which we have at least some hints of his being acquainted with the doctrines of election and reprobation. In one of his books,†† speaking of the different crowns which men of different orders were honoured with, he addresses the Christian after this manner, "But thine order and thy magistracy, and the name of thy court is *the church of Christ: thou art his,* conscriptus in libris vitæ, *written in the books of life.*" And in another place,‡‡ treating of heretics, he says, they were wits of spiritual wickedness, with whom we and the brethren wrestle; the necessary articles of faith merit our contemplation, *ut electi manifestentur, ut reprobi detegantur;* that the elect may be manifested, that the reprobate may be detected." And elsewhere,§§ having cited Isa. xl. 5, 6, he makes this remark, "he distinguishes the issues of things, not substances; for who does not place the judgment of God in a twofold sentence of salvation and punishment? Wherefore *all flesh is grass,* quæ igni destinatur, *which is appointed to the fire,* and *all flesh shall see the salvation of God;* quæ saluti ordinatur, *which is ordained to salvation.*" And as he says upon another account,‖‖ "there can be no election without reprobation." He has indeed a passage, which seems to make election dependent upon the works of men; his words are these,¶¶ "What man is there without sin that God should always choose him whom he never could refuse? Or who likewise without any good work, that God should always refuse him, whom he never could choose? Show a man that is always good, and he will not be refused; show one that is always evil, and he will never be chosen." Hence the learned Scultetus*** charges him with being erroneous in the doctrine of predestination. But this is but a single passage, and seems only to regard the

* Admon. ad Gentes. p. 5.　† Stromat. l. 6, p. 652.　‡ Ibid. l. 7, p. 721.　§ Ibid. p. 765.　‖ Discourse on the Five Points, p. 98; ed. 2. 97.　¶ Ibid. p. 96; ed. 2. 95.　** Vide Hieron. Catalog. Eccles. s. 63.　†† De Corona, c. 13, p. 129; ed. Paris, 1634.

‡‡ De Præscript. Hæret. c. 38, p. 246.　§§ De Resurrect. Carnis, c. 59. p. 427.　‖‖ Ad Nationes, l. 1, c. 10. p. 55.　¶¶ Adv. Marcion. l. 2, c. 23, p. 471.　*** Medull. Patrum, part 1, l. 7, c. 42, p. 243.

different dispensations of divine providence towards good and bad men, on account of which God was censured by the Marcionites, and charged with levity and inconstancy, and not an election to grace and glory.

Dr. Whitby* has a single reference to this writer, which, as the rest that have been before observed, falls under the head of free will, and will be there considered with them.

SECTION VIII

ORIGENUS ALEXANDRINUS. A. D. 230

ORIGEN† of Alexandria, sometimes sirnamed Adamantius, was born about A. D. 185; his father's name was Leonidas, who suffered martyrdom, A.D. 202. He succeeded Clement in the school of Alexandria, was ordained a presbyter at Cæsarea about A. D. 228, and died at Tyre, A. D. 253. He wrote much, and many things are still extant under his name, great part of which are only translations by Rufinus, who took great liberty in altering and interpolating his works; so that it is not easy to know when we read Origen, or when Rufinus. Perhaps many of the errors and mistakes he is charged with may be owing to the ill usage he has met with this way. It is said to be a tenet of his, that souls pre-existed in another state; and that according as they behaved themselves in the other world, they either obtained the order of angels, or were thrust down to the earth, and united to bodies predestinated either to life or death, according to their past merits, which he sometimes calls,‡ *preceding causes* and *more ancient* ones. This notion of his is mentioned by Jerome,§ and rejected by him; who rightly observes, that men are chosen in Christ, not because they were or had been holy, but that they might be so. Origen's sentiments on this head were very peculiar, and are not allowed of on either side of the question before us; and therefore passages of this kind are very injudiciously cited by Dr. Whitby,‖ in this controversy. Indeed it cannot be denied, but that there are other passages in¶ the writings of this father which countenance the doctrine of predestination, upon the foresight of man's future purposes, desires, and actions in this life, which do not accord with his above notion, and shows either that he contradicts himself, or has not had justice done him. And though one might not expect to meet with any thing in favour of the absolute and unconditional scheme in such a writer, yet there are several things said by him which agree with it. And,

1. He agrees with us in his sentiments of prescience and predetermination in general;

he held, that nothing comes by chance, but that all things are appointed by God; yea, that the case of lots is not fortuitous, but according to divine predestination. Thus, speaking of the division of the land of Canaan to the Israelites, he has these words,** "Upon casting lots the inheritance is distributed to the people of God, and the lot moved, *non fortuitu, sed secundum hoc quod prædestinatum est a Deo,* "not by chance, but according to what is predestinated by God." His sense of the prescience of God is,†† that "foreknowledge is not the cause of things future, but the truth he says is, that *to esomenon aition tou toian di einai ten peri autou prognosin,* that a thing being future, is the cause of God's foreknowledge of it; for not because it is known it is future, but because it will be, therefore it is known." To the same puipose he says in another place,‡‡ "Not therefore any thing will be because God knows it to be future, but because it is future it is known by God before it comes to pass." Which entirely accords with what we assert, that God did not decree any thing because he foresaw it, but he foresaw it because he decreed it.

2. He gives plain intimations, as if he thought that there was a certain number of men chosen by God, and given to Christ. By the *elect* in Matt. xxiv. 30, who will be gathered together from the four winds, he understands §§ "all that are loved by God the Father, and preserved in Christ Jesus." God, he says,‖‖ is indeed the God of all, *tes ekloges esti Theos, He* is the God of the election, and much more of the Saviour of the election." And elsewhere mentioning these words in John xvii. 5. *And now, Father, glorify me with thine own self, with the glory which I had with thee before the world was;* he makes this observation,¶¶ "the world here is to be understood of our world above the earth, *apo gar toutou tou kosmou edoke to uio o pater anthropous,* for out of this world the Father hath given men to the Son, for whom alone the Saviour prays the Father, and *not for the whole world of men."* "And again may it be enquired, he says,*** whether *all men* may be called the servants of this king, or *some* truly whom he foreknew and predestinated?"

3. He asserts a predestination to grace, and particularly to faith, which is not consistent with predestination, upon a foresight of it. In one of his books he has these words;†† "It seems that the knowledge of God is greater than to be comprehended by human nature, hence are so many mistakes in men concerning God, but by the goodness and love of God to man, and through wondrous and

---

* Discourse, &c. p. 96; ed. 2. 95.   † Vide Fabricii Bibl. Græc. l. 5, c. 1, s. 26, p. 213.   ‡ Origen. Philocal. c. 21. p. 65. Περι Αρχων, l. 2, c. 9, fol. 133; l. 3, c. 1, fol. 142, &c.; 3, fol. 145; and c. 5, fol. 148.   § Hieron. ad Avitum, tom. ii. p. 51; L. adv. Ruffin. Apolog. p. 68, M. 69; B. Comment. in Eph. p. 90, C. D. E.   ‖ Discourse, &c. p. 98; ed. 2. 96, 97.   ¶ Vide Origin, in Rom. p. 424, 425; ed.

Huet. in Numb. tom. i. fol. 117; in Rom. l. 1, fol. 133, tom. iii. & l. 7, fol. 191, 192.   ** In Josuam Homil. 23, fol. 173, H.   †† Comment. in Gen. p. 8.   ‡‡ In Rom. l. 7, fol. 192, E.   §§ In Matt. Homil. 30, fol. 62, B.   ‖‖ Comment. in Joannem, p. 48.   ¶¶ Com. in Matt. p. 326.   *** Ibid. p. 345.   ††† Contra cells. l. 7, p. 361, 362.

divine grace, the knowledge of God comes *epi tous prognosei Theou pronatalephsthentas,* to them who were before comprehended in the foreknowledge of God; or, according to the version of Gelenius, who to this were *predestinated.*" And in another part of his works, speaking of the conjunction of angels to men, and their care of them, he says,[*] that "an angel begins from the time of a man's conversion and faith to be joined *to prognosthenti kata ton de ton chronon pisteuein kai proristhenti,* to him that is foreknown and preordained to believe at that, even at that very time;" which shows that he held, that some are predestinated to believe, and that at a certain time; and so it has been, and is, that *as many as were ordained to eternal life believed.*

4. It is also manifest, from a certain passage of his, that he held that election does not spring from men's works, but from the mere will and pleasure of God; his words are these;[†] "All these things look this way, that the apostle may prove this;" That if either Isaac or Jacob, for their merits, had been chosen to those things which they, being in the flesh sought after, and, by the works of the flesh, had deserved to be justified; then the grace of their merit might belong to the posterity of flesh and blood also, but now, since, *electio eorum non ex operibus facta sit, sed ex proposito Dei, ex vocantis arbitrio,* "their election does not arise from works, but from the purpose of God, from the will of him that calleth;" the grace of the promise is not fulfilled in the children of the flesh, "but in the children of God; that is, such, who likewise, as they, may be *ex proposito elegantur,* chosen by the purpose of God, and adopted for sons."

SECTION IX

CÆCILIUS THASCIUS CYPRIANUS. A. D. 250

CYPRIAN was an African by birth; he was first a Presbyter, and afterwards Bishop of Carthage : he was made Bishop of that place A. D. 248, and suffered martyrdom A. D. 258, under Valerianus and Gallienus. He ‡ wrote many excellent things, some of which are preserved to this day. The great Augustin thought him to be of the same mind with himself in the doctrine of predestination, which he gathered from those words of his;[§] *In nullo gloriandum quando nostrum nihil sit;* "we must glory in nothing, since nothing is ours;" according to John iii. 27. *A man can receive nothing, except it be given him from heaven.* And 1 Cor. iv. 7, *What hast thou, that thou didst not receive? Now, if thou didst receive it, why dost thou glory as if thou hadst not received it?* Upon which Austin makes this remark;[||] "this Cyprian most truly saw, and most confidently asserted;

per quod utique prædestinationem certissimam pronunciavit, whereby also he hath pronounced predestination to be most certain :" for if we must glory in nothing, since nothing is ours, neither must we glory truly of our most persevering obedience; nor is that to be said to be so ours, as if it was not given us from above; and that itself therefore is the gift of God; which God foreknew that he would give to his own, who are called with the calling of which it is said, *the gifts and calling of God are without repentance,* and must be owned by every Christian; *hæc est igitur prædestinatio, quam fideliter et humiliter prædicamus;* "this is therefore the predestination which we faithfully and humbly preach." And a little after, having repeated the same words of Cyprian, his observation is this; "where, says he, without any ambiguity, he declares the true grace of God, that is, which is not given according to our merits, and which God foreknew that he would give; *his Cypriani verbis procul dubio prædestinatio prædicata est:* in these words of Cyprian, without all doubt, predestination is asserted."

There are some books ascribed to Cyprian, which are called in question by learned men, whether they are his or no, such as those which are entitled, *De Disciplina et bono Pudicitiæ,* and *De Cardinalibus Operibus Christi:* their style is thought, by Erasmus, not to agree with Cyprian's; but Pamelus affirms them to be his:[¶] however, the former of these is allowed to be written by a learned man, and suspected to be done by Cornelius, bishop of Rome, cotemporary with Cyprian; and the latter to be the work, *antiqui et docti autoris,* "of an ancient and learned author," and thought to be written in the age of Cornelius and Cyprian; though in a very ancient copy in the library of All-Souls college in Oxford, it goes under the name of Arnoldus Bonavillacensis;[**] and, therefore, must be the work of far later writer, even of one that lived in the times of Bernard; wherefore, as the genuineness and antiquity of these treatises are questioned, I shall lay no stress upon the testimonies I now produce out of them. In the first of these[††] the author exhorts the saints to chastity, from such considerations as these: " Knowing," says he, "that you are the temple of the Lord, the members of Christ, the habitation of the Holy Ghost; *electos ad spem, consecratos ad fidem, destinatos ad salutem;* elected to hope, devoted to faith, appointed to salvation." And in the latter of these,[§] the compiler of it ascribes the several distinct acts of grace to the persons in the blessed Trinity, and among the rest, particularly *election* to the Father; his words are these: "In this school of divine learning, the Father is he that teaches and instructs, the

---

[*] Comment. in Matt. p. 332.   [†] In Rom. l. 7, fol. 195, G.   [‡] Vide Hieron. Catalog. Script. s. 77; Dallæi Apolog. part 4, p. 768. [§] Cyprian. ad Quirin. l. 3, c. 4, p 373. [||] Aug. de bono Persever. l. 2. c. 14.

[¶] Vide Rivet. Critici Sacri, l. 2, c. 15. [**] James's Corruption of the Fathers, part 1, p. 18.   [††] De bono Pudicitiæ, p. 417. [‡‡] De Baptismo Christi, p. 455.

Son who reveals and opens the secrets of God unto us, and the Holy Spirit who fills and furnishes us. From the Father we receive power, from the Son wisdom, and from the Holy Spirit innocence. *Pater eligit,* 'the Father chooses,' the Son loves, the Holy Spirit joins and unites. By the Father is given us eternity, by the Son conformity to his image, and by the Holy Spirit integrity and liberty." In another place* he speaks of the elect, as of a certain number that shall be saved, when Christ shall return to judge the world: "When, says he, all mankind collected together, shall see the hands they have pierced, the side they have bored, the face they have spit upon, and the irreversible sentence being openly declared, *occurrentibus salvatori electis,* 'the elect meeting the Saviour,' the ungodly shall remain deputed to infinite torments." And, in another part of the same work,† speaking of the manna in the wilderness, he thus expresses himself: "There was," says he, a full measure "through the whole week, the sabbath-day vacant; for which the preceding sixth day, doubling the quantity of the usual food, prefigured the rest of the eighth day, in which, without labour and care, *in deliciis equlabuntur electi,* the elect shall feast with delight, and shall be satisfied in their own land; possessing double, being enriched with an happy perpetuity, and a perpetual happiness of body and soul." There is a passage referred to in the true Cyprian, by Dr. Whitby,‡ to prove that it is in the power of man to believe or not: but since this belongs to the article of *freewill,* the consideration of it must be deferred till we come to it.

SECTION X·

NOVATIANUS. A. D. 250.

NOVATIAN,§ a presbyter of Rome, was contemporary with Cyprian. He is not so well spoken of by some, partly because of his disagreement with Cornelius, bishop of Rome, about the succession in that see; and partly because he held that such who apostatized, though they repented, were not to be received again into the communion of the church; but, in other points, he was judged to be orthodox, and his book, *De Trinitate,* is highly esteemed of; in which stands a full and memorable testimony to the doctrine of predestination of a certain number of men to glory, before the foundation of the world; for, proving the deity and eternity of Christ from John xvii. 5, *Glorify thou me with the glory which I had with thee before the world was,* he shows, that this is not to be understood of predestination, or of Christ's having this glory only in the purpose and decree of God: "For, says he,‖ if he is said to be glorious in predestination, and predestination

was before the foundation of the world, the order must be kept, and before him there will be, *multus numerus hominum in gloriam destinatus,* a large number of men appointed to glory;" for by this appointment Christ will be thought to be lesser than the rest to whom he was pointed out last. For if this glory was in predestination, Christ received this predestination to glory last of all; for Adam will be perceived to be predestinated before, and so Abel, Enoch, Noah, Abraham, and the rest; for since, with God, *personarum et rerum omnium ordo digestus sit,* "the order of all persons and things is digested," many will be said to be *predestinated* before this predestination of Christ to glory, and by this means he will appear to be lesser than other men, who is better and greater, and more ancient, than the angels themselves. His meaning is, that if the passage of Scripture cited, is only to be understood of the predestination of Christ to glory, and not of his having a real glory; then since there is a large number of men who also are predestinated to glory before the foundation of the world, whose predestination, as Adam's, and others after him, *cernetur,* to use his own word, "will be perceived" before the predestination of Christ; not that the act of their predestination itself was before his, but the manifestation of it in time; it would cast some reflection upon him, and make him look as though he was inferior to other men, as a man.

SECTION XI·

ATHANASIUS. A. D. 350

ATHANASIUS was made bishop of Alexandria A. D. 336, and died A. D. 371, who,¶ as he bore an excellent testimony to the deity of Christ against the Arians, so he has left ample proof of his attachment to the doctrines of eternal predestination and election, and of a preparation of grace and glory in Christ before the foundation of the world; as will clearly appear from the following passages:** " The grace of the Saviour to us-ward hath appeared of late, as saith the apostle, when he came to us; *proetoimasto de aute kai priu genesthai emas, mallon de kai pro tes katabotes tou kosmou,* but was 'prepared before, even before we were, yea, before the foundation of the world;' the cause of this is, in some respect, kind and astonishing; for it was not proper that God should, *usteron peri emon bouleuesthai,* afterwards consult concerning us, that it might not appear as if he knew not the things that belong to us; wherefore, the God of the universe creating us by his own word, and knowing our affairs better than we ourselves, and foreknowing, indeed, that we should be made good, but afterwards, become transgressors of the commandment, and for that transgression be cast

---

* De Ascensione Christi, p. 484.   † De Spiritu Sancto, p. 486.   ‡ Discourse on the Five Points, p. 90; ed. 2. 95.   § Vide Hieron. Catalog. Scrip. Eccl. s. 80.   ‖ Novatian, de

Trinitate, c. 24, p. 755.   ¶ Dallæi Apolog. part 4, p. 777.   ** Athanas. Contr. Arian. Orat. 3, p. 245, 246, vol. i.

out of Paradise : he being a lover of mankind, and good, *proetoimazei en to idio logo, di ou kai ektisentemas peri tes soteriodous emon oikonomias*, before prepared in his own word, by whom he also created us for the economy of our salvation ; that though we fall, being deceived by the serpent, we might not utterly remain dead, *all' echontes en to logo ten proetoimasmenen emin lutrosin kai soterian*, ' but, having redemption and salvation before prepared for us in the word, rising again, we might continue immortal." And then, citing those famous and well-known places in scripture, 2 Tim. i. 9, 10, Ephes. i. 3—5, he proceeds thus : *pos oun exelexato prin genesthai emas, ei me, os autos eireken, en outo emen protetupomenoi, pos de olos prin anthropous ktisthenai emas proarisen*, &c., "how therefore should he choose us before we were, unless, as he has said, we were before delineated in him ? how verily, before men were created, should he predestinate us," unless the Son of himself had been founded before the world was, having undertook the economy of salvation for us ? or how, as the apostle says, should *we obtain an inheritance, being predestinated*, unless the Lord himself was founded before the world was ; *that he might have a purpose*, to receive through the flesh for us, the whole lot of condemnation that was against us, and so we at length might be made alive in him ; *pos de kai pro chronon aionion elambanomen, mepo gegonotes all' en chrono gegonotes, eime en to Christo en apokeimene e eis emas phthanousa charis*, " or how should we, not yet made, but made in time, receive before the world began, except the grace that is to come unto us had been laid up in Christ ?" Wherefore, in the judgment, when every one shall receive according to his deeds, he says, *Come, ye blessed of my Father, inherit the kingdom prepared for you from the foundation of the world ; pos oun, e en tini prin genesthai emas etoimasthe, ei me to Kurio*, "how therefore, or in whom should it be prepared before we were, but in the Lord," who was founded for this before the world was ; that we, as stones well fitted together, might partake of life and grace from him ? So it is, as any pious man may in some measure understand, that, as I have before said, rising from a death, which is but for a little while, we shall be able to live for ever ; which men who are of the earth would never be able to do, *ei me pro aionos en troetoimastheisa emin en Christo, e tes zoes kai soterias elpis*, " if the hope of life and salvation had not been prepared for us in Christ before the world was." And a little after * adds : " Having life and spiritual blessings prepared, before the world, for us in the word, according to election ;" so we can have not a temporary life, but for the future continue alive in Christ.

Moreover, seeing, *pro touton, e zoe emon tethemelioto kai etoimaso en Christo*, "before these our life was founded and prepared in

Christ " (for it was not proper that our life should be founded on any other than in the Lord, who existed before the world was, and *by whom the worlds are made*,) hence that being in him we shall also inherit eternal life. For God is good, and being always good wills this, knowing that our weak nature needs his help and salvation ; and as a wise master-builder, purposing to build a house, is likewise desirous that, should it be destroyed, it might afterwards be repaired again ; and willing this, he before provides and gives proper materials for a reparation to the workmen, which is a preparation beforehand. Now, as a fore-preparation of the repair is before the house, *ton auton tropon, pro emon e tes emeteras soterian ananeosis themelioutai en Christo*, " in like manner, before us the reparation of our salvation is founded in Christ," that in him also we may be created again. *Kaie men boule kai e protheois pro tou dionos etoimasthe*, " and the will and purpose was indeed prepared before the world was, but the work was done when necessity required and the Saviour came." A most noble testimony of antiquity this to the doctrine of eternal predestination in Christ. In another place,† he shows that our vocation in time is according to an antecedent will of God ; his words are these : " For even Paul was not at first, though afterwards he was made an apostle by the will of God ; so our calling, which sometimes was not, and now is, *proegoumenen eche boulesin*, hath a preceding will ; for as Paul himself again says, he was made, that is an apostle, *according to the good pleasure of his will*." And elsewhere,‡ he affirms that the foundation of true religion is more ancient than the prophets, and even from eternity ; for speaking of the times in which they prophesied he says, " Not that they laid the foundation of godliness, *en gar kai pro auton kai aei en, kai pro kataboles kosmou, tauten emin o Theos en Christo proetoimasen*, for it was before them, and always was, yea, even before the foundation of the world, this God before prepared for us in Christ." And in another part of his writings,§ where he is giving an account of the epistle to the Ephesians, he observes that " the apostle, in the beginning of it, shows that the mystery respecting us is not new ; but that *exarches kai kataboles kosmou einia tauten eudoman tou Theou, oste ton Christon uper emon pathein kai emas sothenai*, from the beginning, even from the foundation of the world, this was the good will and pleasure of God, that Christ should suffer for us, and that we should be saved." And in his abridgement of the epistle to Titus he has these words :‖ "the apostle, says he, in the first place, gives thanks to God for his piety, and signifies that faith in Christ was not a new thing, *all' ex aionos etoimasthe kai epengelthai para tou Theou touten*, but that this was from eternity prepared and promised by God." Thus did this brave champion for truth at

---

* Athanas. contr. Arian. Orat. 3, p. 447.
† I bid. Orat. 4, p. 511.   ‡ De Synodi

Arimin. & Seleuc. p. 871.   § Synops. Sacr. cript. vol. ii. p. 145.   ‖ [S Ibid. vol. iii. p. 51

once both honour the Father and the Son, by asserting the special and early provision of grace, life, and salvation, made in Christ by the Father before the world began; and by proving and maintaining the eternity and proper deity of the Son, his undertaking, from eternity, to suffer for us, and the satisfaction he has made in time for sin, to the justice of God. Dr. Whitby * refers to one passage in this writer, in favour of free-will, which will be attended to under that article.

SECTION XII

HILARIUS PICTAVIENSIS. A.D. 360

HILARY, bishop of Poictiers, in France, was banished for his orthodoxy, A. D. 354, and died A. D. 371. It † appears from his writings which remain, that he held that there is an election of particular persons to the heavenly glory, and that the number of God's elect is determinate and certain; having cited those words in Isa. lxv. 15, which he reads thus, *Ye shall have your name with joy to my chosen,* he observes,‡ that "the speech is to carnal Israel, with respect to time to come, who are upbraided that they should leave their name to *the elect of God.* I inquire what is that name, to wit, Israel, to whom the word was then? Moreover, I ask, who is Israel now? The apostle truly testifies, that they who are *in the Spirit,* and *not in the letter,* who walk in the rule of Christ, are the Israel of God." And having mentioned the text in Deut. xxxii. 9; *Jacob is the portion of the Lord, and Israel the lot of his inheritance,* he adds;§ "This was *chosen to an eternal inheritance;* and because he was the Lord's portion, therefore the rest were reckoned as unknown; for these were chosen by the privilege of the portion;" which must be understood as before, not of literal, but mystical Israel; since they are said to be chosen to an eternal inheritance. And that there is a certain number of persons thus chosen he clearly asserts, when he says,‖ "we are all, in one, Abraham: and by us, who are all in one, *cœlestis ecclesiæ numerus explendus,* the number of the heavenly church is to be filled up; wherefore every creature waits for the revelation of the children of God; therefore it groans together and grieves, that the number which, by Alpha, is added to Abraham, and which, in Rho, is finished in Sarah, might be filled up by an increase of believers, for the heavenly constitution." And in another place,¶ he says, "that this must needs be understood as referring to the people of the church; he adds, *I will number them, and above the sand shall they be multiplied.* Is their number uncertain, who are written in the book of God? wherefore there is no difficulty in the

number of them whose truth remains in writing." Moreover, nothing is more evident, than that this Christian writer thought that election is an eternal act of God, or that it was from eternity: for which purpose he frequently cites,** or refers to the famous passage in Ephes. i. 4. "The Father, says he,†† absolutely calls the Son of God, meaning in Hosea i. 7, just cited by him, *in whom he hath chosen us before the world began;* and because God is inascible by none, we are given to the Son by God the Father for an inheritance." Again, speaking of the will of the Father and the Son, he has these words, ‡‡ "that he wills the same, he shows without ambiguity, saying, *Father, whom thou hast given me, I will that where I am, they may be with me;* seeing therefore, the Father wills that we should be with Christ, *in whom,* according to the apostle, *he hath chosen us before the foundation of the world;* and the Son wills the same, namely, that we be with him; the will, with respect to nature, is the same, which with respect to nativity, is distinguished in the person willing." Once more, "God, says he,§§ is wonderful in the saints, whom, when he shall have made conformable to the glory of his body, by him who is the Mediator, will also assume unto the unity of the Father's majesty; and whilst the Father is in him by nature, and he again is in us by the society of the flesh, whom he will place to obtain the *kingdom prepared for them before the foundation of the world;* to whom death being swallowed up, he will give an immortal and eternal life."

Vossius,‖‖ and, after him, Dr. Whitby,¶¶ cites a passage from this father, in favour of God's predestinating of men to life, from a prescience that they would live piously, believe, and persevere to the end, which is this, "Because *many are called and few chosen,* therefore, says he,*** there is not a fewness in the invited, but a scarcity in the elect; for in the inviter, without exception, there is the humanity of public goodness: but in the invited, by a right judgment, the election is of probity." To which they might as well have added another passage, occasioned by a citation of the same words, where he says,††† "the elect are conspicuous in the *wedding garment,* and splendid in the pure and perfect body of the *new nativity,* meaning the resurrection; wherefore election is not a thing of undistinguished judgment, but the distinction is made from the consideration of merit." By which, as in the other passage, he means not that election he so often speaks of, as before the foundation of the world, but an election in time, after vocation, and indeed, no other than that distinction and separation which will be made at

---

* Discourse on the Five Points, p. 97; ed. 2. 95.   † Dallæi Apolog. p. 783.   ‡ Hilar. de Trinitate, l. 5, p. 56.   § Enarrat. in Ps. cxliii. p. 629.   ‖ In Matt. Can. 18, p. 301. ¶ Enarrat. in Ps. cxxxviii. p. 610. Vide Etiam in Matt. Can. 9, p. 272, & Can. 10, p. 277. ** Ibid. in Ps. lx. p. 399, and in Ps. lxii. p.

406, & in Ps. vii. p. 437, & in Ps. cxliii. p. 633. †† De Trinitate, l. 4, p. 45.   ‡‡ Ibid. l. 9, p. 143.   §§ Enarrat in Ps. lxvii. p. 439, 440.   ‖‖ Hist. Pelag. l. 6, Thess. 8, p. 543. ¶¶ Discourse on the Five Points, p. 101; ed. 2. 100.   *** Hilar. in Matt. Cau. 22, p. 313. ††† Enarrat. in Ps. lxiv. p. 412.

the day of judgment, in the resurrection morn; when the saints will appear distinct from all others, having on the wedding garment, and in their glorious risen bodies; and so will be singled out from the rest, and placed at Christ's right hand.

SECTION XIII

BASILIUS CÆSARIENSIS. A. D. 370.

BASIL, commonly called the Great to distinguish him from others of the same name, was bishop of Cæsarea; he died A. D. 378. He held the doctrine of predestination, and asserts, that whatever comes to pass, was foreordained by God. Take care, says he,[*] how thou sayest this thing was done by chance, and this comes of its own accord; for *ouden atakton, ouden aoriston*, nothing is unordained, nothing undetermined, nothing is done in vain, nothing is done rashly." He affirms, that not a hand nor an eye are moved, but according to the will of God; the time, state, and condition of this present life, he says, are fixed and determined by God; his words are these,[†] "Consider, that that God, who has formed us, put the soul into us, *idian edoken ekaste psuche tou biou diagogen*, has given to every soul its manner of living; and indeed to others he has fixed other terms of removing hence; for he hath *appointed* this man to abide longer in the flesh, and on the contrary hath *decreed*, that that man should be sooner loosed from the bonds of the body, according to the unspeakable methods of his wisdom and justice." And he not only maintained a predestination of all things in general, but of particular persons, to eternal salvation; citing those words in John x. 16, *Other sheep I have which are not of this fold*. He observes,[‡] that "the Lord is speaking of them, *tou apo ton ethnon proorismenous eis soterian*, who from among the Gentiles, are predestinated unto salvation." And upon mentioning the same words a little after,[§] he has this following note; "the Lord shows that there is some *other fold* truly holy, into which the sheep of Christ are to be gathered; namely, they, *tous apo ton ethnon proorismenous eis soterian*, who, from among the Gentiles are predestinated to salvation; that is, the church in which the true worshippers worship in spirit and in truth." He represents the elect as a particular and distinct people, and as peculiarly blessed. "No man, says he,[‖] calls the people of the Jews blessed, but the people, *ton apo panton ton gaon arisinden exeigmenon*, which is chosen best out of all people; we are the nation, of whom the Lord is our God; we are the people whom he has chosen for an inheritance for himself; a *nation* truly, because we are gathered out of many *nations*: a *people* verily, because we

are called in the room of a *people* cast away, and because *many are called, and few are chosen*; he calls not him that is called, but him that is chosen, blessed; blessed therefore is he whom he hath chosen. What is the cause of this blessedness? the expected inheritance of everlasting good things; or, perhaps, because according to the apostle, *after the fulness of the Gentiles shall be come in*, then *all Israel shall be saved;* first, he calls the fulness of the Gentiles blessed, afterwards Israel, who shall be saved last; but not *every one* shall be saved, only "*the remnant which shall be according to the election of grace*." And in another place,[¶] he says, "*The blessing of the elect*, in the time of retribution, he (Christ) foretold by the parable of the shepherd; *Come*, says he, *ye blessed of my Father, inherit the kingdom prepared for you from the beginning of the world*."

SECTION XIV

CYRILLUS HIEROSOLYMITANUS. A. D. 370.

CYRIL, bishop of Jerusalem, died A. D. 386.[**] There is but little to be collected out of his writings concerning predestination and election. He signifies, that there are some who are elect, distinct from others, when he says,[††] that "*the elect* may not be mixed together, with enemies, he (Christ) *will send his angels with a great trumpet, and they shall gather his elect from the four winds*: he did not despise one *Lot*, should he despise many righteous? *Come ye blessed of my Father*, will he say to them who shall then be carried in the chariots of clouds, and shall be gathered by the angels." And in another place,[‡‡] he says, "the Holy Spirit is the greatest power, it is something divine and unsearchable; for it lives and is rational, sanctifying through Christ, *ton upo Theou gegrammenon a patnon*, all those who are written by God;" that is, in the book of life, or are chosen by God; which agrees with our doctrine, that all those who are chosen by the Father, and are redeemed by the Son, are sanctified by the Spirit.

SECTION XV

GREGORIUS NAZIANZENUS. A. D. 370.

GREGORY, bishop of Nazianzum, in Cappadocia, commonly called *the Divine*, was son of a bishop, of the same name and place, a cotemporary with Bazil, an intimate acquaintance of his, and preceptor to Jerome.[§§] He died A. D. 389. Several of his writings still remain. Austin cites a passage from him in favour of the doctrine of predestination, as held and maintained by him; his words are these :[‖‖] "To these two (meaning Cyprian and Ambrose) who ought to be esteemed suf-

---

* Basil. Homil. in Psalm xxxii. p. 231, vol. i. Vide ibid. p. 205.   † Homil. in Martyr. Julitt. p. 374.   ‡ Homil. in Psalm xxviii. p. 170. § Al. Homil. in ibid. p. 182.   ‖ Homil. in Psalm xxxii. p. 208.   ¶ De Baptismo, l. 1, c. 2, p. 644.   ** Dallæi Apolog. 795. †† Cyril. Catech. 15, sect. 10, p. 216, 217. ‡‡ Ibid. Catech. 16, p. 224.   §§ Hierou. Catal. Viror. Eccles. sect. 127.   ‖‖ Aug. de bono Persever. l. 2, c. 19.

ficient, we may add a third, the holy Gregory; who testifies, that to believe in God, and to confess that we believe, is the gift of God; saying, we pray you confess the Trinity of one Deity; but if ye mean otherwise, say, that he is of one nature, and God will be deprecated, that a voice may be given you by the Holy Ghost; that is, God will be intreated to permit that a voice may be given you, by which ye may be able to confess what ye believe; for I am sure he will give it. He that hath given the first will also give the second; he that gives to believe will also give to confess." Upon which, and some other testimonies of the above-mentioned writers, Austin makes this remark: " Would any one say, that they so acknowledged the grace of God, as that they dared to deny his prescience; which not only the learned, but even the unlearned own? Besides, if they knew that God so gives these things, that they could not be ignorant, that he foreknew that he would give them, and could not but know to whom he would give them; *procul dubio noverant prædestinationem ;* without doubt they were acquainted with predestination; which being preached by the apostles, we laboriously and diligently defend against the new heretics." Gregory writes, indeed, very sparingly of this doctrine, and gives very few hints of it. The most considerable passage I have met with in him is the following;* " Three persons gathered together in the name of the Lord, are more esteemed of by God than multitudes that deny his Deity; would you prefer all the *Canaanites* to one *Abraham ?* or the *Sodomites* to one *Lot ?* or the *Midianites* to Moses, even to these sojourners and strangers ? what, shall the three hundred men that lapped with Gideon, be inferior to the thousands that turned away ? or Abraham's servants, though less in number, than the many kings and myriads of soldiers, whom they, though few, pursued and put to flight ?" How dost thou understand that passage, *If the number of the children of Israel was as the sand of the sea, a remnant shall be saved ?* as also that, *I have reserved for myself seven thousand men who have not bowed the knee to Baal ?* It is not so, it is not, *ouk en tois pleiosin eudokesen o Theos,* " God does not take pleasure in the multitude; thou numberest myriads, but God, *tous sozomenous,* those that are to be saved; thou the unmeasurable dust; but I *ta skeue tes ekloges,* the vessels of election." From whence may be collected, as Gregory's judgment, that there were some persons who were chosen of God, and whom he resolved to save; that the number of them was with him, though that number was very small. In another place,† he speaks of a twofold book of *life* and of *death ;* " Perhaps you have heard," says he, " *tina biblon zonton kai biblon on sozomenon,* of a certain book of the

living, and of a book of them that are not to be saved, where we shall all be written, or rather are *already* written." Though it must be owned, he adds *kat' axian ton ede bebaiomenon ekastos,* " according to the desert of every one that have already lived." And in the same way he interprets Matt. xx. 23, which he reads thus :‡ " *To sit on my right hand and on my left, this is not mine to give,* αλλ' οις δεδοται, but to whom IT IS GIVEN ;" and goes on to ask, " Is the governing mind therefore nothing ? is labour nothing ? reason nothing ? philosophy nothing ? fasting nothing ? watching nothing ? lying on the ground, shedding fountains of tears, are these things nothing ? *alla kata tina apoklerosin kai Ieremias agiaxetai kai alloi ek metras allotriountai,* ' but by a kind of sortition was Jeremiah sanctified, and others rejected from the womb ?' I am afraid lest any absurd reasoning should enter, as if the soul lived elsewhere, and was afterwards bound to this body, and, according as it there behaved, some receive prophecy, and others who lived wickedly, are condemned; but to suppose this, is very absurd, and not agreeable to the faith of the church. Others may play with such doctrines; it is not safe for us." And concludes ; " To those words, *to whom it is given,* add to this, *who are worthy ;* who, that they may be such, have not only received of the Father, but have also given to themselves." The notion he here militates against, is manifestly that of Origen's, of the pre-existence of souls, and their being adjudged according to their former conduct, either to happiness or misery; which Gregory was afraid some might be tempted to give into, and which, in order to guard against, led him into this gloss upon the text, and to make this addition to it.

SECTION XVI

HILARIUS DIACONUS. A. D. 380

THE Commentaries upon the epistles of the apostle Paul, which go under the name of St. Ambrose, are not his. Austin § cites a passage out of them, under the name of Hilary, whom he calls *Sanctus Hilarius,* Saint Hilary ; but this could not be Hilary, bishop of Poictiers, before mentioned, who was earlier, nor Hilary bishop of Arles, who was later, than the author of these commentaries : for whoever he was, he lived in the times of Damascus, bishop of Rome, according to his own words ;‖ wherefore some learned men¶ have thought him to be Hilary, the deacon of the city of Rome, who adhered to the schism of Lucifer Calaritanus. This author continually refers such passages of Scripture which speak of predestination and election, to the prescience of God; nothing is more common with him, than to say,** that God chooses and calls whom he foreknew would believe, would be holy, and devoted to

---

* Greg. Naziauzen. Orat. 32, p. 515, tom. i.
† Ibid. 9, p. 158.   ‡ Ibid. 31, p. 505.
§ Contra duas Epist. Pelag. l. 4, c. 4.
‖ Comment. in 1 Tim. iii. 15, p. 579.

¶ Vide Voss. Hist. Pelag. l. 2, par. 1, thes. 6, p. 168 ; Dallæi Apolog. p. 787.   ** Comment. in Rom. p. 241, 292, 294 ; in Eph. p. 492 ; and in 2 Thess. p. 567.

him : which passages are therefore produced by Vossius,* and Dr. Whitby,† with others, to prove that the fathers held a predestination of men to life, from a prescience that they would live piously, believe and persevere. If by predestination to glory, and not to grace, which is the meaning of the fathers, and of Hilary, we agree with them ; we say also, that such whom God foreknew would believe, and be holy, he predestinated to eternal happiness ; but then we say, the reason why God foreknew that any would believe, and be holy, is because he determined within himself to give them faith, and make them holy, and so prepare them for glory. Neither Hilary, nor any of the fathers, say, that God foresaw that men would believe of themselves, and make themselves holy by their own care, diligence, and improvements of nature, nor that God foresaw that men would believe, and be holy, and therefore predestinated them to faith and holiness ; but having determined to bestow faith and holiness upon them, he foresaw they would believe and be holy, and so through these as means he chose them to salvation. That this is the sense of Hilary, appears partly from his suggesting that some are predestinated to believe. In one place‡ he says, " They believe, who are appointed to eternal life ;" and in another,§ " God of his own grace, of old decreed to save sinners (for God foreknew what would be in man before he made him, and he had sinned,) and *predestinated* how he should be recovered ; in what time, and by whom, and in what way they might be saved : so that they who are saved, are not saved either *by their own merit*, or by theirs by whom they are called, but by the grace of God ; the gift appears to be bestowed through the faith of Christ." And partly this is evident from his account of prescience : " The prescience of God," says he,‖ " is that in which *definitum habet*, ' he has it determined' what shall be the will of every one, in which he is to remain, and through which he may be either damned or crowned." Agreeably to which he says,¶ " By prescience he chooses one and rejects another ; and in him whom he chooses, the *purpose of God* remains ; because another thing cannot happen than what God has known ; *et proposuit in illo*, ' and hath purposed in him,' that he may be worthy of salvation ; and in him whom he rejects, in like manner, ' the purpose which he hath purposed concerning him, remains ;' for he will be unworthy : as foreknowing this, he is no accepter of persons ; for ' he damns no man before he sins, and crowns none before he overcomes.' " To which we heartily subscribe. We say God damns no man but for sin, and crowns none until he has made them *more than conquerors, through Christ.* It is certain, that Hilary or the author of

these commentaries, was of opinion, that there were some predestinated to life who should certainly be *saved ;* and that others were not, who should certainly be *damned ;* for he says,** " The apostle Paul, that he might, by his preaching, *save, homines predestinatos ad vitam,* ' men predestinated to life," was subject to dangers, knowing that he should have the profit of their sought-for salvation." In another place†† he says, " For unbelievers we must not very much grieve, *qui non sunt predestinati ad vitam,* ' because they are not predestinated unto life ;' for the prescience of God has, of old, decreed, that they are not to be saved." And in another place,‡‡ " The law being abbreviated, the remnant of the Jews are saved ; but the rest *cannot be* saved ; *qui per definitionem, Dei spernuntur,* ' because, by the appointment of God they are *rejected,*' by which he hath decreed to save mankind." Again, he says,§§ the apostle Paul, " by his own example, teacheth, that *part* of *Israel* is *saved,* whom God foreknew was to be saved, or yet can be saved ; and that *part* of *Israel, propter jugem diffidentiam perditioni deputatem,* ' for their continual unbelief, is deputed to destruction.' "

SECTION XVII

AMBROSIUS MEDIOLANENSIS. A. D. 380

AMBROSE, bishop of Milain, flourished under the emperors Gratian and Theodosius, and died A. D. 397. Austin,‖‖ who was converted under him, and was acquainted with him personally, as well as with his writings, thought him to be of the same judgment with himself about predestination, and cites¶¶ several passages from him for that purpose, such as these ;*** " Whom God esteems worthy of honour he calls, *et quem vult religiosum facit,* ' and whom he pleases he makes religious.' " And again ; " If he would, *si voluisset ex in-devotis devotos fecisset,* of persons not devoted to him, he could make them devoted." From whence he concludes, that he could be no stranger to the doctrine of predestination, preached by the apostles, and which he defended. Moreover, there are many expressions in his writings which show his sense of this doctrine : on those words of Sarah, *The Lord hath restrained me from bearing,* he has this note ;††† " By which," says he, " you may know, *in predestinatione fuisse semper ecclesiam Dei,* ' that in predestination the church of God always has been ;' and that the fruitfulness of faith is *prepared,* whenever the Lord shall command it to break forth, but by the will of the Lord it is reserved for a certain time." He‡‡‡ owns indeed, that "rewards are proposed not to *the elect* only, but to all, because Christ is all and in all." But he affirms,§§§ that though "all men can *hear,*

---

* Hist. Pelag. l. 6, thes. 8, p. 543.
† Discourse, &c. p. 96 ; ed. 2. 98.
‡ Comment. in 1 Tim. p. 576.   § Ibid. in 2 Tim. p. 592.   ‖ Ibid. in Rom. p. 299.
¶ Ib. p. 298, 299.   ** Ib. in 2 Tim. p. 594.   †† Ib. in Rom. p. 299.   ‡‡ Ib.

p. 302.   §§ Ib. p. 308.   ‖‖ Dallæi Apolog. p. 799.   ¶¶ De bono Persever. l. 2, c. 19.   *** Ambros. in Luc. 9, p. 125. ††† De Abraham, l. 2. c. 10, p. 265.   ‡‡‡ In Luc. 2, p. 28. §§§ Enurrat. in Ps. xlviii. p. 824.

yet all cannot *perceive* with their ears, *nisi electi Dei*, 'only the elect of God :' therefore the Saviour says, *He that hath ears to hear*—all men have not *those* ears." To electing grace, and not to men's works, he refers salvation; " the remnant, he observes,* are saved, not by their own works, but by the *election of grace*." He sometimes, indeed, represents election as a secret with God, and unknown to men : "As no one," he says,† "of whatsoever age, ought to despair, if he is desirous of being converted to the Lord, so none should be secure on the account of faith alone; but should rather fear, through what is added, *many are called but few are chosen*. That we are called by faith, we know; but whether we are elected to eternal life, we know not; so much, therefore, ought every one to be the more humble, as much as he is ignorant, whether he is elected." However, this proves that he held the doctrine of an election of particular persons; and at other times he argues from it, to the great comfort of the saints, with respect to their safety and security. "We must not despair," says he,‡ " that the members can cleave to their own head, *especially* since *ab initio simus præ-destinati*, we are predestinated from the beginning, unto the adoption of the children of God, by Jesus Christ, in himself; which predestination he hath proved, asserting that which from the beginning is before declared, *Therefore shall a man leave father and mother, and shall cleave unto his wife, and they both shall be one flesh*, to be the mystery of Christ and the church."

There is a passage cited from this father by Vossius,§ and from him by Dr. Whitby,‖ as asserting predestination upon the prescience of men's merits; where, explaining the text in Matt. xx. 23, *To sit on my right hand, and on my left, is not mine to give*, he has this note;¶ " He does not say, it is not mine *to give*, but it is not mine to give *to you;* not asserting that he wanted power, but the creature's merit. Take it otherwise: *It is not mine to give you;* that is, it is not mine, who came to teach humility; it is not mine, who came not to be ministered unto, but to minister; it is not mine, who keep righteousness, not grace. Moreover, referring to the Father, he adds, *to whom it is prepared;* that he might show, that the Father also does not use to pay regard to petitions, but to merits, for God is no accepter of persons. Hence the apostle said, *whom he hath foreknown and predestinated;* for he did not *predestinate* before he *foreknew; sed quorum merita præscivit, eorum præmia prædestinavit*, 'but whose merits he hath foreknown, their rewards he hath predestinated.' " But nothing is more evident than that Ambrose is speaking of predestination to glory, which glory he calls by the

name of *rewards;* and we grant, that this follows upon prescience of *merits;* that is, good works done from a principle of grace; but then the prescience of these arises from God's predestination to grace to enable men to perform them, and not predestination to grace from a prescience of merits; for then grace must be given according to merits; a doctrine never known by the ancients before the times of Pelagius. In short, Ambrose's sense is this, and to which we agree, that those whose merits or good works God foreknew, because he had *preordained*, that they should walk in them, and as arising from that grace he determined to give them; these he predestinated unto glory, or prepared rewards of grace for them, which he will certainly bestow on them.

SECTION XVIII

JOHN of Antioch, usually called Chrysostom, or Golden Mouth, from his uncommon eloquence, was bishop of Constantinople : he died in exile at Comma, A. D. 407. Several** volumes of his writings still remain. That he held the doctrine of eternal predestination, will appear from the sense he gives of several places of Scripture relating to this point. That famous passage in Acts xiii. 48, *As many as were ordained unto eternal life believed;* which some, of late, would have understood of the disposition of men's minds unto eternal life, Chrysostom†† interprets of God's *appointment*, or *determination* of men unto it; " *As many as were ordained to eternal life, toutestin, aphorismenoi tou Theou*, that is, says he, '*who were separated* or *appointed by God*' " unto it. And where the apostle Paul says, that he was SEPARATED *unto the gospel of God*, he has this note upon it;‡‡ "To me here he seems not only to intimate *ten apoklerosin*, 'a choice by lot'" (such, I suppose, he means, as was Matthias's,) *all' oti palai kai anothen pros touto en tetagmenos*, "but that he was of old, and from above, ordained to this; as Jeremy says, that God said concerning him, *Before thou camest out of the womb, I sanctified thee, and ordained thee a prophet unto the nations;*" and upon that well-known text in Ephes. i. 4, *according as he hath chosen us in him*, he has these words;§§ "What is the meaning of this, *he hath chosen us in him?* Through faith in him, Christ, he says, has rightly ordered this, *prin e genesthai emas, mallon de prin e ton kosmou katablethenai;* 'before we were born, or rather before the world was founded.' " And on these words,‖‖ *Come, ye blessed of my Father, &c.* he makes this observation; "What honour ! what blessedness do these words contain ! for he does not say, receive,

---

* In Ps. xliii. p. 799. Vide p. 787.
† In Dominic. Septuages. p. 29.   ‡ Epist. l. 5, epist. 37, p. 283.   § Hist. Pelag. l. 6, thes. 8, p. 543.   ‖ Discourse, &c. p. 101; ed. 2. 100.   ¶ Ambros. de fide, l. 5, c. 2, p.

190.   ** Dallæi Apolog. p. 808.
†† Chrysost. in Act. serm. 30, tom. iv. p. 780.
‡‡ Chrysost. in Rom. serm. 1, tom. iii. p. 6.
§§ Ibid. in Eph. serm. 1, tom. iii. p. 766.
‖‖ Ibid. in Matt. homil. 80, tom. ii. p. 494.

but inherit, as your property, as your Father's, as yours, as due to you from above; *prin e gar umas genesthai, tauta umin etoimason kai pro eutrepiso,* 'for before you were born, these things were prepared and made ready for you,' says he; 'for I knew you would be such.' " On the account of the last clause, this passage, with some others, is cited by Vossius,[*] and, after him, by Dr. Whitby,[†] to show that Chrysostom, with other fathers, held predestination according to prescience; which is not denied; the other passages are these: "This did not happen simply," says he,[‡] "but that the prediction of God might be fulfilled by facts, which says, *Jacob have I loved, but Esau have I hated;* for as God foreknew things future, *proanephonese kai toutou ten areten kakeinou tes gnomes mochtherian,* 'he also before declared the virtue of the one, and the evil mind of the other.' " And in another place[§] he observes, that "the apostle casts the whole matter upon the knowledge of God, which none dare militate against, was he never so mad, for, says he, *the children not being yet born, &c.* which shows that the nobility of the flesh profiteth nothing; but inquiry must be made into the virtue of the soul, *en kai pro ton ergon o Theos oide,* 'which God knows, even before any works are done;' for, says he, *the children not being yet born, neither having done any good or evil, that the purpose of God, according to election, might stand; it was said unto her, The elder shall serve the younger.* This is of foreknowledge to be chosen from the same birth; that it might appear, says he, 'the election of God is made according to purpose and foreknowledge; for from the first day he knew and proclaimed him that was good, and him that was not." And a little after,[‖] "Thou knowest, says he, from the end; but he knows clearly before the end." And upon those words, *the people, whom he foreknew,* he thus paraphrases,[¶] *toutestin on edei saphos epitedeion onta kai ten pistin dexomenon;* that is, "whom he clearly knew would be fit, and receive the faith." All which may be very well understood in consistence with the doctrine of absolute decrees; for, as Vossius[**] himself observes, "the fathers who lived before Austin, held, indeed, a decree according to foreknowledge; but then the foreknowledge is of acts performed by the strength of grace;" that is to say, that God knew that Jacob and others would be good, and do that which is good, through the grace he determined to give them, and so appointed them to everlasting happiness; and he also knew that Esau, and others, would be evil and do that which is evil, being left, as he determined to leave them, to their own wickedness, and so for it appointed them to everlasting punishment.

SECTION XIX

HIERONYMUS. A. D. 390

HIERONYMUS, or Jerom, of Stridon, in Dalmatia, was a presbyter of the church; he was born, according to Monsieur Daille,[††] A. D. 340, and died A. D. 420. He lived much of his time in Palestine, at Jerusalem, and especially at Bethelem: he was a man of great learning, and wrote much, though there are many things ascribed to him which are none of his; and in his commentaries it is sometimes difficult to know when he speaks his own or the sense of others. He is allowed, on all hands, to be an eager opposer of the Pelagian principles. And with respect to the doctrines of election and predestination he held,

1. That election was not of whole nations but of particular persons; "for," says he,[‡‡] "the vessels of mercy are not only the people of the Gentiles, but likewise those among the Jews who would believe, and are made one people of believers; hence it appears, that *non gentes eligi sed hominum voluntates,* 'not nations are chosen, but the wills of men.' " And in another place he observes,[§§] " that for this cause all nations are moved, that from their motion might come *electa gentium multitudo,* 'the elect multitude of nations,' which are every where famous;" for instance, *electa de Corintho,* "the elect out of Corinth," because there was *much people of God there. Electa de Macedonia,* "the elect out of Macedonia," because there was a large church of God in Thessalonica, who had no need to be taught *concerning love. Electa de Epheso,* "the elect out of Ephesus;" that they might know the secrets of God, and those mysteries which were before revealed to none. What shall I say more? All nations are moved to whom the Saviour sent the apostles, saying, *Go, teach all nations;* and of the *many* called, *few* being chosen, they built the church of the primitive saints; hence, says the apostle Peter, *The church that is at Babylon, elected, and Marcus, my son, salute you.* And, says John, *The elder to the elect lady;* and who also makes mention of the *children of the elect lady.*

2. He asserted, that those who are chosen of God in Christ, were chosen before the world began; or that election is from eternity; for in one place he says,[‖‖] " It must be affirmed, that according to the prescience and predestination of God, those things are *already done* which are *future. Qui enim electi sunt in Christo ante constitutionem mundi,* 'for they that are chosen in Christ before the foundation of the world,' have been already in former ages." And in interpreting those words in Isaiah xxv. 1, *Thy counsels of old*

---

* Pelag. Hist. l. 6, thes. 8, p. 541, 542.

† Discourse, &c. p. 99, 101; ed. 2. 97, 100.

‡ Chrysost. in Gen. serm. 51, tom. i. p. 401.

§ Ibid. in Rom. serm. 16, tom. iii. p. 140.

‖ Ibid. p. 141.   ¶ Ibid. 18, tom. iii. p. 157.

** Hist. Pelag. l. 6, thes. 8, p. 546.

†† Apolog. p. 4, p. 821.   ‡‡ Hieron. ep. ad Hedib. qu. 10, tom. iii. p. 49, B.

§§ Comment. in Hagg. ii. 6, tom. vi. p. 103, B.   ‖‖ In Eccl. tom. vii. p. 38, I.

are faithfulness and truth ; after he has mentioned the sense of the Jewish writers, observes,* that "others better and more rightly understand them as spoken in the person of the prophet, giving thanks to the Father for the sufferings of the Lord the Saviour; because he had done *wonderful things ; et cogtiationes antiquas veritate compleverit,* 'and had faithfully fulfilled ancient thoughts;' when they that stand at his right hand shall hear these words, *Come ye blessed of my Father, inherit the kingdom prepared for you from the foundation of the world.* Which also Paul understanding, spoke of, saying, *As he hath chosen us in him before the foundation of the world, that we should be holy and without blame."* Which last words of the apostle being elsewhere mentioned by him, he says,† "This we so interpret that we say, that election is not, according to Origen, of them who had been before, but we refer it to the prescience of God: moreover, we say, that we are *chosen that we may be holy and without blame before him,* that is, God; *ante fabricam mundi,* 'before the world was made;' which testifies, that it belongs to the prescience of God, to whom all things future are already done, and all things are known before they be; as Paul himself was predestinated in his mother's womb, and Jeremy in the belly, was sanctified, chosen, and, in the type of Christ, sent a prophet to the nations."

3. He also held that election was irrespective of holiness, as a motive or cause of it, but that it arises from the love, grace, and mercy of God; for in one part of his works, he has these words,‡ "The apostle does not say, he chose us, *before the foundation of the world ; cum essemus sancti et immaculati,* '*when* we were holy and without blame;' but, he chose us, *that we* might be *holy and without blame ;* that is, *qui sancti et immaculati ante non fuimus, ut postea essemus ;* that we, who before were not holy and without blame, might afterwards be so." And a little after he adds, " Paul, and they that are like him, are not *chosen,* ' *quia erant sancti & immaculati,* because they were holy and without blame;' but they are chosen and predestinated, that in their lives following they might become holy and without blame by their works and virtues." And in another place he plainly intimates,§ that predestination springs from the mercy and love of God; for speaking of Jacob he says, "Whiles he was yet in Rebecca's womb, he supplanted his brother Esau, not truly by his own strength, but by *the mercy of* God, *qui cognoscit & diligit quos prædestinavit,* who knows and loves those whom he hath predesti-

nated." It is true indeed, in the first citation I have made from this author, he says, that not nations are chosen, *sed voluntates hominum,* " but the wills of men ;" though what he means by it is not very easy to understand : his meaning cannot be, that God chose such persons whom he knew would of their own free will, by the mere strength of nature, do that which was good ; for this is pure *Pelagianism,* to which Jerom was an enemy ; and is contrary to those principles of grace he was a strenuous defender of. But, if his meaning was, that God chose such to happiness, who he knew would be made willing to obey him in the day of his power, because he had determined to make them so; this entirely agrees with our sentiments. There is another passage cited by Grotius ‖ from this writer, where he says,¶ that God *eligat eum quem interim bonum cernit,* "chooses him whom for the present he knows to be good ;" but it is easy to observe, that Jerom is there speaking, not of God's choice of men to eternal happiness, but of Christ's choosing Judas to the apostleship, who appeared for a while to be good, though he knew he would be wicked. To which may be added another passage produced by Dr. Whitby,** after Grotius,†† and Vossius,‡‡ to prove that election is from a foresight of good works, in which this writer says,§§ that, *dilectio et odium Dei vel ex præscientia nascitur futurorum vel ex operibus,* " the love and hatred of God arises either from the foreknowledge of things future, or from works." But what he means by this disjunctive proposition, is not very evident ; it is very probable, that by the love and hatred of God, he means the effects of them, salvation and damnation, which according to him proceed either according to the prescience of God, or the works of men. As for the citation out of the *Commentary* on the epistle to the Romans made by Vossius and Dr. Whitby,‖‖ I take no notice of, because it is judged by learned men ¶¶ not to be his, but either the work of Pelagius himself, or of some Pelagian writer. I deny not, but that Jerom held election to be according to the prescience of God, to which he refers it in the passages cited by the above writers, out of his commentaries on the epistles to the Galatians and Ephesians; and so do we, in a sense agreeable to the Scriptures; and it is evident that Jerom had the same sentiments of the foreknowledge of God as we have; for, says he,*** *Non enim ex eo quod Deus scit futurum aliquid, idcirco futurum est, sed quia futurum est, Deus novit ;* " not because God knows something to be future, therefore it is future, but because it is future, God knows it, as

---

* In Isa. **xxv.** 1, tom. v. p. 48, F.

† Apolog. adv. Ruffin. l. tom. ii. p. 68, M ; et Comment. in Eph. i. 4, tom. ix. p. 90, C.

‡ Ibid. p. 69, B ; et Comment. in Eph. i. 11, tom. **ix.** p. 90, E.   § Comment. in Hos. tom. vi. p. 21, B.   ‖ Disquisit. de Dogm. Pelagian. p. 11.   ¶ Adv. Pelag. l. 3, tom. ii. p. 100.   ** Discourse, &c. p. 99 ; ed. 2. 97 ;

and Postscript, p. 557 ; ed. 2. 534.   †† Ubi supra, p. 10.   ‡‡ Aist. Pelag. l. 6, thes. 8, p. 544.   §§ Hieron. in Mal. tom. vi. p. 128, H.

‖‖ P. 102 ; ed. 2. 100.   ¶¶ Vide Rivet. Critic. Sacr. l. 4, c. 5, p. 374; et Voss. Hist. Pelag. l. 1, c. 9, p. 12.   *** Comment in Jer. tom. v. p. 162, C.

having a foreknowledge of things to come." And though in the same place, and elsewhere,* he observes, that the prescience of God does not necessitate or force men to do this, or not to do that, but notwithstanding it, the will of man is preserved free in all his actions ; the same we also say, and to this we readily assent.

CHAPTER II

OF REDEMPTION.

Dr. Whitby says,† that the confirmation of the doctrine of universal redemption, from the suffrage of all antiquity, is sufficiently done by Vossius, in his *Historia Pelagiana*, where he lays down these two positions, 1. That " the sense of the ancient church was, that God wills the conversion and salvation of all." 2. That " it was the judgment of the ancient church, that Christ had provided an universal remedy for the universal fault of men, by paying a ransom of infinite value, lest any one should perish through the defect of it." He further observes, that this is more copiously done by Mr. Dally (he means Monsieur Daille) by producing the testimonies of the *ancients* from the *first* to the *twelfth* century ; and concluding thus, " Certainly I do not find one in the first eight ages of Christianity that has said absolutely, and in terms, as is commonly said, that Christ died only for the elect." Here the Doctor rests, and would have his readers trust to and depend upon the conclusions and assertions of these two men. Vossius's Pelagian History must be allowed to be a very considerable performance, and is the fund and magazine of antiquity for the Arminians. Dr. Twisse intended an answer to it, and in one of his books says,‡ he had entered upon it ; but death I suppose prevented his design, at least it never was published ; such a work, by so learned a hand, might have been of great service. But why should we trust to Vossius's account of the judgment of the ancient church in this point, since Dr. Whitby himself would not trust him in another ? namely, original sin ; though he was so very positive as to say, " The catholic church always so judged ;" and the Doctor tells us,§ that " upon an impartial search he found that all the passages he had collected were impertinent, or at least insufficient to prove the point." This gives no encouragement to depend on him. And inasmuch as the several passages cited by Vossius are also, with many others, produced by Monsieur Daille, I shall only attend to the latter, and to those only of the *first four* centuries ; and though he observes, that in these and the *four* following ages, none ever said *absolutely*, and in *express terms*, that Christ died *only* for the *elect ;* yet it does not follow, but that some might say it, in other terms and words equivalent, of the same signification, and which amounted to the same sense. It must be owned, that Monsieur Daille has collected a large number of testimonies indeed ; but when it is considered, that multitudes of them are only expressed in Scripture language, and so capable of the same sense the Scriptures are ; others regard men of all sorts, ranks, and degrees ; others Jews and Gentiles ; others the sufficiency of Christ's death for all ; and others, some general benefit by it, as the resurrection of the dead ; their number will be greatly reduced, and very few left to be of any service to the cause for which they are brought ; besides, it will be made to appear in the following *Sections*, that the ancients often describe the persons for whom Christ died by such characters as cannot agree with all men.

SECTION I

CLEMENS ROMANUS. A. D. 69

Clement, as he believed there was a certain number of elect persons, which has been proved in the preceding chapter, so he plainly intimates, that these are the persons for whom Christ shed his blood ; for having observed, that all *the elect of God* are made perfect in love, he adds,‖ " Without love nothing is well-pleasing to God ; in love the Lord assumed us to himself ; because of the love which Christ our Lord hath towards us, το αιμα αυτου αδωκεν υπερ ημων, he hath given his blood for us, his flesh for our flesh, and his soul for our souls." The sense of which is manifestly this, that the persons for whose sake Christ assumed human nature, and shed his precious blood, are the elect of God, and such who have a special and peculiar share in the love of Christ. And besides his saying,¶ that the blood of Christ was given, υπερ ημων, *for us*, he restrains redemption to them that have faith and hope in God ; for speaking** of the spies that came into Rahab's house, ordering her to hang out a scarlet thread, thereby says he, " making it manifest, *oti dia tou aimatos Kuriou lutrosis estai pasi tois pisteuousin kai elpizousin epi ton Theon*, that through the blood of the Lord there should be redemption for all those that believe and hope in God." Monsieur Daille†† has cited a passage from this writer in favour of general redemption, which is this, " Let us," says Clement,‡‡ " look to the blood of Christ, and see how precious his blood is to God, which being shed for our salvation, *panti to kosmo metanoias Chorin upenegken,* ' hath brought the grace of repentance to all the world.'" But his meaning is evidently this, that the blood of Christ, shed for the salvation of sinners, has laid a foundation for the preaching of the doctrine of repentance

---

* Ibid. in Ezek. tom. v. p. 177, E ; et in Eccl. tom. vii. p. 35, F. † Discourse, &c. p. 193 ; ed 2. 195 : Postscript, p. 566 ; ed. 2. 543. ‡ Riches of God's Grace, against Hord, part 1, p. 83. § Preface to Discourse, &c. p. 4 : ed. 2. p. 2. p. 112. ¶ Ib. p. 52, 54. 30. †† Apol. p. 753. p. 16. ‖ Ep. ad Corinth. ** Ib. p. ‡‡ Ep. ad Cor.

in all ages of the world; for he goes on to instance in the preaching of Noah to the old world; of Jonah to the Ninevites; and in God's declarations of his regard to repenting sinners in the times of Isaiah and Ezekiel; which he closes with this observation, *pantas oun tous agapetous autou boulomenos metanoias metechein,* "God therefore willing that his beloved ones should partake of repentance." In which he suggests, that God's grand design in having the doctrine of repentance preached in all ages was, that those who were the objects of his love might be brought unto it; which is so far from militating against, that it is a confirmation of the doctrine of special grace and redemption through the blood of Christ.

SECTION II

BARNABAS. A. D. 70

BARNABAS was a Levite, of the country of Cyprus,* and a companion of the apostle Paul; there is an epistle extant which goes under his name, and is thought to have been written after the destruction of the temple at Jerusalem, and about A. D. 70,† in which he not only says,‡ "that the Son of God being Lord, and who also shall judge the quick and the dead, *epathen ina e plege autou zoopoiete emas,* suffered that by his stripes he might quicken us;" that he could not suffer *ei me dia emas,* "but for us;" and that he offered the vessels of the Spirit a sacrifice, *uper ton emeteron amartion,* "for our sins," but also introduces Christ § thus speaking of his sufferings, "I see that I shall thus offer my flesh, *uper amartion tou laou tou kainou,* for the sins of the new people; meaning a special and peculiar people that should be taken out from among the Gentiles under the New Testament dispensation, called a *new* people, to distinguish them from God's ancient people the Jews.

SECTION III

IGNATIUS. A. D. 110

IGNATIUS never makes use of any general expressions when he speaks of the sufferings and death of Christ; but either says,‖ that he suffered, *uper emo, di emas,* "for us, that we might be saved;" or *uper amartion emon,* "for our sins;" and sometimes describes the persons he means, as when he says,¶ that "Jesus Christ died for us," *ina pisteusantes eis ton thanaton autou, to apothanein ekphugete,* "that believing in his death, you may escape dying." And in another place he says,** that "Jesus is *e zor ton piston,* "the life of believers." Monsieur Daille has not attempted to give us one instance for general redemption out of this writer, nor the former.

SECTION IV

JUSTIN. A. D. 150

JUSTIN MARTYR, in many places of his writings, limits an incarnation, sufferings, death, and sacrifice of Christ, and redemption by him, to certain persons whom he describes by repenting sinners, believers, &c. when he says,†† that Christ "was born according to the will of God the Father *uper ton pisteuonton anthropon,* for men that believe;" that is, in order to procure salvation, and obtain eternal redemption for such persons, as he elsewhere explains it; saying,‡‡ that he "became man of a virgin, according to the will of the Father, *uper soterias ton pisteuonton auto,* for the salvation of them that believe in him." And in another place,§§ having cited Isa. xxxiii. 16, *Bread shall be given him;* he observes, "that is a prophecy concerning that bread which our Christ hath delivered to us in commemoration of his being embodied; *dia tous pisteuontas eis auton, di ous kai, pathetos gegone,* for the sake of them that believe in him, for whom also he became subject to sufferings." And elsewhere he says,‖‖ that "the offering of fine flour for the leper, was a figure of the bread of the *eucharist,* which Jesus Christ our Lord hath delivered unto us to do in commemoration of his sufferings; which he endured *uper ton kathairomenon tas psuchas apo pases ponerias anthropon,* for those men whose souls are purified from all iniquity;" and this he supposed was done by the blood of Christ; for more than once explaining that text in Gen. xlix. 11, *He washed his garments in wine, and his clothes in the blood of grapes;* he says,¶¶ it "foretold, and manifestly declared the sufferings which Christ should endure, *di aimatos kathairon tous pisteuontas auto,* purifying by his blood them that believe in him." These, he often intimates, share the benefits of Christ's blood, sufferings, and death; "as," says he,*** "the blood of the passover saved them that were in Egypt, so the blood of Christ *tous pisteuontas rusetai ek thanatou,* delivers from death those that believe." In like manner he asserts,††† that Christ was an offering or sacrifice, *uper panton metanoein boulomenon amartolon,* "for all sinners that are willing to repent." Yea,‡‡‡ that *a pallagin de tou thanatou tois metaginoskousin apo ton phaulon kai pisteuousin auto ergazetai,* "he has wrought out deliverance from death for those that *repent* of their evils and *believe* in him." Now had Justin been of opinion that Christ died for every individual of mankind, would he have used such limitations and restrictions, when treating of the extent of his sufferings and death? Monsieur Daille indeed cites §§§

---

* Acts iv. 36.   † Vide Fabricii Bibl. Græc. l. 4, c. 5, p. 173.   ‡ Part 1, s. 6, p. 223. § Ibid. p. 224.   ‖ Ignat. ep. ad Smyrn. p. 2, 5; ad. Polycarp, p. 12; ad. Eph. p. 17; ad. Rom. p. 59.   ¶ Ep. ad Tralles, p. 47. ** Ep. ad Rom. p. 59.   †† Apol. pro

Christ. 1, p. 45.   ‡‡ Ib. 2, p. 86. §§ Dialog. cum Tryph. p. 296, 297.   ‖‖ Ibid. p. 259, 260.   ¶¶ Pro Christ. Apolog. 2, p. 74; Dialog. cum Tryph. p. 273.   *** Ibid. p. 338.   ††† Ibid. p. 259.   ‡‡‡ Ibid. p. 327.   §§§ Page 754, 755.

some passages from him as favouring the doctrine of universal redemption; but his first instance only proves, that Christ was born and crucified *uper tou genous ton anthropon,* " for the generation of men," or for mankind; but not that he was born and crucified for every individual of mankind. Justin's sense in other places is clear, and his meaning is that Christ died for some of all sorts of men; as when speaking of the scarlet thread that Rahab the harlot was directed to bind to her window, he says,[*] it was a " symbol of the blood of Christ, by which are saved the fornicators of old, and unrighteous persons, εκ παντων των εθνων, out of all nations; receiving forgiveness of sins, and sinning no more." And in another place he thus expresses himself,[†] " As Jacob served Laban for the cattle that were spotted, and of various forms, so Christ served even to the cross, υπερ των εκ παντος γενους ποικιλων και πολνειδων ανθρωπων, for men of every kind, of many and various shapes, procuring them by his blood, and the mystery of the cross." Monsieur Daille's second instance only declares that kind and tender manner in which God sent his Son into the world. His third sets forth Justin's sentiments concerning the heathens, which will be considered in a proper place. And his fourth and last only shows, that it is the will of God that all should be saved; meaning, that all men shall be raised from the dead; against those that deny the doctrine of the resurrection; or that it is the will of God that some of all sorts should be saved, referring to the apostle's words and sense in 1 Tim. ii. 4.

SECTION V

ECCLESIA SMYRNENSIS. A. D. 169

THE church at Smyrna wrote a letter to the churches in Pontus, and to the church at Philomelium, as it is thought, about the year 169, giving an account of the sufferings of some martyrs, and particularly of Polycarp, their former bishop; in which they take notice of the stupidity of some persons, who used their interest to prevent the Christians having the dead body of Polycarp given them; lest leaving their crucified Christ, they should begin to worship him; being ignorant, say they,[‡] that we can never leave that Christ, *ton uper tes tou pantos kosmou ton sozomenon soterias pathonta,* " who suffered for the salvation of the whole world of them that are saved, nor worship any other." This passage Monsieur Daille[§] thinks makes nothing to the purpose, since it does not deny that Christ died for others besides those who are really saved. But surely if these pious Christians had believed that Christ died for all men, for them that are saved, and for them that are not saved, they would never have expressed themselves in this restrictive manner; but

would have chose to have carried the extent of Christ's sufferings and death to the utmost, when they were declaring their great regard for him, and the great benefit of salvation men receive by him. Besides, these words manifestly show, in what sense this very ancient church understood those universal phrases, *the world, the whole world,* and *all men,* in Scripture, for whom Christ is said to give himself and die, and for whose sins he is said to be a propitiation; that these design a certain number of men that are and will be saved. As to the version of Ruffinus, urged by this author, rendering the passage thus, " who endured death for the salvation of the whole world;" it is not worthy of regard, since it is an imperfect one, omitting the words *ton sozomenou.* And here I choose to take notice of a citation made by Monsieur Daille,[||] and after him by Dr. Whitby,[¶] out of an epistle of Polycarp, bishop of this church at Smyrna, said to be written A. D. 107, to the Philippians, in which he thus speaks concerning Christ, " who," says he, " will come to judge the quick and the dead; *ou to aima ekzetesei o Theos apo ton apeithounton auto,* whose blood God will require of them that believed not in him;" from whence they conclude, that according to this ancient venerable bishop, Christ died for them that perish, as well as those that are saved. It is something strange, that Monsieur Daille should cite a passage out of an epistle, the genuineness of which he himself[**] has called in question; and, should it appear to be genuine, as it is thought to be by many learned men, it will be of no service to him, or to the Doctor, or to the cause they espoused, since God may be said to require, as he certainly will require, the blood of Christ of the unbelieving Jews who shed it; and indeed of them only, who said, *His blood be on us and on our children;* without supposing that his blood was shed for them; yea, on the contrary it appears, that his blood was not shed for them, both from their final unbelief, and from its being required of them. And of as little service are his citations[††] from Minutius Felix, Athenagoras, Tatian, and Theophilus of Antioch; since they only express the patience, goodness, power, and wisdom of God in creation and providence, and his great regard to repenting sinners; but not a syllable of Christ's dying for men, much less for every individual of mankind.

SECTION VI

IRENÆUS. A. D. 180,

IRENÆUS, when speaking of the incarnation and passion of Christ, and of redemption by his blood, frequently restrains them to certain persons of such and such characters; which evidently shows, that he did not think that these belong to all the individuals of

---

* Dialog. cum Tryph. p. 338.   † Ibid. p. 364.   ‡ Epist. Eccles. Smyrn. apud Euseb. Eccles. Hist. l. 4, c. 15, p. 134.   § Page 945. || Page 754.   ¶ Postscript to the Dis-
course, &c. p. 567; ed. 2. 544.   ** Vide Fabricii Bibl. Græc. l. 5, c. l, s. 14, p. 43.   †† Page 756—758.

mankind in common. Thus, treating of the coming of Christ, and of the end of his coming into the world, he says,* that "he came to save *all* by himself, *omnes inquam, qui per eum renascuntur in Deum*, all, I say, who through him are born again unto God, infants, and little ones, and children, and young men, and old men." And in another place,† taking notice of God's suffering Jonah to be swallowed up by a whale, and of his after deliverance; "So," says he, "God from the beginning suffered man to be swallowed up by the great whale, who was the author of transgression; not that being swallowed up he should wholly perish, but providing and preparing a plan of salvation which is effected by the word, through the sin of Jonah; *his qui eandem cum Jona de Deo sententiam habuerunt*, for them who have the same sentiments concerning God with Jonah; and have confessed and said, I am the Lord's servant, I worship the Lord God of heaven, who made the sea and the dry land; that man enjoying the unhoped-for salvation from God, might rise from the dead and glorify him." And elsewhere proving, that the Father of Christ is the same that was spoken of by the prophets; and that when Christ came, he acknowledged no other but him, who was declared from the beginning. He adds,‡ *a quo libertatem detulit his qui legitime et prono animo, et toto corde deserviunt ei,* "from whom he brought deliverance to them who serve him truly, with a ready mind, and with all their hearts;" but to the despisers of him, and such who are not subject to God, *sempiternam attulit perditionem abscindens eos a vita,* "he hath brought everlasting destruction, cutting them off from life." So far was he from thinking that Christ died to redeem all mankind, that he expressly says, that the death of Christ is the *damnation* of some; his words are these;§ "As they (the Israelites) through the blindness of the Egyptians, so we, through the blindness of Jews, receive salvation; *siquidem mors Domino, eorum quidem qui cruci eum fixerunt et non crediderunt ejus adventum, damnatio est:* seeing the death of the Lord is indeed the damnation of them that crucified him, and did not believe his coming; but the salvation of them *that believe in him.*" And in another place,‖ where he makes Jacob a type of Christ, and Rachel of the church, he confines the obedience and sufferings of Christ to his church: "All things," says he, "he did for the younger Rachel, who had good eyes, *quæ præfigurabat ecclesiam, propter quam sustinuit Christus,* who prefigured the church, for whom Christ endured, that is, sufferings and death." And a little after he has these words,¶ "Christ came not for the sake of them only who believed in him, in the times of Tiberius Cæsar; nor did the Father provide for those men only who now are, but for

all men entirely; *qui ab initio secundum virtutem suam in sua generatione, et timuerunt et dilexerunt Deum, et juste et pie conversati sunt erga proximos, et concupierunt videre Christum et audire vocem ejus;* who from the beginning, according to their virtue or ability, have feared and loved God in their generation, and have righteously and piously conversed with their neighbours, and have desired to see Christ, and hear his voice." The passages cited from this writer, by M. Daille,** for general redemption, have not one word about it, and at most only prove, that man is endued with free will, which, in some sense, is not denied; and that man, and not God, is the cause of his own imperfection, blindness, and destruction, which is readily agreed to.

The citations made by the same author†† out of Clemens Alexandrinus, do, indeed, express, in very general terms, the care of God and Christ over mankind, and their great regard unto and desire after their salvation; and also assert our Lord to be the Saviour of all men, and seem to carry the point further than what is in controversy, even to the salvation of all; which, if it could once be established, we should readily come into the notion of general redemption, though in all these large expressions, Clement seems only to refer to the texts in Jude ver. 3, 1 Tim. ii. 4, and iv. 10, in the first of which the apostle speaks of the *common salvation*, all the saved ones share alike; in the next, of the will of God, that some of *all sorts* should be saved; and in the last, of God, as the preserver of all men, in a way of common, and particularly of believers, in a way of special providence; and after all, Clement‡‡ distinguishes between Christ's being a Saviour of some, and a Lord of others; for he says, that he is *ton pepis teukoton Soter, ton de apeithesanton Kurios,* "the Saviour of them that believe; but the Lord of them that believe not." And in one place§§ he has these words; "Wherefore, he (Christ,) is introduced in the gospel weary, who was weary for us, and promising to give his life a ransom, *anti polton,* in the room of many."

SECTION VII

TERTULLIAN. A. D. 200

TERTULLIAN is a writer, it must be owned, who expresses himself in somewhat general terms, when he speaks of the incarnation, death and sacrifice of Christ, which are yet capable of being understood in a sense agreeable to the doctrine of particular redemption; as when he says,‖‖ that "we who believe that God was here on earth, and took upon him the humility of a human habit, *ex causa humanæ salutis,* 'for the sake of man's salvation,' are far from their opinion, who think that God takes no care of any thing;" which may be truly said, without supposing

* Adv. Hæres. l. 2, c. 39, p. 191.   † Ibid. l. 3, c. 24, p. 289.   ‡ Ibid. l. 4, c. 24, p. 342.   § Adv. Hæres, c. 47, p. 388.
‖ Ibid. l. 38, p. 376.   ¶ Ibid. c. 39, p. 377.

** Page 759.   †† Ibid. p. 760—764.
‡‡ Strom. l. 7, p. 703.
§§ Pædagog. l. 1, c. 9, p. 126.
‖‖ Tertullian. adv. Marcion, l. 2, c. 16, p. 465

that Christ assumed human nature, for the sake of the salvation of every individual of mankind; so when he says, in another place,[*] that "Christ ought to make a sacrifice *pro omnibus gentibus*, 'for all nations;' his meaning may be, that it was necessary that he should be a propitiation, not for the Jews only, but for the Gentiles also;" and elsewhere having observed that the Marcionites concluded from the words of God to Moses, in Exod. xxxii. 10, that Moses was better than his God, he thus addresses them,[†] "You are also to be pitied, with the people, who do not acknowledge Christ, figured in the person of Moses, the advocate with the Father, and the offerer up of his own soul, *pro populi salute*, 'for the salvation of the people;'" by which *people* may very well be understood, the special and peculiar people of God's elect, of whom the people of Israel was a type and figure. Besides, in some places, Tertullian manifestly restrains the death of Christ, and the benefits of it, to some persons only, to the church, and to believers. Thus having cited Deut. xxxiii. 17, *His glory is like the firstling of his bullock; and his horns are like the horns of unicorns; with them he shall push the people together to the ends of the earth*; gives[‡] this interpretation of the words; "not the rhinoceros, which has but one horn, is intended; nor the minotaurus, which has two horns; but *Christ* is signified hereby; a bullock is he called, because of both his dispositions *aliis ferus ut judex, aliis mansuetus ut Salvator*, 'to some fierce as a judge, to others mild as a Saviour,' whose horns would be the extremities of the cross. Moreover, by this virtue of the cross, and being horned in this manner, *nunc ventilat per fidem*, 'he now pushes all the nations;' by faith, taking them up from earth to heaven, and by the judgment, will then push them, casting them down from heaven to earth." And a little after, in the same place, speaking of the brazen serpent, he says, that "it designed the virtue and efficacy of our Lord's cross, by which the serpent the devil was made public, and to every one that is hurt by the spiritual serpents, *intuenti tamen et credenti in eam*, only looking upon it, and believing in it, healing of the bites of sin and salvation are immediately pronounced." And so as he observes in another place,[§] *quod perierat olim per lignum in Adam, id restitueretur per lignum Christi*, what was of old lost through the tree in Adam, that is restored through the tree of Christ." Again he observes,[||] that the apostle says, that *we are reconciled in his body through death;* on which he thus descants : "Yea, in that body in which he could die through the flesh, he died, not through the church, *plane propter ecclesiam*, but verily for the church, by changing body for body,

and that which is fleshly for that which is spiritual." M. Daille[¶] has produced a passage or two from this writer in favour of the universal extent of Christ's death and redemption, in which not one word is mentioned concerning either of them; and only declare, that man was not originally made to die; that God is not negligent of man's salvation; that he desires his restoration to life, willing rather the repentance than the death of a sinner, which, as they do not militate against the doctrine of particular, so cannot serve to establish that of general redemption.

Two testimonies from Hippolitus, bishop of Portua, a disciple of Clement of Alexandria, and a martyr, who is said to flourish about A. D. 220, are next cited[**] at second hand; the first of which is, that "the God of the universe became man for this purpose; that by suffering in passible flesh, our whole kind, which was sold unto death, might be redeemed;" that is, from death, a corporal death; the general resurrection from the dead being thought to be the fruit of Christ's sufferings and death. The other is, that "the Son of God, through flesh, naturally weak of himself, wrought out the salvation of the whole;" which may be understood of the salvation of the whole body of Christ, the church, or of every one of his people, his sheep, his children, and his chosen, and not of every individual of mankind; since all are not saved, as they undoubtedly would be, if Christ had wrought out the salvation of all.

SECTION VIII

ORIGINES ALEXANDRINUS. A. D. 230

ORIGEN is represented[††] as holding, that Christ suffered and died for the salvation of all rational creatures, in heaven and in earth, devils as well as men; and that all in the issue will be saved : and there are passages[‡‡] in his writings which favour this notion. Could our universalists give into, and prove such an assertion, that all mankind will be saved, the controversy about general redemption would soon be at an end. It is no wonder that a writer, who had imbibed such a notion, should express himself in very general terms about the sufferings and death of Christ, and assert him to be the Saviour of all men, which is the substance of the citations out of him by M. Daille;[§§] nevertheless, as it is very probable, he was not always of this mind; and it is certain, that when this notion of his was not in view, he says many things which not only contradict that, but very much countenance the doctrine of particular redemption, as will appear from the following observations.

1. He expressly affirms, that the sufferings and death of Christ are of no use and service to some persons; and that the fruit

* Ibid. adv. Judæos, c. 13, p. 226.
† Adv. Marcion, l. 2, c. 26, p. 474.
‡ Ibid. l. 3, c. 18, p. 192, 193.
§ Adv. Judæos, c. 13, p. 226. || Adv. Marcion. l. 5, c. 19, p. 613.   ¶ Page **765.**

** Adv. Marcion. l. 5, c. 19, p. 765.
†† Vide Hieron. ad Avitum, tom. ii. p. 52.
‡‡ Vide Comment. in Rom. l. 5, fol. 179, B ; et Comment. in Joannem, p. 38.   §§ Apol. p. 765, &c.

and effect of them only belong to others, whom he describes; his words are these :* "The sufferings of Christ, indeed, confer life on them that believe, but death on them that believe not: for though the Gentiles have salvation and justification by his cross, yet is it destruction and condemnation to the Jews; for so it is written in the Gospel; *This child is born for the fall and rising again of many.*" And in another place;† "If any would be saved, let him come to the house," says he, "in which the blood of Christ is for a sign of redemption; for with them who said, *His blood be upon us and upon our children, Christi sanguis in condemnatione est,* 'the blood of Christ is for condemnation;' for Jesus was *set for the fall and rising again of many;* and therefore to them that speak against his sign, *efficitur sanguis ejus ad pœnam,* 'his blood is for punishment;' but to them that believe, for salvation." And elsewhere,‡ mentioning these words, *the Lamb of God which taketh away the sin of the world,* he adds, by way of explanation, *ou panton de e amartia apo tou amnou airetai,* "the sin of all is not indeed taken away by the Lamb, even of those who do not grieve, nor are afflicted until it be taken away."

2. Though he sometimes speaks of Christ's procuring salvation, redemption, and remission of sin, for all men, for the whole world; yet from other passages of his it appears, that he is to be understood of the sufficiency of the price of Christ's blood to procure these things for all men, which is not denied. In one place,§ taking notice of the legal sacrifices, he has these expressions : "Among all these there is one Lamb which is *able* to take away the sins of the whole world; for such was this sacrifice, *ut una sola sufficieret pro totius mundi salute,* 'that that alone was sufficient for the salvation of the whole world.'" And in another place he thus expresses himself,‖ "Until the blood of Jesus was given, which was so precious, *ut solus pro omnium redemptione sufficieret,* 'that it alone was sufficient for the redemption of all;' it was necessary, that they who were brought up in the law, should every one for himself, in imitation of the future redemption, give his own blood," meaning the blood of circumcision.

3. It may be further observed, that Origen, by the *world,* sometimes understands the *church,* for which, he frequently says, Christ suffered and died. The apostle Paul says,¶ that *God was in Christ reconciling the world unto himself;* where, by *the world,* is not to be understood the whole world, that is, those who are in the whole world, as Origen in one place ** observes; and in another place †† having cited the same passage, adds, "the sin of which world Christ has took away,

περι γαρ του κοσμου της εκκλησιας 'for of the world of the church is this word written;'" and immediately subjoins John i. 29, as to be understood in the same sense. And elsewhere,‡‡ in the same work, he not only mentions it as the sense of a certain expositor, that by the world is meant the church, which is the ornament and beauty of the world, and inquires whether it may be called so, and also light, but affirms it to be so, λεγεσθω τοινυν η εκκλησια κοσμος, "therefore," says he, "let the church be called the world, because it is enlightened by the Saviour;" and cites several passages of Scripture, as Matt. v. 14, John i. 29, 1 John ii. 2, 1 Tim. iv. 10, to be interpreted in the same way. And it is easy to observe, that Origen often speaks of Christ's suffering and dying for the church: in one place,§§ speaking of Christ and the church as bridegroom and bride, he says, "First the bride prays, and immediately, in the midst of her prayers she is heard, she sees the bridegroom present, she sees the virgins joined in company with him. Moreover the Bridegroom answers her, and after his words, *dum ille pro ejus patitur salute,* 'while he suffers for her salvation,' the companions answer, until the bridegroom is in bed, and rises from suffering, they will make some ornaments for the bride." And in the same work ‖‖ on these words, *Arise, my fair one,* he thus comments; "Why does he say, arise? Why hasten? I have sustained for thee the rage of tempests; I have received the floods which were due to thee; my soul is made sorrowful unto death for thee." In another place he says,¶¶ "The church of Christ is strengthened by the grace of him who was crucified for her." And elsewhere*** we call the fat, that is, of the sacrifices, the life of Christ, which is the church of his friends, *pro quibus animam suam posuit,* "for whom he laid down his life." Again,††† "He has delivered him for all, not only for the saints, not only for t e great ones, but the Father delivered his own Son for them who are altogether *the least in the church.*"

4. Origen sometimes calls the world for whom Christ died, the *believing* world, and the *people of believers,* and describes those for whom he suffered by such distinguishing characters: his words in one place are these,‡‡‡ "If any one is ashamed of the cross of Christ, he is ashamed of that economy by which these (powers) are triumphant over; for he that knows and believes these things ought to glory in the cross of our Lord Jesus Christ, by which Christ being *stauroumenou to kosmo to pisteuonti,* 'crucified for the world that believes,' the principalities are made a show of, and triumphed over." And in another place,§§§ "because he (Christ) took

* In Lev. homil. 3, fol. 57, D.
† In Joshua, homil. 3. fol. 152, 153, L.
‡ Comment. in Joan. 146.   § In Num. homil. 24, fol. 138. C.   ‖ In Rom. l. 2, fol. 148, B.   ¶ 2 Cor. v. 19.   ** Comment. In Gen. p. 17.   †† Ibid. in Joan. p. 5.

‡‡ Ibid. p. 147.   §§ In Cantic: homil. 1, apud Hieron. tom. iii. fol. 57, G.   ‖‖ Ibid. hom. 2, fol. 61, B.   ¶¶ In Gen. homil. 3, fol. 8, E.   *** In Lev. homil. 5, fol. 67, A.   ††† In Rom. l. 7, fol. 193, A.   ‡‡‡ In Matt. p. 283.   §§§ In Joan. p. 73.

upon him the sins *tou laou ton pisteuonton eis auton*, ' of the people of those that believe in him,' he often says, what he does in Psalm xxii. 1, and lxix. 5." And elsewhere,* speaking of Christ, he says, " This is the live goat sent into the wilderness ; and this is the goat which is offered to the Lord a sacrifice to expiate sin ; and he hath made a true propitiation in himself, *credentibus populis*, ' for the believing people.' " Again,† " The Son of God is come, and hath given himself a ransom ; that is, he hath delivered himself for enemies, and* for them that thirst he hath shed his blood ; *et hæc est credentibus facta redemptio*, ' and this becomes redemption to them that believe." He interprets that text‡ in Matt. xx. 21, " And to give his life a ransom for many," thus, *anti pollon ton pisteusanton eis auton*, " for the many that believed on him." He adds indeed, " And by way of hypothesis, if all believe in him, he gave his life a ransom for all." To which may be added the following passage, " The true purification was not before, but in the passover, when Jesus died *uper ton agnizomenon*, ' for them that are purified,' as the Lamb of God, and took away the sin of the world."§ Monsieur Daille ‖ next cites a passage as from Gregory of Neocæsarea, a hearer of Origen, but the work from whence it is taken is judged by learned men to be none of his ;¶ and this writer himself seems to question it, since he adds, " or whoever is the author of the anathemas which are carried about under his name." And besides, this testimony only shows, that Christ is the " Saviour of the world, and the light of the world ;" which nobody denies, for they are the express words of the Scripture ; but the question is, in what sense these phrases are to be understood.

SECTION IX

CYPRIAN. A. D. 250.

CYPRIAN, in many places of his writings, very expressly limits Christ's sufferings and death to certain persons described by him ; as when he says,** " Though we are many shepherds, yet we feed but one flock ; and ought to gather together and cherish *oves universas quas Christus sanguine suo et passione quæsivit* ' all the sheep which Christ hath sought up by his blood and sufferings ;' nor should we suffer our supplicant and grieving brethren to be cruelly despised and trodden down by the proud presumption of some persons." And in another place he asks, †† " What can be a greater sin, or what a fouler spot, than to stand against Christ, than to scatter his church ? *quam ille sanguine suo præparabit et condidit*, ' which he has prepared and obtained by his own blood ?' "

And elsewhere he says,‡‡ " Christ *is the bread of life ; et panis hic omnium non est, sed noster est ;* and this bread does not belong to all, but is ours ;' and as we say, *our Father*, because he is the Father of them that understand and believe, so we call Christ our bread, *qui corpus contigimus*, ' who have touched his body ;" in which words all but believers are excluded from having any share in Christ, the bread of life. And having in another place§§ mentioned Ezek. ix. 4, where a *mark* is ordered to be set upon the foreheads of the men that sigh and cry for the abominations of Jerusalem, he makes this observation ; "This sign belongs to the passion and blood of Christ ; *et quisquis in hoc signo invenitur*, ' and whosoever is found with this sign shall be preserved safe and whole ?' " which is approved by the testimony of God, saying, *And the blood shall be for a sign upon the houses where you are, &c.* What preceded in type before the Lamb was slain, is fulfilled in Christ, the truth following after ; as there *Egypt* being smitten, the Jewish people could not escape but by the blood and token of the Lamb ; so when the world shall begin to be wasted and smitten, *quisquis in sanguine et signo Christi inventus fuerit, solus evadet,* " whosoever shall be found in the blood, and with the mark of Christ, shall only escape." From whence it is evident, that Cyprian did not think that every individual of mankind is interested in the blood and death of Christ. And a little after, in the same epistle,‖‖ speaking of immortality, he has these words ; "This grace Christ imparts, this gift of his mercy he gives, by subduing death through the victory of the cross ; *redimendo credentem pretio sanguinis sui*, ' by redeeming the believer with the price of his blood ;' by reconciling man to God the Father, and by quickening the dead with the heavenly regeneration." And in one of his tracts,¶¶ animating the saints against the fears of death, he says, " Let him be afraid to die *qui non Christi cruce et passione censetur*, ' who is not reckoned to have any part in the cross and sufferings of Christ ;' let him be afraid to die who will pass from this death to a second death." And a little after,*** " We who live in hope, and believe in God, and trust, *Christum passum esse pro nobis*, ' that Christ has suffered for us, and rose again ;' abiding in him, and rising again by him and in him, why should we be unwilling to depart hence out of this world ? or, why should we mourn over and grieve for our departed friends, as if they were lost ?" And in another place,††† giving an account of our Lord's behaviour before Pilate, makes this remark, " This is he, who when he held his peace in his passion, will not be silent afterwards in his vengeance : this is our God ; *id est, non*

---

* In Lev. homil. 10, fol. 82, D.   † In Rom. l. 3, fol. 155, F.   ‡ Com. in Matt. p. 422.
§ In Joan. p. 372.   ‖ Apolog. p. 768.
¶ Vide Rivet. Critic. Sacr. l. 2, c. 16, p. 220 ; Fabricii Bibl. Græc. l. 5, c. 1, s. 28, p. 252.
** Ep. 67, p. 164.   †† Ep. 72, p. 180.

‡‡ De Oratione Dominica, p. 268.
§§ Ad Demetrianum, p. 283.
‖‖ Page 284.   ¶¶ De Mortalitate, p. 298.
*** Page 299.   ††† De Bono Patientia, p. 319.

omnium, sed fidelium et credentium Deus, that is, not the God of all, but of the faithful and believers." To all which may be added another passage of his, which runs thus,[*] " Writing to the seven churches, and intimating to each of them their sins and transgressions, he said *repent*; to whom? but *quos pretio magno sui sanguinis redemerat*, ' whom he had redeemed with the great price of his blood.' " This last passage is indeed taken out of an epistle which Erasmus thought was not Cyprian's but Cornelius's, bishop of Rome; however, he afterwards judged it to be a learned piece, and not unworthy of Cyprian; Gravius and Palemius affirm it to be his;[†] and if it was Cornelius's, the citation may be properly enough made here, since he was contemporary with Cyprian. The passages cited by Monsieur Daille[‡] from this writer, as being on the side of universal redemption, only set forth either the great encouragement given by God to penitent sinners, or that Christ came to be the Saviour of mankind, to be given unto men, and that he came for the sake of all; which Cyprian explains in the very same passage,[§] of all sorts of men, learned and unlearned, of every age and sex; as in another of them, by a simile taken from the general and equal diffusion of the sun's light, he shows,[||] that Christ, the sun and true day, equally gives the light of eternal life *in sua ecclesia*, " in his own church;" and that the Israelites had an equal measure of the manna, without any difference of age or sex; so the heavenly grace is equally divided to all without any difference of sex or years, and without respect of persons; and the gift of spiritual grace poured forth *super omnem Dei populum*, " upon all the people of God."

Some testimonies are next produced by Monsieur Daille[¶] out of Novatian, Medhodius, and Arnobius; the first of these writers, in one of the passages cited, signifies that, there is hope of salvation for men in Christ: which is not at all against us; for hope is not taken away, but established upon better grounds by the doctrine of particular, than by that of general redemption; since according to the latter, all men are indeed redeemed by Christ, but it was possible that none might be saved by him; whereas the former secures the certain salvation of all the redeemed ones: and in the other of them he suggests, that the anger, hatred, and threatenings of God, are for the good of men, and in order to move upon them, and bring them to that which is right and good; but not a word does he say concerning the death of Christ, and redemption by it. The second of these authors referred to, explains the text in Rom. ix. 21, *one vessel to honour, and another to dishonour*, thus, " not that God makes some good and others evil, but that is to be understood of the power God has of

doing what he will." Nor do we say that God makes any man evil, but that man made himself so; though we think none are good but whom God makes good. This writer indeed suggests, that it is the will of God that all men should be good, virtuous, and faithful, which is true if his approving but not of his determining 'will; and also intimates that all the good things of God are common to all, which in some sense holds good of the common bounties of providence, but not of the riches of grace. The third proposes a pagan objection, formed thus; " If Christ came to be the Saviour of mankind, why does he not, with equal bounty, deliver all alike ?" This objection, supposes, that according to the Christian scheme, all men were not delivered or redeemed by Christ. Arnobius answers to it, not by asserting a deliverance or redemption of every individual of mankind, but by putting another question thus, " Does not he equally deliver, who equally calls all ?" In which he argues indeed, from the extent of the call to the extent of the deliverance; but then the call he speaks of seems to be not of every individual person, but of some of all sorts; a grant from Christ of coming to him to some of all sorts, *sublimibus, infimis, servis, fœminis, pueris*, " high and low, servants, women, and children ;" which are his own words ;[**] and consequently the deliverance he argues from hence must be only of some of all sorts; which is what we contend for.

SECTION X

LACTANTIUS. A. D. 320

LUCIUS COELIUS was callled Firmianus from his country, Firmium in Italy, and Lactantius from his smooth and milky way of speaking; he was an auditor of Arnobius, and preceptor to Crispus, son of Constantine the Great, who died A. D. 326. He wrote seven books of *Divine Institutions*, besides some other treatises, in which he says some things which limit the sufferings and death of Christ, and the benefits thereof, to certain persons. Thus speaking of Christ, he says,[††] " which as he knew what would be, so he would ever and anon say,*oportare se pati atque interfici pro salute multorum*, that he ought to suffer and be slain for the salvation of many ;" and if for the salvation of many, then not of all. And in another place says he,[‡‡] " The Jews use the Old Testament, we the New, but yet they are not different; for the New is the fulfilling of the Old, and in both the same testator is Christ; *qui pro nobis morte suscepta, nos hæredes regni æterni fecit ;* who having suffered death for us, hath made us heirs of the everlasting kingdom, having abdicted and disinherited the people of the Jews." From whence it is plain, that this writer thought that all those for whom Christ died

---

[*] In Epist. ad Novatianum, p. 436, 437.
[†] Vide Rivet. Crit. Sacr. l. 2, c. 15, p. 212.
[‡] Page 768—770.   [§] De Oratione Dominica, 270.   [||] Ep. 76, p. 212.   [¶] Page 770,

771.   [**] Arnobius adv. Gentes, l. 2, p. 109.
[††] Lactant. Divin. Institut. l. 4, c. 18, p. 319.
[‡‡] Ibid. c. 20, p. 327.

are made heirs of everlasting glory : but all men are not made heirs, whence it must follow, that he did not die for all men ; though Lactantius by *us* means the Gentiles, in opposition to the Jews, yet not all the Gentiles, but only some of them, who are called by the grace of God from among them : as appears from a passage of his a little after in the same chapter,* where having mentioned the new covenant made with the house of Judah and Israel, he observes, that "the house of Judah and Israel truly do not signify the Jews, whom he has cast off, but *qui ab ea convocati ex gentibus,* who are called by him (Christ) from among the Gentiles, who succeed in their room in the adoption, and are called the children of the Jews." And elsewhere,† speaking of the crucifixion of Christ, he says, "He stretched out his hands in his passion and measured the world, that he might at that very time show, that *from the rising of sun to the setting of it, magnum populum ex omnibus linguis, et tribubus congregatum,* a large people, gathered out of all languages and tribes, should come under his wings, and receive the most great and sublime sign in their foreheads." And a little after in the same place, having taken notice of the passover lamb, and the sprinkling of its blood upon the door-post, whereby the Israelites were safe, when the Egyptians were destroyed, he observes, that "this was a figure of things to come ; for Christ is a Lamb, white, without spot, that is, innocent, just, and holy, who being sacrificed by the same Jews, saluti est omnibus qui signum sanguinis, id est crucis qua sanguinem fudit in sua fronte conscripserunt, is for salvation to all who have written in their forehead the sign of the blood ; that is, of the cross on which he shed his blood." Monsieur Daille‡ claims this writer on his side of the question, and produces several passages out of him on the behalf of the general scheme ; and true it is that Lactantius says,§ that "the most abundant and full fountain of God is open to all, and the heavenly light arises to all ; but then he adds, *quicunque oculos habent,* who have eyes to see ;" but every individual of mankind has not eyes to see the well of living water the gospel points out, or that heavenly light which breaks forth through it. He also says,‖ that because God is gracious and merciful, that is to say, towards his own (that is, whom he has loved and chosen for himself), he sent him (his Son) to them whom he had hated (that is, the Gentiles, who by his neglect of them in former ages seemed to be the objects of his hatred), lest he should for ever shut up the way of salvation to them ; but would give them free liberty of following God, that they might obtain the reward of life, if they would follow him ; *quod plurimi eorum faciunt atque*

fecerant, which very many of them do, and have done." Again he also says,¶ that "because of this humility, or low estate of Christ, they (the Jews) not knowing their God, entered into detestable counsel to take away his life ; *qui ut eos vivificaret advenerat,* who came that he might quicken them ;" which he might very well say, without having any notion of general redemption ; since many of those who had a hand in the death of Christ, were afterwards converted and quickened by his grace. And in another place, giving the reasons why Christ died the death of the cross, he mentions this in the first place,** that "he who came mean to help the mean and weak, and point out the hope of salvation to all, was to suffer this kind of death, which the mean and weak were wont to do, lest there should be any who could not imitate him." His meaning is this, Christ has humbled himself so low, even to the death of the cross, that all sorts of men might have hope of salvation, even those of the lowest and meanest rank and form ; which well consists with the doctrine of particular redemption ; and accordingly he says,†† that "we of every sex, descent, and age, enter into the heavenly road, because God who is the guide of the way, denies immortality to no man that is born," wherefore all sorts of men may hope for it.

SECTION XI

PAULINUS TYRIUS. A. D. 325

PAULINUS was first presbyter of the church at Antioch, then bishop of Tyre, and after that bishop of Antioch. He died A. D. 328. He composed a *Panegyric Oration* upon the building of churches, in the time of Constantine ;‡‡ in which he says many things concerning the church of Christ, and among the rest, that it was for her sake that Christ assumed human nature, and suffered death in it ; which, had he thought were done for all the world, he would not have mentioned as peculiar favours to her. His words are these :§§ "For it must needs follow, that when her (the church's) shepherd and Lord, *apax ton uper autes thanaton katadexamenou,* 'had once suffered death for her,' and after his sufferings had changed that body which he put on mean and sordid, *charin autes,* 'for her sake,' into a bright and glorious one, and led the flesh that was dissolved out of corruption into incorruption, that she also should enjoy the dispensations of the Saviour," that is, and become glorious also. And elsewhere, in the sameo ration,‖‖ he represents Christ as a Saviour of some particular persons, though of a large number ; as when he calls him "a leader into the knowledge of God, a teacher of true religion, a destroyer of the ungodly, and tyrants, and

---

* Page 328.   † Lactant. Divin. Institut. c. 26, p. 344.   ‡ P. 772.   § Ibid. l. 3, c. 26. p. 225, 356.   ‖ Ibid. l. 4, c. 11, p. 293.   ¶ Ibid. c. 16, p. 314, 315.   ** Ibid. c. 293, 343.   †† Ibid. l. 6, c. 3, p. 440.

‡‡ Vide Vales, Not in Euseb. l. 10, c. 1, p. 189, 190 ; et Euseb. contr. Marcell. l. 1, c. 4, p. 19.   §§ Oratio Panegyr. apud Euseb. Eccl. Hist. l. 10, c. 4. p. 382.   ‖‖ Ibid. p. 373.

ton Sotera emon ton apegnosmenon, 'the Saviour of us, who were in a deplorable and desperate condition,'" and us, who were not only diseased with ulcers, and pressed with putrifying wounds, but lay among the dead, he, *by himself, saved* out of these depths of death; for in none of the heavenly was there such strength, ωs τη των τοσουτων αβλαβωs διακονησαθαι σοτηρια, "as without hurt to procure the *salvation of so many;* he alone touched our miserable corruption, he alone bore our labours, he alone took upon him the punishment of our iniquities."

SECTION XII

EUSEBIUS PAMPHILUS CÆSARIENSIS. A. D. 330.

EUSEBIUS took the name of Pamphilus from Pamphilus the martyr, his intimate friend and acquaintance:[*] he lived in the time of Constantine the Great, and was very dear unto and highly esteemed of by that emperor. He was made bishop of Cæsarea in Palestine about A. D. 315, and died A. D. 339 or 340.[†] He was a man of great learning, and wrote much, and several of his works still remain. Some testimonies are taken from him by M. Daillé,[‡] showing that the sacrifice of Christ was offered up for all mankind, in the room and stead of all men, and is the expiation of the whole world. That he uses such expressions is not denied; but in what sense he used them should be considered. When he says, that the ransom of Christ is for the souls of all men, which he understands equally of Jews and Gentiles, he does not mean every individual of both, only some, as appears from what he immediately subjoins:[§] "by whose (Christ's) divine and mystical doctrine, παντες ημεις οι εξ εθνων, ' all we who are from among the Gentiles,' find the forgiveness of former sins; whence also those of the Jews, *oi eis auton egpikotes,* ' who hope in him' are freed from the curse of Moses." And in another place,[‖] he says, *monois tois dia Christon ex apanton ton ethnon,* "to them only who are taken by Christ out of all nations, can the blessing made to Abraham concerning all nations agree. And as to the Jews, he observes,[¶] that "few of them believe in the Saviour and our Lord, and thereby obtain the promised spiritual redemption; for God did not promise, that the coming of Christ should be salutary to the whole nation of the Jews without distinction; *all' oligois, te komide apantois, tois eis ton Sotera kai Kurion emon pepisteukosin,* but to a few, and very scarce indeed, even to them that should believe on the Saviour and our Lord." Moreover, when he says that the sacrifice of Christ is the expiation of the whole world, it is plain, from other passages

of his, that he means only them that believe; for having cited John i. 29, 1 John ii. 2, 1 Cor. i. 30, he adds,[**] which "teach that his (Christ's) coming is the filling up and finishing of the sin of those who have done wickedly against him; and also the removal and purgation of the sins, and the expiation of the unrighteousness, *ton eis auton pepisteukoton,* of those that should believe in him." And in another place[††] he says, "Wherefore his (Christ's) mighty one left him, willing that he should go down to death, even the death of the cross, and be shown to be the ransom of the whole world, *kai katharsion genesthai ten ton eis auton pisteusanton zoes,* and become the expiation of the life of them that believe in him." Besides, it is abundantly evident that he restrains the incarnation, sufferings, and death of Christ, and the salutary effects thereof, to the church, to them that believe in Christ, fear and obey him. Having mentioned[‡‡] those words in Isa. ix. 6, *To us a child is born,* &c., he puts this question: "To what us, *e tois auton pepisteukosi,* unless to them that believe in him? but to them that *do not believe* in him he is the author of fire and burning." And in another place[§§] he says, that "the cause of Christ's coming is the redemption *ton di autou sothesomenon,* of those that were to be saved by him." And elsewhere[‖‖] he observes, that Isaiah preached the Gospel to the soul that was formerly barren and forsaken of God, or rather, *ten ex ethnon ekklesian,* "to the church from among the Gentiles; for seeing, *ta panta di auten o Christos upemeinen,* Christ endured all things for that, he rightly adds, after what he had foretold concerning him, *Rejoice, O barren,* &c." Again, he, having cited Gen. xlix. 11, makes[¶¶] this note upon it: "See how, as by things hidden, he signifies his mystical sufferings, in which, as in a laver, he hath washed away the ancient filth, *ton eis auton pepisteukoton,* of those that would believe in him." On the text in Mal. iv. 2, he makes[***] this observation: "Whom the Father has begotten he promises shall arise, *ou tois pasin, alla monois,* not to them all, but to them only that fear his name." In another place he says,[†††] "The everlasting High Priest, and who is called the Father's *Christ,* takes the care of the whole, and is consecrated to the Father, *uper ton upekoon apanton,* 'for all them that obey;' and he alone shows himself mild and propitious unto all." It is also very manifest, that Eusebius did not think that the effects of Christ's death reach unto or were designed to reach unto many, or the same all, as the effects of Adam's sin do; since he observes,[‡‡‡] that Christ "became obedient unto death, that as death by one man's sinning has ruled over the whole kind,

---

* Hieron. Catal. Script. Eccl. sect. 91.
† Vide Fabricii Bibl. Græc. l. 5, c. 4, s. 1, p. 30, 31.   ‡ Apolog. p. 773, &c.   § Euseb. Demonstr. Evangel. l. 1, c. 10, p. 37.
‖ Ibid. l. 2, c. 1, p. 45.   ¶ Ibid. c. 3, p. 62, 63.   ** Ibid. l. 8, p. 385.   †† Ibid.

l. 10, p. 495.   ‡‡ Ibid. l. 7, p. 339, 340, et l. 9, p. 440.   §§ Ibid. l. 6, c. 7, p. 265.
‖‖ Ibid. l. 3, p. 101.   ¶¶ Ibid. l. 8, p. 380.
*** Ibid. l. 5, c. 29, p. 254.   ††† Ibid. l. 4, c. 10, p. 164.   ‡‡‡ Euseb. de Eccles. Theolog l. 1, c. 13, p. 75.

so likewise eternal life might reign by his grace *ton eis auton pepisteuonton*, over those that believe in him, and by him commended as known to God and to his Father." Once more, in another work * of his, he takes notice of a law that Constantine made, "that no Christian should serve the Jews; for," says he, "it is not lawful *tous upo tou Soteros lelutromenous*, that those who are redeemed by the Saviour should be under a yoke of bondage to the murderers of the prophets and of the Lord." Whence it appears that he thought the Jews were not redeemed by Christ, only such as are Christians.

As for the article in the creed drawn up by the Nicene fathers A. D. 325, which is next produced by M. Daille,† and is thus expressed; "We believe in one Lord Jesus Christ, the Son of God, who came down and became incarnate, and was made man, *di emas tous anthropous kai dia ten emeteran soterian*, for us men and for our salvation;" it is no other than what every body believes and agrees to; and is so far from militating against the particular scheme, that it is rather a testimony for it, since the phrases *us men and our salvation* design those that believe in Christ the Son of God, to whom they relate. What is next cited‡ from Juvencus, a Spanish presbyter, who flourished under Constantine, about A. D. 330, does not at all serve the general scheme, but the contrary, it being only a paraphrase of John iii. 16, after this manner: "For God loved the world with such a love that his only offspring came down on earth, *credentes Domino vitæ junctura perenni*, to join them that believe in the Lord to everlasting life." Anthony, the patriarch of the Eremites, who died A. D. 358, is next§ mentioned; who, in one of his epistles, says, "that God appointed his only begotten Son for the salvation of the whole world, and did not spare him for our sakes, but delivered him up for the salvation of *us all*," which are almost the very express words of the Scripture in 1 John ii. 2, Rom. viii. 32, to which no doubt he refers, and are capable of being understood in the same sense with them; and that Anthony did not design every individual of mankind, but only some, appears by what he immediately adds :‖ "and hath gathered us by the word of his power, *ex omnibus regionibus*, out of all countries, from one end of the world to the other;" and could he be thought to mean all the individuals of human nature, for whom God appointed and delivered up his Son for the salvation of, yet the general benefit and salvation which all were to have by him, seems, according to him, to be no other than the resurrection from the dead; for a little after, he observes that "Christ is the resurrection of all, destroying him that had the power of death."

SECTION XIII

JULIUS FIRMICUS. A. D. 350

JULIUS FIRMICUS MATERNUS was a native of Sicily. He was brought up in the pagan religion, and wrote some books of astrology, A. D. 336 or 337, being still a heathen. After the year 340, he was converted to Christianity in his old age,¶ and is thought to have wrote his book, *Of the Error of Profane Religions*, about A. D. 350, which is inscribed to the emperors Constantius and Constans; and in it are these words,** speaking of Christ, the Lamb of God: "The reverend blood of this Lamb is shed for the salvation of men, *ut sanctos suos Filius Dei profusione pretiosi sanguinis redimat*, 'that the Son of God, by the pouring out of his precious blood, might redeem his saints;' *ut qui Christi sanguine liberantur*, 'that those who are delivered by the blood of Christ' might be first consecrated with the immortal majesty of that blood." From whence it is evident, that he thought that some, and not all, are redeemed by the blood of Christ, and that those who are redeemed by it are his saints, who were set apart for himself, and are made holy by him, which cannot be said of all the sons and daughters of Adam. M. Daille has indeed cited ††two passages from this writer, as testimonies for general redemption, but neither to the purpose. In the first, Firmicus says,‡‡ "Christ, the Son of God, that he might deliver *humanum genus*, 'mankind from the snare of death, bore all these things;' that he might remove the yoke of the grievous captivity, that he might restore *hominem*, man to the Father, that, mitigating the offence, he might make up the difference between God and man, by a prosperous reconciliation." But he does not say, that Christ delivered or redeemed every individual of mankind, and restored every man to God, and reconciled every man to him : he may be truly said to have redeemed mankind, and to have restored and reconciled man to God, who has redeemed, restored, and reconciled such large numbers of mankind, though not all of them. In the other passage he says,§§ that "so it was by divine disposition, that whatever Adam lost Christ found; for after a long time, in the last age of the world, the Word of God joined himself to a human body, that he might deliver *man*, that he might conquer death, that he might join the frailty of a human body with divine immortality;" but he does not say, that all the individuals of mankind, which were lost in Adam, were found by Christ. By several expressions in the same page we learn, what that was he supposes Adam lost and Christ found; for he says, that Adam, "being deceived by the woman, that is Eve, through the persuasions of the devil, *promissæ sibi gloriæ perdidit dignitatem*, 'lost the dignity

---

* Ibid. de Vita Constantin. l. 4, c. 27, p. 538, 539.

† Apolog. p. 775.   ‡ Ibid. 776.   § Ibid.
‖ Epist. 4, p. 73.   ¶ Fabrici Biblioth. Latin.

p. 147, 149.   ** Julius Firmicus de Error. proph. Relig. p. 40.   †† Page 776, 777.
‡‡ De Error. proph. Relig. p. 40.
§§ Ibid. p. 44.

of the glory promised him.' There was a tree," adds he, "in paradise, *quo promissorum a Deo præmiorum perdidit gratiam*, by which he lost the grace of the rewards promised by God." And a little after, "Adam, being made out of the slime of the virgin earth, through his own transgression, *promissam perdidit vitam*, lost the promised life." Now it was this promised grace, life, glory, and happiness, Adam lost, which, he says, Christ found; but he nowhere says that Christ found this for all the individuals of mankind.

SECTION XIV

ATHANASIUS. A. D. 350

It must be owned that Athanasius, who, as has been observed in the preceding chapter, bore so famous a testimony to the doctrine of eternal election in Christ, has said many things which upon first sight seem to favour the doctrine of universal redemption. M. Daille has cited* a considerable number of testimonies from him to that end, and he might have cited more. But I have the following things to say in vindication of him; first, that when, in the passages referred to, he says that Christ *died for all*, and offered himself a *sacrifice for all*, and died for *the ransom of all*, and that his death is *the ransom of all*, he says no more than the Scriptures do, which are used in this controversy, and so may be understood in the same sense, of *all* the elect, or some of *all* sorts. Secondly, some of the citations only prove that Athanasius believed that Christ, being God as well as man, was *dunatos kai ikanos*, " able and sufficient to suffer for all, and give full satisfaction by his death for all." That Christ was able to redeem all mankind, and that his sufferings and death were sufficient for the redemption of all men, had it been the will of God to have appointed them for that purpose, none will deny. Thirdly, I observe, that in many places he says that Christ assumed a body, became one subject to sufferings, and did endure death *epi te soteria ton panton*, " for the salvation of all;" yea, that by his death, *e soteria tasi gegone*, " salvation is procured for all." Now if by salvation be meant spiritual and eternal salvation, these instances would prove more than they are brought for, namely, universal salvation. But it is easy to observe that Athanasius, in most of these places, is speaking of the resurrection from the dead, which he makes the grand end of Christ's incarnation, sufferings, and death; and if this is what he means by salvation, and by Christ's dying for all, and giving himself for all, this is no more than what some, who are far from giving into the universal scheme, allow of; who suppose that the resurrection from the dead is a benefit which belongs to all men by virtue of the death of Christ. Fourthly, it is very pro-bable that one reason why Athanasius uses those general terms so frequently, is with respect to the Gentile world, among whom a very large number have a special interest in the death of Christ, and redemption by his blood. In one place† he has these words: " What is the fruit of the Lord's death? what the profit of the Jew's conspiracy?" the death of the Saviour hath made the *world* free, that the Gentiles might glorify God; the wrath of the Jews hath destroyed the city with them, and hath blinded them, with respect to the knowledge of God. The death of the Lord hath quickened the dead, but the conspiracy of the Jews hath deprived them of life; for now they are without the Lord, and the cross of the Saviour hath made *ten ekklesian ton ethnon*, " the church of the Gentiles, which was a wilderness, habitable ;" in which he calls the Gentiles the world, in opposition to the Jews; and this world the church of the Gentiles, who enjoy the fruit of Christ's death. This citation is indeed made from a treatise which some‡ learned men have thought is not the genuine work of Athanasius; but inasmuch as M. Daille has made use of it before me, I take the same liberty. But, not to insist on this, there are some things in the genuine works of Athanasius, which manifestly limit redemption by Christ, and the benefits of it to some, as when he says,§ " When was he (Jesus) sent, but when he clothed himself with *our flesh ?* When did he become the high priest of our profession ? but when he offered himself for us, raising the body from the dead, and now he brings and offers to the Father τους προσερχομενους αυτω τη πιστει, those that come unto him by faith, redeeming all, and expiating those things that belong to God for all ;" that is, for all that come unto him by faith. And in another place, he thus expresses himself,‖ " God hath commanded the true Wisdom to take flesh, and become man, and to endure the death of the cross, ινα δια της εν τουτω πιστεως, παντες λοιπον οι πιστευοντες σωζεσθαι δυνωνται, that through faith in him, all henceforth that believe might be saved." The sense of which is that the design and intention of God in the incarnation and death of Christ is not to save all men, but such that believe in him. And elsewhere he says,¶ that Christ "took to himself a body of the virgin Mary; that offering it a sacrifice for all, he might reconcile to the Father παντας ημας, οσοι φοβω θανατου, δια παντος του ζην, ενοχοι ημεν δουλειας, all us, as many as through fear of death were all our lifetime subject to bondage." And a little after, in the same page, he has these words: " The Word was made flesh, that he might offer it for all, και ημας εκ του πνευματος αυτου μεταλαβοντες θεοποιηθεναι δυνησθωμεν, that we partaking of his Spirit might be made like unto God." Again, he observes,** that " as Christ being

---

* Page 777—782.   † In Passion. et Crucem Domini, vol. i. p. 1025, 1026.
‡ Vide Rivet. Critici Sacra, l. 3, c. 5, p. 2, 4, 6.   § Contr. Arian. Orat. 3, p. 377, vol. i.

‖ Ibid. p. 452.   ¶ Synod. Nic. contr. Arian. Decret. p. 262.   ** De Salutar. Advent. Christ. p. 639.

man is God, so being God became man, *kai sozei tous pisteuontas en anthropou morphe,* that he may save those that believe in the form of man." Moreover, and what is full against the universal scheme, having cited the text in Mal. iv. 2, *To you that fear him shall the Sun of righteousness arise ;* he makes this remark on it,[*] *gar panton (emera) aute, alla ton apothanonton te amartia, zonton de to Kurio,* " for this day does not belong to all, but to them who die in sin, and live unto the Lord." By which he means not the day of the week he calls the Lord's day a little before, but the day of grace, which the Sun of righteousness makes when he arises and appears to any in a spiritual saving way, and which is special and peculiar to some persons only.

SECTION XV

MACARIUS ÆGYPTIUS. A. D. 350

MACARIUS was an Egyptian monk, a disciple of St. Anthony. There are fifty homilies of his remaining, out of which M. Daille[†] has a single passage for general redemption ; in which Macarius asserts,[‡] that " Christ would have all men partake of the new birth, because he died for all, and calls all to life ;" but this he could not mean of every individual man, because every one is not called to that life. Besides, there are several things said by him which show, that he thought that Christ came into the world, and suffered, and died, for believers only ; for when he observes,[§] that " it pleased the Lord at his coming to suffer for all, and to purchase them with his own blood," he adds, " and to put the heavenly leaven of goodness *tais pistais psuchiais,* into believing souls, humbled under sin." And again ;[||] " For this cause the Lord came, that he might vouchsafe those spiritual things *tous alethos pisteuontas eis auton,* to those that truly believe on him." And in another place, " we ought," says he,[¶] " to labour and strive very much, for it is not just that the Bridegroom should come to suffer and be crucified for thee, and the bride, *di' en o numphios parageneto,* for whose sake the Bridegroom came, should rejoice and dance." Having elsewhere[**] mentioned the words of the Baptist, *Behold the Lamb of God, which taketh away the sin of the world,* he observes, that " he alone shows this mercy to men, *tois pisteuousin auto,* ' that believe in him,' because he redeems from iniquity ; and to them that always wait and hope, and seek without ceasing, he bestows this unspeakable salvation." And in another place he has this note on the same words.[††] " *Behold the Lamb of God, which taketh away the sin of the world, tes psuches delonoti, pisteusases auto,* namely, of the soul that believes in him, and loves him with all the heart."

SECTION XVI

HILARIUS PICTAVIENSIS. A. D. 363

HILARY of Poictiers abounds in general expressions of God's good will to man, of the universal offer and invitation to all in the external ministry of the word, and of Christ's assuming human nature, and coming into the world for the redemption and salvation of all, many of which are cited by M. Daille.[‡‡] But it is easy to observe, that he sometimes means by these phrases, not the spiritual and eternal redemption and salvation of men, but their resurrection from the dead. There is a remarkable passage of his to this purpose, in which he distinguishes the salvation of some from others, by virtue of Christ's redemption ; " All flesh," he says,[§§] " is redeemed by Christ, that it may *rise again,* and that every one might stand before his judgment-seat ;" yet all have not equal honour and glory of rising again ; to whom therefore only resurrection, and not change is given, they are saved to nothing ; in anger shall those people be led, to whom the salvation of the resurrection is appointed for the sense of punishment, from which wrath the apostle promises we shall be delivered ; saying, *For if when we were yet sinners Christ died for us, much more being justified by his blood, we shall be saved by him from wrath. Pro peccatoribus igitur ad salutem resurrectionis est mortuus,* " for sinners therefore he died, to obtain the salvation of the resurrection ; but those who are sanctified by his blood he will save from wrath." And in another place he says,[||||] " This was the expectation of the saints, *ut omnis caro redimeretur in Christo,* ' that all flesh should be redeemed in Christ,' and we in him might exist the first fruits of an eternal resurrection." Besides, Hilary frequently makes use of limiting phrases when he is speaking of the sufferings of Christ, and redemption by him ; he says,[¶¶] that Christ " is appointed a mediator in himself, *ad salutem ecclesiæ,* for the salvation of the church," which is what he means by the house of David, as the subject of redemption ; when commenting on these words, *Hosanna to the son of David,* he observes,[***] " The words of praise express the power of redemption : for by Osanna in the Hebrew language, is signified the redemption of the house of David." And a little after,[†††] " The high priests envied the cries of the children, and rebuked him (Christ) for hearing them, for he was said to come *for the redemption of the house of David,*" Elsewhere[‡‡‡] he represents all as redeemed by Christ, as kings of heaven, and co-heirs of eternity, which cannot agree with all mankind ; his words are these, speaking of Christ, " He shall remain in the sight of God for ever, having already taken all whom he hath

[*] De Sabbat. et Circumcis. p. 968.
[†] Apolog. p. 782, 683.　[‡] Homil. 30, p. 175.
[§] Ib, 24, p. 137.　[||] Ib. 5, p. 33.
[¶] Ib. 27, p. 156.　[**] Ib. 2, p. 11.
[††] Ib. 44, p. 216.　[‡‡] Apolog. p. 783.

[§§] Hilar. Enarrat. in Ps. lv. p. 386.
[||||] In Ps. lxviii. p. 442.　[¶¶] De Trinitate.
l. 9. p. 116.　[***] In Matt. can. 21, p. 308,
[†††] Ibid. p. 309.　[‡‡‡] In Ps. lx. p. 400.

redeemed, *in reges cœlorum et cohæredes æter-nitatis,* to be kings of heaven, and co-heirs of eternity, delivering them as the kingdom to God the Father." With him a believer in Christ and one redeemed by him is the same. Whoever, he says,* through his insolence, " disdains, provokes, and dishonours a believer in Christ, and one redeemed by Christ, is not a companion of them that fear God."

SECTION XVII.

BASILIUS CÆSARIENSIS. A. D. 370

BASIL of Cæsarea has also many expressions of God's general goodness to men; of his nearness to them, and willingness that all of them should partake of life; and which are therefore, with others, produced by Monseiur Daille,† to countenance general redemption, though there is not one syllable concerning it in them. Nor is Basil very favourable to the universal scheme, when he says,‡ "God is not the God of all, but of them who are joined to him in love, as the God of Abraham, the God of Isaac, and the God of Jacob; for if he was the God of all, he would have given them a testimony as something very excellent." He indeed says, as Monsieur Daille has observed, " The Holy Ghost calls all nations, all that dwell on the earth, to hear the psalm," which is no proof of the point before us; and besides, he explains all nations, and all that dwell on the earth, of *the church,* which he says§ is συνειλεκται, " gathered out of nations of all sorts, of laws and manners." He also speaks of Christ's giving himself a propitiation for the whole world, but in the same place‖ gives a plain intimation that he is to be understood of the sufficiency of Christ's blood and sacrifice to atone for and redeem all mankind; his words are these, " What can a man find of such a nature as he can give for the redemption of his own soul?" Yet here is one thing found out *omoupantonanthroponantaxion,* "worthy of all men alike, even the holy and precious blood of our Lord Jesus Christ, which he has shed for us all." Besides, he frequently describes those who are redeemed by Christ, by such characters as cannot agree with all mankind; for a little after he says,¶ he " that is redeemed by God, who gave a propitiation for him, he indeed labours in this world, but after these things he shall live for ever; verily he shall not see destruction, when he shall see wise men die." Which cannot be said of every individual of mankind. And in another place he says,** " We are all, *oi pisteuontes,* ' who believe,' redeemed from the condemnation of sin by the grace of God, which is through his only begotten Son, our Lord Jesus Christ; who said, *This is my* blood of the new testament, which is shed for many for the remission of sins." Which passage of Scripture is twice cited by him afterwards,†† and applied to *believers,* to whom he says is given the remission of sins. Again, he observes,‡‡ that " where spiritual men are the authors of counsels, and the people of the Lord follow them with unanimity, who can doubt that this is by the communication of our Lord Jesus Christ, *tou to aima autou uper ton ekklesion ekcheontous,* who shed his blood for the churches."

SECTION XVIII

OPTATUS MILEVITANUS. A. D. 370.

OPTATUS, bishop of Milevi in Africa, wrote *six* books, for the seventh is none of his, against the Donatists, in the times of the emperors Valens and Valentinianus,§§ that is, after A. D. 364, and before A. D. 374, in which work stands this passage, which is cited by Monsieur Daille‖‖ in favour of universal redemption; " Christ," says Optatus,¶¶ " is the only redeemer of souls, which the devil possessed before his coming; these Christ our Saviour has redeemed with his own blood, as the apostle says, *Ye are bought with a price.* It is certain that all are redeemed by the blood of Christ." But Monsieur Daille should have read on, and transcribed more, when it would have appeared, that Optatus explains these *all,* of *all that believe;* for thus he proceeds, " Christ has not sold whom he hath redeemed; souls bought by Christ cannot be sold, that they may, as you would have it (speaking to the Donatists), be redeemed again by you. How can one soul have two masters? Is there another Redeemer? Which of the prophets have declared that another is to come? What Gabriel speaks again to another Mary? What virgin brings forth again? Who hath done new or other miracles? If there is none but one, *qui redimit animos omnium credentium,* who redeems the souls of all believers, why do you say, redeem your souls?"

SECTION XIX.

VICTORINUS. A. D. 365

CAIUS MARIUS VICTORINUS, as Jerom calls him,*** was by birth an African, he taught rhetoric at Rome, under the emperor Constance;††† and became so famous in that kind of learning, that the citizens erected a statue for him in the Roman Forum.‡‡‡ He was converted to Christianity in extreme old age, and wrote four books against the Arians, which still remain, from whence Monsieur Daille§§§ has this citation; "The Logos, or Word, is made all things, and in all, and hath

---

* In Ps. cxviii. 1, Heth, p. 480.   † Apolog. p. 792, &c.   ‡ Homil. in Ps. xxix. p. 189. vol. i.   § Homil. in Ps. xlviii. p. 276. ‖ Ibid. p. 280.   ¶ Ibid. p. 282.   ** De Baptismo, l. 1, c. 1, p. 639.   †† Ibid. c. 2, p. 649, 652.   ‡‡ Epist. ad Clericos Nicopolit. ep. 192, p. 977, vol. ii.   §§ Hieron. Catal.

Eccl. s. 120.   ‖ Apolog. p. 794.   ¶¶ De Schism. Donatist. l. 3, p. 80, 81.   *** Hieron. Prœm. in Comment. in Gal. fol. 68, l. tom. ix.   ††† Ibid. Catal. Scrip. Eccles. ε. 111.   ‡‡‡ August. Confess. l. 8, c. 2, s. 2.   §§§ Apolog. p 794.

begotten all things, and hath saved, and hath reigned, existing life eternal in the Spirit :" But of what service this passage can be to the general scheme, I see not; for if it is not to be understood of the concern that Christ the Word has in creation and providence, but of his concern in everlasting salvation, if it favours any scheme it must be that of universal salvation; but from other expressions of his it appears, that he thought that Christ is only the redeemer of, and eternal life to them that believe; "He" (Jesus Christ,) says he,[*] "has performed the mystery of our salvation; he hath made us free; he hath redeemed; *in istum credimus salvatorum nostrum*, 'in him we believe as our Saviour,' according to the cross, and according to the resurrection from the dead." And in another place,[†] Christ is the true life, that is, eternal; *credentibus in se*, to them that believe in him; and is present with God for them that believe in him."

SECTION XX
MARCUS EREMITA. A. D. 390

MARK the Eremite is next produced by Monsieur Daille,[‡] and by him said to be about A. D. 390, though he is placed by Alsted,[§] and the Magdeburgensian Centuriators,[||] in the *fifth* century, about the beginning of it. The testimony from him, cited by the above writer, only signifies, that *God would have all men to be saved, and come to the knowledge of the truth*, which is no other than what the Scripture says; and that evil thoughts or reasonings forbid the will of God, deceive men, and exclude them from salvation. It must be owned, that there is here and there an expression dropped more to the purpose than this; yet in other places he speaks of redemption, and the effects of it, as peculiarly belonging to certain persons: "He who died," says he,[¶] "for our sins, according to the Scriptures, also freely gives liberty, *fideliter et probe ipsi servientibus*, to them that faithfully and honestly serve him," according to Matt. xxv. 21. And in another place he says,[**] "Suretyship proceeds from love, which the Lord Jesus Christ hath showed in all things to us, who in the first place heals the infirmities of our soul, moreover cures every disease, and every sickness; *who takes away the sin of the world; qui puram restituit naturam his qui firmiter credunt ei*, 'who restores a pure nature to them that firmly believe in him,' and gives redemption from death." Again,[††] "Christ is our Lord, both according to essence, and according to the government or administration of the family; for when yet we were not, he made and created us; and being dead in sin, he bought us with his own blood; *et iis qui ita credunt, gratiam suam gratuito largitus est*,

and to them who so believe, he freely gives his grace." And elsewhere he says,[‡‡] *Christus autem credenti sit omnia*, "Christ indeed· is made all things to him that believes."

SECTION XXI
FAUSTINUS. A. D. 390

FAUSTINUS, who was ordained either a presbyter or a deacon of the church of Rome, about A. D. 385, according to Monsieur Daille,[§§] who has transcribed some passages out of a book written by him against the Arians, showing, that God loved the world, and gave his Son for the redemption of the world; and that Christ tasted death not for himself, but for *all;* all which may be said, without supposing that Christ died for every individual of mankind. Besides, Faustinus plainly intimates, that the benefit of Christ's death only belongs to believers; that *many*, and not *all*, are delivered and said by him; "See," says he,[||||] "the love that the Lord of majesty should be crucified on earth for the salvation of the world, who gives eternal life in heaven, *se Filium Dei credentibus*, to them that believe he is the Son of God." And in another place he observes,[¶¶] that "as by the contempt of one many are made sinners, so by the obedience of Christ, which not from infirmity, but from the goodness of the Deity, he yielded for the salutary discipline of men, *multi salvantur*, many are saved." And a little after he says, that "Christ bore the infirmities of body and soul, though without sin, that it might be truly thought he did not take another substance of flesh and blood; and that when in himself he delivers men from infirmities and sufferings, we might believe also, that those are delivered *qui secundum ejus vestigia sectantur*, who follow his steps." The text in Hebrews ii. 9, where Christ is said to *taste death for all*, he says,[***] the apostle interprets in ver. 10, where the *Captain of salvation* is spoken of as bringing *many sons to glory*.

SECTION XXII
CYRILLUS HIEROSOLYMITANUS. A. D. 370

CYRIL of Jerusalem, though a little earlier than some of the former, since he died A. D. 386, according to Monsieur Daille,[†††] is next cited by him as a patron of general redemption, and who indeed does say,[‡‡‡] that Christ took upon him the sins of the *world*, cleanses the *whole world* from sin, has redeemed the *whole world* of men; and that the Father having constituted him the Saviour of the whole world, he came for the salvation of *all*. But these passages will be easily accounted for, when it is observed, that by *the world*, he means, the world of believers. "You have," says he,[§§§] "the twelve apostles witnesses of

---

[*] Victorini adv. Arrian. l. 1, p. 315.
[†] Ibid. l. 4, p. 351.
[‡] Apolog. p. 794, 795.
[§] Chronolog. Thessaur, Chron. 41, p. 419.
[||] Hist. Eccl. vol ii. cent. 5, c. 4, p. 48; c. 18, p. 828. [¶] Marc. Eremit. de Leg. Spirit. p. 60.
[**] Ibid. Exercitoris Disp. p. 119. [††] Ibid.

de Peg. Spirit. p. 61. [‡‡] Ibid. 51.
[§§] Apolog. p. 795. [||||] Faustin. contr.
Arrian. c 2, p. 107. [¶¶] Ibid. c. 3, p. 127.
[***] Faustin. cont. Arrian. c. 4, p. 131, 132.
[†††] Apolog. p. 795. [‡‡‡] Cyrill. Catech. 3,
s. 9, p. 41; et 10, s. 2, p. 124; et 13, s. 1, p. 167.
[§§§] Ibid. 13, s. 19, p. 186.

the cross, and the habitable earth, και του κοσμον των εις τον σταυρομενον πιστευοντων ανθρωπων, and the world of men that believe in him that was crucified." And these, and these only, will be saved by him; for he it is, as he elsewhere says,* "that saves, τους πιστευοντας, 'those that believe' by the word of the cross." Nor need it seem strange that Cyrill should say, that Jesus took upon him τους οικουμενικας αμαρτιας, " the sins of the world," since he talks † " of πασης της οικουμενικης εκκλησιας, of the church of the whole world." Besides, one reason of his using such general expressions, as " the world, the whole world," &c., may be on the account of the extent of Christ's sufferings and death to Jews and Gentiles. "He came," says he,‡ " who has mercy on them, and was crucified and rose again, giving his own precious blood υπερ Ιουδαιων τε και εθνων, both for Jews and Gentiles." Cyrill, indeed, speaks of many ways of eternal life opened for all, which scarce any will agree to; and of human nature being capable of salvation, which none will deny.

As for the words of Diodorus Tarsensis next mentioned,§ declaring " that the Lord being born, showed himself to the Persians before other nations, that grace and salvation might be given by him to those of the magicians and soothsayers that would;" they are so far from bearing a testimony in behalf of universal redemption, that they plainly limit the grace and salvation of Christ τοις εθελουσιν, " to them that are willing;" which none are, but such who are made so by the energy and power of special grace.

SECTION XXIII
GREGORIUS NAZIANENUS. A. D. 370

THE passages cited out of Gregory of Nazianzum, by M. Daille,‖ in favour of general redemption, must be acknowledged to be the most pertinent to his purpose of any produced by him, for Gregory not only says, that Christ took away the sin of *the whole world ;* that his sacrifice was the expiation of the *whole world ;* and that a few drops of his blood restored *the whole world ;* but also, that through his sufferings *all* that partake of Adam, were deceived by the serpent, and died through his sin, *without exception,* are restored; and that his sacrifice was not for a *small part* of the world, nor for a little while, but always continues to be an expiation of the *whole world ;* and that he died for the worst of men, for heretics, yea, for Julian the apostate; nay he affirms that Julian had obtained salvation by him; his words are these,¶ " The first Nebuchadnezzar (meaning Julian) afflicted us, who after Christ was mad against Christ, and therefore he hated Christ, οτι τι αυτου σεσωστω, because he had

been saved by him;" though it may be reasonably thought that he should mean no more than that Julian had enjoyed some temporal mercies, some temporal deliverance and salvation by Christ. And in the same way may his other general expressions be understood; and his sense be, that the whole world, and all men in it, yea, the worst of men, receive some temporal advantages, through the sufferings, sacrifice, and death of Christ; for it is certain, that he sometimes represents a special particular set of men as such for whom Christ died. In one place,** he brings in the people of God to distress complaining after this manner, " O God, why hast thou cast off for ever? thy anger is stirred up against the sheep of thy pasture; remember thy congregation which thou hast possessed from the beginning, ην περιποιησω τοις του μονογενους Λογου σου παθεσιν, ' which thou hast purchased by the sufferings of thine only begotten Word,' to which thou hast vouchsafed thy great covenant, and hast drawn to heaven by a new mystery and the earnest of the Spirit." And in another place, addressing the priests, he says,†† " O ye priests, put on righteousness, or to speak more properly, let us put it on; let us not scatter and destroy the sheep of the pasture, υπερ ων εθηκε την ψυχην ο ποιμην ο καλος, ' for whom the good Shepherd laid down his life; who knows his own, and is known by his own, calls them by name, leads them in, and brings them from unbelief to faith, and from this life to a future rest." And in an epistle to Basil he has these words,‡‡ " We speak concerning the church υπερ ην Χριστος απεθανεν, 'for whom Christ died;' and concerning him that brings and presents the same to God."

SECTION XXIV
DIDYMUS ALEXANDRINUS. A. D. 370,

DIDYMUS of Alexandria was blind from his childhood, so that he never learned letters, and yet was a perfect master of logic and geometry; he was living in the fourteenth year of Theodosus, A. D. 329, being then above eighty-three years of age ;§§ he was the author of many things, and among the rest of a treatise concerning the *Holy Spirit,* translated into Latin by Jerom; in which he says indeed,‖‖ that *Christ tasted death for all ;* and that¶¶ he vouchsafed to come down on earth for the salvation of all; but then he explains these *all* of the children of God and believers in Christ; for citing Isaiah lxiii. 8, which he thus renders, " *He is made salvation to them,* that is," says he,*** " to them, of whom the Lord says, *Are not my people children? And they will not prevaricate ;* for because they do not prevaricate, nor have despised the Father, he is made salvation

---

* Catech· 17, s· 5, p· 245.   † Ibid. 6, s. 1, p. 78.   ‡ Ibid. 14, s. 10, p. 198. § Apolog. p. 796.   ‖ Apolog. p. 796—798. ¶ Greg. Nazianz. Orat. 32, p. 512, tom. i. ** Ibid. 4, adv. Julian. p. 124.   †† Ibid. 9, p.

154.   ‡‡ Ibid. E. p. 22, p. 785.   §§ Hieron. Catalog. Script. Eccles. No. 119, fol. 101, G. ‖‖ Didymus de Spiritu Sancto, l. 2, fol. 181. C, inter opera Hieron tom. ix.   ¶¶ Ibid. l. 3, fol. 183. E.   *** Ibid. A.

to them; or because they are called *chil-dren*, he is made the cause of salvation to them." And a little after, " He is made the occasion of eternal salvation, *cunctis qui in eum credunt*, ' to all that believe in him;' and he is the Saviour of the world, who came to seek what was lost."

SECTION XXV

GREGORIUS NYSSENUS. A. D. 380

GREGORY, bishop of Nyssa, and brother of Basil, died A. D. 395, or 396, according to Monsieur Daille.* There are two volumes of his works extant, in which he sometimes† indeed speaks of *Christ's tasting death for every one*; of his reconciling the world to himself: and of his giving himself for the life of the world. But inasmuch as these scriptural expressions are capable of being understood in a sense which no ways favours the doctrine of general redemption, so they cannot be thought to hold forth explicitly this writer's sentiments upon that subject. Besides, in other places he speaks of the sufferings of Christ, and the benefits of them, as belonging to certain persons; for he not only says,‡ that Christ spilled his blood, and endured sufferings, υπεο ημων, *for us*; but also intimates, that all this was for the sake of such as believe in him; for speaking§ of the cluster of grapes which the spies brought from Canaan, he has these words, " The cluster hanging on the stick, what else was it, but the cluster which in the last days hung upon the tree? *ou to aima poton tois pisteuousi gignetai soteriou*, whose blood is become a salutary drink to them that believe." And in another‖ place he represents the church speaking after this manner to Christ, " How should I not love thee, who hast so loved me, though so black, as to lay down thy life, υπερ των προβατων, for the sheep which thou feedest?" Two passages are cited out of this author by Monsieur Daille,¶ as on the side of the general scheme; the first is this;** " The will of God is the salvation of men;" which nobody will gainsay, for certain it is, that it is owing to the good-will of God that any of the sons of men are saved; and no man would be saved God not willing his salvation. The other is this, where he makes Christ to speak thus,†† " Through the first fruits which I have assumed, I bring in myself all human nature to God the Father." But Gregory, in the place referred to, is showing in what sense Christ is called the *first-born*, and the *first-born from the dead*; and observes, that the human nature which he assumed was the first fruits of all human nature, and that in his resurrection he was the first fruits of them that slept; and suggests, that not only the resurrection

of Christ is a pledge, but a kind of a representation of the general resurrection; which is what he means when he says, " that Christ brought all human nature in himself to the Father, his human nature being the first fruits of the whole." There is another passage in Gregory, which upon first sight may be thought to favour the doctrine of general redemption more than either of these; where he says,‡‡ " that redemption signifies a return from captivity; God gave himself a ransom for those who are held under death by him that has the power of death, and seeing all were in the custody of death, he redeems all from thence by his ransom, so that not one is left under the power of death, after the redemption of every one is made; for it is not possible that any one should be under the power of death; death itself being no more; wherefore the *whole world*, according to its situation, being divided into four parts, no part of it remains without the divine redemption;" and yet, I apprehend, he means no more than this, that as all mankind are subject to a corporal death, and are under the power of it, so they shall be delivered from it, or be raised from the dead in virtue of Christ's ransom; which as a benefit arising from Christ's death, some allow to all mankind, who yet are not in the general scheme.

SECTION XXVI

PACIANUS BARCINONENSIS *vel* BARCILONENSIS. A. D. 380.

PACIANUS, bishop of Barcelona in Spain, died in a very advanced age, under the emperor Theodosius,§§ and before A. D. 391. He wrote many little pieces, in one‖‖ of which stands this passage, produced by M. Daille in favour of universal redemption; " No artificer," says he, " despises his own works, or thinks with himself, that they are faults which he has made; and hence dost thou think, that Christ suffered for sinners, but that he was unwilling to lose what he hath made?" But he does not say, that Christ died for all sinners, and for all that he has made, but for sinners, who being made by him, he was very unwilling to lose. Besides, he intimates in other places, that they are the spiritual seed and offspring of Christ, the church, and particular persons, who are redeemed by Christ, and whom he justifies and saves. "Adam's sin," say she,¶¶ "passed upon the whole kind, as says the apostle, Rom. v. 12, and so hath come upon all men, therefore *the righteousness of Christ, must needs, in genus transeat*, ' pass upon the kind or offspring;' and as he by sin lost his offspring, so Christ by righteousness *genus suum omne vivificat*, quickens all his own kind or offspring." This the apostle urges in Rom. v. 19, 21. Some will say, but the sin

---

* Apolog. p. 798. † Gregor. Nyss. in Ps. c. 16, vol. i. p. 363, in Cant. homil. 7, p. 570; homil. 15, p 697. ‡ Ibid. de Vita Mosis, p. 245. § Ibid. p. 244. ‖ Gregor. Nyss. in Cant. homil. 2, p. 498. ¶ Page 798, 799. ** Greg. Nyss. de Orat. Dominic. orat. 4, p.

741. †† Greg. Nyss. contra Eunom. l. 1, vol. ii. p. 25. ‡‡ Ibid. in Ps. c. 8, p. 279, 980. §§ Hieron. Catalog. Script. Eccl. s. 116. ‖‖ Pacian. contr. Novat. ep. 3, p 112. ¶¶ Pacian. de Baptismo, p. 121.

of Adam deservedly passed to his posterity, because they were born of him; *et nunquid nos a Christo geniti sumus,* and are not we born of Christ, that we might be saved for his sake?" Again,[*] " I will yet," says he, " speak more plainly; the latter people, the poor, the mean, the humble, and modest soul, the soul delivered by Christ, is an image of the church: *hanc venit Dominus salvam facere,* ' this the .Lord came to save,' this he hath not left in hell; ' this is the sheep which is carried on his shoulders." And in another place,[†] having mentioned Rom. v. 9, *We shall be saved from wrath,* adds, " from wrath, indeed, which is due to sinners;" for if he did not suffer the Gentile people to die, *multo magis redemptum non patietur extingui, nec objiciet quos magno redemit,* " much more he will not suffer him that is redeemed to be destroyed, nor will he cast away those whom he has redeemed with a great price, for neither is the loss of servants light to him."

I take no notice of Monsieur Daille's citations from the sermons of Zeno Veronensis, because no mention is made of them by the ancients, they were not extant before A. D. 1508, some things in them cannot agree with the times of the emperor Galienus, under whom Zeno suffered, and, for the major part, are a collection out of divers authors who lived almost two hundred years after his time,[‡] and therefore do not come under our consideration.

SECTION XXVII

HILARIUS DIACONUS. A. D. 380

HILARY the Deacon, or whoever is the author of the commentaries on the epistles of the apostle Paul, commonly ascribed to Ambrose, has furnished Monsieur Daille[§] with numerous instances, urged by him, in favour of the general scheme; though the most that can be made of them is, that God's wills that all men should be saved, and that Christ died for all conditionally, *sub conditione fidei,* " provided they believe," as appears even from several of the citations || made by him out of this writer. And sometimes Hilary expresses the sufficiency of the death and sacrifice of Christ for all; thus, on those words, " any being made perfect," &c., he makes this note,[¶] " It shows what gain is his passion *quæ omnibus credentibus sufficit ad salutem sempiternam* which is sufficient for all believers to everlasting salvation." And in another place,[**] speaking of the offering of Christ once for all, he says, "This offering is once offered up, *sed semper potens est abluere omnes credentes,* ' but is always powerful, or is effectual to wash all believers,' and all that desire to

be cleansed in it." And certain it is, that this writer thought that there are some who in a special sense are redeemed by Christ, otherwise he would not have said as de does, *quotquot redempti sumus,*[††] " As many of us as are redeemed, are redeemed by this sacrifice." He observes,[‡‡] that the word *all,* signifies sometimes only *a part* of a people, either all the good or all the bad, and gives instances of it; and adds, *semper enim duo populi in una plebe,* " for there are always two people in one commonalty." And elsewhere he affirms,[§§] that " all do not obtain grace, nor are all justified by the faith of Christ." He represents those for whom Christ died, and that share in the benefits of his redemption, to be the children of God, believers in Christ, such as love him, and belong to his body. " He (the . apostle) calls God our Father," he says,[||||] " because of the original of things, for from him are all things; but he calls Christ the Lord, because *ejus sanguine redempti,* ' being redeemed by his blood,' we are made the children of God." Again he says,[¶¶] " Christ is crucified for our sins, that destroying death, *credentes sibi liberaret ab ea,* he might deliver from it them that believe in him." Moreover, he observes,[***] that " as to them that love him, *redemptio venturus est Christus,* Christ is to come as the redemption; so to them who love him not, let him be anathema, that is, let him hate and destroy them." Once more "As Adam's sinning," he says,[†††] "found death, and held it, so that all springing from him are dissolved; so likewise Christ not sinning, and hereby conquering death, hath procured life, *omnibus qui sunt ex ejus corpore,* for all who are of that body."

SECTION XXVIII

AMBROSIUS MEDIOLANENSIS. A. D. 380

AMBROSE of Milain is very fruitful of expressions which seem to militate against the doctrine of special and particular redemption. Monsieur Daille[‡‡‡] has collected a large number of them, which Dr. Whitby[§§§] has given himself the trouble to number, and says, they are no less than twenty-eight; and I could help them to as many more of the same kind, and yet all of them will be but of little service to their cause, when it is observed, that Ambrose, by *all* for whom Christ died, and whom he redeemed, means *all sorts* of men, and not every individual: " If," says he,[||||||] " it is related of Ulysses, that the binding him fast to the tree, delivered him from danger, how much more must it be said, what is really fact, that is, that to-day the tree of the cross hath delivered *omne genus hominum,* 'all kind of men,' from the danger

---

* Ibid. contr. Novat. ep. 3, p. 107.   † Ibid. p. 105.   ‡ Vide Rivet. Critici Sacra, l. 2, c. 19, p. 223, 224; and Jame's Corruption of the Fathers, par. I, p. 26.   § Apolog. p. 787, &c.
|| Vide Comment. in Rom. p. 259; in 1 Tim. p. 574; et in Heb. p. 650.   ¶ In Heb. p. 632.
** Ibid. p. 651, 652.   †† Ibid. p. 643.

‡‡ In Rom. p. 257.   §§ Ibid. p. 271, 272.
|||| Ibid. p. 239.   ¶¶ In 2 Cor. p. 458.
*** In 1 Cor. p. 410.   ††† Ibid. p. 402.
‡‡‡ Apolog. p. 799, &c.   §§§ Postscript to Discourse, &c. p. 571; ed. 2. 547. |||||| Serm. 50, in Feria 6, Hebdom. Sanct. p. 70.

of death." And a little after,* "The Lord Christ hung upon the cross that he might deliver *onme genus hominum,* 'all kind of men,' from the shipwreck of the world. And when he says that Christ died for, and redeemed *the world,* such phrases are easily accounted for, since it is abundantly evident that by the world he frequently means *the church.* Having mentioned† those words in Psalm xxiv. 1, *The earth is the Lord's, and the fulness thereof; the world, and they that dwell therein:* he adds, "which the Greeks call οικουμενην, because it is inhabited by Christ, as he says, *Wherefore I will dwell in them;* therefore, what is οικουμενη, the world? *nisi sancta ecclesia,* but the holy church, the temple of God, and habitation of Christ." And in another place he says,‡ "The church is called both *heaven* and *the world,* because it hath saints comparable to angels and archangels; also it hath the greatest part earthly; it is called likewise *orbis terrarum,* the world, which is founded upon the seas, and prepared upon the rivers. Moreover, as the *world* (the church) says, *Look not upon me, because I am black."* And a little after,§ "Is not *the earth the Lord's, and the fulness thereof? Et vere orbis terrarum in ecclesia,* 'and verily the world in the church;' in which not only Jew, nor Greek, nor Barbarian, nor Scythian, nor bond, nor free, but we are all one in Christ." Moreover, Ambrose very frequently observes, that it is the church for whom Christ suffered and died, and which is redeemed by his blood. "The domestic Jews, bought with a price," he says,‖ "are the Gentiles who have believed, *quia pretio sanguinis Christi redempta est ecclesia,* for by the price of Christ's blood is the church redeemed." And in another place he says,¶ "Seeing Christ suffered for *the church,* and the church is the body of Christ, faith does not seem to be exercised on Christ by them (meaning schismatics,) by whom his passion is made void, and his body pulled asunder." And elsewhere,** speaking of the same sort of persons, he says, "They alone are they who would dissolve the grace of Christ, who tear in pieces the members of the church, *propter quam passus est Dominus Jesus,* for which the Lord Jesus suffered." Again he observes,†† that "by the woman the heavenly mystery is fulfilled, being prefigured in her the grace of the church, *propter quam Christus descendit,* 'for which Christ descended,' and has finished that eternal work of man's redemption." Add to all this, that remarkable expression of his, "If Christ," says he,‡‡ "died for all, yet he suffered for us in an especial manner; *quia pro ecclesia passus est,* because he suffered

for the church." Besides, this father makes use of such epithets and descriptive characters, when he is speaking of the persons for whom Christ became incarnate, and whom he redeemed, as can by no means be applied to all the individuals of human nature, such as believers, repenting sinners, Christ's servants, and his own Christian people; thus he explains§§ those words in Isaiah ix. 6, "*To us a child is born; nobis qui credimus,* 'to us who believe;' not to the Jews, who have not believed; to us, not to heretics; to us, not to the Manichees." On these words, *My people shall return hither,* he has this note,‖‖ "What is *hither?* that is, to me, to my equity and righteousness, and to my worship; and *he shall fulfil the days of his life;* both which you may so understand, that the people truly shall be redeemed, *qui crediderit in eo,* which shall believe in him." And in another place he says,¶¶ "The cross of the Lord is a precipice to unbelievers, *sed vita credentibus,* but life to them that believe." Again,*** "The cross is a reproach to the perfidious, but to the believer grace, to the believer redemption, to the believer the resurrection; because Christ has suffered for us." Once more,††† "Christ is salvation to them that believe, but punishment to unbelievers;" yea, he says,‡‡‡ "If thou dost not believe, *non descendit tibi, non tibi passus est,* he did not come down for thee, he did not suffer for thee." Elsewhere he observes,§§§ that "the passion of the Lord is profitable to all, and gives redemption to sinners, *quos flagitii pœnituit admissi,* who repent of sin committed." Again he says,‖‖‖ "Be not the servant of the serpent, the enemy and the adversary, but serve the Lord alone, who in his own love hath redeemed thee, *quia ipse ipse suorum redemptio servulorum,* for he himself is the redemption of his servants." And was in another place, speaking of the man that healed at the pool of Bethesda, he says,¶¶¶ "Then one was cured, not all are healed, or without doubt, *unus solus populis Christianus,* one Christian people only." Once more,**** "The Lord Jesus was alone when he redeemed the world, for not a legate, nor a messenger, but the Lord himself alone, saved his own people." He represents the intercession of the Spirit, and the sufferings of Christ, to be for the same persons:†††† the Spirit intercedes for the saints, *because the Spirit maketh intercession for us, pro quibus enim Christus passus est,* 'for whom Christ suffered,' and whom he hath cleansed by his own blood, for them the Spirit intercedes;" which cannot be said of all men. Moreover, he intimates, as though he thought it im-

* Serm. 53, in Feria 6, Hebdom. Sanct. p. 71. † Enarrat. in Ps. xlviii. p. 823. ‡ Ib. in Ps. cxviii. Lamed, p. 980. § Ib. p. 981. ‖ De Abraham l. 2, c. 11, p. 267. ¶ De Obitu Satyr. p. 316. ** De Pœnitent. l. 2, c. 4, p. 405. †† De Institut. Virg. c. 4, p. 419. ‡‡ In Luc. l. 6, p. 102. §§ Enarrat. in Ps. i. p. 663; et de Fide, l. 3, c. 4, p. 152. ‖‖ Ibid. in Ps. lxxii. p. 855. ¶¶ Ibid. in Ps. cxviii. Samech, p. 1007. *** Ibid. Schin, p. 1079. ††† De Filii Divinitate, c. 8, p. 284. ‡‡‡ De Fide, l. 4, c. 1, p. 163. §§§ De Pœnitent. l. 1, c. 15, p. 399. ‖‖‖ Enarrat. in Ps. xliii. p. 792; et in Ps. xlviii. p. 826. ¶¶¶ De Initiand. c. 4, p. 346. **** Epist. l. 4, ep. 31, p. 262; et l. 6, ep. 51, p. 312. †††† Ibid. l. 5, ep. 40, p. 290.

possible, that any one should be damned for whom Christ died, and whom he has redeemed by his blood; his words are these;* "Can he damn thee, *quem redemit a morte,* whom he has redeemed from death,' for whom he offered himself, whose life he knows is the reward of his own death?" Moreover, many of his general expressions may be understood of the sufficiency of Christ's blood to redeem all men; for thus, in one place,† he expresses himself concerning Christ; "He is free from all, nor does he give the price of redemption for his own soul, the price of whose blood *poterat abundare ad universa mundi totius redimenda peccata,* could abound to redeem all the sins of the whole world." Besides, it may be further observed, that the general benefit which mankind has by the death of Christ Ambrose sometimes explains of the resurrection,‡ though that which is to eternal life he limits § to all Christians, who are the body and members of Christ.

SECTION XXIX

EPIPHANIUS. A. D. 390

EPIPHANIUS was bishop of Salamis, ‖ sometimes called Constance, in Cyprus; he lived to the year 403, and wrote many things in his old age; and the chief of his writings which remain, is a large work against *heresies,* in which are several expressions that are agreeable to the doctrine of particular redemption; as when he calls in question the redemption of some persons, which he could not well do, if he thought that all were redeemed by Christ. Thus, speaking of the Arians, he says,¶ "These rash men again introduce some other passages of Scripture, sowing their opinions of damnation against him who has redeemed them, ειπερ ηγορασθησαν if so be they are redeemed." And elsewhere** having mentioned these words, *Ye are bought with a price, with the precious blood of Christ, a Lamb without spot and without blemish;* he adds, "If therefore ye are bought with blood, ουκ υπαρχεις των ηγορασμενων, thou art not of the number of them that are bought, O Manes, because thou deniest the blood." Besides, the characters which he sometimes gives of the persons for whom Christ suffered and died, do not agree with all mankind; as when he says,†† that "He (Christ) in the last days vouchsafed to be in the womb of a virgin, and formed a body for himself, and was truly born, and really became man, that he might suffer in the flesh for us, and gave his life υπερ των ιδιων προβατων, "for his own sheep."‡‡ Again, "He (the devil) has always heard the prophets declaring the coming of Christ, the future redemption of them that had sinned, και δια Χριστου μετανουντων, and by Christ repent:" and he thought

that he himself should obtain some mercy." Once more, citing those words, *Christ hath redeemed us from the curse of the law, being made a curse for us;* he makes this observation,§§ "Christ is not the curse, but the dissolution of the curse; a blessing indeed *pasi tois eis auton alethos pepisteukasin,* "to all that truly believe in him; so he hath redeemed, he do s not say, he hath *bought.*" Monsieur Daillee‖‖ has cited a single passage from this writer, as countenancing general redemption, where he says,¶¶ that "Christ first offered up himself, that he might abolish the sacrifices of the Old Testament, by giving a more perfect, and a living one," for the *whole world;* which may be very well understood of the Gentiles, since the sacrifices of the Old Testament did not belong to them, but to the Jews only.

As to what is cited*** from Asterius Amasenus, who thought, that if Judas the betrayer had not immediately laid violent hands on himself, but had fallen on his knees and asked mercy, he would not have been afar off from those mercies which are shed over the whole world; this does not prove, that he thought that Christ died for all men, nor for Judas; but that he was of opinion, that had he truly repented, he would have a share in. And whereas it is also observed from him, as his sense of the parable of the man that fell among thieves, that it designs all mankind, naked of piety and virtue, and wounded by enemies, whom Moses and others looking upon, could not heal: but when the Samaritan, who is our Saviour, came, he administered healing; which may very well be allowed; without supposing healing administered to every individual of human nature, which is not true in fact.

SECTION XXX

GAUDENTIUS BRIXIENSIS. A. D. 390

GAUDENTIUS was made bishop of Brixia, a city of Venice, about A. D. 390, and died after A. D. 407.††† There are some tracts of his remaining in which are several passages relating to the subject of redemption. In one place he says,‡‡‡ "We ought, according to the command of God, first to mortify the lusts of the flesh, and so receive the body of Christ, *qui pro nobis servientibus in Ægypto est immolatus,* who is sacrificed for us that serve in Egypt." And elsewhere,§§§ "They (the Jews) not only would not receive him, but they crucified him, who therefore notwithstanding bore up the body that was assumed to die, that by rising again, through his own power, he might both show the omnipotence of his majesty; and that by removing and conquering death, *vitam credentibus redderet,* 'he might restore life to them that believe,'

---

* De Jacob. l. 1, c. 6, p. 317.   † Enarrat. in Ps. xlviii. p. 826.   ‡ In Exod. p. 441. § In Dominic. Resurrect. serm. 55, p. 75. ‖ Vide Act. xiii. 5.   ¶ Contr. Hæres. 66, s. 52, p. 781, vol. 1.   ** Ibid. 66, s. 78, p. 609. †† Ibid. 24, s. 9, p. 74.   ‡‡ Ibid. 39, s.

8, p. 289.   §§ Ibid. 42, s. 8, p. 309.   ‖‖ Apolog. p. 807.   ¶¶ Hæres. 55, s. 4, p. 471.   *** Apolog. p. 807, 808.   ††† Vide Dallæi Apolog. p. 808.   ‡‡‡ Gaudent. de Exodo, tract. 2, p. 46.   §§§ Ibid. tract. 7, p. 57.

and condemn the complete wickedness of the crucifiers." And in another place,* having mentioned Phil. ii. 8, he adds, "By a spontaneous humility, with the Father's will, he (Christ) voluntarily bore the cross, *ut mors ejus fieret vita credentibus*, that his death might become life to them that believe." And elsewhere,† on John xii. 32, he has this note, "To wit, that being lifted up on the cross, *omne seculum ad suam fidem vocaturus esset*, 'he might call every age to faith in himself;' but that he says, *I will draw* omnia, *all things* to myself, and *not* omnes, *all men:* by this, I think," says he, "signified *quod omnia creaturarum genera*, 'that all kinds of creatures,' which were either sacrificed or dedicated to idols, Christ promised should be restored to his blessing, and consecrated to his name." Monsieur Daille cites‡ two passages from this writer, in the first of which Gaudentius says, that Christ took the flesh of righteous men and sinners of the Virgin, and a body not only of the patriarch and prophets, *sed ex totius generis humani massa*, "but of the mass of all mankind" which is very true, Christ's human nature being of the same common lump and mass with, and like to that of others, sin only excepted. But then this writer does not say, that Christ suffered in the flesh, and offered up this body for the whole lump and mass of mankind, and all the individuals of it. True it is, that in the other passage he observes, that Christ died, *pro totius mundi peccatis*, "for the sins of the whole world;" which is no other than the phrase used by the apostle, 1 John ii. 2, to which he doubtless refers, which he understands of Gentiles in distinction from Jews, and is the plain and obvious meaning of the apostle. With much more pertinency might be alleged another passage of this writer in favour of particular redemption, where he says,§ "Let us study to love Christ in the poor, who in all respects loved us; and who, as a good shepherd, laid down his life *pro ovibus suis*, 'for his own sheep;'" not only for *the* sheep, but for *his own* sheep."

SECTION XXXI

JOANNES CHRYSOSTOMUS. A. D. 390,

CHRYSOSTOM often makes use of the apostle's words, *who would have all men to be saved*, and drops many general expressions concerning the love of God to men, and his desire of their welfare; which M. Daille‖ has collected together in favour of the general scheme, though there is not a word in them about the death of Christ, and redemption by it. Chrysostom does indeed say elsewhere,¶ that "the sacrifice (of Christ) was offered for the whole nature *kai ikane pantes en sosai*, and was sufficient to save all."

Which is not denied; but then he immediately observes, that only believers receive any advantage by it; his words are these, *oi de te euergesia chresamenoi oi pisteuontes eisi monoi*, "but they only enjoy the benefit who believe." He also says,** "The rational lamb is offered for the whole world." But then he explains the whole world by such men who are purified, are freed from error, and brought to the knowledge of the truth; for he adds, "the same hath purified the whole world, he has freed men from deception, and brought them to the truth." Indeed on those words, that "he by the grace of God might taste death for all," he observes.†† that "this is not for believers only, but the whole world, for he died for all: What if all do not believe? He hath fulfilled his part." And again, on those words, "Christ was once offered to bear the sins of many," he has this note,‡‡ Why does he say *many* and not *all? epeide me pantes episteusan*, because all do not believe." For all indeed he died, to save all, as to his part, *antirropos gar estin o thanatos ekeinos tes panton apoleias*, 'for that death was equivalent to the destruction of all,' but he did not bear, or take away the sin of all, because they would not." In all which, though he seems to intimate that Christ died intentionally to save all, and makes the effect of Christ's death depend on the will of man; yet what he says confirms the distinction so much used in this controversy, that Christ died for all men as to the sufficiency of his death for all, but not as to the effect of it; for certain it is, that Chrysostom did not think that all Adam's posterity that sprung from him, and died in him, are quickened, or made alive by Christ, in a spiritual sense; his note on those words,§§ "For as in Adam all die, even so in Christ shall all be made alive," is this, "What therefore? tell me, do all die the death of sin in Adam? How then was Noah righteous in his generation? How Abraham? How Job? And how all others? Tell me, "shall all be quickened in Christ?" *pos oi eis geennan apagomenoi*, 'how can they be that are led to hell?' But if this is said of the body, the sense stands good; but if of righteousness and sin, not so." In some places the characters he gives of those for whom Christ died, are such as cannot agree with all mankind: "if," says he,‖‖ "to dig up a church is vile and wicked, much more *naon preumatikon*, 'a spiritual temple;' for man is more venerable than a church, for Christ did not die for walls, *alla dia tous naous toutous*, but for those temples." Again,¶¶ "Dost thou despise *anthropou pistou*, 'a believing man,' who when he was an unbeliever Christ did not despise? What, do I say he did not despise him? Verily, he so loved him, whilst an enemy and deformed,

---

* Ibid. Resp. ad Paul. Diacon. tract. 19, p. 101.
† Ibid. tract. 12, in Joh. xii. 32, p. 78.
‡ Apolog. p. 808. § Gaudent. de Natali Domini, tract. 13, p. 81. ‖ Apolog. p. 808 ad 816. ¶ In Gal. ii. 20, tom. iii. p. 735.

** In Gen. Homil. 47, tom. i. p. 384.
†† In Heb. homil. 4, tom. i. p. 451.
‡‡ Ibid. homil. 17, p. 522. §§ 1 Cor. serm. 39, tom. iii. p. 505. ‖‖ In Rom. serm. 26, ib. p. 210. ¶¶ Ib. serm. 27, p. 216.

os kai apothanein uper autou, as even to die for him." Upon those words,* "And I, if I be lifted up from the earth, will draw all men unto me," he has this note, *toutestin kai tous ex ethno,* that is, and those *of* or *from* among the Gentiles;" by which it appears that by *all,* he only understood *some.* What he says† concerning Julian the emperor, seems to favour the doctrine of general redemption most of any thing cited from this writer, as that "he (Julian) turned from and hated his benefactor and Saviour, and "who did not spare his only begotten Son, *di auton* for him." As for the *imperfect work* upon Matthew, which bears Chrysostom's name, it is none of his ;‡ but is the performance of a much later writer; wherefore what is produced from thence does not come under our consideration.

As for the passages out of Severianus, cited by Monsieur Daille, the first of them only shows, that the gospel of the kingdom is published to the *whole world,* and is made useful to *all sorts* of men, which does not suppose universal redemption ; and the other, that whereas all human things are fallen, Christ has took upon him all things, and by his grace renews them ; which is capable of being understood in such a sense as not at all to favour that doctrine, since it cannot be thought that Christ took upon him more than he renews by his grace, and these are not all men.

SECTION XXXII.

RUFFINUS AQUILEIENSIS. A. D. 390

RUFFINUS was presbyter of the church at Aquileia, and died A. D. 410. He translated much out of the Greek into the Latin tongue, as Eusebius's History, and many of the writings of Origen, of whom he seemed to be a favourer, about which Jerom and he had a sharp contention. Some others of his writings are still extant, as his *Invectives against Jerom,* and his *Exposition of the Creed ;* in the former of which, besides his saying,§ that Christ "was made man, and suffered *for our salvation,* and *for our sins,*" he has these words,‖ "Christ died *for us,* and shed his blood *for our redemption.* Sinners indeed we are, *sed de ipsius grege sumus, et inter ejus oviculus numeramur,* but we are of his flock, and are reckoned among his sheep." From whence it appears, that he thought that those for whom Christ shed his blood, though they are sinners, yet are of his flock, and the sheep of his pasture ; in the latter of these pieces he thus expresses himself,¶ "He alone who knew no spot of sin, hath blotted out the sins of *all ; eorum duntaxat qui sanguine ejus postes suæ fidei signassent,* of them only who should mark the doors of their faith with his blood." Monsieur Daille** has a passage from this author which he thinks favours the general scheme ; in which he says,†† "Therefore Jesus is crowned with thorns, that the first sentence of condemnation might be dissolved ; he is led to the cross, and upon the tree is hung *totius mundi vita,* the life of the whole world." Which character is very true of Christ as the creator of all things, " in whom was life, and that life was the light of men," of every man that comes into the world ; and even of him as a Redeemer and Saviour, who gave his flesh for the life of *the world,* even the whole world of the elect ; but not for the life of every individual person in the world : for it is not true in fact that Christ is the life of every man in a spiritual sense ; every man is not quickened by him, and therefore this could not be Ruffinus's meaning. Besides, a little after, speaking of the water and blood which came out of Christ's side, he says, " it brought forth water, *quæ credentes diluat,* ' that it might wash believers ;' and it brought forth blood, *qui condemnat incredulos,* that it might condemn unbelievers." So far, according to him, was Christ or the death of Christ, from being the life of the whole world in that sense.

Theophilus, bishop of Alexandria, was contemporary with Ruffinus and Jerom, the latter of which translated his three paschal books out of Greek into Latin, from whence M. Daille‡‡ has a citation which he supposes countenances the doctrine of general redemption, and is this,§§ "Now also the living Wisdom of God calls us forth to celebrate the holy *passover (or Easter) omnes cupiens ejus esse participes,* desiring that all might be partakers of it." That is, of the Lord's supper, administered at that time ; but surely it could never be the meaning of Theophilus, that it was the will of Christ that every individual person should partake of it, only all such as were proper subjects, *cunctos Domini timore purgatos,* ' all that were purified in the fear of the Lord ;' these were fit to attend such a solemnity, as he himself says in the same book.‖‖ Monsieur Daille might have picked out a passage more to his purpose than this, as when Theophilus says,¶¶ "that Christ uniting to himself a whole body, and a whole soul, showed in himself a perfect man, *ut perfectam cuntis hominibus in se et per se largiretur salutem,* that he might in and by himself give perfect salvation to all men." But his meaning cannot be, that Christ gives complete salvation to every individual of mankind, for then every man would be *saved,* which is not true ; but that Christ, being perfect man, gives perfect and complete salvation to all men to whom he gives salvation. And it is evident that this

---

* In Joh. xii. 32, tom. p. 840.   † Orat. 1, in S. Babyl. tom. v. p. 439.   ‡ Vide Rivet. Critici Sacr. l. 4, c. 1, p. 349, &c. ; James's Corruption of the Fathers, part 1. p. 87.

§ Ruffin. in Hieron. Invect. l. 1, inter Hieron. Opera tom. iv. p. 87, A. M.   ‖ Ibid. l. 2,

p. 99, B.   ¶ Symbolum, ibid. p. 46, C.
** Page 821.   †† Ibid. M.   ‡‡ Page 821.
§§ Theoph. Pascal. l. 3, inter Opera Hieron. tom. ix. p. 190, E.   ‖‖ Theoph. Paschal. l. 8, inter Opera Hieron. tom. ix. p. 191, A.
¶¶ Ib. l. 1, p. 185. B.

early writer was of opinion, that the sufferings and death of Christ could not be made void, and become of no effect, by any sins or transgressions of men whatever; for speaking of Origen, and his notions, " In vain," says he,* " he dreams that souls ascend to heaven and descend, and now they go forward, and anon tumble down below, that so they often die through innumerable falls, *et Christi passio irrita fiat,* ' and the sufferings of Christ become void ;' for he who once died for us, *æternam nobis victoriæ suæ lætitiam dedit, quæ nulla vitiorum mole extenuetur,* hath given us the everlasting joy of his own victory, which cannot be lessened by any bulk of sins." Whereas if Christ suffered death for all men, and all men are not saved, his sufferings and death must be so far in vain and of no effect.

Monsieur Daillé† next cites Synesius, who was ordained bishop of Ptolemais, A. D. 411, by Theophilus of Alexandria, who only says, " that Christ ought to be crucified υπερ της απαντων αμαρτιας, for the sin of all." But whether he means, that it was necessary that Christ should be crucified for the sins of the Gentiles as well as Jews, for the sins of all sorts of men, for the sins of all the elect, or for the sins of every individual of mankind; which latter sense can only serve the cause for which it is brought, is not certain. This author seems to be of a later date than to come within the time proposed to be considered.

SECTION XXXIII.

HIERONYMUS. A. D. 390.

DR. WHITBY‡ claims Jerom on his side the question, in proof of which he cites two passages out of him ; the first is this, though not as the Doctor has cited and rendered it, which is done very imperfectly. Jerom is speaking of Christ, of whom he says,§ " In no wise either as an ambassador, or as a messenger, but he himself will save them, *qui receperunt salutem,* who have received salvation," not by the merit of their works, but by the love of God ; *for God so loved the world, that he gave his only begotten Son, that whosoever believeth in him, should not perish, but have everlasting life.* But if the prudent reader should with a tacit thought reply, Why are not many saved, if he hath saved them, and loved and spared his sons, and hath redeemed them with his blood, and hath undertook for and exalted them that are assumed ? A plain reason is inferred from hence, " But they have not believed, and have provoked his Holy Spirit, or his Holy One ; which is called in Hebrew, קרשו, wherefore God was willing to save them that desire, that is, to be saved, and hath provoked them to salvation, that the will might be rewarded, but they would not believe." The whole paragraph is intricate and perplexed,

and the meaning of it not easy to come at ; for he suggests, that *many are not saved* whom God *has saved,* and that God is willing to save all that *desire* to be saved, and yet they would not believe ; things which are hard to be reconciled ; and who *the sons* are God has loved, spared, and redeemed, and who the *assumed ones* he has undertook for, and exalted, one cannot very well know, unless he means the Jews. Such an obscure passage cannot yield much advantage to any cause. The second is wrongly translated by the Doctor thus, " John Baptist must lie when he said, *Behold the Lamb of God, who taketh away the sin of the world ;* if there be any yet living for whose sins Christ did not suffer." Now Jerom in the place referred to is taking notice of the heresy of the Cainites, which he says was then revived, and overturns the whole mystery of Christ; for, adds, he,‖ " it says, that there are *some sins, quæ Christus non posset purgare sanguine suo,* ' which Christ could not purge away by his blood ;' and that the scars of former sins were so deep, both in bodies and minds, *ut medicina illius attenuari non queant,* that they cannot be lessened by his medicine." On which he observes, " What else does this mean, but that Christ died *in vain ? Si aliquos vivificare non potest,* ' if there are any he could not quicken ;' and then follow the words referred to, " John the Baptist lies, when pointing out Christ, both by finger and voice, ' Behold the Lamb of God,' behold him ' that taketh away the sins of the world ;' *si sunt adhuc in seculo quorum Christus peccata non tulerit,* if there are any yet in the world whose sins Christ could not bear." The plain and obvious sense of his words, in opposition to the heresy of the Cainites, is this, that there are no sins but the blood of Christ can purge away ; nor any such wounds made by them but *that can* heal them ; nor any persons dead in sin but *he can* quicken if he will ; nor are there now, nor were there ever in any age, such enormous crimes committed but he *could* have bore ; and who will deny this ?

The Doctor next refers us to *ten* other passages to the same effect, cited from Jerom in Monsieur Daillé, whom he always wrongly calls Dally ; and he might have said more than *ten,* but these, as many as they are, only express the will of God to have all men saved, and come to repentance, and the knowledge of the truth ; or Christ's love to mankind, and to a lost world ; and his ability, and the sufficiency of the price of his blood to redeem the whole world ; all which we own agreeable to the Scriptures of truth ; and we will try, if *ten* or *twelve,* or more passages, cannot be found in Jerom's works, in which he either expressly declares, that Christ did not die to redeem all men, or limits his redemption to *certain* persons, whose characters he gives ; as when inter-

---

* Ib. l. 2, p. 188, I.   † Apolog. p. 821.
‡ Postscript to his Discourse on the Five Points, p. 572 ; ed. 2. 548.   § Comment. in Isa. tom.
v. p. 110, F.   ‖ Epist. ad Oceanum, tom. ii. p. 106, B.

preting these words, *bring hither the fatted calf*, he says, " the fatted calf,* *qui ad pœnitentiæ immolatur salutem*, ' which is sacrificed for the salvation of penitents,' is the Saviour himself, whose flesh we daily feed on, whose blood we drink." And a little after,† mentioning these words, *they began to be merry*, " This feast is daily celebrated, the Father daily receives the Son ; *semper Christus credentibus immolatur*, Christ is always sacrificed for believers." And elsewhere he says,‡ ". Therefore the Lord is crucified, *ut et nos qui credimus in eum et paccato mortui sumus*, that we who believe in him, and are dead to sin, might be crucified with him." On those words, *Zion shall be redeemed with judgment ;* he has this note,§ *Non omnes redimentur, nec omnes salvi fient sed reliquiæ*, " not all shall be redeemed, nor shall all be saved, but the remnant, as is said above;" meaning in Isaiah i. 9. And in another place, speaking of spiritual Jacob and Israel, whom he makes to be the first church gathered out of the people of the Jews, he says,‖ " Let him not fear the persecutors, because he is redeemed by the blood of Christ, who has called him by his name ; and because of familiarity, *specialiter appellat populum suum*, he does in a very special manner call him his people." And having in another place¶ taken notice of God's drying up the Red Sea, and causing his people to walk through it, when he drowned Pharaoh and the Egyptians, he thus addresses the Lord, " Thou therefore who hast done these things, now also those who are redeemed and delivered by thy blood, return to Zion, and to the heavenly Jerusalem, or to the church, *quam tibi tuo sauguine præparasti*, which thou hast prepared for thyself by thine own blood." And elsewhere he observes,** that " they should be redeemed, *qui voluerunt credere*, ' who would believe,' not with silver and money, but with the precious blood of Christ, that they may hear by the apostles, *Grace unto you and peace ;* for not for our merits, but for the grace and faith of Christ, we are reconciled to God." He paraphrases those words,†† *As I have sworn that the writers of Noah, &c.*, thus, " To whom I have sworn, that the flood shall in no wise be brought upon the earth, and my engagement has been hitherto kept, nor shall it ever be made void ; so I swear to *my church, quam mihi redemi sanguine meo*, ' which I have redeemed with my blood,' that I will in no wise be angry with them whom I have mercy on." And on those words, *The Redeemer shall come to Zion*, he has this remark,‡‡ " The meaning is," says he, " Christ shall come who shall redeem Zion with his blood. But lest we should think *omnem redimi Sion*, that all Sion, or every one in Sion, is redeemed, and that she is delivered from

her sins, who is defiled with the blood of the Lord, he very significantly adds, *his qui redeunt ab iniquitates si voluerint agere pœnitentiam*, ' to them that return from iniquity, if they would repent ;' in whom our Lord's prayer is fulfilled, *Father, forgive them, for they know not what they do*."

And in another place,§§ having cited Matt. i. 21, *Thou shalt call his name Jesus, for he shall save his people from their sins*, makes this observation ; *Qui salvator credentium*, " He that is the Saviour of believers, is the judge of all, that he may render to every man according to his works ; to the righteous rewards, to sinners everlasting punishment ; and the Lord and Saviour himself, he (the prophet) says, shall call them, or, according to the Hebrew, the *apostles* and *apostolic* men shall call them, *sanctum populum, et redemptum a Domino, qui redempti sunt Christi sanguine*, the holy people, the redeemed of the Lord, who are redeemed by the blood of Christ." And a little after‖‖ he has this note on the words, *The year of my redeemed is come ;* " The year of my redemption cometh, that at the time in which the adversaries are punished, *Dei populus liberaretur, imo redimatur pretioso sanguine agni*, ' the people of God may be delivered, yea, redeemed with the precious blood of the Lamb,' who in the Revelation of John is said to be slain." Those words in Jonah ii. 4, *I will sacrifice unto thee with the voice of thanksgiving, I will pay that I have vowed ;* which he understands of Christ, he paraphrases in this manner,¶¶ " I who am devoured, *pro salute multorum*, ' for the salvation of many,' will sacrifice unto thee with the voice of praise and confession, offering myself ; for Christ our passover is sacrificed, and as a priest and a sheep he offered himself *for us*. And I will confess, says he, unto thee, as I before confessed, saying, ' I confess to thee, Father, Lord of heaven and earth ;' and I will pay the vows which I have made to the Lord, *pro salute omnium, ut omne quod dedisti mihi non pereat in æternum ;* ' for the salvation of all, that all which thou hast given me might not perish for ever." Descanting upon Zeph. iii. 1, which is rendered by the Septuagint, " O illustrious and redeemed city, the dove," he has these words,*** " The illustrious and redeemed city by the blood of Christ, according to what is said above, is clearly meant the *church*, which is called a dove, because of the simplicity of the multitude of believers in it." And a little after,††† " What is so illustrious as the church which is established in the whole world, so redeemed by by the blood of Christ ? And a dove, because of the grace of the Holy Spirit, *ut ecclesia degentibus congregata*, as the church gathered out from among the Gentiles ?" His note on those words,‡‡‡ " And to give his life a

---

* Epist. ad Damasum, tom. iii. p. 42, I.
† Ibid. K.   ‡ Ep. ad Algasiam, tom. iii. p. 52, B.   § Comment. in Isa. tom. v. p. 5, E.
‖ Ib. p. 74, K.   ¶ Ib. p. 86, I.   ** Ib. p. 88, E.   †† Ib. p. 92, I.   ‡‡ Ib. p. 104, F.

§§ Comment. in Isa. tom. v. p. 109, D.
‖‖ Ib. M.   ¶¶ Ib. in Jonam, tom. vi. p. 57, H, I.   *** Ib. in Soph. ib. p. 98, C.
††† Ib. H.   ‡‡‡ Ib. in Matt. tom. ix. p. 28, A.

ransom for many," is this "When he took upon him the form of a servant, that he might shed his blood for the world, he does not say, that he gave his life a ransom *pro omnibus, sed pro multis, id est pro his qui credere voluerunt,* for all, but for many, that is, for those who would believe." Dr. Whitby[*] replies to this citation, by distinguishing between the will of God, that all men should be saved, and the *effect* of it, which depends on the will of man, in which respect Christ died not for all, but for many; as though the will of God depended on the will of man, and could be without effect; and then cites a passage from this father, to prove, that God saves none without their will; which nobody denies; for God makes his people willing "in the day of his power." Again; he elsewhere says,[†] "We were by nature children of wrath as others *omnes sancti ab ira sanguine Christi redempti sunt,* and all the saints are redeemed from wrath by the blood of Christ." Again he observes,[‡] that "without the blood of the Lord Jesus no man can draw nigh to God, because he is our peace; and if Christ is *pax credentinm,* 'the peace of believers,' whoever is without peace consequently hath not Christ." And elsewhere, speaking of the seal of the Spirit, he says,[§] "He that is sealed so as to keep the seal, and show it in the day of redemption pure and sincere, and in no part damaged, may be able, because of that, to be numbered cum his qui redempti sunt, with them that are redeemed." And on those words, "the grace of God hath appeared to all men, he has this remark,[||] "There is no difference of free and bond, of Greek and Barbarian, of circumcised and uncircumcised, of men and women, but we are all one in Christ; we are all called to the kingdom of God, we are all after the offence reconciled to our Father, not by our merits, but by the grace of the Saviour;" where it is plain, by all men he understands persons of every sex, rank, and condition. And a little after, says he,[¶] "Rightly therefore Christ Jesus our great God and Saviour hath redeemed us by his own blood; ut sibi Christianum populum peculiarum facerit, that he might make for himself a peculiar Christian people." More passages of the like nature might be produced, but these may suffice.

As for the many citations by Monsieur Daille[**] out of Maximus Tauriensis, I take no notice of, because the sermons from whence they are taken are *incertæ fide*, "of doubtful credit;"[††] and out of them, many things are ascribed to different authors.

CHAPTER III

OF ORIGINAL SIN, THE IMPOTENCE OF MAN'S FREE WILL, AND THE NECESSITY OF THE GRACE OF GOD, TO EVERY THING THAT IS SPIRITUALLY GOOD.

Austin has proved the doctrine of original sin out of the writings of the fathers that were before him, by producing such clear testimonies of theirs that, as Vossius says,[‡‡] "it is very much to be wondered at, that there were any formerly, or any now to be found, who think that this was a device of Austin's, and would persuade others so; against these," adds he, "we shall show, that even before the times of Austin, *ecclesiam Dei semper in eo conspirasse,* "the church of God always agreed in this," that we sinned in Adam, in whose loins we were virtually contained, and by that sin deserved a privation of original righteousness, temporal death, and an eternal separation from God." The testimonies of Vossius, besides those of Austin, together with an addition of many others, will be given under the following Sections in proof of this point. These early writers did indeed say many things incautiously, and without guard, concerning free will, which are not easily reconcileable to other expressions of theirs, to which they were led by the opposition they made to the errors of Valentinians, Basilidians, Marcionites, Manichees, and others, who held two different natures in man; that some were naturally good, and others naturally evil, and either of them could possibly be otherwise. Now it was common with the fathers, that when they set themselves against one error, they generally went into the other extreme; this is observed[§§] even of Austin himself, "that when he wrote against Arius, he seemed to favour Sabellius; when against Sabellius, Arius; when against Pelagius, the Manichees; when against the Manichees, Pelagius." Moreover, Vossius[||||] has this to say on their behalf, that "those holy martyrs, and other famous doctors, when they ascribe to man freedom to that which is good, either treat only of things natural and moral; or if at any time they speak of works of piety, and such as belong to God, they consider the will of man in common, and indefinitely, not distinguishing what he can do by the strength of nature, and what by the strength of grace, but only attributing that nature to man, by which, before grace, he can do, or not do moral good; and after strength received by grace can believe or not believe, do, or omit works of piety; contrary to which were the opinions of the Bardesanists, Manichees, and the like. If we interpret the fathers otherwise, adds he, we must not only make them contradict one another, but themselves also.

---

[*] Postscript, p. 572; ed. 2. 548. [†] Comment. in Eph. p. 93, C. [‡] Ib. p. 94, B. [§] Ib p. 100, K. [||] Ib. in Tit. p. 112, B. [¶] Ib. C. D. [**] Page 826, &c. [††] Vide Rivet. Critic. Sacr. l. 4, c. 23, p. 430. [‡‡] Hist. Pelag. l. 2, par. 1, thes. 6, p. 150. [§§] Rivet. de Patrum Anthoritate, c. 11, s. 4, p. 68. [||||] Hist. Pelag. l. 3, par. 1, p. 282.

Besides, we shall make it appear in the following Sections, by a variety of testimonies, that they held the weakness and disability of man, without the grace of God, to do any thing that is spiritually good, yea, even that is morally so; and that the will of man is sinful, and the root of sin; and that it is in a state of servitude and bondage to sin, until released by the grace of God: and as to the necessity of the grace of God to the performance of every good action, Vossius[*] asserts and proves what follows, that the Latin writers who were before the times of Pelagius, clearly acknowledged the necessity of grace; both the Africans, as Tertullian, Cyprian, and Arnobius; and the Italians, French, and others, as Lactantius, Hilary, and Ambrose; nor can any one be produced who thought otherwise." Again,[†] "They who deny that the Greek fathers understood the doctrine of the necessity of grace, do them a very great injury, since they often most plainly assert it." The citations made by him in proof of this, with many others, will be given hereafter. I conclude with the words of Vincentius Lirinensis:[‡] "Whoever," says he, "before the profane Pelagius, presumed that there was such a power in free will, as to think the grace of God unnecessary to help it through every act in things that are good? who before his prodigious disciple Cælestius denied, that all mankind are guilty of Adam's transgression?"

SECTION I

CLEMENS ROMANUS.   A. D. 69

CLEMENS was so far from ascribing vocation, conversion, or sanctification, to the will of man, that he always considers it as the effect and produce of the will of God. His epistle to the Corinthians begins thus,[§] "The church of God which dwells at Rome, to the church of God which dwells at Corinth, *kletois egiasmenois en thelemati Theou*, 'to the called and sanctified by the will of God,' through our Lord Jesus Christ." He denies that men are called and justified, and come to honour, glory, and greatness, by themselves, or by their own works, but by the will and grace of God; for thus he expresses himself,[||] "All therefore are glorified and magnified, *ou di auton, e ton ergon auton, e tes dikaiopragias, es katargeisantoi, alla dia tou thelematos auton*, not by themselves or their own works of righteous actions, which they have wrought out, but by his will;" and we also being called by his will in Christ Jesus are justified, *ou di eauton, ou de dia tes emeteras sophias, e suneseos, e eusebeias, e ergon, on kateirgasametha en osioteti kardias*, "'not by ourselves, nor by our wisdom, or understanding, or piety, or the works which we have done in holiness of heart,' but by faith, by which God Almighty hath justified all

from the beginning, to whom be glory for ever and ever. Amen."

SECTION II

BARNABAS.   A. D. 70

BARNABAS in his Epistle[¶] has a passage which sets forth the corruption and weakness of the heart of man before the grace of God is implanted, insomuch that it stands in need of being rebuilt, new made, and created again; it runs thus: "How shall the temple be built in the name of the Lord? Learn; before we believed in God, the habitation of our heart was *phtharton kai asthenes*, 'corrupt and weak,' as a temple truly built with hands; for it was a house full of idolatry, and idolatry was the house of devils, by doing what was contrary to God. It shall be built in the name of the Lord. Attend, that the temple of the Lord may be built glorious. How? Learn; receiving the remission of sins, and hoping in the name of the Lord, we become new, being created again, as at the beginning."

SECTION III

IGNATIUS.   A. D. 110

IGNATIUS was no favourer of the doctrine of free will; he ascribes sanctification and illumination to the will of God. His epistle to the Romans[**] is inscribed, "To the church sanctified and enlightened, εν θεληµασι Θεου τόυ ποιησαντος, 'by the will of God who does,'" or according to another, του θελησαντος, "who wills all things' which are according to the faith and love of Jesus Christ our God and Saviour." He represents repentance as very hard to be obtained, when he warns[††] the members of the church at Smyrna against *beasts* in the forms of *men*, and advises them "not to receive them, and if possible, not meet them, only," says he, "pray for them, if so be they may repent, οπερ δυσκολον, 'which is very difficult;' but Jesus Christ, our true life, has the power of this," that is, of giving repentance. He roundly asserts,[‡‡] that men in a carnal state, have not a power to anything that is spiritual, οι σαρκικοι το πνευµατικα πραωειν ου δυνανται, "They that are carnal," says he, "cannot do the things that are spiritual, nor they that are spiritual do the things that are carnal, as neither faith the things of unbelief, nor unbelief the things of faith." He denies Christianity to be the produce of moral suasion, but the effect of divine power; his words are these,[§§] Ου πεισµονης το εργοναλλαµεγεθους εστιν ο Χριστιανος, "The Christian is not the work of persuasion but of greatness;" that is, of the exceeding greatness of God's power, which is wonderfully displayed in making the Christian, in continuing, preserving, and supporting him as such, especially, as he observes, when he is hated by the world.

---

[*] Ib. thes. 1, p. 267.   [†] Ib. thes. 2, p. 272.
[‡] Commonitor. 1, adv. Hæres. c. 34.
[§] Clement, Ep. 1, ad. Corinth. p. 2.   [||] Ibid.
p. 72.   [¶] Par. 1, s. 12, p. 246.
[**] Page 54, 298.   [††] Ep. ad Smyrn. p. 3.
[‡‡] Ep. ad Ephes. p. 22.   [§§] Ep. ad Rom. p. 299.

SECTION IV

JUSTIN. A. D. 150

JUSTIN MARTYR held the doctrine of original sin; he says,* that "mankind by Adam fell under death, and the deception of the serpent; that † *amartōloi egegoneimen,* 'we are born sinners;' and that‡ we are entirely flesh, and *no good thing dwells in us;* he asserts the weakness and disability of men either to understand or perform spiritual things, and denies that man, by the natural sharpness of his wit, can attain to the knowledge of divine things, or by any innate power in him save himself, and procure eternal life." In one of his treatises, speaking of the doctrines of the Scriptures, he has these words;§ *"Ou de gar phusei onte anthropine ennoia, outo megala kai theia ginoskein anthropois dunaton,* 'for neither by nature, nor by human understanding, is it possible for men to acquire the knowledge of things so great and so divine;' but by a free gift descending from heaven upon holy men, who had no need of the art of words, nor of the contentious and vain-glorious way of speaking, but to exhibit themselves pure to the *energy of the divine Spirit."* And as for himself, he could say,‖ "I do not study to show an apparatus of words by mere art alone, for I have no such power, *alla charis para Theou mone eis to sunienai tas graphas auton edothe moi,* but grace alone is given to me by God to understand his Scriptures." He bids Trypho pray¶ that "above all things the gates of light might be opened to him," for neither are they seen nor known by all, *ei me to Theos do sunienai kai o Christos auton,* unless God and his Christ give them to understand them.'" And in another place he says** "At that time being convicted by our own works that we were unworthy of life, and manifested that of ourselves, *adunaton eiselthein eis ten basileian tou Theou, te duuamei tou Theou dunatoi genethomen,* it was impossible to enter into the kingdom of God, by the power of God we might be made able." And a little after he says, "Having sometime before convinced us *to adunaton tes emeteras phuseos eis to tuchein zoes,* of the impossibility of our nature to obtain life, hath now shown us the Saviour, who is able to save that which otherwise were impossible to be saved." It must be owned, that Justin in many places †† asserts the free will of man; but then it is to be observed, that in all those places, even in those which Dr. Whitby refers to,‡‡ in proof of his being an advocate for free will, he speaks of it as men and angels were possessed of it, *tēn archēn,* "at the beginning of their creation," when

they had full power to do that which is good, and avoid that which is evil; though their natures being mutable were capable both of vice and virtue, and of being turned either way, as the event showed, and which is not denied by us. In like manner are we to understand some passages in Athenagoras §§ and Tatian ‖‖ which the Doctor also refers to,¶¶ where they ascribe free will to men and angels, when created by God, who has a power of doing good and avoiding evil, which clears God from being the author of sin, or being guilty of injustice in punishing of them; for as for Tatian, he clearly asserts the corruption and weakness of human nature; he says, "that at the beginning there was a spirit which lived familiar with the soul, but when it would not follow it, the spirit left it, but retaining *some spark of its power,* though because of the separation, that is, from the spirit, *ta teleia kathoran me dunamene,* 'it is not able to behold things that are perfect,' and seeking after God, through error feigns many gods;" he adds, that the Spirit of God is not with all men, only with such as live uprightly; yea, he plainly intimates, that man through his free will is now become a slave; which is stating in a few words the doctrine of free will, as held by us; for he expressly says,*** *apolesen emas to autezousion, douloi gegonamen oi eleutheroi dia ten amartian emprathemen,* "free will has destroyed us; we who were free are become servants, and for our sin are sold." Theophilus of Antioch also says,††† that God made man possessed of free will, but then he represents him now as impotent and standing in need of the grace of God: "They that know not God, and do wickedly," he says,‡‡‡ "are like to birds who have wings, but are not able to fly; no such men creep upon the ground, and mind earthly things, *katabaroumenoi upo ton amartion,* 'and being pressed down by their sins,' cannot move upward unto God." He expresses his sense which he himself had of the need of divine grace, as well as how necessary it was to others to know the truth, and understand the mind and will of God, when he says,§§§ *ego di aitoumai charin para tou monou Theou,* "I desire grace from God alone,' that I may exactly explain the whole truth according to his will; as also that thou, and every one that reads these things, *odegetai upo tes aletheias kai tharitos autou,* might be guided by his truth and grace."

SECTION V

IRENÆUS. A. D. 180

IRENÆUS is expressly for the corruption of human nature through the sin of Adam,

* Dialog. cum Tryph. p. 316; vide p. 327; et Epist. ad Diognet. p. 502.   † Dialog. p. 327.   ‡ Epist. ad Zenam, p. 506.   § Ad Græcos, Cohort. p. 9.   ‖ Dialog. cum Tryph. p. 280.   ¶ Ibid. p. 225.   ** Epist. ad Diognet. p. 500.   †† Pro Christ. Apolog. l, p. 45, 46; ib. 2, p. 71, 80, 81; Dialog. cum.

Tryph. p. 316, 329, 370.   ‡‡ Discourse, &c. p. 96. 345, 369, 370, 373, 381; ed. 2, 95, 336, 360, 361, 364, 371.   §§ Legat. pro Christ. p. 27.   ‖‖ Contr. Græc. Orat. p. 146.   ¶¶ Discourse, &c. p. 384; ed. 2. 374.   *** Orat. p. 150.   ††† Ad Autolyc. l. 2, p. 103.   ‡‡‡ Ib. p. 96.   §§§ Ib. l. 3, p. 133.

which he calls,* *antiqua serpentis plaga,* "the old plague, blow, or wound of the serpent," from which men cannot be saved otherwise than by believing in Christ. He says,† that " we offended God in the first Adam, not doing his commandment, and which we had transgressed from the beginning;" and that Eve‡ was the cause of death to herself and to all mankind ;" and that man "will bejustlycondemned,§ because beingmade rational, *amittitm veram rationem,* ' he has lost true reason,' and lives irrationally, is contrary to the justice of God, giving himself up to every earthly spirit, and serves all pleasure." Also he affirms,‖ that " we lost in Adam will to the image and likeness of God." Now a very considerable part of this lay in man's free will to that which is good, and therefore this must be lost by sin ; and what free will to that which is spiritually good can there be thought to be in man naturally, who is said by Irenæus¶ to be *lignum aridum,* " a dry tree," which cannot bring forth fruit unless the voluntary rain of the Spirit descends from above upon it ? The weakness of human nature is proved by this writer from Romans vii. 18 ; his words are these ;** " who (Christ) saved them, *qia per seip̄os non habebanti salvari,* ' because they could not be saved by themselves;' " wherefore Paul declaring the infirmity of man, says, " I know that in my flesh dwells no good thing ;" signifying that *non a nobis sed a Deo est bonum salutis nostræ,* " not of ourselves, but of God, is the blessing of our salvation." The inability, yea. the impossibility of attaining to the true knowledge of God, without divine teaching, is plainly asserted by him,†† when after citing some passages in Isaiah, as, " I am God, and before me there is no Saviour," &c. he says, " Neither diversely, nor haughtily, nor in a boasting manner, does he say these things, but because *impossible erat since Deo discere Deum,* 'it was impossible to learn the knowledge of God without him,' he teaches men by his *Logos,* or Word, to know God." And elsewhere he observes,‡‡ the bondage state of man by nature, and that immortality and eternal glory are not of himself, but are the pure free gift of God; " Man," says he, " who was before led captive, is taken out of the power of the possessor, according to the mercy of God the Father," who has pity on his own work, "and restoring it, gives salvation to it by the Word; that is, by Christ; that man may experimentally learn that *non a semeteipso, sed donatione Dei accepit incorruptelam,* not of himself, but by the gift of God, he receives immortality." It is true indeed that Irenæus frequently makes mention of man's free will, and says,§§

that God made him free from the beginning ; that all have a power to do good, or not ; and, that God still preserves the will of man free, not only in works, but even in believing; which passages are produced by Dr. Whitby,‖‖ and others, and may be reconciled to what Irenæus elsewhere asserts, by observing, that in some of them he speaks of free will as man was possessed of it when first created; and in others of the natural liberty of the will, which, in all actions good and bad, is preserved free ; and in none does it appear more so than in spiritual actions, and even in believing, in which men are influenced and assisted by the grace of God. Besides, it is one thing to say, that man has a free will to do spiritual actions, to believe, and the like, from the strength of grace given by God ; and another thing to say that man has a free will and power to do that which is good, and to believe from the mere strength of nature ; the former we allow of, the latter we deny, and which can never be proved to be Irenæus's meaning, for that would be to contradict himself.

SECTION VI.

CLEMENS ALEXANDRINUS. A. D. 190.

CLEMENT of Alexandria, being inclined to the stoic philosophy, it is no wonder that he sometimes speaks of ¶¶ *ta ephi' emin,* "the things that are in our power," and says what seems to favour man's free will ; which passages of his are for this purpose referred to by Dr. Whitby ;*** though it is plain in some places he only speaks of the natural liberty of the will against the Basilidians, and of the power of man to perform the natural and civil actions of life ; however, certain it is, that Clement did not hold free will in such a sense, as to set aside the grace of God, and render that useless and unnecessary : yea, he affirms, that free will, without the wings of grace, can neither rise nor fly. In one place he says,††† "Nor can we obtain the perfection of good without our free choice, nor yet does that wholly lie in our will, such as it shall come to pass, "for by grace we are saved, but not without good works."And in another place he has this observation,‡‡‡ "Whether the Father himself draws unto him, every one that lives purely, and attains to the understanding of happiness, and of the incorruptible nature; or whether our free will coming to the knowledge of that which is good, skips and leaps over the ditches, as is said in the schools, *plen ou chiaritos aneu tes exairetou pteroutai te kai anistatai kai ano ton uperkeimenon airetai psuchir,* yet the soul cannot rise nor fly, nor be lifted up above the things that are on high, without specia.

---

* Adv. Hæres. l. 4, c. 5, p. 322.　† Ib. c. 16, p. 460.　‡ Ib. l. 3, c. 33, p. 301.　§ Ib. l. 4, c. 9, p. 326.　‖ Ib. l. 3, c. 20, p. 982 ; et. l. 5, c. 15, in Fragm. Græc. ad Calcem Irenæi.　¶ Ibid. c. 19, p. 100.　** Adv. Hæres. c. 22, p. 289.　†† Adv. Hæres. l. 4, c. 18. p. 327.　‡‡ Ibid. l. 5, c. 21, p. 469.　§§ Ibid. l. 4, c. 9, p. 326 ; c. 29, p. 349 ; c. 71, p. 416 ; c. 72, p. 417, 418.　‖‖ Discourse, &c. p. 96, 347, 348, 384 ; ed. 2. 95, 338, 339, 374.　¶¶ Stromat. l. 1, p. 311, 314 ; l. 2, p. 363, 370, 387, 388, 390.　*** Discourse, &c. p. 96, 346, 348, 351, 385 ; ed. 2. p. 95, 336, 339, 342, 375.　††† Stromat. l. 5, p. 547.　‡‡‡ Ibid. p. 588.

grace." He says indeed elsewhere,[*] "that we are by nature fit for virtue, yet not so as to have it *ex genetes*, 'from our birth,' but we are fit to possess it." His meaning is, I apprehend, that men have a capacity, which irrational and inanimate creatures have not, of possessing virtue, and receiving the grace of God, of which they are destitute when born, and so in this respect are not like stocks and stones, that are incapable of such things.

SECTION VII

TERTULLIAN. A. D. 200

TERTULLIAN appears from many passages in his writings to have understood the doctrine of original sin, both with respect to the imputation of it to men unto condemnation, and the derivation of a corrupt nature from it; whereby not only man is become filthy and impure, but having lost the image of God, is also impotent to every thing that is spiritual and heavenly. "We call Satan," says he,[†] "the angel of wickedness, the artificer of every error, the interpolator of every age; by whom man from the beginning being circumvented, so as to transgress the commands of God, was therefore delivered unto death, *exinde totum genus de suo semine infectum suæ etiam damnationis traducem fecit*, hence he has also made the whole kind, or all mankind, which springs from his seed, infected, partaker of his damnation." And in another place,[‡] having mentioned John iii. 5, *Except a man be born of water and the Spirit, he shall not enter into the kingdom of God;* that is, says he, he will not be holy. *Ita omnis anima eousque in Adam censetur, donec in Christo recensetur,* "every soul is reckoned so long in Adam until it is re-reckoned, or reckoned again, or renewed *in Christ;* so long unclean, as long as not recounted, sinful indeed because unclean, receiving its own disgrace from its society with the flesh. What crime," says he,[§] "before that of impatience was committed, is imputed to man? He was innocent, the nearest friend to God, and the husbandman of paradise? but when he once gave way to impatience, *desinit Deo sapere, desinit cœlestia sustinere posse,* he ceased to be wise to God, he ceased to be able to bear heavenly things." There are indeed some passages[||] in this writer which seem to countenance the doctrine of free will, and are alleged by Dr. Whitby[¶] on that account; but in these he is to be understood of the natural liberty of the will, which he defended against the Basilidians and Marcionites, and of the power and freedom of the will, about things natural and moral, with which man was at first created, wherein lay the image and likeness of God in man; but Tertullian could never think that this is to be found with man now as then, since he affirms[**] that "the image of God was destroyed by the sin of our first parents;" and it is abundantly manifest, that this writer so held free will as that he believed it was subject to the grace of God; his words are these,[††] "An evil tree will not yield good fruit, if it is not ingrafted; and a good one will yield evil fruit, if it is not dressed; and stones will become the children of Abraham, if they are formed into the faith of Abraham; and a generation of vipers will bring forth fruit to repentance, if they spit out the poison of malignity; *hæc erit vis divinæ gratiæ potentior utique natura, habens in nobis subjacentem sibi liberam arbitrii, potestatem, quod autexousion dicitur,* this will be the power of divine grace, more powerful truly than nature, having free will in us, which goes by the name of *autexousion,* subject to itself."

SECTION VIII

ORIGINES ALEXANDRINUS. A. D. 230

ORIGEN is called by Jerom, writing against the Pelagians, their *Beloved,*[‡‡] their *Master,*[§§] the *Prince,* or author of their error;[||||] and says, that their doctrine is *Origenis ramusculus,* "a sprig of Origen." It need not therefore be thought strange that there are in his writings passages which smell rank of free will in the grossest sense; and especially since many of his works come to us through the hands of Ruffinus, said to be a friend to the Pelagian scheme; and indeed it is no wonder that Origen himself should be somewhat tainted with principles tending that way, seeing he succeeded Clemenis and Pantænus, men both addicted to the stoic philosophy, which obtained in their school, whereby the gospel began to be stripped of its native simplicity. However, notwithstanding all this, it is certain that Origen held the doctrine of original sin, and was sensible of the corruption and weakness of human nature, and of the necessity of the grace and help of God to every good work; and that even to have a will to that which is good, is from the Lord. That he understood the doctrine of original sin, and the guilt and pollution of mankind by it, will appear evident from the following instances; "*In Adam,*[¶¶] as saith the word, *all die, and are condemned in the likeness of Adam's transgression,* which the divine word says not so much of some one, as of all mankind—for *e ara tou Adam koine panton esti,* the curse of Adam is common to all."

Again,[***] "But if you please to hear what other saints have thought of this birth, hear David, saying, *I am conceived in iniquity, and*

---

* Ibid. l. 6, p. 662.   † Tertullian. de Testimon. Animæ, c. 3, p. 82.   ‡ Ib. de Anima. c. 40, p. 342.   § De Patientia, c. 5, p. 162. || Adv. Marcion. l. 2, c. 5 & 6, p. 457, 458; Exhort. Cast. c. 2, p. 665; de Monog. c. 14, p. 686.   ¶ Discourse, &c. p. 96, 346, 348; ed. 2. 95, 337, 339.   ** De Cult. Fœmin.

l. 1, c. 1, p. 170; adv. Marcion. l. 2, c. 5, p. 456.   †† Anima, c. 21, p. 324.   ‡‡ Adv. Pelag. l. 3, p. 102, H.   §§ Ib. l. 1, p. 89, M. |||| Ad Ctesiphont. p. 84, G.   ¶¶ Contr. Cels. l. 4, p. 191.   *** In Lev. homil. 8, fol. 75, A.

in sin my mother brought me forth ; showing, that whatever soul is born in the flesh, *iniquitatis et peccati sorde polluitur,* is defiled with the filth of sin and iniquity." These words he elsewhere says,* David spoke *ex persana omnium nascentium,* "in the person of all born of flesh and blood ;" and therefore it is said, which we have already mentioned above, "for no man is pure from filth, though his life is but of one day." And in the same work,† "Every one that comes into this world is said to be made in some defilement, wherefore the Scripture says, *no man is pure from filth, though his life is but of one day ;* and this defilement," he says, "is in the mother's womb, and that in the mother the child is polluted, even in the very conception." In another place, he says,‡ "The first man, Adam, being wickedly persuaded, through the deceit of the serpent, hath declined from the right way of paradise, to the evil and crooked paths of mortal life ; wherefore consequently, *omnes qui ex ipsius successione in hunc mundum veniunt declinaverunt,* "all who come into this world by succession from him have turned aside,' and are together become unprofitable with him." And in the same commentary he thus argues,§ "If Levi, who was born in the fourth generation after Abraham, is said to be in the loins of Abraham, *multo magis omnes homines qui in hoc mundo nascuntur, et nati sunt, in lumbis erant Adæ, cum adhuc esset in paradiso,* ' much more were all men, who are born in this world, in the loins of Adam, when he was yet in paradise ;' and all men with him, or in him, were driven out of paradise when he was drove from thence ; and by him death, which came to him through his transgression, consequently passed upon them who were reckoned in his loins." Once more, says he,|| "if any one considers this body of humility in which we are born, if any one considers this, *no man is pure from filth, though his life is but of one day, and his months are numbered ;* he will see how *gegenemetha meta akatharsias,* ' we are born with impurity,' and the uncircumcision of our heart." In the same work he has this expression,¶ "In Adam all die, and so *the whole world fell,* and needs rising again, that all men be *made alive* in Christ ;" the devil, he says,** "is called a murderer, not because he killed some one privately, but because he killed all mankind." So elsewhere,†† commenting on these words, *Through the offence of one death reigned by one ;* "This," he says, "shows, that through sin the kingdom is given to death ; nor could it reign in any, unless it receives the right of reigning from sin ; by which seems to be pointed out, that whereas the soul was created free by

God, *ipsa se in servitutem redigat per delictum,* it could reduce itself into bondage through sin." Hence he frequently suggests the weakness of human nature, and its insufficiency to do any thing that is good, and the need it stands in of the assistance of God. "Human nature," he says,‡‡ "is weak, and that it may be made stronger, *divino auxilio indiget,* ' it needs divine help.' We read, *the flesh is weak,* therefore, by what help is it to be confirmed ? Verily, by the Spirit, for the Holy *Spirit is ready, but the flesh is weak ;* he that would be stronger ought to be strengthened only by the Spirit." And in another place,§§ "We in our earth (for it was said to Adam, *Earth thou art*) have need of the strength of God, χωρις δε της δυναμεως τος Θεου, 'for without the power of God' we are not able to perform those things which are contrary to the wisdom of the flesh." Again,|||| "What need is there to say, what wisdom do we want to consider the works of Abraham ? and what power to do them ? η ποιας δυναμεως δεομεθα, ' what power do we need but Christ's,' who is the power of God, and wisdom of God ?" He further observes,¶¶ that "if the branch cannot bear fruit except it abide in the vine, it is evident that the disciples of the word, the intelligible branches, of the true Vine, the Word, *ou dunantai pherein tous karpous tes aretes,* cannot bear the fruit of virtue, except they abide in the true Vine, the Christ of God ;" or, according to another copy, "who is God." And in the same work he says,*** "Because *ouk autarkes emetera proairesis,* ' our free will is not sufficient to have a clean heart, but we are in need of God, who creates such an one ; therefore it is said by him, who knew how to pray, *Create in me a clean heart, O God !*" And a little after,††† "We say, that *ouk autarkes e anthropine phusi,* 'human nature is not sufficient to seek God in any manner,' and to find him purely, unless helped by him that is sought." As he will not allow‡‡‡ what is done by man to be properly good, and no good thing to be done without God,§§§ so he denies that a will to do good is from man, but ascribes it to God ; mentioning those words of Christ, *If any man will come after me,* &c., he makes this observation,|||||| "Hereby is shown, that to will to come after Jesus, and follow him, *ouk apo tou tuchontos andragathematos ginetai,* ' does not arise from any heroic action done by men,' for no man, not denying himself, can follow Jesus." And in another place he says,¶¶¶ "Not only to will, but also to work, as saith the apostle Paul, *ek tou Theos estin,* is of God ; to work, always following to will well, as its yokefellow ;" wherefore this doctrine does not at all discourage diligence and industry, study and

---

* In Luc. homil. 9, fol. 23, C. Vide Comment. in Matt. p. 391, ed. Huet. † In Lev. homil. 12, fol. 85, E. ‡ In Rom. l. 3, fol. 153, A. § Ib. l. 5, fol. 169, C. || In Jer. homil. 5, p. 86. ¶ Ib. homil. 8, p. 96. ** Comm. in Joannem, p. 316. †† In Rom. l. 5, fol. 173, E. ‡‡ In Luc. homil. 11,

fol. 98, H. §§ In Jerem. homil. 8, p. 95. |||| Com. in Joan. p. 296. ¶¶ Contr. Cels. l. 5, p. 239. *** Ib. l. 7, p. 354. ††† Ib. p. 360. ‡‡‡ Com. in Matt. p. 377. §§§ In Psalm, p. 38. |||||| In Matt. p. 287. ¶¶¶ In Joan. p. 312.

endeavour to perform good works in a dependence on divine grace and assistance.

SECTION IX.

GREGORIUS NEOCÆSARIENSIS. A. D. 240

GREGORY, surnamed Thaumaturgus, the *Wonder Worker*, from the miracles said to be wrought by him, was born at Neocæsarea of Pontus, of noble and wealthy parents, heathens; he was converted to Christianity under the preaching of Origen, and was afterwards made bishop of the place where he was born; upon his leaving Cæsarea he made a panegyric oration to a numerous audience, in the presence of Origen, about A. D. 239.* which, and his metaphrase on Ecclesiastes, are the chief writings of his extant, to be depended on as genuine. Could the sermons upon the Annunciation of the Virgin Mary, be thought to be his, which go under his name, they would furnish us with two or three testimonies in favour of original sin; but as they are dubious,† I shall not transcribe them, but refer the reader to them in the margin,‡ however, he has a passage in his oration which gives some plain hints of original sin, and the sad consequences of it; bewailing his departure from Cæsarea, and leaving Origen, " I know not how," says he,§ " through what sufferings, or sinning again, I depart, or am driven hence; what to say I know not, but that as another Adam, out of paradise, I begin to speak—these seem to be sins, της παλαιας απατης, 'owing to the old deception,' the punishments αρχαιων, 'of the ancients' (meaning Adam and Eve) remain *still* on *me;* do I not seem *again* to disobey, daring to transgress the words of God, in which and with which I ought to abide?" He expresses his consciousness of his own weakness, without divine grace and assistance, to attain to any virtue either human or divine, or the knowledge of things spiritual: his words are these;‖ "We neither have, nor are we near any virtue, either human or divine; we need much; these are great and high, and neither of them can be attained or gotten, οτω μη Θεος γε εμπνεοι δυναμιν, 'but to whom God inspires power;' we are not by nature fit nor worthy to enjoy, we still confess." He observes, in another place,¶ that "they that hear the prophets, της αυτης δυναμιος δει¦ προφητευοσι, 'have need of the same power with them that prophesy;' nor can any one hear a prophet, except the same spirit that prophesies gives him an understanding of his words; for there is such an oracle in the holy writings, affirming that he that shuts can only open, and no other." Gregory ascribes his conversion, which was when he was very young, to a divine power, and not to his own free will;

" I first passed," says he,** "to the saving and true word I know not how, *katenagkasmenos mallon eiper ekon,* forced rather than willing." And a little after,†† " Human reason, and the divine reason, or Logos, began together in me, the one helping, *te alelecto men emoi, oikeia de auto dunamei,* by a power indeed unspeakable to me, but peculiar to him, the other helped."

SECTION X.

CYPRIAN. A. D. 250.

CYPRIAN was a strenuous assertor of original sin, as Austin‡‡ has proved by a considerable number of testimonies cited from him; he, and not only, but the rest of his colleagues, who were present at the African synod, to the number of sixty-six bishops, affirm, "that a new-born infant has not sinned at all, unless that after Adam, being born in a carnal manner, it has contracted by its *first birth* the contagion of the ancient death; upon which account it is more easily admitted to receive the remission of sins, because not his own, *sed aliena peccata,* 'but another's sins,' are remitted to it." Yea, he asserted§§ that Adam by sinning lost the image and likeness of God, and consequently the moral liberty of the will, which was one part of that image, must be lost, and is what we contend for. The weakness and disability of man is frequently inculcated by him, and that all our strength and power to do that which is good comes from God, who should be applied to for it. "Whatsoever," says he,‖‖ " is grateful, *non virtuti hominis ascribitur, sed de Dei munere prædicatur,* 'is to be ascribed not to man's power, but to God's gift.' *Dei est, inquam, Dei est omne quod possumus,* 'it is God's, I say, all is God's that we can do;' hence we live, hence we excel, &c." Yea, he says,¶¶ " that in nothing must we glory, *quando nostrum nihil sit,* since nothing is ours." For the proof of which he mentions, John iii. 27, 1 Cor. iv. 7, and "that no man ought to be lifted up with his own works;" which he proves*** from Luke xvii. 7—10. And upon those words in the Lord's prayer, *Lead us not into temptation,* he makes this remark,††† " When we pray that we may not come into temptation, *admonemur infirmitatis et imbecillitatis nostræ,* 'we are put in mind of our infirmity and weakness, whilst we so pray;' lest any one should insolently lift up himself, lest any one should proudly and arrogantly assume to himself, lest any one should reckon the glory either of confession or suffering his own; when the Lord himself, teaching humility, said, *Watch and pray, lest ye enter into temptation; the spirit indeed is willing but the flesh is weak.* Thus while an humble and low confession goes before, and

Vide Fabricii. Græc. l. 5, c. 1, s. 28, p. 247.
† Vide Rivet. Critic. Sacr. l. 2, c. 16, p. 219.
‡ Vide Serm. 1, p. 11, A, 13, D.; et Serm. 2, p. 20, B. § Orat. Panegyr. p. 74, B, C.
‖ Ib. 68, C. ¶ Ib. p. 73, C. ** Ib. p. 55, C. †† Ib. p. 56, A. ‡‡ Contr.

Duas Ep. Pelag. l. 4, c. 8. §§ Cyprian de Bono Patientiæ, p. 314. ‖‖ Ep. 2, ad Donat. p. 6. ¶¶ Test. ad Quirin. l. 3, c. 4, p. 373. *** Ib. c. 51, p. 382. ††† De Orat. Dominica, p. 270.

the whole is ascribed to God, whatsoever is asked in a supplicating manner, with the fear and honour of God, *ipsius pietate præstetur,* "through his tenderness may be given." And, says he, in another place,* or his contemporary Cornelius, "We not only produce words which come from the holy fountains of the Scriptures, but with these words we join our prayers and vows to the Lord, that he would open both to us and you the treasure of his mysteries, *et vires ad implenda quæ cognoscimus tribuat,* and that he would give strength to fulfil what we know." Who also in the same treatise observes,† " that among these things he had been speaking of, yea, and before them, *de divinis castris auxilium petendum est,* 'help is to be asked of God,' for God only is powerful, who vouchsafes to make men, *et plena hominibus auxilia præstare,* and to give sufficient helps to men." Cyprian does indeed in one place say,‡ "that the liberty of believing, or not believing, is placed in man's free will." Which is very true of the natural liberty of the will, which always continues, whether a man believes or does not believe, since no man believes against his will, or disbelieves contrary to it; but is not true of the moral liberty and power of the will, for no man by the strength of nature, without the grace of God, has a power to believe to the saving of the soul. Nor could this be Cyprian's meaning, who in the very same tract says, that "nothing is ours." Besides this passage, Doctor Whitby§ has cited another, from this writer,‖ in favour of man's free will, in which he observes, that Christ said to his disciple, "*Will you go away?* Preserving the law, by which man being left to his liberty, and put in the power of his own will, desires for himself either death or salvation." But this is not to be understood, as though Cyprian thought that the real disciples of Christ were in such a situation, and so left to the freedom of their wills, that they might totally and finally depart from Christ, for his next words are, "Notwithstanding Peter, upon whom the church was built by the same Lord, speaking, one for all, and answering in the church's voice, said, *Lord, whither should we go, thou hast the words of eternal life; andwe believeand know that thou art the Son of the living God;* signifying and showing, that those who depart from Christ perish, through their own fault, but the church which believes in Christ, and which holds that which it hath once known, never at all departs from him; and they are the church who abide in the house of God."

SECTION XI
ARNOBIUS. A. D. 290

ARNOBIUS flourished under Dioclesian, taught rhetoric at Sicca in Africa, and was preceptor

to Lactantius. He wrote seven books *against the Gentiles,* which are his only genuine works extant. There is a Commentary upon the Psalms which goes under his name, but is none of his. Bellarmine thinks it was written by Arnobius junior, who lived about the year 445, and after Pelagianism was broached, of which that writer seems to be a favourer, and either to deny, or at least to extenuate original sin;¶ which was far from the true Arnobius, who asserts the corruption of human nature, and the impotence of men to spiritual things. Thus speaking of the prayers and supplications of the Christians to their master Christ, he observes,** that "these are not made to him for his sake, but for our profit and advantage; non quia proni ad culpas, et ad libidinis varios appetitus, vitio sumus infirmitatis ingenitæ, 'for because we are prone to faults, and to various lustful desires, and are in the vice of inbred weakness,' he suffers himself to be always conceived in our thoughts." And in another place he says,†† "Natural infirmity makes a man a sinner." Addressing himself to the heathens, he thus speaks :‡‡ "You place the salvation of your souls *in yourselves,* and trust that you may be made gods *by your inward endeavour;* but truly we promise ourselves nothing, de nostra infirmitate, 'from our weakness,' looking upon our nature virium esse nullarum, 'to have no strength,' and in every strife about matters to be overcome by its own affections; you, as soon as you shall go away, being loosed from the members of the body, think ye shall have easy wings by which you can fly to the stars and reach heaven; but we dread such boldness, nec in nostra ducimus esse positum potestate res superas petere, nor do we reckon it is in our power to reach things that are above." And elsewhere he says,§§ "that the nature of men is blind, neque ullam posse comprehendere veritatem, 'nor can it comprehend any truth,' nor find out certainly, and know things that are set before their eyes." And a little after he observes,‖‖ that "none but the Almighty God can save souls, nor is there any besides him who can make a long-lived perpetuity, and put a spirit in the room of another, but he who is alone immortal and perpetual, and is not bounded by any circumscription of time." And a little after,¶¶ "It is of our High-priest to give salvation to souls, and to put by or in them a spirit of perpetuity." It is true, indeed, he asserts from Plato,*** that the liberty of the will lies in the power of him that wills, which being understood of the natural liberty of the will, is not denied.

SECTION XII
LACTANTIUS. A. D. 320.

LACTANTIUS embraced and maintained the

---

* De Bono Pudicitiæ. p. 417.   † Ib. p. 421.
‡ Test. ad Quirin. l. 3, c. 52, p. 82.
§ Postscript, p. 561, ed. 2, 538.   ‖ Ep. 55, ad Cornel. p. 116.   ¶ Vide Rivet. Critic. Sacr. l. 2, c. 17, p. 220, 221.   ** Arnob. adv. Gentes, l. 1, p. 25.   †† Arnob. adv. Gentes. p. 42.   ‡‡ Ib. l. 2, p. 83, 84.   §§ Ib. p. 106.   ‖‖ Ib. p. 108.   ¶¶ Ib. p. 109.   *** Ib. p. 110, 111.

same doctrine his master Arnobius did; he seems to be very sensible of the proneness of human nature to sin, and of its weakness and frailty, and how many ways it becomes subject to it. "No man," says he,* "can be without sin as long as he is burdened with the clothing of the flesh, whose infirmity is subject three ways to the dominion of sin, by deeds, words, and thoughts; therefore just men, who can restrain themselves from every unjust work, yet sometimes are overcome through frailty itself, that either they say that which is evil in anger, or upon sight of things delightful, lust after them in secret thought." And to the same effect he says in another place,† "There is none who sins not at all, and there are many things which provoke to sin, as age, oppression, want, occasion, reward, *adeo subjecta est peccato fragilitas carnis qua induti sumus,* 'the frailty of the flesh with which ye are clothed, is so subject to sin, that unless God should spare *this necessity,* very few, perhaps, would live." He sometimes represents man as in a state of blindness and darkness, and suggests, that it is impossible he should have a knowledge of spiritual and heavenly things without divine teachings; "We," says he,‡ "who before as blind men, and as shut up in the prison of folly, sat in darkness, ignorant of God and truth, *are enlightened by God,* who hath adopted us in his covenant, and being delivered from evil bonds, and brought into the light of wisdom, he hath took into the inheritance of the heavenly kingdom." And elsewhere he says,§ that "the mind shut up in earthly bowels, and hindered by the corruption of the body, *aut comprehendere per se potest aut capere veritatem nisi aliunde doceatur,* 'can neither by itself comprehend nor receive truth, unless it be taught from some other person:" yea, he expressly says in another place,‖ that "man cannot himself come to this knowledge, *nisi doceatur a Deo,* 'unless he is taught of God:'" by which he means the knowledge of spiritual and heavenly things; for elsewhere he observes,¶ that "the knowledge of truth, and of heavenly things, *non potest esse in homine, nissi Deo docente, percepta,* 'cannot be perceived in man, unless God teaches it;' for if man could understand divine things, he could do them; for to understand is, as it were, to follow them closely; but he cannot do what God can, because he is clothed with a mortal body, therefore neither can he understand what God has done." There are some things which he denies are in the power of man; "To undertake a thing," he observes, "is** easy, to fulfil is difficult; for when thou committest thyself to a combat and conflict, *in arbitrio Dei, non tuo, posita victoria est,* the victory lies in the will of God, not in thine own." Hence he says in another

place,†† "It is not the part of a wise and good man to will, to strive, and to commit himself to danger, because to overcome, *non est in nostra potestate,* is not in our power." The appeasing of conscience and healing the wounds which sin has made in it, are by him ascribed alone to the power and grace of God; his words are these:‡‡ "It is better therefore either to avoid conscience, or that we should willingly open our minds, and pour out the deadliness thereof through the lanced wound, *quibus nemo alius mederi potest,* 'which no other can heal,' but he alone who has given to the lame to walk, and sight to the blind, hath cleansed spotted members, and hath raised the dead; he will extinguish the heat of lust, he will root out unlawful desires, he will draw away envy, he will mitigate anger, he will give true and perpetual soundness." In one place, indeed, he seems to take too much upon him, and what is beyond the power of a mere man, when he says,§§ "Give me a man that is angry, reproaching, and unruly, with a very few words of God I will make him as quiet as a lamb; give me one greedy, covetous, and tenacious, by and by I will return him to thee liberal, freely giving his money with his own hands, and those full; give me one fearful of pain and death, he shall immediately despise crosses, fires, and Phalaris's bull; give me one lustful, adulterous, a haunter of stews, you shall presently see him sober, chaste, and continent; give me one cruel and thirsting after blood, at once his fury shall be changed into true clemency; give me one unjust, foolish, a sinner, forthwith he shall be just, and prudent, and innocent." But then all this he ascribes to the power of divine grace attending the word and ordinances of the gospel; "for by one laver," adds he, "all wickedness shall be abolished, *tanta divinæ sapientiæ vis est, ut in hominis pectus infusa,* such is the power of divine wisdom, that being infused into the breast of man, at once, by one effort, it expels folly, the mother of sin; to effect which, there is no need of hire of books or lucubrations; these things are done *freely,* easily, quickly, so that the ears be open, and the breast thirsts after wisdom." This he opposes to the maxims, notions, and wisdom of the philosophers, with all the art of moral suasion they were masters of; "their wisdom," says he,‖‖ "the most that it can do, can hide vices, but not root them out; but the few precepts of God so change the whole man, and polishing the old man, make the man new, that you cannot know him to be the same."

SECTION XIII

EUSEBIUS CÆSARIENSIS. A. D. 330.

EUSEBIUS, as he asserts¶¶ that man was at

---

* Lactant. Divin. Institut. l. 6, c. 13, p. 480, 481.   † De Ira Dei, c. 20, p. 660.
‡ Divin. Institut. l. 4, c. 20, p. 328.
§ Ib. c. 24, p. 333.   ‖ Ib. l. 2, c. 3, p. 109.
¶ Ib. l. 7, c. 2, p. 530, 531.   ** Ib. l. 6,

c. 6, p. 452.   †† Ib. c. 18, p. 499.   ‡‡ Ib. c. 24, p. 520.   §§ Ib. l. 3, c. 26, p. 255.   ‖‖ Divin. Instit. l. 3, c. 26, p. 256.   ¶¶ Euseb. Demonstr. Evangel. l. 4, c. 1, p. 144.

first created with a free will, which might be turned to good or evil, which is readily owned, so he signifies,* that man's fall into sin was owing to it, and that through the ill use of it he is not only turned out of the right way, but is become like the beasts that are void of reason; his words are these: having spoken of man as constituted lord of all creatures, and possessed of a free will to that which is good, and the contrary, adds :† "but he not well using his free will, *tes orthes diatrapeis odou, ten enantian ormato,* 'turned out of the right way, and rushed, or was carried, into a contrary one,' considering neither God nor the Lord, nor things holy nor religious, but like the beasts without reason, attempted all kind of actions fierce and intemperate."

The Madgeburgensian Centuriators‡ cite from this writer the following passage, namely, "The liberty of our will in choosing things that are good is destroyed by the devils," which has not so clearly occurred to me. The words of Eusebius,§ which I suppose are referred to, are these: " The devil in his oracles hangs all things upon fate, and taking away that which is in our power, and arises from the self-motion of free will, *anagke de kai touto katadoulosas,* ' brings this also into bondage to necessity.'" Where he seems to have respect not to the fall of man by the temptation of Satan, but to the introduction of the doctrine of fate into the heathen oracles, which is at large confuted by him in the same chapter.

SECTION XIV

MACARIUS EGYPTUS. A. D. 350

MACARIUS frequently asserts the corruption of human nature, as derived from the sin and disobedience of Adam, and the impotence of it to that which is good: " We have received," he says,‖ " within ourselves the vitiosity of the affections, δια της παρακοης του πρωτου ανθρωπου, ' through the disobedience of the first man,' which, by custom and much use, is, as it were, become our nature." And in another place he says,¶ "The whole sinful race of Adam possesses the same condemnation secretly," meaning that which Cain was under ; " for as from one Adam all mankind are multiplied upon the earth, so one certain vitiosity of the affections sits upon the sinful race of men." Again :** " By him (Adam) death hath reigned over every soul, and has destroyed the whole image of Adam, εκ της εκεινου παρακοης, ' through that man's disobedience ;' so that men were turned aside, and came into the worshipping of devils." Moreover he observes,†† that " all that contrariety in things open and secret hath come upon us *apo tes parabaseos tou protou anthro-*

pou, from the transgression of the first man." He farther observes,‡‡ that " as Adam transgressing received into himself the leaven of the evil of the affections, so by participation they that are born of him, even the whole race of Adam, *ekeines tes zumes meteche,* partake of that leaven." Once more, he says,§§ " We are all the children of that dark generation, and all partake of the same evil savour ; wherefore the same suffering that that man (Adam) endured, *pantes ek tou spermatos Adam ontes,* we all, being of the seed of Adam, endure." And elsewhere he says,‖‖ that through " the transgression of the first man, wickedness entered into the soul, and darkened it ;" hence he affirms,¶¶ "that the soul has need of the divine lamp, the Holy Spirit, who beautifies the darkened house, and of that bright Sun of righteousness, that arises upon and enlightens the heart." Nay, he asserts,*** that " as it is not possible that a fish should live without water, or that any one should walk without feet, or see the light without eyes, or speak without a tongue, or hear without ears ; so without the Lord Jesus, *kai tes energeias tes theias dunameos,* ' and the energy of divine power,' it is not possible to know the mysteries and wisdom of God, or to be rich and a Christian." And, as he elsewhere says,††† ."A soul naked and destitute of the Spirit, and under the hard poverty of sin, *ouden dunatai k' an thele,* ' it cannot, even though it would,' bring forth truly any fruit of the spirit of righteousness before it partakes of the Spirit." Or as he expresses himself in another place :‡‡‡ "Without his vessels, that is grace, *adunaton tina to Theo diakonesai,* ' it is impossible that any one should serve God,' that is, be acceptable to him, with respect to his whole will." Agreeable to which are those words of his :§§§ " Without that heavenly leaven, which is the power of the divine Spirit, it is impossible that a soul should be leavened with the goodness of God, and attain to life." And a little after :‖‖‖‖ " That soul that thinks to do any thing of itself with care and diligence, relying alone on its own strength, and thinking that it is able by itself, without the co-operation of the Spirit, to perform a perfect work, *polu planatai,* is greatly mistaken."

He observes,¶¶¶ that those who have the divine law not written with ink and letters, but planted in hearts of flesh, these having the eyes of the understanding enlightened, and always desiring not a sensible and visible hope, but the invisible and intellectual one, are able to overcome the stumbling-blocks of the evil one ; *au' ek tes aettetou dunameos,* "but that is by an insuperable power." They, indeed, who are not honoured with the word of God, nor instructed in the divine law, being vainly puffed up, think, *dia tou idiou*

---

* Ib. c, 9, p. 159.   † Ib. c. 6, p. 155.
‡ Eccl. Hist. cent. 4, c. 10, p. 521.
§ Prepar. Evangel. l. 6, c. 6, p. 242.
‖ Homil. 4, p. 20.   ¶ Ib. 5, p. 32.
** Ib. 11, p. 59 ; vide etiam, p. 61.
†† Ib. 21, p. 131.   ‡‡ Ib. 24, p. 136.

§§ Ib. 30, p. 178.   ‖‖ Ib. 45, p. 220.
¶¶ Ib. 11, p. 58.   *** Ib. 17, p. 118.
††† Ib. 18, p. 118.   ‡‡‡ Ib. 15, p. 118.
§§§ Homil. 24, p. 137.   ‖‖‖‖ Ib. p. 138.
¶¶¶ Ib. 25, p. 139.

autexousiou, " by their own free will," to abolish the occasions of sin, which is condemned by the mystery in the cross only; for the free will which is in the power of man, can resist the devil, but cannot wholly have power over the affections, Psal. cxxvii. 1. For if human nature, " without the whole armour of the Holy Spirit," could "stand against the wiles of the devil," it could not be said by the apostle, what is in Rom. xvi. 20, 2 Thess. ii. 8; wherefore we are commanded to pray the Lord, that he would " not lead us into temptation, but deliver us from evil;" for unless being delivered from the fiery darts of the evil one, *dia tes kreittonos boetheias,* " by a better help," we should have the adoption of children vouchsafed to us, we have our conversation in vain, *os porro tes dunameos tou Theou tugchanontes,* " as being afar off from the power of God." Then he goes on to exhort to seek the powerful help of God, and represents fallen men as comparable to beasts without understanding, as become through disobedience *douloi tes sarkos pathon,* " servants to the affections of the flesh." He sometimes sets forth the case of men by a bird without wings, or having but one; " As," says he,[*] " a bird that has but one wing, cannot fly with that one; so human nature, if it remains naked by itself, and does not receive the mixture and communication of the heavenly nature, *ouden diorthothe,* ' can do nothing aright,' but continues naked and blameable in its nature, with much filth." Yea, though a man may have a will, he denies that he has a power; his words are these :[†] " As when any one sees a bird fly, he would fly also, but he cannot, because he has no wings; so, though to will is with man, to be pure, unblameable, unspotted, and not to have any evil in him, but to be always with God, *to dunasthai de ouk echei,* ' he has not a power;' he would fly into the divine air, and the liberty of the Holy Spirit, but if he does not receive wings, he cannot; let us therefore beseech God, that he would give us the wings of the dove, the Holy Spirit, that we may fly unto him, and be at rest." Yea, he represents man as dead, and so incapable of doing any thing unless quickened; " As the body," says he,[‡] " without the soul is dead, and cannot do any thing, so the soul, without the divine Spirit, is dead from the kingdom, nor can it do any of the things of God, *aneu tou Pneumatos,* without the Spirit." Also he signifies,[§] that " man is so wounded, that it is impossible he should be healed but by the Lord alone, to him only it is possible." And also,[||] that " it is impossible for any man of himself to deliver himself from contrariety, the error of reasoning, the invisible affections, and the machinations of the evil one." And elsewhere, having observed,[¶]

that a man cannot bring forth fruits worthy of the Lord without the wind of the Spirit, and clouds and rains of heaven, he adds; " This is the duty of man, that whether he fasts, or watches, or prays, or does any good thing, that he ascribes all to the Lord; thus saying, Unless God had strengthened me, I could not have fasted nor prayed, nor have left the world."

There are indeed two passages in this writer, cited and referred to by Dr. Whitby,[**] in favour of free will; though they seem to be levelled against such who held, that some men are by nature good, and others evil, and cannot possibly be otherwise, being under a necessity of nature to be one or the other, a doctrine held by none that I know of. However, it must be owned, that Macarius, in those places, says such things of man's free will as are not easily reconciled to his many expressions to the contrary which have been produced.

SECTION XV

ATHANASIUS. A. D. 350.

ATHANASIUS held the doctrine of original sin, and the corruption of human nature through it; whereby man is brought into a state of slavery, out of which he cannot recover himself by his own strength, nor restore the image of God lost by sin; he says,[††] that " Adam transgressing, *eis pantas tous anthropous e apate diebe,* ' the deception passed unto all men ;' and that,[‡‡] when man sinned and fell, through his fall all things were disturbed; death reigned from Adam to Christ; the earth was cursed, hell was opened, paradise was shut, heaven was angry, and at length [*eppthare o anthropos kai apektenothe,* man was corrupted and slain." He observes,[§§] that the apostle in the epistle to the Romans shows, that " otherwise there could be no redemption and grace to Israel and to the Gentiles, *ei me luthe e archaia amartia, e dia tou Adam eis apantas genomene,* " unless the old sin which through Adam came to all men was dissolved;' and that this could not be blotted out but by the Son of God; by whom also at the beginning the curse came, for it was not possible that another should loose the offence." And to the same purpose he says in another place,[||||] that " the devil wrought sin from the beginning in the rational and understanding nature of man; for which reason it is impossible for nature, being rational, and willing, and being under the condemnation of death, *eauten anakalesasthai eis eleutherian,* ' to restore itself to liberty ;' as saith the apostle, " what the law could not do in that it was weak." The weakness of human nature is frequently inculcated by him.[¶¶] The re-implantation of the image of God in man, he represents as a

* Ib. 32, p. 185.   † Ib. 2, p. 11.
‡ Ib. 30, p. 175.   § Homil. 20, p. 128.
|| Ib. 21, p. 132.   ¶ Ib. 26, p. 152.
** Discourse, &c. p. 97, 379, 381; ed. 2. 95, 96, 369, 371.   †† Athanas. contr. Arian. orat.

2, vol. i. p. 358.   ‡‡ Ib. in dictum Matt. xi. 27, p. 150.   §§ Ib. Synops. S. Script. vol. ii. p. 141. |||| Ib. de Salutar. adv. Jes. Christ. vol. i. p. 638.   ¶¶ Athanas. de Incarnatione, p. 63, contr, Arian. orat. 3, p. 436.

thing impossible to be done by either men or angels; his words are these:* "It was not proper that those who once partook of the image of God should perish; what therefore was fit for God to do? or, what should be done? but to renew the image again, that hereby man might be able to know him again: but how could this be done, unless the image of God, our Saviour Jesus Christ, comes? *di anthropon men gar ouk en dunaton*, 'for by men it was impossible,' since they were made after his image; nor by angels, for they are no images; hence the Word of God by himself came, that as being the image of the Father, he might *ton kat' eikona anthropon anaktisai*, 'create man again after his image;' which could not be, unless death and corruption were made to vanish away." And elsewhere, explaining those words, that they may be one in us, among other things he says,† "This phrase in us is the same as if it was said, that they may be made one by the power of the Father and of the Son; *aneu gar Theou touto genesthai aduaton*, for without God it is impossible that this can be done." And a little after he says,‡ *dia ten dedomenen emin charin tou Pneumatos*, "'through the grace of the Spirit given unto us,' we are in him, and he in us; and because he is the Spirit of God who is in us, we likewise having the Spirit are reckoned to be in God; and so God is in us, not indeed as the Son is in the Father;" for the Son does not partake of the Spirit, that thereby he may be in the Father; neither does he receive the Spirit, but rather gives it unto all; nor does the Spirit give the Word to the Father, but rather the Spirit receives from the Word. The Son indeed is in the Father as his own Word, and the brightness of him; we truly without the Spirit are strangers and afar from God, but by participation of the Spirit we are joined to the Deity; so that for us to be in the Father, *me emeterou einai*, "is not ours, or in our power, but the Spirit's, who is in us, and abides in us."

Dr. Whitby § cites a single passage from Athanasius, proving, that man has a free will to incline to that which is good, or turn from it; and it must be owned, that he does in the place || referred to, and elsewhere,¶ speak of man as *autexousios*, "endued with free will;" but then he speaks of man as he was at first created by God, and of the power of his will, with respect to natural and civil actions, which he abused to his hurt, being of a moveable, changeable, and flexible nature; and so capable of being turned from that which is good, and inclined to that which is evil, as the event of things showed.

SECTION XVI

HILARIUS PICTAVIENSIS. A. D. 360

HILARY of Poictiers says many things concerning original sin, and which show the depravity of human nature, its imbecility to do that which is good, yea, its servitude to sin, and the need it stands in of divine grace and assistance. "Sin," he says,** "the father of our body, unbelief, the mother of the soul, began to be in following generations, *ex peccato atque infidelitate primi parentis*, 'from the sin and unbelief of the first parent;' for from these we took our rise, through the transgression of the first parent." And in another place,†† speaking of the parable of the lost sheep, he says, "The one sheep is to be understood of man, and under one man the whole is to be reckoned, *sed in unius Adæ errore*, but in the error of one Adam all mankind went astray." Again, upon mentioning David's confession in Psalm li. 5,‡‡ "Who will boast that he has a pure heart before God? No, not an infant, though but of one day, the original and law of sin remaining in us." And upon a repetition of the same words he has this note,§§ "He knew that he was born *sub peccati origine, et sub peccati lege*, under original sin, and under the law of sin." Hence he represents man as in a state of great ignorance, and as incapable of knowing divine things without divine teachings; "It ought," says he,|||| "to be a doubt to none, that we must make use of divine doctrines to know divine things; neither can human weakness of itself attain to the knowledge of heavenly things; nor can the sense of corporal things assume to itself the understanding of invisible ones." In another place,¶¶ "God cannot be understood unless by God. We must not think of God according to human judgment; for neither is there that nature in us *ut se in cœlestem cognitionem suis viribus efferat*, 'so as that it can, by its own strength, lift up itself to heavenly knowledge.' From God we must learn what is to be understood of God; for he is not known but by himself, the author." Again he says,*** "For the truth of faith, that is, the understanding of God the Father and the Lord, by which especially our justification will be proved, quanta opus est nobis Dei gratia, 'how much of the grace of God do we need,' that we may think rightly." Many more passages††† might be produced to the same purpose. He denies‡‡‡ faith to be *ex nostro arbitro*, 'of our free will;' and affirms§§§, that "we have no love to God the Father but through believing in the Son." He frequently suggests the weakness of man to keep the commands of God or to do his will. "Statues," says he,|||||| "are more

---

* Io. p. 66.   † Ib. contr. Arian. orat. 4, p. 474.   ‡ Ib. p. 477.   § Discourse, &c. p. 97, 381; ed. 2. 95, 371. || Athanas. contr. Gentes, orat. p. 5.   ¶ De Incarnatione Verbi, p. 56.   ** Com. in Matt. can. 10, p. 277. †† Ib. can. 18, p. 301.   ‡‡ Enarr. in Psal. lviii. p. 392.   §§ In Ps. cxix. Tau, p. 522.

|||| De Trin. l. 4, p. 37.   ¶¶ Ib. l. 5, p 53, 54.   *** In Ps. cxix. Aleph, p. 457. ††† Vide de Trin. l. 1, p. 12; in Ps. cxix. Aleph. p. 453, Lamed, p. 489.   ‡‡‡ De Trin. l. 7, p. 93.   §§§ Ib. p. 76. |||||| In Ps. cxix. Aleph, p. 456.

and different, that is, than commands, and are tempered for the observing of each kind of duties; for the keeping of which, *nisi a Deo derigamur, infirmi per naturam nostram erimus,* 'unless we are directed by God, we shall by our nature be infirm;' therefore we must be helped and directed by his grace, that we may follow the order of the statutes that are commanded." In another place he says :* "The prophet freely *ran the way of the Lord,* after he began to have *his heart enlarged ;* for he *could not* run the way of God before he was made a habitation, large and worthy of God." And elsewhere he observes,† that David prays, *Make me to go in the path of thy commandments ;* for," says he, " he knew that his nature was weak, and that he could not attempt that path without a guide." And a little after, 'The prophet refers all to the hands of God, whether that the law of statutes may be appointed for him by the Lord, or that understanding may be given him, or that he may be led in the path, or that his heart may be inclined to the testimonies ;" wherefore he often intimates,‡ what need we stand in of divine assistance upon these and other accounts, which is far from the notion of the power of free will as maintained by Pelagians and Arminians ; yea, he represents man as in a state of bondage and slavery, and his will a servant and not free. " In Peter's wife's mother," says he,§ " an account may be taken of the vicious affection of unbelief, to which adjoins the liberty of the will. She shall be called un-belief, because until she believed *voluntatis suæ servitio detinebatur,* she was held under the bondage of her own will." And in an-other place :‖ "The Gentiles are bound in the bonds of their own sins, from which, through infidelity, they cannot loose them-selves ; according to what is said, *the sinner is holden with the cords of his sins.*" Once more, citing those words in John viii. 34—36, *He that committeth sin is the servant of sin,* &c., he makes this remark,¶ "There-fore we are taken and bound, and serve, not so much in body as in mind;" all which agrees with our sense of free will; though it must be owned, that there are some pas-sages in this writer which cannot well be reconciled to the more frequent expressions of his; two are cited by Dr. Whitby,** and others by Vossius,†† showing that the begin-ning of good is from the will of man, and the finishing and perfecting of it from God.

SECTION XVII

VICTORINUS AFER. A. D. 365

VICTORINUS represents the state of man by nature as most deplorable and wretched, and clearly expresses the necessity of the Holy Spirit, who he speaks of as the alone

sanctifier, from which work of his he takes his name ; "because," says he,‡‡ "men's memory of themselves, and of God, is *obrutam,* overwhelmed or confounded, there is need of the Holy Ghost, if so be that knowledge may come, to understand what is the breadth, &c.—for life was first to be given *mortuis per peccata hominibus,* 'to men dead through sins,' that they might be raised up unto God by faith." The Spirit of God, he says,§§ "is called the Holy Spirit, *quod sanciat, id est sanctos facit,* because he makes holy." And a little after he observes,‖‖ " that " every one that is baptized, and says he believes, and receives faith, he receives the Spirit of truth, that is, the Holy Spirit, *et sanctior fit a Spi-ritu Sancto,* and is made more holy by the Holy Spirit."

SECTION XVIII

OPTATUS MILEVITANUS. A. D. 370

OPTATUS of Milevi owns the original corruption of human nature,¶¶ when he says, "Every man that is born, although he may be born of of Christian parents, *sine spiritu immundo esse non possit,* 'cannot be without an unclean spirit,' which must be excluded and separated from man before the *salutary laver,*" mean-ing baptism. He denies that men, or means, or ordinances, can of themselves remove the pollution of sin. "The filth and spots of the mind," says he,*** "none can wash but he who is the Maker of the mind." Many other things are observed by him in the same chapter against the Donatists, who he thought took that to themselves which belonged to God. He indeed ascribes the willing of what is good to man, not to a natural man, but to a Christian man : mentioning the words of the apostle, 1 John i. 8, "If we say we have no sin, we deceive ourselves, and the truth is not in us," he makes this observa-tion :††† "He that said this wisely reserved himself for the grace of God ; for it is of a Christian man to will that which is good, and to run in that which he wills well, but to man it is not given to perfect— for it is ours to will, it is ours to run, it is of God to perfect."

SECTION XIX

CYRILLUS HIEROSOLYMITANUS. A. D. 370

CYRILL of Jerusalem gives plain intimations of the doctrine of original sin ; he observes twice in one place,‡‡‡ that the sin of Adam brought death into the world : "The wound of the human nature," he says,§§§ "is very great ; from feet to head there is no sound-ness in it." He represents man,‖‖‖ through the fall of Adam, as "deceived, fallen, blinded, lame ; yea, even dead." And as for *free will* itself, he says,¶¶¶ it is *kakon,* evil ; and they

---

* In Ps. cxix. Daleth, p. 468.   † Ib. in He, p. 470.   ‡ Ib. Samech, p. 502, et. in Phe, p. 511.   § In Matt. can. 7, p. 267.   ‖ In Ps. ii. p. 347.   ¶ In Ps. cxxxvi. p. 591.   ** Discourse, &c. p. 378 ; ed. 2. 368.   †† Hist. Pelag. l. 4, par. 2, p. 437, 438.

‡‡ Adv. Arrianos, l. 4, p. 351.   §§ Adv. Arrianos, l. 3, p. 340.   ‖‖ Ib. p. 341.   ¶¶ Adv. Parmen. l. 4, p. 92.   *** Ib. l. 5, p. 103.   ††† Ib. l. 2, p. 51.   ‡‡‡ Catech. 13, c. 1, p. 167.   §§§ Ib. 12, c. 4, p. 151.   ‖‖‖ Ib. 2, c. 3, 4, p. 23.   ¶¶¶ Ib. c. 1, p. 20.

that are holy,* are so, *ou phusei*, "not by nature," but by participation, and by exercise, and by prayer; yea, he affirms,† "that Jesus *to thelein charizetai*, 'gives the will,' and receives the faith, and bestows the gift freely."

Dr. Whitby‡ cites a passage or two from Cyrill in favour of free will, which passages are levelled against the Manichees, who held, that some men are by nature good, and others by nature evil; and that there are two souls in men, one naturally good, the other naturally evil; and that good and evil are respectively done by them through necessity of nature, and not with any freedom of will; and do not militate against our sense of free will, who allow of a liberty of will in all actions good and bad.

SECTION XX

BASILIUS CÆSARIENSIS. A. D. 370

BASIL of Cæsarea very clearly asserts the doctrine of original sin: "No man," says he,§ "can be found pure from filth, though he has been born but one day." Again,‖ "The rose is florid, but it puts shame and sorrow in me; for as often as I see that flower, *tes amartias upomimneskomai tes emes*, 'I am put in mind of my sin,' for which the earth is condemned to bring forth thorns and thistles." And in another place:¶ "I was indeed," says he, "fair by nature, but am now weak, because I am dead in sin, *ex epiboules tou opheos*, through the snare of the serpent." Wherefore, in the same place, he observes, that "beauty may come to the soul, and a power effectually perfective of those things which are necessary, *theias eis touto charitos chrezomen*, for this we need divine grace." Agreeable to this he says,** "We may understand those words, "they that trust in their power, and boast of the multitude of their riches," of the powers of the soul, *os ouk autotelous ouses ou di' autes pros soterian*, as being by no means sufficient of themselves to salvation." And elsewhere he observes,†† that spiritual and enlightened souls "know how impossible it is, by their own strength, to overcome the stumbling-blocks of the evil one, *all' ek tes aettetou duvameos tou Theou*, 'but by the insuperable power of God;' but they who are not honoured with God's word, are vainly puffed up, and think that, by their own free will, they can make void the occasions of sin, which is abolished only by the mystery of the cross." And a little after: "Human nature, without the whole armour of the Holy Spirit, cannot

resist the wiles of the devil." As for free will, he says,‡‡ "the power and liberty of it is the beginning and root of sin." And in another place he affirms,§§ that "every human soul is subject *to ponero tes douleias zugei*, 'to the evil yoke of bondage of the common enemy of all,' and being deprived of the liberty it had from its Creator, is led captive by sin."

Dr. Whitby‖‖ cites two or three passages from Basil in favour of free will, out of a commentary on Isaiah, ascribed to him;¶¶ but it is thought by learned men to be none of his, and therefore deserves no regard.

SECTION XXI

GREGORIUS NAZIANZENUS. A. D. 370

GREGORY of Nazianzum often inculcates the doctrine of original sin in his writings. He represents himself and all mankind as concerned in Adam's first sin, as ruined by it, and most bitterly laments the wretched consequences of it. He affirms,*** that the souls of men sinned in Adam; that all men fell ††† by that sin which was from the beginning; that we are all from the same earth and mass,‡‡‡ and have all tasted of the same tree of wickedness. And of himself he says,§§§ "I am fallen from paradise, I am turned again to the earth from whence I was taken, having for delicious fare this one thing, to know my own evils, *kai anti tes mikras edokes*, 'and for a little pleasure,' and condemned to sorrow without ceasing, and obliged to war against him who got into my friendship to my hurt, and through tasting, drew me into sin; these are the punishments of sin to me; hence I am born to labour, to live, and die: this is the mother of want, want of covetousness, covetousness of wars." In another place he says,‖‖‖ "I fell wholly, and am condemned *ek tes tou protoplas ou parakoes*, through the disobedience of him that was first made, and the theft of the adversary." Elsewhere he cries out,¶¶¶ *pheu tes e emes atheneias, eme gar e tou propatoros*, "'O my weakness! for that of my first parent is mine;' he forgot the commandment which was given him, and was overcome by the bitter taste." And then he proceeds to enumerate the multitude of evils which spring from this root of bitterness: "Beautiful," says he,**** "was the fruit for sight, and good for food, *o eme thanatosas*, which killed me." Hence he calls †††† the eating of it, *geuthis oulomene*, "the destroying taste," which brought bitter punishment upon him; and the tree,‡‡‡‡ *phutonandrophonon*, "the man murdering plant;" and laments §§§§ the heavenly image being des-

---

* Catech. Mystagog. 5, c. 16, p. 300.

† Homil. in Paralyt. s. 2, p. 312.

‡ Discourse, &c. p. 379, 380; ed. 2. p. 369, 370.   § Homil. in Psalm xxxii. p. 202, vol. i.

‖ Ib. 30, de Paradiso, p. 626; vide etiam Hexæm.; ib. 5, p. 61, et concio, 8, de Peccata, p. 61, append.   ¶ In Psal. xxix. p. 193.

** Ib. xlvii. p. 279.   †† De Libero Arbitrio, p. 631.   ‡‡ Homil. quod Deus non est auctor mali, p. 422.   §§ In Psalm xlviii. p. 279.

‖‖ Discourse, p. 97, 388; ed. 2. 96, 370. Postscript, p. 561, 562; ed. 2. 538, 539.

¶¶ Vide Rivet. Crit. Sacr. l. 3, c. 20, 307.

*** Greg. Nazianz. Orat. 51, p. 742, tom. i.

††† Ib. 42, p. 684.   ‡‡‡ Ib. 5, p. 135.

§§§ Ib. 9, p. 158.   ‖‖‖ Ib. 14, p. 221.

¶¶¶ Ib. 38, p. 619; et 42, p. 681.

**** Ib. 43, p. 700.   †††† Ib. carmen 13, p. 86, tom. ii.   ‡‡‡‡ Ib. 47, p. 111.

§§§§ Ib. 4, p. 68.

troyed by the sin of the first man. One so sensible of the sad effects of the fall of Adam, could not fail of observing the weakness of man to all that is good, and the necessity of the Spirit and grace of God, and of divine help, to the performance of that which is truly so. "We are all poor," says he,[*] *kai tes theias charitos epideeis,* "and stand in deed of divine grace." And in another place he observes,[†] that "such is the grossness of the material body, and imprisoned mind, that *me boethoumenon,* 'unless it is helped,' it cannot otherwise have any understanding of God." And elsewhere he says,[‡] "It is by the Spirit of God only that God is heard, explained, and understood. That no man is spiritual without the Spirit.[§] This, says he,[||] "is my sentiment, *oti duslepton men to agathon te anthropine phusei,* that which is good is hard to be received by human nature." He affirms,[¶] that "God both gives a capacity to receive, and strength to perform that which is good. That he has two parts therein, the first and the last, and that *oude Cristoio dicha brotos ichnos aeimei,* 'without Christ a man cannot take one step that way;' and therefore men should be careful not to ascribe too much to themselves, nor trust in their own strength, though never so wise." For, as he observes elsewhere upon those words,[**] "it is not of him that willeth, nor of him that runneth, but of God that showeth mercy: "There are some who are so lifted up with their good works, as to ascribe all to themselves, and nothing to the Creator and Author of wisdom, and Supplier of good things. These words teach them, *oti kai, to boulesthai kalos deitai tes para Theou boetheias,* 'that to will rightly, requires help from God;' or rather, the choosing itself of things needful is something divine, and is a gift of God's good-will to man for salvation, and ought to be both in us and of God: therefore he saith, it is not of him that willeth, that is, not only of him that willeth, "nor of him that runneth only, but of God that showeth mercy; so because *to boulethai para Theou,* 'to will is from God,' he rightly ascribes all unto him; for if thou runnest and strivest never so much, thou standest in need of him who gives the crown, according to Psalm cxxvii. 1." In which passage may be observed, that he asserts not only that divine assistance is requisite to a man's willing that which is good, but that the will itself is of God. Gregory does indeed assert[††] free will in man, as he was at first created by God, and continued in a state of innocence; but at the same time gives plain intimations, that man's free-will is now, through trans-gression, in a state of servitude. "Liberty and riches," says he,[‡‡] "were, or lay in the sole keeping of the commandments; and on the contrary, the transgressions of it is real poverty, *kai douleia,* and slavery."

SECTION XXII

GREGORIUS NYSSENUS. A. D. 380

GREGORY of Nyssa, frequently speaks of the corruption and weakness of human nature. He asserts,[§§] that man is born in sin; that the image of God is lost in man;[||||] that that which is good *choran ouk echen,* "hath no place in him;"[¶¶] and that human nature, being in wickedness through sin, *apokekritai tes kurias tou agathou kleseos,* "is exempted from the proper appellation of good,"[***] or does not deserve the name of good; yea, so faulty is it, that it cannot understand exactly what is naturally good, and what through deceit supposed to be so.[†††] He owns, that man's free will was originally good, and the gift of God, but that it is the instrument of sin;[‡‡‡] yea, the last of evils.[§§§] Moreover he says,[||||||] that "man has changed *ten poneran tes amartias douleian anti tes autexou siou eleutherias,* 'and has, instead of the freedom of the will, the wicked and base slavery of sin;' and has chose rather to be under the tyranny of a corrupting power, than to be with God." Nay, he says,[¶¶¶] "that he who was without lord and master, and of his own free will, *nun upo toiouton kai tosouton kakon kurieutai,* 'is now lorded over by such and so many evils,' as it is not easy to number our tyrants." Hence he observes the impotency of man, and the necessity of the Spirit and grace of God. On Cant. i. 2, he has this note:[****] "In what follows, the soul, the bride, touches a more sublime philosophy, showing *to aprositon te kai achoreton logismois anthropinois tes theias dunameos,* 'that divine virtue is not to be come at and comprehended by human reasonings,' when she says, 'Thy name is as ointment poured forth.'" And in another place he says,[††††] that "the power of human virtue *ouk exarkei kath' eauten,* is not sufficient of itself to raise up souls destitute of grace to a form of life." Yea, he observes,[‡‡‡‡] "that such mischievous evils, and so difficult of cure, are hid in the souls of men, *oste me dunaton einai dia mones tes anthropines apoudes kai aretes,* as that it is not possible, by mere human industry and virtue, to wear them out, and remove them, unless one receives the helping power of the Spirit." And a little after,[§§§§] "The tempter lays many snares for the soul, and human nature is in so bad a condition in itself, that it can-

---

[*] Ib. 16, p. 239, tom. i.   [†] Ib. 42, p. 683.
[‡] Ib. l. p. 17.   [§] Ib. 25, p. 441.
[||] Ib. l, p. 6.   [¶] Greg. Nazianz. carmen 58, p. 136, 137, tom. ii.   [**] Ib. Orat. 31, p. 504, tom. i.   [††] Ib. 1, p. 8, 9; et orat. 16, p. 256; et orat. 38, p. 618; et orat. 42, p. 680.
[‡‡] Ib. 16, p. 256.   [§§] Gregor. Nyss. in Psalm, c. 16, p. 370, vol. i.   [||||] Ib. contr. Eunom. l. 11, p. 282, vol. ii.   [¶¶] Ib. Orat.

Funebr. Pulcher. p 955.   [***] Ib. contr. Eunom. l. 10, p. 264.   [†††] De Beatitud. orat. 5, p. 801.   [‡‡‡] Ib. in Eccles. homil. 2, p. 338, vol. i.   [§§§] De Beatitud. homil. 8, p. 459.   [||||||] Ib. de Orat. Dominic. orat. 5, p. 754.   [¶¶¶] De Beatitud. orat. 3, p. 785.   [****] Ib. in Cant. homil. 1, p. 485.   [††††] Ib. de Scopo Christ. p. 372, vol. ii.   [‡‡‡‡] Ib. p. 734.   [§§§§] Ib. p. 736.

not get the victory of him." He argues the weakness of human nature, and the necessity of divine grace and assistance, from the several petitions in the Lord's Prayer; "What," says he,* "does that petition mean, *Hallowed be thy name, thy kingdom come ?* but this, *oti asthenes esti pros agathou tinos ktesin e anthropine phusis,* 'that human nature is weak to procure any thing that is good;' and therefore none of the things that we are seeking diligently after befall us, unless the divine help works that which is good in us." And a little after,† "He that says in prayer, *hallowed be thy name,* prays thus, *genoimen te sunergeia tes ses boetheias,* 'O that I might, by thine help and assistance,'be unblameable, righteous, godly, abstaining from every evil work, speaking truth, working righteousness, &c.; for God cannot otherwise be glorified by man, unless his virtue witness, that the cause of good things is through the divine power." Then he goes on to set forth the wretched condition that human nature is in by reason of sin, and adds,‡ "Well do we pray, that the kingdom of God may come upon us; for we cannot otherwise put off the wretched government of corruption, unless the quickening power takes the dominion over us." Again, on that petition, *Thy will be done,* he asks,§ "Why do we pray, that we may have a good will from God? *oti asthenes e anthropine phusis pros to agathon estin,* because human nature is weak to that which is good." And a little after he observes,‖ that "there is in us such a bias to that which is evil, that we have no need of an assistant, seeing wickedness perfects itself of its own accord in our will; but if the inclination is made to that which is better, *tou Theou chreia ten epithumian eis ergon agontos,* 'we have need of God to bring the desire into action.' Therefore we say, because thy will is temperance, but I am carnal, sold under sin, "by thy power form aright this good will in me; the same of righteousness, godliness, the alienation of the affections. And yet after all this it cannot be denied, that Gregory drops several expressions which seem to favour free will; and among others of the like nature, that is said¶ by him, which is cited by Dr. Whitby,** that "it is in men's power to be the children of the day, or of the night; and that they are the children of God by virtue, and of the enemy by vice; which must be reckoned among his unguarded expressions, in which he carries the power of man's free will too far; unless the patrons of that doctrine can reconcile them to the numerous testimonies to the contrary produced here and elsewhere. To which may be added, that prayer of his at the close of one of his treatises;†† "The Lord give us *power, eis to ekklinein apo kakon, kai poiein agathon,* 'to decline from evil, and to do that which is good,' through the grace and philanthropy of the Lord and God, and our Saviour Jesus Christ."

SECTION XXIII

HILARIUS DIACONUS.   A. D. 380

HILARY the Deacon, or the author of the Commentaries on the Epistles of the apostle Paul, formerly thought to be Ambrose's, very plainly asserts the doctrine of original sin, the impotency of man to fulfil the law, or do that which is spiritually good, and the necessity of divine grace. "It is manifest," says he,‡‡ "that *in Adam all sinned; quasi in massa,* 'as in the lump;' for he being corrupted by sin, all whom he begat are born under sin; wherefore from him we are all sinners, because we are all of him." Again :§§ "It is right and plain, that we ought not to obey the invention of Adam, who acted carnally, and who first sinning hath left death unto us, *hæreditatis titulo,* by way of inheritance." Likewise speaking of sin, being condemned by the cross of Christ; hence, says he,‖‖ "The authority as it were of sin was taken away, by which it held men in hell *propter delictum Adæ,* for the sin of Adam." And elsewhere,¶¶ to the same effect: "Being delivered from a state of darkness, that is, pulled out of *hell,* in which we were held by the devil, tam ex proprio quam ex delicto Adæ, 'both for our own and the sin of Adam,' who is the father of all sinners, we are translated by faith into the heavenly kingdom of the Son of God." Once more, "Adam," says he,*** "sold himself first, and hereby all his seed are subject to sin, wherefore man is weak to keep the commands of the law, nisi divinis auxilius muniatur, 'unless he is fortified by divine aids;' hence it is," he says, "the law is spiritual, but I am carnal, *sold under sin;* that is, the law is firm and just, and without fault, but man is frail, and subjected by his father's sin; so that he cannot use his power in obeying the law, and therefore must fly to the mercy of God to escape the severity of the law." And a little after:††† "What is commanded by the law is pleasing, and there is will to do, but power and strength are wanting to fulfil; because man is so pressed with the power of sin that he cannot go where he would, nor can he gainsay, because another is master of his power." And a little farther :‡‡‡ "It was impossible for us to fulfil the law, because we were subject to sin."

SECTION XXIV

AMBROSIUS MEDIOLANENSIS. A. D. 380

AMBROSE of Milain abounds with testimonies to the doctrine of original sin, and the depravity and weakness of human nature: "We

---

* Ib. Orat. Dominic orat. 3, p. 784.
† Ib. p. 735.   ‡ Ib. p. 736.
§ Ib. Orat. 4, p. 742.   ‖ Ib. p. 743.
¶ De Beatitud. contr. Eunom. l. 2, p. 95, vol. ii.   ** Discourse, &c. p. 97; ed. 2. p. 96.

†† Ib. in Christ. Resurrect. orat. 2, p. 848, vol. ii.   ‡‡ Comment. in Epist. Rom. p. 269.
§§ Ib. p. 289.   ‖‖ Ib. p. 287.
¶¶ In Col. p. 535.   *** In Rom. p. 283.
††† In Rom. p. 283.   ‡‡‡ Ib. p. 286.

have all," says he,* "sinned in the first man, and through a succession of nature, a succession also of the fault is transfused from one to all. Adam is in each of us, for in him human nature failed, because through one sin passed upon all." Again :† "The species of mankind may be considered in one : Adam was, and in him all were; Adam perished, *et in illo omnes perierunt,* and in him all have perished." And in another place he says,‡ "All men are born under sin, *quorum ipse ortis in vitio est,* whose very beginning itself is in sin, according to Psalm li. 5." And elsewhere he thus expresses himself :§ "I am fallen in Adam, I am cast out of paradise in Adam, am dead in Adam ; how could· he call me back, unless he had found me in Adam, as obnoxious to fault in him ? A debt to death, so justified in Christ." Once more, says he,‖ "We are all begotten in bondage. Why dost thou assume the arrogance of liberty in a servile condition? Why dost thou usurp the titles of nobility, O servile inheritance! Thou knowest not that the fault of Adam and Eve has bound thee to servitude." Yea, he says,¶ *antequam nascamur maculamur contagio,* "'before we were born we are spotted with the infection;' and before the use of light we receive the injury of its original; we are conceived in iniquity;" with more that follows to the same purpose. It would be too tedious to transcribe all the passages of this father which speak of this doctrine; I shall therefore refer the learned reader to the places in the margin,** which he may consult at his leisure. Hence he frequently inculcates the inability of man to do any good thing of himself, and the necessity of divine grace and assistance. "We often talk," says he,†† "of avoiding this world; I wish the affection was as cautious and careful as the talk is easy; but what is worse frequently the allurement of earthly lust creeps in, and a flood of vanities seizes the mind, that what you study to shun, that you think of, and roll over in your heart; which to beware of is difficult to men, to put off, impossible. Moreover, that this is a matter rather of wish than affection, the prophet testifies, saying, *Incline my heart to thy testimonies, and not unto covetousness: Non enim in potestate nostra est cor nostrum,* 'for our heart is not in our own power.' Who is so happy as always in his heart to ascend? But how can this be without divine help? Truly by no means, according to Psalm lxxxiv. 5." Again :‡‡ "Who can ascend from earthly things to heavenly, from the shadow to clearness, from the exemplar to the inner chambers of truth, by human steps, *sine divino ductu,* without divine guidance?" And in another place he says,§§ "Because human nature without divine aid is weak, it requires God a helper to heal it." Elsewhere he says,‖‖ "Neither can any say, that man can procure more for himself than what is bestowed upon him by a divine gift." Having mentioned the complaint and conduct of the apostle Paul, in Rom. vii. 23—25, he makes this observation,¶¶ "that if he that was stronger did not commit himself to his own strength, that he might escape the body of death, but sought help from Christ, *quid nos facere oportet infirmiores,* what should we do who are more infirm ?" He ascribes men's having a will to that which is good, and the beginning of every good action, unto God. "He that follows Christ," he observes,*** "being asked why he should be a Christian, may answer, it seemed good to me; which, when he says, he does not deny that it seemed good to God; *a Deo enim preparatur voluntas hominum,* 'for the will of men is prepared by God ;' for that God is honoured by a saint is owing to the grace of God." Again :††† "you see that everywhere the power of God co-operates with human endeavours; no man can build any thing without the Lord; nemo quidquam incipere sine Domino, no man can begin any thing without the Lord." As for man in a state of unregeneracy, Ambrose was so far from supposing that he has a free will to that which is good, that he represents him in a state of bondage and slavery; "The soul," says he,‡‡‡ "is fastened as with nails to corporal pleasures, and when it is once immersed in earthly lusts, it sticks fast, so that it is difficult to fly back on high, from whence it descends, *sine favore Dei,* without the grace of God." Again :§§§ "Every passion is servile, for *he that commits sin is the servant of sin ;* and what is worse, *multorum servus est,* 'he is the servant of many;' he that is subject to vices has given himself up to many lords, so that he can scarcely come out of the service." Once more :‖‖‖ "He that is in sin cannot be said to be *free,* but a servant, whom the grievous bonds of sin hold." I do not remember that either Vossius or Dr. Whitby has either produced or referred to one single passage in this father in favour of free will.

SECTION XXV

EPIPHANIUS. A. D. 390

EPIPHANIUS does indeed assert a free will in man, and argues for it, against the pharisaical fate, and destiny of men by birth, owing to the stars; which is equally denied by us in a passage Dr. Whitby ¶¶¶ has cited or referred

---

* Apolog. David. 2, c. 12, p. 519, 520.
† In Luc. l. 7, p. 169.   ‡ De Pœnitent. l. 1, c. 3, p. 388.   § De Fide Resurrect. in obit. satyr. p. 322.   ‖ De Jacob. l. 1, c. 3. p. 314.   ¶ Enarr. in Psalm l. p. 835.
** De Noe, c. 12, p. 194 ; de Jacob, l. 1, c. 3, p. 313, Apolog David. 1, c. 5, p. 496, et c. 8, p. 512; de Tobia, c. 6, p. 589, c. 23, p. 601; Enarr. in Ps. xlviii. p 825, 826, in Ps. cxix. Zad. p. 1052, Koph, p. 1057, Res. p. 1065 ; in Luc. l. 4, p. 72, l. 7, p. 133; de Initiand. c. 6, p.

347; vide plura in Aug. contr. duas Epist. Pelag. l. 4, c. 11.   †† De Fuga Seculi. c. 1, p. 351.   ‡‡ Enarr. in Psalm cxix. Gimel, p. 894.   §§ Expos. in Isa. apud Aug. contr. duas Epist. P. lag. l. 4, c. 11.   ‖‖ De Paradiso. c. 5, p. 116.   ¶¶ De Abraham, l. 2, c. 6, p. 251.   *** In Luc. l. 1, p. 8.   ††† Ib l. 2 p. 38.   ‡‡‡ Ib. l. 4. p. 71.   §§§ De Jacob. l. 2. c. 3, p. 327.   ‖‖‖ Enarr. in Psalm xxxvi. p. 689.   ¶¶¶ Discourse, &c. p. 97, 346, 352; ed. 2. 95, 337, 343.

to no less than three times; yet he affirms, that man is wholly under the power of sin, and, in a state of nature, weak, yea, dead. "Our life," says he,* "came, and again showed light unto us, when he found us wandering; for we were immersed in pride and blasphemies, by the images of idols, and impieties of spirits, *kakon panton epitagian*, under the government of all evils." And a little after,† mentioning those words, "Come unto me, all ye that labour and are heavy laden, and I will give you rest," he adds, "Therefore when *ego ethenoun dia tes sarkos*, 'I was weak through the flesh,' a Saviour was sent to me in the likeness of sinful flesh, fulfilling such a dispensation, that he might redeem me from bondage, from corruption, from death." And a little further:‡ "As many as are accounted to death, these are called *natural* or *carnal;* wherefore he commands us to reject the works of the flesh, as being the munitions of sin, and mortify the members of death by his grace, and receive the Holy Spirit, which he had not, *to zoopoioun eme ton palai tethnekota*, 'who quickens me that was formerly dead,' whom if I had not received I should have died; *dicha gar Pneumatos autou pas nekros*, for without his Spirit every one is dead."

<h3 style="text-align:center">SECTION XXVI</h3>
MARCUS EREMITA. A. D. 390

MARK the Eremite acknowledges, that all mankind are guilty of Adam's sin, and under condemnation on the account of it; that they cannot of themselves remove that or any other sin from themselves, or do any thing that is good, being dead in sin; and that, notwithstanding their free will, they are as brutish as the beasts of the field. "Let us suppose," says he,§ "that some are found free from these things, and as soon as born are strangers to all vice, which indeed cannot be, since Paul says, *we have all sinned*, &c. Yet though they were such, nevertheless they have their original from Adam, *cuncti que peccato transgressionis fuerunt ideoque capitali sententia condemnati*, 'and have been all guilty of the sin of transgression, and so condemned by a sentence of death;' insomuch that without Christ they cannot be saved." "Wherefore," as he elsewhere observes,‖ "we must not think that *Adæ peccatum certaminibus amputandum posse*, 'the sin of Adam can be removed by our strivings;' nor even our own sins, which befall us after baptism, unless by Christ; for how could we, who were dead in sins, a nobis ipsis boni quippiam agere, 'do any good thing of ourselves,' unless the Lord had quickened us by the laver of regeneration, and had bestowed upon us the grace of the Holy Spirit?" Again, says he,¶ "Let none of those who study virtue,

think, se suapte duntaxat facultate boni quippiam fecisse, 'that they have, by their own power alone, done any good thing;' 'for a good man out of the good treasure of the heart bringeth forth good things;'" where he calls the Holy Spirit hid in the heart of believers a treasure. This writer does indeed in some places ** speak of man as endued with free will, and yet, notwithstanding this, his opinion of him was, that he was sunk below the beasts of the field. "We," says he,†† "who are adorned with free will above all animals, are more savage than wild beasts, and appear less rational than the brutes."

<h3 style="text-align:center">SECTION XXVII</h3>
JOANNES CHRYSOSTOMUS. A. D. 390

CHRYSOSTOM, though he has been thought too much to favour the Pelagian scheme, yet clearly asserts the condemnation of all mankind for Adam's sin; the corruption and weakness of human nature; the slavery man is in by sin, and the necessity of divine grace to his deliverance. "If," says he,‡‡ "a Jew should say to thee, How can the world be saved through one Christ doing well? you may reply to him, *Pos enos parakousantos tou Adam e oikoumene katekrithe*, 'How could the world be condemned through one Adam sinning?'" Again :§§ "What is the meaning of that, *in whom all have sinned? he falling*, they also who do not eat of the tree, *gegonasin ex ekeinou pantes thnetoi*, all become mortal through him." Some have observed, that Chrysostom's sense of original sin was only this, that our bodies only are become mortal by it, but that our souls receive no damage on account of it; but the contrary will appear by what follows, "for along with death" he says,‖‖ *kai o ton pathon epeitelthen ochthos*, "a multitude of affections also entered in; for when the body became mortal, it necessarily received lust, anger, grief, and all the rest." And in another place he observes,¶¶ "that before the coming of Christ, our body was easily overcome by sin; for with death, *kai polus pathon epeiselthen esmos*, 'likewise a vast swarm of the affections came in;' wherefore neither was it very light to run the race of virtue, neither was the Spirit present to help, nor baptism, which is able to mortify; *all' osper tis ippos duoenios*, but 'as an unbridled horse,' it ran, and frequently went astray; the law indeed showing, what was to be done, and what not, but brought in nothing besides a verbal exhortation to them that strove; but after Christ came, the combats were made more easy; wherefore greater ones are set before us, as being partakers of greater help." Once more :*** "When Adam sinned, his body became mortal and passible, and received many natural vices; *kai baruteros kai dusenios o ippos*

* Lib. Ancorat. s. 64, p. 67, vol. ii.
† Ib. s. 65, p. 68.   ‡ Ib. s. 66, p. 70.
§ De Pœnitentia, p. 77.   ‖ Ib. de Baptismo, p. 87; vide etiam p. 88.   ¶ De Baptismo, p. 86.
** De Leg. Spirit. p. 50, 63; de Baptismo. p.
80, 81, 87, 93.   †† De Pœnitentia, p. 73.
‡‡ Homil. 10, in Rom. tom. iii. p. 72.
§§ Ib. p. 71.   ‖‖ Ib. 13, p. 99.   ¶¶ Ib. 11, p. 82.   *** Ib. 12, p. 91.

kateste, ' and the horse became more heavy and unbridled ;' but when Christ came, he made it lighter for us by baptism ; *en to ptero diegeiron tou Pneumatos,* raising it up with the wings of the Spirit." Moreover he says,*, when sin entered, *elumenato ten eleutheriav,* " it destroyed the freedom and corrupted the privilege of nature, which was given, *kai ten douleian epeisegagen,* and introduced slavery." And in another place,† " We ourselves were weak, but by grace are made strong." " Nor is it of human strength," says he,‡ " that we are delivered from all these things, but the grace of God, who will and can do such things. And that you may know that it is not from their good will alone, *alla kai tes tou Theou charitos to pan gegonen,* ' but that the whole is done by the grace of God ;' he says, ' Ye have obeyed from the heart the form of doctrine into which ye were delivered ;' for obedience from the heart shows free will; and to be delivered, *ten tou Theou boetheian ainittetai,* intimates the help of God." And though he frequently asserts free will, yet, such as it is after the grace of God is bestowed ; "he has left," says he,§ " all in our free will, *peta ten anothen charin,* after the grace which is from above." And elsewhere he asserts, that all evil things are from our will only,‖ and all good things, from our will, *kai tes autoropes,* " and his impulse." Chrysostom has indeed been blamed by many writers, both Papists and Protestants, for too highly extolling the power of man's free will; and particularly our Bradwardine¶ not only says, that he approached near Pelagius, but said the same he does : and it must be owned, that there are many of his expressions which look this way, some of which Dr. Whitby ** has cited, and more might be; but then, as Vossius observes,†† it should be considered, that when he extols the power of man, he does not speak of it as *without,* but *with* and *under* the grace of God; and it is worthy of notice, that the same writer remarks,‡‡ that when Chrysostom, being in exile, and near to his death, heard of Pelagius's fall into error, he lamented it in these words : " I am exceedingly grieved for Pelagius the monk : consider therefore what account they are worthy of, who bravely stand, when men who have lived with so much exercise and constancy appear to be so drawn away."

SECTION XXVIII

HIERONYMUS. A. D. 390

JEROM asserted the doctrine of original sin, which not only appears from his saying,§§

that " all men transgressed in paradise, are obnoxious to the sin and punishment of offending Adam, and fell with him from paradise into the captivity of this world :" but from that famous passage of his, in which he has put together many of the principal texts of Scripture we make use of in proof of this doctrine ; upon which account, and especially for the sake of his sense in Psalm li. 5, I shall transcribe it at large. His words are these ;‖‖ " The world lies in wickedness, and the heart of man from his youth is bent to that which is evil; nor is the human state without sin one day, from the beginning of its birth; hence David confesses in the Psalms, " Behold, I am conceived in iniquities, and in sins my mother conceived me ;" *non in iniquitatibus matris meæ, vel certe meis, sed in iniquitatibus humanæ conditionis,* 'not in the iniquities of my mother, or truly in my own, but in the iniquities of the human condition.' Hence the apostle says, " Death reigned from Adam to Moses ; even over them that sinned not after the similitude of Adam's transgression." The weakness of man to fulfil the law he ¶¶ proves thus, " For that no man can fulfil the law, and do all the things which are commanded, the apostle elsewhere testifies, saying, " For what the law could not do," &c. On those words, " The sin of Judah is written with a pen of iron," &c., he has this note,*** " If this be so, where is that, that the doting old woman (meaning Pelagius) devises, that a man may be without sin, if he will; and that the commands of God are easy ?" And elsewhere ††† directing himself to Pelagius, " You say," says he, " that the commands of God are easy, and yet you cannot produce one man that has fulfilled them all ; answer me, are they easy or difficult ? If easy, produce the man that has fulfilled them ; if difficult, how durst thou say, the commands of God are easy, which no man hath fulfilled ?" Yea, he affirms, that man can do nothing that is good of himself ; " Man," says he,‡‡‡ " from the beginning of his creation, makes use of God as his helper ; and seeing it is of his grace that he is created, and of his mercy that he subsists and lives, *nihil boni operis agere potest absque eo,* 'he can do no good work without him ;' who hath so given free will, that he may not deny his own grace in every work ; lest the liberty of the will should redound to the injury of the Creator, and to the hardening of him who is so made free, that without God he knows that he is nothing." And elsewhere he observes,§§§ that "without the Holy Ghost there is no strength;" that is, to do any thing that is good. More-

* In Gen. homil. 29, tom. i. p. 233.
† In Rom. homil. 27, p. 213.　‡ Ib. 11, p. 83.　§ In Gen. homil. 22, p. 155.
‖ In 2 Tim. homil. 8, tom. iv. p. 868.
¶ De Causa Dei, l. 2, c. 36, p. 605.
** Discourse, &c. p. 92, 347. 378, 382; ed. 2. 96, 337, 369, 372.　†† Hist. Pelag. l. 4, par. 2, p. 441.　‡‡ Ib. l. 1, c. 3, p. 5.
§§ Comment. in Oseam, tom. vi. p. 11, G, H;

in Jonam, p. 58, B; in Micheam, p. 62, I; Epitaph. in Nepotian. tom. i. p. 8, A; Adv. Pelag. l. 3, tom. ii. p. 102, F.　‖‖ Commeut. in Ezech. tom. v. p. 259, M. 260, A.　¶¶ Ib. in Gal. tom. ix. p. 75, M.　*** Ib. in Hierem. tom. v. p. 141, B.　††† Ad Ctesiph. adv. Pelag. tom. ii. p. 85, B.　‡‡‡ Ad Cyprian. Explan. Ps. lxxxix. tom. iii. p. 32.　§§§ Com. in Eph. tom. ix. p. 96, L.

over he declares,* that "this is the chief righteousness of man, to reckon that whatsoever power he can have, non suum esse, sed Domini qui largitus est, ' is not his own, but the Lord's who gives it.'" Yea, he pronounces† the man "accursed, who not only puts his hope in man, but him *that makes flesh his arm*, that is, his own strength; and whatsoever he does, non Domini clementiæ, sed suæ putaverit esse virtutis, does not think it is owing to the clemency of the Lord, but to his own power." He denies that the understanding of the Scripture, and utterance to declare the mind of God, are in the power of man, "for," says he,‡ "unless all things which are written were opened by him, who has the key of David, "who opens, and no man shuts; who shuts, and no man opens;" nullo alio reserente pandentur, "they could be opened by no other." And in another place he says,§ "The opening of the mouth, is not in the power of man, but of God; as Paul says, "A great door and effectual is opened unto me, and there are many adversaries; wherefore God is called he that opens." The whole work of conversion, repentance, and spiritual knowledge, is clearly ascribed by him to the power of God, and not man. He represents ‖ man as being much in the same case the poor woman was, whom Satan had bound eighteen years, so that she could not look up to heaven, but always on the earth; so man is bound down, et se erigere non possit, "and cannot raise himself up, because he is bound by the devil." On these words, "I will give them an heart to know me," he makes this remark:¶ "This is like to that of the apostle, "God is he that worketh in you both to will and to do;" for not only our works, but our will, Dei nitatur auxilio, depends upon the help of God." And on those words, "Turn thou me, and I shall be turned," he has this note;** "We cannot fulfil this, that we repent, unless we lean on the help of God; for after thou shalt convert me, and I shall be converted unto thee, then shall I know that thou art the Lord my God, and that my errors and sins shall not slay me; vide quantum sit auxilium Dei, et quam fragilis humana conditio, ' see how great is the help of God, and how frail the condition of man;' that we cannot by any means fulfil this, that we repent, unless the Lord first convert us." And in another place †† having cited John vi. 44, he thus descants upon it; "When he says, *no man can come to me*, he breaks the proud liberty of free will; for if ever he would come to Christ unless that is done which follows, "except my heavenly Father draw him; nec quicquam cupiat, et frustra nitatur, he

can desire nothing, and in vain he endeavours." And on these words, which he thus reads, "I will give them thought and sense, that they may know me," he argues.‡‡ "If thought and sense are given by God, and the understanding of the Lord spring from him who is to be known, ubi est liberi arbitrii tantum superba jactatio, where is the proud boasting of free will?" And having mentioned Psalm lxxvii. 10, which he renders thus; "Now have I begun; this is the change of the right hand of the Most High;" makes this remark upon it,§§ "It is the language of a righteous man, who after meditation in sleep, and distress of conscience, at last says, Now have I begun either to repent or to enter into the light of knowledge; and this change from good to better, non mearum virium sed dexteræ et potentiæ Dei est, 'is not owing to my own strength, but to the right hand and power of God." He frequently argues against the power of free will, from this consideration, that upon a supposition of this there is no need of prayer, "for," says he, "if only the grace of God lies in this, that he hath made us endued with free will, with which we are content, nor do any longer stand in need of his help, lest if we should, our free will would be destroyed; ' then we ought by no means to pray any longer,' and thereby engage the goodness of God, that we may daily receive, what, being once received, is in our power; for we pray in vain," adds he, "if it is in our will to do what we will. Why should men pray for that from the Lord, which they have in the power of their own free will?" He farther argues ‖‖ against the power of free will from the grace of God, and the help and assistance which he affords to man; "Where," says he,¶¶ "there is grace, there is no reward of works, but the free gift of the donor; that the saying of the apostle may be fulfilled, "It is not of him that willeth, nor of him that runneth, but of God that showeth mercy;" and yet to will and nill is ours, but that which is ours, is not ours, sine Dei miseratione, without the mercy of God." And elsewhere he observes,*** that "where there is grace and mercy, free will in part ceases : for it is only by that we will, desire, and give an assent to things that are liked; but it is in the power of the Lord, that that which we desire, labour for, and endeavour after, we are able to fulfil, illius ope et auxilio, by his help and assistance." And in another place he says,††† "If not one, nor few, nor many, but all, are governed by their own will, ubi erit auxilium Dei, 'where will be the help of God?" Then how did you explain Psalm xxxvii. 23, Jer. x. 23, John

---

* Adv. Pelag. l. 1, tom. ii. p. 88, H.
† Com. in Hierem. tom. v. p. 141, D.
‡ Ad Paulin. tom. i. p. 36, D.   § Com. in Joel, tom. 6, p. 25, C,   ‖ Ib. in Isa. tom. v. p. 6, E. F.   ¶ Ib. in Hierem. ib. p. 150, C.
** Ib. p. 158, I.   †† Adv. Pelag. l. 3, tom. ii. p. 100, L.   ‡‡ Ib. l. 2, p. 98, I.   §§ Ib.
p. 97, B.   ‖‖ Ad. Ctesiph. adv. Pelag. p. 84, I; adv. Pelag. l. 1, p. 88, I, K, l. 2, p. 96, E, F, G, p. 102.   ¶¶ Ad Demetriad. tom. i. p. 23, M.   *** Adv. Pelag. l. 1, tom. ii. p. 101, A.
††† Ib. l. 1, p. 91, B; vide etiam Ep. ad Ctesiph. adv. Pelag. p. 84, B.

iii. 27, 1 Cor. iv. 7, &c. ?" And again,* he asks, "Where are they that say, that man may be governed by his own will? That such a power of free will is given, that the mercy and justice of God are taken away? Let them be ashamed that say so." He allows of and pleads for such a free will, as is consistent with, and depends upon the grace and power of God; "not that," says he,† "free will is taken away from man by the grace of God, but the liberty itself, Dominum habere debeat adjutorem, ought to have God for its helper." He owns,‡ that "it is ours to will and to run; but, that our willing and running may be accomplished, belongs to the mercy of God; and it is so brought about, that in our willing and running, free will may be preserved, and in the consummation of our will and race, Dei cuncta potentiæ relinquantur, all things may be left to the power of God." Yea, he argues that the Pelagians, and not such as himself, destroyed free will; "They boast," says he,§ "up and down, that free will is destroyed by us; when, on the contrary, they ought to observe, that they destroy the liberty of the will, who abuse it, contrary to the grace of the donor. Who destroys free will? He who always gives thanks to God, and whatsoever flows in his rivulet, he refers to the fountain? Or, he who says, ' Depart from me, for I am clean, I have no need of thee?'" Thou hast once given me freedom of will, that I may do what I will, why dost thou thrust in thyself again, that I can do nothing unless thou completest thine own gifts in me?" Once more, he observes,‖ "that it is not in this we differ from brute beasts, that we were made with a free will; but in this, that this free will depends upon the help of God, illiusque per singula ope indiget, ' and stands in need of his assistance in every action;' which you (Pelagians) do not mean; but this you mean, that he that once hath free will, does not want God for his helper." From hence we may better understand Jerom's meaning, when he is speaking in favour of free will, as he does in many places; though it is easy to observe that he¶ sometimes considers free will, as man was endued with it at his first creation; at other times he speaks** of the power of it, with respect to natural and civil actions, to which also he supposes the power of God was necessary;†† and very often of the freedom of it, as opposed ‡‡ to force and violence, which it cannot admit of. He also observes,§§ that it is not always the same, and is to be regarded according to the mode, time, and condition of man's frailty.

Now in one or other of these senses are the passages to be taken which Dr. Whitby has cited ‖‖ from this writer in favour of free will. It must be owned, that Jerom sometimes drops some things incautiously, and without guard, which are not easily reconciled to his avowed principles; but then these passages should not be urged against his declared opinion and sentiments.

CHAPTER IV

OF EFFICACIOUS GRACE

DR. WHITBY¶¶ affirms, "that the fathers generally teach, that God doth only persuade, and by his Spirit assist, those that are willing to be good; but leaves them still to neglect and resist his persuasions, not laying them under a necessity to be good; because that would destroy the virtue and reward of being so." In proof of which he produces but two or three testimonies, which will be hereafter considered. And in another place he says,*** "As for the antiquity of irresistibleness of grace, he (Dr. Edwards) hath only one, St. Austin, to produce, against a hundred testimonies of the fathers cited by Vossius, to prove that God laid no necessity upon man's will to act; as he must do, if he acts irresistibly upon it, that being necessary which cannot be otherwise." All which pains might have been spared, for none say, that God lays any necessity of coaction or force upon the wills of men; but that by the power of his grace he moves upon them, and influences them to that which is good according to their nature. Besides, Vossius, after he had made the citations referred to, and which regard the article of free will already considered, observes,††† that these writers were far from Pelagianism; and that, according to them, the will remained free, and all things are ascribed to grace; which he undertakes more fully to explain; and among the rest, says, "Every good work, as such, is positively from the Holy Spirit, because whatsoever hath a being, as good and supernatural, that it has from grace. From the free will indeed it is only privately, as it does not resist grace, when it could resist; that it can resist, it has of itself; that it can will to resist, it has from grace." And elsewhere he says,‡‡‡ "I would not have it so taken, as if nothing, could be produced from them (the fathers) which may seem to intimate, that grace is bestowed from an absolute will to convert ;" and then mentions a passage from Basil, cited by Petrus Diaconus, and others; "Thou canst do all things, and there is none can contradict thee; for when thou wilt thou

---

* Com. in Hierem. tom. v. p. 133, D, E, p. 134, F.   † Com. in Ezech. tom. v. p. 196, K.
‡ Adv. Pelag. l. 1, 87, K.
§ Ad Ctesiph. adv. Pelag. p. 84, M.
‖ Ad Ctesiph. adv. Pelag. p. 85, G, H.
¶ Ad Damasum, tom. iii. p. 43, H; Comment. in Zeph. tom. vi. p. 121, E; ib. in Eccl. tom. vii. p. 37, E.   ** Ib. in Isa. tom. v. p. 4, H; ibid. in Ezech. ibid. p. 231.   †† Ad Ctesiph. adv. Pelag. p. 85, A.   ‡‡ Ad Deme-

triad. tom. i. p. 24, B; adv. Jovinian. tom. ii. l. 2, p. 25, C; ad Damasum, tom. iii. p. 41, K; ad Hedibiam, ib. p. 46, C, 49, H; Comment in Eccl. tom. vii. p. 34, D; ibid. in Philemon, tom. ix. p. 116, B.   §§ Adv. Pelag. l. 3, p. 101.
‖‖ Discourse, &c. p. 384. Postscript, p. 562; ed. 2. 374, 536.   ¶¶ Discourse, &c. p. 296; ed. 2. 259, 260.   *** Postscript, p. 565; ed. 2. 542.   ††† Hist. Pelag. l. 7, par. ii. p. 717, 718.   ‡‡‡ Ib. l. 6, thes. 10, p. 553, 554.

savest, and none resists thy will." And adds, "Also memorable is that of Ambrose, God calls whom he pleases, and whom he will he makes religious." In the following Sections I shall make it appear, that it was the sentiment of the ancient writers, that regeneration, conversion, sanctification, faith, &c., are wrought in the soul through the energy of the Spirit of God, and the powerful and insuperable efficacy of divine grace, and are not the fruits and effects of mere moral suasion.

SECTION I

CLEMENS ROMANUS. A. D. 69

CLEMENT was an admirer of the grace of God in vocation and sanctification, for he not only speaks of grace in general as God's gift, when he says,* " Let us be joined to them, to whom *e charis apo tou Theou dedotai*, grace is given from God; and in the free pathetic manner takes notice of the goodness of God in the free donation of them, saying, "How blessed and wonderful are the gifts of God, O beloved! Life with immortality, splendour with righteousness, truth with freedom, *pistis en pepoithesei, eykrateia en agiasmo*, faith with confidence, continence with holiness." Of which last he elsewhere says,† "He that is chaste in the flesh, let him not be proud or insolent: knowing that *eteros estin o epichoregon auto egkratean*, it is another who furnishes him with the gift of continence." And a little after, in the same page, having mentioned the blessings which God has prepared for us before we were born, draws this inference ; "Therefore since we have all these things from him, we ought *kata para* in all things to give thanks to him, to whom be glory for ever and ever. Amen." In the conclusion of his epistle‡ he prays, "that God would give to every soul that calls upon his great and holy name, faith, fear, patience, long-suffering, continence, chastity, and sobriety, that they may rightly please his name."

SECTION II,

BARNABAS. A. D. 70

BARNABAS speaks of the work of grace as a new creation, or as a formation of man again, which requires Almighty power ; his words in one place are these,§ "Wherefore having renewed us by the remission of our sins, *epoiesen emas allon tupon, os paidion*, 'he hath made us of another form, as a little child,' to have a soul as though he had made us again ; for the Scripture says concerning us, as he said to the Son, 'Let us make man after our image, and after our likeness.'" Again, says he, "I will show thee how in the last days he hath made δευηεραν πλασιν, ' a second formation for us ;' the Lord saith, Behold, I will make the last as the first :

behold, therefore, *emeis anapeplasmetha*, ' we are made again ;' as he again says in another prophet, *Behold*, saith the Lord, *I will take out their stony hearts, and I will put in them fleshly ones.*" And in another place,‖ speaking of the sanctification of the sabbath-day, he expresses himself thus ; " When we receive the righteous promise, of sin being no more, *gegonoton de kainon panton upo Kurio*, ' being made all new by the Lord,' then shall we be able to sanctify it, being first sanctified ourselves." And a little after says he,¶ "Receiving the remission of sins, and hoping in the name of the Lord, *egenometha kainoi, palin ex arches aptomenoi*, we become new, being created again as at the beginning." Repentance, spiritual wisdom and knowledge, are, according to him, pure gifts of the grace of God ; for, says he,** he "dwells in us, who were under the servitude of death, opening to us the door of the temple, which is the mouth ; *metanoian didous emin*, ' and giving repentance to us ;' introduces us into the incorruptible temple." He observes,†† that " Christ chose his apostles to preach the gospel, *ontas uper pasan amartian anomoterous*, ' being more sinful than all sin itself ;' that he might show he came *not to call the righteous, but sinners to repentance.*" And in another place he says,‡‡ " See how well Moses gave the law, but whence is it that they know and understand these things ? We therefore justly understanding the commandments, speak as the Lord hath willed ; wherefore he hath circumcised our ears and hearts, *ina suniomen tauta*, that we may understand these things." Wherefore he blesses the Lord for what knowledge and understanding in divine things he is pleased to give, saying,§§ " Blessed be our Lord, *o sophian kai noun themenos en emin ton kruphion autou*, who hath put in us wisdom and understanding of his hidden things." To which may be added that prayer of his,‖‖ " God, that governs all the world, *doe umin sophian*, ' give you wisdom,' understanding, prudence, and knowledge of his commandments, with patience."

SECTION III.

JUSTIN. A. D. 150,

JUSTIN MARTYR asserts the necessity of the grace of God to the right understanding of the Scriptures ; *ei oun tis me metameyales charitos tes para Theou laboi*, "' unless,' says he,¶¶ ' any therefore should undertake with the great grace which is from God,' to understand the things which are said and done by the prophets, it will be of no advantage to him to seem to read the words or facts, unless he can render a reason for them." And in another place, speaking to Trypho the Jew, and those that were with him he says,*** "Do you think, O men, that we could ever have been able to have under-

* Ep. ad Corinth. 1, p. 68.   † Ib. p. 78.
‡ Ep. ad Corinth. 1. p. 130.
§ Barnab. Ep. Far. 1, sect. 5. p. 221. 222.
‖ Ibid. sect. 11. p. 224.   ¶ Barnab. Ep.
Par. 1. sect. 12. p. 246.   ** Ibid. p. 247.

†† Ibid. sect. 4. p. 218.   ‡‡ Ibid. 8. p. 233.
§§ Ibid. 5. p. 221.   ‖‖ Ibid. Par. 2, sect.
3, p. 253.   ¶¶ Dialog. cum Tryph. p. 319.
*** Ibid. p. 346.

stood these things in the Scriptures, ει μη θεληματι που θελησαντ۞ αυτα ελαβυμεν χαριν του νοησαι, unless by the will of him that wills these things, we had received grace to understand them." Addressing himself to the same men, he says,* " Cease to deceive yourselves, and them that hear you, and learn of us, των σοφισθεντων απο της του Xρισου χαριτος, ' who are made wise by the grace of Christ." And having mentioned the text in Matt. xi. 27, he adds,† " Therefore he hath revealed all things to us, which from the Scripture, δια της χαριτος αυτου νενοηκαμέν, " through his grace we have an understanding of, knowing him to be the first-born of God, and before all creatures." Yea, says he,‡ " to us is given to hear, and to understand, and to be saved by this Christ. and to know all the things of the Father." Nay, Eusebius says,§ that he openly declares in his Dialogue with Trypho, "how, η θεια χαρις αυτον εωι τον της πισεως ωαρωρμηδε λογον, " the grace of God impelled him to the doctrine of faith ; that is, powerfully wrought upon him to embrace and make a profession of it ; which expresses the efficacy of divine grace in its irresistible and unfrustrable operations upon his heart, which Justin had an experience of.

Dr. Whitby‖ cites ʻa passage from this writer, in which he says, "That God sent his Son into the world, ως πεισθων, ου βιαζομεν۞, ' as persuading, but not compelling man to be good." But no such words are to be found in the place he refers to. Justin there says,¶ that "To be from the beginning is not our's ; but us, who choose by the rational powers which he gives, to follow those things, which are grateful to him, πειθει τε και εις ωισιν αγει ημας, ' he persuades and leads to faith.' " That God persuades men to believe, nobody denies ; nor does any say that he compels them to believe, or to be good against their wills ; but the question is, whether his persuasions are merely moral ? or whether they are attended with an internal, powerful, and unfrustrable operation of his grace ? It looks as if Justin meant the latter, since he adds, " What human laws could not effect, that the Λολ۞, or Word, being divine, has performed." Now human laws, working only by moral suasion, are deficient ; but the divine Word, or Son of God, working in a way of irresistible grace, produces that which they cannot.

SECTION IV

IRENÆUS. A. D. 180,

IRENÆUS, in many places, shows that the Spirit and grace of God are necessary to the knowledge of God, to our performance of good works, and bringing forth good fruits of righteousness ; for, says he,** "the Lord

hath taught us, that no man can know God, nisi Deo docente, hoc est, sine Deo non cognosci Deum, unless God teaches him, that is, God is not or cannot be known without God." And in another place :†† " Him we rightly show is known by none, unless by the Son, and such to whom the Son will reveal him ; for the Son reveals him to all to whom the Father would be known, et nique sine bona voluntate Patris, neque sine administratione Filii cognoscet quisquam Deum, and neither without the good will and pleasure of the Father, nor without the administration of the Son, can any one know God." And in the same place he represents men in a state of nature as comparable to stones, in whom Christ, by the mighty power of his grace, works the same kind of faith as was in Abraham : for having cited Matt. iii. 9, he makes this observation: " This Jesus did, drawing us off from the religion of stones, and translating us a nostris duris et infructuosis cogitationibus, et similem Abrahæ fidem constituens, from our hard and unfruitful thoughts, putting in us faith like to that of Abraham." Very observable, and much to our purpose, is the following passage of this ancient writer : "As," says he,‡‡ " of dry wheat, one lump, or one loaf, cannot be made without moisture, so neither we, being many, can be made one in Christ Jesus, sine aqua quæ de cœlo est, without the water which is from heaven." And as the dry earth, if it receives not moisture, does not "bring forth fruit, so likewise we, lignum aridum existentes primum, nunquam fructificaremus vitam, sine superna voluntaria pluvia, hoc est Spiritu Sancto, being first a dry tree, can never bring forth fruit unto life, without the rain which comes freely from above, that is, the Holy Spirit." And a little after, having compared the Spirit of God to dew, adds, qua propter necessarius nobis est ros Dei, "wherefore the dew of God is necessary for us, that we be not burnt up, nor become unfruitful." And when he elsewhere says,§§ Facere proprium est benignitatis Dei, fieri autem proprium est hominis naturæ, "To make, belongs to the kindness or grace of God ; to be made, is the property of man's nature." What else does he suggest, but that God is active, and men passive, as in the old, so in the new creation ?

Dr. Whitby,‖‖ to prove that the fathers taught, that God only persuades men, and leaves them under a power to neglect and resist his persuasions, cites a passage from Irenæus,¶¶ in which he says, that " God redeems his from the apostate spirit, non vi sed suadela, not by force, but by persuasion, quemadmodum decebat Deum suadentem et non vim inferentem accipere quæ vellet, as it became God to receive what he would by persuasion, and not by force." But upon

---

* Ibid. p. 250.   † Ibid. p. 326.   ‡ Ibid. p. 350.   § Eccles. Hist. l. 4, c. 18. p. 140.   ‖ Discourse on the Five Points, p. 266, Ed. 2. 260.   ¶ Apolog. 2. pro Christian. p. 58.   ** Adv. Hœres. l. 4, c. 14, p. 331.

†† Ib. c. 19, p. 333.   ‡‡ Ib. l. 3, c. 19, p. 280.   §§ Ib. l. 4, c. 76, p. 422.   ‖‖ Discourse, &c. p. 226 ; ed. 2. 260.   ¶¶ Adv. Hæres. l. 5, c. 1, p. 432.

examining the place, it will appear, that Irenæus is speaking not of God's operation upon the hearts of men, but of Christ's redeeming his from the apostate spirit rationally, in a way of righteousness, mildly, gently, and not by *force* and *violence ;* and that the *persuasion*, whatever Irenæus means by it, is used not with the persons redeemed, but with the apostate spirit who had usurped dominion over them.

SECTION V

CLEMENS ALEXANDRINUS. A. D. 190

CLEMENT of Alexandria must be reckoned among the assertors of the necessity of the grace of God to perform that which is good; and of the power and efficacy of it in the hearts of men producing faith, &c.; for in one place he says,* that " men ought to have a sound mind, which does not repent of a studious search after that which is good; *pros oper malista tes theias chrezomen charitos,* ' in order to which especially, we stand in need of divine grace,' of right doctrine, of a pure affection of mind, *kai tes tou Patros pros auton olkes,* and of the Father's drawing to himself." And in another place he observes,† that " few knew the Son of God as Peter did, whom he pronounces blessed, because *flesh and blood* hath not revealed the truth to him, but his Father which is in heaven; plainly signifying, that a man is a gnostic, or endued with knowledge, so as to know the Son of the Almighty, not by his flesh, which was conceived, *alla di autes tes dunameos tes Patrikes,* but by the Father's power." He strongly‡ disputes against the Basilidians, who held that faith was natural and proper to men, and arose from some preceding natural necessity; whereas he affirms it to be something that comes from above, that is divine, and springs from the grace of God; his words are these ;§ " Faith is not to be calumniated, *os eukolon te kai pandemon,* ' as easy and vulgar, and what every one has.' I say, therefore, that faith, whether it is founded on love or on fear, as the adversaries say, *theion ti einai,* is something divine." And elsewhere he says,‖ " The conjecture of truth is one thing, and truth itself another; the likeness of it one thing, and that itself another; the one comes by learning and exercise, the other by power and faith; *dorea gar e didaskalia tes theosebeias, charis de e pistis,* for the doctrine of godliness is a gift, and faith a grace." Again he says,¶ " It remains, that *theia chariti,* ' by divine grace,' and by the world alone, which is from God, we understand that which is unknown."

SECTION VI

TERTULLIAN. A. D. 200

TERTULLIAN ascribes all that a man has and does, in a spiritual way, to the grace of God, and the whole work of grace to his mighty power. At the beginning of his Treatise on Patience, he confesses, that he was very unfit to write on that subject, as being homo nullius boni, ' a worthless man; 'and observes,** " that as evil things, so some good things are of such a prodigious magnitude, that, ad capienda et præstanda ea, sola gratia divinæ inspirationis operetur, only the grace of divine inspiration can work in us to receive and perform them." The virtue of continence he makes to be the gift of God, on the account of which none should boast in themselves, but give God the glory; his words are these :†† " And if the virtue of continence is bestowed by God, why dost thou glory as if thou hadst not received it; and if thou hadst received it, what hast thou that is not given to thee ? But by this it is plain, that it is not given to thee by God, because thou dost not ascribe it to him alone." And in another place, speaking of the knowledge of God and Christ, he expresses himself thus :‡‡ " By whom is truth found out without God ? To whom is God known without Christ ? By whom is Christ explored without the Holy Spirit ? To whom is the Holy Spirit applied without the mystery of faith?" Elsewhere he says,§§ " When a renewed soul comes to believe through the second birth, ex aqua et superna virtute, 'which is of water and power from above,' the curtain of former corruption being drawn, beholds all its own light." Again having mentioned a passage in Psalm xlv. 4, which he reads, *Thy right hand shall lead thee wonderfully,* makes this note on it :‖‖ " Virtus scilicet gratiæ spiritualis, qua Christi agnitio deducitur, namely, the power of spiritual grace, by which the knowledge of Christ is brought on." And a little after, speaking of the name of Jesus, as a name under which the Jews did not expect the Messiah, adds,¶¶ " For neither though we, per Dei gratiam, ' through the grace of God,' obtain an understanding of his mysteries, also acknowledge this name as appointed for Christ, therefore will the thing be known to the Jews, from whom wisdom is taken away." And in the same chapter he says,*** that " the possession of eternal life is not by Moses, that is, not by the discipline of the law, but comes by Jesus, that is, per evangelii gratiam, by the grace of the gospel." And a little after, upon the types and figures of Christ, he makes this observation,††† " that the more incredible any thing is, the more offensive, if it is nakedly preached; and the more magnificent it is, the more is it to be overshadowed, ut difficultas intellectus gratiam Dei quæreret, that the difficulty of the understanding may seek after the grace of God." Citing Luke xi. 40, he observes,‡‡‡ that " Christ by this saying

---

* Stromat, l. 5, p. 548.   † Ib. l. 6, p. 680.
‡ Ib. l. 2, p. 363.   § Ib. l. 2, p. 372.
‖ Ib. l. 1, p. 288.   ¶ Stromat. l. 5, p. 588.   ** Tertull. de Patientia, c. 1, p. 1, 9.
†† De Virgin. Veland c. 13, p. 202.

‡‡ De Anima, c. 1, p. 304.   §§ Ibid. c. 41, p. 343.   ‖‖ Adv. Marcion, l. 3, c. 14, p. 489.   ¶¶ Ib. c. 16, p. 490.   *** Ib. p. 491.
††† Adv. Marcion, c. 18, p. 492.
‡‡‡ Ib. l. 4, c. 27, p. 548.

plainly demonstrates, ad eundem Deum pertinere munditias hominis exterioris et interioris; that the cleansing both of the outward and inward man belongs to the same God, whose they are both." And in another place,* having mentioned Eph. ii. 10, he has this note : "It is one thing to make, and another to crèate, but both he gives to one; man is the workmanship of the Creator, the same therefore who hath made, hath created in Christ. With respect to substance, he hath made him; quantum ad gratiam condidit, 'with respect to grace, he hath created him." Inspect the context. To which may be added that saying of his,† Fiunt non nascuntur Christiani, "Men are made, not born Christians."

SECTION VII

ORIGINES ALEXANDRINUS. A. D. 230

ORIGEN, though a very unguarded writer, and though a very considerable part of his works have been interpolated by Ruffinus, said to be a favourer of Pelagius, yet has many passages in his writings which shows that he thought that regeneration, and all that is truly and spiritually good, are owing to the grace and power of God. "It must be known," says he,‡ "that all that men have is from the grace of God, for they have nothing of debt; for who hath first given to him, and it shall be recompensed to him again? Wherefore it is grace, whatever he has, who was not, and is a receiver from him, who always was, and is, and will be for ever." He intimates, that all good thoughts are from the Spirit of God. "We pray," says he,§ "that the light of the knowledge of the glory of God might shine into our hearts, the Spirit of God being present with our imaginative faculty, *kai phantazontos emas ta tou Theou*, and suggesting to us the things of God." He represents all manner of virtues, as wrought in us by a divine hand, and not as the produce of nature. "Images dedicated to God, and becoming him," says he,‖ "are not such as are prepared by mechanic artificers; but what are planned by the Logos or word of God, *kai morphoumena en emin, ai aretai*, 'and formed in us, even those virtues' which are the images of the first-born of every creature, in whom are examples of righteousness, temperance, wisdom, godliness, and the rest of the virtues." Yea, he ascribes the duties and actions of the saints to the energy of the same divine person : "As," says he,¶ "the soul quickens and moves the body, which of itself has no living motion; so the Logos or Word, *kinon epi ta deonta kai energon*, 'inciting with energy to things which ought to be done,' moves the whole body, the church, and every member of them that are of the church, doing nothing without the Word." Whatever

knowledge men have of God in a spiritual way, springs from divine grace according to him. "Those words in Matt. xi. 27," he says,** " manifestly show, that God is known *theia tini chariti*, 'by a certain divine favour or grace,' which is infused into the soul, not without God, but by a sort of an afflatus, or inspiration." And in another place he observes,†† that "God opens the mouth, the ears, and eyes, that we may speak, perceive, and hear the things that are God's." He must be a stranger to Origen's writings, who knows not that he frequently suggests the necessity of the grace and assistance of God to understand the Scriptures. I need not give instances. The work of sanctification he attributes to the Spirit of God. "Let us endeavour," says he,‡‡ "that we may be unworthy of this so great and sublime an understanding, that is, of the mystical sense of the shew-bread; but that our soul may first be made a holy place, and in the holy place we may take in holy mysteries, through the grace of the Holy Spirit, ex quo sanctificatur omne quod sanctum est, by whom is sanctified every thing that is holy." And in another place,§§ "The grace of the Holy Spirit is present, that those things which are not substantially holy, may be made holy by the participation of him. Seeing therefore first, that they may be, they have from God the Father. Secondly, that they may be rational, they have from the Word. Thirdly, that they may be holy, they have from the Holy Spirit." The change that is made in man in conversion, he denies to be the effect of moral suasion, but ascribes it to the power and efficacy of divine grace. . Having mentioned these words in Matt. iii. 9, *Think not to say*, &c., he observes,‖‖ that "they teach us that unbelievers, who are called *stones*, because of their stony hearts δυναμει Θεου μεταβαλειν οιους τε ειναι, may be changed, by the power of God, from *stones*, to children of Abraham." "Celsus," says he,¶¶ "may laugh at what is said, or the Jew, whom he introduces; yet it must be said, that many, as if unwilling, have come to Christianity, πνευματος τινος τρεψαντος αυτων το ηγεμονικον αιφνιδιον, 'a certain spirit suddenly turning their intellectual faculty,' from hating the Logos or Word, to die for him." And in the same work he has these words :*** "The doctrine of those who were first sent, and laboured to constitute churches, and their preaching, were indeed with persuasion; but not such as is among the professors of the wisdom of Plato, or any other philosophers, who have nothing more than human nature; but the demonstration of the apostles of Jesus, given by God, had a force of persuading them the Spirit and power; wherefore their word, or rather God's, ran swiftly and sharply, and thereby changed many of them, who were by nature and cus-

---

* Ib. l. 5, c. 17, p. 609.   † Apolog. c. 18, p. 18.   ‡ Origen in Rom. l. 10, fol. 223, B.   § Contr. Cels. l. 4, p. 227.   ‖ Ib. l. 8, p. 389.   ¶ Ib. l. 6, p. 309, 310.   ** Contr. Cels. l. 7, p. 361.   †† In Exod. hom. 3, fol.

32, C.   ‡‡ In Lev. hom. 13, fol. 88, H.   §§ Περι Αρχων, l. 1, c. 3, fol. 118, A.   ‖‖ Comment. in Joan. p. 115.   ¶¶ Contr. Cels. l. 1, p. 35.   *** Ib. l. 3, p. 152.

tom sinners, whom no man could change by any punishment whatsoever; the Word transformed them, shaping and forming them according to his will." Again he observes,* "The divine Word says, that what is said, though it is in itself true, and is fit to persuade, yet is not sufficient to reach the human soul, εαν μη και δυναμις τις Θεφ εκδοθη, unless a certain power is given from God to him that speaks,' and grace flourishes in what is said: and this is not without God, in them who speak with energy." To which may be added the following expressions of his :† "Now the word of his preaching is known to all, so that it is received by very many, almost in all the world; that they may understand what are believed, not by persuasory words of wisdom, but by *demonstration of the Spirit and power;* wherefore they may conclude they are brought to faith and credulity, *cœlesti virtute imo etiam plusquam cœlesti,* by a heavenly power, yea, by more than a heavenly one." Once more: "This," says he,‡ "is a new thing, that those who are *strangers from the covenants of God, aliens from the promises,* and afar off from the truth, δυναμει τινι θεια, by a certain divine power receive it." Yea, sometimes he expresses himself as though he thought some sort of force and violence were used with men in the conversion and salvation of them. "The only begotten Son of God is present," he says :§ "he defends, he keeps, he draws us to himself: hear how he speaks; "And lo, I am with you unto the end of the world ;" but neither is it sufficient that he is with us, "sed quodam modo vim nobis facit, ut nos pertrahat ad salutem," 'but in some sort he forces us, that he may draw us unto salvation;' for he says in another place, "When I shall be lifted up, I will draw all unto me." You see, how that he not only invites the willing, but draws those that delay." And a little after, "The Lord himself, the Father, does not neglect the dispensation of our salvation, for he not only calls us to salvation, but he draws; for so the Lord says in the gospel, "No man comes to me, but whom my heavenly Father draws." But the Father of the family, who sent his servants to invite his friends to the marriage of his Son, after they who were first invited excused themselves, says to the servants, "Go forth to the highways and alleys, and whomsoever ye find, compel them to come in;" so therefore we are not only invited by God, sed et trahimur et cogimur ad salutem, but we are drawn and compelled unto salvation." Moreover he signifies, that this call of God to the participation of his grace, entirely arises from his sovereign will and pleasure. "The God of gods," he says,|| "calls from the east and west to partake of himself by Jesus Christ, ous bouletai, whom he pleases." Wherefore

there should be no boasting in the creature, but all glorying should be in God. "There are," he observes,¶ "some among the Gentiles, of good manners and honest behaviour, who yet do not refer what they have to God, nor acknowledge the grace given to them by him; but either ascribe it to their own industry, or glory in their masters and instructors; but the apostle shows to us, that all that is good is from God, and given by the Holy Spirit; as the apostle James says, chap. i. 17, "that he that glories, may glory in the Lord." "That which is worthy of boasting," he says,** "ouk emeteron alla doron esti Theou, 'is not ours, but is the gift of God;' from him is wisdom, from him is strength, and so of the rest." To all which may be added the following words of his,†† which not only express his own, but the sense of the whole church at that time : "It is the united sense of the whole church, that all the law is indeed spiritual; yet these things which the law breathes out are not known to all, but to them only to whom the grace of the Holy Spirit is given, in the word of wisdom and knowledge."

SECTION VIII
CYPRIAN. A. D. 250

CYPRIAN clearly expresses his sense of the efficacy of divine grace in the sanctification of a sinner, and of the continuance of it, for the carrying on and perfecting of that work, as well as of the need the saints always stand in of the aids of it for the performance of every good work. In one of his‡‡ epistles he seems surprised at his own conversion, and wonders how it was possible that it should be; when he had lain in darkness, was first a stranger to light and truth, so implicated in the errors of a past life; and so obsequious to sin and vice; this he ascribes to *divine grace* in his *second birth,* which *desuper lumen infudit, postquam cœlitus Spiritu hausto in novum hominem reparavit,* "infused light from above, and after the Spirit was derived from heaven repaired him a new man :" and then goes on to beat down all boasting in the creature, and to give the whole glory to God. In his *Treatise of the Lord's Prayer,* he says many things which confirm this. Upon the first clause in that prayer he makes this remark,§§ "A new man, a regenerated person, and one restored to his God, *per ejus gratiam,* 'through his grace,' says, in the first place, *Father,* because now he begins to be a son." And a little after,|||| "Most beloved brethren," says he, "we ought to consider and understand not only this, that we call *Father which is in heaven,* but we add and say, *Our Father,* that is, of them that believe; of them, who being sanctified by him, *et gratiæ spiritualis nativitatæ reparati,* 'and repaired through the

---

* Contr. Cels. l. 6, p. 276; vide l. 1, p. 21, et l. 5, p. 231.   † Περι Αρχων, l. 4, c. 1, fol. 151, D.   ‡ Contr. Cells. l. 8, p. 405.

§ In Num. homil. 20, fol. 131, 132, I. K.

|| Contr. Cels. l. 8, p. 381.   ¶ In Rom. l.

9, fol. 211, E.   ** Comment. in Matt. p. 227; vide Περι Αρχων, l. 3, c. 1, fol. 139. B.

†† Περι Αρχων, l. 1, Præm. fol. 112, C.

‡‡ Ep. 2, ad Donat. p. 6.   §§ De Oratione Dominica, p. 265. |||| Ib. p. 266.

birth of spiritual grace,' begin to be the children of God." And upon the first petition, *Hallowed be thy name*, he has this observation,* "Not that we should desire of God, that he may be sanctified by our prayers, but that we should request of him, that his name may be sanctified in us. Moreover, by whom is God sanctified, *qui ipse sanctificat*, 'who himself sanctifies?' But because he says, *Be ye holy, for I am holy;* this we desire and ask, that we who are sanctified in baptism, might persevere in that which we begin to be; and this we daily pray for, *opus est enim nobis quotidiana sanctificatione*, 'for we have need of daily sanctification,' that we who daily sin, may purge away our sins by daily sanctification; which sanctification is what is bestowed upon us *de Dei dignatione*, through the favour of God." And a little after, "This we ask night and day, that sanctification and vivification, *quæ de Dei gratia sumitur, ipsius protectione servetur*, which proceed from the grace of God, might be preserved by his protection." Upon the third petition, *Thy will be done in earth, as in heaven*, he has this note;† "We add and say this, not that God may do what he will, but that we may do what God wills; for who hath resisted God that he may not do what he will? But because we are withstood by the devil, that our minds and actions might not in all respects obey God, we pray and desire, that the will of God may be done in us; which that it may be done in us, *opus est Dei voluntate, id est, ope ejus et protectione*, 'there is need of the will of God, that is, of his help and protection;' for no man is strong, *suis viribus*, 'by his own strength,' but is safe through the grace and mercy of God." And a little after, speaking of the combat between the flesh and the Spirit, he adds, "Therefore we earnestly desire, that an agreement may be made between these two, *ope et auxilio Dei*, 'by the help and assistance of God;' that whilst the will of God is done both in the spirit and in the flesh, the soul may be saved, *quæ per eum renata est*, which is regenerated by him." And in another treatise of his, concerning *Patience*, he thus speaks :‡ "This virtue we have in common with God; from hence patience begins; from hence its glory and worth take their rise; the original and greatness of patience spring *Deo auctore*, from God the Author."

SECTION IX
EUSEBIUS CÆSARIENSIS. A. D. 330

EUSEBIUS represents conversion as a wonderful change wrought in the soul through the power of divine grace; "Who should be those Canaanites," says he,§ "but we, who before were *aliens;* and who, out of all nations, that

were formerly profane and ungodly, are preserved sheep for Christ; *oi kai dia tes autou charitos metabeblemetha*, 'who also are changed by his grace;' and understanding the things before prophesied of, have received the true knowledge of the word of the Lord." And in another place he breaks out in a pathetic exclamation, after this manner,‖ "Who is he that is not amazed at this surprising affair, when he sees such who from the beginning worshipped stones, wood, devils, brutes, demons, reptiles, &c.—who in their manner of living suffered nothing from the savage beasts, *nuni dia tes tou soteros emon entheou dunameon metablethentes kai osper ex eteron eteroi gegonotes*, now through the divine power of our Saviour changed, and, as it were, become other men." All which he supposes was brought about, not by moral suasion, or merely by the ministry of the word; but by a secret, unspeakable, and almighty power, which attended it; to which he always¶ ascribes the success of the Gospel: "You have," says he,** "plain and evident demonstrations, that is, in prophecy, from whom the Gospel should begin, even from Christ himself; by whom it should be preached, namely, by his apostles; besides also, *poia dunamei kratesei, oti me anthropeia*, 'with what power it should obtain or overcome; that it should not be by that which is human." It would be too tedious to transcribe all the passages of this kind which are observable in this writer; I shall only add, that he considered sanctification as the peculiar work of the Spirit of God, as appears from his following words;†† "Wherefore the Holy Spirit dwells in a friendly manner with the saints only, being imparted by the Son to those whom the Father would approve of, *kai tout' an eie ergon autou to pantas agiazein*, and this is his work, to sanctify all, to whom he gives some one or more of his gifts."

SECTION X
ATHANASIUS. A. D. 350

ATHANASIUS acknowledges the necessity of divine grace, and the efficacy of it in sanctification, when he says,‡‡ "As the Son, the giver of the Spirit, does not disdain to say, that as man *he cast out devils by the Spirit;* so likewise the same being the giver of the Spirit, disdains not to say, *The Spirit of the Lord is upon me, because he hath anointed me*, with respect to his being made flesh, as John says; that he might show that we are in both respects such, *oi kai en to agiazesthai deomenoi tes tou Pneumatos charitos*, who in sanctification stand in need of the grace of the Spirit; and also are not able to cast out devils without the power of the Spirit." And a little after, "So likewise David shows, *oti ouk an allos metegomen tou Pneumatos kai*

* Ibid. † De Oratione Dominica, p. 267. ‡ De Bono Patientiæ, p. 313. § Demonstr. Evangel. l. 10, p. 484. ‖ Præparat. Evangel. l. 1, c. 5, p. 21. ¶ Vide Eccl. Hist. l. 2, c. 1, p. 39; c. 3, p. 41; c. 14, p. 52; l. 3, c. 37,

p. 109. Preparat. Evangel. l. 1, c. 4, p. 10; l. 2, c. 4. p. 68. ** Demonstr. Evangel. l. 3, Prœm. p. 89. †† De Eccles. Theolog. l. 3, c. 6, p. 174. ‡‡ Athanas. contr. Arian. orat. 2, vol. i. p. 257.

egiasthemen, 'that we could otherwise partake of the Spirit, and be sanctified,' unless the Word himself, the giver of the Spirit, had said, that he would be anointed by the Spirit for us." And in another place he argues after this manner, in favour of the Deity of Christ;* "Otherwise, if the Son was a creature, there being one and the same nature of rational creatures, no help could be given to a creature by a creature, *dia to pantas deisthai tes para Theou charitos,* inasmuch as all stand in need of the grace of God." That the image of God, imparted to man, and whatsoever holiness he has, is not from nature, but is owing to the grace and power of God, is owned by him, when he observes,† that "God being good, hath imparted his image, our Lord Jesus Christ, to men; and hath made them according to his image and likeness, that they, *dia tes toiautes charitos,* 'through such grace,' understanding the image, the Word of the Father, might be able, through him, to receive the knowledge of the Father; and so knowing the Creator, might live a truly happy and blessed life." And elsewhere he says of Christ,‡ that "he only is the true and natural image of the Father; for though we are made again after his image, and are called the glory and image of God, *all' ou di' eautous,* 'but not because of ourselves; but because that the true image and glory of God, which is the Word of God, dwells in us, who being at last made flesh for us, *tautes tes kleseos echomen ten charin,* we have the grace of this vocation." And much to the same purpose he says in another place,§ "We are made sons, but not as he, by nature, and in truth, *alla kata charin tou kalesantos,* but according to the grace of him that calleth." And men, who are of the earth, are called gods, but not as the true God, or his Word, but as God pleases, who gives this, that is grace, to them. So likewise we are made merciful as God, but not equal to him, *oude phusi, kai alethinoi euergetai ginomenoi, ou gar emon eurema euergetein, alla tou Theou eis emas kata charin ginomenon,* nor by nature, or true benefactors, are we made; nor is it our invention to do well; but this is according to the grace of God to usward." That sanctification is a creation-work, and so a work of almighty power, is asserted by him, when having mentioned these words, *Except a man be born again,* he says, "not hereby signifying generation by women, but showing, that the soul is regenerated, *kai anaktizomenen,* and *created again* according to his image, the image of God." And especially in these words,‖ "Every intelligent hearer knows, that to sanctify is to create: when we hear, *Create in me a clean heart, O God!* what else do we understand but this, Sanctify a clean heart in me, O

God?" And a little after, "To create is the work of God, but it is not greater than to sanctify, for it is written, *Holy Father, sanctify them through thy truth.*" Yea, he adds, that "to sanctify is *greater* than to create." This last passage is indeed cited from a tract which is thought¶ by some learned men not to be the work of Athanasius, but of Maximus, who lived many years after him. Theodore Beza, who has given us a Latin translation of the whole, says,** that in the margin of the first dialogue, in the copy he made use of, were written by another hand these words, "Some say this present dialogue is Athanasius's, others that it is Maximus's;" however, since not only these dialogues are allowed by all to be pious, learned, and worthy to be read, but also by Beza said to have nothing in them unworthy of Athanasius, or unsuitable to his times, I have ventured to make the above citation from them.

SECTION XI

MACARIUS ÆGYPTIUS. A. D. 350

MACARIUS, the Egyptian, ascribes regeneration and sanctification to the Spirit and grace of God; he says,†† it is "through the participation of the Holy Spirit that men are born again of God, and counted worthy to be the children of God in truth and power." And again :‡‡ "As God is love, joy, peace, kindness, and goodness, so the new man is made *kata charin,* by grace." And in another place he says,§§ "The five rational senses of the soul, if they receive the grace from above, and the sanctification of the Spirit, are truly virgins." And elsewhere he observes,‖‖ that "as many as are the children of the light, and of the ministry of the New Testament by the Holy Spirit, learn nothing of men; for they are taught of God, for *aute e charis,* 'grace itself' writes the laws of the Spirit in their hearts." Again: "Never think," says he,¶¶ "that thou preventest the Lord by virtue, according to Phil. ii. 13 :" it is certain he both owns the preparing, preventing, and subsequent grace of God; for he speaks*** of the Holy Spirit, *etoimasanti,* 'as preparing the soul' to be a seat and habitation for himself; and of some††† whom the gifts and graces of the Holy Spirit *proapantosi,* 'prevent.' "God," he says,‡‡‡ "requires of men labour, fatigue, and working; but unless there appear the heavenly cloud, *kai uetoi charitos,* ' and the rains of grace,' the labouring husbandman will profit nothing." In short, he ascribes all that the saints enjoy now, or shall hereafter, to divine grace. "The glory and beauty of Christians," says he,§§§ "and the heavenly riches, are unspeakable, and are obtained with la-

---

* Ib. 3, p. 412.   † De Incarnat. Verbi Dei, p. 63, 64.   ‡ Contr. Arian. orat. 4, p. 463, 472.   § De Incarn. p. 66.   ‖ De S. Trinitate, dialog. 3, vol. ii. p. 232.   ¶ Vide Rivet. Critic. Sacr. l. 3, c. 6, p. 254, 255.   ** Præfat. p. 137, ed. Commelin.

†† Homil. 5, p. 33.   ‡‡ Ib. 2, p. 12.
§§ Homil. 4, p. 19.   ‖ Ib. 15, p. 87.
¶¶ Ib. 37, p. 199.   *** Ib. l. p. 2.
††† Ib. 29, p. 171.   ‡‡‡ Ib. 26, p. 148.
§§§ Ib. 5, p. 33, 34.

bour, and sweat, and trials, and agonies; *to de olon chariti Theou*, but the whole is owing to the grace of God." Particularly he observes,[*] that "the knowledge of God in truth is through the power of God, and energy of grace." He represents the work of grace and conversion as a new creation, and the effect of divine power, and which cannot be done without it. "Our Lord Jesus Christ," he says,[†] "came to change and transform nature, and to renew *kai anaktisai*, 'and create again the same soul,' which was subverted by the affections, through the transgression, mixing it with his own Spirit." And a little after,[‡] "Seeing the soul that truly believes in Christ must be translated and changed from this present evil state into another good state, and from this present mean nature into another divine nature; also it must be made new, *dia tes dunameos tou Agiou Pneumatos*, 'by the power of the Holy Spirit,' that so it may be fit for the heavenly kingdom." And whereas it may be thought difficult, if not impossible, that men should be converted, or turned from their sins, he advises[§] to remember what Christ did when he was here on earth; how he cured the blind, and raised the dead, and the like; intimating, that that power which wrought in the one was able to effect the other. He speaks[||] of the fire of the Spirit which rekindles hearts, enlightens souls, makes devils to flee, takes away sin, and gives immortality.

SECTION XII

HILARIUS PICTAVIENSIS. A. D. 360

HILARY of Poictiers affirms, that all good things spring from the grace of God: "What room," says he,[¶] "is left for boasting in us, when we remember that *all things are of God?*" "The services of our tongue and mouth, he says,[**] "are not sufficient to give praise to God; we have changed crimes for innocence, vices for virtue, ignorance for knowledge, destruction for immortality; *et hoc a Dei gratia*, and this is from the grace of God." Faith in Christ, the knowledge of him, he frequently[††] intimates, are the gifts of God. He ascribes regeneration to the secret and powerful, yea, irresistible efficacy of divine grace; "Obtaining," says he,[‡‡] "the faith of my regeneration, I am ignorant; and what I know not I now hold, *sine sensu enim meo renascor*, for without my perception I am born again." And in another place he says,[§§] "The operation of God hath *raised Christ from the dead, et hæc eadem Dei operatio*, and the same operation of God quickens us with Christ." And elsewhere he says,[||||] "We are indeed children to God, but by the workman-

ship of the Son; for we were sometime children of wrath, but are *made* children to God by the spirit of adoption. We were not born so, but *made*; not generated, but acquired." He represents the grace of regeneration as making persons new, and without which they cannot receive new things. On Luke v. 36, 37, he has this note:[¶¶] "Souls and bodies infirm through the oldness of sins, do not take in the mysteries of the new grace, for the rent will be worse, and the wine being shed, the old bottles will perish; for the guilt of such will be double, since besides the oldness of their sins, they will not bear the power of the new grace; and therefore the pharisees, and the disciples of John, could not receive new things, *nisi novi fierent*, unless they were made new;" which they could not be without the power of God, to which all things are possible, and so this; for, as he says,[***] "What is so possible to the power of God, than that he can save through faith? That he can regenerate by it?" And, indeed, such is his power, that it is not to be resisted, which is proper and peculiar to him; for as this father somewhere observes,[†††] "To God alone it agrees to do all things which he wills; for sole perfect power is hindered by none, so that he could not do what he wills; and no difficulty occurs to him from whom are all things."

SECTION XIII

BASILIUS CÆSARIENSIS. A. D. 370

BASIL of Cæsarea asserts, that sanctification is the work of the Holy Spirit, and entirely owing to the preventing grace of God. Speaking of the Holy Spirit, he says,[‡‡‡] that "there is no sanctification without him; and that[§§§] we have learnt concerning him by the divine writings, *auto estin o tous agious, agiou epoiese*, that he it is who makes the saints saints, and gives divine life to them that ask God by him.'" And in another place,[||||||] "The Spirit is not a creature, but the character of God's holiness *kai pege tois pasin agiasmou*, 'and the fountain of holiness to all,' as the apostle teacheth; we are called in the holiness of the Spirit; makes us a new creature, abiding for ever." And elsewhere,[¶¶¶] "It was impossible to be born again *me prolabouses charitos tou Theou*, without the preventing grace of God." "Faith," he says, "is the work of God," and he means not what God requires of us, but what he works in us. "If our faith in the Son," says he,[****] "is the work of God, for this is the work of God, that ye believe on him whom he hath sent, he himself, that is the Son, cannot be the work of God." Moreover he says,[††††] that "faith is not in us

---

* Ib. 24, p. 138.   † Ib. 44, p. 215.
‡ Ib. p. 217.   § Ib. 4, p. 28, 29.
|| Ib. 25, p. 143, 144.   ¶ Enarr. in Psalm cxxiii. p. 540.   ** Ib. cxxv. p. 547.
†† De Trinitate, l. 6, p. 74; l. 11, p. 174. Comment. in Matt. can. 16, p. 296; in Ps. cxix. Vau, p. 472.   ‡‡ De Trinitate, l. 12, p. 197.

§§ Ib. l. 9, p. 119. |||| Ib. l. 12, p. 185.
¶¶ In Matt. can. 9. p. 271.   *** Ib. can. 20, p. 305.   ††† In Psal. cxxxiv. p. 581.
‡‡‡ De Spirit. Sancto, c. 16, p. 180.
§§§ Contr. Eunom. l. 5, p. 139, vol ii.
|||||| Ib. p. 117.   ¶¶¶ De Baptismo, l. 1, c. 2, p. 650.   **** Contr. Eunom. l. 4, p. 99.
†††† In Ps. cxv. p. 313.

through geometrical proofs, but *tais tou Pneumatos energeis*, by the effectual operations of the Spirit." Again; he affirms,* that "is to be held for certain, and to be confessed, that the grace of every good thing, and so the patience of those things which we suffer for the sake of Christ, *para Theou uparchein*, are from God:" for the proof of which he cites John iii. 27 ; 1 Cor. iv. 7 ; Eph. ii. 8, 9 ; Phil. i. 29. He frequently ascribes the whole of salvation to the free grace of God, to which he gives all the glory, and rejects boasting in the creature. "Let no man," says he,† "praise my industry, by which I am saved from dangers ; for salvation is not in the power or wisdom of man, but in the grace of God." And elsewhere,‡ "Nothing is left for thee, O man, of which thou canst boast, whose glorifying and hope lie in this, that thou mortify all thy will, and seek life to come in Christ, of which we having in these things the first fruits, entirely live by the grace and gift of God. Phil. ii. 13. Why therefore, I pray thee, dost thou extol thyself as if thou hadst good things of thine own, when thou shouldest give thanks for gifts to the giver of them ? 1 Cor. iv. 7. God is not made known to thee by thy righteousness, but thou to God by his goodness. Gal. iv. 9. Thou hast not apprehended Christ by thine own power, but Christ thee by his coming. Phil. iii. 12."

SECTION XIV

GREGORIUS NAZIANZENUS. A. D. 370.

GREGORY of Nazianzum was an advocate for the grace of God. "If any one" say he,§ "is a child of light, or a man of God, or is near to God, or a man of good desires, or is worthy to be called by any such names, with which the scripture honours men divine and exalted, and that have a right to that portion which is above; *touto men ede doron Theou, kai phaneros uper ten axian ten emeteran*, this is verily the gift of God, and manifestly beyond our desert." He acknowledges,‖ that "it is of God that we are, *kai to eidenai Theou*, 'and that we know God,' and that we have what we offer to him ;" and calls upon others to make the same confession : "Acknowledge," says he,¶ "from whence thou hast that thou art, that thou breathest, that thou hast an understanding mind ; and what is the greatest of all, *to ginoskein Theou*, "that thou knowest God;' hopest for the kingdom of heaven, equal honour with angels, and a sight of glory." He makes God to be the author and finisher of all that is good,** *παρ' ου καλον απαν και αρχεται και εις τελος ερχεται,,* "by him, that is God, every good thing both begins and comes to an end." Regeneration is ascribed by him to the Spirit of God,

παρα μεν του Πνευματος εμιν η αναγεννσις, from the spirit we have regeneration," says he,†† "from regeneration reformation, from reformation knowledge of the worthiness of him that forms us again ;" and this, with the Scripture, he makes necessary to a man's enjoyment of the heavenly glory. "Assure yourselves," says he,‡‡ "that no man can either see or receive the kingdom, unless he is born from above by the Spirit, and is cleansed from the first birth." It is easy to observe, that Gregory does in these passages frequently represent the work of grace as a creation, and by a being formed again. "The Spirit," he says,,§§ *το ποιησαν το ανακτιζον,* ' is he that forms, that creates again by baptism,' by the resurrection ; the Spirit knows all things is he that teacheth, and breathes where and as much as he pleases," And in another place,‖‖ speaking of his Father he has these words : "He came to that regeneration which is by water and the Spirit, by which we confess to God *μορφωσιν τε και τελειωσιν,* "the conformation and perfection of the man, according to Christ, *και μεταθεσιν και αναπλασιν,* and the change and reformation of that which is earthly to the Spirit." And elsewhere,¶¶ mentioning those words, *and it was winter,* that is, adds he, "of unbelief, and Jesus was present, God and the temple, the eternal God, the new temple, to-day dissolved, and in three days raised again, and abiding for ever ; that I might be saved, and be called again from the old fall (meaning the fall of Adam), and being *αναπλαττομενος,* "formed again,' through such philanthropy, might be made a *new creature.*"

SECTION XV

DIDYMUS ALEXANDRINUS. A. D. 370

DIDYMUS of Alexandria, in his treatise concerning the *Holy Spirit*, says many things of *his* grace and power in the sanctification of men : "The Holy Spirit," says he,*** "is by the confession of all, the immutable sanctifier, the giver of divine knowledge, and all good things ; and that I may speak more briefly, he is subsisting in those good things, which are given by the Lord, according to Matt. vii. 11 ; Luke xi. 13 ; from whence it appears, that the Holy Spirit is the fulness of the gifts of God, and that those things which are ministered by God do not subsist without him ; for all advantages which are received from the grace of the gifts of God flow from this fountain." And a little after he calls him the giver of sanctification,††† and says that it is impossible any one should obtain the grace of God si non habeat Spiritum Sanctum, "'if he has not the Holy Spirit ;' in which we prove, that all the gifts of God consist." And again, says he,‡‡‡ "No one ever receives the spiritual blessings of God, nisi præcesserit Spiritus Sanctus, 'unless the

---

* Moral. Reg. 55, p. 331, vol. ii.

† In Ps. xxxiii. p. 215.

‡ De Humilitate, p. 550.   § Greg. Nazianz. orat. 6, p. 137, tom. i.   ‖ Ib. 9. p. 153.

¶ Ib. 16, p. 253.   ** Ib. 12, p. 198.

†† Ib. 37, p. 609.   *‡ Ib. 44, p. 714.

§§ Ib. 37, p. 610.   ‖‖ Ib. 19, p. 294.

¶¶ Ib. 43, p. 698.   *** Didymus de Spiritu Saucto, l. 1, fol. 176, B, inter Hierom. opera, tom. ix.   ††† Ib. C & M.

‡‡‡ Ib. fol. 177, D, E.

Holy Spirit goes before;' for he that receives the Holy Spirit consequently will have blessings, that is, wisdom and understanding, and the rest;—wisdom and understanding which are in the Holy Spirit are given by God:— God the giver of good things, will give the hope which he has promised, in the power of the Holy Ghost to them that have him."

SECTION XVI

GREGORIUS NYSSENUS. A. D. 380

GREGORY of Nyssa attributes all virtue, and every good thing that is in us, or done by us, to God, and to his grace. Upon Cant. iv. 12, he has this note,* "Hence we learn, *aretas de einai ten tou Theou phuteian*, 'that virtues are the plantation of God,' about which the intellective power of our souls being employed, is sealed with the character of truth, and formed with a habit to that which is good." Yea, he asserts,† that *pan aretes onoma te kai noema eis ton Kurion ton areton anapheretai*, "every name and thought of virtue is referred to the Lord of virtues." And in another place he observes,‡ that "what food and drink is to the body, that is to the soul, to look to what is good, *kai touto os alethos doma esti Theou to enatinozein Theo*, 'and this is truly the gift of God, to look intently unto God." And a little after, "He that looks to that which is good, has the gift of God in all his labour; and this is it, always to look to that which is good." And elsewhere,§ having mentioned Gal. ii. 20, he takes notice, that "the apostle says, that evangelical good works were *not his*, but he ascribes them to the grace of Christ, that dwelt in him." And a little after, "The sum of all good things is subjection to God —and this is to be referred to him that lives in us; for if there is any thing excellent, it is his, *kai ei ti anathon par autou*, 'and if there is any good thing, it is from him;' as says one of the prophets; if therefore subjection is excellent and good, it appears to be his, since his is every good thing, from whom the nature of all good comes." To which agrees what he says in another place,‖ "Whatsoever is good, *doreon meris esti*, is a part of the gifts of the Holy Spirit." Particularly he observes,¶ that "to be dead unto sin, and to be quickened by the Spirit, is *doron Theou*, the gift of God." Regeneration is by him ascribed to the Spirit and grace of God. "This benefit," says he,** speaking of regeneration, "the water does not give, for it would be above or higher than the whole creation, but the order of God, *kai e tou Pneumatos epiphoitesis*, and the coming of the Spirit upon us." And in another place he says,†† "They that are born of the Spirit are

the children of God, for so expressly does he bear witness, *to Agio Pneumati ton tou Theou teknon ten genesin*, that the birth of the children of God is owing to the Holy Spirit, according to John iii. 6." The change in regeneration heexpresses thus;‡‡ "We were once the trees of Lebanon—but he hath made us a chariot for himself, *metastoicheiosas tou xulou ten phusin dia tes palingenesias eis to argurion*, transforming the nature of the word by regeneration into silver and gold, &c." This therefore must require an almighty power; and to this does Gregory ascribe it, when he says,§§ that "Christ is made king over them, who are born and made kings, in whom is the rod of iron, that is, *e atreptos dunamis*, 'the immutable power,' which breaking in pieces that which is earthly and frail, *eis ten akeraton phurin metestoicheiosen*, transforms into a nature incorrupt." And elsewhere speaking of the power and energy of God in regeneration, he says,‖‖ "it is *akataleptos kai atechnologetos*, 'incomprehensible and inexpressible by art,' easily producing whatsoever it will."

SECTION XVII

HILARIUS DIACONUS. A. D. 380

HILARY the Deacon, or the author of the Commentaries on Paul's Epistles, which are among the works of Ambrose, ascribes regeneration to the grace and power of God. "Man," he says,¶¶ "is the work of God by creation; and he is again the work of God, *dum reformatur per regenerationem*, whilst he is re-made by regeneration." And in another place he says,*** "That good thing which seems to flourish in Christians, arises from the root of divine grace; for God of his mercy saves us by Christ, by whose grace being regenerated, we receive the Holy Ghost abundantly; that we may endeavour after good works, he helping us in all, that through these we may attain to the inheritance of the kingdom of heaven; wherefore with all devotion we ought to obey him, and comply with his commands; *quia quicquid in nobis pulchrum est*, 'because whatsoever is beautiful in us,' he paints with spiritual lineaments." Again, he observes,††† that "it is manifest, that grace is the gift of God; not a reward due to works, but is granted in a free way, mercy intervening." In particular, he says,‡‡‡ "Faith is the gift of God's mercy, that those who are made guilty by the law may obtain pardon, wherefore faith works joy." And in another place,§§§ "The grace of faith is given that believers may be saved. True it is, because all thanksgiving for our salvation is to be referred to God, who gives his mercy to us, that he might call back

---

* Greg. Nyss. in Cantic. homil. 9, p. 608, vol. i.   † Ib. in Eccl. homil. 8, p. 464.
‡ Ib. p. 467.   § Ib. Orat. in 1 Cor. xv. 28, p. 850, 851.   ‖ Greg Nyss. contr. Eunom. l. 1, p. 67, vol. ii.   ¶ Ib. in Eccl. hom. 6, p. 433, vol. i.   ** Ib. in Baptism. Christ. p. 801, vol. ii.   †† Ib. contr.

Eunom. l. 1, p. 60.   ‡‡ Ib. in Cantic. homil. 7, p. 537, vol. i.   §§ Ib. in Psalm, c. 8, p. 308.   ‖‖ Ib. in Baptism. Christ. p. 803, vol. ii.   ¶¶ In Epist. Rom. p. 326.   *** In Tit. p. 606.   ††† In Rom. p. 309.   ‡‡‡ In Rom. p. 263.   §§§ In Eph. p. 496.

wanderers to life, and those who do not seek the true way; wherefore we must not glory in ourselves, but in God, who hath regenerated us in the heavenly birth, through the faith of Christ." And upon those words, *no man speaking by the Spirit of God calls Jesus accursed*, he makes this observation,* "Whatsoever truth is said by any one, *a Spiritu Sancto dicitur*, is said by the Holy Ghost."

SECTION XVIII

AMBROSIUS MEDIOLANENSIS. A. D. 380

AMBROSE of Milain frequently suggests, that every thing that is good is from God, as good thoughts, virtues, faith and obedience. "There is none," says he,† "who has not some sort of image, that is, either of holiness or sin; we walk in the image of God, quando cogitationes bonæ quæ nobis a Deo insitæ sunt, 'when good thoughts, which are put into us by God,' remain in us, and lead us on to good works." In another place citing John iii. 21, he makes this observation,‡ "Lo here we read, that the works of men are wrought in God, and yet we cannot refer them to the divine substance; but we know, either that they are made by him, according to Col. i. 16, 17, or as the reading of the present testimony teaches, we ought to reckon that those virtues through which the fruit of eternal life is obtained, are made in or by God, as charity, piety, religion, faith, and others of the like kind, which are wrought in or by the will of God; therefore as in or by the will and power of God the Father, so likewise of Christ, they are made, according to Ephesians ii. 10." And elsewhere speaking of the faith of the centurion, he says,§ "this is not of man, sed potestate Dei, 'but by the power of God." Again, discoursing of Eve's subjection to her husband, he makes this remark,‖ "in which I evidently perceive," says he, "the mystery of Christ and the church; for the future conversion of the church to Christ, and that religious servitude subject to the word of God, which is much better than the liberty of this world, are designed. Moreover it is written, 'Thou shalt worship the Lord thy God, and him only shalt thou serve;' hæc igitur servitus Dei donum est, wherefore this servitude is the gift of God. Regeneration, from whence spiritual obedience springs, of which faith and other graces are parts, is often referred by this pious father, to the Spirit, grace, and power of God. That we are according to grace, born again of the Spirit, he observes,¶ "the Lord himself witnesses, John iii. 6—8, wherefore it is clear, that the Holy Spirit is the author also of spiritual regeneration,

because we are created after God that we may be the sons of God; therefore when he shall take us to his own kingdom by the adoption of holy regeneration, do we deny him what is his own? he hath made us heirs of regeneration which is from above, we claim the inheritance, do we disprove the author? But the benefit cannot remain when the author is excluded; neither is the author without the gift, nor the gift without the author; if you claim the grace, believe the power; if you disprove the power, do not seek after the grace." And a little after, "The more excellent regeneration, Sancti Spiritus opus est, 'is the work of the Holy Spirit;' and the Spirit is the author of the new man, which is created after the image of God." And in another place he says,** "There is no carnal man in Christ; but 'if any man is in Christ, he is a new creature:' non naturæ novitate formatus, sed gratiæ, not formed by newness of nature, but of grace." And this grace, to which he frequently ascribes the new creation and formation of man, is all from the Spirit of God; for, as he observes,†† "How can there be grace, sine Spiritu, 'without the Spirit,' since all divine grace is in the Spirit?" Wherefore in the same work he says,‡‡ "We cannot call to the Father or the Son without the Spirit, 'for no man calls Jesus Lord, but in the Holy Ghost:' upon which account he elsewhere says,§§ 'To pray to God is spiritual grace.'" And again,‖‖ "This common life does not keep the heavenly command, but that which is supported by the eternal gift, through the operation of spiritual grace." Moreover, he observes,¶¶ "that to whomsoever the Spirit of grace is present, nothing is wanting; and in whom the Holy Ghost is infused, there is a fulness of great virtues;" all which he represents as the effect of almighty power, and as flowing from the sovereign will and pleasure of God. "What," says he,*** "is impossible by human desires, that can be possible per divinam gratiam solam, by divine grace alone;" for, as he expresses himself elsewhere,††† "Who can change nature, but he who hath created nature? to put off the bridles of lusts from minds infected with vices," says he,‡‡‡ "and amend, is not only of perfect virtue, but also of heavenly grace; for to amend things to come, is of human attention; but to damn things past, is of divine power;" which power is put forth by the Lord as he pleases,§§§ for "God, whom he thinks fit, he calls, et quem vult religiosum facit, 'and whom he pleases he makes religious;' and could, if he would, of persons not devoted to him, make them devoted; and so he does when it seems good in his sight." Thus Ambrose, speaking of the Spirit of God,

---

* In 1 Cor. p. 387. † In Symbol. Apost. c. 16, p. 99. ‡ De Fide, l. 3, c. 3, p. 150. § In Luc. l. 5, p. 91. ‖ De Aaradiso, c. 14, p. 130. ¶ De Spiritu Sancto, l. 3. c. 9, p. 242. ** Epist. l. 8, ep. 61, p. 327; vide etiam Enarr. in Ps. cxix. Jod, p. 959; et in Luc. l. 10. p. 217. †† De Spiritu Sancto,

l. 1, c. 11, p. 227. †† Ib. c. 10. §§ Expos. Isa. apud Ang. contr. duas Epist. Pelag. l. 4, c. 11. ‖‖ Enarr. in Ps. cxix. Mem. p. 974. ¶¶ In Luc. l. 1, p. 13. *** In Ps. cxix. Heth, p. 935. ††† Epist. l. 5, ep. 37, p. 284. ‡‡‡ In Ps. cxix. Tau, p. 1080. §§§ In Luc. l. 7, p. 125.

says,* " who, when he pleases, into whom he pleases, and as many as he pleases, and as much as he pleases, he inspires by his own proper will; therefore he fills with his grace whom he pleases, and as much as he pleases; he himself is not filled; he gives, he does not receive perfection; he sanctifies, but he himself is not sanctified." And in another place he says,† " The grace of the Lord is given, not as from merit of reward, sed quasi ex voluntate, ' but as of will,' according to 1 Cor. xii. 11, as *he will*, he says, not as is *due* ;" wherefore there is no room nor reason for boasting in the creature. " Let no man," says Ambrose,‡ " boast that he has a pure heart; but he that glories, let him glory in the Lord, qui sanctis suis cor mundum creare dignatus est, who vouchsafes to create a clean heart in his saints." And, as is elsewhere observed by him,§ " Whether thou art numbered among the angels, thou oughtest always to speak in justification of God; and the glory which thou hast obtained, thou shouldest not arrogate to thine own merits, sed divinæ misericordiæ semper ascribas, ' but always ascribe it to divine mercy ;' lest it should be said to thee, as in 1 Cor. iv. 7, for every creature, whatsoever good things it hath, it receives from Christ, who is the author of the whole creation.

SECTION XIX

MARCUS EREMITA. A. D. 390

MARK the Eremite ascribes every good thing to God as the author of it; he denies that he can be prevented by any good works of men, or that his grace is given in proportion to them; but affirms, that salvation is entirely of grace. " First of all," says he,‖ " we certainly know, that God is the author, both beginning, middle, and end, of all good. Moreover, it is impossible that we should do any good thing, or believe but by Christ Jesus and the Holy Spirit." Again,¶ " The author and beginning of all virtue is God, as the sun is of daily light; as often as ye do any virtuous action, remember him who said without me ye can do nothing." In another place he affirms,** that "a man's own work does not save him, but he who gives the power of working, therefore never think, that prævenisse Dominum in virtute, 'thou hast prevented the Lord by thy virtue," according to his judgment who says, it is God which worketh in you both to will and to do of his good pleasure." And elsewhere he observes,†† that " what is given by grace we ought not now to measure, according to the manner and merit of preceding weakness, since then grace would not be

grace but believing in God Almighty, let us come to him with a heart single, and void of care, who through faith bestows the communications of the Spirit, non ex proportione operum naturæ, 'not in proportion to the works of nature; for, he says, ye have not received the Spirit by the works of the law, but by the hearing of faith." And it is a conclusion of this writer's,‡‡ that "the salvation of them that are saved arises from grace, not from nature ;" wherefore he advises,§§ " not to seek the perfection of the law in human virtues, for no man is found perfect in them, seeing the perfection of the law is hid in the cross of Christ."

SECTION XX

JOANNES CHRYSOSTOMUS. A. D. 390

CHRYSOSTOM, in many places, freely owns, that our calling, faith, will, and power to do good, are to be ascribed to the grace and power of God, and the energy of the Spirit; " Not you labouring," says he,‖‖ " have found God, but living in error, αυτος δε υμας επεπιασατο, he himself hath drawn you out;" that is, of a state of sin and misery. Again, says he,¶¶ " To be called and to be cleansed are of grace; and he that is called and clothed with a pure garment should continue to keep so. Diligence belongs to them that are called; for since to be called, *ouk apo tes axias gegonen alla apo tes charitos*, is not of merit, but of grace, therefore something ought to be returned for that grace." Again,*** "Thou hast nothing of thine own but what thou hast received from God:—not thine are those good deeds, *alla tes tou Theou charitos*, ' but are owing to the grace of God.' Shouldest thou name faith, this is from calling ; shouldest thou mention remission of sins, or gifts, or the teaching word, thou hast received all from thence." " Hence " says he elsewhere,††† " we should reckon nothing ours, *opouge kai auti e pistis ouk emeteron*, seeing faith itself is not ours, but rather God's. Hear Paul saying, 'and this not of ourselves, it is the gift of God.' " And in another place he observes,‡‡‡ that " the apostle does not say, vessels of well doing, nor vessels of liberty, but vessels of mercy; showing *oti to pan este tou Theou*, that the whole is of God." Upon Phil. ii. 13, he has this note,§§§ *kai prothumian autos emin didosi kai ergasian*, " and he himself gives the readiness of mind; that is, to do good, and the doing of it itself." He asserts,‖‖‖ that " a man brings nothing to the aforesaid things," meaning ordinances, "and the administration of them, *alla to pan tes tou*

---

* In Symbol. Apost. c. 4, p. 90.   † De Exhort. ad Virgin. p, 437.   ‡ In Psalm cxix. Jod, 966.   § Iv. Samech, 1012, 1013.
‖ Marc. Eremit. de Leg. Spirit. p. 51.   ¶ Ib. p. 53.   ** Ib. p. 50.   †† Ib. p. 49.
‡‡ Marc. Eremit. capitula de Temperantia, p. 104.   §§ Ib. de Leg. Spirit. p. 52.
‖‖ Comment. in Gal. iv. 9, tom. iii. p. 744.

¶¶ In Matt. xxii. hom. 69, tom. ii. p. 438.
*** In 1 Cor. iv. 7, hom ii. 12, tom. iii. p. 313, 314.   ††† In Act. homil. 30, tom. iv. p. 783.
‡‡‡ In Rom. ix. 23, homil. 19, tom. iii. p. 144.   §§§ Homil. 8, tom. iv. p 46.
‖‖‖ In 1 Cor. iii. 1, 2, homil. 8, tom. iii. p. 291.

Theou dunameos ergon esti, but all is the work of God's power." Yea, he affirms,* that "it is impossible that a man should be able to have conversation with God," he means in prayer, "or to pray unto him, *aneu tes energeias tou Pneumatos*, without the energy of the Spirit."

SECTION XXI

HIERONYMUS. A. D. 390

JEROM was a warm defender of the grace of God, against Pelagius and his followers; he asserts, that all the good things we enjoy are from the free grace of God : "All things," says he,† speaking to and of God, are thine ; and whatever good thing there is, sine te cujus est, dari non potest, 'cannot be given without thee, whose it is ;'—for God only is he who can instruct his people, and who can give diversitates gratiæ, 'diversities of grace,' to them that wait upon him." And elsewhere,‡ having observed God's different dispensations towards men, and his leaving of them to their own wills, that they may receive the reward or punishment thereof, he adds, "Not that all that shall come to pass shall be of man, but of the grace of him that gives all things ; for so the liberty of the will is to be preserved, ut in omnibus excellat gratia largitoris, 'that in all things the grace of the giver may excel, according to Psalm cxxvii. 1, Rom. ix. 15." And a little after he asks, "Where then is the power and judgment of man's own free will without the grace of God ?" Upon Jeremiah xxxii. 40 he has this note,§ "So he gives free will, that notwithstanding the fear which is bestowed, gratia permaneat largitoris, the grace of the giver might remain." In another place, says he,‖ "Whatever thou hast, thou thinkest non tuæ esse virtutis sed ejus misericordiæ, is not owing to thine own virtue, but to his mercy." And explaining Eccl. ix. 11, he thus expresses himself ;¶ "He that is light, and his soul is not oppressed, nevertheless cannot come to the goal, absque Deo ajutore, unless God is his helper. And seeing the battle is against contrary powers, of which it is written, *sanctify the battle ;* though a man may be strong, yet he cannot conquer, propriis viribus, by his own strength. Also one that is perfect and wise among the children of men cannot have the living and heavenly bread, but through wisdom inviting, *Come, eat of my bread.* And because that riches are not wanting, of which the apostle says, 1 Tim. vi. 18, 1 Cor. iv. 5, it must be known, that a prudent man cannot gather those riches, nisi eas a Domino acceperit, "unless he receives them from the Lord.' Grace also, unless it accompanies knowledge, and is granted by God, though a learned man, he cannot

find it." He frequently inculcates the necessity of divine grace to the understanding of the Scriptures. The knowledge of the Scriptures he represents** as "a watered garden, or a paradise of divers trees, sed qui absque gratia spirituali est, 'but he that is without spiritual grace' does not so much as bring forth herbs." And in another place†† he speaks of some, who though "they did not depart from the head, Christ, yet held things contrary to their head ; who promise themselves by their own judgment, a knowledge of the Scriptures, absque magistro et gratia Domini, without a master and the grace of the Lord." Particularly he observes,‡‡ that "the whole epistle to the Romans wants interpretation, and is involved in such obscurities, that to understand it, Spiritus Sancti indigeamus auxilio, we stand in need of the help of the Holy Spirit ;" especially the ninth chapter, and the doctrines contained in it. Yea, he signifies, that all the doctrines of the gospel are unsearchable by man's own diligence and industry ; for explaining Ephesians iii. 8, he has this observation,§§ "Those things which are in their own nature unsearchable to man, these are known, *Deo revelante,* 'God revealing them ;' for it is one thing to attain to a secret through one's own curiosity, which after it is found out ceases to be unsearchable, aliud propria diligentia, nequaquam posse comprehendere sed per gratiam cognoscere Dei, 'another thing in nowise to be able to comprehend it through one's own diligence, but to know it by the grace of God ;' which, when thou knowest, and hast also shown it to others, nevertheless remains unsearchable, since it was a secret to thee, as much as in thee lay before it was shown." He asserts the necessity of the Spirit's assistance, and the grace of God to the right performance of every good action, to which he refers it, when he says,‖‖ "It is in our power to do any thing, or not to do it ; so only that whatsoever good work we will, desire and fulfil, ad Dei gratiam referimus, ' we refer to the grace of God,' who, according to the apostle, gives us *both to will and to do.*" And again,¶¶ "The divine Word bid and commanded the prophet, saying, *Stand upon thy feet ;* sed sine auxilio Dei et adventu Spiritus Sancti stare non poterat, ' but without the help of God and the coming of the Holy Spirit he could not stand ;' wherefore he entered into him, or took and raised him up, that he might stand firm, and be able to say, *He hath set my feet upon a rock.*" Yea, he affirms, that the best of men stand in need of the grace of God ; thus, explaining the names of Hilkiah, Jeremiah, Shallum, and Hanameel, he says,*** "Hilkiah is by interpretation the portion of the Lord, Jeremiah the height of the Lord : for rightly the height of the Lord is born from the portion

---

* De Precatione, hom. ii. tom. vi. p. 759.
† Hieron. Comment. in Hieremiam, tom. v. p. 138, K, L.   ‡ Ib. p. 143, A, P.   § Ib. p. 162, I. K.   ‖ Comment. in Ezech. p. 256, K.
¶ Ib. in Eccl. tom. p. 39, K, L.   ** Ib. in Isa. tom. v. p. 5, E.   †† Ib. in Mich. tom.
vi. p. 72, G.   ‡‡ Epist. ad Hedib. tom. iii p. 48, H   §§ Comment in Ephes. tom. ix. p. 95, K.   ‖‖ Com. in Hieremiam, tom. v. p. 152. D.   ¶¶ Ib. In Eccl. tom. vii. p. 177, C.
*** Ib. in Hieremiam, v. p. 160, K.

of the Lord ; Shallum may be translated peace or peaceable, Hanameel the gift or grace of God ; nor shall we wonder that peace and grace are joined together, when the apostolic epistles begin thus, *Grace be unto you, and peace ;* for, first, we obtain the peace of God, and after peace grace is born in us ; quæ non in possidentis, sed in arbitrio donantis est, which is not in the will of the possessor, but in the will of the giver." The grace of God carries the purchase to him who is set in high places, that though he may be seen high, tamen gratia Dei indigeat, yet stands in need of the grace of God." And elsewhere he says,* that " though a man be righteous, yet whilst he is in this flesh he is subject to vices and sins, et majore præsidio indiget, and is in need of a greater succour." He very plainly and clearly asserts, that the work of sanctification is the work of God, and owing to his grace ; yea, that it is a work of his mighty power, and what he even works irresistibly. "Faith," he says,† " flows from the free will of a man's own mind (which I suppose he means of the acts and exercise of faith being performed with freedom of will from the strength of grace; but, adds he,) sanctification is sometimes begun without our will, ex sanctificantis largitate, by the free gift of the sanctifier." And a little after he says,‡ " As God being good, according to his essence and nature, nos communione sui effecit bonos, ' hath made us good by the communion of himself :" and speaks to Israel, *Be ye holy, for I am holy ;* so he himself being blessed makes us blessed." Upon Ephesians ii. 8—10, he has these words ;§ " This faith is not of yourselves, but of him that calleth you : this therefore is said, lest, perhaps, a secret thought should creep into us, if we are not saved by our works, surely either by faith we are saved, and it is ours in another kind that we are saved ; therefore he adds, and says, fidem quoque ipsam non nostræ voluntatis esse sed Dei muneris, ' that this faith itself also is not of our will, but of God's gift ;' not that he takes away free will from man ; but since the liberty of the will has God for its author, all things are to be referred to his grace ; seeing he even permits us to will that which is good; all this is therefore lest any one should glory in himself, and that he is not saved by God." He goes on, and observes, that " God gives reasons why *we are saved by grace, through faith, and that not of ourselves, but of the gift of God ;* saying, *for we are his workmanship,* that is, that we live, that we breathe, that we understand, et credere possumus, ' and are able to believe." And that the work of grace is a work of almighty power, he declares‖ in his note on Jeremiah xiii. 23, " That which is impossible to men is possible to God, so that the Ethiopian or leopard

can in nowise seem to change their nature, but he who works in the Ethiopian and leopard, according to Phil. iv. 13, 1 Cor. xv. 10, Gal. ii. 20, 1 Cor. iv. 7 ; for which reasons, " let not the wise man glory in his wisdom, nor the strong man in his strength, nor the rich man in his riches, nor the chaste man in his chastity ; knowing that in all these, Christi virtus sit, is the power of Christ, not theirs who glory in their own virtues." And that he thought, that God when he works, works irresistibly, so as that which he works shall be accomplished, appears from these expressions of his ;¶ " We men will to do most things by counsel, but the effect in nowise follows the will ; but no one *can resist him* so that he cannot do all that he wills : he wills whatsoever things are full of reason and counsel ; he wills that all may be saved, and come to the knowledge of the truth ; but because no man is saved without his own will, for we are endued with free will, he wills, that we will that which is good, that when we have willed, velit in nobis et ipsius suum implere consilium, he also wills in us to fulfil his own counsel."

CHAPTER V

OF PERSEVERANCE

DR. WHITBY says,** " it were easy to confirm this doctrine (of the saints' apostacy) from the concurrent suffrage of the ancient fathers ; but this seems to him unnecessary, after the confession of the learned Vossius, communem hanc fuisse antiquitatis sententiam, ' that this was the common judgment of antiquity, or of the ancients ;' and that antiquitas tota indeficibilitati adversatur, ' all antiquity was contrary to this doctrine,' of the indefectibility of the saints." But it should be known, that Vossius, who sets himself with all his might to prove these assertions, not only in the same place †† owns, that the holy fathers (Austin and Prosper) held, " that God decreed from eternity to bring some by infallible means to eternal life, whose faith and love therefore should either never fail, or being lost, should be restored before the end of life ; seeing God's purpose of saving them whom he hath once chosen to life, can by no means be made void." In which Austin thought the writers before him agreed with him, as appears from his book De Bono Perseverantiæ ; but Vossius also in his next thesis observes,‡‡ that the fathers distinguished faith into three degrees, the last of which they call a perfect, solid, rooted one ; and this they say can by no means be lost. He also farther observes,§§ that " when the holy fathers teach that justifying faith may fail, and sometimes does really fail, they understand this with respect to acts which flow from the power and habit of faith ; for this power, which we may call

---

* Ib, in Eccl. tom. vii. p. 36, L.

† Comment. in Eph. tom. ix. p. 89, L.

‡ Ib. M.   § Ib. p. 93, H, I.   ‖ Ib. in Hieremiam, tom. v. p. 137, G, H.   ¶ Ib.

in Ephes. tom. ix. p. 91, E.   ** Discourse, &c. p. 489 ; ed. 2. 468.   †† Hist. Pelag. l. 6, thes. 12, p. 565.   ‡‡ Ib. thes. 13, p 571, 572.   §§ Ib. p. 575.

the seed of actual faith, they own, is not utterly taken away, at least in the elect." What is the sense of these ancient writers may be better judged of by what will be produced under the following Sections.

SECTION I

CLEMENS ROMANUS. A. D. 69

CLEMENT of Rome gives plain hints of the firmness of true faith, and the perseverance of the saints in it to the end. When addressing the members of the church at Corinth, he says,* " Who has dwelt among you, that has not had an experience of, or proved, *ten panareton kai bebaian umon pistin,* your all-powerful, and firm or stable faith?" He also observes,† that "whereas it is the will of God, that all whom he loves should partake of repentance, and so not perish with the unbelieving and impenitent, *esterizen to pantokratoriko boulemati autou,* 'he has established it by his almighty will.' But if any of those whom God wills should partake of the grace of repentance, should afterwards perish, where is his almighty will ? And how is this matter settled and established by such a will of his ?"

SECTION II

BARNABAS. A. D. 70

BARNABAS, an apostolic man, bears testimony to the doctrine of the saints' final perseverance, when he says,‡ that "he that hopes in Christ, *sterean petran,* 'the firm and solid rock,' shall live for ever;" which he afterwards repeats in answer to a question, why the wool and the wood were used in the legal ceremonies: "Because," says he,§ "the kingdom of Jesus depends upon the tree (he means the cross,) wherefore they that hope in him shall live for ever." And in another place, he cites ‖ the following words as a passage of Scripture, *And there was a river drawing,* or running, *on the right hand, and out of it sprung up beautiful trees, and whosoever eats of them shall live for ever ;* upon which he observes, that "this he says, because we go down into the water (meaning in baptism) full of sins and filth, and we come up out of it bringing forth fruit; having in the heart fear and hope in Jesus through the Spirit, 'and whosoever eats of these shall live for ever;' this he says, that whosoever hears the things that are said, *kai pisteuse,* and believes, shall live for ever."

SECTION III

IGNATIUS. A. D. 110

IGNATIUS also is a witness to this most comfortable truth of the gospel, when he exhorts¶ the saints to "avoid those evil excrescences which bring forth deadly fruit, of which who-

ever tastes dies; for they are not the Father's planting;" for if they "were, the branches of the cross would appear, *kai en auto karpos auton aphthartos,* 'and their fruit would be incorruptible;' whereby through his sufferings he hath called you, being his members, *ou dunatai ouk kophale choris gennethenai aneu melon,* for the head cannot be born, or be, without the members." And in another place he says,** " No man professing faith, sins ; nor having obtained love, hates. The tree is known by its fruit. · So they that profess to be Christians shall be seen by what they do ; for now it is not the business of a profession, *all' en dunamei pisteos ean tis eurethe eis telos,* but it is through the power of faith, if any one is found to the end." By which he intimates, that such is the strength and virtue of true faith, that such who have it are preserved and continued Christians to the end, and are then found to be so. His epistle to the Philadelphians†† is directed to them as a church firmly settled in the harmony of God, as being an everlasting and permanent joy; and their bishops, elders, and deacons, such whom Christ, according to his own will, *esterixen en bebaiosune,* "had firmly established, through his Holy Spirit."

SECTION IV

IRENÆUS. A. D. 180

IRENÆUS has several passages in his writings which favour this doctrine. Allegorizing the history of Lot's wife, he thus expresses himself :‡‡ "The church, which is the salt of the earth, is left in the confines of the earth, suffering the things which are human ; and whilst whole members are often taken away from it, *perseverat statua salis quod est firmamentum fidei, firmans et præmittens filios ad Patrem ipsorum,* 'the pillar of salt continues, which is the firmament of faith, confirming and sending before the children to their Father." He speaks of the grace of love as an abiding one: "Love," says he,§§ " perfects the perfect man ; and he that loves God is perfect both in this world, and in that which is to come ; *nunquam enim desivimus diligentus Deum,* for we never cease loving God, but the more we look upon him, the more we love him." He also represents the Spirit of God as never leaving the man he has taken up his residence in; for, he says,‖‖ "The breath of life is one thing, which makes the man animal, and another the quickening Spirit, which makes him spiritual. That which is made is different from him that makes it, wherefore the breath is temporal, *to de Pneuma aennaon,* the Spirit eternal." The breath indeed is vigorous for a little while, and remains some time, after which it goes away, leaving it breathless where it was before; but the Spirit encompasses man within and without, *ate aei paramonimon*

---

* Ep. 1, ad Cor. p. 2.   † Ib. p. 20.
‡ Barnab. Ep. par. 1, c. 5, p. 220.   § Ib.
c 6, p. 227.   ‖ Ib. c. 9, p. 235, 236.
¶ Ignat. Epist. ad Tralles, p. 52.   ** Ep.

ad Ephes p. 25.   †† Ep. ad Philadel. p. 38,
39.   ‡‡ Iren. adv. Hæres. l. 4, c. 51. p. 392.
§§ Ib. c. 25, p. 342.   ‖‖ Ib. l. 5, c. 12,
p. 450 ; vide Fragm. Græc. ad Calcem Irenæi.

oudepote kataleipei auton, as always abiding, and never leaves him." Yea, he represents it as blasphemy to say, that the members of Christ shall not be saved, but destroyed; for he makes this observation on 1 Cor. iii. 17, *If any one defile the temple of God,* &c.: *Templum igitur Dei in quo Spiritus inhabitat Patris, et membra Christi non participare salutem, sed in perditionem redigi dicere, quomodo non maximæ est blasphemiæ?* Therefore to say, that the temple of God, in which the Spirit of the Father dwells, and the members of Christ, shall not partake of salvation, but be brought down to destruction, is it not the highest blasphemy ?" Vossius* refers to a chapter in Irenæus,† as militating against the doctrine of the saints' final perseverance, in which are these expressions : " All are of the same nature, and able to retain and do good, and able to lose it again, and not do it." And a little after,‡ "Disobedience to God, and loss of good, are indeed in the power of man." But it should be known and observed, that Irenæus is disputing against those heretics who held, that some men were by nature good, and others evil; whereas, he says, they are all of the same nature, as at first created by God, capable of doing good and evil. Besides, he speaks only of the loss of natural and moral good in the natural man, and not of the loss of spiritual good, or of supernatural grace in the regenerate man. Moreover, Irenæus has a passage in the very same chapter§ which seems to favour the saints' perseverance ; for he says, that "the Lord bore all these things for us, that by all things being learned in all, we might be cautious for the future, et perseveremus in omni ejus dilectione, and persevere in all love to him."

SECTION V

EPISTOLA MARTYRUM GALLIÆ. A. D. 180

THE letter of the Martyrs in France I place here, because it is thought by some learned men ‖ to have been drawn up by Irenæus, who was first a presbyter, and then bishop of the church at Lyons. In what year it was written is not certainly known ; it must be after the death of Pothinus, predecessor to Irenæus, since it gives an account of his martyrdom. The letter is written in a truly grand, noble, Christian spirit ; it begins thus : " The servants of Christ dwelling in Vienna, and Lyons in France, to the brethren in Asia and Phrygia, which have the same faith and hope of redemption with us, peace, and grace, and glory, from God the Father, and Christ Jesus our Lord." In it they give an account of the sufferings and martyrdom of many excellent and godly persons in those parts, how bravely they endured, persevered, and held out to the end ; which constancy

and perseverance they all along ascribe to the grace and power of God. Among other expressions they have these :¶ " When," say they, "we were not only driven from houses, baths, and markets, but were entirely forbid to appear in any place, *antistrategei de e charis tou Theou,* 'the grace of God fought for us against the adversary,' and delivered the weak, and set against him firm or solid pillars, able, through patience, to draw upon themselves the whole force or power of the wicked one." And a little after ** they make mention of others, "who were bitterly tormented, insomuch that it seemed as though they could not live, notwithstanding every kind of medicine they made use of ; they remained in prison, destitute indeed of the help and care of men, but *anarronumenoi upo tou Kuriou kai endunamoumenoi kai somati kai psuche,* 'being afresh strengthened by the Lord, and enabled or assisted in body and soul,' they stirred up and comforted the rest." And of Blundina, in particular, they say,†† that "though she was little, and weak, and despicable, yet, *megan kai akutagoniston athleten Christon endedumene,* 'being clothed with that great and invincible champion, Christ,' many a time overcame the enemy, and through the combat is crowned with the crown of immortality." And after having taken notice of some who had denied the faith at first, afterwards, beyond the expectation of the heathens, made a confession of it ; whereby Christ was greatly glorified, and all they were added to the number of the martyrs. They speak of others after this manner :‡‡ " But they remained without, *oi me de ichnos popote pisteos,* 'who never had the least appearance of faith,' nor sense of the wedding garment, nor understanding of the fear of God, but through their whole conversation caused the way to be blasphemed ; that is to say, the sons of perdition." From whence it appears, that these early pious Christians, as they observe that such as had the true grace of God held out to the end, which they ascribe to the power of God ; so such as finally and totally fell away, were such who never had the root of the matter in them.

SECTION VI

CLEMENS ALEXANDRINUS. A. D. 190

CLEMENT of Alexandria frequently suggests the stability and permanency of such as have received the grace of God. Thus allegorizing Isaac's sporting with Rebecca his spouse, whom he makes to signify the church; "which has," says he,§§ " a firm and solid name put upon her, *upomone,* 'patience ; either because she only *eis tous aionas menei,* 'abides for ever,' always rejoicing ; or because she consists of the patience of believers,

---

* Hist. Pelag. l. 6, thes. 12, p. 566.
† Adv. Hæres. l. 4, c. 72, p. 417.   ‡ Ib. p. 418.   § Adv. Hæres. l. 4, c. 72, p. 419.
‖ Vide Vales. Annot. in Euseb. Eccl. Hist. l. 5, c. 1, p. 86 ; Fabricii Bibl. Græc. l. 5. c. 1, p.

74.   ¶ In Euseb. Eccl Hist. l. 5, c. 1, p. 155.   ** Ib. p. 159.   †† Ib. p. 162.
‡‡ Ib. p. 163.   §§ Clement.Pædagog. l. 1, c. 5, p. 90, 91.

who are the members of Christ, and the testimony of them *ton eis telos upomeinanton*, that endure the end." And in another place he says,* "David cries out, "The righteous shall not be moved for ever," neither by deceitful words, nor by deceitful pleasure; hence neither shall he be moved from his own inheritance, nor shall he be afraid of evil tidings, nor of vain calumny, nor of false opinion that is about him." And elsewhere,† speaking of a devout and religious person, he says, that "such a soul *ou diorizetai pote tou Theou kat' oudena kairon*, shall never at any time be separated from God." Having cited Psalm xlviii. 12, he gives this sense of the words :‡ "It signifies, I think, that such who have received the word from on high, shall be high as towers, *kai bebaios en te te pistei kai te gnosei stesesthai*, and shall stand firmly in faith and knowledge." Both which, namely, faith and knowledge, he often represents as abiding and durable : of the former he has these expressions :§ "The life of Christians, which we are now giving some instructions about, is a certain system of rational actions, that is, of those things which are taught by the Logos, or Word, *adiaptotos energeia*, 'a never-failing energy,' which we indeed have called faith." And in another place,‖ "Faith, I say, whether it is founded on love or on fear, is something divine, *mete upo alles philias kosmikes diaspomenen, mete upo phobon parontos dialuomenen*, which cannot be pulled assunder by any other worldly friendship, nor be dissolved by present fear." And elsewhere,¶ "Faith is *ischus eis soterian, kai dunamis eis zoen aionion*, strength unto salvation, and a power unto everlasting life." Yea, he observes,** "The power of faith is such, that it exceeds every thing that is contrary to it, *kai auton olou enistamenou tou kosmou*, and even the whole world itself that it stands in the way of it." To which may be added another passage of Clement's †† : "I am persuaded that *neither death*, which is inflicted by persecutors, *nor the life* which we here live, *nor angels*, the apostate ones, *nor principalities*, the principality of Satan, which is the life he chooses, for such are the principalities and powers of darkness, according to him ; *nor things present*, among which we are in this time of life, as the hope of the soldier, the gain of the merchant ; *nor height, nor depth, nor any other creature*, by an operation proper to men, *resists the faith* of him who makes a free choice. *Creature*, synonymously, is called operation, being our work, and such an operation *cannot separate us from the love of God which is in Christ Jesus our Lord*. And as to the continuance of true spiritual knowledge he thus expresses himself :‡‡ "Divine instruction," says he,

"*ktema estin eis aei paramenon*, is a possession that abides for ever." Yea, he speaks of it as what cannot be lost :§§ "To him that has by exercise, proceeding from knowledge," says he, "got that virtue which cannot be lost, the habit of it becomes natural, and as heaviness to a stone, *outos toude e episteme anapobletos*, 'so his knowledge cannot be lost,' neither unwillingly nor willingly ; by the power of reason, knowledge, and providence, it is so established that it cannot be lost ; through a godly fear it becomes so as that it cannot be lost. The greatest thing therefore is the knowledge of God, because this is so preserved that virtue cannot be lost." This perseverance of the saints is ascribed by Clement, not to themselves, but to the power and kindness of their Lord. "We shall not fall," says he,‖‖ "into corruption, who pass through into incorruption, *oti anthexetai emon autos*, 'because he sustains us ;' for he hath said, and he will do it." And a little after he says,¶¶ that "his, that is, Christ's goodness towards them, who through hearing have believed, is *ametakinetos se kai arrepes*, immoveable, and turns neither one way nor another." Vossius*** refers to this writer as favouring the saints' apostacy ; who does indeed, in the book††† referred to, cite Heb. x. 26, and observes, that those who go on sinning and repenting, repenting and sinning, do not at all differ from such who never believed ; and that he knows not which is worse, to sin wilfully, or to repent for sin, and sin again ; but then he gives no intimations, that he thought that such had ever received the true grace of God, who go on at this rate, and were now fallen from it. I have produced two passages out of the same book in proof of the doctrine of perseverance.

SECTION VII

TERTULLIAN. A. D. 200

TERTULLIAN was no stranger to the doctrine of the saints' final perseverance. " Satan," he says,‡‡‡ "cannot do anything against the servants of the living God, unless he permits, *ut aut ipsum destruat per fidem electorum in tentatione victricem, aut homines ejus fuisse traducat, qui defecerint ad eum*, ' either that he may destroy him through the faith of the elect, which overcomes in temptation, or that he may openly show that the men were his, who fell off to him." You have an example in Job. So he desired power to tempt the apostles, not having it but by permission ; since the Lord in the Gospel says to Peter, *Satan hath desired that he might sift thee as wheat ; but I have prayed for thee, that thy faith fail not ; ne tantum Diabolo permitteretur, ut fides periclitaretur*, ' lest only it should be permitted to the devil, as that

---

* Ib. Stromat. l. 6, p. 655.   † Ib. 670.
‡ Ib. l. 7, p. 749   § Ib. Pædagog. l. 1, c. 13, p. 136.   ‖ Ib. Stromat. l. 2, p, 372,
¶ Ib. p. 284.   ** Ib. l. 6, p. 647.
†† Clement. Strom. l. 4, p. 512.   ‡‡ Ib. Pædagog. l. 1, c. 7, p. 109.   §§ Ib. Stromat,

l. 7, p. 726.   ‖‖ Ib. Pædagog. l. 1, c. 9, p. 125.   ¶¶ Ib. p. 126.   *** Hist. Pelag. l. 6, thes. 12, p. 566.   ††† Stromat. l. 2, p. 385.   ‡‡‡ Tertull. de Fuga in Persecut. c. 2, p. 690.

faith should be in danger;' whereby it showed, that both are with God, and shaking of faith, and the protection of it; since both are desired of him, shaking by the devil, protection by the Son; and seeing the Son of God has the protection of faith in his own power, which he requested of the Father, from whom he receives all power in heaven and in earth; how can the devil have the shaking of faith in his own hand?" And a little after he observes,* that "the legion of devils had had no power over the herd of swine, unless they had obtained it of God; *tantum abest ut in oves Dei habeat,* ' so far are they from having any over the sheep of God.' The devil seems now to enjoy his own power, *si forte in eos qui ad Deum non pertinent,* though perhaps over them who do not belong to God." Moreover, against the household of God he can do nothing of his own power; for when he is allowed, the instances in Scripture demonstrate from what causes it is; for either the power of tempting is granted to him, provoked or provoking, for the sake of probation, as in the cases above; or for the sake of reprobation, is the sinner delivered to him as to an executioner for punishment, as Saul;—or for the sake of restraint, as the apostle relates, that there was given him *a staff, a messenger of Satan to buffet him.* Nor is this kind permitted to the devil, for the humbling of the saints, by afflicting the flesh; *nisi simul ut et virtus tolerantiæ scilicet in infirmitate perfici possit,* "unless that also, at the same time, the power of patience might be made perfect, namely, in weakness." He elsewhere suggests,† that it is impossible the elect of God should be destroyed by Satan, notwithstanding all the signs and wonders done by him. "God forbid," says he, "that we should believe that the soul of any saint, much less of a prophet, should be drawn out by the devil, who are taught, that Satan may be transfigured *into an angel of light;* not only into a *man* of light; yea, that in the end he will affirm himself to be *God,* and will do more wondrous signs, *ad evertendos si fieri possit electos,* to destroy the elect, if possible."

Moreover, Tertullian asserts, that the work of God cannot be lost, extinguished, or cease; "for what is of God," says he,‡ "is not so extinguished, as it is overshadowed; for it may be overshadowed, because it is not God; it cannot be extinguished, because it is of God." And if this is true of natural good, which God puts into men, of which he seems to speak, it must be much more so of supernatural good infused into them. And in another place § he asks, "How is it, that though Satan is always working, and adding daily to the wicked wits of men, opus Dei aut cessaverit aut proficere destiterit, that either the work of God should cease, or stop going forward." Vossius‖ indeed refers us

to two places in this writer, in favour of the saints' defectibility from the grace of God. In the first of them are these words :¶ "And is this to be wondered at, that any who have been proved for the time past should afterwards fall? Saul, a good man, above the rest, is overthrown by envy; David, a good man, according to the Lord's heart, is afterwards guilty of murder and adultery; Solomon, endued with all grace and wisdom by the Lord, is by women induced to idolatry: for to the Son of God alone was it reserved *to abide without sin.* What if, therefore, a bishop, a deacon, a widow, a virgin, a doctor, yea, even a martyr, should fall from the rule, shall heresies on that account seem to obtain truth? Do we prove faith by persons, or persons by faith? No man is wise, but a believer; no man of great name, but a Christian; no man a Christian, but he who shall persevere to the end." All which amounts to no more, than that the best of men may fall into sin; that none are exempt from it but the Son of God; therefore we should not think ill of the doctrine of faith, because of the falls of the professors of it; no man being a true Christian but he that shall persevere to the last; for such who do not, were never true Christians; to all which we heartily subscribe. Tertullian, both before and after this passage, says such things as are so far from destroying, that they serve to strengthen the doctrine of perseverance. Before it he observes, that "heresies prevail through the infirmities of some, which would not prevail at all, *si in bene valentem fidem incurrant,* had they attacked one whose faith was sound and well." And after it he has these words, which gave great light into his sense and meaning; "*The Lord knows them that are his,* and the plant which the Father has not planted he roots up, and of the first shows the last, and carries the fan in his hand to purge his floor. Let the chaff of light faith fly away with every breath of temptation, as much as can fly, *eo purior massa frumenti in horrea Domini reponetur,* ' so that the more pure mass of wheat may be laid up in the Lord's garners.' Shall not some of the learners, being offended, turn away from the Lord? Yet the rest should not therefore think of departing from following him; but they that know that he is the Word of life, and came from God, *persevera-verunt in comitatu ejus usque ad finem,* ' have persevered in his company unto the end,' when he mildly offered to them to depart if they would. It is a lesser matter if such as Phygellus, Hermogenes, Philetus, and Hymenæus, leave his apostle. The betrayer of Christ was of the apostles. We wonder at his churches, if they are deserted by some, when these things show us Christians, what we suffer after the example of Christ himself; *They went out from us,* says he, 1 John ii. 19, *for they were not of us,*" &c. In the other **

---

* Tertull. de Fuga in Persecut. c. 2. p 691.
† Ib. de Anima, c. 57, p. 356.   ‡ Ib. c. 41, p. 342.   § Tertull. de Virgin. Veland. c.

1, p. 192.   ‖ Hist. Pelag. l. 6, thes. 12, p. 567.   ¶ De Præscript. Hærat. c. 3, p. 230; 231.   ** De Pœnitentia, c. 6, p. 144.

place referred to stands this passage : " Do not many afterwards fall? Is not the gift taken away from many? These are they, namely, who creep in by stealth ; who, attempting the faith of repentance, place their house, about to fall upon the sands." But Tertullian is manifestly speaking of such who never had the true grace of God, or built upon a right foundation, from whom was taken away that which they seemed to have ; having fallen, not from true faith they never had, but from a profession of it : so he sometimes * calls Simon Magus a believer, because he professed to be one ; though he afterwards says, that he was cursed by the apostles, and cast out from the faith, that is, from the church of God, and a profession of faith in it. So when he speaks † of some ready to perish after baptism, he is to be understood of such who have not, and never had, oil in their lamps." Or, when he speaks of true believers losing their faith, he does not mean that they shall finally and totally perish ; " for," says he,‡ " though such an one may be said to perish, it will be of such kind of perdition as to be recovered again ; because the sheep perishes, not by dying, but by wandering, and the piece of silver, not by decaying, but by lying hid ; so that may be said to perish which is safe ; wherefore also a believer, falling into a sight of the charioteer's fury, the fencer's blood, the filthiness of the stage, &c., perishes ;" yet he observes, that he ought to be sought after and fetched back.

SECTION VIII

ORIGINES ALEXANDRINUS. A. D. 230

ORIGEN has many things in his writings which countenance the doctrine of the perpetuity of grace in the saints, and their final perseverance. "To me," he says,§ " those things seem firmer which are by grace, than those which are of the law ; because those are without us, they are within us, and these consist in frail matter, so as that they may easily decay, but they are written by the Spirit of God, and being impressed in the inward chambers of the soul, firmitatem perpetuitatis obtinent, obtain the firmness of perpetuity." Again, he observes,‖ " that the grace and gift of our Saviour," referring to John iv. 10, 14, *anaphairetos kai me analiskomene, mede phtheiromene,* " cannot be taken away, nor consumed, nor destroyed in him that partakes of it." Particularly he observes, agreeably to the Scripture, that " charity, or the grace of love, never fails ; wherefore," adds he,¶ " the apostle being confident that he had received it entire, said, Who shall separate us from the love of God? shall tribulation, &c., for from charity never failing, were those words of his," Rom. viii.

35. In another place** he takes notice of a twofold light, the light of the ungodly, which will be put out, and the light of the righteous, quæ permanet in æternum, "which abides for ever ;" and then argues thus : " Our soul is enlightened either with the true light, quod nunquam extinguetur, 'which shall never be put out,' which is Christ ; or if it has not in it that light which is eternal, without doubt it is enlightened with a temporal and extinguishable light, by him who transforms himself into an angel of light." Moreover, having observed, as before, that "charity never falls ; so," says he,†† "the possession and house of the saints never falls, is never taken away, is never separated from their right ; for how can that house be separated from the priest, which *is built upon the foundation of the apostles and prophets, in which Jesus Christ is the chief corner stone?*" He often argues the inexpugnableness and safety of the saints, and church of Christ, from their being built upon a foundation, and upon a rock. "The church," he says,‡‡ " as the building of Christ, who builds his own house wisely upon a rock, *anepidektos esti pulon adou,* 'cannot admit of the gates of hell ;' which indeed prevail against every man *without* the rock and church, but can do nothing against *it.*" And a little after,§§ " No gate of hell can prevail against the rock, or the church which Christ has built upon it." Hence he asserts, that none that belong to Christ, even the least, can ever perish, or the elect be deceived ; his words are these ;‖‖ after citing the passage in Matthew xviii. 10, he adds, " He that is now a little one, can neither be offended nor perish, for great peace have they which love the name of God, and nothing shall offend them. Even he that is the least of all the disciples of Christ, *ouk an apoloito,* cannot perish, and therefore he is great, and may say this, Who shall separate us from the love?" &c. And elsewhere,¶¶ referring to Matthew xxiv. 24, he says, " If it be possible, is a word of exaggeration ; for he does not affirm, or say, that the elect also *may be deceived ;* but would show that the words of heretics are frequently very persuasory and powerful to move even them that hear wisely." Satan, as powerful an adversary as he is, is represented as unable to hurt and destroy those that fear the Lord. "We do not deny," says he,*** "that there are many devils on earth ; we say there are, and that they are powerful in the wicked because of their wickedness ; but can do *nothing* to those who have *put on the whole armour of God,* and have received *strength to stand against the wiles of the devil.*" And a little after :††† " Others, who through ignorance subject themselves to them, may suffer by them ; but the Christian, the true Christian, who sub-

---

* De Idolatria, c. 9, p. 109.　　† Scorpiace, c. 6, p. 623.　　‡ De Pudicitia, c. 7, p. 722, § In Rom. l. 4, fol. 162, C.　　‖ In Joan. p. 206.　　¶ In Matt. hom. 23, fol. 43, A.
** In Jud. homil. 1, fol. 177, C ; et in Matt.

homil. 30, foi. 60, E.　　†† In Lev. homil. 15, fol. 91, A.　　‡‡ In Matt. p. 276.　　§§ Ib. p. 277.　　‖‖ Ib. p. 33.　　¶¶ In Matt. homil. 30, fol. 59, D.　　*** Contr. Cels. l. 8, p. 400.　　††† Ib. p. 401.

jects himself to God only, and to his word, cannot suffer anything by the devils, being greater than them; and he cannot suffer or be hurt by them, because *the angel of the Lord encamps round about them that fear him.*" And a little after he adds,* "So that the contrary angels, nor the prince of them, who is called *the prince of this world,* can do nothing effectually against those who are devoted to God." The power of sustaining the combat with our spiritual enemies, and the obtaining the victory over them, he ascribes† not to the power of man, but to divine grace and assistance.

I own there are some passages in the writings of this father which are not agreeable to this doctrine, though frequently suggested by him: as when he supposes‡ Judas to be a true believer, and observes,§ that though none can *pluck* Christ's sheep out of the hands of God, yet they may *fall out* of them through their own negligence, or by setting themselves afar off from the hand of God. As also when he intimates,|| that the Spirit of God is sometimes in the saints, and sometimes not; though this may be understood of the gifts of the Spirit, bestowed at certain times for peculiar service; or of the graces of the Spirit not being always in exercise, though in being. And in the first passage referred to by Vossius, where Origen says,¶ that the Holy Spirit is taken away from persons unworthy, and that he who is now worthy of the participation of him, and turns back, is really guilty of blasphemy against him, he is to be understood of the *gifts,* and not of the *grace* of the Spirit. His second passage is not to be met with, there being no such chapter in the book he cites. In his third reference are plain intimations of the doctrine of perseverance; he says,** that they, of whom the apostle says they *made shipwreck of faith,* were indeed *called,* but not *justified;* and observes,†† that neither the death of the body, nor the life of sin, nor the vain glory of this world, nor the prince of the world, and other powers, though they desire and endeavour, they cannot separate any from the love of God. It is true, he adds,‡‡ if love is perfect, and rooted and grounded; and so it is in every true believer, as to the principle, though not as to the degree and exercise of it.

SECTION IX

CYPRIAN. A. D. 250.

CYPRIAN must be reckoned among the assertors of the final perseverance of the saints, and of the indefectibility of true believers,

as will appear from the following passages§§ in his writings. He makes this observation on Romans viii. 35, "Who shall separate us, &c. "Nihil horum potest separare credentes, ' none of these things can separate believers;' nothing can pull them away that cleave to his body and blood." And to the same purpose he speaks in another place,|||| "The church, that is, the people fixed in the church, faithfully and firmly persevering in that which they have believed, nothing can separate from Christ, quo minus hæreat semper et maneat in individua dilectione, that they should not always continue and remain in individual love." Again he observes,¶¶ that "the Lord, the protector and defender of his people, will not suffer, *triticum de area sua diripi,* ' the wheat to be taken from off his floor,' but the chaff only can be separated from the church." Agreeable to which he elsewhere says,*** "He that is not planted in the precepts and admonitions of God the Father, solus poterit de ecclesia ille discedere, he only can depart from the church." And again,††† "The church which believes in Christ, and which holds that which it has once known, never departs from him at all; and they are the church who remain in the house of God; but there is a plantation which is not planted by God the Father, whom we see are not made firm and solid with the stability of wheat, but are winnowed like chaff with the breath of the scattering enemy; of whom John in his epistle says, They went out from us," &c. Here presents faith‡‡‡ as inexpugnable, and says,§§§ that "the strength of believers remains immoveable, and that integrity continues stable and strong with those who fear and love God with their whole heart." To which may be added the following expressions of his,|||||| "The strength of hope, and firmness of faith, are vigorous with us, and we have a mind erect, virtue immoveable, patience ever joyful, and a soul secure of its own God, amidst the ruins of a decaying age; as the Holy Ghost, by the prophet, speaks and exhorts, strengthening with a heavenly voice the firmness of our faith and hope, Although, says he, the fig-tree shall not blossom," &c. He denies, "that a man of God, and a worshipper of him, leaning on the truth of hope, and founded on the stability of faith, can be moved by the troubles of this world and age." Once more he says,¶¶¶ "To whom remission of sins is given, to them the name of children is ascribed, and to them eternity is promised, according to John viii. 34, 35. Now this perseverance of the saints, Cyprian considered as the gift of God's grace, and owing to his almighty

---

* Contr. Cels. l. 8, p. 402.   † In Exod. homil. 6, fol. 376; Πρχι Αρχων, l. 3, c. 2, fol. 143, D, 144, D.   ‡ In Joan. p. 392.
§ In Jer. homil. 18. p. 166; et in Joan. p. 265. || In Num. homil. 6, fol. 100, C, D, 101, E, F.   ¶ Hist. Pelag. l. 6, thes. 12, p. 566.   ** Περι Αρχων, l. 1, c. 3, fol. 117, C, D.   †† In Rom. l. 7, fol. 192, B.
‡‡ Ib. fol. 194, A, B, C.   §§ Cyprian. Ep.
8, ad Clerum, p. 24. |||| Ib. Ep. 63, ad Cæcilium, p. 149.   ¶¶ Ib. Epist. 69, ad Florentium, p. 172.   *** Cyprian. Ep. 49, ad Cornelium, p. 91.   ††† Ib. Epist. 55, ad eundem, p. 116; vida etiam ep. 69, ad Florentium, p. 172.   ‡‡‡ Ib. Epist. 9, ad Martyres, p. 26,   §§§ Ib. Epist. 52, ad Antonianum, p. 94. |||||| Ib. ad Demetrianum, 282, 283.
¶¶¶ Ib. de Oratione Dominica, p. 266.

power; hence, says he,[*] "This we desire and entreat, that we who are sanctified in baptism, might persevere in that which we have begun to be." And a little after, "This we request night and day, that sanctification and vivification which proceeds from the grace of God, ipsius protectione servetur, might be preserved by his protection." Which passages, with others, are cited by Austin[†] for the same purpose to show the sense of this great and good man, who not only held the doctrine, but had the grace of perseverance unto the end; for when the proconsul put the question to him, "Dost thou then persevere in this mind, that thou wilt not sacrifice?" he answered, Bona voluntas, quæ Deum novit mutari non potest, "A good mind which knows God cannot be changed.'" which were some of his last words, as Pontius his deacon relates:[‡] Vossius[§] refers to three places in Cyprian, showing that the saints may lose the true grace of God, and finally and totally perish. The two || first of them regard one of the same case, that of Solomon's, of whom he says, that "while he walked in the ways of the Lord, he enjoyed the grace of the Lord, but when he left them he lost it." Where, by the grace of the Lord, I apprehend he means the discoveries of the love and favour of God to him, which he enjoyed whilst he walked in his ways, and lost when he departed from them; since he adds, "and the Lord raised up Satan, or an enemy, to Solomon.". Which may be the case of a true believer, and yet not fall from grace, as in the heart of God, or as implanted in his own heart, much less finally and totally perish; nor does Cyprian suggest any such thing concerning Solomon. Besides, in one of the places where this case is mentioned, he says many things which confirm the doctrine we plead for. Thus speaking of the saints, he observes,[¶] that "He (Christ) says, that they are strong and stable, and founded upon a rock of a mighty bulk, and that they are solidly settled with an immoveable and unshaken firmness against all the storms and tempests of the world." Again,[**] says he, "Let no man think, bonos de ecclesia posse discedere, 'that good men can depart from the church.' The wind does not take away the wheat, nor does a storm root up the tree that is founded with a solid root; empty chaff is carried away with a tempest; weak trees are overturned at meeting a whirlwind; these the apostle John curses and strikes at, first epistle, chap. ii. 19." Once more, "The Lord chose Judas," says he,[††] "though Judas afterwards betrayed the Lord, non tamen idcirco apostolorum fides et firmitas cecidit, 'yet the faith and firmness of the apostles did not fall,' because Judas, the betrayer, fell from their society;

so here, the holiness and dignity of confessors are not immediately broke to pieces, because the faith of some is broken. The blessed apostle in his epistle speaks, saying, "For what if some of them fell from the faith?" &c. Now, supposing that in the case before us, Cyprian had expressed himself a little incautiously, must this instance prevail against so many testimonies which have been produced to the contrary? In the other place,[‡‡] referred to by Vossius, are these words, "And on the contrary oftentimes, some of those who are baptized in health, if afterwards they begin to sin, are shaken by the unclean spirit returning; so that it is manifest, that the devil, who is excluded in baptism by the faith of the believer, returns, si fides postmodum defecerit, if faith should afterwards fail." But then let it be observed, that Cyprian does not assert, only supposes the failing of faith after baptism; and had he asserted it, Vossius [§§] himself has taught us how to understand the fathers, when they say that faith may fail, and sometimes really does; by which they mean, not the habit or seed of faith, but the acts which flow from it; and that true faith, as to the acts and exercise of it, may fail, is not denied by us.

SECTION X

LACTANTIUS. A. D. 320

LACTANTIUS clearly asserts the perpetuity of virtue or grace, when he affirms, that where it once is, it can never remove; his words are these,[||||] "virtue is perpetual, without any intermission; nec discedere ab eo potest, qui enim semel cepit, 'nor can it depart from him who has once received it;' for if it has any interval, if we can at any time be without it, vices immediately return, which always oppose virtue; nor is it therefore laid hold on, if it leaves, if it at any time departs; but seeing it has placed for itself a stable habitation, it must needs be conversant in every act; nor can it truly repel vices, and cause them to flee away, unless it fortifies the breast where it has its seat, perpetua statione, 'with a perpetual station;' wherefore the perpetuity of virtue shows, that the human mind, if it has received virtue, continues, because virtue is perpetual, and the human mind only is capable of it."

SECTION XI

EUSEBIUS CÆSARIENSIS. A. D. 330

EUSEBIUS observes,[¶¶] that Christ foretold, that "the church gathered out of all nations should be aetteton kai akatamacheton, 'unconquerable and inexpugnable,' and never to be overcome by death itself; but should

---

* Ibid.   † Aug. de Corrupt. et Gratia, c. 6, de Bono Perseverantia, l. 2, c. 2 and 21.
‡ In Vita Cypriani.   § Hist. Pelag. l. 6, thes. 12, p. 567. || Ep. 7, ad Rogatianum, p. 20. D; et de Unitate Ecclesiæ, p. 259.
¶ De Unitate Ecclesiæ, p. 235.   ** Ib. p.

256.   †† Ib. 259.   ‡‡ Ep. 76, ad Magnum, p. 213.   §§ Hist. Pelag. l. 6, thes. 13, p. 575. |||| Lactant. Institut. Diviu. l. 7. c. 10, p. 562.   ¶¶ Prep. Evangel. l. 1. c. 3, p. 7, 8.

stand and abide unshaken, being established by his power, and fixed as upon an immoveable and unbroken rock." And elsewhere,[*] he affirms it to be a matter out of question, and "without controversy, that a new nation has appeared, not small, nor situated in a corner of the earth, but of all nations most populous and religious to this day, *anoletron kai aetteton e kai esaei, tes para Theou boetheias tugchanei*, not being liable to ruin, but insuperable, because it has always help from God." And in another place,[†] having mentioned Psalm xlvii. 9, he. observes, that "this shows yet more clearly, that the princes of the church of Christ, among the Gentiles, are translated into the inheritance of the prophets, formerly dear to God: and these being strengthened by the power of our Saviour, are lifted up very high *oudenos anthropon katabalein autous kai tapeinosai dedunemenou*, 'insomuch that no man is able to cast them down and lay them low,' because of the right hand of God that lifts them up, and strengthens them." Once more, he says,[‡] "The Lord himself being both shepherd and Lord of the flock, is said to feed it by himself in strength, so that the sheep being kept with a mighty hand, and a high arm, *meden ti pathein deinon pros ton ephedreuonton autois agrion kai apenon therion*, suffer no evil from the wild and savage beasts which lie in wait for them."

SECTION XII

CHRONOMATIUS. A. D. 335

CHRONOMATIUS was, as we learn from Jerome,[§] bishop of Aquileia; he is said to flourish about A. D. 335,[||] and therefore must live to a great age, as appears from Jerom's knowledge of him, and acquaintance with him. He wrote upon the Beautitudes, and some other passages in the fifth chapter of Matthew, and part of the sixth. Vossius[¶] refers to a passage in this writer as militating against the perseverance of the saints; who indeed observes,[**] that "they are infatuated, who, when once taught by faith, and the heavenly wisdom, and ought to remain faithful and stable, leave the faith and divine wisdom, and either fall into heresy, or return to the folly of the heathens." But it is plain that he is speaking of nominal Christians, and of their leaving the doctrine of faith they were once instructed in, and professed, but not of their losing the grace of faith, which they never had. He instances in Judas, "who," he says,[††] "was of these sort of salts, but afterwards he rejected that divine wisdom, and of an apostle became an apostate; not only could not be profitable to others, but became miserable and unprofitable to himself." And a little after, "Judas, of the

household of faith, became an enemy of the truth." All which only regard the office to which he was called, the external gifts bestowed upon him, and outward profession of faith he made, and the character he bore in the esteem of others, from which he sadly fell. But this is no proof of the apostacy of a true believer. Besides, Chronomatius observes in the same work,[‡‡] "as salt, when it operates in any flesh, it does not admit of corruption, it takes away ill smells, it purges out filth, it does not suffer worms to be generated; so the heavenly grace of faith, which was given through the apostles, in like manner works in us; for it takes away the corruption of carnal concupiscence, it purges out the filth of sin, it excludes the odour of an evil conversation, and does not suffer the worms of sin to be generated, that is, lustful and deadly pleasures to rise out of the body. And as salt indeed is put without, but inwardly operates by virtue of its own nature, so the heavenly grace penetrates through the outward and inward parts of the man; et *totum hominem, integrum a peccato incorruptumque conservat*, and preserves the whole man entire, and incorrupt from sin." Which may be considered as a testimony for the doctrine of the saints' perseverance.

SECTION XIII

ATHANASIUS. A. D. 350

ATHANASIUS expressly asserts the stability of the church, and the safety of believers, as they are established upon the rock Christ Jesus. Having cited Matt. xvi. 18, he makes this observation upon it:[§§] "Faithful is the saying, and immoveable the promise, *kai e ekklesia aettetos*, 'and the church invincible,' though hell itself should be moved, and the rulers of darkness in it." And in another place he says,[||||] "A faithful disciple of the gospel, that has grace to discern spiritual things, builds his house of faith upon a rock, *kai esteken edraios kai asphales apo tes touton apates diamenon*, and stands firm, and abides safe from their deceit;" that is, from the deceit of false christs and false prophets he had been speaking of before. And having elsewhere[¶¶] mentioned some instances in the Psalms, he adds, "Wherefore it is manifest, that we being made one, are able, in the name of the Father, and of the Son, *bebaion echein tes agates ton sundesmon*, to hold the bond of love firm." He suggests, that the reason why Christ receives grace for men, is, that it might remain safe for them. "He, the Lord," says he,[***] "received, that the gift residing in him, *bebaia e charis diamene*, 'grace might remain firm;' for if men only had received, it was possible that it might be taken away again, which is shown in Adam,

---

* Hist. Eccl. l. 1, c. 4, p. 15.
† Demonstr. Evangel. l. 6, c. 2, p. 260.
‡ Ib. l. 7, c. 2, p. 344.   § Hieron. ad Ruffin. tom. ii. fol. 66, A; Comment. in Amos, l. 3, prœm. tom. vi. fol. 44. || Vide Magdeburg. Centuriator. cent. 4, c. 10, p. 693.

¶ Hist. Pelag. l. 6, thes. 12, p. 567.
** Chronomatius de 8 Beatitud. concio. l. p. 376   †† Ibid.   ‡‡ Ib. p. 375.
§§ Athanas. Orat. unum esse. Christum, vol. i. p. 667. |||| Ib. contr. Arian. orat. i. p. 287, ¶¶ Ib. orat. 4, p. 474.   *** Ib. p. 490.

for what he received he lost; *ina de anaphairetos e charis yenetai kai bebaia phu-
gachthe tois anthropois,* ' now that this grace
might not be taken away, but be kept safe
from men,' therefore he made this gift his own,
and says, that he received power as man,
which he always had as God.'' He also represents* it as the effect of Christ's redemption, that the redeemed die no more;
for thus he introduces Christ's speaking: "I
have finished the work, which thou, Father,
gavest me; the work is finished; for the
men that are redeemed from sin, *ouketi
menousi nekroi,* no longer remain dead.'' But
if any of them should perish who are redeemed
by Christ, how would this end of redemption
be answered in such persons, or the effect of
it appear in them? Vossius† appeals to
a passage in Athanasius,‡ as militating
against this doctrine, which is this : " When
any one falls from the Spirit, through some
wickedness, grace indeed remains irrevocable,
with those who are willing; though a man
falls, he may repent; but such an one that
falls is no longer in God, because the Holy
Spirit, the Comforter, which is in God, departs from him; but the sinner is in him, to
whom he has subjected himself, as in the
case of Saul; for 'the Spirit of God departed
from him, and an evil spirit afflicted him.' "
But this must be understood of the external
gifts of the Spirit, as the instance of Saul
directs us to observe, and not of the special
grace of the Spirit in effectual vocation; for
Athanasius, in the very same page, says, that
it never fails, is without repentance, and being
once bestowed, is never revoked. His words
are these: " That phrase, *as we are one,* referring to John xvii. 22, means nothing else,
than that the grace of the Spirit which the
disciples had, might be *adiaptotos kai ameta-
meletos,* ' never-failing and irrevocable ;' for,
as I said before, what the Word had by nature to be in the Father, he desires might be
irrevocably given us by the Spirit ; which
the apostle knowing, said, ' Who shall separate us from the love of Christ ? For the
gifts of God, and the grace of calling, are
without repentance.' "

SECTION XIV

MACARIUS ÆGYPTUS. A. D. 350

MACARIUS gives plain intimations, that such
who are truly born again shall never perish,
but have everlasting life. " The true death,"
he says,§ is inbred in the heart, and is
hidden, and the inward man is become dead;
if therefore any one passes from this death
unto the life which is hidden, verily he shall
live for ever, *kai ouk apothneskei,* and not
die." Again :|| " The soul shall be kept by
the power of the Lord, which, as much as it
is able, restrains itself, and turns from every
worldly lust; and so it is helped by the Lord,

that it may be truly kept from the aforesaid
evils ; for whenever the Lord sees any one
bravely declining the pleasures of life, dis-
tractions, gross cares, earthly bonds, and the
wanderings of vain reasonings, he grants the
peculiar assistance of grace, *aptoton diateron
len psuchen ekeinen,* preserving that soul from
falling.'' Once more :¶ " The humble man
never falls, for from whence should he fall
who is under all ?'' And in another place,
speaking of Mary, he observes, that a divine
power filled her heart ; and adds,** " That
power, wherever it is necessary, becomes permanent, *os ktema anaphaireton,* as a possession that cannot be taken away." Once
more he says,†† that a soul " calling upon
the Lord is able to continue *en pistei adisakto,*
in faith, without doubting." Vossius‡‡ refers to several Homilies of this writer, as
containing in them passages which militate
against the saints' perseverance. Out of the
fourth homily referred to, I have produced an
instance in favour of it : in it, he does indeed
make mention of the *foolish virgins,* but then
he supposes them to be such who were in a
state of nature, were never regenerated by
the Spirit of God, and were destitute of the
oil of grace ; and in it also he represents God
as not ashamed to receive such that fall, provided they repent, turn to him, and desire
help of him. In the fifteenth, these questions are put: Whether a man having grace
can fall ? whether grace remains after man is
fallen ? To which he replies, that he may
fall if he is negligent, which may prove a loss
to him, but he does not say that grace itself
may be lost. And out of the same homily I
have cited a passage in proof of the doctrine
contended for. In the twenty-fourth homily
referred to, I do not meet with any thing
that looks like the doctrine of the saints' final
and total apostacy. In the twenty-sixth he
says, that many who think they have attained
to perfection wander from the grace they have,
by which he means gifts; for he supposes
that a man may have this grace, and yet his
heart not purified, or be a Christian; for as for
Christians, he says, though Satan wars against
them without, they are inwardly safe by the
power of God, and care not for Satan. In
the twenty-seventh homily he indeed cites
Hebrews vi. 4—6, and makes this remark
upon it: " Behold, they that are enlightened,
and have tasted, fall;" which nobody denies.
And in the same page he has these words,
" He that has these things," meaning *gifts,*
" falls; but he that has charity, or love,
aptotos estin, cannot fall."

SECTION XV

HILARIUS PICTAVIENSIS. A. D. 350

HILARY of Poictiers says many things which
favour the doctrine of the saints' perseverance : he often speaks of faith as invincible

---

* Ib. p. 476.   † Hist. Pelag. l. 6, thes.
12, p. 566.   ‡ Contr. Arian. orat. 4, p.
477.   § Homil. 15, p. 96. || Ib. 4. p. 18.

¶ Ib. 19, p. 126.   ** Ib. 12, p. 72.
†† Ib. 21, p. 131.   ‡‡ Hist. Pelag. l.
6, thes. 12, p. 566.

and immoveable. " This is the mystery of divine revelation," says he,* "not only to say, but also to believe, that Christ is the Son of God :—this faith is the foundation of the church, through this faith the gates of hell against it are weak." Again,† " When he (Christ) asked Martha, praying for Lazarus, whether she believed that those that believed in him should never die; she spake out the faith of her own conscience, saying, *Yea, Lord, I believe,* &c. Confessio hæc æternitas est et fides ista non moritur, this confession is eternity, and this faith dies not." In another place he says,‡ " We do not depend on uncertain and idle hopes, as mariners, who, sometimes sailing rather by wishes than in confidence, the wandering and unstable either drive or leave; but we have insuperabilis fidei spiritus dono unigeniti Dei permanens, " the insuperable spirit of faith, through the gift of the only begotten of God,' abiding, and leading us by an unalterable course to the quiet haven." Much the same he says of hope as he does of faith : " By him " (Christ), he observes,§ " we are brought into the hope of eternity, and in this hope we are not confounded; because this same hope, nobis fortitudinis turris est facta, ' is made unto us a tower of strength.' Through this hope we sustain the force of the devil and his snares, being hedged about tutissima fidei munitione, ' with the most safe munition of faith,' against him and his spiritual wickednesses." Hence he represents the case of believers to be such, that there need be no hesitation about enjoying eternal happiness. " The kingdom of heaven," says he,‖ " which the prophets declared, John preached, our Lord professed was in himself, he wills should be hoped for, sine aliqua incertæ voluntatis ambiguitate, ' without any doubtfulness of an uncertain will,' otherwise there is no justification by faith, if faith itself should be doubtful ;" for, as he observes a little after, " In the sayings of God is truth, and all the efficiency of created things is in the Word; wherefore neither what he has promised is doubtful, nor what he speaks is ineffectual." He further intimates, that such as are built upon the foundation, Christ, can never be moved or perish. Commenting on Matthew vii. 24, he says,¶ " By the which the Lord makes himself the strong foundation of a high building, and that he who from him grows up into a sublime work, cannot be moved, either by rains, or floods, or wind; by *rains,* he means the allurements of flattering pleasures, and which sensibly slide into the open chinks, whereby faith is first made wet ; after that, a run of torrents, that is, of motion, of grievous lusts, rush in ; and then the whole force of the winds blowing about, rages ;

namely, the whole breath of devilish power is brought in; but the man built upon the foundation of the rock, insistet, nec moveri loco suo poterit, will stand, nor can he be moved out of his own place." Again, he says,** " A house reared up by men's works does not abide; nor does that stand which is instituted by the doctrines of the world; nor will it be kept by the empty labour of our care; it is to be built up otherways, it is otherways to be kept : it is not to be begun upon the earth, nor upon the fluid sliding sand, but its foundation is to be laid upon the prophets and apostles; it is to be increased with living stones; it is to be held together by the corner-stone ; it is to be built up by the increase of mutual connexion, into a perfect man, and into the measure of the body of Christ : and also to be adorned with the form and beauty of spiritual grace ; this house, so built by God, that is, by his doctrines, *non concidet,* shall not fall." On these words, *the Lord keepeth them that love him,* he has this note,†† " He will save by keeping them, that is, by reserving them to be partakers of the everlasting kingdom ; but they are those who will fear, pray, and love." Once more, he observes,‡‡ that " this is the constitution of invariable truth, in the beginning of the words of God is truth, that the new man, regenerated in Christ, vicat deinceps æternus, ' may henceforth live eternal,' according to the image of the eternal God, that is, of the heavenly Adam."

SECTION XVI.

BASILIUS CÆSARIENSIS. A. D. 370.

BASIL gives plain intimations, that such who are redeemed by Christ, and are truly gracious souls, shall never perish. " He," says he,§§ " that has chosen the narrow and laborious way, before the smooth and easy one, shall not see everlasting corruption : namely, the affliction that shall endure for ever." And a little after, " Persuasions of knowledge, falsely so called, give occasion of death to them that receive them ; which death he shall not see who is redeemed by him, whom it hath pleased *by the foolishness of preaching, to save them that believe.*" Virtue, grace, righteousness, holiness, faith, and such like, he represents as what always remain, and can never be destroyed. "Virtue," he says,‖‖ "is the only possession, *anaphaireton,* ' that cannot be taken away,' and continues with a man living and dying." Again,¶¶ " Holiness and righteousness, which are brought in the room of them (sins), are easy and light ; *kai ouk eidota kumasi kaluphthenai tisi,* and which cannot be covered or borne down by any floods." And elsewhere he observes,*** that " the preaching of the gospel

---

* De Trinitate l. 6. p. 74.   † Ib. p. 78.
‡ Ib. l. 12, p. 182.   § Enarr. in Psalm lx. p. 399, 400.   ‖ Comment. in Matt. can. 5, p. 261, 262.   ¶ Comment. in Matt. can. 6, p. 266.   ** Enarr. in Psalm cxxvi. p. 550.
†† In Psalm. cxliv. p. 638.   ‡‡ In Psalm

cxix. Res, p. 519, 520.   §§ Homil. in Psalm xlviii. p. 283.   ‖‖ Homil. de Legend. Libr. Gentil. p. 575.   ¶¶ Ib. non Adhærend. Reb. Secular. p. 563.   *** Ib. in Psalm xliv. p. 254.

has great power of leading and drawing unto salvation, and every soul is held by its immoveable doctrines, and is by grace confirmed *pros ten adaleuton eis Christon pistin,* in the unshaken faith of Christ." And in another place* the question is asked, " What is the property of faith ?" The answer is, " An undoubted full assurance of the truth of the divine word, which by no reason induced by natural necessity, or having the appearance of piety, διασαλευομενη, can be moved." Once more he observes,† " that because God is in the midst of his own city, he gives it το ασαλευτον, ' stability,' whether this name of a city agrees with the Jerusalem that is above, or the church which is below." Vossius‡ refers us to several of the homilies of this father, as militating against this doctrine of the saints' perseverance ; but in some of them that are referred to, there are very strong expressions in favour of it ; in the first of them he thus says,§ " These words, *I have loved because the Lord hath heard the voice of my prayer,* seem to be equivalent to the words of the apostle, and to be said with the same affection by the prophet as by the apostle, *Who shall separate us from the love of Christ! Shall tribulation,* &c. Therefore I have loved all those things, knowing that I can bear those dangers for the sake of godliness." And a little after, says he, " Not that I can by my own power strive against those sorrows ; but because I have called upon the name of the Lord." In the second stands this passage,‖ " Prudence itself will give to one that builds a house to lay the foundation upon a rock ; that is, to found it in the faith of Christ, *ωστε ασειστον διαμενειν,* that it may abide immoveable and firm." And in the last of them, he observes,¶ " that we are not angels, but men, and fall and rise again, and that often in the same hour ;" and instances in David and Peter ; and of the latter he says, that " though he was a rock, yet he was not a rock as Christ ; for Christ truly is the immoveable rock ; but Peter so, because of the rock." In the third of them he does indeed say,** that " sin abolishes the grace given us by the washing of regeneration ; and that sin precedes the loss of grace, which is given through the humanity of our Lord Jesus Christ." But what he means by that grace is not very evident. And in the fourth†† he says, that " the Spirit must needs excel them that receive, and are sanctified by him, when he comes ; but are corrupted, he leaving them ; he himself always being the fountain of everlasting life." But then this must be understood of such who receive him not aright, for, as he elsewhere‡‡ expresses himself, " The saints receive water springing up unto eternal life,

which *opes gignetai en tois kalos labousi* in them that receive it rightly, it becomes so."

SECTION XVII

GREGORIUS NAZIANZENUS. A. D. 350

GREGORY of Nazianzum has several expressions in his writings which favour the doctrine of the saints' perseverance. He says,§§ " A man may possess such a habit of virtue, *oste kai schedon adunaton, genesthai ten peri ta geiro poran,* so as that it is almost impossible that he should be carried away to that which is evil." And as for the grace of faith, he says,‖‖ " that only of all things is *αναλωτον* inexpugnable." And elsewhere,¶¶ for the consolation of the people of God under reproaches and afflictions, he thus expresses himself ; " Are we reproached ? Let us bless them that do ill. Are we spit upon? Let us study to have honour from God. Are we made to fly ? Not from God, *τουτ' ουκ αφαιρετον γε των παντων μονον,* this alone of all things cannot be taken away." With what exultation and joy does he express himself in a view of interest in Christ ! " O, my Christ," says he,*** " thou art my portion, which to have is better than to have all things else, *monon bebaion ktematon kai eleutheron,* this is the only firm and free possession." Those who fall off from a profession of faith, and desert the interest of Christ and religion, he represents††† as such " who never were sown *epi ten sterean petran kai aseiston,* ' upon the firm and unshaken rock, but upon dry and barren land ;' these are they who come to the word in a superficial way, and are of little faith ; and because they have no depth of earth, suddenly arise, and looking to please others, after a short assault of the evil one, and a little temptation and heat, are withered and die." Vossius‡‡‡ refers to a passage in this writer§§§ as militating against this doctrine ; in which Gregory advises such as are cleansed " to keep themselves, lest the issue of blood should flow again, and they not be able to lay hold on Christ ; and such who have been made whole to sin no more, lest a worse thing should befal them, and should appear to be evil, after having received a great and considerable benefit ; and such who had heard that great voice, " Lazarus, come forth ;" and were come forth, to take heed lest they die again, when it would be uncertain, whether they would be raised again until the last and common resurrection." These expressions, it must be owned, do seem to intimate, that persons may be purged, and yet perish ; be made whole, and yet lost ; be quickened, and yet die again. But then they must be imputed to this author's great zeal for the good of souls, and care of them,

---

* Moral. c. 22, p. 386.   † Hom. in Psalm xlv. p. 270.   ‡ Hist Pelag. l. 6, thes. 12, p. 566.   § Homil. in Psalm cxiv. p. 307.   ‖ Ib. in Princip. Prov. p. 461.   ¶ Ib. de Pœnitentia, p. 618, 619.   ** Ib. in aliquot Script. loc. p. 546.   †† Contr. Eunom. l. 5, p. 139.   ‡‡ Homil. in Psalm. xxviii. p.

173.   §§ Greg. Nazianzem. orat. 31, p. 508, tom. i.   ‖‖ Ib. orat. 4, p. 133.   ¶¶ Ib. Carmen. Jambic. 21, p. 234, tom ii.   *** Ib. p. 252.   ††† Ib. orat. 3, p. 53, tom. i.   ‡‡‡ Hist. Pelag. l. 6, thes. 12, p. 566.   §§§ Orat. 40, p. 662, tom. i.

and concern for them, and to his earnestness in cautioning of them against sin, and advising them to that which is good.

SECTION XVIII
GREGORIUS NYSSENUS. A. D. 380

GREGORY of Nyssa gives plain intimations of the security of the saints, and the perpetuity of grace where it is once implanted. Having taken notice of Balaam's being sent for to curse Israel, which he was not able to do, he makes this remark on it;* "Hence we understand that no enchantment is effectual against those who live virtuously; but such being satiated through divine assistance, *pases uperischuein epiboules*, prevail over every snare." And in another place he observes,† that "the earth first apostatized through sin, but now, through the knowledge of God has a firm standing; we are all God's earth, who were first unstable in that which is good, and therefore became a curse; but afterwards, being delivered from the curse, we again obtain a standing in that which is good." And a little after, he makes this observation on Psalm xcvii. 1, "Beautifully he calls the souls of them that show *to edraion te kai ametatheton*, 'firmness and immoveableness in temptations, isles ;' whom the salt waters of wickedness surround on every side, and yet dash not against them with so much strength *os kai salon tina to pagio tes aretes empoiesai*, as to cause any fluctuation in the firmness of virtue." Psalm lii. 8, he explains of such an one‡ "that is rooted in the house of God as a fruitful olive tree, *kai to edraion te kai ametakineton tou kata ten pistin stereomatos en eauto bebaiosas*, and has the firm and immoveable ground of faith established in himself." He more than once represents the grace of faith as permanent and lasting. The good of the sons of men, which Solomon desired to see, he says,§ "appears to him to be no other than the work of faith, whose energy is common to all; being equally set before them that will, and is *pantodunamos kai diarkos te zoe paramenousa*, all-powerful, and abides in life continually." And elsewhere,‖ speaking of the saints' spiritual armour, among other things he observes, that "the shield, which is a piece of armour that covers, is, *e arrages pistis*, faith that cannot be broken." He says the same of all other graces: explaining the *beams of the house* in Cant. i. 17, "These," says he,¶ "should be the virtues, which do not admit the floods of temptations within themselves, *sterrai te ousai kai anendotoi*, 'being firm, solid, and not giving way,' and preserve in temptations from being softened into wickedness." And in another place,** says he, "He describes the house of virtue, whose matter for covering is cedar and cypress, which are not susceptible of rottenness and corruption; by which he expresses *to monimon te kai ametableton tes pros to agathon scheseos*, the permanency and immutability of the habit to that which is good." Now all this he ascribes, not to the saints themselves, but to God; he observes,†† that "David says, *Theou ergon to en eusebeia kratunein ton anthropon*, 'it is the work of God to confirm a man in piety;' *for thou art my strength and my refuge*, says the prophet, and *the Lord is the strength of his people ;* and, *the Lord will give strength unto his people.*"

SECTION XIX
HILARIUS DIACONUS. A. D. 380

HILARY, the deacon, puts perseverance upon the foot of election, and intimates, that the reason why any persevere, is because they are elected; and that if any who have thought to have been believers do not persevere, it is a plain case that they never were elected. "Those," says he,‡‡ "whom God foreknew would be devoted to him, them he chose to enjoy the promised rewards; that those who *seem* to believe and *do not* continue in the faith begun, may he denied to be God's elect; quia quos Deus eligit apud se permanent, for whom God hath chosen, they continue with him." And a little after, "Whom God foreknew to be fit for himself, these continue believers, quia aliter fieri non potest, 'for it cannot be otherwise,' but that whom God foreknows, them he also justifies, and so hereby glorifies them, that they may be like the Son of God. As to the rest, whom God has not foreknown, he takes no care of them in this grace, because he has not foreknown them; but if they believe, or are chosen for a time, because they *seem* good, lest righteousness should be thought to be despised, they do not continue that they may be glorified; as Judas Iscariot, or the seventy-two, who, being chosen, afterwards were offended, and departed from the Saviour." Again,§§ "Whom God is said to call, they persevere in faith ; hi sunt quos eligit ante mundum in Christo, 'these are they whom he has *chosen in Christ before the world began*,' that they may be unblameable before God in love." And in another place he observes, that some persons may seem to be in the number of good men, when, according to God's prescience, they are in the number of evil men ;‖‖ "Hence God saith to Moses, *if any one sins before me, I will blot them out of my book.* So that, according to the righteousness of the judge, he then seems to be blotted out, when he sins ; but according to prescience, nunquam in libro vitæ fuisse, 'he never was in the book of life.' Hence the apostle John says of such, *They went out from us, but they were*

---

* Greg. Nyssen. de Vita Mosis, vol. i. p. 250.
† Ib. in Psalm, c. 9, p. 316.   ‡ Ib. c. 13, p. 339.   § Ib. in Eccles. homil, 2, p. 395.
‖ Ib. 8, p. 463.   ¶ Ib. in Cant. homil. 4, p. 523.   ** Ib. homil. 6, p. 557.

†† Gregor. contr. Eunom. orat. 1, p. 68, vol. ii.   ‡‡ Comment. in Rom. p. 294 ; vide p. 304.   §§ In Ephes. p. 492.   ‖‖ In Rom. p. 299.

not of us, &c. 1 John ii. 19." He represents a believer's love to Christ as insuperable, and the love of God in Christ to him as inseparable. Of the former he says,[*] "no torments overcome the love of a firm Christian." And of the latter,[†] "there is *nothing that can separate us from the love of God which is in Christ Jesus*." "This confidence," he says,[‡] "arises from the engagement of Christ, by which he has promised to help in tribulation that faith which is devoted to him." And as to *faith* itself, he says it is[§] res æterna "an everlasting thing," written by the Spirit, that it may abide. To which add another observation of his,[‖] "Because God hath promised to give the heavenly kingdom to them that love him, et det necesse est, 'and he must needs give it,' because he is faithful; therefore he is present with them that are afflicted for him; nor will he suffer so much to be laid upon them as cannot be borne; but will either make the temptation to cease quickly, or if it should be long, will give power to bear it, otherwise he will not bestow what he has promised; because he that suffers will be overcome; for man is subject to weakness, and there will be none to deliver; but because God is faithful who has promised, he helps, that it may fulfil what he has promised." Vossius[¶] refers us to the commentary of this writer upon the ninth of the Romans, but therein does not appear any thing against, but for the saints' perseverance, as has been already cited out of it.

SECTION XX.

AMBROSIUS MEDIOLANENSIS. A.D. 380

AMBROSE, of Milain, says many things in favour of the saints' perseverance; he speaks of it as a thing certain, and not at all to be doubted of. "There is nothing," says he,[**] " we may fear can be denied us, nothing in which we ought to doubt of the continuance of divine goodness; the abundance of which has been so daily and constant, as that first he should predestinate, then call, and *whom he calls he justifies*, and *whom he justifies them he also glorifies*. Can he forsake those, whom he follows with such benefits of his own, even unto rewards? Among so many blessings of God, are the snares of the accuser to be feared? But who dare accuse them, who in the judgment are counted the elect? Can God the Father himself rescind his own gifts, who has bestowed them, and banish them from the grace of paternal affection, whom he, by adoption, has received? But it is feared, lest the judge should be more severe. Consider what judge thou must have; the Father hath given all judgment to Christ. ' Can he damn them whom he has redeemed

from death?' For whom he offered himself, whose life, he knows, is the reward of his own death?" And in another place he observes,[††] that "*many waters cannot quench love ;* so that thy love cannot be lessened by any persecution, which many waters cannot exclude, nor floods overflow. Whence is this? Consider that thou hast received the spiritual seal, the spirit of wisdom and understanding, the spirit of counsel and might, the spirit of knowledge and piety, the spirit of holy fear; and keep what thou hast received. God the Father hath sealed thee; Christ the Lord hath confirmed thee, and hath given the pledge of the Spirit in thine heart." Again he says[‡‡] "The righteous man falls sometimes, but if he is righteous, *though he falls he shall not be confounded*. What is of nature falls, what is of righteousness rises again; for God does not forsake the righteous, but confirms his hands." And in another place,[§§] " His (the good man's) soul does not perish for ever; neither does any one snatch it out of the hand of the Almighty, Father or Son; for the hand of God, that established the heavens, quos tenuerit non admittit, does not lose whom it holds." *Faith* he not only represents as firm itself, but says,[‖‖] that it is the stable foundation of all virtues; and speaks of grace in general as perpetual. " This," says he,[¶¶] " is the alone possession, which being obnoxious to no tempests, brings forth the fruit of perpetual grace." And though the church of Christ, saints, righteous ones, true believers, are liable to many afflictions, temptations, and trials, yet he intimates that he shall be preserved in the midst of all. " *Zebulon shall dwell by the sea*," he observes,[***] " that he may see the shipwrecks of others, whilst he himself is free from danger; and behold others fluctuating in the straits of this world, who are carried about with every wind of doctrine, whilst he perseveres immoveable in the root of faith; as the holy church is rooted and founded in faith; beholding the storms of heretics, and shipwrecks of Jews, because they have denied the governor they had." And in another place,[†††] " The ship is the church, which though this world is a sort of a troublesome sea to it daily, it is not dashed against the rock, nor sunk to the bottom." Again,[‡‡‡] "The soul, which deserves to be called the temple of God, or the church, is beaten with the floods of worldly cares, but not overturned; it is stricken, but not destroyed." Once more,[§§§] " The righteous, placed in the house of God, and intent on the word of God, are indeed tried by worldly afflictions, but not estranged from the house of God, and from the keeping of the heavenly commands." All which preservation from evil, and continuance from

---

* Ib. p. 295.   † Ib. p. 296.   ‡ Ibid.
§ In 2 Cor. p. 419.   ‖ In 1 Cor. p. 379.
¶ Hist. Pelag. 1, thes. 12, p. 567.
** Do Jacob. l. 1, c. 6, p. 317.   †† De
Initand. c. 7, p. 349.   ‡‡ Enarrat. in Psalm
xxxvi. p. 700.   §§ In Psalm cxix. Nun, p.

1002.   ‖‖ In Psalm xl. p. 753.   ¶¶ De
Cain et Abel, l. 2, c. 3, p. 154.   *** De
Benedict. Patriarch, c. 5, p. 408.   ††† De
Salomone, c. 4, p. 1093.   ‡‡‡ De Araham. l.
2, c. 3, p. 247.   §§§ Ib. c. 5, p. 249.

grace, he ascribes not to the power of man, but to the grace of God. "Perseverance," says he,* " is neither of man that willeth or runneth ; non est enim in hominis potestate, ' for it is not in the power of man,' but it is of God that showeth mercy, that thou canst fulfil what thou hast begun." There are many other passages † which countenance this doctrine I forbear to transcribe.

SECTION XXI

JOANNES CHRYSOSTOMUS. A. D. 390

CHRYSOSTOM represents the church, and all the people of God, as invincible, and the graces of faith and hope as always abiding. "He calls the church," says he,‡ "a mountain, *to ton dogmaton akatagoniston,* ' being as to its doctrines inexpugnable;" for a thousand armies may encamp against mountains, bending their bows, wielding their shields, and using stratagems, but cannot hurt them, and when they have destroyed their own power go away; so likewise all they that war against the church, *tauten men ouk eseisan,* cannot move her." Again,§ " Neither the tyrant, nor the populace, nor *battalias* of devils, nor the devil himself, *perige esthai auton ischusen,* are able to prevail against them, the saints." He not only observes,‖ that faith is a foundation, and the rest the building; but ¶ calls it *tes petras tes arragous,* " the unbroken rock;" and adds, "neither rivers nor winds falling upon us can do us any hurt, for we stand unshaken upon the rock." And elsewhere,** " Well does he say, *in which we stand ;* for such is the grace of God, that *ouk echei telos, ouk eide peras,* it has no end, it knows no bounds." And in another place he observes,†† that the apostle "rightly calls faith a *shield,* for as that is cast about the whole body, being as a wall, so is faith, *panta gar aute eikei,* ' for all things give way to it ;' *wherewith,*" says he, " *ye shall be able to quench all the fiery darts of the evil one ; ouden gar dunatai touton ton thureon diakopsai,* seeing nothing is able to cut this shield in pieces." And elsewhere he asks,‡‡ " Are our good things in hopes ? In hopes, but not human ; these fail, and often make the man that hopes ashamed ; or he dies, who is expected to do these things ; or if he lives, he changes ; ours are not such, *alla bebaia kai akinetos e elpis,* but our hope is firm and immovable." There are two or three places in this writer referred to by Vossius,§§ against the saint's perseverance, which have not occurred to me ; and the last of these references is to

a homily, which, and many others with it, he owns is none of his, but a collection from him ; and, as he observes,‖‖ is not to be depended upon as genuine ; it being usual with such collectors to add things foreign to the doctrine of Chrysostom, and out of other authors.

SECTION XXII.

HIERONYMUS. A. D. 390

JEROM says many things which countenance the doctrine of the perseverance of the church, of righteous persons, true believers, and regenerate ones. Upon Amos ix. 14, he has this note,¶¶ " From hence we understand, that the church, to the end of the world, will be shaken indeed with persecution, sed nequaquam posse subverti, ' but can in nowise be overthrown;' will be attempted but not overcome ; and this will be, because the Lord God omnipotent, or the Lord God of it, that is, of the church, hath promised that he will do it." And in another place says,*** " We know that the church, in faith, hope and love, is inaccessible and inexpugnable, there is none in it immature, every one is docible ; impetu irrumpere vel arte illudere potest nullus, no one by force can break in upon it, or by art illude it." And elsewhere he observes,††† that " as the islands are indeed smitten with frequent whirlwinds, storms, and tempests, but are not overthrown, for an example of the evangelic house, which is founded upon a rock of a mighty bulk ; so the churches which hope in the law, and in the name of the Lord the Saviour, speak by Isaiah, saying, I am a strong city, a city which is not assaulted;'. that is, so as to be taken and destroyed. Much like to this is his remark‡‡‡ on Isa. li. 5, " The right hand and arm of the Lord is he who saves for himself those who first were lost, ut nullus periret de his quos ei Pater dederat, ' that none of them might perish whom the Father had given to him ;' for that either the souls of the saints, who in the midst of the persecutions of this world, arma in Deum solididatæ sunt fide, ' are established with a firm faith in God,' or the multitude of churches among the Gentiles, are called isles, we have frequently declared." Having mentioned§§§ Prov. xxiv. 17, he puts these questions, " If he falls, how is he just ? If just, how does he fall?" which he answers thus, "but he does not lose the name of a just man, who by repentance, always rises again :" moreover, having cited Psalm xcii. 12, he explains it after this manner,‖‖‖ " They that are planted in the

---

* In Psalm cxix. Jod, p. 963.   † Vide Euarrat. in Ps. xl. p. 762 ; in Ps. xliii. p. 790 ; in Ps. cxix. Daleth, p. 903 ; in Prov. c. 31, cap. 3, p. 1099.   ‡ Comment. in Isa. ii. 2, tom. i. p. 1030.   § In Rom. 8, homil. 15, tom. iii. p. 131.   ‖ In Heb. 6, homil. 8, p. 431.
¶ In 1 Tim. vi. 20, homil. 18, tom. iv. p. 326.
** In Rom. v. 2, homil. 9, tom. iii. p. 66.
†† In Eph. vi. homil. 24, tom. iii. p. 888.

‡‡ In Rom. v. 5, homil. 9, tom. iii. p. 67.
§§ Hist. Pelag. l. 6, thes. 12, p. 566, 567.
‖‖ Vide Rivet. Critic. Sacr. l. 4, c. 1, p. 355.
¶¶ Hieron. Comment. in Amos, tom. 6, p. 50,
*** Ib. adv. Jovinian. l. 1, tom. ii. p. 7,
††† Hieron. ad Algasiam, tom. iii. p. 51,
‡‡‡ Ib. comment. in Isa. tom. v. p. 86,
§§§ Ib. ad Rusticum, tom. i. p. 76, E.
‖‖‖ Ib. adv. Pelag. l. ii. tom. ii. p. 97, C.

M. D. L, M. C.

house of the Lord are just men in ecclesia conformati, 'established in the church;' but they, not at present, but hereafter shall flourish in the courts of the Lord, where there is a pure and safe possession." And, says he,[*] in another place, "Dost thou say that the resurrection is of the soul, or of the flesh? I answer, Which with the soul is regenerated in the laver; *Et quomodo peribit quæ in Christo renata est*, And how shall that perish which is regenerated in Christ?" And elsewhere he observes,[†] that "he who with his whole mind trusts in Christ, though as a fallen man he was dead in sin, fide sua vivit in perpetuum, by his faith lives for ever." Once more, "The building," says he,[‡] "which is laid upon the foundation of Christ, of which the apostle speaks, as a wise master builder, I have laid the foundation, nunquum destruetur, sed permanebit in perpetuam, shall never be destroyed, but shall abide for ever." He asserts the security of the saints, notwithstanding all the efforts and attempts of Satan by his power and policy to destroy them. "He" (the devil,) says he,[§] "will endeavour to enter into Judah, that is, the house of confession, and frequently, through them who are negligent in the church, he will come up even to the neck, desiring to suffocate believers in Christ; and he will stretch out his wings, filling the whole country of Immanuel, sed non poterit obtinere, quia habet Judas præsentem Deum, but cannot obtain, because Judah has God present with him." Upon Isaiah xiv. 16, he makes this remark,[||] "He shook, he does not overthrow; hence one of them that were shaken, and yet did not fall, says, my feet were almost gone; and the apostle speaks to believers to take the armour of God, and stand against the snares of the devil. The house indeed which is founded on a rock, is not shaken by any tempest; that is, so as to be overthrown. He has another passage to the same effect.[¶] "When," says he, "the devil shall come, who is, by interpretation, the reprover and corrector, upon the land and country of believers, and of them whom the Lord shall feed, in the strength and in the majesty of the Lord his God; and he, the devil, shall tread upon them through various tribulations, and as a proud man shall ascend and depress the houses of our souls, that is, our bodies, et tamen nihil nos a Christi charitate separaverit, yet nothing shall separate us from the love of Christ." The grace of love he more than once represents as that which shall abide, and never be lost. Upon Matthew xxxiv. 12, he has this note;[**] "He does not deny the faith of all, but many, *for many are called, but few chosen;* for in the apostles, *et similibus eorum, permansura est charitas*, 'and them that are like them, love remains;' concerning which it is written in Cant. viii. 7, Rom viii. 35." And in another place he expresses himself thus;[††] "And, because love never fails, he who is in the soundness of love," that is, as he explains it in the same place, "who loves the Lord with all his soul, with all his heart, and with all his strength, nunquam et ipse corruit, he himself also never falls,' according to Romans viii. 35."

Now this perseverance and continuance in grace he denies is owing to the free will of man, but is to be ascribed to the mercy and power of God; which he concludes[‡‡] from 2 Thess. iii. 3, ergo non liberi arbitrii potestate sed Dei clementia conservamur, "therefore," says he, "we are preserved, not by the power of free will, but by the clemency of God." And a little after,[§§] having mentioned the words of Christ to Peter in Luke xxii. 32, he thus addresses the Pelagians; et certe juxto vos in apostoli erat positum potestate, si voluisset, ut non deficeret fides ejus, "but truly, according to you, it was in the power of the apostle, if he would, that his faith should not fail." Jerom does indeed sometimes[||||] speak of the Spirit of God being taken away and quenched; but then, by the Spirit, he means the gifts of the Spirit, such as are mentioned in 1 Cor. xii. 8—10. The text in Eccl. vii. 15, he understands,[¶¶] not of one that is really just, but of one who seems to himself to be so. It must be owned that there are some expressions of Jerom's here and there, which are not easy to be reconciled either with himself or this doctrine; as when he seems[***] to make the perpetuity of God's gifts to depend upon the worthiness of men, and men's continuance of grace to lie in the power of their wills, contrary to what he at other times asserted, which has been already observed; as also when he says that "God indeed has[†††] planted, and no man can root up his plantation; but because this planting is in his own free will, no other can root up, nisi ipsa præbuerit assensum, unless that assents to it." And in another place he says,[‡‡‡] that "though no one can pluck out of the hand of God, yet he that is held may fall out of the hand of God, propria voluntate, by his own will." And again, that "he who is like an adamant stone, which cannot be hurt or overcome by any, yet may be dissolved by the alone heat of deadly lust." And this he says[§§§] after he had expressed the doctrine of the saints' perseverance in a very strong manner. Moreover, he asserts,[||||||] that the Ethiopians may, upon repentance, become the children of God;

---

 * Ib. adv. Error. Joan. Hierosol. p. 60, E.
 † Ib. ad Minerium, tom. iii. p. 62, 1.
 ‡ Ib. Comment. in Hieremiam, tom. v. p. 160, F; vide etiam Comment. in Oseam, tom. 6, p. 20, K, p. 21, G. § Ib. Comment. in Isa. tom. v. p. 17, F. ‖ Ib. p. 37, E.
 ¶ Hieron. Comment. in Mich. tom. vi. p. 68, C. ** Ib. in Matt. tom. ix. p. 33, B, C.

 †† Ib. in Tit. p. 110, M. ‡‡ Ib. adv. Pelag. l. 1, tom. ii. p. 9. 95, E. §§ Ib. p. 96, F.
 ‖‖ Ib. ad Hedib. tom. iii. p. 49, L. p. 50, C.
 ¶¶ Ib. Comment. in Isa. tom. v. p. 50, B.
 *** Ib. in Hieremiam, tom. v. p. 150, G.
 ††† Ib. in Matt. tom. ix. p. 23. B. ‡‡‡ Ib. in Oseam, tom. vi. p. 10, L. §§§ Hieron Comment. in Amos, p. 47, A. ‖‖‖ Ib. p. 50, C.

and the children of God, by falling into sin, may become Ethiopians; and yet in the same leaf stands a testimony to the doctrine of perseverance, which is cited above. But these must be reckoned among Jerom's unguarded expressions, by which we are not to form a judgment of his sentiments against the numerous testimonies produced to the contrary.

CHAPTER VI

OF THE HEATHENS

To the doctrine of the ancients, concerning the necessity of grace to the performance of every good work, the Pelagians objected the virtues and famous actions of the heathens. These Vossius, a favourite author of Dr. Whitby's* has largely proved, under various theses or propositions, to want all the conditions requisite in good works; such as doing them according to the law of God, in love to him, from faith in him, and with a view to his glory; and that " though some few of the ancients were of opinion, that the more virtuous among the heathens, such as Socrates and others, were saved, yet this notion was condemned of old by the other *fathers*, especially in the time of Austin." The collection which Dr. Whitby† has made out of the *fathers*, is very little to the purpose, chiefly relating to the endowments of nature, the blessings of providence, and temporal favours bestowed on heathens in common with others, denied by none. The principal testimonies in favour of the good works and salvation of the heathens are taken from Justin Martyr, Clement of Alexandria, Chrysostom, and Jerom; but these, as Dr. Edwards observes,‡ at least some of them, had been bred in a philosophical way themselves, and so had retained a charity for that sort of men, yea, thought better of them than they deserved. Besides, should these testimonies be examined, they will not be found so full and express as they are thought to be; and other passages of these writers may be produced, contradicting of them. As to Justin Martyr, when he says, that such as Socrates and Heraclitus were Christians, he does not mean, as a learned man of our nation has observed,§ that they were perfectly, only in part so; that is, as they were partakers of and lived according to the *logos*, or *reason*, which Christ, the Word and Son of God, imparts to every man. And as to Clement of Alexandria, Vossius has clearly shown,‖ that he could not say or think, that any could be saved without faith, and without the knowledge of Christ; which he supposed the heathens had

through Christ's descent into hell, and preaching to them there. Nor that he could mean that the philosophy of the Greeks was sufficient to salvation, only at most, that it was one degree towards, or what had a tendency to lead to Christ. And though Chrysostom says, that before the coming of Christ, they that did not confess him might be saved, yet he elsewhere affirms,¶ that the works of men ignorant of God, are like to the garments of the dead, who are insensible of them; his words are these; " They that labour in good works, and know not the God of piety, are like *leipsanois neeron*, ' to the remains of the dead, who are clothed with beautiful garments but have no sense of them.' " And though Jerom talks in one place,** of " the knowledge of God being by nature in all, and that no man is born without Christ, and hath not in himself the seeds of wisdom and justice, and other virtues; whence many without faith, and the gospel of Christ, do some things either wisely or holily;" yet in another place he says,†† " Let us bring forth that sentence *(The just shall live by faith)* against those who, not believing in Christ, think themselves to be strong, wise, temperate, and just; that they may know that no man liveth without Christ, *sine quo omnis virtus in vitio est*, without whom all virtue is to be reckoned for vice." To which I shall add two or three testimonies more, showing that the virtues of the heathens were not properly good works, but had only a show of them, and were insufficient to salvation, and conclude, says Origen,‡‡ " if a conversation of good manners were sufficient to men for salvation, how is it that the philosophers among the Gentiles, or many among heretics, *continenter viventes nequaquam salvantur*, ' who live soberly, are not saved?' but because the falsity of their doctrine darkens and defiles their conversation." Again he observes§§ from Peter in Clement, " that good works which are done by unbelievers profit them in this world, *non et in illo ad consequendam vitam æternam*, but not to obtain eternal life in the other." Cyprian has these words;‖‖ " The philosophers also profess to follow this (patience), but as their wisdom is false, so is their patience: for how can he be either wise or patient, *qui nec sapientiam nec patientiam Dei novit*, who neither knows the wisdom nor patience of God?" Ambrose¶¶ expresses himself in this manner, " Virtues, without faith, are leaves; they seem to be green, but cannot profit; they are moved with the wind, because they have no foundation. How many heathens have mercy, have sobriety! but they have no fruit, *quia fidem non habent*, because they have no faith."

---

* Hist. Pelag. l. 3, par 3, p. 358 ad 379.
† Discourse, &c. p. 550, &c.; ed. 2. 527, &c.
‡ Veritas Redux, p. 439. § Bulli Judicium, Eccl. Cathol. de necess. credendi quod Christ. sit Deus, append. ad c. 7, p. 201, &c.
‖ Hist. Pelag. l. 3, par. 3, p. 376, 377.

¶ Serm. de Fid. et Leg. Nat. tom. vi. p. 838.
** Comment. in Gal. p. 70, M.   †† Ib. p. 76, B.   ‡‡ In Matt. hom. 27, fol. 53.
§§ Ib. 35, fol. 74; vide etiam Comment. in Rom. l. 2, fol. 142. ‖‖ De Bono Patientiæ, p. 313.   ¶¶ Enarrat. in Ps. i. p. 665.

A TABLE

OF THE

ANCIENT WRITERS CITED IN THIS FOURTH PART

WITH THE

EDITIONS OF THEM MADE USE OF IN IT

AMBROSE *Ed.* Paris 1661.
ANTHONY, *in Bibl. patr. Ed. Tertia,* Paris 1610, *per marg, de la Bigne.*
ARNOBIUS, Hanov, 1503, *cum notis Elmenhorst.*
ATHANASIUS, Colon 1686.
ATHENAGORAS, *ad calcem Justini,*
BARNABAS, *ad calcem Ignatii.*
BASIL, Paris 1618,
CHRONOMATIUS, Eton 1612, *a Savilio*
CHURCH at Symrna, *apud Euseb. Hist. Eccl.*
CLEMENT of Alexandria, Paris 1631.
CLEMENT of Rome, Oxon, 1669.
CYPRIAN, Paris 1643.
CYRIL, Oxon, 1703, *a Milles.*
DIDYMUS, *inter opera Hieronymi.*
EPIPHANUS, Colon, 1682.
EUSEBIUS, *Hist. Eccl.* Mogunt 1672. *Preparat. Evangel. et. Demonstr. Evang.* Colon, 1688. *juxta Ed,* Paris 1628.
FAUSTINUS, Oxen, 1678,
FIRMICUS, Oxen, 1662,
GAUDENTIUS, *in Bibl. patrum.* Paris 1610,
GREGORY of Nazianzum, Paris 1628
GREGORY of Neocaesarea, Paris 1621,
GREGORY of Nyssa, Paris, 1615,
HILARY of Poictiers, Basil 1570.
HILARY the Deacon, *inter Ambrosii opera.*

JEROM, *per Erasmus.*
IGNATIUS, Lond. 1680. *a Vossio.*
IRENÆUS, Paris 1675.
JUSTIN, Paris 1636.
LACTANTIUS, Genev. 1630.
MACARIUS, Paris 1621,
MARK the Eremite, *in Bibl. patrum,* Paris 1610.
The MARTYRS of France, *apud Euseb. Eccl, Hist*
MIMUTIUS FELIX, Oxon, 1662,
NOVATIAN, *inter opera Tertullian,*
OPTATUS, Paris 1679.
ORIGEN, *Opera Lat. per Merlin,* Paris 1512, *Gr. .Lat. ab Huetio.* Colon 1685, *Contr. Cels. a Spencero.* Cantabr. 1670.
PACTANIUS, *in Bibl. patr.* Paris 1610.
PAULINUS, of Tyre, *apud Euseb. Hist. Eccl.*
POLYCARP, *apud Euseb. Hist. Eccl.*
RUFFINUS, *inter opera Hieronymi,*
TATIAN, *ad calcem Justini.*
TERTTULLIAN, Paris 1634.
THEOPHILUS of Alexandria, *inter opera Hieronymi,*
THEOPHILUS of Antioch, *ad calcem Justini,*
VICTORINUS *in Bibl, patr,* Paris 1610,

A VINDICATION

OF A BOOK ENTITLED

THE CAUSE OF GOD AND TRUTH

PART IV

RELATING TO THE SENSE OF THE ANCIENT CHRISTIAN WRITERS, ABOUT SOME THINGS IN CONTROVERSY WITH THE ARMINIANS, FROM THE CAVILS, CALUMNIES, AND DEFAMATIONS OF MR. HENRY HEYWOOD, &c.

HAVING published, some time ago, an Answer to the Birmingham Dialogue-Writer's Second Part, I annexed a postscript to it, relating to some charges brought against me by one Mr. Henry Heywood, in an introduction of his to a translation of *Dr. Whitby's Treatise of Original Sin.* This postscript, containing my answer to the said charges, it seems, is not relished by him and his friends, and has produced a defamatory pamphlet, wrote either by himself or some of his party, entitled *A Defence of Dr. Whitby's Treatise of Original Sin,* &c. I say, wrote either by himself, or some of his party—for I greatly suspect that this piteous performance is done by some other person or persons, and published under his name; since, if my information is right, this man was gone for Carolina some months before the publication of this pamphlet; which, had it been drawn up and finished by himself before his departure, might have been published in *ten days'* time. The temper and genius of a certain person, not very remarkable for candour and good-nature, are pretty visible in it; but, whoever be the author or authors, revisers and editors of it, they ought to look upon themselves concerned in the guilt and shame arising from the blunders and scandal which are manifestly in it, as will appear by the following examination of it :—

I. The *first* charge brought against me is mistranslation, of which *three* instances are given, and to which I have replied ; the sum of the difference between us is, I have rendered *plaga*, in Irenæus, *plague ;* this man, sometimes *wound ;* and, at another time, *sore*, and sometimes *disease ;* I have interpreted *recenseatur*, in Tertullian, *re-reckoned*, or *reckoned anew ;* he, *enrolled anew ;* I have translated *damnatio*, in the same author, *damnation*, he *condemnation*. I shall not contend with him about words : the reader may choose and prefer which translation he pleases. What is more material, is the pertinence of these passages to the point in hand, the sense of them, and whether any injury is done thereunto. And,

1. As to the passage in Irenæus, whether *antiqua serpentis plaga* be rendered *the old blow*, or *stroke*, or *wound*, or *sore*, or *plague*, or *disease of the serpent*, it certainly intends some hurt or mischief done by the old serpent, the devil, to our first parents, and to all mankind. This man says that Irenæus, by this *pestilential disorder* (and which surely, then, must be a *plague*,) with which the old serpent has *infected* mankind, understands not *original corruption*, or the *vitiosity* whereby man's nature is depraved, but only *death and mortality*. But let the words of Irenæus[*] be produced and considered, which are these : " Men cannot else be saved from the old wound (the pestilential disorder) of the serpent, *nisi credant in eum*, except they believe on him, who, in the likeness of sinful flesh, was lifted up from the earth, on the tree of martyrdom, who draws all things to himself, and quickens the dead." Now, are they that believe in Christ saved by him from mortality and death ? Are they not as liable to mortality ? And do they not labour under the same diseases of body, and die a corporal death, as other men do ? Are these the persons only that will be cured of this mortal disorder, the disease of death, by a resurrection from the dead ? Will there not be a resurrection of the just and unjust, believers and unbelievers ? Who then can conceive that this should be the meaning of Irenæus ? As to the passage which Dr. Whitby cites in

favour of the sense this author from him has espoused, it makes more against him than for him ; for Irenæus[†] does not say that *plaga*, the disorder itself, but *dolor plagæ*, " the pain of it," or what arises from it, " with which men was stricken in the beginning, *in Adam inobediens*, 'being disobedient in Adam ;' this is the death which God will cure, by raising us from the dead, and restoring us to our forefathers' inheritance." So that corporeal death, according to Irenæus, is not the blow, the disorder itself, but what arises from it is the fruit and effect of it. Besides, how he, or any other man, can imagine that even mortality and death should be inflicted on men for Adam's disobedience, unless they are involved in the guilt of it, or that is reckoned to them, which is what we contend for, is unaccountable. And further, it may be observed, that we have here another testimony from this ancient writer in favour of our sentiments, when he says, " man was disobedient in Adam," as elsewhere,[‡] " he offended in him," which is entirely agreeable to, and confirms our sense of, Rom. v. 12, *in whom all have sinned :* for the reason which [§] Dr. Whitby gives of his use of such phrases, "because we were born of Adam after he was overcome by sin, we receive our name from him," is exceeding trifling, and ridiculous to the last degree, Upon the whole, since our Lord Jesus Christ saves those that believe in him, not from mortality and a corporeal death, but as from their actual transgressions, so from original sin ; from the corruption and vitiosity of their nature ; from the damning power of it, by his death ; and from its governing influence by his Spirit and grace ; there is the strongest reason to conclude that this is the sense of Irenæus ; and in this I am supported by such great names as Austin,[||] Vossius [¶] Polyander, Rivet, Walæus, and Thysius ;[**] nay, even F euardentius the Papist,[††] though otherwise a strenuous advocate for free will, insists upon it, that this passage of Irenæus is a proof that the doctrine of original sin was held by the ancients before the time of Austin ; and since then, Irenæus means the same which the Scripture calls [‡‡] the *plague* of a man's heart, no injury is done him by my translation.

2. The first passage out of Tertullian is owned by Dr. Whitby[§§] to be more to the purpose than some he had been considering ; nor has he anything to object to the former part of it, for which it is chiefly cited ; in which Tertullian[||||] says, " Every soul is reckoned in Adam, until it is reckoned anew, or registered in Christ ; so long unclean, until it is thus registered." Nor does our author object to the pertinence of this testimony, which clearly expresses that the souls of men, whilst unregenerate, are not only

---

* Adv. Hæres. lib. 4, c. 5, p. 322.
† Ib. c. 34, p. 500.   ‡ Ib. c. 16, p. 460.
§ Treatise of Original Sin, p. 269.
|| Adv. Julian. lib. i. c. 11.   ¶ Hist. Pelag, par. 1, lib. 2, thes. 6, p. 152.   ** Synops. Pur.

Theolog. disp. 15, thes. 8, p. 150.   †† Annotat. in Irenæum, p. 323.   ‡‡ 1 Kings viii. 38.
§§ Treatise, p. 176 |||| De Anima, c. 39, p. 342.

reckoned in Adam, as belonging to him, and under him as their head; but are also reckoned unclean in him, being partakers of the sinful pollution, which he, by his transgression, brought upon all mankind. Pamelius makes this to be the argument and summary of the chapter wherein this testimony stands; Tamdiu enem animam ex carnis societate, in Adam immundam censeri, et peccatricem, tam animam, quam carnem dici; "So long as the soul, through society with the flesh, is reckoned unclean in Adam, both soul and body are said to be sinful;" which shows that he thought that Tertullian's sense was, that not only the soul is reckoned unclean in Adam, but that both body and soul are sinful, being defiled in him; though Dr. Whitby says, his commentator makes a doubt of it, whether, when he adds, "sinful because unclean, receiving its disgrace from society with the flesh," he attributes this disgrace of the soul from its society with the flesh, in respect of its mere original, or because it made use of it as an instrument of sinning.

3. The other passage in Tertullian is,[*] "Man being at the beginning circumvented by Satan, so as to transgress the commandment of God, and he being therefore given up to death, has defiled all mankind which spring from him, and has also made them partakers of his damnation." This man finds fault with me for translating in my book, totem genus, "his whole kind," instead of "his whole race or offspring;" but is not Adam's whole kind the same with all mankind? and are not all mankind his offspring? or, are any his offspring but mankind? He calls this an egregious blunder in me; but everybody will see that this is egregious trifling in him. A greater oversight is committed by neglecting to translate infectum, which expresses the pollution of nature all mankind are tainted with by Adam, and which exposes them to the same condemnation with him. But, since I have rendered damnatio in this passage damnation, the principal controversy about it is, though this writer says it will not bear any dispute, whether this relates to a bodily death and condemnation only, which he suggests is Tertullian's sense in this and in all other places; or also to the sense of condemnation and death which passed on Adam, body and soul, for his disobedience, and on all mankind in him, on account of the same. That Adam, according to Tertullian, was assigned

to a corporal death, and such a sentence of condemnation passed on him, is out of question. The passages cited by this author, to which more might be added,[†] will be allowed to be proofs of this. But then, this was not all that came upon him, nor the whole of the sentence which was pronounced on him; for, according to this ancient writer, he was not only subject to a corporal death, but also the image of God in him was destroyed; which lay not, as this man suggests is the sense of other ancient writers, in the immortality of the body, but in the soul, its powers and faculties, and especially in the power and freedom of the will, as appears from these following words of his :[‡] "I find that man was created by God, free, and possessed of his own free will and power, observing in him no image and likeness of God more than the same form of state: for not in the face and lineaments of the body, so different in mankind is he made after God, who is of one form or essence, but in that substance which he has derived from God, that is, of the soul, answering to the form of God, and is sealed with the liberty and power of his free will." And a little lower he says, "The image and likeness of God ought to be of his own free will and power, in which this itself, the image and likeness of God, may be thought to be, namely, the liberty and power of free will." He not only affirms that the image of God in man is defaced; but that also, by his sin, he has lost communion with God: "By not having faith," he says,[§] "even that which he seemed to have is taken from him, the favour of paradise, and familiarity with God, whereby he would have known all the things of God, had he been obedient." Now, the deprivation of the image of God, and of communion with him, through the fall, are what we call a mortal or spiritual death. Moreover, in the very passage in dispute, Adam is said "to render all mankind polluted," and so they become partakers of his condemnation, soul and body; hereby they become loathsome and abominable to God, and consequently liable to, and deserving of, his everlasting wrath and displeasure; which is no other than the second death; and that such a sentence of death passed on Adam for his offence, according to Tertullian, is clear from the following passages :[||] "For though, because of the condition of the law, Adam is given up to death, yet there is good hope for him, since the Lord says, Adam is become as one of us; namely, concerning

* De Testimon. Animæ, c. 3, p. 82.

† Vide Tertullian. de Resurrect. c. 6, p. 383; c. 18, p. 891; c. 26, p. 597; c. 52, p. 421.

‡ Liberum et sui arbitrii, et suæ potestatis invenio hominem a Deo institutum, nullam magis imaginem et similitudinem De illo animadvertens, quam ejusmodi status formam; neque enim facie et corporalibus lineis tam variis in genere humano, ad uniformem Deum expressus est, sed in ea substantia, quam ab ipso Deo traxit, id est, animæ ad formam Dei respondentis et arbitrii sui libertate et potestate signatus est.—Tertullian adv. Marcion. lib. 2, c. 5, p. 457. Oportebat igitur ima-

gineum et similitudinem Dei, liberi arbitrii, et suæ potestatis institui. in qua et hoc ipsum, imago et similitudo Dei deputaretur, arbitrii, scilicet libertas et potestas.—Ib. c. 6.

§ Ideoque non habendo fidem, etiam quod videbatur habere ademptum est illi, paradisi gratia et familiaritas Dei, per quam omnia Dei cognovisset si obedissst.—Ib. c. 2, p. 454.

|| Nam etsi Adam propter statum legis deditus morti est, sed spes ei salva est, dicente Dominoque, ecce Adam factus est tam quam unus ex nobis, de futura scilicet ad lectione hominis in divinitatem.—Ib. c. 25, p. 473.

the future assumption of the man into union with the Deity." Now, of his being delivered from a bodily death there was no hope, for the sentence of that not only passed, but was executed on him; but of his being delivered from the second death there is hope, through the sacrifice and satisfaction of the Second Adam; hence he elsewhere* condemns Tatian as a heretic, for asserting that "Adam could not obtain salvation; as if," says he, "the branches could be saved, and not the root." And in another place he has these words :† "God, after so many and such great offences of human indiscretion deliberately committed by Adam, the father of mankind, after man was condemned, with the dowry (the sin) of the world, after he was cast out of paradise, and subject to death, seasonably received him to his mercy, and immediately renewed repentance within himself; that is, as Rigaltius‡ explains it, as God repented that he had made man, he also repented that he had condemned him; wherefore, having rescinded the sentence of former wrath, or the former sentence of wrath and vengeance, he agreed to forgive his workmanship and image." Now, pray what was *sententia irarum pristinarum,* "the former sentence of wrath," said to be rescinded? Could it be the sentence of bodily death? Was that rescinded? Did not Adam die that death, as do all his posterity? Could it be any other than the sentence of eternal death and damnation, which, though it passed, was not executed on him, through the grace and forgiveness of God? Since then, according to Tertullian, this was the sentence pronounced on Adam, and he has made all his posterity partakers of it, I have done him no injury by my translation; besides, in the place before us, Tertullian is speaking to and of the soul, and not the body; for he immediately adds,§ "Thou art sensible of thy destroyer." And a little after, "We affirm that thou wilt remain after this life is ended, and wait for the day of judgment; and, according to thy deserts, shall be assigned either to torment or rest, both which will be for ever." Upon the whole, we see that this writer had no reason to say, that Tertullian everywhere declares the sentence of a bodily death alone to be what was pronounced on Adam in the beginning; or that he ever supposes the divine sentence of condemnation pronounced against man in the beginning, to concern the body and bodily death only, and never supposes it to respect the eternal death of body and soul hereafter.

This writer, unwilling to let slip an opportunity, or seeming one, of reproaching me, says, that I have ventured to translate a passage of Dr. Whitby's but not without a mistake; whereas I have not pretended to give an exact translation of the passage, but only the sense of it, and in that, it seems, I am mistaken: How so? I say, "the learned Doctor was of opinion, that what he has wrote in the treatise was almost above the capacities of the common people." This man says his words are these: "Seeing these things which I shall say of original sin, for the most part, exceed the capacity of the vulgar." Well, if they, *for the most part,* exceed, then surely they must be *almost* above the capacity of the vulgar. Should a person meet with this passage in Terence, *fere ruri se continet,* which this author mentions, and should render it, "he keeps almost always in the country," would it not be all one as if it was rendered, "he keeps for the most part, or usually, in the country?" And so, if he should on this scrap of Latin, *ut fere fit,* and translate it, "as it almost always falls out;" would it not be the same as if it was translated, "as it usually, or for the most part, falls out?" A man that can be grave in such observations as these, whatever opinion he may have of himself, as a very learned critic, must be set down for a *solemn trifler.*

I pass on (having nothing to do with his reasons for translating Dr. Whitby's book, nor with the translation itself) to,

II. The next charge exhibited against me, which is *impertinence,* pretending I have alleged testimonies from the ancients beside my purpose, and particularly from Clemens, Barnabas, Ignatius, Justin, and Lactantius, which shall be re-examined. And,

1. Clemens addressed the Corinthians, to whom he writes, as persons "called and sanctified by the will of God;" which translation of his words is censured as inaccurate, though perfectly agreeable to the version of Patricius Junius, a man of great erudition, revised by that very learned hand, Dr. John Fell, bishop of Oxford, who renders them, as I have done, vocatis et sanctificatis voluntate divina; yet this poor creature has the assurance and vanity to suggest, that his own translation is most exact, and this very loose, obscure, and inaccurate; but it is plain what makes him uneasy with this version, because he observes, it "makes it look as if both the calling and sanctification were ascribed here to the will of God;" and truly so it does, and that very rightly: and why should the man boggle at this, since Clemens, in the passage next cited by me, expressly says of the Corinthians, that they were "called by the will of God in Christ Jesus?" whence it is clear, that not only sanctification, but vo-

---

* De Præscript. Hæret. c. 52, p. 254.

† Nam Deus post tot, et ac tanta delicta humanæ temeritatis a principe generis Adam auspicata, post condemnatum hominem, cum seculi dote, post ejectum Paradiso mortique subjectum, quum rursus ad suam misericordiam maturavisset, jam inde in semetipso pœnitentiam dedicavit, rescissa sententia irarum pristinarum, ignoscere

pactus operi et imagini suæ.—Ib. de Pœnitentia, c. 2, p. 139, 140.   ‡ Observ. in loc. p. 38.

§ Sentis igitur perditorem tuum, affirmamus te manere post vitæ dispunctionem et expectare diem judicii. proque meritis aut cruciatui destinari aut refrigerio, utroque sempiterno.—Ib. de Testimon. Animæ, c. 3, p. 82.

cation, is ascribed by him to the will of God. But then, it seems, this vocation is to be understood, not of internal, effectual calling, but of the outward call of the gospel. To which may be replied, that persons may be called externally, by the preaching of the gospel, who are never sanctified; but then those who are sanctified, are internally called, are called with a holy calling, or are sanctified in and by their effectual vocation; and since these Corinthians were sanctified as well as called, their vocation cannot be understood of a mere outward call, by the ministry of the word; but of an eternal, efficacious call, by the Spirit and grace of God. If this will not do, it is suggested, that sanctification, in this passage, does not design regeneration, conversion, or any internal work of the Spirit of God upon the soul; but expiation and pardon of sin, through the sacrifice of Christ; the words of Clemens being an allusion to, and the sense of the same, with Heb. x. 10. Though one should rather think that Clemens, writing to the Corinthians, as the apostle Paul had done before, should copy after him, and in his addresses to them make use of the same characters, and in the same sense, as he does 1 Cor. i. 2, where we find both these words, *kletois* and *egiasmenois*, called and sanctified; and the rather, because Clemens had this epistle in his view when he wrote, makes mention of it, and exhorts the Corinthians to consider it.* It is therefore most natural to conclude, that Clemens, using the same words as the apostle did, in an epistle written to the same persons, should design the same things by them, namely, their effectual calling to be saints, and their sanctification through the Spirit and grace of Christ; and then what is become of the charge of impertinence? why, truly, this passage is still nothing to the point, since none of the Remonstrants pretend that any person can be sanctified, but by the will of God: to which I have made answer, that they will not affirm, that any person can be sanctified by the will of God, without the co-operation of man's will, by which, according to them, grace becomes effectual; whereas Clemens attributes vocation and sanctification entirely to the will of God: when I add, that

the Remonstrants affirm, that the difference of calling grace in man lies not so much in the will of God as in the will of man; and that it is no absurdity to say, that a saint is distinguished from an unregenerate man by his own will; in affirming which, this writer says I say what is weak and false, and which no Remonstrant ever used; but in all these I am supported by the following testimonies out of their own mouths; they affirm that† "the holy Scriptures requires especially, to the opening of the heart, the co-operation of man; that co-operation which proceeds from preventing grace, for if God commands man to open his heart in conversion, it is certain that that operation is not effected by God, without the consent of man's will." Corvinus, the Remonstrant, asserts that,‡ "supposing all the operations which God uses to work conversion in us, yet conversion so remains in our power, that we may not be converted." He denies§ "that the difference of calling grace is not so placed in the will of man as in the will of God; and expressly uses these words,‖ "It is no absurdity that a man should be distinguished by his own will from an unbeliever." Grevinchovius, the remonstrant, affirms,¶ that "it is not foreign from Scripture and truth, if any one should assert that believers, not indeed of themselves, or by themselves, yet do distinguish themselves." And in reply to these words, "Who hath made thee to differ? he says,** I make myself to differ, since I could resist God and divine pre-determination, and yet have not resisted, and why may not I glory in it as my own?" The same writer also says, that "the effect of grace ordinary depends on some act of the will, as a previous condition, sine qua non;" and that†† "no other common cause of the whole complex together can be given beside the liberty of the will." And again,‡‡ that "the will of itself alone, by a certain prievous motion, determines grace: when we say," adds he, "that the will determines grace, we mean nothing else than that the will freely performs its concourse with co-operating grace; or that the will so co-operates, as that it might not co-operate, and so, by not so co-operating, hinder the co-operation of grace."

---

* Epist. p. 106.　　† Sacra Scriptura imprimis ad istam cordis apertionem requirit συεργιαν, et co operationem humanam, inquam, eam, quæ ex gratiæ prævenientis-vi proficiscitur, nam si homini præcipitur a Deo, ut is in conversione cor suum aperiat, certum est, operationem istam non effici a Deo sine consensu humauæ voluntatis.—Coll. Hag. art. iii. & iv. p. 274.

‡ Positis omnibus operationibus, quibus ad eam in nobis efficiendam Deus utitur, manet tamen ipsa conversio ita in nostra potestate, ut possimus non converti.—Corv. ad. n. Boger par. ii. p. 263.

§ Negatur discrimen gratiæ vocantis non tam in hominis arbitrio positum esse quam in Dei voluntate.—Ib. contra Tilen. p. 264.

‖ Non est absurdum hominem sua voluntate discerui a nou credente.—Ib. p. 136.

¶ Non alienum est a Scriptura et veritate, si quis affirmat, fideles non quidem ex seipsis aut per

semetipsos, sametipsos tamen discernere.—Grevinchov. contr. Ames. p. 219. Quis te discernit? in promptu causa est, ego meipsum discerno, quum enim Deo ac prædeterminationi divinæ resistere possem, non restiti tamen, at qui in eo quid ni liceat mihi tanquam de meo gloriari?—Ib. p. 253.

** Imo ut confidentius agam, dico effectum gratia ordinaria lege pendere ab actu aliquo arbitrii ut prævia conditione sine qua noa.—Ib. p. 198.

††† Totius simul complexi causam communem dari non posse aliam præter libertatem voluntatis. —Ib. p. 204.　　‡‡‡ Arbitrium ex se solo, prævia quadam motione determinet gratiam. Eo quo diximus sensu arbitrium determinare gratiam, nihil aliud est quam arbitrium libere præstare concursum suum gratiæ co-operanti, vel arbitrium ita co-operari, ut possit non co-operari, adeoque non co-operando impedire co-operationem gratiæ. —Ib. p. 206.

Many more citations of the like kind might be made, but these may suffice. Since, then, they ascribe conversion, or calling grace, so much to the will of man, as to give it the turning point in it, as to make conversion dependent on it, for so Grevinchovius* allows, "you will say," observes he, "that in this way of working, even God himself, in some measure, depends upon the will. I grant it," he replies, "as to the act of free determination." It therefore cannot be saying either a weak or false thing of the Remonstrants, that they may make the difference of calling grace to lie not so much in the will of God as in the will of man.

The other passage cited by me out of Clemens being, in that clause of it for which I cite it, the same with the former, since that is pertinent to my purpose, this must be also, and I therefore need not say any thing more about it; only whereas I have once (not more than once, as this man says) elsewhere cited it, to prove that according to Clemens good works are unnecessary in point of justification. This writer is pleased to make a digression from his subject, and observe, that this passage is full against the doctrine I embrace, will not serve my purpose against the person I opposed; and on the contrary, is a strong bulwark in defence of the Remonstrants, who hold that persons are not justified by works without faith, nor by faith without works; but by faith accompanied with, and productive of, good works. To all which I reply, that this passage of Clemens is not, in the least, against any doctrine I embrace, but entirely agreeable: the doctrine of justification by faith, in the Scripture sense of it, is what I hold and maintain; nor are any thoughts and sentiments of mine concerning justification inconsistent with it. The passage is also full to my purpose for which I cited it, against my antagonist, which was to show, that good works were not necessary to salvation, as the antecedent to the consequent: but, above all, it is surprising that the passage should be thought to be a strong bulwark in defence of the Remonstrants, since Clemens expressly says, "We are justified not by our piety, nor by our good works, which we have done in holiness of heart; but by that faith, by which the Almighty God hath justified all from the beginning;" by which expressions he excludes all works from our justification; yea, such as believers themselves perform, which spring from the best principles, from holiness of heart, and are done in the best manner, even works which spring from faith, and are produced by it: for, can there be holiness of heart where there is no faith, any more than there can be faith where there is no holiness of heart? If the Remonstrants have no stronger bulwarks than this, they are most miserably defended in this article.

2. Barnabas is the next ancient writer mentioned, from whom I have cited a passage, to prove the weakness and corruption of human nature before faith; and here a hideous outcry is raised, of an egregious blunder, false translation, want of sense, and I know not what, through a repetition of the word idolatry; and all this is aggravated by its being in my fourth volume,† and re-tained in my postscript, after I had revised the translation; whereas, upon examination, it will appear the blunder is his, and not mine; and that he has not consulted the original Greek of Barnabas, but the old Latin translation. The Greek of Barnabas, as it stands in the edition of the very learned Isaac Vossius, is as follows :—*Pro tou emas pisteusai to Theo, en emon to katoiketerion tes kardias phtharton kai asthenes—oti en pleres men eidololatrias oikos, eidololatria en oikos diamonion, dia to poiein osa en enantia to Theo ;* which I must again render, "Before we believed in God, the habitation of our heart was corrupt and weak ; for it was a house full of idolatry, and idolatry was the house of devils; wherefore we do, or did, such things as were contrary to God." Indeed the word *idolatria* is omitted in the old Latin version of Barnabas, which is this : *Antequam crederemus Deo erat habitatio nostra corrupta et infirma—quia pleni eramus adorationibus idolorum et srat domus dæmoniorum, propter quod faceremus, quæ Deo essent contraria.* Now where is the egregious blunder ? and who is the blunderer ? or, where is the impertinence of the passage? Does it not clearly and fully express the corruption and weakness of man before he believes, or has the grace of God implanted in him, for which purpose it was cited? He next finds fault with the version of the latter part of the passage, and in a very magisterial way says, the words will never bear such a translation, without giving any reason for his so saying; but why should not *dia to poiein* be rendered 'wherefore we do,' or did, rather than 'forasmuch as we have done,' since the verb is of the present, and not of the preterperfect tense. The reason of his being uneasy with my translation is pretty evident, because it leaves his charge of impertinence utterly insupportable. One would think he might have made use of softer words than those railing ones, of ignorance and dishonesty; but such is modern charity ! As for the passage in Barnabas he refers me to, when he says, "When God has received us by the remission of our sins, he then gives us another form, so as to have souls like the soul of an infant :" this is only to be understood in a comparative sense, in like manner, as Matt. xviii. 3, and xix. 14, 1 Cor. xiv. 20, and clearly expresses the power and efficacy of divine grace, in forming the new creature in regeneration ; for which purpose I have cited it in this my fourth Part.

3. Ignatius comes next under consideration, from whom I have cited a passage which agrees with those out of Clemens Romanus, and which is allowed to be so by this

* Dices in hoc operandi modo, Deum etiam quodam modo dependere a voluntate? Concedo, quoad actum determinationis liberæ.—Ib. p. 279.

† The first edition was in four volumes, &c.

author, and since they are to my purpose, as has been proved, this must be also : but whereas there are *three* other passages besides, which are produced by me, this man has thought fit to examine them likewise. In the first of these, Ignatius advises the church of Smyrna to avoid some very wicked persons he describes as beasts in the shape of men, and " only to pray for them, if so be they may repent, which is very difficult ; but Jesus Christ, our true life," says he, " has the power of this ;" which words are cited, not only to show the difficulty of such wicked persons obtaining repentance, and which this author allows, even such a difficulty as amounts to an impossibility ; an impossibility as great as is in the Ethiopian to change his skin, or the leopard his spots ; but also to show that Christ, who is our life, who has quickened us, and given us repentance unto life, or we had never had it, has the sole power of it ; and who, as he has given repentance to such who may not have been such notorious sinners, or they would never have repented of themselves ; so he is able to give it to the most profligate wretches, and which, therefore, is the argument or encouragement to pray for such. The next passage of Ignatius is, " They that are carnal, cannot do the things that are spiritual ; nor they that are spiritual, do the things that are carnal ;" from whence, this writer says, I infer, that men in a carnal state have no power to do any thing that is spiritual : it is very right, so I do, and that justly : but then, it is said, the former part of the citation cannot intend this, and more than the latter part of it can mean, that a spiritual man has no power to do a wicked action ; and therefore can never intend, that a carnal man cannot cease to be carnal and become spiritual, and then do spiritual things. To which I reply, that a carnal man has nothing that is spiritual in him, and therefore can do nothing that is spiritual ; but a spiritual man has both flesh and spirit in him, that which is carnal and that which is spiritual. Now when the carnal part prevails, it puts a man upon doing of carnal things, as in the case of David referred to ; but then this same man, as spiritual, and when in a spiritual frame, and in the exercise of spiritual grace, according to Ignatius, cannot do carnal things ; and which is the sense of the apostle John, 1 John iii. 9, *Whosoever is born of God doth not commit sin, for his seed remaineth in him, and he cannot sin, because he is born of God.* We do not deny that a carnal man may cease to be carnal, become spiritual, and then do spiritual things ; but then we affirm that he cannot cease to be carnal, become spiritual, and do spiritual things, but by the grace of God, and not by his own power and strength. The last citation from Ignatius, and which is no marginal reading, but stands in the body of Vossius's edition, is, that " the Christian is not the work of persuasion, but of greatness ;" that is, as I explain it, of the exceeding greatness of God's power, referring to

Ephesians i. 19, to which I am inclined to think Ignatius refers ; where the word *mege-thos*, used by him, is to be taken in this sense ; our author, from Mr. Whiston and Archbishop Wake, interprets it of fortitude and courage in times of persecution. The place referred to, as a parallel one, to support this sense, is not to the purpose, where Ignatius says, " They that profess themselves to be Christians, shall be seen by what they do ; for now it is not the business of a profession, but it is through the power of faith, if any man is found to be *a Christian* to the end ;" by which he means, that it is not by a mere outward profession, but by the power and strength of faith, that a Christian continues and perseveres to the end. Nor is there any mention of *peismone*, or *megethos*, or any thing that answers to them, in the passage. But when this author suggests that I have left out these words, " especially when he is hated by the world ;" and if purposely, he says, it will be a full proof that I am not overstocked with integrity ; he is guilty of a vile piece of slander, and is a glaring proof of his having a very small share of integrity himself : what guilt, shame, and confusion, must rise up in him, when I have produced the whole passage, as it stands in my book, thus : " The Christian is not the work of persuasion, but of greatness, of the exceeding greatness of God's power, which is wonderfully displayed in making the Christian, in continuing, preserving, and supporting him as such, *especially*," as he observes, " *when he is hated by the world !*"

4. Justin Martyr is another ancient writer from whom I have cited passages, showing that the Scriptures, and the doctrines contained in them, are not to be understood without the Spirit and grace of God. The first of these I freely own, and I never gainsaid it, does most clearly express, that the doctrines of the sacred writings are such as could never be discovered by the light of nature, nor without the inspiration of the Holy Spirit ; but then, since these writings contain *such great and divine things*, as Justin says, exceeding the natural knowledge and understanding of men, it follows, that they can only be spiritually discerned, through the assistance of the Spirit of God, the dictator of them ; which, as it is the sense of the apostle Peter, 2 Peter i. 20, 21, so it is of this holy martyr, as will fully appear from what he elsewhere says, notwithstanding what this man has said to the contrary ; for, in the very next citation from him, Justin declares that " he understood the Scriptures by the grace of God alone, which was given to him, and not through any natural or acquired parts of his." This man believes that the word *charis*, which he renders *favour*, and I have translated *grace*, for which he charges me with unskilfulness, how justly, let others judge, never signifies, throughout Justin's works, the operations or assistances of the Spirit : but his faith and judgment in this matter are of very little weight and signifi-

cance. The learned Scultetus * believed otherwise, and so did the famous Vossius, and whom the men of his party cite with great applause, when they meet with any thing in him that serves their turn: his words are these,† "Justin, in his dialogue with Trypho, asserts, that the outward preaching of the word, or reading of the Scriptures, is not sufficient, but that besides them, the internal illumination of the Holy Spirit is requisite; for thus he writes, Do ye think, O men, that we could ever have understood the things contained in the Scriptures, unless by the will of him that wills these things *elabomen charin tou noesai*, we had received grace to understand them?" And in some other place before this he had said the same; "Unless one should take upon him, *meta megales charitos tes para Theou*, ' with that great or wonderful grace which is of God,' to understand the things which are said or done by the prophets; it will not avail him, to seem to relate their words or facts, unless he can also give a reason of them." These, with some others of the like nature, I have cited in my book,‡ and have referred him to them in my postscript, of which he has not taken the least notice, being, no doubt, convinced in his own mind, that they were clear testimonies against him. Besides, were *charis* to be rendered *favour*, what could that favour be, to understand the Scriptures, but the illumination of the blessed Spirit?

The third passage cited by me, which directs to pray that " the gates of light, that is, the Scriptures, might be opened, since they are not seen or known by all, except God and his Christ give an understanding of them." This he owns sounds something more to the purpose, though he afterwards says, most probably it has no such meaning, at least it is very uncertain whether it has or not. But that this also may not pass without some reproachful censure, he represents me as here blundering on according to custom, because I took these words to be an address of Justin's to Trypho; whereas, he says, they are Justin's advice to a Gospel preacher. Now, who is most likely to blunder in this matter, he or I? Is it probable that Justin should give such advice to a gospel preacher, one that was more knowing than himself at that time, and who was then instructing him? or, is it not much more likely that he should thus address Trypho, the blind, ignorant Jew, with whom he was conversing, and relating some matters of fact respecting himself? But, indeed, the truth of the case is this, the words are not spoken by Justin at all, either to Trypho or to a gospel preacher; but they are the words of a Christian man, whether a gospel preacher is

not so manifest, to Justin himself, whilst a heathen philosopher, who had been instructing him in the Christian religion, and closes with these words; upon which Justin immediately observes, that this man having said these, and many other things, which he had not then time to relate, departed from him, charging him to pursue those things, and he never saw him any more; which, with what he had said before, made such an impression on him, as to engage his affections to the prophets and Christians, and issued in his conversion.

Two other passages being cited by me out of an epistle of Justin's to Diognetus, showing the impossibility of obtaining life and salvation of ourselves, by our own works, or any other way than by Christ; this man represents this epistle as doubtful and uncertain, whether it was Justin's or no; whereas Sylburgius§ formerly thought it savoured of Justin's spirit and genius: and the very learned‖ Fabricus of late could see no reason why it should not be thought to be his; and the famous Scultetus¶ says, that with the common consent of all, that, and also the epistle to Zenas, which this man blunderingly calls the epistle of Zenas, and which he likewise represents as dubious, were ascribed to Justin; by which learned writer also the passage out of the epistle to Zenas is twice** produced, and that for the same purpose for which I have cited it.

5. Lactantius is the last of the ancients excepted to by our author under this head, from whom I have cited three passages, to prove that man is in such a state of blindness and darkness, that it is impossible he should have a knowledge of spiritual things without divine teachings. And the first of them fully expresses that such is the condition and situation of the mind, or soul of man, that "it cannot of itself apprehend or receive the truth, unless it be thought by some other;" where Lactantius is speaking, not of the inability of the mind to discover truth without a revelation, but to *comprehend*, or *apprehend*, *receive*, or *embrace* truth when it is revealed; wherefore he argues, that the teacher must be heavenly, and not earthly, and have both virtue and knowledge. The second of them, in which he says, that "man cannot, of himself, come to the knowledge of the truth, unless he is taught of God," the excellent†† Scultetus understands as I do, to intend, not the necessity of a revelation to lead men to a knowledge of the truth, but of divine teachings to understand the revelation made; his words are these: "Concerning the understanding of the Christian religion, very remarkable is that saying of his, *Man of himself cannot come to this knowledge, unless he*

---

* Medulla Patrum, par. 1, lib. 1, c. 14, p. 29.

† Justinus dialogo cum Tryphone docet, externam verbi prædicationem aut Scripturarum lectionem minime sufficere, sed in super requiri internam Spiritus Sancti illuminationem sic enim scribit, &c.—Voss. Pelag. Hist. par. 1, lib. 3, thes. 2, p. 272.   ‡ Cause of God and Truth,

part 4.   § Annotat. in Justin. p. 43.

‖ Bibliothec. Græc. vol. v. lib. 5, c. 1. s. 15, p. 58.   ¶ Medulla Patrum, par. 1, lib. 1, c. 1, p. 2.   ** Page 32, 38.   †† De intelligentia religionis Christianæ præclara ejus vox est, homo per seipsum, &c.—In lib. 10, c. 11, p. 341.

is taught of God." The third of them, in which Lactantius asserts, that the knowledge of truth, and of heavenly "things, cannot be perceived by man, unless God teaches him," is of the same kind with the former, and expressed in almost the same words, and is to be understood in the same manner.

But, it seems, did these passages of Justin and Lactantius prove ever so clearly the necessity of grace, or the assistance of the Spirit to understand the Scriptures, they must still be impertinent; since the Remonstrants never deny this, nor will they contest such a proposition. This is not a slip of his pen, but what 'e repeats over and over, and most manifestly betrays his ignorance of the writings and sentiments of the Remonstrants, who have very openly expressed themselves on this head, in the following manner :* "Such is the clearness and perspicuity of the Scriptures, in doctrines, especially which are necessary to be understood in order to everlasting salvation, that all readers, not only learned men but private persons (that are but endued with common sense and judgment,) may sufficiently attain the meaning of them, provided they do not suffer themselves to be blinded with prejudice, vain confidence, and other evil affections." And when the Anti-Remonstrants† charged this passage with smelling rank of Pelagianism and Socinianism, and urged that they confounded the literal and spiritual sense of the Scripures, the Remonstrants‡ reply, by arguing after this manner, that if there is "a sense of Scripture superinfused, it cannot be the sense of the words of Scripture, but the sense of the Spirit of God : or if it is the sense of the words of Scripture, how or wherein does it differ from the literal sense ? To what purpose is it superinfused ? Is it that the sense may be understood, which is understood already ? This is trifling. Is it that it may be more clearly understood ? But the sense lies in something indivisible ; should you say, this light of the Holy Spirit is pre-requisite to understand the true sense, you increase the absurdity." Episcopius, a leading man among the Remonstrants, says§ many things

to the same purpose ; hence it most clearly appears, that all such passages of the ancients, which express the necessity of grace and the assistance of the Spirit to understand the Scriptures, are most pertinently alleged, being diametrically opposite to the sentiments of these men.

When I say, that the Remonstrants and Dr. Whitby allow of no supernatural grace infused, or supernatural aid requisite to conversion and good works, besides objective evidence, respecting truth to the understanding, and bringing it to remembrance ; this man asks, with what face I could say this, when the Remonstrants and Dr. Whitby assert supernatural grace in words and terms as express as any of my party. Strange ! why then has a controversy about it been continued for so many years ? But this is but a further proof, that he is utterly unacquainted with the writings and tenets of those of his own party. The Remonstrants expressly deny that any grace is infused in order to conversion, either into the understanding, or will, or affections. "As to the distinction," say they,‖ "of *habitual* and *actual* grace, this is rejected by us ; since by habitual grace is meant such an infusion of faith, hope, and love, into the will, as that a man may be said to obtain those habits without any intervening operation of the will ; there is no such thing in Scripture, this is a device of the schoolmen." Again, they say,¶ that "faith cannot be called the gift of God, unless in respect of the actual infusion of it into our hearts, as the brethren, that is, the Anti-Remonstrants, profess they understand it ; that, indeed, we utterly deny." Corvinus,** a noted one among them, expresses himself thus : "Infusion of habits, or virtues, whether into the will, or into the understanding and affection, if you regard ordinary conversion, is contrary to the use of means, by which God would produce a new life in man." And, says Grevinchovius,†† another of them, "That there be any intrinsic form, or any supernatural habit infused, raising and determining the natural faculty by its own power and efficacy, this figment I do

---

* Tanta est claritas ac perspicuitas in sensibus imprimis ad æternam salutem intellectu necessariis, ut omnes lectores, non docti tautum sed et idiotæ (communi quidem sensu ac judicio præditi) quantum satis est, mentem eorum adsequi possiut, modo præjudicio, vona confidentia, aliisque pluris affectionibus sese occæcari non sinant.—Remonstr, Confessio, c. 1, s. 14, p. 6.   † Censura Confessioni, c. 1, s. 14, p. 23, 24.

‡ Sensus ille superinfusus non erit sensus verborum Scripturæ, sed sensus Spiritus Dei, aut si est sensus verborum Scripturæ, quomodo et qua re differt a sensu grammatico ; Quorsum super infunditur ? An ut intelligatur sensus, qui jam intelligitur ? Nugæ. An ut clarius intelligatur ? At sensus in indivisibili consistit : si dicas, lumen hoc Spiritus Sancti prærequiri, ut verus sensus intelligatur, auges absurditatem.—Examen. Censuræ, c. 1, s. 14, p. 34.   § Disput. de Perspicuitate S. Script. thes. 1 & 3.

‖ Quod attinet distinctionem illam gratiæ

habitualis et actualis, ea a nobis rejicitur ; siqidem per habitualem gratiam intelligitur talis fidei, spei, charitatis in voluntatem infusio, ut citra ullam intervenientem voluntatis operationem eos habitus adipisci dicatur homo. Nihil tale in Scriptura, scholasticorum hoc figmentum est, &c. —Declaratio Sentent. Remonstr. circa art. iii. & iv. p. 15.   ¶ Eam non posse donum Dei appellari, nisi respectu actualis iufusionis in corda nostra, prout id fratres se intelligere profitentur, id vero nos exserte negamus.—Coll. Hag. art. iii. & iv. p. 308.   ** Infusiones habituum seu virtutum, tum in voluntatam, tum in intellectum et affectus (si ordinariam conversionem spectes) repugnant mediorum, quibus Deus in homine novam vitam operari vult, administrationi.—Corvinus adv. Walachros, p. 56.   †† Formam quandam intrinsicum sive habitum quendam supernaturalem infusum, potentiam naturalem elevantem ac determinautem vi et efficacitate sua, non admitto hoc figmentum.—Grev. contr. Ames, p. 286.

not admit of." They do indeed own,* "that a supernatural power is conferred on the will, and that hereby God immediately acts on the will, provided this action does not necessitate the will antecedently, and take away the liberty and power *non valendi*, of not willing or nilling," which this man has falsely translated *willing*. So that notwithstanding this supernatural power, the will remains indifferent to will or not will, to act or not act, believe or not believe, do well or not, and by this power it is only enabled to bring into act its innate faculty of willing and nilling; for thus they say,† "Though God may so affect the will by his word, and the internal operation of his Spirit, and confer the power of believing and supernatural aid, and cause a man actually to believe, yet man can of himself reject this grace and *not believe*, and so even perish through his own fault." What kind of supernatural power or aid must this be? And as for Dr. Whitby, he affirms‡ that *supernatural and infused habits*, or Christian virtues, are never styled *grace* in Scripture; and he humbly conceives,§ that the inward operation of the Holy Spirit consists in these two things, in representing divine truths, and in bringing them to our remembrance; and further observes,‖ in a passage I referred this author to, though he has thought fit to take no notice of it, "that any *supernatural habits* must be infused into us in an instant, or that any other *supernatural aid* is requisite to the conversion of a sinner, besides the fore-mentioned illumination of the Holy Spirit, and the impression which he makes upon our hearts by the ideas which he raises in us, is that which my hypothesis by no means will allow; which ideas, though they are raised by a *physical* operation, yet they are *moral* in their operations; even as a man's tongue, in speaking to persuade or dissuade another, performs a physical operation, though the effect of it is only moral."

The reader will easily see from hence in what sense Dr. Whitby is to be understood, when he says, as this author has cited him, that "we become new creatures, is, indeed, effected by the supernatural aid of the Spirit;" and with what face I could, and still say, that the Remonstrants and Dr. Whitby, besides the moral suasion of the word and Spirit, allow of no supernatural grace infused, or supernatural aid requisite to conversion and good works.

This writer seems uneasy with me for representing the Remonstrants and Dr. Whitby as meaning no more by the aids of the Spirit, and the grace of God, which they allow to be necessary to conversion and good works, than what Pelagius called the *grace of nature*, or moral suasion; and produces a large citation, which it is very probable somebody or another has helped him to, showing in what manner the Remonstrants at the synod of Dort endeavoured to clear themselves from the charge of Pelagianism; from whence, it is manifest, that such a charge was exhibited against them; and, notwithstanding all the colour and artifice they made use of, they were not able to convince that venerable body of men to the contrary, who continued to charge them with introducing Pelagianism; and particularly, that they meant no more by *grace*, than *external calling* by the word, and internal *moral suasion* by the Spirit, as appears from the Act of that Synod,¶ and which is fully evident from these men's own writings: "If the word of the gospel," say they,** "is not the sole and only ordinary means of conversion; but the internal and efficacious, or irresistible action of the Spirit must concur; then it follows, that that, together with the word, is the means of conversion, or collaterally works along with the word, by a distinct action from the action of the word; or the one is subordinate to the other; neither of which can be asserted." Again, after the power is conferred on the will, before-mentioned, they say,†† "We confess, that no other grace is owned by us to be necessary, to draw out an act of faith, than that which is *moral*, or that which uses the word as an instrument to produce faith." Once more, they‡‡ say, "It may be disputed whether that is not the most noble action respecting man, which is performed by persuasion and admonitions; and, whether it is expedient that any other power should be used with man, maintaining the properties of the human nature; and moreover, whether such an operation as Satan uses, would not be strong enough." And, says§§ Grevinchovius, "What hinders, but that *moral grace alone* may make natural men spiritual ones?" These men, indeed,

---

* Declaratio. Sentent. Remonstr. circa art. iii. & iv. p. 17.

† Licet ita voluntatem afficiat verbo et Spiritus sui operatione interna Deus, ut et potentiam credendi sive vires supernaturalis conferat et hominem actu credere facit, tamen potuit homo ex se gratiam istam adspernari et non credere, eoque etiam sua culpa perire.—Ib. p. 2.

‡ Discourse, &c. p. 211.   § Ib. p. 226.

‖ Ib. p. 231.   ¶ Acta Synod. Dordrecht. p. 243, 261, 306, 307.   ** Si verbum evangelii non est solum et unicum conversionis medium ordinarium, sed actio Spiritus Sancti interna et efficax sive irresistibilis concurrere debeat, tum sequitur, id quod una cum verbo medium conversionis est vel collateraliter juxta verbum per actionem distinctam ab actione verbi; vel alterum alteri subordinari; at qui nutrum horum dici potest.—Defensio Sentent. Romonstr. circa art. iv. p. 128, 129.   †† Fatemur aliam a nobis ad actum fidei eliciendum necessarium gratiam non agnosci quam moralem sive eam, quæ verbo tanquam instrumento ad fidem efficiendam utitur.—Ib. p. 62.   ‡‡ Posset quoque et hoc (ut a nonnullis fit) disputari, an non nobilissima sit actio ea circa hominem, quæ fit per inductionem et monelas et an expendiens sit, alia aliqua circa hominem vi uti, servatis humanæ naturæ proprietatibus ac proinde an non satis vehemens foret operatio, si talis esset, quali Satan utitur.—Coll. Hag. art. iii. & iv. p. 291.   §§ Quid enim obstat, quominus vel sola gratia moralis istos ψυχικους, spirituales reddat?—Grevinch. contra Ames, p. 297.

sometimes talk of special and supernatural grace; but can that be *special*, which they say is *universal* and *common* to all men? Or *supernatural*, which produces no supernatural effects, and which may be overcome and made of no effect, by that which is natural? But after all, it seems the holy fathers of the Christian church always speak of God's grace just as the Remonstrants do: and that I have not cited, nor am able to cite, a single father who has said more than the Arminians; whereas in Part IV., of the *Cause of God and Truth*, chap. 4, I have produced not only one but many, who speak of regeneration and conversion, as owing entirely to powerful and efficacious insuperable and unfrustrable grace, and not to moral suasion; to which I refer him and the reader. And thus, having done with his impertinent charge, I go on.

III. To consider his next charge of weakness, in citing passages from the ancients, which only prove that "by the fall of Adam, men are become prone to sin, and subject to a corporeal death:" but supposing no more is proved by such passages; a proneness to sin is a corruption of nature, and if a bodily death is inflicted as a punishment, than which there is not a greater corporeal punishment on Adam's posterity for his sin, they must be involved in the guilt of it, or that must be imputed to them; otherwise, how should they be liable to such a punishment of death for it? Now the derivation of a corrupt nature from Adam, and the imputation of the guilt of his sin to his posterity, are the very things in the controversy we contend for; and if the Remonstrants will accede to these things, they in a manner give up their cause. Should it be said, that though they allow of a proneness to sin, yet not such a general corruption of nature as we plead for; and though they own that 'men are become subject, through Adam's sin, to a corporeal death, yet not to death in soul and body. I have cited passages from the ancients, and referred this man to them, showing that men by the fall have lost the image of God, even true reason, moral goodness, righteousness, and holiness; that they are born sinners, yea, infected with sin before they are born; that they are under a spiritual darkness and death, and held by the devil in hell for the sin of Adam, the fault of which is transferred to them. To which this author has chiefly replied by referring me to Dr. Whitby's *Treatise of Original Sin*, particularly respecting the passages of Origen, Macarius the Egyptian, Athanasius, Basil, Cyrill, and Optatus. Whose replies to these passages, as well as to some others of Origen and Chrysostom, about which this man elsewhere so much blusters, are mere shifts and evasions, and chiefly lie in setting other passages against them.

It will not be denied, nor is it to be wondered at, that there are some passages in those writers which may seem to militate against this doctrine; for no controversy being moved about it, they wrote without guard; but, if it was entirely unknown till the times of Austin, it is much there should be any thing of it in their writings; wherefore, upon *these considerations*, I say again, and which was before my sense, that one *full* testimony in favour of it, before the controversy was moved, is of more weight than ten which may *seem* to be against it.

But to go on: this author replies to the passages referred to by me, partly by saying of others of them, as those of Hilary of Poictiers, Victorinus Afer, and Gregory Nazianzen, that they are nothing to the purpose; **if** the reader pleases to take his *ipse dixit*, his bare word for it; though the first of these affirms, that sin and unbelief arise from the transgression of our first parents; that all mankind are to be considered under the first man, and went astray when he did; and that man is born under original sin, and the law of it; and the *other* represents man in a state of nature, as *dead* through sin; and the *third* asserts, that all men sinned in Adam, fell by his sin out of paradise, were condemned through his disobedience, and lost the heavenly image. The passages of the ancients referred to which he has ventured to make some remarks upon, are those of Justin, Irenæus, Hilary the Deacon, Ambrose, and Mark the Eremite, which will be attended to.

1. Justin Martyr affirms,[*] that "we were born sinners:" which words this man says in one place I have translated to a false sense; but in some pages after, when he had forgot what he had said before, says, it may be translated either way; either "we were, *or* were made, *or* were born sinners:" but be this as it will, the question, he says, will return, in what sense Justin uses the word *sinners*, as it is now the question between us, in what sense St. Paul uses the word, Romans v. I answer, Justin does not use the word *sinners* for *sufferers*, in which sense our modern Arminians, silly enough, make the apostle to use it in the above place; and I can scarcely think our author has front enough to assert this, when he reads the passage in Justin, which stands thus; "We, who by him (Christ) have access to God, have not received the carnal, but spiritual circumcision, which Enoch, and those like him, kept; but we, seeing *we were born sinners*, have received it by baptism, through the mercy of God."

2. Irenæus[†] has such a passage as this referred to by me, "Christ hath granted us salvation, that what we lost in Adam, that is, to be after the image and likeness of God, we might receive in Christ Jesus;" which this man, after Dr. Whitby, would have to be understood of the immortality of the body, which is only a part of that image; whereas Irenæus[‡] elsewhere makes this likeness to be in the whole man, body and soul, and par-

---

* Dialog. cum Tryph. p. 261.
† Adv. Hæres. l. 3, c. 20, p. 282.

‡ Ib. l. 5, c. 6, p. 441.

ticularly to consist in the reason of man, and the freedom of his will, which, he says, he has lost; his words are these;* " Man being rational, *et secundum hoc similis Deo,* ' and in this respect like to God,' and being made free in his will, and of his own power, is himself the cause why he may become sometimes wheat, and sometimes chaff; wherefore he will be justly condemned, because being made rational, he hath lost true reason; and living irrationally, he acts contrary to the righteousness of God, giving himself up to every earthly spirit, and serving all sorts of pleasures:" Feuardentius,† Irenæus's annotator, interprets *image,* in the place in dispute, of the excellent gifts of grace, righteousness, and godliness, bestowed on man in his creation; it is therefore no piece of weakness, to cite or refer to such a passage, showing that man has lost by the fall the image of God, which chiefly lies, according to this ancient writer, in the freedom of his will, and the exercise of right reason.

3. Hilary, the Deacon, is another ancient writer cited and referred to by me, to prove that men are held in hell by Satan for the sin of Adam: and here I am gravely reprimanded for translating *inferi* " hell," and not hades; but supposing the word *inferi* should not be used by Hilary, and that these phrases *apud inferos* and *in inferis* are not to be met with in the passages referred to, as this man has put them, as indeed they are not; with what shame and confusion must he appear, who makes such large pretensions to accuracy, and takes every slight occasion, and indeed where there is none at all, of charging others with blunders! Hilary's words are these, speaking of sin being condemned by the cross of Christ; " Hence," says he, " the authority, as it were, of sin was taken away, by which it held men (not *apud inferos,* as this man says, but) *de inferno,* in hell for the sin of Adam." Again, " Being delivered," says he, " from a state of darkness, that is, pulled (not *inferis* but) *de inferno,* ' out of hell,' in which we were held by the devil, both for our own, and the sin of Adam, who is the father of all sinners; we are translated by faith into the heavenly kingdom of the Son of God, that God might show us with what love he loves us, when he lifts us up *de imo tartari,* ' out of the lowest hell,' and introduces us into heaven with his own real Son." Now, let Hilary mean what he will by *infernus* and *imum tartari,* it is certain, that according to him, men are in the custody of the devil, and are in some sort of punishment, *propter delictum Adæ,* "for the sin of Adam." which is what the passages were cited for. This writer, after Dr. Whitby, and which he has taken from him, cites a passage of Hilary's in which he says,‡ that " we do not endure the second death in hell for Adam's sin, but only by occasion thereof it is exacted for our sins:" and I could direct him to an-

other in the same commentary,§ where he says, *delicto Adæ multi tenentur a morte secunda in inferno inferiori;* many are held by the second death in the lowest hell for the sin of Adam."

4. Ambrose is allowed to say some things of men's deriving pollution and corruption from Adam, and it is owned that some passages in him do declare that he thought mankind defiled in Adam, and that they are undone and destroyed in him: but Ambrose not only declares that a corrupt nature is derived from Adam, but also, that the fault of his transgression is transferred or imputed to his posterity, as appears from what I have cited from him. As to what Ambrose says concerning infants going to heaven, which he makes a doubt of, and being freed from punishment; it is to be hoped they may, through the pardoning mercy of God, the blood of Christ, and the regenerating grace of the Spirit, notwithstanding the corruption of their nature, and the imputation of Adam's sin to them.

5. Mark the Eremite is the last upon the list excepted to; who says, that " all men have been guilty of the sin of Adam's transgression, and have therefore been condemned to death, so that without Christ they cannot be saved." Our author desires to know where the Latin word for *guilty* is to be found in this passage: Mark's words are these, *cunctique peccato transgressionis fuerunt;* which being literally rendered is, " all have been in the sin of his transgression;" and is not the sense the same? If they were *in* it, they must be *guilty* of it; for if not guilty, how should they be condemned on account of it? for Mark adds, *ideoque capitali sententia condemnati,* " and therefore have been capitally condemned," or condemned to die, insomuch that without Christ they cannot be saved; not merely from a corporeal death by the resurrection from the dead, which wicked men will partake of, and yet not be saved; but from the second death, from wrath to come, which none will escape, but such who are saved by Christ with a spiritual and eternal salvation.

The fourth charge brought against me by this writer, is great partiality in reciting all the passages of Vossius which relate to original sin, without taking notice of Dr. Whitby's replies to them. To which I have answered, by observing and proving, that I have not recited all the passages of Vossius relating to this point, nor has he all the passages I have cited; and that Dr. Whitby has not replied to all the citations of Vossius, and has passed over many passages of the ancients which he refers to. This author being shut up on every side, betakes himself to this miserable subterfuge, " that I have mistaken his meaning;" which was, he says, that I have recited all the passages of Vossius concerning original sin, which I have recit-

---

* Adv. Hæres. l. 4, c. 9, p. 326.
‡ Comment on Rom. v. p. 209.
† Annotat. in Irenæum, p. 285.
§ Comment on Rom. v. p. 272.

ed, without taking any notice of Dr. Whitby's answers; which would have been true if I had not recited one of Vossius's citations; but certain it is, that he would have had the reader understand, that I have recited every individual citation of Vossius; for in his margin he observes, that I have copied him even to his mistakes, which he affirms, without pointing out one single instance to support it.

The reply to my answer to his fifth charge has nothing in it worthy of any notice; only I would observe, that to refer to passages of the ancients which seem to favour the Arminian scheme, if not transcribed at length, is at one time chargeable with unfairness, and at another time it is weakness to the last degree, to cite such passages from them, in which they seem to agree with their tenets, and not denied by us. So determined is this man to cavil at any rate!